Technology in Western Civilization

TECHNOLOGY IN

Technology
in the Twentieth Century

WESTERN CIVILIZATION

Volume II

EDITED BY

MELVIN KRANZBERG

CARROLL W. PURSELL, Jr.

EXECUTIVE EDITORS
PAUL J. GROGAN
DONALD F. KAISER

New York
OXFORD UNIVERSITY PRESS
London   Toronto   1967

Preface

This is the second of two volumes dealing with the development of technology in Western civilization. The first, subtitled *The Emergence of Modern Industrial Society*, carried the story from the beginnings of mankind through 1900; the present volume continues the story of man's evolving mastery over his physical environment into our own times.

The fact that the first volume covers several millennia while the second describes only the events of the last sixty-odd years is significant. Like so many other elements in recent historical experience, technological innovation is increasing at an exponential rate; that is, the more changes there are, the faster they occur. The chronological imbalance of these two volumes, therefore, merely illustrates the fact that technology has changed both itself and ourselves within the last two generations. In addition, this volume focuses primarily on American developments, not because of any parochial outlook by the authors or editors, but because the industrial leadership of the world passed to America during the 20th century and because the major technological developments which have had worldwide influence became dominant in America, even when they did not originate there.

The project which gave rise to this history of technology originated with the United States Armed Forces Institute for a text, to be prepared under the auspices of the University Extension, University of Wisconsin, to explain the critical role of technology in our present society. A balance was sought among various factors: the nature of the subject matter itself, the dictates of organization for a course comprising a certain number of weeks and requiring viable assignments for the students, and the interests of the authors, all of whom stress the importance of their own particular field of specialization. The editors have endeavored to provide coherence and unity throughout the text which has, because of its collaborative nature, differences in individual styles, emphases, and interpretations.

The editors have accepted what seems to us to be the clear responsibility to place the many inventions with which we deal in their social context. For machines do not simply evolve out of the logic of their mechanism and the genius of their inventors, nor do they miraculously appear in response to some real or imagined social need. Their importance lies in the control which they give us over our environment and, hence, in the influence which they exert upon society. In this volume we have tried to give primary attention to such questions as: How does an invention produce innovation—in other words, how does a new machine or process come to make a difference in the way people think and do things? In what way does society encourage or resist innovation? How is technology diffused, and how does an idea or a value in one field spread to other areas of human concern? And finally, is the machine the master or the servant of man—or, perhaps, is this question meaningless?

The rationalization of production, automation, the balancing of military and civilian technical needs, the sharing of technology with developing countries, and the crisis of abundance—many of these innovations and their social effects are in process rather than finally complete. Historians are loath to approach the present too closely, even though that is the very point at which the future becomes the past. Nevertheless, the rewards of understanding appear to us to far outweigh the dangers of shortened perspective. Calling upon our colleagues in economics, sociology, and the other social sciences, we have attempted to explain how it is that we have arrived at the place we are, in the belief that a people who know whence they have come will be best prepared to choose their own course for the future.

Case Western Reserve University,   MELVIN KRANZBERG
   Cleveland
University of California, Santa Barbara   CARROLL W. PURSELL, JR.
July 1967

Contents

PART I

INTRODUCTION

1 / The Promise of Technology for the Twentieth Century   3
CARROLL W. PURSELL, JR., AND MELVIN KRANZBERG

2 / Technological Trends in the Twentieth Century   10
PETER F. DRUCKER

3 / Technology and Society in the Twentieth Century   22
PETER F. DRUCKER

PART II

RATIONALIZATION AND ITS CONSEQUENCES

4 / The Rationalization of Production   37
JOHN B. RAE

5 / The Rationalization of Management   52
ROBERT H. GUEST

6 / Technology and Labor in the Twentieth Century   64
JACK BARBASH

7 / The Organization of Distribution and Marketing   77
THEODORE F. MARBURG

8 / The Social Effects of Mass Production   91
CHARLES R. WALKER

9 / The Crisis of Abundance   103
ROBERT THEOBALD

PART III

TRANSPORTATION

10 / The Internal-Combustion Engine on Wheels   119
JOHN B. RAE

11 / Rail and Water Transport   137
ERNEST W. WILLIAMS, JR.

12 / The Development of Aviation   153
THOMAS M. SMITH

PART IV

MATERIALS AND STRUCTURES

13 / Man Makes His Materials   183
EDUARD FARBER

14 / Building with Steel and Concrete   196
MELVIN M. ROTSCH

15 / The Home Environment   217
MELVIN M. ROTSCH

PART V

ENERGY RESOURCES

16 / Developing the Energy Inheritance   237
BRUCE C. NETSCHERT

17 / Man Harnesses the Atom   256
RICHARD G. HEWLETT

18 / Energy Resources for the Future   275
J. A. DUFFIE

PART VI

ELECTRONICS AND COMMUNICATIONS

19 / Electronic Communications   293
BERNARD S. FINN

20 / Origins of the Computer   309
THOMAS M. SMITH

21 / The Impact of Mass Communication   323
ROBERT C. DAVIS

PART VII

THE FOOD REVOLUTION

22 / Scientific Agriculture   337
WAYNE D. RASMUSSEN

23 / Mechanization of the American Farm   353
REYNOLD M. WIK

24 / Pest and Disease Controls   369
AARON J. IHDE

25 / Food Processing and Packaging   386
GEORG BORGSTROM

26 / Food from the Sea   402
GEORG BORGSTROM

27 / Food for the Future   414
WAYNE D. RASMUSSEN

PART VIII

LAND USE AND RESOURCES

28 / The Resource Revolution   431
J. L. PENICK, JR.

29 / Regional Planning and Development   449
FOREST G. HILL

30 / Urban Planning and Development   461
ROY LUBOVE

PART IX

TECHNOLOGY AND THE STATE

31 / Technology and Public Policy   487
MORGAN B. SHERWOOD

32 / The Problem of Social Control   499
LESLIE H. FISHEL, JR.

33 / The Challenge of Underdevelopment   516
JACK BARANSON

PART X

TECHNOLOGY IN WAR

34 / Organization of Military Research   535
DONALD C. SWAIN

35 / The Mechanization of War, 1880-1919   548
EDWARD L. KATZENBACH, JR.

36 / Three-Dimensional Warfare: World War II   561
RALPH SANDERS

37 / The Contemporary Spectrum of War   578
EUGENE M. EMME

38 / Technology and Strategy   590
I. B. HOLLEY, JR., AND THEODORE ROPP

39 / The Transfer of Military Technology to Civilian Use   601
RICHARD S. ROSENBLOOM

PART XI

SCIENTIFIC RESEARCH, TECHNOLOGY, AND AUTOMATION

40 / Industrial Research and Development   615
W. DAVID LEWIS

41 / The Development of Automation   635
JAMES R. BRIGHT

42 / The Impact of Cybernation   655
DONALD N. MICHAEL

PART XII

SPACE, CULTURE, AND TECHNOLOGY

43 / The Challenge of Space   673
EUGENE M. EMME

44 / The "Two Cultures"   686
KENNETH E. BOULDING

45 / Technology's Challenge   695
MELVIN KRANZBERG AND CARROLL W. PURSELL, JR.

Readings and References   709
Contributors   741
Subject Index   747
Name Index   767

Part **I**
Introduction

1 / The Promise of Technology for the Twentieth Century

CARROLL W. PURSELL, Jr., AND MELVIN KRANZBERG

At the threshold of a new century, men are inclined both to look back into the past and to peer into the future. The retrospective view as the year 1900 dawned encouraged confidence and optimism about the prospects ahead. The idea of progress, first clearly enunciated in the Enlightenment philosophy of the 18th century, had been fortified in the 19th century by the Darwinian concept of evolution, so that man's past appeared to be a long struggle upward from the primal ooze, through the Stone Age and progressive stages, to the comforts of the Victorian age. Material evidence of this doctrine of progressive evolution abounded in the products of technology, which attested to man's ever-growing control over his environment. To most men the coming century held forth the promise of still greater achievement.

THE ACCELERATION OF TECHNOLOGY

What is more, there was confident expectation that material progress through the advance of technology would come more rapidly than in the past. Historical evidence seemed to support the idea that technological development progressed not on an *arithmetic* scale, by accumulation of machines or the steady improvement of those already in existence, but that the process was *geometric* or even logarithmic in growth.

In 1800 a man travelled only as fast as a horse or a sailing ship could carry him, and these speeds were not significantly greater than they had been a thousand years earlier. But within the succeeding hundred years, man developed the steamboat, the railroad, the automobile, and stood at last on the threshold of powered flight. Whereas throughout most of human history a man could be heard only as far as his voice would carry, by 1900 sound could be carried over wires for long distances. A man's voice no longer died when he did; by 1900 it could be recorded for posterity by means of the phonograph; even his actions

3

could be depicted and preserved for the future through the medium of motion pictures.

Because so many technological advances had occurred only since the Industrial Revolution, it was widely held that the material progress of mankind would develop at an accelerated pace in the future. Indeed, the 20th century has witnessed technological growth of such magnitude that it can be said to have equalled or surpassed, both quantitatively and qualitatively, all previous technological developments throughout history.

PROGRESS OF KNOWLEDGE AND THE SPIRIT

Progress in technology during the 19th century was accompanied by a flowering of science. After centuries of alchemical activity, chemistry moved within a single century from the work of such 18th-century pioneers as Lavoisier and Priestley, who made it a modern science, to that of the Curies and Josiah Willard Gibbs. Physics, geology, astronomy, and medicine all made strides which staggered the imagination in the 19th century. To men who saw themselves at the evolutionary pinnacle, and who tended to view the entire past as a long struggle to become the present, it was clear that the prejudices, ignorance, and stupidity of thousands of years of darkness had been cast off in the marvelous century just past.

The catalogue of new machines, industrial processes, and scientific laws propounded was, indeed, impressive. Nor was this idea of progress limited to material things: in the moral and social realms the same rapid rate of improvement was detected. Within a few decades the institution of slavery, which went back farther even than biblical times, had been abolished throughout most of the world. The role of women was raised, if not to equality, at least to the level of respect and dignity. A new humanitarian concern was given to the treatment of drunkards, the insane, and the indigent—a whole body of the population once known as defective and dependent. Furthermore, the freedom from world war after the defeat of Napoleon in 1815 held out the hope that war itself, the oldest and most terrible barbarity, might eventually be eliminated. Even liberal political institutions, seen in few countries in 1800, seemed to be spreading to all the great nations of Europe.

Fundamental to this advance was the increasing ability, through the development and proper use of technology, to exploit the natural resources of the earth and to turn them to man's use. However wasteful the exploitation might have been, the capacity to use those resources was absolutely necessary to the progress which had come to be expected almost as a natural law in itself. The burst of utopian literature toward the end of the 19th century, especially as it came from the minds of such men as the American author Edward Bellamy and the English author H. G. Wells, pointed out how the next centuries might witness the fulfillment of the technological promise of their time—the further development of mechanization and the extension of its benefits to an ever larger proportion of the population.

"THE AMERICAN CENTURY"

The geographical focus of Western civilization has constantly been changing. In antiquity the Mediterranean littoral was the scene of the origins of Western culture; Northern Europe was sparsely populated, and then only by tribes scarcely above the level of barbarism. During the Middle Ages, the major sphere of influence shifted to the western and central portions of Northern Europe. By the 19th century Britain had emerged as the most powerful nation in the world, with a far-flung colonial empire, tremendous wealth and productive power, and a preponderant influence on international affairs. As the 20th century opened, the focal point was again moving westward, to the New World: America was beginning to emerge as the dominant power.

To a technological determinist—that is, one who believes that technological developments determine the course of human events, including the nature and distribution of political power—these shifts might seem to follow advances in technology. To others who do not share this belief in the historical force wielded by technology, it might appear that technological development was the result rather than a cause of the changes in the focus of Western civilization. In either case, it is evident that technological developments paralleled political, cultural, and social changes of the first magnitude, and that the countries with the greatest international military and political power were also the leaders in technology. Certainly it was no accident that Britain, the home of the Industrial Revolution and the technological leader throughout the 19th century, was also the most powerful and wealthy nation of that era.

As the 19th century drew to a close, it was clear that Britain's industrial lead was being challenged; not that her great industrial productivity was declining —for indeed, it was rising—but that of other nations, particularly Germany and the United States, was increasing so rapidly that it threatened Britain's long-held primacy as the world's largest steel producer. The United States, throughout the 19th century, had largely been an "importer" of technology, obtaining much of its technical personnel, machinery, processes, and capital for industrial development from abroad, largely from England. By the beginning of the 20th century, this situation had begun to change, and America was moving into a position of industrial leadership.

The 20th century has been called "the American century" for two reasons. First, because America in this century has become a dominant force in international affairs, exporting characteristic elements of its political and value systems to the rest of the world; also, because the 20th century is a "technological century" and it was in the United States that many of the major technological developments which were to characterize the age were either invented or developed. Technology helped make America the wealthiest nation in the world, measured both in terms of industrial production and standards of living; hence it is not surprising that the optimistic outlook characteristic of the year 1900 was found especially in America, the young nation which was just then beginning to feel its growing industrial power.

THE OPTIMISTIC OUTLOOK

The very first years of the new century showed signs of the political and social changes coming to balance the changing industrial character of society. In 1901, Queen Victoria, the symbol of British primacy throughout most of the 19th century, died; her successor, King Edward VII, created new and closer ties between the monarchy and the common people. Even more significant in terms of the changing political picture was the formation of the Labour Party, devoted to the interests of the working class, and soon to exert a major influence on British politics. In the United States, when President McKinley was assassinated shortly after his re-election, Vice President Theodore Roosevelt succeeded him and began what has come to be called the Progressive era. Even in autocratic Russia there were signs of change when a revolution in 1905 resulted in the embryonic development of some constitutional organs in a politically and socially backward country just beginning its industrial development.

The technological success of the 19th century and the response of political institutions to that success had, for the first time in history, created the means whereby the common man might enjoy a decent life. Religion had long promised a spiritual heaven after the apocalypse. More recently, Karl Marx had promised a socialist millennium after the Armageddon of class warfare. The tremendous advances in technology, however, and resultant increases in individual productivity, finally held out the possibility of a utopian millennium immediately available within the liberal-democratic-materialistic context of Western civilization.

THE DOUBTING AND DISSENTING MINORITY

Despite all these enormous accomplishments of technology, some men remained unconvinced that the future held such shining promise. There were and are those who would agree with the English author G. K. Chesterton, who said that nothing fails like success. It is true that in solving so spectacularly a great many of the problems of the 19th century, science and technology raised new ones for the 20th.

Another who responded with doubt and confusion to the new technology and science was the American author and historian Henry Adams. Adams, son of an ambassador to the Court of St. James, grandson of one President and greatgrandson of another, walked the corridors of the Paris International Exposition of 1900 in the company of Samuel P. Langley, secretary of the Smithsonian Institution and a leading astronomer and experimenter with the problems of flight. Adams confided in his autobiography that "the dynamo became a symbol of infinity." And, referring to himself, he continued, "As he grew accustomed to the great gallery of machines, he began to feel the forty-foot dynamos as a moral force, much as the early Christians felt the Cross." Adams was, of course, familiar with the steam engine, but "between the dynamo in the gallery of machines and the engine-house outside, the break of continuity amounted to abysmal fracture for a historian's objects . . . . The forces were interchangeable if not reversible, but he could see only an absolute *fiat* in electricity as in faith. Langley could not help him. Indeed, Langley seemed to be worried by the same trouble . . . ." Even more upsetting to this close and sympathetic student of the 19th century was the recent discovery of radioactivity. Radium, Adams explained, "denied its God—or, what was to Langley the same thing, denied the truths of his Science. The force was wholly new." As though in a bad dream, Adams "found himself lying in the Gallery of Machines at the Great Exposition of 1900, his historical neck broken by the sudden eruption of forces totally new."

The cosmic discontinuity which Adams, and some intellectuals in other fields, felt in 1900 was accompanied by a list of specific grievances. At the Exposition, Langley showed Adams "the automobile, which, since 1893, had become a nightmare at a hundred kilometres an hour, almost as destructive as the electric tram which was only ten years older . . . ." It took decades before the general public began to realize the dangers of which he spoke then, and of others not then foreseen. Recently the critic and historian of technology Lewis Mumford has suggested that the automobile, "the Sacred Cow of the American Way of Life[,] is overfed and bloated; that the milk she supplies is poisonous; that the pasturage this species requires wastes acres of land that could be used for more significant human purposes; and that the vast herds of sacred cows, allowed to roam everywhere, like their Hindu counterparts, are trampling down the vegetation, depleting the wild life, and turning both urban and rural areas into a single smudgy wasteland, whose fancy sociological name is Megalopolis."

Some of these warnings have come, it is true, from people who reject mechanization altogether, and hark back to a pastoral time. Of greater moment were those critics (of whom Mumford is one) who distinguished between the machine and its system, and who insisted that those human values which justify mechanization and define progress should not be lost sight of in the course of their efficient pursuit.

THE TECHNOLOGICAL FOUNDATIONS OF THE OPTIMISTIC HOPES

At the turn of the century, it was difficult to take even the most sober critic seriously—the technological promise of the new century was altogether too overwhelming. To the vast majority of men, technological progress was "a good thing," indeed, almost an end in itself. Once men, through technology, could satisfy their basic needs for food, clothing, and shelter, somehow, it was thought, all the other ills of mankind would disappear. Although many of our most spectacular developments, such as space travel and atomic energy, were still in the realm of science fiction, others were already present, though embryonic.

In the area of transportation, the automobile was already a success. Thousands of these new machines were in operation, and it was only the beginning. Although the airplane had not yet been "invented," all its important elements had been developed and the theory of flight had been proposed. Dozens of skilled experimenters were at work on the problem, and it was only a matter of time until one of them hit the right combination of design and luck. Locomotives were becoming heavier and faster, and ocean vessels, soon to be powered by steam turbines and diesel engines, were similarly transformed. But again, these were merely extensions of known technologies.

In the field of communications, the telegraph had been thoroughly explored but telephony was in its infancy, and the new field of wireless telegraphy was a babe of enormous potential. The phonograph and the motion picture had been put on the market, though engineering development and commercial exploitation of them had hardly begun. The United States Bureau of the Census had recently introduced, in the census of 1890, the use of machines to sort and tabulate data on punched cards, thus opening up a tremendously fertile field of development in the area of information storage and manipulation.

The field of energy production was in a somewhat different position. Although the discovery of radioactivity had caused excitement in a large segment of the scientific community, the harnessing of this energy for useful purposes, especially in large quantities, was contemplated only by the most imaginative writers of science fiction. For the hard-headed engineer and industrialist, the future seemed to lie in the development of more efficient ways of consuming the limited mineral coal deposits of the earth and, more important, in the wider exploitation of hydroelectric power—a source of huge quantities of power only recently brought to public attention by the Niagara Falls development.

Agriculture, too, promised much at the start of the 20th century. The new science of genetics was radically changing the prospects for improved crops and animal breeds, while the recent development of the germ theory of disease made veterinary medicine a more successful practice. The growing body of data concerning the interrelations of water and soil resources had many implications for conservation. Perhaps most important, the development of the gasoline tractor, a device already beginning to compete with the horse and the steam traction engine, for the first time put efficient and flexible power in the hands of the individual farmer. It caused a power revolution in the history of agriculture. The growth of a reclamation movement in the United States and the development of an American chemical industry promised water and fertilizers to a much larger proportion of the nation's farmers.

In the construction sector of the economy, the two great monuments of the 20th century, the skyscraper and the suspension bridge, were already well understood, and there was no doubt in 1900 that such structures would, in the future, be built even higher and longer. The study of materials had just received a boost with the discovery of X-rays, and an increasingly sophisticated understanding of the chemical and crystalline structure of metals led to ever-improved alloys and more carefully calculated matching of material to use. The beginnings of a chemical plastics industry raised the whole question of how far synthetic materials might go toward providing the perfect material for every need.

At the beginning of the 19th century the wedding of science to technology had been a philosopher's ideal, based on Francis Bacon's notions of two centuries earlier; but by the beginning of the 20th the marriage had been consummated and its offspring were increasingly numerous. More important, the union had been institutionalized in the industrial research laboratory. This new type of institution had arisen first in Germany in the last half of the 19th century, and in the United States it was foreshadowed by Thomas Edison's laboratory at Menlo Park. Soon after the turn of the century the General Electric Laboratory was established and it became, almost immediately, the archetype of the research laboratory. Here, and in increasing numbers of other such establishments, large numbers of scientists, mathematicians, engineers, and technicians co-operated to provide an entire industry with everything from fundamental research into the laws of nature to quality control of current products.

The development of Scientific Management by Frederick W. Taylor opened a new dimension in the area of employer-employee relations and in the whole field of administration. It had long been recognized, though sometimes only half-consciously, that the "American system" of manufacture, which had scored such successes in the 19th century, was something more than just the sum of its constituent machines. The rational arrangement and balancing of these machines were also important. Taylor's idea of Scientific Management—that interpersonal, man-machine, and other relationships could be placed upon a firm scientific footing—held great promise. Furthermore, the system, with its emphasis upon efficiency, came to have meaning for areas of human life far removed from the technology of the factory or machine shop.

The idea of rational management appeared in industry, agriculture, and in resource management before the turn of the century. Within a few years it was applied also to the planning of cities and the social development of whole regions. Even the government itself, it was believed, could be made more efficient. Governments had always served special interests with patents, tariffs, tax rebates, research information, and so forth. Now it was hoped that the government could, guided only by the facts and their scientific application, serve the public interest in an ever wider range of problems.

Thus, the technological prospect at the turn of the century could hardly have been brighter. Wherever one looked—to transportation, communications, materials, energy, agriculture, resource development, industrial research, industrial management—the 19th century had brought forth a whole range of exciting new inventions, theories, discoveries, techniques, and insights which promised to transform the new century.

The optimistic enthusiasm of most people was based on the belief that man would use his new-found power well. Despite clear signs of colonial exploitation, class warfare, and international rivalries, it was possible to believe, looking back to the past hundred years of freedom from world war, that the barbarity of war was something that man had outgrown. It was not just that war was becoming unthinkably horrible. A rising standard of living on both sides of the Atlantic fed the hope that the lot of the working class might become respectable and even comfortable, with hunger and insecurity done away with. The spread of liberal-democratic institutions gave rise to the expectation that the peace-loving masses of people of the world were taking control of their own destinies and could be expected to cultivate the arts of peace rather than the craft of war. And finally there was the hope that, with economic well-being and the spread of liberal institutions, education, and scientific knowledge, man might also develop and realize his full capacity. This was the dream of the new man. Believing his own animal nature firmly disciplined and the forces of nature securely chained by science and technology, man stood on the threshold of the 20th century confident of his own destiny.

2 / Technological Trends in the Twentieth Century
PETER F. DRUCKER

Technological activity during the 20th century has changed in its structure, methods, and scope. It is this qualitative change which explains even more than the tremendous rise in the volume of work the emergence of technology in the 20th century as central in war and peace, and its ability within a few short decades to remake man's way of life all over the globe.

This overall change in the nature of technological work during this century has three separate though closely related aspects: (1) structural changes—the professionalization, specialization, and institutionalization of technological work; (2) changes in methods—the new relationship between technology and science; the emergence of systematic research; and the new concept of innovation; and (3) the "systems approach." Each of these is an aspect of the same fundamental trend. Technology has become something it never was before: an organized and systematic discipline.

THE STRUCTURE OF TECHNOLOGICAL WORK

Throughout the 19th century technological activity, despite tremendous success, was still in its structure almost entirely what it had been through the ages: a craft. It was practised by individuals here, there, and yonder, usually working alone and without much formal education. By the middle of the 20th century technological activity has become thoroughly professional, based, as a rule, on specific university training. It has become largely specialized, and is to a very substantial extent being carried out in a special institution—the research laboratory, particularly the industrial research laboratory—devoted exclusively to technological innovation.

Each of these changes deserves a short discussion. To begin with, few of the major figures in 19th-century technology received much formal education. The typical inventor was a mechanic who began his apprenticeship at age fourteen or earlier. The few who had gone to college had not, as a rule, been trained in technology or science but were liberal arts students, trained primarily in Classics. Eli Whitney (1765-1825) and Samuel Morse (1791-1873), both Yale graduates, are good examples. There were, of course, exceptions such as the Prussian engineering officer Werner von Siemens (1816-92), who became one of the early founders of the electrical industry; also such university-trained pioneers of the modern chemical industry as the Englishman William Perkin (1838-1907) and the Anglo-German Ludwig Mond (1839-1909). But in general, technological invention and the development of industries based on new knowledge were in the hands of craftsmen and artisans with little scientific education but a great deal of mechanical genius. These men considered themselves mechanics and inventors, certainly not "engineers" or "chemists," let alone "scientists."

The 19th century was also the era of technical-university building. Of the major technical institutions of higher learning only one, the École Polytechnique in Paris, antedates the century; it was founded at the close of the 18th century. But by 1901, when the California Institute of Technology in Pasadena admitted its first class, virtually every one of the major technical colleges active in the Western world today had already come into being. Still, in the opening decades of the 20th century the momentum of technical progress was being carried by the self-taught mechanic without specific technical or scientific education. Neither Henry Ford (1863-1947) nor the Wright brothers (Wilbur, 1867-1912; Orville, 1871-1948) had ever gone to college.

The technically educated man with the college degree began to assume leadership about the time of World War I, and by the time of the Second World War the change was essentially complete. Technological work since 1940 has been done primarily by men who have been specially educated for such work and who have earned university degrees. Such degrees have almost become prerequisites for technological work. Indeed, since World War II, the men who have built businesses of new technology have as often as not been university professors of physics, chemistry, or engineering, as were most of the men who converted the computer into a saleable product.

Technological work has thus become a profession. The inventor has become an "engineer," the craftsman, a "professional." In part this is only a reflection of the uplifting of the whole educational level of the Western world during the last 150 years. The college-trained engineer or chemist in the Western world today is not more educated, considering the relative standard of his society, than the craftsman of 1800 (who, in a largely illiterate society, could read and write). It is our entire society—and not the technologist alone—that has become formally educated and professionalized. But the professionalization of technological work points up the growing complexity of technology and the growth of scientific and technological knowledge. It is proof of a change in attitude toward technology, an acceptance by society, government, education, and business that this work is important, that it requires a thorough grounding in scientific knowledge, and, above all, that it requires many more capable people than "natural genius" could produce.

Technological work has become increasingly specialized, also, during the 20th century. Charles Franklin Kettering (1876-1958), the inventive genius of General Motors and for thirty years head of G. M. Research Corporation, represented the 19th-century type of inventor, who specialized in "invention" rather than in electronics, haloid chemistry, or even the automobile. Kettering in 1911 helped invent the electric self-starter, which enabled the layman (and especially women) to drive an automobile. He concluded his long career in the late 'thirties by converting the clumsy, wasteful, heavy, and inflexible diesel engine into the economical, flexible, and relatively light-weight propulsion unit that has become standard in heavy trucks and railroad locomotives. In between, however, he also developed a non-toxic freezing compound which made household refrigeration possible and, with it, the modern appliance industry; and tetra-ethyl lead which, by preventing the "knocking" of internal-combustion engines using high-octane fuel, made possible the high-performance automobile and aircraft engine.

This practice of being an inventor characterized the 19th-century technologist altogether. Edison and Siemens in the electrical industry saw themselves as "specialists in invention," as did the father of organic chemistry, Justus von Liebig (1803-79) of Germany. Even lesser men showed a range of interests and achievements that would seem extraordinary, if not unprofessional, today. George Westinghouse (1846-1914), for instance, took out important patents on a high-speed vertical steam engine; on the generation, transformation, and transmission of alternating current; and on the first effective automatic brake for railroad trains. The German-born Emile Berliner (1851-1929) contributed heavily to early telephone and phonograph technology and also designed one of the earliest helicopter models. And there were others.

This kind of inventor has not yet disappeared—there are many today working as Edison, Siemens, and Liebig worked a century ago. Edwin H. Land (1909-   ), of Polaroid fame, quit college to develop polarizing glass, and has ranged in his work from camera design to missiles, and from optics and the theory of vision to colloidal chemistry. He deliberately describes himself in *Who's Who in America* as an "inventor." But such men who cover the spectrum of applied science and technology are not, as they were in the 19th century, the center of technological activity. There we find instead the specialist who works in one increasingly narrow area—electronic circuit design, heat exchange, or high-density polymer chemistry, for instance.

This professionalization and specialization have been made effective by the institutionalization of work in the research laboratory. The research laboratory —and especially the industrial research laboratory—has become the carrier of technological advance in the 20th century. It is increasingly the research laboratory, rather than the individual, which produces new technology. More and more, technological work is becoming a team effort in which the knowledge of a large number of specialists in the laboratory is brought to bear on a common problem and directed toward a joint technological result.

During the 19th century the "laboratory" was simply the place where work was done that required technical knowledge beyond that of the ordinary mechanic. In industry, testing and plant engineering were the main functions of the laboratory; research was done on the side, if at all. Similarly, the government laboratory during the 19th century was essentially a place to test, and all the large government laboratories in the world today (such as the Bureau of Standards in Washington) were founded for that purpose. In the 19th-century college or university, the laboratory was used primarily for teaching rather than for research.

Today's research laboratory had its origin in the German organic-chemical industry. The rapid rise of this industry from 1870 on rested squarely on the till then unheard of application of science to industrial production. However, even those German chemical laboratories were at first given mainly to testing and process engineering, and it was not until 1900 that they were devoted primarily to research. The turning point came with the synthesis of aspirin —the first purely synthetic drug—by Adolf von Baeyer (1835-1917) in 1899. The worldwide success of aspirin within a few years convinced the chemical industry of the value of technological work dedicated to research alone.

Even Edison's famous laboratory in Menlo Park, New Jersey—the most productive research center in the whole history of technological discovery and innovation—was not altogether a modern research laboratory. Although devoted solely to research, as is the modern research laboratory, Menlo Park was still primarily the workshop of a single inventor rather than the team effort that characterizes the industrial or university research laboratory of today. Many of Edison's assistants became successful inventors in their own right, for instance, Frank J. Sprague (1857-1934), who developed the first practical electric streetcar. But these men became productive technologists only after they had left Menlo Park and Edison's employ. While there they were just the great man's helpers.

After the turn of the century, new research laboratories suddenly appeared on both sides of the Atlantic. The German chemical industry rapidly built great laboratories that helped to give Germany a worldwide monopoly on dyestuffs, pharmaceuticals, and other organic chemicals before World War I. In Germany, too, shortly after 1900, were founded the big governmental research laboratories of the Kaiser Wilhelm Society (now the Max Planck Society), where senior scientists and scientific teams, free from all teaching obligations, could engage in research alone. On this side of the Atlantic C. P. Steinmetz (1865-1923) began, at about the same time, to build the first modern research laboratory in the electrical industry, the great research center of the General Electric Company in Schenectady. Steinmetz understood, perhaps even better than the Germans, what he was doing, and the pattern he laid down for the General Electric Research Laboratory is by and large that followed by all major industrial and governmental research centers to this day.

The essence of the modern research laboratory is not its size. There are some very large laboratories, working for governments or for large companies, and also numerous small research laboratories, many employing fewer technologists and scientists than did some 19th-century establishments; and there is no apparent relationship between the size of the research laboratory and its results. What distinguishes today's research laboratory from any predecessor is, first, its exclusive interest in research, discovery, and innovation. Secondly, the research laboratory brings together men from a wide area of disciplines, each contributing his specialized knowledge. Finally, the research laboratory embodies a new methodology of technological work squarely based on the systematic application of science to technology.

It is a great strength of the research laboratory that it can be both "specialist" and "generalist," permitting an individual to work alone or a team to work together. Quite a few Nobel Prize winners have done their research work in industrial laboratories such as those of the Bell Telephone System or the General Electric Company. Similarly nylon (1937), one of the first building blocks of today's plastic industry, was developed by W. H. Carothers (1896-1937) working by himself in the DuPont laboratory during the 'thirties. The research laboratory provides an individual with access to skills and facilities which greatly increase his capacity. It can at the same time, however, organize a team effort for a specific task and thus create a collective "generalist" with a greater range of skills and knowledge than any individual, no matter how gifted, could possibly acquire in one lifetime.

Before World War I the research laboratory was still quite rare. Between World War I and World War II it became standard in a number of industries, primarily the chemical, pharmaceutical, electrical, and electronics industries. Since World War II research activity has become as much of a necessity in industry as a manufacturing plant, and as central in its field as is the infantry soldier for defense, or the trained nurse in medicine.

THE METHODS OF TECHNOLOGICAL WORK

Hand in hand with changes in the structure of technological work go changes in the basic approach to and methods of work. Technology has become science-based. Its method is now "systematic research." And what was formerly "invention" is "innovation" today.

Historically the relationship between science and technology has been a complex one, and it has by no means been thoroughly explored nor is it truly understood as yet. But it is certain that the scientist, until the end of the 19th century, with rare exceptions, concerned himself little with the application of his new scientific knowledge and even less with the technological work needed to make knowledge applicable. Similarly, the technologist, until recently, seldom had direct or frequent contact with the scientist and did not consider his findings of primary importance to technological work. Science required, of course, its own technology—a very advanced technology at that, since all along the progress of science has depended upon the development of scientific instruments. But the technological advances made by the scientific instrument-maker were not, as a rule, extended to other areas and did not lead to new products for the consumer or to new processes for artisan and industry. The first instrument-maker to become important outside of the scientific field was James Watt, the inventor of the steam engine.

Not until almost seventy-five years later, that is until 1850 or so, did scientists themselves become interested in the technological development and application of their discoveries. The first scientist to become a major figure in technology was Justus von Liebig, who in the mid-19th century developed the first synthetic fertilizer and also a meat extract (still sold all over Europe under his name) which was, until the coming of refrigeration in the 1880's, the only way to store and transport animal proteins. In 1856 Sir William H. Perkin in England isolated, almost by accident, the first aniline dye and immediately built a chemical business on his discovery. Since then, technological work in the organic-chemicals industry has tended to be science-based.

About 1850 science began to affect another new technology—electrical engineering. The great physicists who contributed scientific knowledge of electricity during the century were not themselves engaged in applying this knowledge to products and processes; but the major 19th-century technologists of electricity closely followed the work of the scientists. Siemens and Edison were thoroughly familiar with the work of physicists such as Michael Faraday (1791-1867) and Joseph Henry (1791-1878). And Alexander Graham Bell (1847-1927) was led to his work on the telephone through the researches of Hermann von Helmholtz (1821-94) on the reproduction of sound. Guglielmo Marconi (1874-1910) developed radio on the foundation Heinrich Hertz (1857-94) had laid with his experimental confirmation of Maxwell's electromagnetic-wave propagation theory; and so on. From its beginnings, therefore, electrical technology has been closely related to the physical science of electricity.

Generally, however, the relationship between scientific work and its technological application, which we today take for granted, did not begin until after the turn of the 20th century. As previously mentioned, such typically modern devices as the automobile and the airplane benefitted little from purely theoretical scientific work in their formative years. It was World War I that brought about the change: in all belligerent countries scientists were mobilized for the war effort, and it was then that industry discovered the tremendous power of science to spark technological ideas and to indicate technological solutions. It was at that time also that scientists discovered the challenge of technological problems.

Today technological work is, for the most part, consciously based on scientific effort. Indeed, a great many industrial research laboratories do work in "pure" research, that is, work concerned exclusively with new theoretical knowledge rather than with the application of knowledge. And it is a rare laboratory that starts a new technological project without a study of scientific knowledge, even though it does not seek new knowledge for its own sake. At the same time, the results of scientific inquiry into the properties of nature—whether in physics, chemistry, biology, geology, or another science—are immediately analyzed by thousands of "applied scientists" and technologists for their possible application to technology.

Technology is not, then, "the application of science to products and processes," as is often asserted. At best this is a gross over-simplification. In some areas—for example, polymer chemistry, pharmaceuticals, atomic energy, space exploration, and computers—the line between "scientific inquiry" and "technology" is a blurred one; the "scientist" who finds new basic knowledge and the "technologist" who develops specific processes and products are one and the same man. In other areas, however, highly productive efforts are still primarily concerned with purely technological problems, and have little connection to science as such. In the design of mechanical equipment—machine tools, textile machinery, printing presses, and so forth—scientific discoveries as a rule play a very small part, and scientists are not commonly found in the research laboratory. More important is the fact that science, even where most relevant, provides only the starting point for technological efforts. The greatest amount of work on new products and processes comes well *after* the scientific contribution has been made. "Know-how," the technologist's contribution, takes a good deal more time and effort in most cases than the scientist's "know-what"; and though science is no substitute for today's technology, it is the basis and starting point.

While we know today that our technology is based on science, few people (other than the technologists themselves) realize that technology has become in this century somewhat of a "science" in its own right. It has become "research"—a separate discipline having its own specific methods.

Nineteenth-century technology was "invention"—not managed or organized or systematic. It was, as our patent laws of two hundred years ago still define it, "flash of insight." Of course hard work, sometimes for decades, was usually required to convert this "flash" into something that worked and could be used. But nobody knew how this work should be done, how it might be organized, or what one could expect from it. The turning point was probably Edison's work on the electric light bulb in 1879. As his biographer Matthew Josephson points out, Edison did not intend to do organized research. He was led to it by his failure to develop through "flash of genius" a workable electric light. This forced him, very much against his will, to work through the specifications of the solution needed, to spell out in considerable detail the major steps that had to be taken, and then to test systematically 1600 different materials to find one that could be used as the incandescent element for the light bulb he sought to develop. Indeed, Edison found that he had to break through on three major technological fronts at once in order to have domestic electric lighting. He needed an electrical energy source producing a well-regulated voltage of essentially constant magnitude; a high vacuum in a small glass container; and a filament that would glow without immediately burning up. And the job that Edison expected to finish by himself in a few weeks required a full year and the work of a large number of highly trained assistants, that is, a research team.

There have been many refinements in the research method since Edison's experiments. Instead of testing 1600 different materials, we would today, in all probability, use conceptual and mathematical analysis to narrow the choices considerably (this does not always work, however; current cancer research, for instance, is testing more than 60,000 chemical substances for possible therapeutic action). Perhaps the greatest improvements have been in the management of the research team. There was, in 1879, no precedent for such a team effort, and Edison had to improvise research management as he went along. Nevertheless he clearly saw the basic elements of research discipline: (1) a definition of the need—for Edison, a reliable and economical system of converting electricity into light; (2) a clear goal—a transparent container in which resistance to a current would heat up a substance to white heat; (3) identification of the major steps to be taken and the major pieces of work that had to be done—in his case, the power source, the container, and the filament; (4) constant "feedback" from the results of the work on the plan; for example, Edison's finding that he needed a high vacuum rather than an inert gas as the environment for his filament made him at once change the direction of research on the container; and finally (5) organization of the work so that each major segment is assigned to a specific work team.

These steps together constitute to this day the basic method and the system of technological work. October 21, 1879, the day on which Edison first had a light bulb that would burn for more than a very short time, therefore, is not only the birthday of electric light; it marks the birth of modern technological research as well. Yet whether Edison himself fully understood what he had accomplished is not clear, and certainly few people at the time recognized that he had found a generally applicable method of technological and scientific inquiry. It took twenty years before Edison was widely imitated, by German chemists and bacteriologists in their laboratories and in the General Electric laboratory in the United States. Since then, however, technological work has progressively developed as a discipline of methodical inquiry everywhere in the Western world.

Technological "research" has not only a different methodology from "invention"; it leads to a different approach, known as "innovation," or the purposeful and deliberate attempt to bring about, through technological means, a distinct change in the way man lives and in his environment—the economy, the society, the community, and so on. "Innovation" may begin by defining a need or an opportunity, which then leads to organizing technological efforts to find a way to meet the need or exploit the opportunity. To reach the moon, for instance, requires a great deal of new technology; once the need has been defined, technological work can be organized systematically to produce this new technology. Or "innovation" can proceed from new scientific knowledge and an analysis of the opportunities it might be capable of creating. Plastic fibers, such as nylon, came into being in the late 1920's after curiosity about what economic opportunities might result from the application of the new understanding of "polymers" (that is, long chains of organic molecules) that chemical scientists (mostly in Germany) had gained during World War I.

"Innovation" is not a product of the 20th century; both Siemens and Edison were "innovators" as much as "inventors." Both started out with the opportunity of creating big new industries—the electric railway (Siemens), and the electric lighting industry (Edison). Both men analyzed what new technology was needed and went to work creating it. Yet only in this century—and largely through the research laboratory and its approach to research—has innovation become central to technological effort.

In innovation, technology is used as a means to bring about change in the economy, in society, in education, warfare, and so on. This has tremendously increased the impact of technology. It has become the battering ram which breaks through even the stoutest ramparts of tradition and habit. Thus modern technology influences traditional society and culture in underdeveloped countries (see the following chapter). But innovation means also that technological work is not done only for technological reasons but for the sake of a non-technological economic, social, or military end.

Scientific "discovery" has always been measured by what it adds to our understanding of natural phenomena. The test of invention is, however, technical—what new capacity it gives us to do a specific task. But the test of innovation is its impact on the way people live. Very powerful innovations may therefore be brought about with relatively little in the way of new technological invention.

A very good example is the first major innovation of the 20th century, mass production, initiated by Henry Ford between 1905 and 1910 to produce the Model T automobile. It is correct, as has often been pointed out, that Ford contributed no important technological invention. The mass-production plant, as he designed and built it between 1905 and 1910, contained not a single new element: interchangeable parts had been known since before Eli Whitney, a century earlier; the conveyor belt and other means of moving materials had been in use for thirty years or more, especially in the meat-packing plants of Chicago. Only a few years before Ford, Otto Doering, in building the first large mail-order plant in Chicago for Sears, Roebuck, used practically every one of the technical devices Ford was to use at Highland Park, Detroit, to turn out the Model T. Ford was himself a highly gifted inventor who found simple and elegant solutions to a host of technical problems—from developing new alloy steels to improving almost every machine tool used in the plant. But his contribution was an "innovation": a technical solution to the economic problem of how to produce the largest number of finished products with the greatest reliability of quality at the lowest possible cost. And this innovation has had greater impact on the way men live than many of the great technical inventions of the past.

THE SYSTEMS APPROACH

Mass production exemplifies, too, a new dimension that has been added to technology in this century: the systems approach. Mass production is not a thing, or a collection of things; it is a concept—a unified view of the productive process.

It requires, of course, a large number of "things," such as machines and tools. But it does not start with them; they follow from the vision of the system.

The space program today is another such "system," and its conceptual foundation is genuine "innovation." Unlike mass production, the space program requires a tremendous amount of new invention and new scientific discovery, also. Yet the fundamental scientific concepts underlying it are not at all new —they are, by and large, Newtonian physics. What is new is the idea of putting men into space by a systematic, organized approach.

Automation is a "systems" concept, closer to Ford's mass production than to the space program. There had been examples of genuine automation long before anyone coined the term. Every oil refinery built in the past forty years has been essentially "automated." But not until someone saw the entire productive process as one continuous, controlled flow of materials did we see "automation." This has led to a tremendous amount of new technological activity to develop computers, program controls for machines, materials-moving equipment, and so on. Yet the basic technology to automate a great many industrial processes had been present for a long time, and all that was lacking was the "systems approach" to convert them to the innovation of automation.

The systems approach, which sees a host of formerly unrelated activities and processes as all parts of a larger, integrated whole, is not something technological in itself. It is, rather, a way of looking at the world and at ourselves. It owes much to *Gestalt* psychology (from the German word for "configuration" or "structure"), which demonstrated that we do not see lines and points in a painting but "configurations"—that is, a whole, and that we do not hear individual sounds in a tune but only the tune itself—the "configuration." And the systems approach was also generated by 20th-century trends in technology; the linking of technology and science, the development of the systematic discipline of research, and "innovation." The "systems approach" is, in fact, a measure of our newly found technological capacity. Earlier ages could visualize "systems" but they lacked the technological means to realize such visions.

The "systems approach" also tremendously increases the power of technology. It permits today's technologists to speak of "materials" rather than of steel, glass, paper, or concrete, each of which has, of course, its own (very old) technology. Today we see a generic concept—materials—all of which are arrangements of the same fundamental building blocks of matter. Thus it happens that we are busy designing materials without precedent in nature: synthetic fibers, plastics, glass that does not break and glass that conducts electricity, and so on. We increasingly decide first what end use we want and then choose or fashion the material we want to use. We define, for example, the specific properties we want in a container and then decide whether glass, steel, aluminum, paper, one of a host of plastics, or any one of hundreds of materials in combination will be the best material for it. This is what is meant by a "materials revolution" whose specific manifestations are technological, but whose roots are to be found in the systems concept.

We are similarly on the threshold of an "energy revolution"—making new use of such sources of energy as atomic reaction, solar energy, the tides, and so forth; but also with a new systems concept: energy. Again this concept is the result of major technological developments—especially, of course, in atomic power—and the starting point for major new technological work. Ahead of us, and barely started, is the greatest "systems" job we can see now: the systematic exploration and development of the oceans.

Water covers far more of the earth's surface than does land. And since water, unlike soil, is penetrated by the rays of the sun for a considerable depth, the life-giving process of photosynthesis covers infinitely more area in the seas than it does on land—apart from the fact that every single square inch of the ocean is fertile. And the sea itself, as well as its bottom, contains untold riches in metals and minerals. Yet, even today, on the oceans man is still a hunter and a nomad rather than a cultivator. He is in the same early stage of development as our ancestors almost ten thousand years ago when they first tilled the soil. Comparatively minor efforts to gain knowledge of the oceans and to develop technology to cultivate them should therefore yield returns—not only in knowledge, but in food, energy, and raw materials also—far greater than anything we could get from exploiting the already well-explored lands of the continents. Oceanic development, rather than space exploration, might well turn out to be the real "frontier" in the next century. Underlying this development will be the realization brought about by such technological developments as the submarine, and in turn sparking such new technological efforts as the Mohole project to drill through the earth's hard crust beneath the ocean, namely, the concept of the oceans as a "system."

There are many other areas where the "systems approach" is likely to have a profound impact, where it may lead to major technological efforts, and through them, to major changes in the way we live and our capacity to do things. One such example is the modern city—itself, as the next chapter will show, largely a creation of modern technology.

As an earlier chapter in this present history of technology (Volume I, Chapter 19) has recounted, one of the greatest 19th-century inventions was invention itself. It underlay the explosive technological development of the years between 1860 and 1900, "the heroic age of invention." It might similarly be said that the great invention of the early 20th century was innovation: it underlies the deliberate attempt to organize purposeful changes of whole areas of life which characterizes the systems approach.

Innovation and the systems approach are only just emerging. Their full impact is almost certainly still ahead. But they are already changing man's life, society, and his world view. And they are profoundly changing technology itself and its role. To sketch these changes in 20th-century technology has been the purpose of this chapter. As a result of these changes, technology has come to occupy a different place in a society which it is busy making over, and a discussion of the new meaning of technology for modern man and his society requires a chapter of its own.

3 / Technology and Society in the Twentieth Century
PETER F. DRUCKER

THE PRE-TECHNOLOGICAL CIVILIZATION OF 1900

Modern man everywhere takes technological civilization for granted. Even primitive people in the jungles of Borneo or in the High Andes, who may themselves still live in the Early Bronze Age and in mud huts unchanged for thousands of years, need no explanation when the movie they are watching shows the flipping of a light switch, the lifting of a telephone receiver, the starting of an automobile or plane, or the launching of another satellite. In mid-20th century the human race has come to feel that modern technology holds the promise of conquering poverty on the earth and of conquering outer space beyond. We have learned, too, that it carries the threat of snuffing out all humanity in one huge catastrophe. Technology stands today at the very center of human perception and human experience.

On the other hand, at the beginning of the 20th century modern technology barely existed for the great majority of people. In terms of geography, the Industrial Revolution and its technological fruits were largely confined, in 1900, to the small minority of mankind that is of European descent and lives around the North Atlantic shores. Only Japan, of the non-European, non-Western countries, had then begun to build up a modern industry and modern technology, and in 1900 modern Japan was still in its infancy. In Indian village, Chinese town, and Persian bazaar, life was still pre-industrial, still untouched by the steam engine and telegraph, and by all other new tools of the West. It was, indeed, almost an axiom—for Westerner and non-Westerner alike—that modern technology was, for better or worse, the birthright of the white man and restricted to him. This assumption underlay the "imperialism" of the period before World War I, and it was shared by such eminent non-Westerners as Rabindranath Tagore (1861-1941), the Nobel Prize winning Indian poet, and Mahatma Gandhi (1869-1948) who, just before World War I, began his long fight for Indian independence. There was indeed enough apparent factual support for this belief to survive, if only as a prejudice, until World War II. Hitler, for instance, made the Japanese "honorary Aryans" and considered them "Europeans in disguise" primarily because they had mastered modern technology. And in the United States the myth lingered on in the widespread belief, before Pearl Harbor, that the Japanese, not being of European stock, were not proficient in handling such weapons of modern technology as planes or battleships.

Still, in the West, indeed even in the most highly developed countries in 1900—England, the United States, and Germany—modern technology played only a minor role in the lives of most people, the majority of whom were then still farmers or artisans living either in the countryside or in small towns. The tools they used and the life they led were pre-industrial, and they remained unaware of the modern technology that was so rapidly growing up all around them. Only in a few large cities had modern technology imposed itself upon daily life—in the street railways, increasingly powered by electricity after 1890, and in the daily paper, dependent upon the telegraph and printed on steam-driven presses. Only there had modern technology crossed the threshold of the home with electric lights and the telephone.

Even so, to Western man in 1900, modern technology had become tremendously exciting. It was the time of the great international exhibitions in every one of which a new "miracle" of technical invention stole the show. These were also the years in which technological fiction became a best-seller from Moscow to San Francisco. About 1880, books by the Frenchman Jules Verne (1828-1905) such as *Journey to the Center of the Earth* and *Twenty Thousand Leagues under the Sea*, became wildly popular. By 1900 the English novelist H. G. Wells (1866-1946), whose works included the technological romance *The Time Machine* (1893), had become more popular still. And, as stated earlier in this volume, there was virtually unbounded faith in the benevolence of technological progress. All this excitement was, however, focused on *things*. That these things could and would have an impact on society and on the way people behaved and thought had not occurred to many.

The advances in technology in this century with which most of the succeeding chapters in this volume will deal are indeed awe-inspiring. Nevertheless, it can be argued that the foundations for most of them had been well laid by 1900, and certainly by 1910. The electric light, the telephone, the moving picture, the phonograph, and the automobile had all been invented by 1900 and were indeed being sold aggressively by prosperous and growing companies. And the airplane, the vacuum tube, and radio telegraphy were invented in the opening years of the new century.

The changes technology has wrought in society and culture since then could hardly have been anticipated by the men of 1900. The geographical explosion of technology has created the first worldwide civilization; and it is a technological civilization. It has already shifted the power center of the world away from

Western Europe thousands of miles to both West and East. More important still, modern technology in this century has made men reconsider old concepts, such as the position of women in society, and it has remade basic institutions— work, education, and warfare, for example. It has shifted a large number of people in the technologically advanced countries from working with their hands to working, almost without direct contact with materials and tools, with their minds. It has changed the physical environment of man from one of nature to the man-made big city. It has further changed man's horizon. While it converts the entire world into one rather tight community sharing knowledge, information, hopes, and fears, technology has brought outer space into man's immediate, conscious experience. It has converted an apocalyptic promise and an apocalyptic threat into concrete possibilities here and now: offering both the utopia of a world without poverty and the threat of the final destruction of humanity.

Finally, in the past sixty years man's view of technology itself has changed. We no longer see it as concerned with *things* only; today it is a concern of man as well. As a result of this new perspective we have come to realize that technology is not, as our grandparents believed, the magic wand that can make all human problems and limitations disappear. We now know that technological potential is, indeed, even greater than they thought. But we have also learned that technology, as a creature of man, is as problematical, as ambivalent, and as capable of good or evil, as is its creator.

This chapter will attempt to point out some of the most important changes which modern technology has brought about in society and culture, and some changes in our own view of and approach to technology thus far, in the 20th century.

TECHNOLOGY REMAKES SOCIAL INSTITUTIONS

Twentieth-century history, up to the 1960's, can be divided into three major periods: the period before the outbreak of the First World War in 1914—a period culturally and politically much like the 19th century; the First World War and the twenty years from 1918 to the outbreak of World War II in 1939; and from World War II until today. In each of these periods modern technology has shaped basic institutions of Western society. And in the most recent period it has started to undermine and remake, also, many of the basic institutions of non-Western society.

1. *Emancipation of Women.* In the years before World War I technology, in large measure, brought about the emancipation of women and gave them a new position in society. No 19th-century feminist, such as Susan B. Anthony, had as strong an impact on the social position of women as did the typewriter and telephone. If the "Help Wanted" advertisement of 1880 said "stenographer" or "telegrapher," everybody knew that a man was wanted, whereas the

ad of 1910 for a "stenographer" or "telephone operator" was clearly offering a woman's job. The typewriter and the telephone enabled the girl from a "decent" family to leave home and make a "respectable" living on her own, not dependent on a husband or father. The need for women to operate typewriters and switchboards forced even the most reluctant European governments to provide public secondary education for girls, the biggest single step toward granting women equality. The flood of respectable and well-educated young women in offices then made heavy demands for changes in the old laws that withheld from women the right to enter into contracts or to control their own earnings and property, and for another change which finally gave women the vote almost everywhere in the Western world by 1920.

2. Changes in the Organization of Work. Technology soon began to bring about an even greater transformation about the time of World War I. It started to replace the manual work that had always provided a livelihood for the great majority of people—as it still does in technologically "underdeveloped" countries. The starting point was the application of modern technological principles to manual work, which went under the name of Scientific Management and was largely developed by an American, Frederick Winslow Taylor (1856-1915).

While Henry Ford made the systems innovation of mass production, Taylor applied to manual operations the principles that machine designers during the 19th century had learned to apply to the work of a tool; he identified the work to be done; broke it down into its individual operations; designed the right way to do each operation; and finally he put the operations together, this time in the sequence in which they could be done fastest and most economically. All this strikes us today as commonplace, but it was the first time that work had been looked at; throughout history it had always been taken for granted.

The immediate result of Scientific Management was a revolutionary cut in the costs of manufactured goods—often to one-tenth, sometimes to one-twentieth of what they had been before. What had been rare luxuries inaccessible to all but the rich, such as automobiles or household appliances, rapidly became available to the broad masses. More important, perhaps, is the fact that Scientific Management made possible sharp increases in wages while at the same time lowering the total cost of the product. Hitherto lower costs of a finished product had always meant lower wages to the worker producing it. Scientific Management preached the contrary: that lower costs should mean higher wages and higher income for the worker. To bring this about was indeed Taylor's main intent and that of his disciples, who, unlike many earlier technologists, were motivated as much by social as by technical considerations. "Productivity" at once became something the technologist could raise, if not create. And with it, the standard of living of a whole economy might be raised, something totally impossible—indeed, almost unimaginable—at any earlier time.

At the same time, Scientific Management rapidly changed the structure and composition of the work force. It first led to wholesale upgrading of the labor force. The unskilled "laborer" working at a subsistence wage, who constituted the largest single group in the 19th-century labor force, became obsolete. In his place appeared a new group, the machine operators—the men on the automobile assembly line, for instance. They themselves were no more skilled, perhaps, than the laborers, but the technologist's knowledge had been injected into their work through Scientific Management so that they could be paid—and were soon being paid—the wages of highly skilled workers. Between 1910 and 1940 the "machine operators" became the largest single occupational group in every industrial country, pushing both farmers and laborers out of first place. The consequences for mass consumption, labor relations, and politics were profound and are still with us.

Taylor's work rested on the assumption that knowledge, rather than manual skill, was the fundamental productive resource. Taylor himself preached that productivity required that "doing" be divorced from "planning," that is, that it be based on systematic technological knowledge. His work resulted in a tremendous expansion of the number of educated people needed in the work force and, ultimately, in a complete shift in the focus of work from labor to knowledge.

What is today called "automation" is conceptually a logical extension of Taylor's Scientific Management. Once operations have been analyzed as if they were machine operations and organized as such (and Scientific Management did this successfully), they should be capable of being performed by machines rather than by hand. Taylor's work immediately increased the demand for educated people in the work force, and eventually, after World War II, it began to produce a work force in advanced countries like the United States in which educated people applying their knowledge to the job are the actual "workers," and outnumber the manual workers, whether laborers, machine operators, or craftsmen.

The substitution of knowledge for manual effort as the productive resource in work is the greatest change in the history of work, which is, of course, a process as old as man himself. This change is still in progress, but in the industrially advanced countries, especially in the United States, it has already completely changed society. In 1900 eighteen out of every twenty Americans earned their living by working with their hands, ten of the eighteen as farmers. By 1965, only five out of twenty of a vastly increased American labor force did manual work, and only one worked on the farm. The rest earned their living primarily with knowledge, concepts, or ideas—altogether, with things learned in school rather than at the workbench. Not all of this "knowledge" is, of course, advanced; the cashier in the cafeteria is also a "knowledge worker," though of very limited extent. But all of it is work that requires education, that is, systematic mental training rather than skill in the sense of exposure to experience.

3. The Role of Education. As a result, the role of education in 20th-century industrial society has changed—another of the very big changes produced by technology. By 1900 technology had advanced so far that literacy had become a social need in the industrial countries. A hundred years earlier literacy was essentially a luxury as far as society was concerned; only a handful of people —ministers, lawyers, doctors, government officials, and merchants—needed to be able to read and write. Even for a high-ranking general, such as Wellington's partner at Waterloo, the Prussian Field Marshal Bluecher, illiteracy was neither a handicap nor a disgrace. In the factory or the business office of 1900, however, one had to be able to read and write, if only at an elementary school level. By 1965 those without a substantial degree of higher education, more advanced than anything that had been available even to the most educated two hundred years ago, were actually becoming "unemployable." Education has moved, from having been an ornament, if not a luxury, to become the central economic resource of technological society. Education is therefore rapidly becoming a center of spending and investment in the industrially developed society.

This stress on education is creating a changed society; access to education is best given to everyone, if only because society needs all the educated people it can get. The educated man resents class and income barriers which prevent the full exercise of his knowledge, and because society requires and values the services of the expert it must allow him full recognition and rewards for his talents. In a completely technological civilization "education" replaces money and rank as the index of status and opportunities.

4. Change in Warfare. By the end of World War II technology had completely changed the nature of warfare, and altered the character of war as an institution. When Karl von Clausewitz (1780-1831), the father of modern strategic thought, called war "a continuation of policy by other means" he only expressed in an epigram what every politician and every military leader had known all along. War was always a gamble. War was cruel and destructive. War, the great religious leaders always preached, is sin. But war was also a normal institution of human society and a rational tool of policy. Many of Napoleon's contemporaries, including Clausewitz himself, considered him wicked, but none thought him insane for using war to impose his political will on Europe.

The dropping of the first atomic bomb on Hiroshima in 1945 changed all this. Since then it has become increasingly clear that major war no longer can be considered "normal," let alone "rational." Total war has ceased to be a usable institution of human society because in full-scale, modern technological warfare, there is no "defeat," just as there is no "victory." There is only total destruction. There are no "neutrals" and no "noncombatants," for the risk of destruction extends to the entire human race.

5. A Worldwide Technological Civilization. After World War II modern technology established a worldwide technological civilization. Modern inventions had of course been penetrating the non-Western world steadily since

1900: bicycle, automobile, truck, electric lights, telephone, phonograph, movie and radio, and so on. In most areas, these remained culturally surface phenomena until the 1940's. The Bedouin on the Arabian Desert took to carrying a battery radio on the camel; but he used it mainly to receive the Muezzin's call to evening prayer direct from Mecca. World War II brought modern technology in its most advanced forms directly to the most remote corners of the earth. The airplane became as familiar as the camel had been. All armies required modern technology to provide the sinews of war and the instruments of warfare. And all used non-Western people either as soldiers in technological war or as workers on modern machinery to provide war material. This made everyone in the world aware of the awful power of modern nuclear technology.

This, however, might not have had a revolutionary impact upon older, non-Western, non-technological societies but for the promise of "scientific management" to make possible systematic economic development. The new-found power to create productivity through the systematic effort we now call "industrialization" has raised what President John F. Kennedy called "the rising tide of human expectations," the hope that technology can banish the age-old curse of disease and early death, of grinding poverty, and ceaseless toil. And whatever else this may require, it demands acceptance by society of a thoroughly technological civilization.

The shift of focus in the struggle between social ideologies shows this clearly. Before World War II free enterprise and Communism were generally measured throughout the world by their respective claims to have superior ability to create a free and just society. Since World War II the question is largely: which system is better at speeding economic development to a modern technological civilization? India offers another illustration. Until his death in 1948, Mahatma Gandhi opposed industrialization and sought a return to a pre-industrial technology, symbolized in the hand spinning wheel. His close comrade and disciple Jawaharlal Nehru (1889-1964) was forced, however, by public opinion to embrace "economic development," that is, forced-draft industrialization emphasizing the most modern technology, as soon as he became the first Prime Minister of independent India in 1947.

Even in the West, where it grew out of the indigenous culture, technology has in the 20th century raised fundamental problems for society and has challenged—if not overthrown—deeply rooted social and political institutions. Wherever technology moves it has an impact on the position of women in society; on work and the worker; on education and social mobility; and on warfare. Since this is the case, in the non-Western societies modern technology demands a radical break with social and cultural tradition; and it produces a fundamental crisis in society. How the non-Western world will meet this crisis will, in large measure, determine what man's history will be in the latter 20th century—even, perhaps, whether there will be any more human history. But unless the outcome is the disappearance of man from this planet, our civilization will remain irrevocably a common technological civilization.

MAN MOVES INTO A MAN-MADE ENVIRONMENT

When, by 1965 the number living on the land and making their living off it had dwindled to one out of every twenty, man had become a city-dweller. At the same time, the man in the city increasingly works with his mind, removed from materials. Man in the 20th century has thus moved from an environment that was essentially still nature to an environment, the large city and knowledge work, that is increasingly man-made. The agent of this change has, of course, been technology.

Technology, as has been said before, underlies the shift from manual to mental work. It underlies the tremendous increase in the productivity of agriculture which, in technologically developed countries like the United States or those of Western Europe, has made one farmer capable of producing, on less land, about fifteen times as much as his ancestor did in 1800 and almost ten times as much as his ancestors in 1900. It therefore enabled man to tear himself away from his roots in the land to become a city-dweller.

Indeed, urbanization has come to be considered the index of economic and social development. In the United States and in the most highly industrialized countries of Western Europe up to three quarters of the population now live in large cities and their suburbs. A country like the Soviet Union, that still requires half its people to work on the land to be adequately fed, is, no matter how well developed industrially, an "underdeveloped country."

The big city is, however, not only the center of modern technology; it is also one of its creations. The shift from animal to mechanical power, and especially to electrical energy (which needs no pasture lands), made possible the concentration of large productive facilities in one area. Modern materials and construction methods make it possible to house, move, and supply a large population in a small area. Perhaps the most important prerequisite of the large modern city, however, is modern communications, the nerve center of the city and the major reason for its existence. The change in the type of work a technological society requires is another reason for the rapid growth of the giant metropolis. A modern society requires that an almost infinite number of specialists in diverse fields of knowledge be easy to find, easily accessible, and quickly and economically available for new and changing work. Businesses or government offices move to the city, where they can find the lawyers, accountants, advertising men, artists, engineers, doctors, scientists, and other trained personnel they need. Such knowledgeable people, in turn, move to the big city to have easy access to their potential employers and clients.

Only sixty years ago, men depended on nature and were primarily threatened by natural catastrophes, storms, floods or earthquakes. Men today depend on technology, and our major threats are technological breakdowns. The largest cities in the world would become uninhabitable in forty-eight hours were the water supply or the sewage systems to give out. Men, now city-dwellers, have become increasingly dependent upon technology, and our habitat is no longer a natural ecology of wind and weather, soil and forest, but a man-made ecology. Nature is no longer an immediate experience; New York City children go to the Bronx Zoo to see a cow. And whereas sixty years ago a rare treat for most Americans was a trip to the nearest market town, today most people in the technologically advanced countries attempt to "get back to nature" for a vacation.

MODERN TECHNOLOGY AND THE HUMAN HORIZON

Old wisdom—old long before the Greeks—held that a community was limited to the area through which news could easily travel from sunrise to sunset. This gave a "community" a diameter of some fifty miles or so. Though each empire—Persian, Roman, Chinese, and Incan—tried hard to extend this distance by building elaborate roads and organizing special speedy courier services, the limits on man's horizon throughout most of the 19th century remained unchanged and confined to how far one man could travel by foot or on horseback in one day.

By 1900 there were already significant changes. The railroad had extended the limit of one day's travel to 700 miles or more—the distance from New York to Chicago or from Paris to Berlin. And, for the first time, news and information were made independent of the human carrier through the telegraph, which carried them everywhere practically instantaneously. It is no accident that a very popular book of technological fiction to this day is Jules Verne's *Around the World in Eighty Days*. For the victory of technology over distance is, perhaps, the most significant of all the gifts modern technology has brought man.

Today the whole earth has become a local community if measured by the old yardstick of one day's travel. The commercial jet plane can reach, in less than twenty-four hours, practically any airport on earth. And unlike any earlier age, the common man can and does move around and is no longer rooted to the small valley of his birth. The motor vehicle has given almost everyone the power of mobility, and with physical ability to move around comes a new mental outlook and a new social mobility. The technological revolution on the American farm began in earnest when the farmer acquired wheels; he immediately became mobile, too, in his mental habits and accessible to new ideas and techniques. The beginning of the Negro drive for civil rights in the American South came with the used car. Behind the wheel of a Model

T a Negro was as powerful as any white man, and his equal. Similarly, the Indian worker on the Peruvian sugar plantation who has learned to drive a truck will never again be fully subservient to the white manager. He has tasted the new power of mobility, a greater power than the mightiest kings of yesterday could imagine. It is no accident that young people everywhere dream of a car of their own; four-wheeled mobility is a true symbol of freedom from the restraints of traditional authority.

News, data, information, and pictures have become even more mobile than people. They travel in "real time," that is, they arrive at virtually the same time as they happen. They have, moreover, become universally accessible. The radio brings to anyone in possssion of a cheap and simple receiving set news in his own language from any of the world's major capitals. Television and movies present the world everywhere as immediate experience. And beyond the earth itself the horizon of man has, within the last two decades, extended out into stellar space. It is not just a bigger world, therefore, into which 20th-century technology has moved the human being; it is a different world.

TECHNOLOGY AND MAN

In this different world technology itself is seen differently; we are aware of it as a major element in our lives, indeed, in human life throughout history. We are becoming aware that the major questions regarding technology are not technical but human questions, and are coming to understand that a knowledge of the history and evolution of technology is essential to an understanding of human history. Furthermore, we are rapidly learning that we must understand the history, the development, and the dynamics of technology in order to master our contemporary technological civilization, and that unless we do so, we will have to submit to technology as our master.

The naive optimism of 1900 which expected technology somehow to create paradise on earth would be shared by few people today. Most would also ask: What does technology do *to* man as well as for him? For it is only too obvious that technology brings problems, disturbances, and dangers as well as benefits. First, economic development based on technology carries the promise of abolishing want over large parts of the earth. But there is also the danger of total war leading to total destruction; and the only way we now know to control this danger is by maintaining in peacetime a higher level of armaments in all major industrial countries than any nation has ever maintained. This hardly seems a fitting answer to the problem, let alone a permanent one. Also, modern public-health technology—insecticides above all—has everywhere greatly increased man's lifespan. But since birth rates in the underdeveloped countries remain at their former high level while the death rates have declined, the world's poor nations are threatened by a "population explosion" which not only eats up all the fruits of economic development but threatens world famine and new pestilence. In government, modern technology and the modern economy founded on it have outmoded the national state as a viable unit. Even Great Britain, with fifty million inhabitants, has been proven in recent decades to have too small a productive base and market for independent economic survival and success. Nationalism is still the most potent political force, as developments in the new nations of Asia and Africa clearly show; yet the revolution in transportation and communication has made national borders an anachronism, respected by neither airplanes nor electronic waves.

The metropolis has become the habitat of modern man. Yet paradoxically we do not know how to make it habitable. We have no effective political institutions to govern it. Urban decay and traffic jams, overcrowding and urban crime, juvenile delinquency and loneliness are endemic in all modern great cities. No one looking at any of the world's big cities would maintain that they offer an aesthetically satisfying environment. The divorce from direct contact with nature in work with soil and materials has permitted us to live much better; yet technological change itself seems to have speeded up so much as to deprive us of the psychological and cultural bearings we need.

The critics of technology and dissenters from technological optimism in 1900 were lonely voices. Disenchantment with technology did not set in until after World War I and the coming of the Great Depression. The new note was first fully struck in the novel *Brave New World* by the English writer Aldous Huxley (1894-1964), published in 1932, at the very bottom of the Depression. In this book Huxley portrayed the society of the near future as one in which technology had become the master and man, its abject slave, was kept in bodily comfort without knowledge of want or pain but also without freedom, beauty, or creativity, indeed, without a personal existence. Five years later the most popular actor of the period, the great Charlie Chaplin (1889-   ), drove home the same idea in his movie "Modern Times," which depicted the common man as the hapless and helpless victim of a dehumanized technology. These two artists have set the tone: only by renouncing modern civilization altogether can man survive as man. This theme has since been struck with increasing frequency, and certainly with increasing loudness. The pessimists of today, however, suffer from a bad case of romantic delusion; the "happier society of the pre-industrial past" they invoke never existed. In the late 13th century, Genghis Khan and his Mongols, whose raids covered an area from China to Central Europe, killed as many people—and a much larger proportion of a much smaller population—as two 20th-century world wars and Hitler put together, yet their technology was the bow and arrow.

However much justice there may be in Huxley's and Charlie Chaplin's thesis, it is sterile. The repudiation of technology they advocate is clearly not the answer. The only positive alternative to destruction by technology is to make technology work as our servant. In the final analysis this surely means mastery by man over himself, for if anyone is to blame, it is not the tool but the human maker and user. "It is a poor carpenter who blames his tools," says an old proverb. It was naive of the 19th-century optimist to expect paradise from tools and it is equally naive of the 20th-century pessimists to make the new tools the scapegoat for such old shortcomings as man's blindness, cruelty, immaturity, greed, and sinful pride.

It is also true that "better tools" demand a better, more highly skilled, and more careful "carpenter." As its ultimate impact on man and his society, 20th-century technology, by its very mastery of nature, may thus have brought man face to face again with his oldest and greatest challenge: himself.

Part **II**
Rationalization and its Consequences

4 / The Rationalization of Production
JOHN B. RAE

Already in this volume, mass production has been listed among the major technological trends of the 20th century. From an American point of view this has special significance because mass production is a most distinctive American contribution to modern technology. In no other field of technology did the United States owe so little to Europe, even though, as we shall see, some of the basic ideas were foreshadowed in European experiments with techniques of production.

Yet even among Americans the real nature of mass production is widely misunderstood. It is commonly equated with cheap production, that is, with the manufacture of vast amounts of goods of inferior quality. Nothing could be farther from the truth. Mass production is a technique for producing large quantities of goods at a low unit cost. The achievement of this objective requires an elaborate and systematic organization of the manufacturing process, designed to eliminate waste effort and motion and to maintain a smooth and efficient flow of materials through the plant. It must be a mechanized process in order to attain the requisite volume of output. Furthermore, mass production calls for highly specialized machines and tools and a minute division of labor, and since large numbers of units are being worked on, standardization and interchangeability are indispensable.

The fundamentals of mass production have been defined as precision, standardization, interchangeability, synchronization, and continuity—to which must be added the qualification that all these elements must be present and functioning in combination in order to achieve true mass production. In addition, constant accurate cost accounting and supervision of standards of quality are also implied in this definition; they are essential to the economic success of the system. To achieve low cost at the end of the process, a heavy investment in plant, machinery, and tools must be made at the beginning. The technique cannot be economically employed under any and all conditions; the investment

37

is justified only if a mass market exists. In other words, mass production and mass consumption are completely interdependent; one cannot exist without the other, although one may create the other. Finally, it is seldom appreciated that the commodities turned out by this process are not only cheaper than what could be made by handicraft methods; they ordinarily embody a degree of precision and accuracy unattainable by human hand and eye, no matter how skillful or highly trained.

EARLY EXPERIMENTS

The advantages of a rational organization of production were always perfectly obvious to any individual concerned with the manufacture and sale of commodities, and it is possible to go through history and pick out innumerable examples of experiments which could be claimed as foreshadowing modern mass production. For our purposes it is sufficient to point out that experimentation in this direction goes back more than 500 years, with clear evidence of understanding of the potentialities of the division of labor (specialization), the orderly flow of materials, and even of interchangeability. We have, for example, this account of the fitting out of Venetian galleys in the 15th century:

And as one enters the gate there is a great street on either hand, and one side are windows opening out of the houses of the Arsenal, and the same on the other side, and out came a galley towed by a boat, and from the windows they handed out to them, from one the cordage, from another the bread, from another the arms, and from another the balistas and mortars, and so from all sides everything which was required, and when the galley had reached the end of the street all the men required were on board, together with the complement of oars, and she was equipped from end to end. In this manner there came out ten galleys, fully armed, between the hours of three and nine.

The analogy to the modern automobile assembly line, with the finished cars being driven off at the end, is self-evident.

In the same era Johannes Gutenberg was making his name as the inventor of printing. There has since been a good deal of scholarly dispute as to what Gutenberg actually invented, since it was not the press, or type, or paper, all these having existed for centuries previously. The consensus works out that Gutenberg's claim lies in his technique of casting the type so that it was not only movable but interchangeable, so that any letter from a given font would fit into place as easily as any other.

The concept of flow of materials reappears in iron manufacturing. The process can be observed in the recently reconstructed Hammersmith Ironworks in Saugus, Massachusetts, which, when built in the mid-17th century, represented the most advanced technology of the time. There was a linear progression through the works, from blast furnace to forge to rolling and slitting mills, ending at the dock where the finished iron products were loaded for shipment.

With the acceleration of industrialization in the 18th century came more definite anticipations of mass production. Indeed, at the beginning of the century a Swedish engineer named Christopher Polhem displayed remarkable insight. He is quoted as saying:

Gain may be secured in all things but most especially in industrial installations by saving labor so that the products need not be so costly, for nothing increases demand so much as low prices; therefore, there is great need of machines and appliances which will, in one way or another, diminish the amount or intensity of heavy manual work. This result can be most adequately achieved by the substitution of water power for handwork with gains of 100 or even 1,000 per cent in relative costs.

About 1700 Polhem established a factory in Sweden for making iron goods in accordance with his ideas. It was successful enough, but Polhem was just a little too far ahead of his time. Had he possessed the machine tools that were developed within a half-century after his death (1751), he might well have become the father of mass production instead of being left in an undeserved obscurity.

Another forgotten man appeared at the end of the 18th century. About all we know of him is that his name was Blanc; that he was a superintendent in the French royal arsenals; and that by 1785 he had worked out in every respect the technique, later introduced into the United States, of making muskets by machine manufacture of interchangeable parts. When Thomas Jefferson was Minister to France he became interested in Blanc's work and tried to persuade him to move to the United States. It is probable, although there is no direct evidence, that Jefferson's reports gave Eli Whitney and his contemporaries the basic ideas they later developed. Blanc succeeded in persuading the French government to equip an arsenal for production by his methods. It was maintained by the revolutionary governments until 1797, when pressure from the gunsmiths forced its closing.

Meanwhile, in Great Britain the Industrial Revolution was opening new fields for quantity manufacturing and thereby drawing some attention to the organization of production. Richard Arkwright, for example, owes his place in history far less to his technical skill (his claim to the invention of the water frame is very dubious) than to his organization of factory operations on the basis of rigid scheduling and discipline. One enterprise in particular, however, may be identified as containing some of the components of genuine mass production. This was a factory established by three fascinating individuals to make pulley blocks for the Royal Navy. The three were: Samuel Bentham, a naval inspector and brother of Jeremy Bentham, the founder of utilitarian philosophy; Marc Isambard Brunel, a brilliant French refugee engineer; and Henry Maudslay, the great tool-maker whose achievements are discussed in the first volume of this work. Since a ship of the line required some 1400 blocks, the incentive to quantity production was strong. Maudslay designed and built 44 machines, all powered by a single thirty-two-horsepower steam engine, operating in a planned sequence so that hand work was eliminated in the making of the blocks and sheaves. The factory employed ten unskilled men whose output was estimated as equal to that of 110 skilled craftsmen. During its peak year in 1808, the plant turned out over 130,000 blocks. It was a remarkable achievement, but two qualifications should be made: first, working with wood was easier than working with metal; and second, some precision could be sacrificed because the pulley blocks did not require exactly identical dimensions. However, with the end of the Napoleonic Wars the large-scale market for pulley blocks disappeared, and the three entrepreneurs turned their talents in other directions.

THE AMERICAN PRELUDE

These early European gestures in the direction of rationalized large-scale production were isolated phenomena which eventually disappeared with little perceptible after-effects. It was left for the United States to continue the development which would reach fruition finally in the 20th century. Various reasons can be offered, all partially valid, none complete in itself, to explain the success of the system in the United States. First, the United States was a fast-growing country, with more work to be done than there were people available to do it, so that there was an incentive to devise methods and techniques to substitute for human labor. Skilled labor was more expensive in the United States than in Europe, so that there was a marked advantage in using mechanical processes. And there were no strongly entrenched crafts or long-standing traditions to inhibit innovation.

In point of time, the first outstanding American contribution came from the versatile genius Oliver Evans, who in 1787 built a grist mill near Philadelphia. It was history's first recorded application of a mechanized continuous-flow process: power was supplied by water wheels; and grain was fed in at one end and passed by a system of conveyors and chutes through the various stages of milling and refining, emerging as finished flour at the other end. Evans's system was widely imitated in American milling.

American pioneering in standardization and interchangeability is perhaps better known. Credit for introducing this technique is usually given to Eli Whitney, but Captain John N. Hall probably anticipated Whitney's achievement in the machines and methods he employed at the United States Arsenal at Harpers Ferry. Whitney seems to have turned to machine fabrication of parts for his muskets chiefly to cut costs by using unskilled labor, admittedly one of the advantages of the system. Yet another to use the system was his Connecticut neighbor Simeon North, who made pistols. North stated his purpose thus: "The component parts of the pistols are to correspond so exactly that any limb

Fig. 4-1. Interior view of the Colt Company's armory shop, 1880, showing lines of machine tools. (C. H. Fitch, "Interchangeable Mechanism," *United States Census: Report on the Manufacturers of the United States.* Tenth Census, 1880, II, Washington, D. C., 1883)

or part of one pistol may be fitted to any pistol of the twenty thousand" he had contracted to make for the federal government.

Standardization and interchangeability first appeared in the manufacture of firearms because it was a commodity for which there was a large market. The technique was subsequently applied to the making of clocks by Eli Terry and Chauncey Jerome. They, like Whitney, North, and Samuel P. Colt, worked in Connecticut, but their system spread rapidly from the Nutmeg State. By the middle of the 19th century the mechanical fabrication of standard parts was referred to in the Western world as "the American system of manufacture."

Further developments followed. The meat-packing industry employed an overhead conveyor to carry carcasses through the plant—a procedure Henry Ford later credited with giving him the general idea of the moving assembly line. The work of Frederick W. Taylor and others on Scientific Management

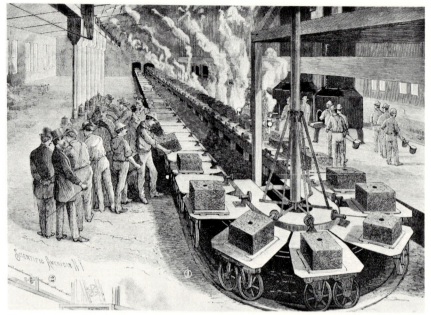

Fig. 4-2. The Westinghouse foundry in Pittsburgh, 1890. (*The Bettman Archive*)

stimulated further interest in the systematic organization of production. The concept of the mass market (Volume I, Chapter 42) stimulated the imagination of American businessmen. It was more than a dream, however; by the close of the 19th century, the mass market was a reality made possible by the high American standard of living. Even after a century of growth this system of production remained peculiarly American. In the 1890's a group of German visitors reported admiringly on a conveyor they observed in the Westinghouse foundry in Pittsburgh. What they saw was simply an endless chain of tables which carried materials between the moulding room and the foundry—a type of mechanical operation that was certainly no novelty in American industrial processes. Yet it is significant that as late as the 1890's Europeans could still consider it worthy of special notice.

THE AUTOMOBILE REVOLUTION

If this account has taken long to reach the 20th century, it is with deliberate intent, for it is important to realize that rationalized mass production did not come about as the result of a single stroke of inspiration. Rather, it was created by many minds over a long span of years, and by an assortment of step-by-step advances in a variety of industrial fields. This in no way detracts from the achievement of those who finally reached the goal: great discoveries frequently consist in seeing how to combine separate existing items of knowledge.

The revolution in production techniques took place in the American automobile industry. Later in this volume we will deal with the development of the motor vehicle as a means of transportation; however, for present purposes it is sufficient to state that the gasoline automobile, with which we are concerned, was invented in Europe in the 1880's and "re-invented" in the United States a decade later. When it first appeared it was either greeted with derision ("Get a horse") or dismissed as a plaything for the rich, with no significant commercial implications.

The idea that the horseless carriage might be made an item of mass consumption and use was clearly and unmistakably American. As is usual with great novel ideas, the evidence is vague as to when it originated and with whom. Henry Ford claims to have envisioned a "car for the great multitude" when he began his automotive experiments in the 1890's. Ford's recollections with regard to his own achievements were notoriously unreliable, but in this case there is nothing in the record to contradict him. The first attempt to apply the concept is another matter; and here the glory definitely belongs to Ransom E. Olds and the one-cylinder, curved-dash buggy which became the "Merry Oldsmobile." Olds began to build these in Detroit in 1901 and in 1904 reached the then phenomenal output of 5000 cars a year, at which point a dispute between Olds and his partners terminated the operation. In the following decades, other men were to add to and refine the basic techniques.

The difficulty was not in having the idea of the mass-produced car but in executing it. Even at that time an automobile was a complicated mechanism, far more difficult to produce in quantity and at low cost than, let us say, railroad rails or ready-to-wear clothing. Making identical rails is a comparatively simple technique, and ready-to-wear clothing need only be approximately the right size. But a motor vehicle is assembled from hundreds of parts and components, and for mass production all of them must fit exactly on whatever vehicle they are installed. Moreover, a large proportion of these parts have always been fabricated by firms independent of the companies that assemble the cars.

American automobile manufacturers were thus fortunate in being able to operate in an industrial system where standardization and interchangeability were already well established and understood, as was the technique of assembling the final product from parts fabricated by others. For example, William C. Durant, the founder of General Motors, was a successful carriage manufacturer before he turned to automobiles; his Durant-Dort Carriage Company of Flint, Michigan, which was one of the country's largest producers of horse-drawn vehicles (Studebaker was the largest), had something like a dozen separate factories in Flint making parts for its carriages, including one plant devoted exclusively to the manufacture of whip sockets.

The automobile men elaborated on and improved these techniques, using them, significantly, for high-quality as well as low-priced cars. The personification of precision and interchangeability in the formative period of the automobile industry is not Henry Ford but Henry M. Leland, founder of the Cadillac Motor Car Company. Alfred P. Sloan related how, when he was a young man just starting the Hyatt Roller Bearing Company, he had to go to Detroit to investigate a complaint from Leland. Leland showed him a pile of rejected bearings, demonstrated by micrometer measurement where they varied from specifications, and said, "Young man, Cadillacs are made to run, not just to sell. You must grind your bearings. Even though you make thousands, the first and last should be precisely alike." This, reports Sloan, gave him an insight into what mass production really meant. What Leland's rigorous standards of accuracy produced in practice was shown in 1908. The British distributor for Cadillac had three of his cars taken apart at the Royal Automobile Club's test track, the parts piled up and scrambled, and then 90 of them chosen at random by club officials to be replaced from stock. Mechanics then reassembled the three Cadillacs, which immediately performed perfectly in a 500-mile test run —a display that astonished the British.

The ability of American industry to reach this degree of accuracy in the use of interchangeable parts was prerequisite to the attainment of mass production, but more needed to be done in order to find a method which would combine quantity output and low cost in building automobiles. Olds organized his labor force into work gangs, each of whose members had a specific task to perform, and he tried to control the flow of materials so as to eliminate delays. He was on the right track; had production of the Oldsmobile buggy continued he might well have surpassed Henry Ford. On the other hand, Olds and his numerous imitators were concentrating on making vehicles which could be produced cheaply but which were basically too small and flimsy to satisfy the needs of the potential buying public.

This was an error which Henry Ford avoided. In fact, his greatest single contribution to mass production technology was his realization that the development of the "car for the great multitude" was a two-step process: first, to design a suitable car, meaning durable, mechanically simple, and inexpensive to operate and maintain; second, to find a means of building such a car in quantity and at low cost. The first was achieved when the Ford Motor Company put the famous Model T—the "Tin Lizzie" or "Flivver"—on the market in 1908. The second step took longer. Ford believed that he could reach the mass market if the selling price of his car did not exceed $600; it reached this figure in 1912 but then production could not keep pace with demand. Ford himself knew what should be done; the question was how to do it. As early

Fig. 4-3. A Model T Ford, 1908. (Courtesy of *Automobile Manufacturers Association*)

as 1903, the year the Ford Motor Company was founded, he told John W. Anderson, one of his partners, "The way to make automobiles is to make one automobile like another automobile, to make them all alike, to make them come from the factory just alike—just like one pin is like another pin when it comes from a pin factory." Since Ford had a number of talented assistants working on the production problem with him, various individuals have claimed the honor, or had it claimed for them, of making the key proposal of a moving assembly line. The evidence points to Clarence Avery, who had been Edsel Ford's manual training teacher in high school, as the man who made the initial suggestion, but a more likely explanation is offered by Charles E. Sorensen: "The essential tooling and the final assembly line resulted from an organization which was continually experimenting and improving to get better production."

At any rate, early in 1913 the Ford Motor Company installed experimentally a moving assembly line for magnetos. Previously, each magneto was assembled entirely by one man, and the maximum performance was one magneto every 18 minutes. The assembly line had 29 men, each performing a single operation, with the immediate result that each magneto was assembled in 13 minutes. Subsequent improvements cut this time to five minutes. This success was convincing, and in less than a year the system was extended to the assembly of the entire car. To begin with, a chassis was pulled down a line 250 feet long with rope and windlass while tests were made on assembly techniques. When the mechanized assembly line was installed, using an endless chain drive, it was

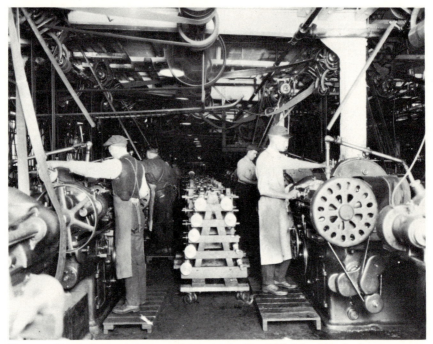

Fig. 4-4. Crankshaft grinding machines in the Ford Highland Park plant. (Courtesy of *Automobile Manufacturers Association*)

possible to complete a chassis in an hour and 33 minutes as against twelve and a half hours under the system of stationary assembly. Similarly, assembly time of engines was cut from twelve hours to six.

None of this process was as easy as it may sound. There had to be exhaustive experimentation to determine the proper heights and speeds of the assembly lines and the most efficient subdivision and mechanization of the various assembly operations. Since the times needed to assemble engine, chassis, and components all varied, the several assembly processes had to be co-ordinated and synchronized. The influence of current ideas on Scientific Management seems apparent in all this careful calculation, although Ford never acknowledged any indebtedness of this kind. At any rate, at the beginning of 1914 Model T's were being driven off the assembly line, and the Ford Motor Company was displaying to the world the first complete system of true mass production.

The results were phenomenal. According to the company's production reports, the output of Model T passenger cars in the United States rose from 170,000 in 1912 to over 300,000 in 1914, crossed the half-million mark a year later, and in 1923 and 1924 reached a peak of close to two million annually.

By that time, half the motor vehicles in the entire world were Model T Fords. Meanwhile prices dropped steadily, subject to occasional fluctuations, until an all-time low was reached in 1924, when a new Ford touring car could be bought for $290. These reductions in price were aided by supplementary features of the Ford system, conspicuously the establishment of branch assembly plants which permitted substantial lowering of transportation costs.

It is important to emphasize that the separate features of the assembly-line process—the conveyor, the specialization of labor, interchangeability—had all been used before and for the most part were well established in American industrial practice. What was achieved by combining all these features into a closely co-ordinated system turned out to be more complex than anyone could have anticipated. When production shot upward the parts suppliers, of necessity, had to keep pace, and this frequently meant converting to assembly-line methods. Moreover, for the automobile assembly lines to keep functioning efficiently there had to be an adequate and regular flow of parts. Since stockpiling in large quantities was wasteful inventory practice, it became increasingly necessary for the automobile manufacturer to supervise the flow of materials in considerable detail, frequently by acquiring the supplier firms. Henry Ford himself envisioned a completely integrated vertical trust in which every component of the Ford car would be produced within his own organization, with the whole so efficiently co-ordinated that no single item—from raw material to finished vehicle—would stop moving and require storage. It was an unattainable ideal—and subsequent experience showed that it was sometimes better to rely on independent suppliers—but the idea embodies the logic of wholly rationalized production.

Impressive as this achievement was, it was a beginning and not an end; and Henry Ford's failure to realize this later caused trouble for his company. The system as developed in 1914 and practised until the mid-1920's was elementary. It depended on a rigid uniformity in the product: a single chassis, no accessories, and identical fixtures and styling, all summed up in a remark attributed to Henry Ford, "The customer can have the car any color he wants as long as he wants it black." It was at this point that Ford contributed to his own defeat by failing to see that automotive technology had to advance beyond his great achievement. Of the fifteen million Model T's built by his company, the last five million—on a rough approximation—were obsolete even before they left the assembly line. Tin Lizzie should have been discarded about five years before she was actually discontinued in 1927.

The refinements of later years made it possible to control assemblies and sub-assemblies so as to permit the customer an almost infinite latitude of choice, not only in color, but in chassis, model, equipment, and styling. Moreover, while the Ford assembly systems of 1914 sent finished chassis rolling off the assembly line, the bodies were installed outside the plant. An observer in a modern automobile

Fig. 4-5. Ford body assembly, 1919. (Courtesy of *Automobile Manufacturers Association*)

plant will see body and chassis lines converge at a point where the body is dropped onto the chassis with split-second precision.

THE EXTENSION OF MASS PRODUCTION

Henry Ford's dramatic demonstration that mass production was both feasible and highly profitable had widespread repercussions. As might be expected, his system was promptly adopted by would-be competitors, although none was able to match his success until William S. Knudsen, himself a product of the Ford Motor Company, was put in charge of the Chevrolet Division of General Motors in 1922.

In the 1920's major changes also took place in industries that supplied components for motor vehicles. Two of these provide vivid examples of new production techniques that resulted from the insatiable automotive demand. Glass-making in the United States underwent a rapid mechanization after 1880, especially in the manufacture of bottles and lamp bulbs, but until 1920 the production of plate glass, the type required for automobiles, was still a somewhat laborious batch process. Faced with short supply and rising prices the Ford Motor Company turned its attention to glass and devised a method of pouring the glass in an endless strip onto a moving table, which carried it through the processes of rolling, grinding, and polishing. Within a few years this became the standard American technique for making plate glass. With steel, the demand for sheet steel caused by the general adoption of all-steel automobile bodies in the 1920's made it economically practical for the steel industry to adopt the continuous-strip mill, in which sheet steel is rolled in an endless strip.

The mass-production technique was also rapidly adopted for the commodities classified as durable consumers' goods—such items as refrigerators, washing machines, and sewing machines—that have in common with the automobile the properties of being somewhat complex mechanically and requiring precise and accurate assembly. It is significant that the Frigidaire, the first really successful electric refrigerator (the name almost became a generic term for all electric refrigerators), should have been made by General Motors, even though the acquisition of Frigidaire was a whim of William C. Durant's rather than a piece of deliberate policy-planning.

The spectacular achievements of American industry attracted attention elsewhere, along with some misinterpretation. During the 1920's and 1930's in Europe there was a movement to keep pace with America by adopting American production methods. The English term was "rationalization"; the Germans called the process "Fordismus." Throughout industrial Europe there were efforts to utilize American techniques of mechanization and the orderly organization of production; at the time, these efforts met with only qualified success despite the fact that European industry had ample technical skill to enable it to match American performances. The vital point that was overlooked was one that Henry Ford had grasped when he instituted the five-dollar day (that is, paying his workers a minimum wage of $5 per day) in 1914 with the completion of the assembly-line system: namely, that mass production presupposes mass consumption. If the former is to succeed, the latter must either exist or be capable of being created.

THE EXTRACTIVE INDUSTRIES

While the rationalization of production has been most pronounced in the manufacturing industries, especially those in which assembly is the culminating process, it has by no means been limited to this field. The components of rationalization—systematic control of the flow of materials and the use of machines to the exclusion of manual work—can be employed in any situation where the volume of output justifies the investment. A good example is provided in changes in mining techniques which occurred at the same time as the general adoption of mass production in the assembly industries.

Since petroleum technology is considered in detail elsewhere (Volume I, Chapter 41) it will be omitted here, except to observe that the petroleum industry must be rated as one of the first to employ continuous flow and fully automatic controls on a large scale in its production facilities. The mining of metallic ores offers an example of the growth of a rationalized mechanical technique that is less well known than the assembly line but which has some features in common with it. The system introduced into mining was, like its assembly-line counterpart, a combination of separate technologies into an organic whole.

Mining has been in the anomalous situation of being one of the earliest of all industrial operations to use machine power (see Volume I, Chapter 21), while at the same time it remained basically dependent upon a craft technique. In other words, commercially successful mining for centuries rested, in the last analysis, on the skill and experience of the individual miner, and on his ability to select and extract with a minimum of waste matter ores of a quality suitable for economic utilization. The technical advances of the 19th century, such as pneumatic drills and dynamite, were seen as aids to the individual miner rather than as the beginning of mechanization of the process.

To some extent the mining industry was forced into rationalization by the depletion of high-grade ore deposits. It became necessary to develop methods of concentrating or "beneficiating" low-grade ores, but after this was accomplished, it was no longer essential to be as highly selective in the extraction of the ores. It therefore became practical and profitable to employ mass techniques such as open-pit or strip mining with power excavators, or mechanical devices for breaking, loading, and conveying ores underground.

The power excavator offers an excellent illustration of an independently evolved technology which contributed to the rationalization of mining. The steam shovel was introduced by William Smith Otis in 1835 for use in the building of canals and railroads. It saw no important use in mining until the 1890's, when steam shovels were employed on the Mesabi Range, where the thin topsoil and the concentrated deposits of high-grade iron ore made power excavation practical. These were the so-called "railroad" shovels, which had to operate on tracks and could swing in a very limited arc. More general open-pit mining had to wait for the appearance of the full revolving shovel in 1915 and the mounting of excavators on caterpillar tracks in the early 1920's. During the same period diesel-powered and electric shovels came along to offer greater efficiency than steam.

Coal mining clung to its traditional techniques somewhat longer. Strip mining for coal was still something of a rarity in the 1930's, but in the ensuing years the competition of alternative fuels and sources of energy pushed the extraction of coal in the same direction as that of metallic ores. Thus mining processes came to follow an ordered and mechanized sequence, the first step being the establishment of geological data to determine what techniques of extraction and processing can be most effectively used. Then comes the extraction itself, increasingly a job for operators of machines rather than for skilled miners. Third is the processing of the product, also highly mechanized. This is the stage at which the desired levels of quality are obtained.

CONCLUSION

The social and economic consequences of the rationalization of production will be described in the chapters that follow. In order to understand them, however, it is necessary to keep in mind the real nature of 20th-century mass production. It began as much more than a technique for achieving quantity output of low-priced goods, and above all it did not sacrifice quality to quantity. It is unfortunate that the first dramatic example of the process, the Model T Ford, should have lent itself to a considerable amount of low-grade humor which distorted appreciation of the technological revolution behind the Tin Lizzie.

The features of mass production have been enumerated previously as precision, standardization, interchangeability, synchronization, and continuity. Two others should be added. One is complete mechanization, the elimination of all manual work. The machine can reach levels of accuracy unattainable by manual skill, and thus, automatic controls and automation are the logical consequences of mass production. The other component is control. It is the essence of a rational system, whether philosophical or industrial, that there should be no loose ends or imperfections. Mass production will function as it should only when the same rigorous standards are applied at every stage of the process. It is therefore necessary to have an elaborate mechanism of inspection and testing. The Ford Motor Company was among the first large industrial organizations to gauge and test by means of Johannson blocks (steel blocks machined to a very fine tolerance, developed by a Swedish machinist in the late 19th century). This and other techniques for controlling quality are an integral feature of mass production. Control is, interestingly, one of the variable costs in the process that is likely to rise rather than fall with an increase in the scale of production, since with more units to be produced and more components to be assembled, the more elaborate must be the inspection and supervision. The investment is too heavy to risk losses that would be incurred by a flaw at any one point.

Mass production, rationalized production, is an American export. One of the greatest tributes to its effectiveness has been the eagerness of others to copy it. In spite of the disappointing results of "Fordismus" during the 1920's and 1930's, mass-production methods were enthusiastically adopted in industrial societies after World War II and contributed greatly to the astonishing economic recovery of Europe and Japan. Technology, however, does not stand still. By that time the rationalization of production was moving rapidly toward automatic controls and automation. This story will be told in later chapters.

5 / The Rationalization of Management
ROBERT H. GUEST

Few men in the history of American technology have had greater impact on the organization of work than Frederick W. Taylor (1856-1915), the father of Scientific Management. What Eli Whitney and others did to lay the ground-work of mass production in the 1800's, later perfected in the continuous-flow technology of Henry Ford in the 20th century, Frederick Taylor applied to the motions of men at work. Today's large fraternity of industrial engineers, systems and methods experts, work-standards specialists, and a whole host of management experts in a very real sense owe their jobs and allegiance to Taylor. While many would credit America's great industrial leap forward in the 20th century in large measure to the work of this man, others—especially in the trade union movement—would condemn Taylor for "making man just another machine."

THE RISE OF TAYLORISM

In the closing decades of the 19th century Taylor became concerned with vast inefficiencies he found in the burgeoning industries of the period. In many industrial occupations the need for craft skills was disappearing. Basic industries that were formerly isolated and small-scale grew in size and complexity. In steel, for example, there were large concentrations of production facilities operated by unskilled and semi-skilled manpower in the Bessemers, open hearths, rolling mills, and in the fabricating segments of the industry. The technical processes determined the character of the jobs, the pace at which men worked, and the degree of control workers could exercise over their jobs. The work itself was becoming hardly more than the use of muscle power to feed the furnaces and operate the machines. Taylor watched at close range how the workers performed and became convinced that most were working at a low degree of efficiency.

As a disciplined and methodical thinker well versed in engineering logic, Taylor, in effect, asked the simple question, "Why can we not apply the same principles of efficiency to the hand and muscle of man that we apply to the design of machines?" In one of his first experiments in the steel industry late in the 1890's, he tackled the case of a hardworking but unskilled pig-iron handler. Taylor's own words show vividly his own thinking as he described the incident later.

"Now, Schmidt, you are a first-class pig-iron handler and know your business well. You have been handling at a rate of 12½ tons per day. I have given considerable study to handling pig iron, and feel sure that you could do a much larger day's work than you have been doing. Now don't you think that if you really tried you could handle 47 tons of pig iron per day, instead of 12½ tons?"

What do you think Schmidt's answer would be to this?

Schmidt started to work, and all day long, and at regular intervals, was told by the men who stood over him with a watch, "Now pick up a pig and walk. Now sit down and rest. Now walk—now rest," etc. He worked when he was told to work, and rested when he was told to rest, and at half past five in the afternoon had his 47½ tons loaded on the car. And he practically never failed to work at this pace and do the task that was set him during the three years he was at Bethlehem; and throughout this time he averaged a little more than $1.85 per day, which was the ruling rate of wages at that time in Bethlehem. That is, he received 60 per cent higher wages than were paid to other men who were not working on task work. One man after another was picked out and trained to handle pig iron at the rate of 47½ tons per day until all of the pig iron was handled at this rate, and the men were receiving 60 per cent more wages than other workmen around them.

In this example one can see the raw data from a single experiment that were to become the rudiments of the great Scientific Management movement. Taylor had observed and timed all of Schmidt's movements to determine which motions were necessary to perform the tasks and which were not. By instructing the worker in the precise motions required, with adequate time for rest, the operation could be performed more efficiently in a machine-like manner. Taylor proved here, and in many applications that followed, that it was possible to manipulate human activity and to control it by logical procedures in much the same way that physical objects could be measured and controlled.

In deciding to make work "scientific," Taylor had been influenced not only by the tendency of workers to avoid hard work, but also by the current practices of trying to force men to work. As a plant supervisor himself, Taylor had become dissatisfied with the usual methods of threatening workers with discharge or with other types of persuasion. And until he attempted the experiment described above he had been frustrated by the seeming ability of groups of workers to "peg" the pace at which they worked. Contrary to what critics have since said about Taylor, he placed the blame not on the worker as a person, but rather on the procedures that were expected of him in performing the task. Once the proper procedures were established, it would be easy to perform the work, Taylor thought. He also felt that the rate at which work ought to be done could be determined scientifically.

The hallmarks of the Taylor method were job analysis and time study. Job analysis depended upon one's being able to break down a series of operations into elements made up of simple constituent motions. The elements of the operation would be analyzed to determine which were superfluous and which were essential for the job. These elements could then be arranged, and rearranged, so long as the sum total added up to the total operation for the worker. In the total complex of a worker's operation, Taylor discovered that much time was wasted by improper tools and equipment. In mining operations, for example, if a worker had to take time to sharpen his cutting tool, this delay constituted "down time" which was a waste. Taylor thus decided that such operations were more properly jobs for someone else. Careful examination showed many other elements of the job that could be taken out and delegated elsewhere. In short, Taylor was applying at the immediate job level the same principle of division of labor that had been applied to the factory or industry as a whole.

The other ingredient of Taylor's system was time study. Once the job had been broken down into its constituent parts and extraneous motions eliminated, the remaining operations could be timed. The timing was done by a stopwatch, a device which, in addition to serving its utilitarian function, later became to workers a symbol of suspicion and distrust. Taylor was able to take each element of the job, time it, and then calculate how much time was involved in the work cycle. In machining operations, for example, some of the elements he timed were functions of the machine tool itself, while others were physical motions of the operator's own functions. Thus, when the worker was merely supervising and adjusting the machine while it operated, the machine time was recorded. But when the operator was setting up the work and removing it, these elements were considered part of the handling time.

Taylor was realistic in his recognition that certain allowances had to be made for unanticipated problems, both in the machine and in the worker. Although Taylor claimed that these allowances themselves were subject to time and motion study, they were, in fact, usually arbitrary and based upon general experience. Moreover, individual differences between workers were not considered. When Taylor was questioned about who should be timed he gave different responses: "Select a good, fast man," or "Give me an average, steady man." Furthermore, when asked who was capable of making the time study, his usual reply was, "Give me a man with experience." He did insist that all of the technical aspects of work should be standardized and put at the highest level of efficiency before the stopwatch was applied. Taylor made simplistic assumptions with respect to the psychological motivations of the individual and his needs as a member of a human work group. Indeed, Taylor insisted on doing everything to exclude those factors that make up what we now regard as the total environment of a job. It should be emphasized, however, that some of Taylor's greatest contributions resulted from his insistence that technical operations themselves, apart from the human element, be standardized, synchronized, and operated efficiently.

THE WORKER ON THE ASSEMBLY LINE

The principal criticism of Taylor and the work rationalization concept is that it ignored the workers' feelings and motivations. Taylor himself vigorously denied this, believing that men would respond favorably to the obvious logic of its benefits. Taylor expected the worker to appreciate the elimination of wasteful and unproductive motions; to be happy to have tasks simplified so as not to have to make complicated decisions; and to welcome guidance in the "best way" of performing the task. The worker would be given the right tools to do the job, and the machines would be kept in proper adjustment. Furthermore, the worker would be paid fairly for his effort. Wage incentives could be established on a piecework basis to give extra compensation for extra effort. The worker, like any normal human being, would respond to man's natural desire to benefit himself economically—at least Taylor thought so.

One way to illustrate how some of Taylor's assumptions might be questioned is to look at the job which represents an extreme form of work rationalization: assembly-line operations, and more specifically, those in the automobile industry. As has been pointed out, "The extraordinary ingenuity that has gone into the construction of automobile assembly lines, their perfected synchronization, the 'all but human' or 'more than human' character of the machines, the miracle of a car rolling off the conveyor belt each minute under its own power— all this has caught and held the world's imagination. . . . On the other hand, the extreme subdivision of labor (the man who puts a nut on a bolt is the symbol) conjoined with the 'endlessly moving belt' has made the [automobile] assembly line the classic symbol of the subjection of man to the machine in our industrial age."

Utilizing the two basic principles of standardization and interchangeability, Henry Ford was able to work out and apply three additional "principles" of progressive manufacture in pioneering the automobile assembly line: (1) the orderly progression of the product through the shop in a series of planned operations so arranged that the right part always arrives at the right place at the right time; (2) the mechanical delivery of these parts to the operators and the mechanical delivery of the product from the operators, as they are assembled; and (3) a break-down of operations into their simple constituent motions.

These principles are purely mechanical. Extended to the human component of the total work-flow system, and when combined with the Taylor principle, they mean the following for the worker: (1) a mechanically controlled work pace; (2) repetition of simple motions; (3) minimum skill requirements; (4) predetermined operating procedures; (5) a small fraction of the total product worked on; and (6) superficial mental attention.

How does the man on the line react? Here is one worker's response. It is typical of hundreds which this observer and others have heard in the course of their research.

THE CASE OF AN AUTO WORKER

The worker is J. D., a graduate of a public vocational training school, thirty-seven years old, married, with two children. He makes good wages and is buying his own home. He is being interviewed at home. [Parts of interview reprinted from *Personnel*, with permission of American Management Association.]

"Some years back I heard that they were hiring people for the assembly plant. Must have been thousands of fellows lined up for the job. The word got around that they were paying real good money. It was a big outfit, too. No fly-by-night affair.

"Figured I'd get any job and then, with a little electrician experience I had in vocational school, I could work my way up to a good job. And the idea of making automobiles sounded like something. Lucky for me I got a job and was made a spot welder on the front cowling. There wasn't much to the job itself. Picked it up in about a week. I tried to get into the Maintenance Department as an electrician, but there was no opening, so I went back to the line—we call it the iron horse. They made me a welder again, and that's what I have been doing ever since."

The worker then went on to describe his job:

"My job is to weld the cowl to the metal underbody. I take a jig off the bench, put it in place and weld the parts together. The jig is all made up and the welds are made in set places along the metal. Exactly twenty-five spots. The line runs according to schedule. Takes me one minute and fifty-two seconds for each job. I walk along the line as it moves. Then I snap the jig off, walk back down the line, throw it on the bench, grab another just in time to start on the next car. The cars differ, but it's practically the same thing. Finish one—then have another one staring me in the face.

"I don't like to work on the line—no man likes to work on a moving line. You can't beat the machine. Sure, maybe I can keep it up for an hour, but it's rugged doing it eight hours a day, every day in the week all year long.

"During each day I get a chance for a breather ten minutes in the morning, then a half-hour for lunch, then a few minutes in the afternoon. When I'm working there is not much chance to get a breather. Sometimes the line breaks down. When it does we all yell 'Whoopee!' As long as the line keeps moving I've got to keep up with it. On a few jobs I know some fellows can work like hell up the line, then coast. Most jobs you can't do that. If I get ahead maybe ten seconds the next model has more welds to it, so it takes ten seconds extra. You hardly break even. You're always behind. When you get too far behind, you get in a hole—that's what we call it. All hell breaks loose. I get in the next guy's way. The foreman gets sore and they have to rush in a relief man to bail you out.

"It's easy for them time-study fellows to come down there with a stop watch and figure out just how much a man can do in a minute and fifty-two seconds. There are some things they can see and record with their stop watch. But they can't clock how a man feels from one day to the next. Those guys ought to work on the line for a few weeks and maybe they'll feel some things that they never pick up on the stop watch.

"I like a job where you feel like you're accomplishing something and doing it right. When everything's laid out for you and the parts are all alike, there's not much you feel you accomplish. The big thing is that steady push of the conveyor—a gigantic machine which I can't control.

"You know, it's hard to feel that you are doing a good quality job. There is that constant push at high speed. You may improve after you've done a thing over and over again, but you never reach a point where you can stand back and say, 'Boy, I done that one good. That's one car that got built right.' If I could do my best, I'd get some satisfaction out of working, but I can't do as good work as I know I can do.

"My job is all engineered out. The jigs and fixtures are all designed and set out according to specifications. There are a lot of little things you could tell them but they never ask you. You go by the bible. They have a suggestion system, but the fellows don't use it too much because they're scared that a new way to do it may do one of your buddies out of a job.

"There's only three guys close by—me and my partner and a couple of fellows up the line a bit. I talk to my partner quite a lot. We gripe about the job 90 per cent of the time. You don't have time for any real conversation. The guys get along okay—you know the old saying, 'Misery loves company.'

"My foreman's an all right guy. I see him once in a while outside, and he's 100 per cent. But in the shop he can't be. If I was a foreman nobody would like me either. As a foreman he has to push you all the time to get production out so that somebody above won't push him. But the average guy on the line has no one to push—you can't fight the line. The line pushes you. We sometimes kid about it and say we don't need no foreman. That line is the foreman. Some joke."

The worker then discussed the general working conditions in the plant—the lighting, ventilation, safety conditions, cafeteria facilities, and the plant hospital. He thought these conditions were all good, but then added:

"But you know it's a funny thing. These things are all good, but they don't make the job good. It's what you spend most of the time doing that counts.

"My chances for promotion aren't so hot. You see, almost everybody makes the same rate. The jobs have been made so simple that there is not much room to move up from one skill to another. In other places where the jobs aren't broken down this way, the average fellow has something to look forward to. He can go from one step to another right up the ladder. Here it's possible to make foreman. But none of the guys on the line think there's much chance to go higher than that. To manage a complicated machine like that, you need a college degree. They bring in smart college boys and train them for the better jobs."

Interviewer: "What does your wife think about your job?"

At this point his wife spoke up: "I often wish he'd get another job. He comes home at night, plops down in a chair and just sits for about fifteen minutes. I don't know much about what he does at the plant, but it does something to him. Of course, I shouldn't complain. He gets good pay. We've been able to buy a refrigerator and a TV set—a lot of things we couldn't have had otherwise. But sometimes I wonder whether these are more important to us than having Joe get all nervous and tensed up. He snaps at the kids and snaps at me—but he doesn't mean it."

The worker was then asked if he had considered working elsewhere:

"I'll tell you honest. I'm scared to leave. I'm afraid to take the gamble on the outside. I'm not staying because I want to. You see, I'm getting good pay. We live according to the pay I get. It would be tough to change the way we live. With the cost of living what it is, it's too much of a gamble. Then there's another thing. I got good seniority. I take another job and I start from scratch. Comes a depression or something and I'm the first to get knocked off. Also they got a pension plan. I'm thirty-seven and I'd lose that. Course the joker in that pension plan is that most guys out there chasing the line probably won't live till they're sixty-five. Sorta trapped—you get what I mean?"

The subject of the worker's relationship to his union came up in the course of the interview:

"The union has helped somewhat. Before they organized, it was pretty brutal. The bosses played favorites—they kept jacking up the speed of the line every time after they had a breakdown. But the union can't do much about the schedule and the way a job is set up. Management is responsible for that.

"We'd had a walk-out last year. They called it an unauthorized strike. Somebody got bounced because he wouldn't keep up his job on the line. The union lost the case because it should have gone through the grievance procedure. The company was dead right to insist that the union file a grievance.

"But it was one of those things it's hard to explain. When word got around that the guy was bounced—we all sort of looked at each other, dropped our tools and walked. Somehow that guy was every one of us. The tension on the line had been building up for a long time. We had to blow our top—so we did. We were wrong—the union knew it and so did the company. We stayed out a few hours and back we came. We all felt better, like we got something off our chests.

"Some of these strikes you read about may be over wages. Or they may be unions trying to play politics. But I sometimes think that the thing that will drive a man to lose all that pay is deeper than wages. Maybe other guys feel like we did the day we walked out."

Toward the end of the interview, the worker spoke of the company he worked for:

"They are doing what they can—like the hospital, the safety, the pay, and all like that. And the people who run the plant I guess are pretty good guys themselves. But sometimes I think that the company doesn't think much of the individual. If they did they wouldn't have a production line like that one. You're just a number to them. They number the stock and they number you. There's a different feeling in this kind of a plant. It's like a kid who goes up to a grown man and starts talking to him. There doesn't seem to be a friendly feeling. Here a man is just so much horsepower. You're just a cog in the wheel."

Notice, first, that this worker's dissatisfaction was not due primarily to the things that are usually considered important to a job. This man's pay was good. His job was secure. He worked for a sound company. He had substantial seniority. He had a pension, hospitalization and disability benefits when he became sick, and a good boss; at least he did not blame his boss for the kind of job he had. Working conditions, heating, lighting, cafeteria facilities, and safety conditions were as good as—if not better than—the average found in industrial plants. Yet J.D. despised his job.

The simple fact is that the impact of "sound" engineering principles, when translated into human experience, had a profound effect on J.D.'s view of the meaning of work. Both the technical setup and the application of work rationalization principles made this man feel like hardly more than an extension of the machine. The sense of anonymity implicit in much of what he said can be traced back to some of the basic characteristics of his immediate job, which we can compare with the assembly-line principles mentioned earlier: (1) the conveyor belt determined the pace at which he worked. He had no control over his work ryhthm. (2) Because the task was broken down into simple motions, the job was highly repetitive; (3) simple repetitive motions meant that there was little need to draw upon a variety of skills; and (4) the tools and the work procedures were predetermined. And when techniques changed, it was the engineer or time-study man—not the worker—who controlled the change. (5) J.D. worked on a fraction of the product, which meant also that he never felt a sense of the "whole." Finally (6) some attention was required—too much to allow him to daydream or carry on any sustained conversation with others, but not enough to allow him to become absorbed in the work itself. The technical setup determined the character of his work relationships. J.D. identified himself with the partner who worked with him on the opposite side of the line, but beyond that he displayed almost no identification with a work group as such. Men on the line work as an aggregate of individuals, each man performing his operation more or less independently of the others. The lack of an intimate group awareness appeared to reinforce the same sense of anonymity fostered by the conveyor-paced, repetitive character of the job itself.

The worker's comments about promotion and job aspirations are also pertinent. He saw little hope for advancement because most of the production jobs paid about the same. By applying principles of work rationalization, the industrial engineer, in the best interests of efficiency, had simplified the tasks so that differences in skill from one job to the next were all but eliminated. It was difficult for the average worker to move vertically through a series of distinct steps in promotion.

This case is only one of over four hundred actual work careers that were studied in one research project. Only a few had experienced any substantial change in job classification during a period of from twelve to fifteen years. Collectively, all the workers had improved their overall economic status; individually, few had experienced much change in their relative job status. The net effect of this condition was to increase the de-personalization of the job.

True, the case of an automobile assembly-line worker is in many respects an extreme case in the application of the principles of work rationalization. There are many types and conditions of work in which the degree of dissatisfaction is not expressed as strongly as it was in this case. Nevertheless, the evidence shows that work in highly repetitive, conveyor-paced jobs is looked upon as a meaningless end in itself.

THE UNDERLYING ASSUMPTIONS OF SCIENTIFIC MANAGEMENT

We have thus far described the rationale of the Scientific Management movement as seen by its original founder, F. W. Taylor. We have also shown, through the experience of a worker, how some of these principles appear in practice. In the latter case, not only were we looking at the application of the Taylor principles but also the rational application of principles of progressive manufacturing. Let us look for a moment at some of the underlying assumptions of these principles, assumptions which have been seriously challenged not only by experienced practitioners of management but also by social-science researchers.

The basic assumption Taylor made was that men were motivated by the desire to maximize economic gain. Anything done to make their work more efficient would make workers produce more to get more money. Therefore, the worker would be happy and satisfied on his job. A second assumption was one that seemed quite consistent with the long tradition of "individualism" in American industry. It held that the worker's world was focused on the individual worker and that the group of people with whom he works was not important to him. Hence the worker's relationship to his fellow workers, to his boss, and to the total organization, were virtually ignored. Because of this the further assumption was made that man, being the logical extension of the machine, could have not only his physical motions but his thinking processes standardized. It assumed that there was only one correct way to do a job, and that that way was determined by the requirements of the machinery. All one had to do to have a "standard" worker was to standardize his motions, his hours, his basic wages, and the entire routines of his work life. The result was that the worker became hardly more than a passive agent of the machine process.

The inadequacy of these assumptions was reflected in one form of worker response, namely, the growth of unionism. The union movement was an organized recognition not only that men had to be protected from arbitrary action by management, but that workers had, indeed, a need for expression as members of social groups. It recognized, too, that the motives or norms of the groups are not always directed toward the maximization of work and efficiency. In fact, one of the most common phenomena in the history of work is the powerful force that workers can generate in work restriction or "doing as little as one can get away with."

THE HUMAN RELATIONS MOVEMENT

The first serious research to expose the limited assumptions of Scientific Management was that inspired by Elton Mayo (who has been called America's first industrial sociologist) during the 1920's. These studies, frequently hailed as the beginnings of a counter-movement against Scientific Management, opened up the era of what is commonly called the human relations movement.

Mayo's study took place at the Hawthorne plant of the Western Electric Company, just outside of Chicago. The researchers began their studies in much the same way that Taylor began his, except that they were interested in problems of physical fatigue among the workers. During World War I the British Medical Research Council had done considerable work on fatigue among factory workers. Now, a few years later, the Hawthorne group sought to discover first, the relationship between the workers' efficiency (as measured in parts produced) and the amount of illumination that would affect the performance of their tasks. They chose two groups of employees with similar backgrounds working under similar conditions. The plan was to have one experimental group and vary the intensity of the light under which they worked in order to determine whether it had any effect on their output. Conditions for the "control" group were to be held constant.

The first shocking revelation was that there did not seem to be any relationship between rate of production and changes in the amount of lighting. The researchers were curious about this fact; they thought perhaps there was something wrong with their experimental design, or that there might be factors other than illumination.

Mayo, who had earlier performed research in textile mills in Philadelphia, was convinced that the problem was not simply physiological, or the amount of light and its effect upon the workers' vision. Rather, he believed that there were also psychological factors at work. The researchers therefore switched the experiment slightly in order to get at these; they told the workers that the light bulbs had been changed (although they had not been), and implied that the illumination would be brighter. The workers responded by saying they liked the "increased" illumination. This in turn was proof to the researchers that something other than physiological conditions was needed to explain the paradox.

The experiment continued in hopes that the researchers would still investigate the problem of the illumination as such and isolate the psychological factors. To do so, the researchers decided to make some other changes related to rest pauses and the hours of work. They further reasoned that if they could isolate the workers they could identify other physical conditions of work which might explain output behavior. A new group was then organized and placed in a separate room. The six girls chosen were average workers assembling a not-too-complicated telephone relay component. The job cycle was approximately one relay per minute. Thus, any changes in output would be clearly measurable. By this time, and from past experience, the investigators expected that they would probably not be able to identify any single factor, such as illumination. However, they were curious about other kinds of conditions and attitudes related to the work experience. In carrying out the experiment, the researchers kept careful records of the time of day when defects might occur. Weather conditions, temperature, and humidity in the test room were also controlled; and medical examinations were held periodically. Activities outside of working hours and types and amount of food eaten were also considered. Through direct observation the investigators watched carefully every aspect of worker behavior hour by hour. They also took notes of conversations. These later proved one of the keys to the "great discovery" that pointed to the importance of social factors at work.

After the experiment had been under way for some time, it was decided to call the girls in when changes were contemplated. More than that, their own comments were encouraged, and they were even allowed veto power over any change that was made or proposed. They were also encouraged to work at a natural pace and not to push themselves too hard just to satisfy the experiment.

The researchers felt that over an extended period of time it would be possible to find out what made for the most satisfactory output both in terms of quantity and quality. In the first experimental period no change was made in the working conditions and the hours stayed the way they always had been. This period had been preceded by a two-week period when production records were kept without the girls' knowledge. In the third series of weeks the method of payment was changed so that each girl was paid more closely in relation to her own effort. Several weeks later, efforts were made to alter the rest pauses, varying them in frequency and length. In some phases of the experiment, the rest periods lasted as much as half an hour each day.

These experiments went on for a year, with the experimenters becoming frustrated over the fact that the results were not what they had expected. Instead of changes that could be related directly to various types of changes in rest periods, they discovered that there had been a steady increase in output throughout the year. Even when they reverted to the original conditions of work with no rest pauses, including no special lunch period, the daily and weekly production rose to a point higher than it ever had been before. The physiological experimental work thus went down the drain because of this mysterious and unexplained continued rise in output.

The girls' own comments eventually suggested the key to the puzzle: they looked upon the experiments as fun. They also enjoyed not being told by their boss what to do, and being able to share ideas with the experimenters. More important, the girls had the feeling that they were part of an experiment that could lead to improvements in working conditions for all the workers. It was, in other words, the girls' *involvement* which improved their output, not the specific conditions of their work environment. The Hawthorne studies paved the way for literally hundreds of other experiments since that time by many researchers. All of them led to the conclusion that the measurement of work itself and the application of Scientific Management principles ignored the importance of the human group and the motivation associated with group behavior.

CONTRIBUTIONS OF SCIENTIFIC MANAGEMENT

Despite the subsequent modification of Scientific Management, Taylor's work stands as an inevitable though unique contribution to modern industrial technology. When all other resources were being rationalized, labor could not hope to escape. Paradoxically, improvement over the years has come in two opposite directions. First, it is now recognized that many of Taylor's "scientific" findings were, in fact, mere rationalizations of the class interests of management rather than necessary conditions implicit in the work itself. At the same time, the abandoning of the more extreme claims of Scientific Management and the recognition of psychological factors, through the introduction of human relations studies, have actually made the approach more "scientific" over the years.

What will be required in the future will be a combination of the advantages of Scientific Management with the contributions of behavioral science to the understanding of the nature of human work. In an automated society where we will be less concerned with the efficient use of hand and brawn our efforts will need to be directed toward releasing the great potential of the mind. This is the challenge for tomorrow's enlightened management.

6 / Technology and Labor in the Twentieth Century
JACK BARBASH

In the 20th century the industrial worker has had to face technology in the form of both increasing mechanization and sophisticated managerial technique. To some extent, the workers have utilized legislative enactments, and management has used the administration of the personnel function, to deal with technology. But the institution that workers have organized as their own most effective response to both forms of technology has been the union. Through unionization workers have been able to use collective bargaining to protect themselves against the harsh blows of technological change.

The workers of every industrializing country have had to come to terms with technology in one form or another. Just as England of the 19th century became the classic testing ground for workers' response to the Industrial Revolution, so the United States is the classic environment for the first two thirds of the 20th century in the unfolding of technology and its consequences for the working classes. Looking ahead, the developing nations of Asia and Africa are likely to become the historically critical areas for technology in the final third of the 20th century.

Milestones in the American workers' encounter in this period with technology and technological change are: (1) the rejection and later modification of Scientific Management; (2) the rise and consolidation of industrial unionism; (3) the emergence of specialized personnel administration; (4) the "automation" impact on collective bargaining; and (5) the labor movement's recourse to politics and legislative enactments.

LABOR AND SCIENTIFIC MANAGEMENT

Frederick W. Taylor's system of Scientific Management represented a rationalization of management technique, and one of its major purposes was, as Taylor himself said very early, "to render labor unions and strikes unnecessary." Taylor deliberately designed his system to transfer control over the work task from the worker to the scientific manager, who would substitute the efficient, "one best way" for the traditional and customary ways of the worker.

The first phase of the union reaction to burgeoning Taylorism in the decade after 1910 was an outright assault on the premises and practice of Scientific Management. The union attack spurred a widening public discussion that ultimately brought Taylor and his faithful disciples—the Taylor "revisionists," who were trying to assimilate the union objections into the basic Taylor system— face to face with government, in the persons of administrators and congressmen. This last reached its high point in two events: the appointment of Professor Robert F. Hoxie of the University of Chicago by the U. S. Commission on Industrial Relations to investigate Scientific Management, and the unions' successful quest in 1916 for amendments to a Navy appropriations bill outlawing both the stopwatch and premium and bonus plans in federal establishments. These restrictions remained on the books until 1949.

The direction of union criticism remained unaltered in this period. As N. P. Alifas, a spokesman for the International Association of Machinists, put it in 1914:

The [principal] objection [to the stopwatch] is that in the past one of the means by which an employee has been able to keep his head above water and prevent being oppressed by the employer has been that the employer didn't know exactly what the employee could do. The only way that the workman has been able to retain time enough in which to do the work with the speed with which he thinks he ought to do it, has been to keep the employer somewhat in ignorance of exactly the time needed. . . . We don't want to work as fast as we are able to. We want to work as fast as we think it's comfortable for us to work. We haven't come into existence for the purpose of seeing how great a task we can perform throughout a lifetime. We are trying to regulate our work so as to make it an auxiliary to our lives and be benefited thereby. . . . Most people walk to work in the morning, if it isn't too far. If somebody should discover they could run to work in one third the time, they might have no objection to have that fact ascertained, but if the man who ascertained it had the power to make them run, they might object to having him find it out.

The most sophisticated formulation of the grounds for the union position on Scientific Management at this time came from Professor Hoxie. In summary form, the unions, in Hoxie's view, were not opposed to "science in management"— improvements resulting from improved machinery and efficient management; rather, they were opposed to Taylorism as a "cult." The labor movement denounced the sweating and speedup practice Scientific Management encouraged because it "looks upon the worker as a mere instrument of production and reduces him to a semi-automatic attachment to the machine or tool." Scientific Management was "undemocratic," and a "reversion to industrial autocracy," attempting "to gather up and transfer to the management all the traditional knowledge, the judgment and skill of the workers" and to deprive the workman of a "voice in hiring or discharge, the setting of the task, the determination of the wage rate or the general conditions of employment." Scientific Management was neither genuinely scientific nor efficient, the labor movement charged, and it led to "industrial unrest," "displac[ing] harmony and cooperation among the working group by mutual suspicion and controversy."

After World War I the attitude of the American Federation of Labor (founded in 1886) became more favorable to Scientific Management—a result in the first instance of the amicable relationship between labor and management leaders that had developed in the climate of common wartime objectives. Samuel Gompers (1850-1924) tried to capitalize on this good will to extend union influence in American industry by persuading businessmen rather than by organizing more workers. As part of this strategy, Gompers and his successor as head of the AFL, William Green, undertook to create an image of the labor movement as management's partner in promoting industrial efficiency through the private enterprise system. This was more a piece of expediency than a fundamental ideological commitment; the simple fact was that organizing *workers* in the mass-production industries was almost impossible in this period, and thus the AFL embarked on this campaign to enlist workers by organizing their employers. The AFL found favor in all quarters except among those employers whose employees the unions were actively seeking to organize. Except for a venturesome handful, most employers pursued their traditional policy of pursuing industrial efficiency without union help. And although a handful of corporations did institute promising plans that brought the unions into partnership in production, these pioneering systems proved unable to survive the drastic economic contraction which began in 1929.

The period from the inception of Scientific Management (the closing years of the 19th century) to the Great Depression was, then, mostly one of verbal exchanges spiced by a few isolated but celebrated experiments in management-labor co-operation. More successful encounters had to wait for the unionization of the mass-production industries, the heartland of Scientific Management. In short, industrial unionism had to develop before a realistic exchange could take place among workers, unions, and management.

INDUSTRIAL UNIONISM

By industrial unionism is meant inclusive unionism. The industrial union admits and bargains for all or almost all classes of workers in a given industry or plant; it is a union of the *skilled and unskilled*. This inclusiveness is in marked contrast to craft unionism, which caters primarily to the skilled worker.

The skilled craft unions are as old as the United States and have been historically strongest in the building trades, railroads, and printing industries.

Although changes in machines and materials have had an impact on the established crafts, not until recently have they had to face the full thrust of modern technology. Indeed, the skilled unions have not up to the present had to yield on the major lines of craft demarcation to the onrush of technology.

Industrial unions, too, existed for many years but did not emerge as a national power until the combined forces of the New Deal, in the specific form of the Wagner Act (1935), and John L. Lewis, head of the United Mine Workers, gave the spark of life to the Committee for Industrial Organization, later the Congress of Industrial Organizations. The CIO's great achievement was the penetration of the mass-production industries starting in the mid-1930's.

In many respects, this rise of industrial unionism has been the most significant development in the workers' assimilation of the effects of technology. Only industrial unionism, with its organization around the factory-environment of work and its roots sunk deeply in the loyalties of factory workers, could react with relevance to workers' fears of technological change. At the same time, industrial unionism could also confront factory management from a stance of power based on near-total worker support.

Integral to the role of the industrial union in the factory is the grievance procedure, a joint union-management mechanism based on a written contract for handling complaints of workers. A graduated grievance procedure typically begins with the union steward, elected by the workers in a plant department, to whom the workers address their complaints. The steward takes up the grievance with his opposite number on the management side, usually the foreman. If the grievance remains unsettled it moves up in sequence two additional stages (usually), manned on either side by successively higher level union and management personnel. If, after all of this, the grievance remains unresolved it is common for an outside impartial arbitrator, in effect a private judge agreed to by union and management, to render a final and binding judgment.

The most numerous class of complaints, on all the evidence, has been and continues to be the grievances dealing with the changes in factory jobs produced almost daily by changing technology. These relate to job classification, timing of jobs, job shifts, wage rates, layoffs, and so forth—the real stuff of technology's ongoing effect on worker's lives in modern industry. The steward has enabled the union presence in the shop to have meaning to the individual worker and, incidentally, to confront management with the need for rationalizing its handling of worker grievances.

The grievance procedure has in large part become a kind of probing instrument for the continuous and orderly adjustment of the individual worker's life to technological change. It handles other problems, but those arising out of technology are increasingly assuming the greatest importance. The grievance machinery, as has been noted, is based upon a grant of authority commonly established in the collective agreement (union contract). The cases processed by the grievance machinery have become a kind of common law which in turn has influenced the provisions of later agreements.

MUTUAL ACCOMMODATION

When the industrial union became established as a going concern in the factory the union-management exchange over Scientific Management took on a new character. Whereas in the early decades of the 20th century the controversy had been conducted on the level of debate, as industrial unionism began to take shape in the factories the controversy rose to a level of *action* with different results from those in the first encounter.

World War II provided the conditions for functional interaction between unions and management on the question of Scientific Management. The circumstances were these: (1) unionism had taken hold in the mass-production industries and so could speak both from a position of power and from practical experience with Scientific Management systems; (2) the cost-plus method of financing war production eased the cost pressures on management, making possible greater flexibility of administration and better earning opportunities; (3) the government's wartime wage-stabilization policy favored increases arising out of wage-engineering programs, which presumably increased productivity. Finally, there was one condition which promised much for the longer pull: the National Labor Relations Board (NLRB) interpreted the employer's statutory obligation to bargain under the National Labor Relations Act so as to include the obligation to furnish on request whatever supporting data (on wage or job determination) were necessary to help the union negotiate effectively.

From the time of World War II on, union and management have agreed to *negotiate* the main features of the wage-determination system, in contrast to Taylorism's earlier insistence upon unilateral determination by management. The unions have not, however, abandoned their formal philosophic objections; they continue to criticize the principles of Scientific Management which, by this time, cover time studies, job evaluation, wage incentives, and merit rating, to mention those of chief concern to the unions. Their grounds of criticism have been: (1) that the main objective of engineered wage systems is to exclude important aspects of the determination of rates, earnings, and the intensity of effort from the collective bargaining process and therefore from union influence; (2) that there is still a large margin of human error and fallibility in all of the work-measurement techniques associated with industrial engineering; (3) that industrial engineering has introduced excessive competitiveness within the work group, to the deterioration of the workers' morale and their sense of solidarity; and (4) that these schemes have not demonstrably resulted in efficiency improvements. Indeed, it would be difficult to see how unions could endorse these systems openly when much of their early success in organizing was based on a fear of the "speedup" effects of industrial engineering. However, the unions and their members have learned to live with work-engineering systems by using collective bargaining to alter undesirable features, by making plans "pay off" for their members, and by maintaining their skill at the bargaining table.

The union strategy in bargaining over the engineering systems of wage determination is fourfold: (1) to make sure that no system is installed without union acquiescence, although most unions do not wish to collaborate with management in the actual installation of a system; (2) to make secure the union's right to "grieve" about any individual rate, classification, time, or standard set by management; (3) to regulate the terms under which management may change rates, times, and classifications; and (4) to develop competent stewards at the shop level to deal with the daily problems, augmented by a professional staff at the national union-headquarters level to backstop the local union leadership.

When unions arrive at the point where they can hold up their end of the bargaining, their spokesmen tend to recognize positive virtues in systematic wage determination. As one union spokesman from the rubber workers said in relation to incentive systems: "It affords us an orderly way of establishing work measurements. . . . It establishes an orderly way for a worker to perform his job. I think it establishes an orderly flow of production through a mass production plant, and I think, too, that it enables the worker to work easier if the incentives are properly employed." Similarly, a spokesman for the steelworkers observed that the current job-evaluation and classification system in effect as a result of industry-union negotiation was materially superior to the former "crazy-quilt patchwork system" of rate determination based on the foreman's rule of thumb. Long before job evaluation developed in the steel industry, the union "had only one idea in mind and that was they wanted uniform rates for the same job wherever it might be in the steel mills." The job-evaluation program which the management and the union jointly developed replaced five thousand separate job designations in the steel industry with thirty-two grades. Wage- and work-rationalization systems are likely, moreover, to become part of a general system of efficient management providing for sound safety practices in the plant, an agreeable work place, well-planned layout, and flow of materials.

AUTOMATION AND COLLECTIVE BARGAINING

The union role in ameliorating the effects of technology on the worker is evident in another important area—that in which labor-saving machinery displaces workers and radically transforms work and job circumstances, the so-called "automation" effect. The crafts have been most significantly affected here. Labor-saving machinery was developed on a large scale in the 1950's in craft-union (or craft-like) fields, notably in railroads, airlines, and printing. Dieselization threatened the jobs of railroad firemen; the jet plane made the flight engineer redundant; and in printing, "automated" typesetting weakened the position of the typographer.

An industrial union can offset some of its losses from this sort of technological change by job shifts within the plant or between other plants in the same industry because its union's occupational lines are not as rigid as craft lines, and in any case, wherever the individual union member works in the plant or company he will likely remain in the same union. In the craft unions, on the other hand, a major technological change can wipe out an entire occupation, as in the case of railroad firemen and flight engineers. Union resistance understandably becomes more stubborn and last-ditch obstruction more supportable when the very survival of the union as an institution is at stake.

Examples of sporadic craft obstruction to partial changes have, in past years, included the granite cutters' restriction of the hand surfacer, the steamfitters' prohibition against pipe-cutting and threading machines at the job site, the limitation of the use of spray guns by painters, and of pre-glazed windows by the glaziers, the ban on handling of pre-cut and pre-packed meats by meat cutters' union locals, and the typographical union restrictions on the use of the teletypesetter. More recently, in order to maintain the long-distance hauling of assembled automobiles by trucks (driven by union members), rather than having such transport diverted to railroads, East Coast Teamsters locals instructed drivers "not to deliver trailers to . . . railroad units for "piggyback" loading, that is, the carrying of trucks on railway flatcars. Union obstruction of technological change is still, however, the exception rather than the rule. A more characteristic strategy is to try to slow down the pace of worker displacement. As displacement inevitably occurs, the union acts to ease the burden of change on the displaced worker. The means through which the union seeks to achieve this objective are the specific provisions of the collective agreement.

The following is the general pattern union adjustment to technological change seems to be taking. The specific measures negotiated by unions and managements in any given situation are determined (among other factors) by the prosperity of the industry and employer undergoing technological change, the magnitude of saving to be achieved by the change, the quality and temper of the collective bargaining relationship, and the personal and social characteristics of the displaced workers, that is, their age, sex, color, geography.

Job and income maintenance for current employees is a characteristic first line of union defense. In one form, unions negotiate explicit productivity gain-sharing; for example, an "annual improvement factor" where wage rates rise in line with a predetermined rate of productivity increase. Any increase in real wages and wage supplements (negotiated health, welfare, and pension programs, and supplementary unemployment benefits) and reduction in hours without loss in earnings results from sharing the gains of productivity. In this sense, the entire rising level of real wages in the United States is a consequence of technological advance.

Layoffs due to technological change are frequently slowed down by contract requirements that: (1) prohibit reduction in the number of men scheduled for the performance of a given task; (2) guarantee *current* employees against job and income loss; and (3) offset net job and income losses through job and income gains, as in the reduction of weekly hours, increases in paid leaves (holidays, vacations, "sabbaticals," and so forth) of one sort or another.

When worker displacement does come, collective bargaining sets in motion new forces to moderate the impact of displacement which act to: (1) induce voluntary separations by raising pensions for early retirees; (2) tide workers over to the next job through separation allowances; (3) aid the displaced worker to find another job in the same company by enlarging the seniority unit within which the worker can legitimately claim employment rights, or by a relocation allowance to permit the displaced worker to move to a company plant in another area; and (4) provide effective job retraining opportunities.

Procedures to encourage advance planning for technological change have been incorporated in contract provisions, requiring (variously) advance notice of major labor-saving changes and consultation between unions and management in planning the displacement. Most recently, unions and management have joined to develop study committees, frequently with participation by neutral outsiders, to explore the problems of work displacement *before* the bargaining climate of crisis sets in. The general principle which collective bargaining seems to have established is that the employee displaced by technology has an equitable interest in his job; and in the event of material impairment of this interest, the employee has a legitimate claim against his employer to offset—in whole or in part—the losses suffered as a consequence of impairment.

PERSONNEL ADMINISTRATION

Unionism, and especially industrial unionism, has hastened the flowering of personnel administration. Union demands that management share power in its traditionally exclusive employment function induced management to reconsider and then replace hit-and-miss practices with a rationally tenable program. Moreover, union efforts to enlist employee support caused management to devise techniques for reaching employees on the basis of consent and understanding, rather than solely by authority.

Of course, other factors have motivated managements to institute more systematic administration of the elements affecting employment policies. The manager's growing sensitivity to the human needs of employees, the increasing prosperity of enterprise, the emergence of personnel administration as a movement, and the growing possibility that these policies were not only more humane but more efficient, all contributed to the growth of personnel administration.

Personnel administration has sought to extend standards of rational management over the entire range of the employment process, from recruitment to retirement. Although the idea of orderly employment management can be traced back as far as Robert Owen (1771-1858), the industrialist and utopian socialist of the early years of the 19th century, personnel management as an established function in industrial enterprise (excluding Scientific Management) probably originated in the years immediately prior to World War I when corporations began to add safety engineers to cut down the cost of accident insurance. Not long after, the personnel function was enlarged to include training directors, employment managers, and industrial physicians.

Personnel administration took on new vigor in the 1920's when the union offensive of World War I and the immediate postwar period was still well remembered. Even as the union threat began to decline the personnel movement, motivated largely by the desire of employers to deter the advance of unionism, continued to grow until the Great Depression of 1929. A survey made in the 1920's covering a broad range of industries showed these characteristic personnel activities in the area of employment: interviews, medical examination for selection, and clerical and stenographic tests; and in the area of employee welfare: first aid stations, lunch rooms, employee magazines, libraries and recreation rooms, benefit associations, group life insurance (including accident), and pensions and health insurance. The post-1933 period in personnel administration was tuned largely to the implications of the union demands for a larger voice in management. Corporate industrial relations departments grew rapidly, and within these departments bargaining, grievance handling, wage and work engineering, and insurance, became major functions.

During World War II government controls over wages and manpower utilization additionally influenced the expansion of personnel administration as a professional field. During this period, and continuing in the postwar years, management was increasingly attracted to human-relations techniques for enlisting the support of employees. Training of supervisors, executive development, employee attitude surveys, and counselling all became accepted techniques which management experimented with to strengthen the bonds of employee loyalty to the company. By this time, most managers had begun to think of the union upsurge of the 1930's as a reflection on the quality of the managerial performance of the period; and they were determined not to repeat those mistakes in dealing with the most prominent employment problem of the 1950's and 1960's: the rapidly growing white-collar work force.

Thus, the combination of union demands, government regulation, and management's own "efficiency-mindedness" has resulted—one can say without too much exaggeration—in a "technology" of personnel and industrial relations. The technology of modern employment administration consists of an integrated system of specializations spanning the employee's relations to the enterprise from recruitment to retirement and beyond. A corps of psychologists, engineers, lawyers, sociologists, physicians, and, in a few instances, "industrial chaplains" has been employed in personnel departments to staff these specialties. This technology goes beyond enterprise boundaries to enlist university schools of business administration, professional associations, learned journals, and consultants in a massive movement of discussion, research, education, and training.

In the contemporary period, beginning about the mid-1950's, management industrial-relations policy has taken its posture from the impact of major technological change on employment. The present management position differs from that of the past in one fundamental respect: it no longer waits for union demands before acting. Now there is an initiating, experimental, pragmatic quality to management industrial relations, as shown by the American Motors profit-sharing plan, the Armour automation study committee, the human-relations committee in the basic steel industry, and the mechanization and modernization program in the historically volatile West Coast longshore industry.

LEGISLATION

When collective bargaining provides insufficient remedies for the impact of technology on the worker, the labor movement turns to legislation and to influencing public policy, especially at the national level, to protect the job interests of its constituents.

Political action by workers and unions to achieve legislative objectives is more than a century old, but *mass* political action in the 20th century developed only as the industrial unions perceived that the job interests of their members were inextricably intertwined with a public policy based on full employment. The industrial unions led the way in widespread political action programs aimed at bringing into power legislators and administrations favorable to full employment objectives. This political and legislative action of the labor movement was put to energetic use in the period following the 1957-58 recession to promote comprehensive public programs directed at the consequences of technology on employment. More concretely, union spokesmen have pressed for systematic economic policies, both domestic and international, designed to increase employment opportunities and programs of guidance, education, training, rehabilitation, and labor-market organization, as well as anti-poverty programs and anti-discrimination programs. The sharpest focus and the most intense efforts are being directed at programs to deal with "structural" unemployment, that is, unemployment among youth, the unskilled, and the uneducated—groups that do not share proportionately in the fruits of the expanding economy.

WORKERS' MOVEMENTS OUTSIDE OF THE UNITED STATES

Industrial societies do not all respond in identical ways to the impact of technology on workers, although all industrial societies have confronted the same problems. The pattern of interaction between the worker and technology in the United States in comparison to other societies has differed in several respects, showing: (1) a greater reliance on the process of autonomous collective bargaining between unions and management to determine the worker's reaction to technology; by contrast, other countries have relied more on public policy and legislative enactment; (2) a greater depth of penetration of American collective bargaining into management practice in regulating the effects of technology on employment; the extent of involvement of the American trade unionist in the regulation of work and wage standards is without equal anywhere; and (3) a greater degree of managerial rationalization of the employment function. Most basic to the American worker's response has been (4) the advanced stage of development of industrialization and of the supporting systems of education, law, and government and the intensity of economic aspirations among the people.

The American worker's response to technology has thus been unique among the industrial societies of the world in his relatively greater emphasis on private collective bargaining between autonomous unions and highly organized business enterprise with a relatively lesser dependence on government policy. In the countries of Western Europe including the United Kingdom, collective bargaining by autonomous unions is important, and increasingly so, but not so important as in the United States. In Western Europe, too, the role of the state is substantially more important in regulating working conditions.

Another order of industrial systems is represented by the so-called underdeveloped countries in Asia and Africa, excluding for the moment Communist China. In those countries, attempts at rapid industrialization under state planning have been going on for perhaps a decade and a half. These are also systems in which massive foreign aid has been available at the same time that nationalism and anti-colonialism have been interwoven with industrializing objectives. Unionism in these settings exists largely under the tutelage of the government in power. Consequently, collective bargaining functions only in a very elementary way, for the most part in the handling of grievances. Government legislation performs most of the protective functions. If unionism went unregulated by public policy, it is generally held it could seriously endanger the growth objectives of the state.

There is finally the Communist model, where unionism is explicitly a part of the state administrative apparatus. As an arm of the state, an important part of the union's function is to promote productivity among workers and to campaign against worker practices that interfere with efficiency.

The various types of industrial revolutions which these contemporary societies are newly experiencing evoke worker protest. But, unlike the United States and Western Europe, this protest does not for the most part take the form of unions of the Western type. Indeed, such unions do not exist in these societies for reasons which are profoundly rooted in their development. Some scholars have concluded that industrialization in the present period is not generating the kind of bitter protest and class struggles that broke out in the comparable stage of Western industrial development. Instead, labor and social legislation and a more sophisticated management utilizing Western managerial techniques are blunting the feeling of outrage on the part of the masses of workers that marked Western industrialism more than a century earlier.

Industrialization in these countries in the present period is caught up with overriding movements of nationalism, anti-colonialism, nationhood, and socialism, which provide the main outlet for social protest and organization. In this setting, the focus of industrial authority is not primarily on the middle-class managers typical of the West but on a military, a monarchical, or a one-party state power structure, depending upon the society.

Worker protest and resistance to industrialization do occur; but instead of routine strikes and collective bargaining restrictions, the workers' protests in these countries take the form of sporadic demonstrations and wildcat walk-outs, excessive turnover, absenteeism, sabotage, and thievery. In part this represents conscious protest and in part understandable frictions in the adjustments of a rural-oriented work force to a new urban industrialized environment.

Comparisons among industrial systems and the workers' responses to technology under these systems must, of course, take account of major differences in the supporting systems of education, law, and government and the intensity of economic aspirations among the masses of people. Technology does not function in a cultural vacuum.

THE "HUMANIZATION" OF WORK

Any assessment, no matter how cursory, of the interaction between technology and the workers in 20th-century America must give first place to the increasing humanization of the work situation. Work is less physically demanding—the drudgery has almost been eliminated; the manager is more conscious of the human problems of the worker; and by and large the job pays enough to the worker to permit him and his family to live decently. The total work situation is, in general, more compatible with the physical, moral, and economic needs of the worker as a complete human being.

But the conditions of earning a living are not yet utopian, even in the United States, where the process of work humanization has advanced the farthest. The work place is still primarily a hierarchical order in which someone gives the orders, and those below him follow; most work is still performed as a job, that is, as a small piece of the whole; and economic uncertainty is still a nagging concern. Menial and ill-paid work is becoming the unchanging lot of a caste of workers, based upon their color and ethnic origin.

The major breakthrough in the enhancement of the worker's condition has come perhaps in the last quarter-century or so. Although bosses still boss, there are checks and balances on their authority, which make their power more bearable. If a job is still a job, there are currents in the wind looking toward planned work enlargement as against greater work specialization; a new "ergonomic" work science is attempting to explore work effort in relation to the "biosocial" characteristics of the worker. Though unemployment persists at uncomfortable levels, unemployment compensation, retraining, and education protect the worker from an engulfing hopelessness.

No *one* great cause is responsible for the long-run improvement in conditions for workers. We do know this—the wellsprings of improvement do not stem from individual and unilateral benefaction but from the fluid interaction of power forces in a free society. The manager and the engineer respond to competition to produce more efficient machines and techniques. The workers organize informally and in unions to shield themselves from undiluted efficiency. The autonomous workers' organizations confront managements with their demands for greater satisfaction in jobs and more equitable treatment. The managers in turn have to keep orienting management techniques to the willingness of workers to tolerate them and to the willingness of consumers to buy their product in the competitive marketplace. This interplay becomes even more complex when, at some point, government enters the contest. The upshot is that the combination of the benevolence of nature, pressures for achievement, the free play of human beings, and human institutions, has made possible an era of plenty; and once the end of hunger is in sight, it will be possible to contemplate and act on a fuller conception of the human relationship to work.

7 / The Organization of Distribution and Marketing
THEODORE F. MARBURG

The increasingly rational and efficient organization of labor, management, and production in the early 20th century would have availed little had not distribution and marketing kept pace. The present abundant economy in the United States has been made possible by the fact that, with some exceptions, they have kept pace.

In surveying these changes in marketing organization since 1900, we can distinguish between adaptive response to changes already introduced elsewhere in the economy and creative changes originating in this sector. This distinction was articulated by the Austrian-American economist Joseph A. Schumpeter, who characterized the creative response—or innovation—as occurring when a firm does something that is outside the range of existing practice. Both types of response have taken place in marketing management since 1900. An example of a clearly adaptive response is the expansion of retailers, or the organization of more retail stores to distribute, in the accustomed manner, increased quantities of mass-produced goods to an expanding and increasingly affluent population. Creative response occurred when merchants developed new approaches in marketing, such as mail-order sales through catalogs, the self-service supermarket, or improved inventory handling and control by means of automated equipment and electronic data processing. We regard such responses as constructive when they contribute to more effective distribution of goods or to a more effective means of enabling manufacturers to provide the type of goods consumers want.

MARKETING, EMPLOYMENT, AND PRODUCTIVITY

Statistics on employment suggest that labor-saving methods and technology were introduced more slowly in marketing than in production. The arresting statistic is the nearly fourfold increase between 1900 and 1960 in the number of people employed in trade (see Table 7-1). This stands in sharp contrast to an increase of only about 50 per cent in commodity-production employment and transportation employment.

These shifts in the labor force reflect a pattern that is general in Western civilization. As economies develop, and as living standards rise and capital and technology contribute to more economical production, there is generally a decrease in the proportion of labor engaged in producing food and raw materials; a rise and then a levelling off in the proportion engaged in manufacture; but a sustained increase in the proportion of labor engaged in services such as trade, teaching, and maintenance. This increase in the number of employees in trade and service implies a low rate of productivity growth in marketing, although this is probably overstated unless we also measure the change in output.

Table 7-1   Employment in trade compared to employment in other activities, 1899-1957*

	1899 (IN THOUSANDS)	1957 (IN THOUSANDS)
Commodity Production (Including farm employment)	15,936	24,065
Construction	1,315	4,259
Trade	2,892	13,178
Transportation	1,908	2,867
Other Services (Including government and miscellaneous)	4,690	20,565
Total Civilian Economy	26,741	64,943

* Source: Adapted from John W. Kendrick, *Productivity Trends in the United States* (Princeton: Princeton University Press for the National Bureau of Economic Research, 1961), p. 308.

There is no common agreement as to the proper measure of marketing output. Although in most of our discussion in this chapter we refer primarily to retailing, it goes without saying that intermediary middlemen and the transportation agencies also perform a necessary function in getting the right goods from the mine, farm, or factory to industrial users or retailers. The various intermediaries for the period we are studying include assemblers, wholesalers, jobbers, brokers, and manufacturers' wholesale branches. In a recent study the costs of these intermediary services have been tallied, together with the costs of retailer services and all other goods distribution services, and found to constitute approximately one fifth of the national income in the period 1929-63. This study tells us what was paid for marketing and indicates that the share of national income paid did not change; but it does not measure this cost against a separately computed estimate of output.

Such a quantitative estimate of the rate of increase in marketing productivity is, however, available for a narrower segment of distribution of goods sold through retail channels to consumers. As shown in Table 7-2, the distribution output per person engaged in this industry increased at the rate of 0.1 per cent per year between 1909 and 1949. This low rate of increase was in part due to a shortening of hours. The output per man-hour rose at an annual rate of 0.9

per cent. These rates are compared with the greater rates of growth in commodity-production output for the same period in Table 2. It is clear that output per man-hour has been rising, even though at a rate only one third that of commodity-production output. Two technological innovations that have contributed to this modest rise in marketing productivity have been the introduction of better handling equipment in warehouses and the growth of larger retail establishments.

Table 7-2　Output, output per man, and output per man-hour in commodity production and distribution, 1909-1949. Mean annual per-cent rate of change.°

	COMMODITY PRODUCTION	DISTRIBUTION
Output	+ 2.7	+ 2.8
Output per man engaged	+ 2.6	+ 0.1
Output per man-hour	+ 3.0	+ 0.9

° Source: Harold Barger, *Distribution's Place in the American Economy since 1869* (Princeton: Princeton University Press for the National Bureau of Economic Research, 1955), p. 39.

The large increase in marketing employment and the more modest increase in transportation and commodity-production employment all contributed, along with technological innovations and investment in productive equipment, toward making possible a great increase in goods available to retail consumers. Between 1900 and 1960 the dollar amount of retail sales increased from less than ten billion dollars to over two hundred billion dollars. If we consider the population increase, we see that the dollar amount of retail sales to the average consumer increased almost ten times. Even after the necessary adjustment for price rises it can be estimated that the average retail consumer of 1960 received two and one half times as many goods at retail as his 1900 counterpart. This rise in the amount of goods purchased from retail stores reflects the rise in real income that was possible because of the effectiveness of the economy. Yet the rise in real income, permitting consumers to spend less of their money on bare necessities, also gives us some measure of the increase in the magnitude and complexity of the marketing task since 1900.

MARKETING ORGANIZATION IN 1900

In 1900 most retail firms were small. Urban department stores and the few chain-store systems and mail-order houses were both exceptional and small by today's standards.

Since most of the customers in 1900 lived on farms or in towns of less than

2500 population, and since customers were not so mobile as the automobile owners of today, they did most of their buying from retail stores located in villages or county-seat towns. Rural consumers generally made most of their purchases at country general stores close by, or at dry goods and hardware stores and variety or specialty shops in the county-seat towns. In small towns or villages there were feed stores, also, where a farm wife might sell surplus cream or eggs to be shipped to creameries in larger towns or cities. Lumber yards supplied the rural market with building materials. There were franchised dealers of farm equipment—cultivators, mowers, binders, and other planting or harvesting equipment; these set the pattern for later distribution of automobiles.

People who lived in the city bought coffee, tea, spices, and packaged goods at grocery stores. They purchased some of their fresh fruits and vegetables in public markets, but increasingly they looked for these, too, in retail stores. They bought their meat from local butchers, who were increasingly doing less of their own slaughtering and were distributing the products of large packing plants.

City buyers could still turn to such single-line stores as dry goods firms and hardware stores and to specialty shops of the type that had been available in the cities during most of the 19th century. The type of goods being sold, however, had changed from earlier years. Dry goods stores and specialty shops sold the ready-to-wear clothing that was increasingly demanded and increasingly available. The boot and shoe, millinery, and haberdashery shops carried factory-made merchandise. The hardware stores and various specialty shops offered such items as bicycles, tools, and kitchen utensils, available from the growing factories.

The major innovation in retailing of the 19th century had been the department store, located in the downtown shopping district of the larger cities. This type of retail unit, combining many lines of goods under one roof, was particularly suited to serve the changing tastes of consumers. In 1900 such firms as John Wanamaker in Philadelphia and R. H. Macy in New York City had sales on the order of ten million dollars. The department stores were in a position to benefit from the market growth in urban population during the first decade of the century and from the new transportation facilities within the cities in the form of an expanded network of electric streetcars. Service from suburbs and nearby towns was provided by both the steam railroads and a rapidly expanding system of inter-urban electric companies.

The management of retailing in 1900 was already undergoing some changes from earlier practice. The sale of goods at a price that was the same to all customers was customary in some establishments in the middle of the 19th century or earlier. The practice was not general in all stores, however, and the small retailers objected to it; but they were gradually forced to adopt this prac-

Fig. 7-1. A grocer's view of the consequences of fixed retail prices. (From *The Grocer and Country Merchant,* March 10, 1905)

tice, no doubt by the competition from larger firms that advertised their prices in the newspaper. A cartoon depicting the practice and lamenting the loss of the opportunity to haggle over prices is reproduced from a 1905 issue of *The Grocer and Country Merchant.*

Another practice that had been adopted by some stores by 1900 was the more general sales of goods for cash. A half-century earlier, R. H. Macy had claimed that his policy of selling for cash was the main reason why his goods were cheaper. By 1900 many urban stores made a good portion of their sales for cash.

Most retail firms in 1900 secured their goods from wholesalers, who performed a very necessary role in stocking the goods, furnishing them in the assortments and quantities needed, and extending credit to the retailers. In some cases the new department stores and the emerging chain-store systems and mail-order houses managed to bypass the wholesalers and purchase directly from the manufacturers. In such cases they had to assume the wholesaling functions of warehousing and providing stock in the quantities needed for retail stores.

When manufacturers started advertising directly to consumers, they became less dependent upon the wholesalers' and retailers' promoting the sale of their product. It was generally observed at the turn of the century that, in order to give their customers what they wanted, retailers were obliged to sell advertised goods, even though the mark-up was less than on other goods. In 1901 a study in the *Journal of Political Economy* pointed to an extreme example of how advertising could cut down profit margins of retailers: the well-advertised Pear's soap was being retailed for close to the price retailers paid. It was also an indication of the effectiveness of advertising in channelling consumer demand.

MAIL-ORDER HOUSES

The mail-order house was the retailing institution that most left its mark on the first quarter of the 20th century. As developed by such firms as Montgomery Ward, Sears, Roebuck, and several smaller houses, it was a response to the marketing opportunities outside the range of pre-existing practice. In looking back upon the development from today's perspective, we can recognize a number of conditions which were necessary for mail-order selling, although none of them would have been sufficient to cause it to take the character that the leaders of the industry gave to it.

A high level of literacy among consumers was a first requirement, so that they could read the mail-order catalog. A similar role was played by newspapers that carried promotional advertising to acquaint customers with the mail-order products and invite them to send for catalogs. Other necessary conditions were dependable postal service and express and rail freight service reaching the small communities in rural regions. The introduction of Rural Free Delivery of mail by the federal government in 1896 and the introduction of parcel post service in 1913 further aided mail-order selling.

One negative factor that contributed, paradoxically, to make the conditions favorable to some new marketing pattern, was the relatively limited marketing service offered the farmer by country general stores or retail stores at the county seats. Normally, these rural retail merchants made purchasing trips only once or twice a year, and they stocked, chiefly, staple items that were not subject to style change. Their pricing policies differed from one community to another, depending upon the competition; in villages with only one or two stores, the storekeeper may have calculated that he would not add much volume to his business by selling a bit cheaper. This combination of policies contributed to a relatively low turnover of stock in country stores. The unsatisfactory state of this retail trade is reflected in the fact that urban department stores in 1900 were making mail-order sales as an accommodation to customers, and some even printed catalogs for this purpose. The department stores appear to have been indifferent and in due course some of them discontinued their catalogs. However, single-line and specialty firms, such as the Cash Buyers Union and E. C. Allen, solicited business by mail and did so aggressively.

It was discovered by such firms as Ward and Sears that prosperous and literate farmers were ready to buy great quantities of a general line of merchandise by mail if it was effectively described, advertised, and offered at a low price. Montgomery Ward is the older firm. Aaron Montgomery Ward in 1871 started the firm in Chicago for the express purpose of selling a general line of goods through handbills sent by mail. In 1874, he issued a pamphlet catalog of eight pages. In subsequent years he issued a larger catalog and included illustrations of the merchandise. He had the business well under way by 1900, when sales were approaching nine million dollars.

Richard W. Sears organized Sears, Roebuck in 1893, together with A. C. Roebuck. Sears was shortly afterward joined by Julius Rosenwald, who assumed control of the firm upon Sears's retirement in 1908. Since Sears had earlier sold watches by mail, Rosenwald envisioned the possibilities of catalog selling from the start. He spent generously on magazine advertising designed to interest the reader in some particular new product. He quickly expanded his line of goods from watches and jewelry, to include bicycles, sewing machines, clothing, sporting goods, harnesses, and even buggies. By 1900, net sales were over ten and a half million dollars.

The growth of mail-order selling after 1900 may be traced in the histories of these two general catalog mail-order houses. Still, it should be pointed out that the method was also used by many other sellers. Many specialty firms and a variety of so-called "clubs" grew up, making their sales entirely by mail. Nowadays the consumer may subscribe, for example, to book-of-the-month, fruit-of-the-month, or phonograph record-of-the-month clubs.

The role filled by mail-order houses can be illustrated from some of the activities of Sears, Roebuck. The products offered in the Sears catalogs reflect the ever-widening consumer use of mechanical devices and the availability of those devices at a price the farmer or small-town customer was willing to pay. To the bicycles and sewing machines of the 1890's, there have been added many new items through the years. In 1903 an electric belt was offered that was purported to relieve backache and headaches; and in 1905 there were electric insoles for shoes. For leisure-time activity, one could choose the gramaphone, the stereoscope, and a magic lantern picture projector. For saving labor on the farm, there were the cream separator and the washing machine. Today one can find anything from a vitamin capsule to a high-powered cabin cruiser, from utility items to oil paintings by well-known artists, in the Sears catalog.

The Sears method of merchandising cream separators provides an illustration of the manner in which mass merchandising could open the way for mass production of a product. Prior to Sears's entry into this market, cream separators had been sold through individual agents who also gave instructions for use; and the prices on them had ranged from $60 to $125. Sears offered separators at $27, $35, and $39.50. He was able to arrange for mass production at costs that made these prices possible because of the volume in which he was going to move the separators; but there was also a saving in his method of distribution.

Sears knew that the sale of separators by mail would be difficult unless he could destroy the myth that agents were necessary to instruct buyers in the use of separators. In order to convince potential buyers that his product could be operated easily from the accompanying instructions, he offered to pay one thousand dollars to the manufacturer of any separator that could outperform his; and he offered to pay the agent of the competing manufacturer an additional one hundred dollars. He stated his confidence in the customer's operation of his separator as follows: "We are perfectly willing that the expert agent run the other machine and you run the Economy, which you can do easily by following the simple directions which we send with each machine." Sales of cream separators rose from barely more than a quarter-million dollars in 1902 to almost two million dollars in 1906. The net profit on these separators in 1906 was 13.1 per cent of sales; in 1908 it was 28.5 per cent of sales.

This same bold approach was taken in merchandising many other new items which were sold in quantities that made mass production possible. For example, as automobiles became popular, the Sears catalog included automotive equipment and supplies. Also the 1909 catalog advertised an automobile entitled the "Sears motor buggy." This venture, however, did not prove profitable, and after several years the automobile was withdrawn from the catalog.

Mail-order sales increased during the prosperous decade 1910-20. The Sears catalog reflects, to some extent, the changes in type of goods carried. In 1905 the catalog had been 1100 pages; in 1910 it was 1348; by 1915 it was 1636. The greatest amount of space in 1915 was given over to women's, misses', and girls' ready-to-wear apparel. Furniture was second, and men's and boys' clothing, third. There were fourteen pages given over to the gasoline-engine department and another fourteen to the automobile-supply department. By 1920, twenty-six pages were used for the automobile-supply department. Among lines added between 1910 and 1917 which proved profitable and brought new technology to the rural customers were: electric household appliances, electric lighting plants, automobile accessories, marine supplies, building plans, dairy barn equipment, and machine-made houses. The 1920 catalog advertised a gasoline-powered washing machine for $107.50 and an electric washer selling for $85. A good many of the durable goods such as washers, vacuum cleaners, furnaces, electric light plants, and "modern homes" were available on installment purchase plans. The homes were, in fact, sold on credit even prior to World War I.

In the five-year period 1915-20, the sales volume of Sears and of Ward more than doubled. The year 1920 was a temporary peak, however, and the next year brought a sharp slump; in the following five years mail-order sales grew only modestly. The automobile, which Sears had failed to market successfully, was destined to affect mail-order business adversely.

Table 7-3   Growth in mail-order sales, 1915-1925°

SALES IN MILLIONS OF DOLLARS

YEAR	SEARS	WARD	NATIONAL BELLAS HESS
1915	$106.2	$ 49.3	$17.4
1920	245.4	101.7	47.7
1925	243.8	170.6	46.7

° Source: Boris Emmet and John E. Jeuck, *Catalogues and Counters: A History of Sears, Roebuck and Company* (Chicago: The University of Chicago Press, 1950), p. 204.

CHAIN STORES AND ADAPTATION OF MAIL-ORDER HOUSES

The decade of the 1920's has been called the chain-store era. This organizational form in retailing had already been developed in the grocery and limited-price variety-store lines prior to the First World War. Merchandising through chain stores, as it was developed by the managers of the Atlantic and Pacific Tea Company, F. W. Woolworth, J. C. Penney, and others, filled an important role in town and city retailing. By the 1920's the major mail-order firms were also in the process of opening retail chain stores.

Two characteristics of the economy of the 1920's were propitious for retail chain-store expansion, and both these characteristics involved technological developments. First, the population had become more than half urban by 1920, and thereafter the urban population continued to grow faster than the rural population. Second, with increased ownership of automobiles, the farmer was ready to go some distance for his retail purchases. While the representative distance travelled in 1900 had been five or six miles, this came to be thirty miles or more in the 1920's.

The organization of the chain-store system provided for a degree of centralized management, particularly in purchasing, determining store layout, and in accounting control. By providing mass distribution of goods, chain-store merchandisers could arrange for mass production at low cost and could bargain for low prices. When these retailers merchandised goods under their own brand names, so-called "private" brands, they further strengthened their power to bargain with the manufacturers.

By 1929 the Great Atlantic and Pacific Tea Company had retail sales of over a billion dollars, and F. W. Woolworth, sales of three hundred million. The sales of J. C. Penney were just over two hundred million dollars. In 1929, almost two fifths of grocery sales and nine tenths of variety five-and-ten-cent-store sales were made by multi-unit stores. More than one fifth of all retail store sales were made by such stores.

In the years following 1929 the chains continued to increase their sales, although because of the rise in retail sales generally, the chains' share of the total has not grown. Chain systems continue to be very important in the variety-sales field: by the 1960's chain stores made just over two fifths of all sales of groceries and in the tire, battery, and auto-accessory field. Regional chains assumed importance in both of these lines.

Counter developments to the growth of chains include the rise of co-operative wholesaling initiated by retail member stores and wholesaler-initiated voluntary chains, both of which, by the 1960's, account for nearly half of all grocery sales. In a number of states, punitive taxation was enacted against chains during the Depression years, under which the tax rate increased as the number of stores increased. At the federal level, the Robinson-Patman Act, passed in 1936, attempted to make it more difficult for large buyers to purchase goods at prices lower than those paid by the small buyers. Perhaps the ultimate accolade to chain-store efficiency was bestowed by the Ohio Farm Bureau, which, in December 1964, sponsored a resolution authorizing a comprehensive study of the possibility of purchasing stock control of the Great Atlantic & Pacific Tea Co.

By the 1960's the leading retail firms either were chains or included chains in their operations. The ten top firms in 1963, with over a billion dollars in sales, were all in this category. Sears, Roebuck and Montgomery Ward were among the ten top retailers in 1963, but by that time mail-order business held a subordinate place even in these firms, accounting for only one eighth of Ward's sales and one fourth of Sears's. In addition to their retail stores and mail-order sales, both these firms used their catalogs in making non-mail sales. In the 1930's, they instituted a system in larger cities for accepting telephoned orders made from catalogs; in small communities, catalog offices were established, which did not stock goods but simply took orders. In 1963 Ward operated 818 such catalog stores. In addition, both firms, after a halting start in the 1920's, expanded their retailing operations. Today they operate a total of over one thousand such department stores in cities of intermediate size. In large cities, they operate complete department stores which differ from the usual downtown department stores in that they are located in outlying neighborhoods, where land values are lower and parking space is more easily available.

SUPERMARKETS

The supermarket was the most conspicuous retailing innovation of the 1930's. Supermarkets are, essentially, large, departmentalized, self-service food stores that achieve a high volume of sales of both food and non-food items. Initially, in the early 1930's, they achieved high volume by offering goods at low prices in low-rental quarters, such as empty factories or warehouses, and on a cash-and-carry basis. As a consequence, such a market was called a "cheapy" on the eastern seaboard. On the West Coast, however, where the drive-in aspect was featured, someone with a more dramatic flair called the new markets "supers." The designation "supermarket" is more appropriate, since these stores now attract customers primarily because of their wide assortment of goods and convenient one-stop shopping, with adequate parking space.

Two concepts that anticipated the supermarket were cash-and-carry and self-service. By the 1920's, a greater portion of the grocery trade was conducted on a cash-and-carry basis than had been the case in 1900. Some impetus in this change may have come from the Atlantic and Pacific Tea Company's "economy stores," which operated on a cash-and-carry basis after 1912. Also in 1912 Clarence Saunders opened the first Piggly Wiggly self-service store in Memphis. By 1929 there were nearly 3000 self-service stores operated under the Piggly Wiggly franchise. Other self-service systems were soon in operation. In some cases the self-service units were parts of chains and in others they were independently owned stores operating under patented systems, using special equipment supplied through central buying services. Additionally, the limited-price variety stores, such as F. W. Woolworth, had a semi-self-service system under which goods on display were selected by the customer. The workability of all such systems depended upon customer familiarity with the products offered for sale, and with brand names through advertising, so that the goods could "sell themselves."

Increased consumer ownership of automobiles and electric refrigerators was a development that partly preceded and partly paralleled the major growth of supermarkets in the 1930's and after World War II. Ownership of both automobiles and refrigerators was prerequisite to the spread of once-a-week shopping. The automobile was, by 1930, both a necessity and a status symbol for many families in the vast middle class. In 1930 there were over twenty-three million registered passenger cars, nearly three times as many as in 1920. The number doubled in the subsequent thirty years. There was a comparable increase in the ownership of electric refrigerators, an innovation of the 1920's, which, by 1950, were to be found in almost nine-tenths of urban households. Technological developments which made possible open display of refrigerated fresh meats and even frozen foods without danger of spoilage were also important for the complete self-service supermarket.

The Super Market Institute has defined a supermarket as "a complete departmentalized food store with a minimum sales volume of one million dollars a year and at least the grocery department entirely self-service." Other studies have been based on merely a criterion of a minimum volume of $375,000 sales per year. This latter, broader definition includes just over one eighth of all grocery stores which, in 1960, made 69 per cent of total United States grocery sales. The success of the largest stores in attracting customers is reflected in their larger volume of sales per square foot of floor space. In 1960 the supermarkets with under half a million dollars' worth of yearly sales averaged 3722 square feet of sales area; they averaged $2.19 weekly sales per square foot of sales area. By contrast, the largest stores, with over two million dollars' worth of yearly sales, averaged $4.79 weekly sales per square foot of sales area. These modern, large markets offered consumers a choice of some 8000 items, compared with the 800 appearing on grocers' shelves in 1930.

SHOPPING CENTERS

The deliberate planning of space use to provide convenience as well as coordinated unity, orderliness, and beauty was the creative contribution of the shopping center developers. The shift of the automobile-owning consumers to suburban residences provided a pre-condition for the development of such coordinated centers on the periphery of major metropolitan areas. Sites were available at these locations on which land use could be planned from the start.

In a negative sense, the absence of adequate provision for vehicular traffic and parking in the central business district created a need for some new approach. The lag in road construction and parking provisions behind the increase in auto sales has been glibly designated the "affluence gap." The unco-ordinated development of shopping districts outside the downtown core provided conspicuous evidence of failure of the central area to provide for traffic and parking needs in the automobile age. These outlying districts occasionally became eye-sores, and sometimes changing traffic routes and the construction of freeways caused them to be bypassed by traffic and hence the business which they sought to attract.

Comprehensive planning, although often initially resisted by businessmen, was clearly called for. The basic need has been for conveniently located areas in which provision for access roads and adequate parking is regarded as an integral part of the land-use pattern. Some planned shopping centers are designed to serve only a limited neighborhood. In these, a departmentalized variety store and a supermarket are major tenants. Other centers are designed to serve a larger region, and in these one or more department stores constitute major tenants, while specialty stores are located in the line of pedestrian traffic. Beyond the element of store location, careful planners worked toward more than provision of store space, with the result that shopping centers today meet many of the needs formerly met by downtown areas. They offer opportunities for social life and recreation with their theaters, bowling lanes, auditoriums, and fine restaurants, as well as their carefully and attractively designed courts or parks. By the early 1960's there were more than 4500 such co-ordinated, planned shopping centers in the United States.

The impact of these centers upon the downtown department stores and the central business district specialty shops has been difficult to gauge fully. In almost all cases, the department store tenants in shopping centers are merely branches of the major department stores located in the core area. Stock comes from a common warehouse. Their billing is through the central office. Sales of such branches accounted for over half the gross of major retail firms for the first time in the year ended January 31, 1965. The long-established central business district department stores have found this new development just one more of the many problems faced since the Second World War. Other problems have included the rise of discount houses and the upgrading of variety stores to serve as junior department stores. Central business district retailers have assumed initiative, along with other interested groups, in promoting urban-core redevelopment. The tasks are large in both major cities and in moderately large cities.

HANDLING OF GOODS

The warehouse is a key element in the distribution of goods, and here, too, technology has produced significant changes. The use of trucks in freight hauling has facilitated relocation of warehouses on the periphery of major metropolitan centers where space is not at a premium. Modern warehouses on such sites are one-story buildings built to accommodate palletized loads put in position by fork-lift trucks. The use of electric or gasoline-driven trucks for materials-handling within the warehouses themselves became common in large part after the 1920's. As early as 1915 there were over one thousand electric trucks in use for materials-handling, but these were used mostly in industry. The now-familiar fork-lift was offered for sale a few years later, and subsequently, a wide variety of conveyor systems came into use.

Warehouse operation in the 1960's, by contrast with that of the 1920's, goes beyond mechanical handling of materials and, in some cases, includes automated equipment for selecting items, maintaining inventory records, and reporting when stocks fall to reorder points. Automated and computer-controlled warehousing opens the way for economies to retail systems that provide a standard selection of merchandise to many retail outlets, such as Sears and Ward. Sears practices "pooled-stock warehousing" which permits stores to carry smaller inventories. Montgomery Ward opened a service center for 121 retail and catalog stores at Detroit in 1958, in which 6700 types of goods were placed in stock, and from which these items were withdrawn as needed to fill orders, all through a computerized system. Perhaps one measure of the performance of this system is the fact that twenty-four trucks and ten freight cars can be simultaneously unloaded with all items moving directly to proper location and all inventory continuously recorded. The Detroit installation is reported to be just the beginning of a major change in Ward's materials-handling and recording system.

CONSUMER CREDIT

Consumer credit, which underlies much of the new economy of mass consumption in the 20th century, took a greater variety of forms than the pervasive open-book credit of the 19th century. Department stores and some specialty stores continued to charge goods, but with monthly billing. The charge privilege was similarly extended by oil companies, for example, to all purchases from their stations. At a later time such organizations as American Express and Diners Club provided a charge service on a great variety of purchases. The administration of such programs was facilitated by the "charge-plate" which the customer carried in his wallet and which bore his name and address embossed in such a way that these would be printed on his bill by a simple press made available to retailers honoring such cards or plates.

A different approach was initially taken in the sale of durable goods such as automobiles and refrigerators, which was comparable to the time-payment plans used by the mail-order houses during World War I. A modest downpayment secured possession of the appliance or automobile; the balance of the price, plus interest and service charges, was then paid in monthly installments. It was not until the customer's final payment that title was passed from the seller to the buyer. As early as 1929 this installment plan was used for nearly two thirds of all automobile sales and nearly one half of household-appliance sales.

Variations in department store and mail-order house charge accounts provided the convenience of both these types. There are ninety-day charge accounts and also revolving charge accounts, under which the customer is obligated to make monthly payments constituting some fixed proportion of the amount due. Administration of these programs has been facilitated by appropriate accounting, bookkeeping, and computing machines.

The widespread use of installment credit in the prosperous 1920's left some consumers overextended with the onset of the Depression years, and their goods were repossessed by the sellers or by the finance companies to whom they still owed money on the item purchased. Consumer credit was contracted during the ensuing Depression, and again during World War II, when consumers had cash and no durable goods were available. At the end of the war, consumer credit stood at five billion dollars. In the twenty years since the end of the war, consumer credit ballooned to seventy-four billion dollars. Easy financing has enabled a greater number of consumers to acquire new types of goods more promptly than would have been the case without credit.

CONCLUSION

The changes in distribution and marketing which we have surveyed have contributed toward facilitating the flow of goods to consumers. This increased distributive service has been the counterpart of the increased commodity production and the increased provision of services in our growing and affluent economy. In marketing, as in the services generally, increased performance heretofore has called for increased manpower.

Today, however, marketing management and market research may be on the threshold of new applications in the use of the computer and other technological devices. *Business Week* quoted a leading executive as saying, "In none of the major functions of American business has the impact of the computer been so lightly felt. Yet in none of the major functions is its potential so great."

It should be noted that the changes in distribution and marketing in the past have depended—and will depend in the future—in large measure upon technological developments within those fields and in other fields. Increases in production made possible mass consumption, while mass consumption necessitated increased production. Technological devices such as the automobile changed population patterns, distribution channels, and buying habits. In few other fields has the interdependence of technology and the consumer economy been so clearly shown as in the distribution and marketing of goods.

8 / The Social Effects of Mass Production
CHARLES R. WALKER

Writing more than twenty years ago, a Census Bureau expert, Dr. Alba Edwards, commented:

The most nearly dominant single influence in any man's life is probably his occupation. . . . A man's occupation not only tells for each workday, what he does during one half of his waking hours, but it indicates, with some degree of accuracy, his manner of life during the other half—the kind of associates he will have, the kind of clothes he will wear, the kind of house he will live in . . . and, in some degree, the cultural level of his family.

The technologies of mass production in their impact on occupations strongly affect men's lives in all the ways noticed by Dr. Edwards, and in many more. These technologies have their social effects on men and women in both industry and government, and at all levels, from supervisor to worker. In this chapter we shall emphasize the impact of the direct thrust of mass-production technologies on man at work in our industrial society and on man in his leisure time as well, especially in the lower echelons of industry, where it has been more drastic and in sharper contrast to pre-mass-production times. Possibly as the effects of automatic techniques increase, other ranks of our society will be even more exposed than the workers to these effects, but that is a subject for other investigators.

MASS PRODUCTION

Exactly what is mass production? A group of top executives in one of the largest American corporations, when asked by the author to define mass production, spent an hour in hot discussion, emphasizing first one aspect and then another of this widely used term. For the purposes of this chapter, however, we shall adopt a very simple and broad definition: mass production is volume production of a standardized product for mass consumption.

For Americans, and also for much of the rest of the world, the supreme symbol of mass production—in all aspects of its influence—has been the automobile. Writing for the *Encyclopaedia Britannica,* Henry Ford, the father of the mass-produced automobile, said:

Mass production is not merely quantity production for this may be had with none of the requisites of mass production. Nor is it merely machine production, which also may exist without any resemblance to mass production. Mass production is the focussing upon a manufacturing project of the principles of power, accuracy, economy, system, continuity, speed, and repetition. The normal result is a productive organization that delivers in continuous quantities a useful commodity of standard material, workmanship and design at minimum cost. The necessary precedent condition of mass production is capacity, latent or developed, of mass consumption, the ability to absorb large production. The two go together. . . .

Nowhere in economic history can one find so swift and pervasive a technological revolution as occurred in the automobile industry in the first half of the 19th century. In 1910 there was one passenger car for every 265 person in the United States, in 1928 there was one for every six, and by 1962, one for every two and a half persons. The widespread ownership of automobiles has transformed our material civilization, altering the nature of our towns, cities, and countryside and impinging on nearly every aspect of modern living; its revolutionary role in abolishing class lines and social stratification has often been celebrated, also. Throughout history an unbridgeable social distance had prevailed, separating the man who rode a horse or drove a carriage from the man who walked; within twenty-five years the automobile had abolished this distinction forever. A study made in 1928 in an urban community found that 29 per cent of all passenger-car sales were to laborers, firemen, artisans, and motormen. On the farm and in rural communities the Model T had become ubiquitous by 1920.

Henry Ford listed the fundamental steps in mass production in these words:

. . . the keyword to mass production is simplicity. Three plain principles underlie it: (a) the planned, orderly and continuous progression of the commodity through the shop; (b) the delivery of work instead of leaving it to the workman's initiative to find it; (c) an analysis of operations into their constituent parts. These are distinct but not separate steps; . . . All three fundamentals are involved in the original act of planning a moving line production.

Essential to the whole concept, as Ford went on to point out, is not merely the final assembly line but a multitude of sub-assembly lines, producing hundreds of parts to be delivered for final assembly. Thus, the machines are never idle; the workman, instead of moving from one to another, stays in one place doing his assigned job or jobs; materials are brought to him and the product taken away on the moving line; and the total job is broken down into a series of simple, repetitive tasks which the individual performs over and over again as the line moves by him.

Much in Ford's system was not new, the principle of division of labor being as old as Adam Smith, and the transfer of skills from men to machines—upon which mass production depended—being the essence of most technological progress. For at each step in the invention of new machines, skill was taken from the workman and built into the tool until, as a perceptive observer wrote many years ago: "The true significance of the Industrial Revolution was that it carried the transfer of skill to such a degree as to make the worker an adjunct to the tool, whereas formerly the tool was an adjunct to the skill of the worker."

THE WORK ENVIRONMENT: THE ASSEMBLY LINE

By 1949 when the Yale Technology Project began its studies of automobile assembly lines, these two principles—division of labor and transfer of skills—had reached the point that clearly produced a new *work environment* for modern man. The Yale Technology Project sought to investigate this environment.

Within this environment the Yale studies isolated the characteristics of the average assembly-line job as follows:

1. Mechanical pacing of work. The worker must time his operations to fit the speed of the moving line, finishing his assigned job or jobs on one part before the next arrives. In some jobs this requirement made for a more rigid schedule than others; in general, the assembly jobs on the main line required a more rigid pace of work than on sub-assemblies.

2. Repetitiveness. This feature of assembly-line work is perhaps most familiar

and most frequently commented on. There is, however, some difference between jobs. A job requiring the performance of five simple operations is repetitive, but less so than a job requiring only one operation. Out of a sample of 180 men studied, 57 performed one operation, 23 performed two operations, and the rest did three or more.

3. Minimum skill requirement. Nearly all assembly-line jobs are officially classified as "semi-skilled." A few may require months to learn, but many take only a few hours. Most mass-production jobs do not call for any skill in the traditional sense of judgment, experience, and varied dexterity of eye and hand. Quite often they call for a great deal of concentrated practice. Indeed, "practice" and "knack" would appear more appropriate words than "skill." Most jobs, except those of utility man and repairman, take relatively little time to learn.

4. Predetermination in the use of tools and techniques. This is the essence of assembly-line and indeed any kind of mass-production work. Any kind of individual control over, or choice of, tools or methods of work is eliminated for all except certain repair jobs.

5. Subdivision of the product worked on. As jobs are broken down into a few simple operations assigned to each worker, so is the product, into a multitude of small, seemingly meaningless parts. There are workers with as much as ten or twelve years' experience on the final assembly who have never seen a completed car roll off the line.

6. Surface mental attention. Although the work is repetitive in automobile assembly plants most of it requires a high degree of surface attention. Assembly jobs in some industries are such that the operator can think of other things while his fingers do the job mechanically, but in the automobile factory the line moves too fast to allow the worker to think—or to daydream.

Despite differences in both the jobs and the individual's reaction to them, the findings of social scientists both in the United States and abroad suggest that a majority of automobile assembly workers dislike their immediate or intrinsic jobs and that this dislike is often reflected in high turnover, in absenteeism, and in the quality of work done. Here is a social effect largely traceable to certain characteristics of mass-production technology. Rotation among jobs, some redesigning of the jobs themselves by industrial engineers, and "job enlargement," or a joining together of smaller job elements into a larger whole, are some of the methods that have been recommended to counter these negative effects. But it is important to notice, of course, the positive results of these same technologies. They make possible the payment of high wages for work demanding little skill, a great improvement in working conditions, and the extraordinary level of mass consumption from which the workers as well as most of the rest of the population benefit.

Mass-production technologies clearly impinge on the worker not only through the immediate content of his daily work but by moulding and modifying the social structure of the in-plant environment in which he spends his working hours. These technologies, of which the auto assembly line is an extreme example, tend to limit the amount of interaction and personal contact a man may have with his fellow workers, his supervisors, or other members of management. This is in contrast to certain other types of modern production—for example, the process industries, basic steel, oil and chemicals, and so forth. Lower ranks of management in these industries have sometimes important and frequent contacts with the blue-collar worker; but under assembly-line conditions, the lower managers tend to carry out their duties impersonally, thus confirming the worker's conviction that he is only a number or an adjunct to his machine.

The wage structure and the system of promotion also tend to reinforce a sense of impersonality. Because many mass-production jobs, although different in detail, are much the same from management's point of view, the companies greatly limit the number of pay classifications. In the auto industry, for example, the spread between the lowest paid assembly worker and the highest is, in most cases, only a few cents.

The same forces of mass production that simplify and standardize jobs and wages clearly influence the character of the promotion system in a mass-production plant. The production worker is on a "wage floor" which, although relatively high in certain industries, is also "flat." Unlike pre-mass-production times, there is no recognized ladder of progression to jobs of greater skill and responsibility as well as income. This characteristic, though not emphasized by all modern technologies, strikes at one of the strongest social incentives and also at the American cultural tradition of individual success and "rising in the world."

It is important to remember—especially when considering the social effects of mass-production technologies—the enormous diversity of American industry. For there are still a few important industries where crafts dominate, as in large portions of the printing and construction industries. Also, while the great process industries—basic steel, oil, and chemicals—come under our general definition of mass production since they produce in volume for a mass market, the social effects of their technologies are often quite different from those in the automobile or other assembly-line industries.

THE TEXTILE INDUSTRY

Before turning to the process industries, however, we shall look first at the textile industry, which has several unique features. The first is its long history as a mechanized industry, and the second is its geographical concentration in the South. Both in England and in this country the textile industry is the oldest factory industry, its history being almost synonymous with the rise of industrialism. It is, for this reason, the earliest industry to reflect many of the social consequences of technology and technological change. As historians of the Industrial Revolution have recorded, the unemployment and loss of skill that marked the transformation of handicrafts into the factory system gave rise to bitter protests by the workers, culminating in the famous Luddite riots of machine-wrecking which took place in England in 1811, and which were believed by some to be directed against the introduction of machines to take the place of hand labor. The end of the Napoleonic Wars and the depressed economic conditions that followed increased working-class misery and unrest.

In this country, New England, with its many streams available for water power, became the early American center for the manufacture of cotton and woolen goods and so remained throughout the 19th century. Although a few textile mills were opened in the South as early as 1880, it was only after World War I that the major migration of textiles from New England to the South took place. The move continued during the Depression years of the 1930's, encouraged by the availability of "cheap and docile labor" in small southern towns. Today 90 per cent of all cotton mills in this country and 50 per cent of our woolen mills are in the southern states. In these mills 40 per cent of the workers are women, nearly all of them being employed at low-skilled jobs. Maintenance and a few specialized occupations employ men, but even among male employees, only about 17 per cent can properly be classified as skilled workers.

Although textile manufacturing has no true assembly lines, workers have little freedom to determine the techniques of their work or to vary the sequence of timing of their jobs. Because textiles was originally a handicraft industry the transfer of human skill to the machine is nowhere more strikingly exemplified. Furthermore, any decisions not incorporated into the machine itself are made through work design or by supervisors and management. In the old days of handicraft production the weaver and, to a lesser degree, the spinner were skilled craftsmen, learning their trade in a long and strict apprenticeship; the weaver, especially, enjoyed considerable prestige among his fellows. Even with the introduction of the power loom a residue of skill and prestige still clung to the weaver's job. But with the automatic looms of today all skill resides in the machine. The weaver's and the spinner's jobs have been subdivided into a series of repetitive machine-tending tasks. Their low-skilled incumbents have become loom-cleaners, battery hands, doffers, and so forth.

The pacing of his job also has been taken away from the worker. Since there is no assembly line to determine the speed of work, this responsibility has been placed in the hands of supervisors; and as machines have grown more automatic and the workers' jobs routinized, there has been, as one might expect, a tendency to increase the number of machines that the worker is expected to tend. As a result, by the 1930's and 1940's what was called the "stretchout" in textiles came to be as bitterly resented as the "speedup" on the assembly line and, indeed, became a major grievance in the industry. Solomon Barkin, formerly an economist of the Textile Workers Union, has commented on some of the continuing fears of the textile workers, most of which have an economic or technological origin:

Most moves to increase the number of machines tended by operators create new fears, anxieties and pressure—the cumulative effects of which have bred the historic hatred of the "stretchout." Tension increases among workers as they face both new patterns and the larger machine assignments with the fear that they may not be able to handle the new job. . . . The worker's greatest fear is that machines will stand idle waiting for him. . . . Not to be "on top" of the job is a mark, to his peers, of inferior performance as well as an invitation for criticism and reprimand by his superiors. This constant state of alertness to breaks and stops creates a high degree of stress. . . .

In a pioneering study of work fatigue in a textile mill conducted by Elton Mayo in the early 1920's, rest periods were found to be extraordinarily effective in reducing physical and psychological fatigue and all but eliminating absenteeism. Yet in the late 1950's a researcher in a typical southern mill found that workers were allotted only one fifteen-minute break for smoking during an eight-hour shift. Machine pressure forced many operatives to eat lunch while working or to wait until they had "caught up with the machine."

As in many automobile plants, the textile worker has no recognized job ladder. He rarely rises to more responsible jobs as he grows older:

It is the job that is paid for . . . rather than the man, for the length of time with the company and the amount of experience do not count in calculating wages. As workers grow old and are unable to keep up with the fast moving machines, they are shifted to jobs requiring less speed and consequently their wages are reduced.

It is true, of course, that social influences other than technological ones determine the character of work and leisure for the southern textile worker. The working force is composed mainly of "poor whites" often brought down from their native hills to live in company villages; husband, wife, children, and close relatives frequently work in the same mill. As a result, strong loyalties of kinship and neighborhood develop. The pattern of submission to authority, represented by the church in their rural homes and by the employer in their new factory environment, has created a subculture that is quite distinct from any other working group in America today.

Many poor white families of roughly the same background migrated to Detroit in the boom days of the 'twenties, and again during World War II, and soon became absorbed into the larger northern community. Similarly, the small enclaves of Poles, Slavs, and other European workers in Pennsylvania steel towns have been "melted" into a mass-production society. Yet, except for migrant agricultural workers, no group in America has continued to experience the same kind of isolation as the southern textile worker. That situation is now changing. Most companies have sold their housing and no longer directly control the workers as landlords. Glenn Gilman, writing in 1956, stated that the caste system for the mill worker is passing. Other observers have found this hope too sanguine, but with the increasing industrialization and growth of urban communities in the South it is predictable that the extreme isolation of the southern textile worker will someday be a thing of the past.

THE PROCESS INDUSTRIES

For our final illustrations of the social influence of mass production as defined in this chapter, we turn to the great bloc of "process industries," chemicals, oil, and basic steel, among others. Since the First World War, and increasingly after World War II, these industries have been producing standardized products—gasoline, fertilizers, paper, drugs, and so forth—in enormous volume and for very large mass markets. Although assembly-line techniques are inappropriate here, technologies in these industries have been thoroughly modernized from year to year. Automatic controls were common in some of them, as in the oil industry, many years before the word "automation" was invented. In several important ways process technologies have produced quite different social effects than those we reviewed in machine industries like automobiles and textiles. We turn to several outstanding examples:

1. Time is less important than in the other industries we have examined; there is no speedup or stretchout. Instead, these processes demand of the operator continual vigilance, alertness, and responsibility.

2. Many, though not all, of the process industries offer greater security and continuity of employment. The labor costs in oil refineries, for example, are a relatively small fraction of the total cost, so that even in business recessions, maintaining trained and reliable crews is more important than saving money through layoffs.

3. The jobs have somewhat greater variety and call for a wider span of attention than do jobs in other types of mass-production technology.

4. In some of these industries there is a closer relationship between the ranks of management and of blue-collar workers.

5. In some process industries, such as basic steel, there are close-knit crews of men at work, so that part of the personal satisfaction of the job is membership in a smooth-working team. In others, as in the now thoroughly automated oil industry, operators frequently work in isolation in front of consoles or control boards. Such men must have a strong sense of responsibility since they exercise power over a variety of processes and expensive machinery.

6. Finally, some companies do offer the possibility for progressive advancement, in sharp contrast to assembly lines and most of the textile industry. In these companies many more workers can expect to grow in skills, responsibility, and income over the years.

Robert Blauner, in a study contrasting the impact of varied technologies on the worker, comments as follows on the process industries:

Continuous-process technology reduces the powerlessness of the blue-collar worker by giving him control over his immediate work process. The technology, work organization, and social structure of these industries also counteract tendencies toward meaninglessness. The result is that workers in continuous-process industries have more of a sense of purpose, understanding, and function in their work than workers in machine-tending and assembly-line technologies.

The impact of automation on the mass-production industries is such an important question that an entire later chapter is given over to the principal effects of automatic technologies. We will, therefore, only point out that automation introduces special social opportunities as well as special social problems. It is important to emphasize, however, that the so-called age of automation does not replace the age of mass production; in some ways it speeds it up, enhancing the efficiency of former mass-production technologies as well as their social effects. In other ways, such as through the introduction of the computer into the office and "numerical control" into the factory, it brings into the industrial economy wholly new influences, whose full social significance we have hardly begun to explore. We are living, in short, in an age of transition and in an age of mixed technologies, which are having profound but not as yet thoroughly understood social effects.

LEISURE

One of the most important social effects of mass production on our mass culture is the changing relation between work and leisure. This includes not only the "new leisure," its amount and its quality, but the reciprocal relationship between work and leisure activities. The promise and the problems implied were already being experienced before the advent of automation. They are now greatly emphasized.

In 1850 the average number of working hours in non-agricultural industries was 65.7 a week; in 1960 this had dropped to 38, but as Sebastien de Grazia in his recent study for the Twentieth Century Fund has pointed out, neither the jobs nor the hours were the same in 1960 as in 1850. In 1850 the workman was usually paid by the day—which was long, ten or twelve hours—but he then worked at his own pace. Thus, although his work day had no formal "rest periods," it was broken up by interchanges with his fellow workers, his foreman, and sometimes, the top boss. If he lived near enough, he often went home for lunch; if he brought a lunch pail, work usually stopped for the lunch period so that it was a real break with time for social exchanges. Time itself mattered much less; considerable leisure, in short, was built into the job.

By 1950 and indeed earlier in many industries, job time, although shorter, had become more costly. An enormous overhead investment in machines and plant and the functional rise of the cost accountant meant that every minute, even every second, was of prime importance. In automobile plants, for instance, the hour was divided into ten-minute periods and wages calculated accordingly, so that the so-called hourly wage-earner found his paycheck at the end of the week figured not on hours but on one sixth of each hour. Rest pauses and lunch periods were carefully regulated and had become a major issue in collective bargaining negotiations. Whether through the mechanism of the moving line or the speed of highly automated machinery, the pace of work was no longer under the worker's control.

In some industries reduction in hours netted great gains for workers, as well as for lower and middle management, by relieving pressure and fatigue. Until the 1920's, for example, workers and supervisors in basic steel worked a twelve-hour day, seven days a week; and every two weeks when they changed from night to day shift they worked twenty-four hours around the clock. The work was hot and physically exhausting. The growth of mass-production technologies which, along with collective bargaining and government intervention, helped to bring about the eight-hour day, enormously lightened the burden and increased the real leisure time of the average employee in these jobs and many similar ones in industry.

However, as factory hours have decreased, much of the time gained has been absorbed in other ways so that the net increase in "free" time is not what it first appears to be. In 1850 the average worker lived a short distance away from the plant and walked to work. Today, long bus journeys, crowded highways, or packed commuter trains add an estimated eight and a half hours a week to the hours spent in the plant. They also add a varying amount of nervous and physical fatigue. Homes and their equipment are more complicated; the worker in 1850 did not have to worry about repairs to electrical and plumbing equipment. Today's technology has given the worker all this, but he now has to earn money to keep them in repair or learn how to make the repairs himself. The worker sometimes "moonlights," as the practice of a second job is called, in order to add to his income. Moreover, in 1850 few married women worked, so that few men concerned themselves with household chores. Today it has become common practice for most husbands to help working wives with the dishes, the weekend marketing, and other chores connected with house or children. As a result, according to the Twentieth Century Fund study, the present-day worker who is head of a family has only slightly more net free time than his 19th-century counterpart.

Nevertheless it cannot be denied that the average worker in mass production has weekends off and vacations, social dividends that the factory worker of a hundred years ago never dreamed of. In the use of this time technology appears in a new role, as television, radio, and above all the automobile, play key roles in his leisure. The automobile takes him not only to work and to the supermarket, but gives him mobility to spend his weekends visiting relatives, taking his family to the mountains or the beach, or himself to the public golf course. For such purposes, the automobile is more than "transportation." It is a source of power, freedom, and satisfaction that almost every American from the age of sixteen has come to consider his birthright. It is often noted, usually unsympathetically, that the slum family who can afford few of life's amenities often has surprisingly expensive cars. It is easy to see why: the automobile in America today is not only a status symbol but the symbol of a free and better life, and to no man more than to the one who spends eight hours a day making them. In an important sense the man behind the wheel is "anyone's equal."

According to a study made in 1956 by the Opinion Research Corporation of Princeton, New Jersey, 37 per cent of the manual workers interviewed had taken vacations of a week or more during the previous year, most of them in the family car. Another 21 per cent had taken such vacations sometime in the previous five years. Other leisure activities of industrial workers as found by this study included watching competitive sports (27 per cent), participating in them (20 per cent), engaging in non-competitive sports (38 per cent), social recreational, political, or athletic clubs (7 per cent), or fraternal organizations (15 per cent). Outings and picnics were listed as favorite recreational pastimes by 7 per cent, and 6 per cent mentioned gardening. Increased leisure is, of course, a dividend of modern technologies for the whole population, not solely for the worker. All income groups at every educational level, with the exception only of the very old and of young couples without children, spend an average of 5 to 6 per cent of their income on recreational activities and equipment. But such a figure represents only a minimum; it has been estimated, for instance, that one third to one half of the purchase price and upkeep of all automobiles goes for pleasure and recreation.

Some of the most challenging questions raised by the new character of leisure acquired from mass-production technologies and automation are these: Do all of these changes add up to a real displacement of work from the central place it has traditionally occupied in the life of man? Will the worker in the future derive his most important satisfactions not from a work career but from occupations pursued in his free time? Clearly it is too soon to give definite answers, but it is not too soon to say that the character of both work and leisure and the relationship between them have been profoundly altered by the new technologies.

A CASE STUDY IN CHANGE

We have already concluded that we are in an age of transition between the typical mass-production technologies of the 'twenties, 'thirties, 'forties, and early 'fifties and something new that we loosely term automation. To illustrate some of the problems of this transitional period we shall turn briefly to a study of the installation of the first semi-automatic pipe mill in the United States, made in a plant of the US Steel Corporation from 1947 to 1955. The study thus began at a time when almost no one was using the word "automation" and ended when it was beginning to be discussed as the wave of the future.

From the standpoint of the social effects of mass production in this age of transition, the new equipment: (1) increased enormously the volume and quality of an already standardized product—in this case seamless pipe—for an already large market; (2) cut down, as automatic equipment frequently does, the number of men employed while doubling the quantity of product, thus creating at first the fear and later the fact of technological displacement; (3) greatly lightened the physical load of the job for workers and supervisors and increased the demand for new mental skills for some of them; (4) left certain jobs untouched by automatic controls or partially affected others, while it completely transformed the content of some jobs; and finally (5) it suggested, but did not solve, new problems of psychological adjustment, training, and education for all groups—engineers, managers, and white- and blue-collar workers.

The technological—and consequent social—changes which took place in this pipe mill may stand for a large segment of the now rapidly transforming American economy. With the aid of new machines and new arrangements fewer men produce more goods. Some jobs are upgraded so that retraining or more formal education is demanded; other jobs are wiped out, meaning that alternative employment must be found.

MASS PRODUCTION AND MASS CONSUMPTION

Since mass production demands mass consumption, we are faced with the necessity of creating a society in which consumption must be maintained even though work declines. Our moral philosophy has tended to relate the right to consume with the need for long and hard work; hence the demand for mass consumption is difficult to absorb into our ethical system and makes great demands on our social fabric as well. For the mass production required by mass consumption means that education becomes even more important to bring workers up to the skilled or even professional levels; and the ability to produce more with less work means keeping youths from entering the work force until they are older and taking middle-aged people off the work force sooner by earlier retirement—a prospect which, coupled with greater life expectancy, raises enormous problems of leisure. One is reminded of what Henry Ford II said in a talk before the American Society of Mechanical Engineers shortly after becoming president of the Ford Motor Company:

Machines alone do not give us mass production. Mass production is achieved by both machines *and* men. And while we have gone a long way toward perfecting our mechanical operations, we have not successfully written into our equation whatever complex factors represent Man, the human element.

9 / The Crisis of Abundance
ROBERT THEOBALD

In recent years, economists have reached rather general agreement about the critical factor necessary to secure a continuing high rate of economic growth in the rich countries of the world: people and institutions must be provided with the means to purchase all the production put onto the market. This is in accordance with the work of John Maynard Keynes, the famous British economist. Economists disagree, however, over how this purchasing power is to be created and especially as to whether future purchasing power can match the rapidly increasing flow of goods produced by modern technology.

If we are to determine probable developments for the future we must examine how much production is presently available and how rapidly we can expect it to increase the national income. The value of goods and services produced in the United States in 1966 was approximately $725 billion, which amounts to an average income of some $7000 per family unit. Although this chapter concentrates on the situation in the United States, developments in Europe can be expected to follow much the same path, although at a later date. Determination of the relevant issues for America will also illuminate the policy facing European countries.

THE RATE OF PRODUCTIVITY

Knowing the production that was achieved in 1966, we must now go on to determine the rate of increase which may be achieved in production, and, therefore, the amount of goods and services available for consumption. The 1966 Presidential Commission on Automation, Technology and Economic Progress (Automation Commission) has provided its answer to the question. It has estimated that "In the 35 years before the end of the Second World War, output per man-hour rose at a trend rate of 2 per cent a year. . . . Between 1947 and 1965 productivity in the private economy rose at a trend rate of about 3.2 per cent a year." In other words, the amount that each worker in the private economy could produce rose by 2 per cent in the earlier period and by 3.2 per cent in the later period. Using this data, the Automation Commission assumed that we could anticipate that productivity would continue to rise at about the postwar average rate over the coming decade at least. Because the Automation Commission's report was signed by leaders in all segments of the society and because there were no really significant dissenters from the tenor of the documents, the Commission represents the general consensus of conventional thinking about the technological revolution.

At first sight a 3.2 per cent rate of increase scarcely appears dramatic. However, the consequences of compound interest are such that a growth rate of 3.2 per cent means a doubling of production in about 22 years. Thus, if the Automation Commission is right about productivity rates, and their assumption remains valid beyond the period 1965-76, family income would be about $14,000 in the second half of the 'eighties, $28,000 around the year 2010, and some $224,000 a century from now.

THE COMPUTER

Many analysts believe, on the other hand, that the report of the Commission is excessively conservative in its estimates. These analysts focus their case on the potential impact of the computer, which was dismissed by the Automation Commission in a single sentence:

It is beyond our knowledge to know whether the computer, nuclear power and molecular biology are quantitatively or qualitatively more "revolutionary" than the telephone, electric power and bacteriology.

In the opinion of these men no new means of adding to and controlling production has ever been introduced so rapidly as was the computer. The first commercial computer was installed in 1950; the number of computers operating in the United States had grown to 5000 by 1960, and is conservatively estimated to reach 70,000 by 1970. During the decade of the 'sixties, the technique of time sharing will come into general use: it is even today well beyond the experimental stage. Because time sharing allows several people to use the same computer at the same time without even leaving their offices, it greatly increases the usefulness of each computer, enabling it to function closer to its capacity. In addition, major improvements are being made in the handling of information, both in terms of the efficiency of the computer itself and also in the programmer's ability to provide the computer with information in the form most suitable to its capacities.

It is, of course, difficult to develop figures for the effects of these last two developments, but it may be helpful to provide even extremely crude estimates.

Thus, it is probably conservative to estimate that an average of ten people will use each computer simultaneously in 1970, as compared to one in 1960; it is equally conservative to estimate that the average computer in 1970 will handle information 1000 times more efficiently than in 1960. When one multiplies these two figures by each other and by the increase in the number of computers during the decade, one arrives at an estimate for the increase in computer information handling capacity of 140,000 times. Most of the impact of this increase in capacity will make itself felt between 1965 and 1970. No slowing down of the pace of introduction of computers is foreseeable at the present time.

It can be expected that this increase in computer capacity will have wider consequences than are yet generally understood. The prime results of the introduction of the computer are to force rationalization of operations, and to minimize the possibility for organizations to carry people who do not contribute to the efficient operation of the system. Charles de Carlo, Corporate Director of Advanced Systems Research for the International Business Machines Corporation, described this effect in an article in the magazine *Campus Dialogue:* ". . . the information processing system represents a different phenomenon in the history of machine development, being the ultimate extension of physical implementation of a way of thinking about, and controlling, other machines and devices for transforming the physical environment."

Given this reality of increasing rationalization, we can expect additional pressure to limit production staffs and also employees in the middle levels of organizations, whether engaged in management, engineering, accounting, banking, or legal services. For any job that is structured, that is to say, one where the decision-making rules can be set out in advance, it will be possible to replace an individual with a computer; and as wage and salary costs rise and machine-system costs fall it will be more and more profitable to do so. The certainty of this development for middle management was recently documented in a report entitled "Automation and the Middle Manager," issued by the American Foundation on Automation and Employment.

Computer-controlled machine systems will not only be inherently more productive in the future but they will almost literally force men out of structured activity. Thus there is the potential not only for rapid increases in output but also for rapid declines in manpower needed. The combination would result in an increase in productivity per man-hour, meaning that the availability of goods and services would grow considerably faster than predicted by the Automation Commission.

PRESENT RESOURCE DISTRIBUTION

At first sight such a possibility appears completely favorable: to achieve the highest possible output of goods and services. However, the present method of distributing the growing quantity of goods and services requires us to examine several questions before we can be certain that continued growth in production will necessarily improve the position of the individual and the society.

We must first recognize that it is inherently difficult to measure the availability of goods and services; also, it is not necessarily true that an increase in available goods and services results in an increase in economic welfare, let alone social welfare. Our faith in present statistics is such that we consider an increase in national income as necessarily good without any further examination. This is unrealistic, for our methods of calculation are most peculiar. We can see just how odd they are by examining the effect of a rebuilding program. Such programs cost tenants and those in neighboring buildings money; however, payments for moving from one building to another and for additional cleaning, repainting, and so on, made necessary by the demolition, appear by some alchemy as an *addition* to and not a *subtraction* from the national income. Given today's methods of calculation, any *expenditure* increases the national income. We urgently need new methods of calculation that will reflect more accurately real changes in wealth. We should be able to calculate which uses of goods and services represent additions to economic welfare and which—such as costs of transit to and from jobs or anti-pollution moves—should either not be counted at all or should appear as costs rather than as benefits.

In addition, we must recognize that there is no theory in economics which makes it possible to argue that an increase in economic welfare necessarily results in an increase in social welfare or an improvement in the general way of life. This is an assumption of economics which cannot be proved and which is increasingly being challenged by other social-science disciplines.

The problems of measurement, however, are not the only ones which need concern us. We must recognize also the implications of our present socioeconomic system, which is organized in such a way that it will not function satisfactorily unless all available production is purchased; if this does not occur, a proportion of the population will be deprived of a share of the ever-growing volume of production which becomes available each year. It is important to recognize the full implications of this statement. Our present socioeconomic system depends upon a very simple resource-distributing mechanism: in effect, it is assumed that it is possible for the overwhelming proportion of those seeking jobs to find them and that the incomes received from these jobs will allow the job-holder to live with dignity. Our present system therefore requires for its satisfactory operation that we are able to find jobs for all those who seek them. This situation occurs only when people are willing to purchase everything that is produced. As we will see later in this chapter, even when this is the case, it may still be a problem to provide jobs for those less skilled and educated.

One consequence of the economic situation has been that businesses increasingly feel compelled to strengthen their efforts to persuade the consumer to buy, for they have recognized that it is not a lack of productive capacity that limits their output, but rather their inability to sell all the goods and services produced. Similarly, governments have ceased to be passive observers of the economic situation and have moved instead to balance the national economic system. Meno Lovenstein, an economist, has summarized the evolution in an essay in *The Guaranteed Income:* "This responsibility of the Federal government [for assuring economic stability] is widely accepted, but the policies are still thought of as providing a *favorable environment* for private enterprise. In a sense, they do, but with the continuous large budgets of the Federal government, the growing ones of the state and local governments, and the added responsibility for economic growth, would it not be more descriptive and insightful and honest to speak of these policies and actions as guaranteeing the national income."

We must therefore face up to two matters. First, even assuming that society desires to absorb all the goods and services which can be produced, will we have enough wisdom to ensure that the ability to purchase available goods will mesh with the types of goods capable of being produced? Second, the Automation Commission study shows that the present rate of increase in production exceeds the fastest rate of increase in demand recorded in the past.

It should be emphasized that there would be no serious difficulty in writing an economic program to ensure that all goods and services would be used. All economists would agree that policy measures can be devised to use all competitive resources. There is no *economic* problem in achieving full use of competitive resources for a considerable time into the future; the problem here is political. And while it is now part of conventional wisdom to argue that there are massive unmet economic needs among the American poor, massive unmet social needs in America, and massive requirements for goods and services elsewhere in the world, it is surely clear that American society is not yet ready for the major restructuring of its institutions that would be required for an all-out attack on the causes of poverty, both internal and external, and an all-out attempt to build an attractive environment. Whether one believes that the necessary rethinking will take place as fast as will be required to keep up with technological change depends upon one's personal judgment and must be decided by each reader individually.

LIMITS ON CONSUMPTION

Yet the question of whether we will be able to use all the available production is certainly less important than whether we should be willing to continue to accept the present socioeconomic system, which operates satisfactorily only if we use all the available production. The conventional economic reply to this point states simply that tastes are insatiable, and that is is irrelevant to discuss the possible limitation of consumption since people will desire everything that can be produced.

We have already seen that such an argument is certainly overstated, for there must come a point at which we will want to restrict consumption. The economist Robert Heilbroner made the point dramatically, if inelegantly, in the *New York Review of Books*. After examining the feasible rate of increase in production to $224,000 per family a century from now, he continued: "Is it beyond human nature to think that at this point (or a great deal sooner) a ceiling will have been imposed on demand—if not by edict, than tacitly? To my mind, it is hard not to picture such a ceiling unless the economy is to become a collective vomitorium." The question we need to discuss, therefore, is how soon we can expect a drive toward limitation of consumption and production, either because of developments in individual attitudes or changes in social requirements.

Arguments about the need for and the desirability of limiting consumption have, in the past, been based primarily on the social undesirability of life patterns that emphasize consumption. Analysis along these lines has had little appeal for a society that has always basically believed that "enough" is $1000 more than present income. Recent experimentation, however, has confirmed the significance of the problem of sensory overload, that is, an inability to absorb more than a certain amount of experience in a given time. Sensory overload results in a deadening of all the senses. This can be illustrated on one level by a new anesthesia technique, used particularly in dentistry, of providing earphones to the patient and then raising the level of sound to the point where pain ceases to be felt. A similar phenomenon occurs during rapid world tours: it becomes impossible to absorb more sights or sounds. The implications of this understanding of sensory overload are critical because there is increasingly general agreement that creativity depends upon a period of low sensory activity, in other words, upon an opportunity to reflect. As individuals come to realize the reality of sensory overload, they can be expected voluntarily to restrict their input of sensory perceptions; this will inevitably force limits on purchases and on travel.

In addition, society will be forced to limit waste by changing its pattern of rewards and sanctions. This argument cannot be based successfully, in my opinion, on the assumed shortage of raw materials, for man's ability to produce new materials through physics and chemistry could grow at least as fast as his need for materials. Rather, the need for limiting waste—whether caused by exaggerated rates of obsolescence, the development of a "throw-away" culture, the acceptance of polluting by-products, or other reasons—will be based upon awareness of the necessity to limit the degree of change in the environment if man is to survive, part of our growing knowledge of ecology.

Even if the previous arguments were conceded, which is not generally the case, many people would feel that the needs of the poor countries were so great that we could not afford to cut back on production—whatever we do not need can be employed abroad. It should be recognized that this argument is often advanced as a last-ditch attempt to avoid making the change required by abundance. However, the argument is invalid even when this is not used as the basis. It is, of course, valid to argue that we should provide the developing countries with all the resources they can effectively absorb; but it is totally unjustified to leap from this statement to the argument that poor countries can absorb anything the rich countries do not need. Given present levels of aid and our lack of knowledge of how to use massive aid to improve, rather than to damage, conditions in the poor countries, it seems unlikely that as much as 10 per cent of the annual increase in production in the rich countries could be used effectively to support higher levels of aid programs.

Dennis Gabor, a British physicist, has indicated the implications of the need to limit growth. After pointing out the fact that under present conditions all curves are exponential, he continues: ". . . exponential curves grow to infinity only in mathematics. In the physical world they either turn around and saturate or they break down catastrophically. It is our duty as thinking men to do our best towards a gentle saturation, instead of sustaining the exponential growth, though this faces us with very unfamiliar and distasteful problems."

EMPLOYMENT

The extensiveness of the changes required would be affected still further with a profound shift in the demand for labor, which many analysts expect will occur. It now seems extremely probable that we are entering what I call a "reverse-leisure society"—one in which those with the most creativity and imagination, and therefore the capacity to enjoy leisure, will have very little spare time, while those with little education will be unable to find meaningful activity—unless we change our socioeconomic system dramatically.

This causes severe problems at both ends of the ladder. First, we must examine how we are to economize the time of those people who will be in increasingly short supply as the system demands higher and higher levels of imagination and creativity. There is already substantial evidence to show that the degree of overload on those engaged in trying to determine appropriate directions for society is excessively great and is certain to increase further.

As the load on those directing society increases, a different problem appears to be emerging for those with inadequate education and skills. This view of the problem is challenged by conventional analyses, however, for the position accepted by most economists is that the pace of improvement in educational accomplishments will counterbalance the increase in the efficiency of machines, and that special education and retraining programs will be adequate to deal with the relatively few people who require further help. Unfortunately, however, there is no economic theory or contemporary evidence to justify this conclusion. The theorizing of the last part of the 19th century and the beginning of the 20th assumed that men and machines would augment one another's capacities, whereas today they are competitive. Keynes's writings, which are used as the justification for the assertion that demand and supply can be kept in balance, and jobs provided for all, are improperly used for this purpose because Keynes excluded from his analysis the very factors that now threaten massive unemployment: "We take as given the existing skill and quantity of available labor, the existing quality and quantity of available equipment, the existing technique." In effect, therefore, economists have no valid theoretical structure to support their contention that the problem of ultimate unemployability can be avoided by counterbalancing increases in demand for products and services which will keep everyone gainfully employed.

The application of economic theory to today's world suggests that, on the contrary, unemployability is inevitable for an ever-growing number of people unless the socioeconomic system is changed. At the present time the minimum wage is rising while the cost of machine systems is declining; one estimate suggests that a present-day dollar's worth of computer time will cost only three cents in 1970. Application of the fundamental law of supply and demand shows that machine systems will inevitably become more attractive than great numbers of potential employees.

This expected theoretical relationship can already be supported by developments in employment statistics. As is well known, Negro unemployment rates remain obstinately twice as high as those of whites. This cannot justifiably be ascribed to problems of discrimination, for the relative position of the Negro has worsened at the same time that the degree of discrimination has lessened. The President's 1964 manpower report emphasized this deterioration, stating: "The disparity between non-white and white unemployment since 1955 . . . has been much broader than it was between 1947 and 1955." The most disturbing element in the picture is that the Negro teenage unemployment rate remains about 25 per cent and has not fallen throughout the 1960-66 boom; and this figure has been arrived at by considering those active in programs under the War on Poverty either as being employed or outside the labor force —a complete reversal of the statistical practice of the 1930's, which would have counted them as unemployed.

The most disturbing information available thus far on this subject came from a special census report of the South Los Angeles area following the rioting in Watts in 1965. During the boom period of 1960-66, when general economic conditions in the United States were improving at an unprecedented rate, conditions in South Los Angeles were no better than static, and some key indicators actually showed declines. For example, the male unemployment rate for South Los Angeles was 11.3 per cent in 1960 and 10.1 per cent in 1965 while nationally the unemployment rate for non-white males dropped from 12 per cent to 6 per cent during the same period. Median family income in South Los Angeles actually declined during a period in which the typical American family's rose substantially.

A severe problem of unemployability thus appears to be emerging. Certain types of workers have insufficient capacities to be worth employing at any job for the prevailing wage rate. Under the circumstances, employers can be expected to claim that there is a severe shortage of workers even at times when large numbers of people assert that they cannot find jobs. Also, it is still not recognized that the problem of ultimate unemployability is not confined to blue-collar workers. A recent *Wall Street Journal* story stated that even amid the present boom a substantial number of middle-management personnel are finding it impossible to keep up with the new knowledge required for effective administration. The lead sentence of the article set the tone: "Today's fast-changing business methods are spawning a new breed of executive—the obsolete executive." In particular, companies that rely ever more heavily on computers find it necessary to give responsibility to younger people who have an understanding of computer management, thus limiting the prospects of older employees who would normally have continued to move up the management ladder. A recent survey by the American Foundation on Automation and Employment indicated that the problem could be expected to spread rapidly.

THE PROBLEM

At this point a summary of the arguments thus far would probably be helpful. Economists now agree that it is possible to achieve a rapid increase in production in the rich countries so long as people and institutions are allowed to obtain the goods which are produced. They disagree on three prime issues: (1) the rate at which the ability to produce goods and services will increase, and though the differences in percentage terms appear small, they are significant because of the impact of compound interest; (2) the desirability of additional goods and services; or to put it differently, when the individual has enough and when the system should not be forced to produce more. It is argued on one side that wants are unlimited, on the other, that there is already a necessity for limiting production and consumption; and, finally (3) the prospect of ultimate unemployability for a substantial number of employees as computers and machine systems continue to develop.

As might be expected, these differences in values and assumptions result in fundamentally different approaches to solving the problems of a mass-production society. The conventional approach was clearly set out in the program of the Automation Commission, which included the following points:

1. For those with obviously usable skills and no other serious competitive

handicaps, ample job opportunities and adequate incomes can be assured by management of the total demand for goods and services.

2. For those less able to compete in the labor market, productive employment opportunities adapted to their abilities should be publicly provided.

3. Under the best of circumstances, there will be some who cannot or should not participate in the job economy. For them there should be an adequate system of income maintenance, guaranteeing a floor of income at an acceptable level.

As the Commission is the most authoritative source which has proposed a set of programs to deal with the problems of technology, it is perhaps worth citing its justification for each of the points made above at somewhat greater length. The first point on stimulating overall demand was stated in the following way: "It is the unanimously held conviction of the Commission that the most important condition for successful adjustment to technological change is an adequate level of total employment and income. We recognize that this is not the end of economic policy, but we are confident it is the beginning. . . . Some combination of tax reduction (leading to higher private spending) and increased public expenditure will be required to stimulate the economy when stimulus is needed. The choice between them depends upon our national priorities: a balanced policy will in the long run surely include both."

The second point on availability of jobs for all was advanced in the following way: "We take seriously the Employment Act of 1946 to provide 'useful employment opportunities for all those able, willing, and wishing to work.' . . . The principle of . . . public service employment has been implicitly endorsed in existing programs. We recommend that the concept be expanded and made explicit as a permanent, long-term program. . . . We therefore recommend (1) that public service employment opportunities be provided to those unsuccessful in the competition for existing jobs; (2) that a 5-year program be established, with the amount of public service employment increased each year, depending upon previous experience and labor market conditions; (3) that an initial sum of $2 billion be appropriated to provide about 500,000 additional full-time public service jobs."

The third recommendation for new methods of income maintenance was argued in the following terms: "We are convinced that rising productivity has brought this country to the point at last when all citizens may have a decent standard of living at a cost in resources the economy can easily bear. We believe that nearly all should, and wish to, earn their own support, for the dignity and self-respect that come from earning one's own living can hardly be achieved otherwise. . . . We suggest that Congress give serious study to a 'minimum income allowance' or 'negative income tax' program."

The Commission's report has been challenged primarily on the grounds of its underlying assumption that most citizens desire, and should desire, to earn their own support; those who question this assumption feel that men should not need to work for their living at a time when machines can increasingly produce the goods and services required by the society.

A SUGGESTED SOLUTION: BASIC ECONOMIC SECURITY

Individuals advancing this latter view, and I am among them, argue that the first appropriate step at present would be to provide every individual with a guaranteed income, or Basic Economic Security (BES), as I have called it in my writings. Indeed, it would appear that we will need to go further: if we are to deal with the threat of the ultimate unemployability of those who presently have adequate incomes, some form of income maintenance will be essential.

Supporters of BES recognize that the key element in the proposal is an absolute, constitutional guarantee. While the additional funds made available would have some short-run benefits even if a constitutional guarantee were not adopted, the long-run effect would be disastrous, for the payment of benefits would become a weapon to force conformity. Moreover, if the right to an income is not absolutely guaranteed, some method of determining eligibility for the guaranteed income would have to be introduced; and those applying the eligibility rules would have overwhelming power. It is better, therefore, to permit some people to abuse the guaranteed income—as some would in the early stages—rather than provide any government with such potential for tyranny. Such a position is, of course, only logical if the percentage of those who would choose to be idle is small. Available studies of many groups—from those on welfare to those in middle management—show that idleness is greatly feared and that the vast majority of Americans do not want to be mere cultural spectators but rather hope to fulfill some societal role. But, it should be noted, this is not the same as being forced to work in order to earn a living.

Those arguing for BES claim that full employment does not promise the full achievement of America's potential; rather, that people will act more creatively if they have the right to an income and are challenged to develop themselves and their society. They claim that BES is not merely one possible solution to the problem of cybernation, which can be compared with many others, but that, on the contrary, it is the prerequisite to other policies which must be developed to deal with emerging problems. They argue further that there is in American society today a vast amount of human energy that cannot be employed because of a lack of available independent financial resources, and that the provision of BES would lead to cultural, social, and political advance on an unprecedented scale.

For society at large, and especially for those creative individuals now shackled by the absence of BES, the situation appears analogous to the introduction of limited liability in the 19th century. Limited liability was introduced to encourage risk-taking by those investing in companies. The concept of a joint venture was replaced by the concept that the stockholder's liability for company debts no longer puts a lien on his total wealth but only on the amount he invested in the company. Limited liability was a pre-condition for the taking of risks; it did not insure risk-taking or innovation but it did make them possible, thus allowing the economy and society to benefit from the self-interested acts of individuals.

Similarly, BES provides the individual with the ability to do what he personally feels to be important. This allows risk-taking and innovation in areas where the existing and emerging needs of society are not being met by an otherwise efficiently functioning free enterprise market system. And since the minimum income is not mediated through the offices of any individual or organization within the market system it consequently does not carry any built-in pressures for the recipient to continue doing what is already being done through the market system.

BES will perhaps have its greatest importance in the development of education, which will become vital to life. We shall recognize in the very near future that mere extension of the period of education will not be enough; that we shall need major changes in concepts of education to meet the new challenges; and that today's school and university were designed to serve the requirements of the passing industrial age. If we are to educate for the future, we must find ways to develop creativity and enlarge the capacity of the individual to think in terms of his own uniqueness. We shall have to teach people to think for themselves rather than merely to absorb and regurgitate, with maximum accuracy, the theories of past thinkers.

If we adopt the idea of BES, we will have far more "unemployment" in the future than there is today, but we would come to perceive unemployment as favorable rather than unfavorable. The individual and society now fear unemployment for it usually implies an inadequate income and threatens cessation of all meaningful activity while encouraging anti-social activity. When we provide adequate incomes to all and develop each individual's uniqueness so that he knows what he wants to do, unemployment (which will then be redefined as the condition of *not* holding a job) will be seen as highly desirable.

These long-run arguments in favor of BES need to be paralleled by an argument from short-run necessity. BES would appear to provide a partial answer to the problem of ultimate unemployability, for it would at least provide minimal funds. It would not, however, automatically provide meaningful activity to those no longer able to find jobs and would, therefore, meet only half of the problem. There are many people who wish to be employed, but who do not have the capacity to develop their own lives within the freedom provided by BES. It is extraordinarily unfortunate that many of those ultimately unemployable within the existing job-structured productive system seem likely to be those most in need of structured activity to make their lives meaningful. This is true both for blue-collar workers and for middle management and similar groups with high levels of professional training.

The upbringing and education of those most immediately threatened by cybernation have limited their horizons so severely that they cannot fully benefit from the potential abundance which their own work has created. Society crippled these people in order to get them to produce efficiently. As their productive efforts are no longer required, society must not only provide them with rights to adequate incomes but must also provide new types of activities that will give them a sense of satisfaction in their lives.

This can be done only through new types of organization, and BES will greatly simplify the provision of new work roles for individuals who will not have to be paid wages. We can anticipate the organization of what I have called "consentives": productive groups formed by individuals who come together on a voluntary basis, simply because they wish to do so. Articles made by these consentives will not compete with mass-produced goods available from automated factories; the consentive will normally produce the "custom-designed" objects that have been vanishing from the present economy.

This type of productive unit will continue far into the future, for skilled handwork is one of the most satisfying of occupations. But the proportion of the population that spends most of its time in production will decline as education in its fullest sense takes an ever more central position and other activities come to seem more challenging. For the present, however, it is essential to recognize that we face an acute transitional problem. We may reasonably hope to change the educational process so that those still within it will understand that toil is unnecessary and will accept the freedom made possible by cybernation. It will be far more difficult to bring an older generation that was raised within the Protestant ethic of America to this point of view. Will we have to develop political policies to preserve jobs for the older members of society while challenging the young to work in non-structured situations? And if this is indeed necessary, what social norms can we develop to prevent a profound generational split?

SOLVING ABUNDANCE

Despite the radical divergence of the two strategies set out above, initial policies under the two strategies would be remarkably similar: both would include an income floor for all and would set up new techniques of providing structured activity for those who cannot find jobs within the present system. Their long-term goals, however, are radically divergent.

The strategy of the Automation Commission is designed to preserve full employment: to preserve a situation where most individuals can only live with dignity if they can find a job. It argues that men are needed in jobs and that they need jobs. On the other hand, the proposal that we should use BES as the new philosophical grounding for income distribution in a cybernated era assumes that we should strive toward full unemployment. Obviously, this would require a profound shift in our views of rights and responsibilities. To-day a man has first, the responsibility to obtain an income and then, the right to "pursue happiness"; under the new system a man would be provided with his income as a right but would need to feel a duty to develop himself and his society.

Given this extreme divergence of ultimate goals, it can be expected that the believer in one of these strategies must find the other unrealistic and, indeed, dangerous. This is, in fact, the case. Those who accept that we should continue to strive for full employment fear the effects of a guaranteed income on incentive; they believe that people will be unwilling to work if they receive an income without holding a job. Those in favor of providing an income to all answer this argument on two levels: first, that most Americans today have an almost pathological desire to toil; and second, that the best work is not done for money but because of other motivations. Those who argue that we should strive for full *un*employment claim, too, that those who wish to perpetuate full employment have lost sight of the original purpose of increasing productivity, which was to free men from the necessity of meaningless and degrading toil. This argument is also answered on two levels: first, that it is too early to aim at the eminently desirable goal of freeing men from toil; second, that men would not be able to benefit from such freedom.

In the end, therefore, the arguments about the potential inherent in man's increasing productive powers turn out to be part of the far more general question posed by man's increasing power over all his environment. We now have the ability to order our socio-economy and our environment in a variety of ways. The questions we must therefore face are: what do we want to do with the available technology, and how do we ensure that the necessary changes take place? It is now agreed that we have the power to order what we wish to a far greater extent than ever before in human history. Doubts about the future are in terms of man's ability to use this growing power to ensure that we improve our condition. The issues posed by rapidly increasing productive power must be solved within this framework.

Part **III**
Transportation

10 / The Internal-Combustion Engine on Wheels

JOHN B. RAE

Few technological developments of the last hundred years have had more far-reaching social and economic consequences than the motor vehicle. It transformed transportation by land and changed the living habits of people throughout the world. Through the automobile the technique of mass production was finally worked out to create what, in effect, was a new industrial revolution. In the United States the manufacture of motor vehicles became the nation's largest industry, and automotive output became the prime index of the state of the economy. By its mere existence the motor vehicle created a need for innovations in highway design and construction and compelled efforts to meet that need; it expedited the movement of population from cities to suburbs, and by making people more mobile, it thereby uprooted them. It made itself economically indispensable and an integral part of modern culture, but it brought with it problems of traffic congestion and atmospheric pollution.

THE ORIGINS OF THE AUTOMOBILE

The modern automobile is, almost without exception, powered by an internal-combustion engine. Other types of propulsion are possible, and the internal-combustion engine was, in fact, a late arrival in the field. The self-propelled highway vehicle that was dreamed of for centuries became a practical possibility only with the advent of the steam engine. As early as 1769 a French artillery officer, Nicholas Joseph Cugnot, designed a steam-powered carriage for the purpose of pulling artillery pieces. Considering that this was the year James Watt patented his steam engine, Cugnot performed a rather remarkable technical feat, but his vehicle unfortunately was clumsy and failed to attract the interest of the French government.

The development of steam highway vehicles was left to British engineers, if we except Oliver Evans's feat in 1805 of putting a steam-powered dredge on wheels and propelling it through the streets of Philadelphia. However, the Commonwealth of Pennsylvania refused to allow Evans to operate steam coaches on its highways. The British engineers eventually suffered the same fate. In the mid-19th century there were several successful experiments with steam-driven omnibuses on British highways. On some routes regular schedules were maintained over periods of years, and on occasion speeds of thirty to forty miles an hour were reached, an astonishing performance on roads that were not built for heavy, powered vehicles. Railway and stagecoach companies met this threat by securing legislative restrictions on the omnibuses, culminating with the Red Flag Law of 1865, requiring that self-propelled vehicles on public highways limit their speeds to four miles an hour and be preceded by a man on foot carrying a red flag. A promising development was thus short-sightedly brought to a halt, but the concept of the steam highway vehicle survived.

In the meantime the internal-combustion engine came along to offer a potentially lighter power plant. Étienne Lenoir (Volume I, Chapter 40) built and operated a carriage using his engine in the 1880's, but this experiment brought no further development. A Viennese named Siegfried Marcus has been claimed as the inventor of the automobile because he is supposed to have run a vehicle with an internal-combustion engine during the 1860's. The evidence that he actually had a workable motor carriage this early is, however, dubious. And though in 1879 an American patent attorney, George B. Selden, filed an application for a patent on a "road engine," using a modification of the Brayton internal-combustion engine which he had seen at the Philadelphia Centennial Exposition in 1876, Selden did not at that time build a vehicle conforming to his patent specifications.

The men who first successfully put the internal-combustion engine on wheels were Karl Benz and Gottlieb Daimler, both of whom achieved this feat in Germany in 1885. There has been a considerable controversy over which one should be considered as *the* inventor of the automobile, but like most such controversies it is not worth pursuing. Daimler is entitled the credit for seeing that a high-speed motor offered the best prospect for using an internal-combustion engine on a highway vehicle; and Benz introduced spark ignition. Both Daimler and Benz carried on as manufacturers of motor vehicles; Daimler's engine was adopted by Armand Peugeot and the firm of Panhard and Levassor in France in 1890.

Following the German and French lead, American and British inventors moved into the field. The first American-built gasoline automobile was the work of the brothers Charles and Frank Duryea; it made its public appearance in Springfield, Massachusetts in 1893. Following the Duryeas came Elwood Haynes (1894), Hiram Percy Maxim (1895), Charles B. King, Henry Ford, and Alexander Winton (all 1896), and Ransom E. Olds (1897). British ex-

Fig. 10-1. Duryea, 1893, the first American-built gasoline automobile. (Courtesy of *Automobile Manufacturers Association*)

perimentation was inhibited until the Red Flag Law was finally repealed in 1896. In that year a British Daimler Company was formed, and the great automotive engineer F. W. Lanchester built the first all-British gasoline automobile.

As was to be expected, most of these early efforts were crude affairs, with noisy and inefficient one-cylinder engines mounted on buggy or bicycle frames, with two exceptions. In 1891 Emile Constant Levassor produced the prototype of the modern automobile: the body designed for a self-propelled vehicle, the engine in front where its weight would help to hold the car on the road, and a sliding gear transmission. Lanchester's car followed the same pattern.

THE HORSELESS-CARRIAGE ERA

At the close of the 19th century the motor vehicle had a tenuous foothold in industrial society. Manufacture was well established in France and Germany, although still on a small scale, and it was just beginning then in the United States and Great Britain. For its rapid advance the automobile owed much to its immediate predecessor in the technology of road transportation, the bicycle. The invention of the "safety" bicycle by J. K. Starley of Coventry, England, in 1885 (the modern low-wheeled, geared bicycle, replacing the earlier high-wheeled velocipede) paved the way for the motor car by putting people on the highways by the thousands, and creating a public demand for better roads. The bicycle also contributed to the automobile steel-tube framing, ball and roller bearings, differential gearing, acetylene lamps, and above all, the pneumatic tire, invented in 1888 by a British physician, John B. Dunlop. Many of the early automobile firms, in addition, started out in the bicycle business: Opel in Germany; Humber, Riley, Rover (Starley's company), and Morris in Great Britain; Winton, Willys, Pope, Peerless, and Rambler in the United States.

The automobile industry grew very rapidly once it got started. During the pioneering days it was not especially difficult to get into the business. Cars were assembled in small shops from parts made by other companies, and the builder could finance himself, or at any rate try to, by buying his parts on credit and selling to his dealers for cash. (The cash sale to the dealer is still an integral feature of the American automobile business.) In the United States alone there are records of over 3000 different makes of cars having been produced by some 1500 separate firms, most of which rose and fell before World War I.

The technological variations were almost infinite, showing an understandable uncertainty about what the vehicle of the future would turn out to be. The four-cycle engine was most commonly used, but two-cycle models were reasonably numerous. Both water- and air-cooled engines were tried; the former gradually gained in popularity, although an American car with an air-cooled engine, the Franklin, stayed on the market until 1932 and air cooling experienced a revival after World War II in the Volkswagen and some of its imitators. Steering was chiefly by tiller until after 1900; the steering wheel became a superior method only with the invention of the steering knuckle by Sterling Elliott in 1902; this device permits both front wheels to turn while the axle remains rigid. There was also a wide choice among transmission systems. The H-slot transmission was in the lead by 1900, but there were experiments with electric drive, and at least one American automobile, the Cartercar, whose company was dissolved in 1910, used a friction drive; the Model T Ford used planetary gearing.

In general design the customer's basic choice was between the continuing buggy-type vehicle with a one- or two-cylinder engine—the real horseless carriage—and the Levassor-Lanchester design of the true automobile, which after the turn of the century, was being equipped with four- and six-cylinder engines. Larger motors were designed for racing cars, which embodied the sum total of research and testing done by the industry at the time.

Fig. 10-2. Thomas A. Edison and Mrs. Edison in an early Baker electric car. (Courtesy of *Automobile Manufacturers Association*)

In the horseless-carriage days it was not even certain that the car of the future would be driven by an internal-combustion engine. Steam and electricity were active competitors. Indeed, during the 1890's the electric automobile enjoyed a greater popularity than the gasoline car. It was clean, quiet, and easy to operate. When Hiram Percy Maxim went to Hartford in 1897 as chief engineer of the newly created Motor Carriage Department of the Pope Manufacturing Company, he found to his dismay that the company intended to give priority to the development of electric cars because, as Colonel Albert A. Pope said, "You cannot get people to sit over an explosion." Yet the fundamental weakness of the electric automobile was already apparent; it could not go fast or far without running down its battery.

The steam car was a more dangerous competitor since it was more powerful than the early gasoline cars and did not require the complex transmission of the internal-combustion engine. The one great drawback, the twenty minutes or so needed to get up steam, was eliminated when a French engineer, Leon Serpollet, invented the flash boiler in 1889, although it was not generally adopted for another ten years. Experimental steam automobiles (as distin-

Fig. 10-3. A Stanley Steamer. (Courtesy of *Automobile Manufacturers Association*)

guished from the heavy steam omnibuses previously mentioned) appeared in Europe and the United States throughout the last half of the 19th century but did not come into commercial production until the 1890's. The most famous American manufacturers of steam automobiles, the Stanley brothers of Newton, Massachusetts, began operations in 1897 and two years later drove one of their cars up Mount Washington. The White Motor Company of Cleveland, Ohio, was the first American firm to use the flash boiler.

The technical merits of the steam-powered automobile have caused much speculation as to why it lost to the gasoline-powered competitor, and no really complete and satisfactory solutions can be offered. On the technological side the basic problem was the high pressure (600 psi) required to make a steam engine of adequate power small enough for an automobile. The fear of boiler explosions, which inhibited purchases of steam cars, was unfounded; there is no record of any serious accident of this kind, and the manufacturers of gasoline cars would certainly have publicized any such incidents. Nevertheless the high pressures did create mechanical problems beyond the capability of the ordinary motorist or mechanic to handle. Except for the Stanley brothers, who continued until after World War I, the builders of steam automobiles either gave up or turned to the internal-combustion engine by 1910.

THE AUTOMOTIVE REVOLUTION

The date when the horseless-carriage period ended and the automobile era began has to be approximated. One might say 1903, when the Ford Motor Company was founded, or 1904, when R. E. Olds gave up his curved-dash Oldsmobile buggy. Of the possible choices the year 1908—when the Model T Ford was put on the market and William C. Durant founded General Motors —heads the list. From this point the production and use of motor vehicles expanded phenomenally. In 1909 American output reached six figures for the first time, and the million mark was passed only five years later. Along with this explosion of numbers went marked technological advance in the cars themselves, as well as in the processes of manufacture.

Before this potential for growth could be fully realized the American automobile industry had to settle a vital question of patent claim. As mentioned above, George B. Selden had filed a patent application for a "road engine" in 1879. Loopholes in the patent laws enabled him to keep his application alive until 1895, when he received United States patent No. 549,160, valid until 1912. It specified a vehicle propelled by a liquid hydrocarbon engine, with a

Fig. 10-4. The Selden "Road Engine," patented in 1895. (Courtesy of *Automobile Manufacturers Association*)

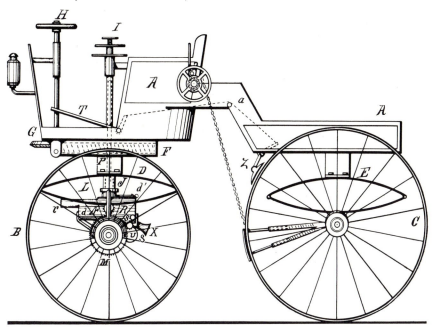

device for disengaging the motor from the driving wheels, and a receptacle for the fuel. Selden, who had never been able to get support for his ideas though they were sound enough technically, sold his patent in 1899 to a syndicate of financial promoters, organized as the Electric Vehicle Company. When its initial project for operating electric cabs failed, the Electric Vehicle Company tried to obtain some financial gains from its ownership of the Selden patent. Negotiations with the principal automobile firms resulted in the formation of the Association of Licensed Automobile Manufacturers (ALAM), which had the right to award licenses to manufacture autos under the Selden patent and hoped to use this power to stabilize the industry.

The patent was challenged by Henry Ford and others in a lawsuit which dragged through the courts for eight years. Ford lost most of his allies when the lower court ruled against him, but he stuck to his position, and in 1911 the Court of Appeals ruled that he had not infringed upon the Selden patent, which was valid only for cars using Selden's adaptation of the Brayton two-cycle engine. The prolonged legal battle convinced the industry that patent conflicts were undesirable. As a consequence, a cross-licensing agreement was adopted in 1915 under the supervision of the National Automobile Chamber of Commerce, successor to the ALAM and predecessor of the Automobile Manufacturers Association. It was not complete—Henry Ford, who had no use for patents, abstained—but it worked well enough to eliminate patent suits among automobile firms. In addition, the program of technical standardization which the ALAM had initiated during its brief and stormy life was continued by the Society of Automotive Engineers after the demise of the former organization.

With this difficulty resolved, the way for expansion was open. In the twenty years after 1908 production climbed to the point where 85 per cent of the world's automobiles were made in the United States, and where, with 24 and a half million registered motor vehicles in 1928, it was possible to move the country's entire population by car at one time. (On summer Sunday afternoons it frequently appeared that this was actually being done.)

Technical advance was equally rapid, although it was predominantly a development or refinement of existing automotive knowledge. The multicylinder, four-cycle engine became standard, and the Model T Ford used a 20-horse-power, four-cylinder motor. On the more expensive makes, however, bigger engines were offered. The first American car with a V-8 engine was built in 1907 by Edward R. Hewitt, son of Abram S. Hewitt and grandson of Peter Cooper. It was not a commercial success; and the general adoption of the V-8 in luxury cars dates from the 1919 Cadillac. Straight-eight engines appeared in high-priced cars in the 1920's, and some luxury models, like the Marmon, eventually went to twelve and sixteen cylinders. The eight-cylinder engine for low-priced cars came from what Charles E. Sorensen has described as "the elder Ford's last great mechanical triumph," the V-8 engine installed in the 1932 Ford. It was made possible by casting the entire block and crankcase as a unit, a gamble in foundry technique which paid off.

The one major variation in basic gasoline-engine design was the sleeve-valve motor, patented by Charles Y. Knight in 1911. Known as the "Silent Knight," its valve ports were operated by a sleeve outside the cylinder, providing a smoother and quieter motor than the poppet-valve engines of the period. On the other hand, the Knight was more expensive to build and maintain. The last car to use it, the Willys-Knight, went out of production in 1932, by which time it offered no real advantage in performance over the poppet-valve engine.

After the pioneering inventions, probably the greatest single step toward promoting general use of the gasoline car was electric starting, developed jointly by the Cadillac Motor Car Company and Charles F. Kettering, and introduced in 1912. Since cranking a gasoline engine by hand was difficult at best and sometimes dangerous, various experiments were made to obtain mechanical starting, including some with clockwork, compressed air, and electric devices. The key problem to electric starting—designing a motor powerful enough to turn the engine over and still small enough to put in the car—was solved by Kettering on the basis of experience designing electric cash registers for the National Cash Register Company. Kettering's success lay in recognizing that the motor need not be built to carry a constant load. The Bendix drive for engaging and disengaging the starting mechanism came along in 1913 to complete the system. It would be difficult to exaggerate the importance of electric starting. In one step it removed what was perhaps the greatest single drawback to the employment of the internal-combustion engine as an automotive power plant, and it greatly increased the utility of the gasoline car by making it as easy for a woman to drive as a man.

Stopping the car is, of course, as important as starting it, probably even more so. The most notable advance in this field was the invention of a hydraulic four-wheel brake system in 1918 by Malcolm Loughead of the aviation family who later spelled their name Lockheed. Hydraulic brakes were at first a feature only of high-priced cars. Four-wheel mechanical brakes, however, were virtually standard equipment by the early 1930's.

Other technical features which can be classified as useful but not essential owed their adoption largely to competitive pressure for sales. The institution of the annual model change made it desirable to offer something that would differentiate between the new and the secondhand car, and that would either add prestige value or could be advertised (as during the Depression days of the 'thirties) as contributing to efficiency and economy of operation. To these motives can be attributed the introduction of free wheeling (1930), overdrive (1934), and the automatic transmission (1937).

None of these changes represented any drastic technological innovation; most were ideas which had been thought of and experimented with earlier but had not in their initial stages proved commercially practical. What was happening to the passenger automobile was a constant process of refinement and improvement. Engines became more efficient and more powerful. The average horsepower of American passenger-car engines in the 1920's was twenty; by 1950 it had risen to a hundred, and it continued to climb until the growing popularity of the "compact" car slowed down the process somewhat. The gains in engine performance were the result of a variety of factors, including metallurgical advances, higher compression ratios, and improved fuels. By the 1960's there were prospects of major technological change in automotive power plants, either by adoption of the diesel engine, already widely used in commercial vehicles, for passenger cars, or, more drastically, by conversion to the gas turbine. Both were experimented with; in the 1950's the German Mercedes-Benz used diesel engines for passenger cars, and in 1963 Chrysler turned out some pilot models of cars with gas-turbine engines in the United States.

Even in the absence of radical technical changes, the development of the automobile in the years following World War II has been phenomenal. The American automobile industry, after an almost complete conversion to military production during the war, resumed normal operations rapidly, and despite the temporary interruption of the Korean War, reached a record output of more than nine million vehicles in 1955. The vital place of the industry in the American economy is vividly illustrated by the fact that a subsequent decline in the demand for new cars precipitated a sharp, if temporary, depression.

Even more striking is the expansion of automobile production in other parts of the world, especially in Europe. Using mass-production techniques developed in the United States, but concentrating on small cars, easy to maneuver in crowded streets and with low fuel consumption, European manufacturers have not only become vigorously competitive in the world market but have also been able to invade the American market with telling effect. In the early 1950's American passenger cars were getting steadily bigger, heavier, more powerful, and more expensive; pressure from the European competition was then directly responsible for the introduction of the "compact" car in the latter part of the decade.

The most dramatic success story is that of the German Volkswagen. It was initially projected during the Nazi regime as a low-priced car for the German masses, but the coming of World War II made necessary a change of plans and the Volkswagen emerged as a military vehicle comparable to the American jeep. The end of the war left the builder, Dr. Ferry Porsche, with shattered factories and his original idea. Nevertheless, the revived Volkswagen appeared in 1948, a well-designed light car (1600 pounds) with a four-cylinder, air-cooled, 36-horsepower engine, mounted in the rear. It soon became the leading seller among European cars, accounting by the early 1950's for half of Germany's automotive production and making a significant contribution to Germany's economic recovery. Great Britain, France, Italy, Sweden, and Japan also showed a substantial increase in automobile production; the automotive revolution begun in the United States half a century earlier had become worldwide.

COMMERCIAL AND SPECIALIZED VEHICLES

Recognition of the potentiality of the motor vehicle as a commercial carrier of passengers and freight came early. Crude trucks and buses appeared during the 1890's. In the United States Alexander Winton's first manufacturing effort was an order for omnibuses to operate on Shore Drive in Cleveland—cancelled when the promoters were threatened with lawsuits for frightening horses. Under Hiram P. Maxim's supervision, the Pope Manufacturing Company of Hartford, Connecticut, built a number of gasoline-powered tricycles for local package delivery, and finding no buyers, operated a delivery service itself. Progress with commercial vehicles was somewhat slower than with passenger cars, partly because of the crudeness of the vehicles, but still more because of the inadequacy of existing roads. Highway transport could not compete with the railway either in long-distance travel or in carrying heavy loads.

World War I brought a major change. The taxicabs that carried French soldiers from the Paris garrison to defeat the Germans in the Battle of the Marne (1914) and the endless lines of trucks rolling along the "Sacred Way" to carry food and supplies to the beleaguered French forces at Verdun (1916) have been woven into the story of the war. Less dramatic, but in the long run more important, was the demonstration of what highway transport could do to relieve overburdened railway systems. During the winter of 1917-18 some 30,000 trucks were driven from factories in the Midwest to Baltimore for shipment overseas, each carrying a load of freight with it. The operation required a detailed survey of usable routes and close co-operation by local authorities to keep them open, but it proved conclusively that large-scale movement of traffic by road had become practical. At the same time, the development by the Goodyear Tire and Rubber Company of a pneumatic tire for trucks (1916) opened up vast new possibilities. As long as heavy trucks had to rely on solid rubber tires there was a limit to their size and carrying capacity; beyond it they pounded the roads, the loads, and themselves, to pieces.

Improvement was such that after the war highway competition began to cut noticeably into rail traffic. The decline of railroad passenger business and the virtual extinction of street and interurban lines was due mainly to the private passenger automobile and partly to buses. In the case of freight there was a definite loss of railroad short-haul and less-than-carload shipments to trucks. With subsequent developments in automotive technology plus a steady increase in the mileage of good roads, commercial highway transport rapidly expanded its role.

An important advance in bus design was the introduction of the Twin Coach by the Fageol brothers of Kent, Ohio, in 1927. Buses previously were essentially bus bodies on truck chassis. The Fageol design put the engine underneath so that the whole body of the vehicle was available for payload, and the driver was at the front where he had maximum vision. In 1934 the White Motor Company improved on the design with a "pancake" engine having twelve horizontally opposed cylinders. White also adapted this same basic idea to trucks by being the first to introduce the "cab-over-engine" truck.

The greatest benefit to commercial highway transport (apart from the expansion of highway systems) was the revolution in diesel technology which occurred during the 1930's. The development of the diesel engine itself has been described in Volume I, Chapter 40. As a power plant it had the advantages of high thermal efficiency, no ignition system, and low cost fuel; but its high ratio of weight to power inhibited its use for locomotion on land. Both European and American diesel-engine manufacturers applied their talents to these problems and, until the 1930's, European diesel technology led the American efforts. In that decade, however, a major change occurred. Charles F. Kettering persuaded General Motors to go into the diesel-engine business and he devoted his own rather considerable genius to the improvement of the diesel. While Kettering is not entitled to exclusive credit for the results, he clearly contributed a substantial share. Two changes were vital to solving the weight-power difficulty and curing the diesel's propensity to malfunction. One was to make it a two-cycle engine. The other was to design and make a fuel-injection system capable of feeding exactly measured amounts of fuel and air into the cylinders through capillary-thin tubes.

The initial impact of the diesel revolution was on the railroads rather than the highways (see Chapter 11), and not until after the Second World War did diesel-powered trucks and buses begin to appear in appreciable numbers. When they did, however, they raised highway transport to a new level of effectiveness. Diesel engines permitted high power and speed to be combined with economy of operation. Buses and trucks could be made larger to carry bigger loads. The feasibility of increasing the size and carrying capacity of trucks led, in the larger designs, to a separation of the power unit and the cargo-carrying unit, the latter becoming usually a semi-trailer coupled to a swivel mount on the tractors when it was in use but capable of being detached for loading or unloading while the tractor went to work elsewhere. Where road conditions permitted, larger combinations of truck and full trailer in tandem were employed, most commonly in the wide reaches of the American West. These vehicles require air brakes and transmissions with as many as fifteen gear shifts.

The growth of commercial highway transportation in the United States can be illustrated by a few figures. In 1905, the earliest year in which registrations

Fig. 10-5. A modern V-8 diesel engine for heavy-duty trucks. (Courtesy of *Automobile Manufacturers Association*)

of commercial vehicles appear separately from those of private automobiles, 1400 trucks and buses were registered. This figure rose to 350,000 when the United States entered World War I and passed the million mark in 1920. By 1962 the total had grown to 140,000 buses and over twelve million trucks. Of the latter, about 60 per cent were classified as "light," the variety of trucks carrying loads of less than four tons.

The social and economic efforts of this development of highway transportation require separate consideration. They can merely be summarized here by saying that the motor truck brought to the movement of goods on land a degree of flexibility never previously experienced. It brought economic viability to farms and communities which did not have ready access to rail transport, and it gave the shipper of small lots a means that could be tailored to his needs. And if the truck became a serious competitor of the railroad, it also proved to be an invaluable adjunct; many railroad companies, in fact, organized their own trucking subsidiaries as an effective means of providing comprehensive and co-ordinated freight service.

The role of the motor bus has been less important because the great bulk of passenger traffic moves in private automobiles. Nevertheless, because of their greater flexibility in traffic and economy of operation, buses superseded the street railway and became the sole agency of public transportation in all but a few metropolitan centers. They replaced the interurban electric railway entirely and have almost replaced the regular railroads as the carrier of short-haul passenger traffic, the exception again being the great metropolitan centers where heavy commuter traffic continues to move by rail. The development of diesel power and the multiplication of express highways after World War II put the bus effectively into the long-haul passenger business. Big, high-powered vehicles, offering as much in the way of comfortable travel as the regular railroad coach, were able on many routes to offer long-distance schedules as fast as those offered by all but a few top-flight trains.

The greater freedom of movement offered by the bus affected other facets of American life; for example, the one-room rural schoolhouse became extinct when pupils could be carried by bus to larger and presumably better consolidated schools, and even in urban areas bus transportation of school children became commonplace. Churches also found it increasingly useful and relatively inexpensive to provide bus service for parochial-school pupils and for parishioners who would otherwise have been unable to attend services.

The motor vehicle was quickly and readily adapted for such specialized duties as fire engines and ambulances. These were not novelties; they existed before the automobile and were simply remodelled to use an internal-combustion engine. Fire engines in earlier days were drawn by man- or horse-power and had a separate pumping mechanism. The advantage of the motorized fire truck, apart from its ability to get to the scene of action faster, was that the same power plant could be used for both propelling the vehicle and for pumping water or raising ladders. Other uses of the engine for the motorization of warfare will be described in later chapters (35, 36). In American automotive history, however, a special place has to be reserved for the jeep.

The first four-wheel drive American motor vehicle was built by Otto Zachow and William Besserdich in Clintonville, Wisconsin, in 1908. It was technically successful but too far ahead of its time for commercial production. The creator of the jeep, as far as one may give credit to one individual, was Colonel Arthur W. S. Herrington, an English-born engineer who served as a military transport officer during the First World War. This experience led him to experiment with all-wheel drive vehicles, and in 1931 he and the Marmon brothers formed the Marmon-Herrington Company in Indianapolis to build trucks of this type. The prototype of the jeep, designed by Captain Robert G. Howie, was demonstrated by Herrington at Fort Benning, Georgia, in March 1940. In one of several short-lived efforts made about that time to put a small car on the American market, the American Bantam Car Company was selected to build the vehicle. However, the demand for jeeps soon outran the company's facilities, and Willys-Overland and Ford were brought into the picture. The three combined to produce 660,000 jeeps for war use. Subsequently Willys-Overland (later Kaiser Motors) continued the jeep as a peacetime vehicle; after a few years, indeed, jeeps in various models were the company's sole remaining automotive product.

DIRT ROAD TO FREEWAY

Repeated references have been made in this chapter to the importance of the road system in the development of travel by motor vehicle. It is self-evident that highway transport can flourish only if there are highways capable of being used with economy and efficiency. By and large such roads did not exist when the automobile was born. The great advances in highway engineering of the previous century—the work of McAdam and Telford (see Volume I, Chapter 12)—were predicated on relatively light and slow-moving vehicles and not on the automobile. Even so, builders in the Western world knew how to build better roads than they actually did. The superiority of rail transport during the 19th century removed much of the incentive to put money or effort into the improvement of highways. France alone had a national road system of good quality when the 20th century arrived, and it is significant that France had the most rapid early development of motor vehicles. At the opposite end of the spectrum the United States had conspicuously poor roads. In 1900 there were only about 200 miles of hard-surfaced road in the country, excepting the cobbled streets of the major cities.

Here, as in other matters, the bicycle played an important preliminary role. It is tempting but not quite true to say that the bicycle paved the way for the automobile; the popularity of bicycling did, however, attract public attention to the highway problem. In the United States the League of American Wheelmen enjoyed some limited success in getting state and local authorities to improve their roads and even persuaded Congress to appropriate ten thousand dollars in 1893 for a study of improved techniques of road-building to be conducted by the Department of Agriculture. This department later became the administrator of federal highway programs, first because rural roads were most urgently in need of improvement, and second, because at the time it was politically expedient for federal activity in this field to be justified on the ground that it would help the farmers.

After the turn of the century the rapid increase in automobile ownership created a strong body of public opinion agitating for more and better roads. The automobile industry naturally gave its wholehearted support, and public authorities were gradually won over, largely by the discovery that the motor vehicle could be made to pay for its own roads by the simple device of taxing automobile fuels. The acceptance of highway development as a desirable public policy was signallized in the Road Aid Act of 1916, which set up the

Bureau of Public Roads in the Department of Agriculture as the administrator of a system of grants-in-aid for the construction of "farm-to-market" roads. A subsequent act of 1921 provided for more financial aid and attempted to create a national highway system by requiring the recipient states to designate seven per cent of their road mileage as "primary," that is, for major highway arteries between large population centers. Yet the great bulk of highway funds came from local governments; expenditures in the 1920's were on the order of two billion dollars a year.

It was one thing to find the money for roads and another to decide how to spend it. It was easy enough to determine that the automobile required a hard surface to ride on, but not so easy to decide whether concrete or compounds with an asphalt base gave the most satisfactory results for the expenditure. A major source of trouble was that at the beginning most of the money and effort was used to improve existing roads and streets which had not been designed for automotive traffic. Main roads ran through the middle of towns and villages, so that through traffic was added to the congestion of local traffic, but proposals to bypass a community were likely to be vigorously resisted by its merchants.

The need to control the flow of vehicles led to the general introduction of traffic lights in the early 1920's, at first changing at fixed intervals, then regulated by the volume of traffic through plates in the roadway which activated the light when depressed by passing cars. In many large cities lights were eventually synchronized so as to permit constant movement at a predetermined speed.

By the mid-1920's steps were being taken to build roads designed for use by motor vehicles. Main arteries were constructed with three and four lanes, although the three-lane road quickly lost favor because of the calamitous frequency with which drivers going in opposite directions would elect to use the passing lane at the same time. The four-lane roads were a great improvement over their predecessors, but they still suffered from inadequate control of the flow of traffic. They seldom had dividers to separate lanes, and they had frequent intersections and cross traffic. The proper technique of highway design was foreshadowed in the 1920's by the beginning of metropolitan parkway systems, with the Hutchinson River Parkway leading north out of New York City as the prototype. The intent of the parkways was to reduce congestion by providing routes on which commercial vehicles were banned and private cars could therefore move more smoothly and expeditiously. They also introduced, in somewhat preliminary form, the concept of limited access.

By the 1930's highway engineers were generally aware that the most promising solution to their problems was the limited-access express highway, with traffic in opposite directions rigorously separated and cross traffic interdirected. The obstacles were economic, not technical, in that the cost of this kind of construction was high, although it may be questioned if it was any higher than the overall social cost of traffic congestion and accidents caused by inadequate roads. The first such highways to be built were the Italian *autostrade,* constructed in the 1920's as expressways linking major cities. Hitler's Germany undertook a more ambitious program for a national system of *autobahnen,* ostensibly to stimulate employment and economic recovery but also with an obvious military motive. In the United States the Commonwealth of Pennsylvania undertook the Pennsylvania Turnpike as a public-works project to combat depression conditions. The section from Harrisburg to Pittsburgh, completed in 1940, was built on a long-abandoned railroad right-of-way, including seven tunnels through the Alleghenies. To finance the project, Pennsylvania revived the old practice of charging tolls. In this situation the tolls were no burden on the traffic because of the economy of operation resulting from the elimination of the frequent stopping and starting on ordinary highways.

After World War II other states followed Pennsylvania's example, until the United States had by the 1960's some 3000 miles of toll roads. By 1960 it was possible to drive from New York City to Chicago without having to stop, except for food, fuel, and toll gates. Experience showed that some features of the first express highways needed revision. Divider fences had to be made stronger or median strips wider so that cars that lost control travelling at excessive speeds would not cross over into the oncoming traffic. The elimination of curves was found to have its drawbacks; long straight stretches of road without change created a condition known as "highway hypnosis."

While the toll roads were being built, metropolitan centers were trying to solve their traffic problems by constructing the limited-access express highways known as freeways, beginning with Los Angeles in the late 1940's. The costs (never less than a million dollars a mile) were met by gasoline taxes rather than tolls, fundamentally because in areas like these the traffic load was such that stopping to pay tolls would have caused far worse congestion than the express highways could have relieved.

A nationwide system of express highways was provided for by the federal Interstate Highway Act of 1956. It envisaged a network of 41,000 miles of limited-access, toll-free expressways. The cost, initially estimated at $40 million but subsequently revised upward, was to be met by excise taxes on automotive fuels and tires, with the federal government paying ninety per cent of the total. Within four years close to a third of the projected mileage was completed, and about a fifth more, including toll roads incorporated into the system, was open to traffic; by 1967 the system was well on its way to completion.

THE IMPORTANCE OF THE AUTOMOTIVE INDUSTRY

Some idea of what the combination of motor vehicles and improved highways has meant can be gained by citing figures. In 1960, just about three quarters of a century from the first practical efforts to put the internal-combustion en-

Fig 10-6. Aerial view of a freeway interchange. (Courtesy of *Automobile Manufacturers Association*)

gine on wheels, the world had approximately 120 million motor vehicles: 93 million passenger cars, 26 million trucks, and one million buses. About 74 million of these were in the United States, 62 million being passenger cars. Three out of four American families owned at least one automobile.

The heavy concentration in the United States was reflected in the fact that one out of every six businesses in the United States was related to the automobile industry when the decade of the 1960's opened. Included in this list were 3000 manufacturers of automotive parts; 3500 producers of petroleum products, tires, and batteries; 65,000 dealers in new and used cars; 115,000 repair shops; 205,000 service stations; 40,000 motels; 8000 trailer courts; and many other establishments such as drive-in theaters and car rental agencies. It is perfectly clear that the impact of automotive technology on American life has been all-pervasive. Until the coming of World War II the rest of the Western world was less intensely affected, but in ensuing years most of the industrial states were rapidly duplicating the American experience, and even in the non-industrial areas, the motor vehicle had become the agent of significant cultural change.

11 / Rail and Water Transport
ERNEST W. WILLIAMS, Jr.

As the 20th century dawned, sailing vessels were still performing cargo transportation in marginal trades, although the steam vessel had long since become competitive in most types of ocean carriage. And railroads in North America and in Western Europe had, for the most part, reached the end of their great period of extensive development. Since the networks were largely laid down, new construction slowed, and a period of intensive development in the more densely populated and industrialized areas began. Both line-haul and terminal capacities required rapid increase in those areas, and capacity at times fell behind demand. Rapid application of technological improvements became necessary in order to keep abreast of growing traffic densities. Although single-track lines were converted into double track, and double track in some cases to triple or quadruple track, much of the added capacity had to be provided by increasing the load-hauling ability of trains and by increasing their frequency over given track segments.

STEAM LOCOMOTIVES

The capacity of the steam locomotive increased with great rapidity between 1900 and 1920. By 1900 the type of locomotive that relied on saturated steam (which began to condense in the cylinders before all of its latent capacity could be secured) had come close to its capacity. Superheating, developed first in Europe, began to be applied extensively to new locomotives soon after the turn of the century. Its purpose was greatly to raise the temperature of the steam and convert it from a moist to a dry condition. Eventually temperatures as high as 850 degrees were reached in steam locomotives, and there were even higher temperatures in marine and stationary installations.

The superheater was a comparatively simple device, a series of pipes having return bends which were inserted into the fire tubes of the boiler. The effects realized from its use were, however, great. The effect is illustrated by the comparison between the Pennsylvania Railroad H-8 Consolidation (2-8-0)[*] loco-motive of 1907 and the H-10 S seven years later. The latter was superheated and with the same boiler was able to supply larger cylinders, with the result that tractive effort increased by 17 per cent with no significant increase in the size or weight of the locomotive. The ability to work superheated steam ex-pansively during part of the piston stroke enabled more work to be done using the same boiler capacity and at lower fuel consumption rates. It brought an end to compounding (putting the steam through more than one cylinder), a process on which considerable experimentation had been conducted during the first decade of the century.

Another solution to securing increased power in the locomotive unit in the face of limitations of clearances, curvature, and track conditions was the artic-ulated locomotive, that is, where two sets of cylinders and their drive mech-anisms share a common boiler. While various types of articulated steam loco-motives have been employed elsewhere in the world, only the Mallet was used in quantity in America. This was a French development which permitted a single boiler to supply two engines, each of which had its own frame and set of driving wheels. The boiler was rigidly joined to the frame of the rear engine, while the front engine frame was connected with a pin and was thus able to swing radially under the smokebox end of the boiler (the smokebox is the front end of the locomotive, directly under the smokestack). Such locomotives spread their weight over an increased number of driving wheels—more than could have been accommodated in a rigid wheel base—to hold axle loadings down. They were also flexible and had good curving capabilities. The first such locomotive in the United States was "outshopped" (a railroadman's term mean-ing that the engine was completely finished in the builder's shop and sent out to do its work) in 1904. With six pairs of driving wheels, compared to four pairs on contemporary Consolidation engines, this locomotive developed 50 per cent more tractive effort than the heaviest Consolidations then being built. Like all true Mallets it was a compound, working steam at boiler pressure in the rear engine and exhausting thence into the much larger low-pressure cylinders of the front engine where the steam was worked expansively.

Further refinement of the steam locomotive was accomplished by the addition of numerous devices designed to increase capacity and enhance efficiency. The

---

[*] Railroadmen refer to locomotives by the number of wheels performing different functions. The first digit is the number of wheels on the leading truck (a truck con-sists of an axle and the frame connecting it to the main body of the locomotive), which enables a long locomotive to go around curves; the second digit indicates the number of main driving wheels; the third refers to the trailing truck (which supports the fire-box at the end of the locomotive). In some later—and massive—engines four digits are used, the two middle numbers referring to two separate sets of driving wheels re-quired for these powerful monsters. A 2-8-0 locomotive would be one with 2 front wheels, 8 driving wheels, and no trailing truck, hence a fairly small one.

Fig. 11-1. "Cid Maud," the first Mallet locomotive (0-6-6-0) placed in service on an American railroad, 1904. (Courtesy of *Baltimore & Ohio Railroad*)

wide firebox carried over a trailing truck behind the driving wheels was originally intended to permit use of low-grade coals and lignites by expanding the grate areas. It became a necessary fixture of high-capacity locomotives in both passenger and freight work. The mechanical stoker permitted larger firing rates, which were necessary as boiler pressures increased and steam-consumption rates grew. Feed water heaters and exhaust-steam injectors permitted exhaust steam to perform useful work in forcing water into the boiler and raising its temperature. The brick arch (brick lining of the firebox to increase its heat capacity) and the thermic syphon (which kept the boiler water circulating) notably increased the efficiency of the firebox.

By 1926 all of these elements were being incorporated in new designs of more efficient, high-horsepower locomotives which the Lima Locomotive Works called "super power." By 1914 tractive effort had been raised from the 40,000 pounds characteristic of the freight locomotives built in 1900 to 120,000 pounds in large Mallets. But these were slow, ponderous machines. Acceleration of freight and passenger service required larger driving wheels, lightweight rods and valve gears, and abundant steam capacity. Not much further increase of tractive effort was secured, the maximum being reached at 148,000 pounds; but horsepower at speed (the capacity to improve the engine's tractive efforts at higher speeds) was sharply increased and fuel efficiencies improved. Late in the steam era the articulated locomotive was revived, but it took the form of the single-expansion engine with four high-pressure cylinders and large

Fig. 11-2. One of three Union Pacific 4000-class locomotives placed in freight service in 1941. (Courtesy of *Union Pacific Railroad*)

driving wheels. It reached its acme in the Union Pacific 4000-class, first out-shopped in 1941. These magnificent locomotives of the 4-8-8-4 wheel arrangement weighed, with tenders (a tender is an auxiliary car attached to the locomotive and carrying the fuel and water for the engine), in excess of 600 tons, developed 135,375 pounds tractive effort, and with their 68-inch driving wheels, were capable of speeds of 70 miles per hour.

PERMANENT WAY, STRUCTURES, AND SIGNALLING

The necessity to run heavier and faster trains compelled improvements in all elements of railroad technology. Most often motive power led the way, but increasing the total weight and axle loadings of locomotives then forced improvement of track and bridges, while their increased length necessitated the installation of longer turntables and the enlargement of engine houses. Motive power of higher capacity also made possible the running of longer and heavier trains, thus permitting an increase in the volume of business done by a given number of train units. The efficient handling of these longer trains required, in turn, the lengthening of passing sidings and of receiving and departure tracks in yards.

One necessity was an improved rail which had deeper flanging sections and more metal in the head, so that heavier loads and increased traffic densities could be handled without undue rail damage or too rapid a changeout period because of wear. Rail sections employed in heavily trafficked main lines moved upward from 85 and 90 pounds to the yard to 131 pounds, and on some of the heaviest density trackage, 152 pounds. All of these sections were redesigned and further improved after World War II.

Both the increasing traffic and the growing scarcity of good timber demanded a new preservative treatment for ties, and pressure creosoting had the effect of prolonging the life of soft wood ties by two to three times, given adequate tie plating and careful handling in track. Track ballasting and drainage were also improved, and mechanical ballast-cleaning devices were developed to permit economical maintenance of a good, clean ballast section. Frogs, switch points, and other special trackwork were made more durable under increasing loads by the more extensive use of manganese steels. Finally the problem of transverse fissures, a major cause of rail breaks, was brought under control by having a fleet of flaw-detector cars and, ultimately, by the development of the controlled cooling process for rails in 1936. In the late 1930's important steps were taken to strengthen the track structure at its weakest points, the rail joints, by end hardening of rails, the building up of worn rail ends in track, and the development of continuous-welded rails, in which rail is installed in track in continuous welded lengths up to one mile, thus eliminating joints except where these long sections are joined.

Higher train speeds, longer and heavier trains, and increased train frequency also necessitated improvements in signalling and train control. The right of way was divided into sections known as blocks; the signal system, usually a semaphoric device, indicated whether the block or blocks ahead were clear of other trains. The automatic block signal, as well as mechanical interlocking systems at junctions and terminals, was already in use at the turn of the century. These underwent rapid extension, and electropneumatic systems came to characterize the larger installations. Semaphore signals gave way to color light and position light signals which provided greater sighting distances; four-aspect signalling was developed to permit closer headway on heavy traffic lines, and block signal systems were adapted to provide protection from following trains in either direction on single-track lines. Automatic train control was applied to a considerable amount of mileage in the early 1920's to provide for application of the brakes if the engineer failed to respond to a restrictive signal. In addition, cab signalling, which repeated the wayside signal inside the cab, was adopted on some lines, thus reducing problems of visibility.

Finally, perhaps first in 1926, centralized traffic control was developed. Under this system trains were operated by signal indication only, and all signals and switches on a railroad line were remote-controlled from the dispatcher's office, where their position and the location of all trains was displayed on an illuminated track diagram. The system not only cut expenses by eliminating telegraph operators along the route, but it also expedited train movements and permitted as much as a 75 per cent increase in line capacity.

PASSENGER AND FREIGHT CARS

At the turn of the century the all-steel railroad car was virtually unknown, the first hopper cars of such construction having been outshopped only in 1898. Both freight and passenger cars were predominantly of wood, although steel underframes were beginning to be applied. Heavier and longer trains, however, required greater strength in cars to stand the pull and buffing stresses generated. Hence, not only were new freight cars provided with steel underframe construction, but thousands of older cars were upgraded by the application of steel underframes. All-steel construction became the norm for gondola, hopper, and flatcars by 1914, but the steel-sheathed boxcar was not widely built until the 1920's.

In passenger service, for reasons of safety, transition to the all-steel car in main line service was comparatively rapid. Since it brought an increase of about 50 per cent in the weight per seat, it was a factor of great importance in stimulating the design of passenger locomotives of greatly increased capacity. Although the automatic coupler and the air brake were in wide use at the opening of the century, both required further development to cope with greater loads and higher speeds. Among those developments, the design and testing of the air brake valve in 1931 was one of the more important. This valve, which provides much more rapid and even application and release of brakes in long trains, is only now beginning to be superseded.

ELECTRIFICATION

The reciprocating steam engine was almost the sole motive power of railroads the world over in 1900. Experimental electrification had been tried and, in the first 15 years of the century, electrification was resorted to in special circumstances, such as where there was a need for smoke abatement in large cities and a necessity to improve conditions in tunnels. For these respective reasons, the suburban lines entering Manhattan and many in the Philadelphia area were electrified, and the Elkhorn grade and tunnel of the Norfolk and Western and the Cascade Tunnel were increased in capacity and safety by this method, for it was now possible to send long, heavy, slow-moving trains through these lengthy tunnels without asphyxiating the crew or passengers with smoke fumes. Various systems of electrification were employed, but 640-volt d.c. using third rail and 11,000-volt a.c., delivered by overhead wire, became the most common systems.

Electrification moved out of the specialty category when, in 1932, the Pennsylvania Railroad began electrification of its New York-Washington service and later extended the electrified system to Harrisburg on the main line west. These routes then showed some of the heaviest traffic densities to be found anywhere in the world.

Electrification involves a large investment in power transmission lines and in catenary or third-rail construction to conduct power to locomotives or self-propelled cars. Electric locomotives are compact, flexible, and comparatively easy to maintain. Since their power is limited not by the capacity of a power source carried on the engine, but only by the power available from the trolley and speed with which motors will overheat, for short periods they can work at substantial overload. They also enjoy constant torque, that is, they deliver power continuously throughout the revolution of the driving wheel rather than in four impulses as is the case with the reciprocating steam engine.

High investment cost, however, has limited electrification to lines of exceptional traffic density and special circumstances. Not only has no new electrification been added since 1940, but the electrification of the Milwaukee Line across the Rockies, Bitterroots, and Cascades; that of the Great Northern through the Cascade Tunnel; and those of the Virginian and Norfolk and Western railroads have been abandoned. Some hold that, as the merger movement among railroad systems continues, and as larger volumes of traffic are concentrated upon particular lines of railroad, electrification may again become important. Since 1950 the ignition and solid-state rectifiers have permitted great improvement in electric locomotives using a.c. current off the trolley.

DIESEL LOCOMOTIVES

While electrification has been at a standstill, the steam locomotive has been completely ousted from American railroad service and brought to the position of a curiosity in public parks, on a few short line and logging railroads, and in museums. Incredibly, this complete turnover from steam to diesel locomotives occurred primarily in the period from 1945 to 1960. Already third-generation diesel locomotives are now going into service representing considerable improvement in capacity, performance, and efficiency.

In 1925-26 some small diesel switching locomotives were placed in service at locations where steam locomotives were unsatisfactory. In the early 'thirties diesel switching power began very slowly to replace steam in some classes of work while efforts were made to adapt the diesel prime mover successfully to passenger service, first in rail motor cars designed to replace local and branch line trains, and later as high-speed units for the upgrading of long-distance passenger services. The first diesel-powered, streamlined, articulated passenger train was built for the Union Pacific in 1934 and was followed shortly by the first Burlington *Zephyr*. These trains ushered in an era of dieselization in pas-

Fig. 11-3. The nation's first diesel-powered main line locomotive, General Motors 103, shown shortly after leaving the Electro-Motive Division plant at La Grange, Illinois, on the morning of November 25, 1939, to begin an 11-month, 83,000-mile test run. (Milwaukee Journal Photo. Courtesy of *General Motors Corporation*)

senger service which was accompanied by the complete re-equipping and acceleration of many important long-distance trains and the placing in service of some new long-distance streamliners to augment existing schedules.

Although the diesel was adapted to freight service last, it is here that it has had its greatest impact. The first General Motors road freight diesel was given road tests in 1940 and became the prototype for a large number of such locomotives built over the next ten years. It was composed of four units of 1350 horsepower each, which could be used in any desired multiples. These, and virtually all diesels built for service in the United States, employ electric drive, which is why they are sometimes called diesel-electric locomotives. The diesel engine is directly connected to a generator which supplies current for the traction motors mounted on the trucks, one motor for each driving axle. Unlike steam locomotives, the driving wheels are not connected, and each pair therefore requires a wheel-slip indicator or a device to cut power to the axle when the drivers slip.

The advantages of the diesel in freight service proved to be very great; any desired number of units could be coupled together and controlled in unison by one engine crew. With their constant torque and very high starting tractive effort, they enabled train weights to be significantly increased and better running time to be made under almost all conditions of profile (the gradient, or hilliness of the line). Their fuel economy was also noteworthy, since the early freight diesels delivered in power at the driving-wheel rims about 26 per cent of the energy embodied in the fuel as compared with 8 to 11 per cent for steam locomotives. Since they required no boiler water, they were largely assigned during the Second World War to western railroads operating through desert country. Complete dieselization permitted elimination of boiler-water supply and treatment facilities, water-pipe lines and standpipes, coaling stations, and ash pits. Much higher availability was also credited to the diesel locomotive, that is, it could spend more hours out of the average day in active service and fewer hours in idleness for servicing and maintenance. Diesel freight locomotives showed dollar savings of up to 30 per cent per annum on the investment compared with steam locomotives.

One of the great contributions of the diesel locomotive builders was the high degree of standardization which they provided for the railroads. Each builder, and there were usually only three active builders of diesels, developed a line of standard types much as automotive manufacturers do. Whereas thousands of different types of steam engines had to be designed to meet the varying requirements of different terrains and traffic conditions, these same variations could readily be met simply by varying the number of standard diesel units employed. The road switcher, and later the versatile "hood" unit, became an all-purpose type of locomotive unit capable of doing switching work, way freight service, drag or manifest road freight service, as well as handling all but the fastest passenger schedules. Thus, the railroads handled almost as many ton miles of freight traffic in 1956 as in 1944, but they owned only 13,000 locomotives in that year, compared with 43,000 in 1944.

Diesel locomotives have been steadily improved, higher horsepowers are currently being supplied (for the most part in the 2000-3000 h.p. range), and maintenance requirements have been reduced. No startling changes have taken place, but replacement and upgrading of older locomotives have steadily improved the quality of the fleet. The first major change to be experimented with has been in the transmission of power. Mechanical drive has been employed extensively on small locomotives, especially in Europe. Hydraulic transmission has also made considerable progress in Europe on larger locomotives. In 1961 the Southern Pacific imported for testing a group of Krauss-Maffei locomotives with hydraulic transmission, and an American manufacturer was subsequently induced to develop a comparable design. Thus far, other railroads have not shown active interest in the type, and only a limited number are employed on the Southern Pacific. Another variant which employs a different type of prime mover is the gas-turbine locomotive, first outshopped for the Union Pacific in 1948. These locomotives have had considerable success, primarily in freight service west of Cheyenne. The latest group were of 8500 horsepower capacity.

They, too, have not found employment on other roads, and there is little to indicate any radical motive power changes in the near future.

The diesel came to the rescue of the railroads in the postwar period when they faced a cost squeeze resulting from rising wages and prices on the one hand, and a loss of freight traffic and inability to make comparable increases in freight rates on the other hand. This last was the result of growing competition from other forms of transport, especially truck and inland barge. The economies to be secured by dieselization put locomotive purchases in first place in the capital budgets of railroad corporations, and this single development, more than any other, saved the rail lines from a financial crisis of major proportions. Other cost-saving devices contributed in a major way—the least well-known but most important being the thoroughgoing mechanization of track maintenance work. Much was also accomplished in the reduction and mechanization of clerical work.

The competitive struggle also induced important changes in the freight service which were made possible by technological developments. Piggyback (now more often known as TOFC [trailer-on-flatcar] service) was not new. Wagons had been put on flatcars in the early days of railroading, the circuses had employed end loading of their wagons on flatcars, and trucks and truck trailers had been handled in a piggyback-type service by railroads as early as 1926. It was not until the early 1950's, however, that the handling of highway trailers on flatcars as a major competitive device was begun in earnest.

Originally standard flatcars were provided with runways, bridge plates to connect one car with another, and chains and turnbuckles to secure the highway trailers onto the car. These makeshift arrangements soon gave way to specially designed TOFC flatcars of 85- and later 89-foot length, capable of handling two 40-foot highway semi-trailers. Retractable trailer hitches were devised to secure trailers to the car by fastening onto the trailer kingpin. Thus no special equipment was required on the trailer itself, and tie-down was greatly expedited. Automatic trailer hitches are now under test. Not only circus-type loading over the car ends, but the use of gantrys and straddle carriers is becoming common.

Piggyback enables the low line-haul cost of the railroad to mesh with the flexibility of the truck—the ability to give service direct to the premises of shippers and receivers, and the relatively low operating costs in terminal areas. It has become an important competitive tool for regaining truck traffic in rail service and for rendering a type of service, generally on hauls in excess of 500 miles, that can sometimes be superior to all-truck service in speed, reliability, and freedom from loss and damage. Piggyback car loadings have grown from about 180,000 in 1955 to over 1,000,000 in 1965.

Piggyback experience led to another important development—the bi- and tri-level auto rack installed on a piggyback type of flatcar. These enable a single car to carry 12 conventional or 15 compact automobiles in place of the four which could be loaded in the standard automobile car of a decade ago. Whereas in 1959 railroads handled only 8 per cent of the new automobile traffic, the auto rack has enabled them to build this up to about 45 per cent by 1966.

A multitude of new freight car designs, many within the last decade, have also contributed heavily to the efforts of railroads to hold their position against competition. For example, the range of specialized tank cars has increased, and size has moved up rapidly. The 8000- and 10,000-gallon cars are being replaced by "jumbo" cars ranging up to 33,500-gallon capacity. Indeed, one car has been built to 59,000-gallon capacity. The covered hopper car for dry bulk commodities has increased in size, and also been changed in form; the center-flow car dispenses with the center sill and, in some cases, has been equipped with air-slide or pressure-differential systems to expedite the unloading of such commodities as cement and flour. Grain is increasingly moved in covered hopper cars rather than in boxcars, and the tendency to move commodities in bulk rather than in bags or barrels is at present very strong.

Railroads have reduced freight rates in return for heavier car loading as a means of improving the efficiency of rail service, extending part of the benefit to shippers, and meeting competition. The large capacity car is an important tool to this end, so boxcars are also becoming larger, with more cubic capacity, and are being built for 70-ton rather than 50-ton loads. At the same time, much has been done to protect ladings against shock and thus to make feasible heavier loads without undue expense for bracing and dunnage or excessive loss and damage to freight. The cushion underframe, a type of draft gear with 18 to 30 inches of travel, is a noteworthy example.

Much of the delay to rail freight movement, as well as much of the rough handling which causes damage to freight, occurs in classification yards and terminals. Where traffic volumes permit, hump yards are customarily used. A hump yard is a switching yard with a small hill, with one track leading up one side of the hill and meeting at the top a number of tracks fanning out in various directions; the switch engine pushes a line of freight cars to the top of the hill, where the freight cars are uncoupled and roll by gravity onto their proper tracks, coupling with other cars having the same destination. Early in the century these required large numbers of switch tenders and car riders. Remote-controlled power switches have eliminated the switch tenders, and car retarders have superseded riders. Today there is more precise control of cars and the so-called electronic yards eliminate much labor. Small computers are used to receive the switch list, to line up the switches accordingly and to compute and slow down the cars, depending upon how many are already on the track in question, the weight of the car, temperature, and other conditions. The cars are slowed down by retarders—30-foot long sections of track which pinch the flanges of the car wheel as it goes by, thereby retarding its speed; there can be more than one set of these retarding devices. Radar measurement of the actual speed of the car as it leaves the master retarder permits correctives to be applied in the secondary retarder pressure.

THE OCEAN TRADES

Just as great technological progress has been made in the railroad industry, so have astonishing advances occurred in ocean shipping, many of which are the waterborne counterparts of similar developments on land. In 1900 the blue ribbon of the Atlantic was held by the Hamburg American Line's *Deutschland*, a twin-screw vessel of 16,502 gross tons and 23-knot speed produced by quadruple-expansion reciprocating engines. The steam cargo vessel, both liner and tramp, came into its own in the 1880's and gradually pushed the sailing vessel into less and less remunerative trades, almost eliminating sail altogether from ocean routes. Tramp ships, of 3000-4000 tons deadweight and 8 to 9 knots speed, built for general cargo work and not operating on a definite schedule, were the characteristic vessels of ocean commerce. Tramp steamers in the great British merchant fleet were important to its coal export trade and grain import trade.

In the express-liner trades the first of a series of important developments was about to occur. At the time when reciprocating steam engines had been pushed almost to the limits of their capacity, the Parsons steam turbine had been demonstrated and had received naval application. The ever-conservative Cunard Line, determined to test the usefulness of the new turbine on large ocean vessels, in 1904 launched two similar 20,000-tonners, one having the usual quadruple-expansion engines, and the other equipped with turbines. The turbine vessel developed approximately one-knot greater speed. Turbine power plants were more compact, had fewer moving parts, and were simpler to maintain; but their great advantage was the potential they offered for further increasing the horsepower that could be installed on shipboard, thus setting the stage for rapid increases in size and speed. In 1907 the ill-fated *Lusitania* and the *Mauritania* were launched, 24-knot ships of 32,000 tons. The latter held the blue ribbon of the Atlantic until superseded by the *Bremen* in 1929.

Of greater economic significance was the shift from coal to oil that began just before World War I. This eliminated the fire-room gang and reduced the space required for coal bunkers, permitting also odd space and the space be-

Fig. 11-4. The *Queen Elizabeth*. (Courtesy of *The Mariners Museum*, Newport News, Va.)

tween double bottoms to be used for the new oil bunkers. Substantial space was thus released for cargo-carrying purposes. When the marine diesel was introduced in large vessels in the early 1920's still further savings of space and weight were achieved, and as in rail applications, thermal efficiency more than doubled, and bunkers were accordingly reduced and the boiler room eliminated. Every saving in space or weight required for machinery, fuel, and crews' quarters made available additional revenue capacity and thus improved the economies of the ship. The early marine diesels were large and heavy, but gradual improvement in weight-horsepower relationships were effected to make the advantage of diesel power greater in all but the largest ships. Since both turbines and diesel engines, unlike reciprocating steam, are ideally constant-speed units, reduction gears, hydraulic couplers, or electric drive were required; however, the resulting power assemblages were increasingly compact and efficient.

While the standard cargo ship between World War I and II was 2000-3000 tons larger than earlier ships and one to two knots faster, the development of the ocean tanker was perhaps the most noteworthy change in the cargo-ship picture. These vessels, however, remained of moderate size. The principal advances in size occurred in express-passenger and large combination vessels, culminating in the *Queen Mary* (80,750 tons) in 1936 and the *Queen Elizabeth* (83,650 tons) in 1940. The *United States* in 1952, although smaller (53,330 tons), became the fastest of the great merchant ships with a speed in excess of 35 knots. Because of growing competition from transoceanic airlines, the great

Fig. 11-5. The *United States*. (Courtesy of *The Mariners Museum*, Newport News, Va.)

passenger liners have been compelled lately to turn to holiday cruising service, for which ships of more modest size and speed are desirable. It is possible, therefore, that we have seen the last of the express liners built solely for transatlantic trade.

Since 1950 a veritable revolution in cargo shipping has taken place. The developments were spurred by the changing character of world trade; by the Suez crisis (1956), which closed the canal and compelled vessels to make the long voyage around the Cape of Good Hope; and by the increasing degree to which bulk cargo movements are regularly part of the continuing raw materials requirements of giant industrial concerns. In 1937 world seaborne trade approximated 480 million tons, of which 105 million were liquid (primarily crude and refined petroleum). In 1958 the total was 930 million, of which 440 million were liquid. Iron ore, which had been negligible in 1937, reached 101 million tons in 1960. The development of enormous regular flows of ore and petroleum pushed out the small and general-purpose tramps and led to the development of specialized cargo vessels of ever-increasing size. As a result, unit transport costs have declined as vessel size has increased, largely because no comparable increase in crew size is required, but partly because the larger hulls require less horsepower per ton at given speed.

The era of the supertanker has arrived and, whereas a 16,500-ton tanker had been considered large in 1945, tonnages have climbed steadily, so that the *Man-*

hattan of 1962 measured 137,068 tons and the *Idemitsu Maru* of 1966, 205,000 tons. Ore ships have followed a similar course of development, although not reaching such great size. Specialization is the order of the day. Most large cargo ships carry loads in one direction only. Special vessels have been built for liquid sulfur, various chemicals, and liquefied petroleum gas. In the general cargo trade conventional design has persisted, although higher speeds are now possible and cargo-handling gear has been greatly improved.

In the domestic coast and intercoastal service and increasingly on overseas trade routes, the high costs of handling general cargo on and off vessel is being attacked by containerization. Vessels built new, or modified as container ships, have cellular structures in the holds to permit containers to be stacked one on top of another in the cells. Special cranes on shipboard handle the containers. An all-container ship may turn around in port in one day as compared with six or more days for a conventional ship handling non-containerized freight.

The next step is automation, permitting engines to be controlled directly from the bridge. Although we have only seen the beginning of this, some of the new automated cargo vessels require a crew of but 32 compared with 56 for a conventional ship. Despite the fact that the nuclear-powered *Savannah* was placed in service on an exhibition basis, commercial experience with the atomic-powered vessel is still lacking and the economics of this type of propulsion has yet to be proved.

Fig. 11-6. The nuclear-powered *Savannah*. (Courtesy of *The Mariners Museum*, Newport News, Va.)

At the turn of the century American river transport was at a low ebb. In the 1920's, however, channel improvements undertaken by the federal government paved the way for a new era of growth. Improvements in barges and towboats made economical bulk transport by river tow possible. The old wooden-hulled, stern-wheel towboat powered by a reciprocating steam engine gave way to the steel-hulled propeller vessel. Quadruple screws (four propellers) became common on large boats, and Kort nozzles were used behind the propellers to direct the propeller stream and increase efficiency in shallow water.

Towboats on the Mississippi push rather than pull their tows, the barges being lashed together rigidly ahead of the boat. Great maneuverability is secured by an unusual number of rudders, sometimes as many as twelve—four at the bow, four ahead of the propellers, and four astern, while additional control may be had by reversing, that is, making the port engines turn the tow to port. Diesel power has replaced steam with resulting fuel economy and a marked reduction in crew size. Steel barges, including many of specialized design, have become the rule. It is not uncommon for these to tow up to 20,000 tons, and the largest boats can move 40,000 tons at acceptable speeds. However, uncertain water levels in the Upper Mississippi and the Missouri still limit navigation, and the limited size of lock chambers at some points require tows consisting of several barges to be taken through in segments. Radar and ship-to-shore telephones have been other great aids to the navigation of rivers and restricted waters.

In the 1960's some interesting devices for water transportation were in a trial state. One such device was the hydrofoil, the hull of which has extended flat fins, like skis, which greatly reduce water resistance, thereby permitting the boat to travel at high speeds. This boat was rendering passenger service on a limited scale. Great interest was also aroused by the hovercraft, a vehicle which could travel a few feet above the water (or level land) on a cushion of compressed air.

CONCLUSION

Table 11-1, showing the proportions of domestic commerce carried by the several modes of transportation, 1939-65, gives a fair picture of some of the changes in this field. First, the total quantity has risen rapidly, and this alone has forced technological change by the strain upon facilities. Second, although water transport percentage figures have held their own, those of the railroads have fallen sharply from 62 per cent in 1939 to only 43 per cent in 1962. Oil pipelines have picked up some of this loss, but motor vehicles (Chapter 10) got the lion's share.

Table 11-1   Domestic inter-city freight traffic
(All figures in millions of ton-miles)

	1939		1945		1962		1965	
	Volume	Per cent	Volume	Per cent	Volume	Per cent	Volume	Per cent
Railroad	338,850	62.34	690,809	67.26	599,977	43.04	704,600	42.87
Motor Vehicle	52,821	9.72	66,948	6.52	331,900	23.81	370,800	22.56
Inland Water	96,249	17.71	142,737	13.90	223,089	16.00	256,000	16.28
Oil Pipe	55,602	10.23	126,530	12.32	237,723	17.05	310,149	17.49
Airway	12	0.002	91	0.009	1,182	0.085	1,910	0.12
Total	543,534		1,027,115		1,393,871		1,643,459	

The railroads have, nevertheless, clung to the major portion of transport, and for the past five years their share has been relatively stable, so that they have participated in total traffic growth. The present (mid-century) crisis of the railroads, marked as it is by declining service and more frequent mergers, can probably be solved only by more radical technological development preceded by changes in government policy. Research and development in the industry are still given low priority, although the research efforts of suppliers have been considerably stepped up. Because water and rail transport will undoubtedly continue to be the main arteries of American commerce, it is clear that future changes in this field will take place, just as they have in the past.

12 / The Development of Aviation
THOMAS M. SMITH

The history of aviation is the triumphant story of how a few hundred men during the first two thirds of the 20th century mastered the skies and brought the other side of the earth, hitherto always weeks or months away, to within a few hours' distance. Scientific research and engineering know-how made these achievements possible. Mathematics, experimental testing, financial and industrial enterprise, university research facilities, and governmental regulation and encouragement brought them to pass.

THE MILITARY STIMULUS

In the face of the stunning success story of the rise of aviation in less than one man's lifetime, it is a rueful irony of history that the major cause of the success of aviation has been the airplane's usefulness as an instrument of war. The root cause, however, lies not in the usefulness of the airplane as a destructive weapon but in the special emphasis nations have given the conduct of military affairs. Believing that military preparedness is essential to their very survival, the industrialized countries have called for ever better warplanes at whatever cost. A consequence has been the dramatic design progress of military aviation since 1910, at dollar costs only governments can incur.

Because the stakes are so much higher in the conduct of military than of peaceful affairs, the United States Congress has, for example, over the decades financed military aviation on an utterly lavish scale compared to its direct dollar support of civil aviation. Hence the advance of aviation technology has resulted primarily from scientific and engineering activities paid for by millions of military dollars. Civil aviation has, of course, taken quick advantage of the costly gains in aircraft performance that only military budgets could finance, with the result that civilian air travel since 1945 has vaulted out of the "horse-and-buggy" stage into an era of all-weather, day and night flights, in comfortable, temperature-controlled, pressurized cabins, at faster and faster speeds.

THE CONTRIBUTION OF RESEARCH AND DEVELOPMENT

The spending of thousands of millions of dollars to improve airplanes year after year, decade after decade, is only one element responsible for the progress from wood, cloth, and guy-wire contraptions to aluminum and steel, semi-monocoque fuselage and sandwich-wing-construction monoplanes. The other element is the refinement of a technique for mastering nature unique in human history and less than two centuries old: a special combination of scientific *research* and engineering *development*.

Research and development have enabled aircraft designers and builders to move back and forth, as the necessity arises, from the scientific study of phenomena in order to understand them to the application of this understanding in ways that will control and manipulate the phenomena to man's advantage. The airplane was not improved simply because numbers of men devoted endless hours of persistent effort to it, although this was indeed necessary. Rather, it was improved because practical engineering know-how was combined with fundamental scientific research, and this created the scientific technology distinctive of modern aviation—and lacking in the technology of building private homes or in such traditional enterprises as the fabrication of ready-to-wear garments. In short, the practical and the theoretical men assisted one another.

THE WRIGHT BROTHERS

The breakthrough that made the airplane possible occurred when Orville (1871-1948) and Wilbur (1867-1912) Wright—behaving not as bicycle mechanics but as the gifted practitioners of the research and development process that they also were—appraised the status of man's attempt to fly before 1900. Earlier intermittent efforts of such talented men as Gayley, Henson, Stringfellow, and Lilienthal had been marred by recurring failures and spurred by tantalizing near successes. The details of these practical and theoretical contributions compose a separate story too long to recount here, but they nevertheless deeply impressed the Wrights.

After careful study, the Wright brothers came to the shrewd (and to them, obvious) engineering conclusion that propulsion offered no problems. Perceiving that the piston-engine motors already in existence possessed sufficient power to move a glider large enough to carry a man, they turned to the problem of *controlled* flight, only to learn that efficient propellers had never been designed to translate the engine's power into the thrust necessary for flight.

Their solution to the control problem was not easy to arrive at. After much analysis, paper work, searching of the technical literature, and preliminary testing with models, between 1896 and 1903, they designed a biplane (for strength) that was deliberately as inert, aerodynamically unstable, and unresponsive to aerodynamic forces—except those providing lift—as they could make it, until the pilot twisted the wing tips. They did not want the airplane to fly itself at the start; they wanted to isolate the control problem and place control of the flight attitudes of their glider thoroughly in the hands of the pilot.

When the pilot simultaneously twisted the wing tips up at one end and twisted down at the other end, the resulting aerodynamic loads caused the Wrights' glider to go into a roll. Deflection of a small horizontal panel out ahead of the wing nosed the glider up or down. With these basic corrective movements under control and with rudder corrections added for stability, the Wrights' powered glider could be directed anywhere through the air at the pilot's will. The Wright brothers had mastered, at last, the art of flying in a powered, heavier-than-air craft.

Just when this momentous event took place is not so easy to determine as one might imagine, for technical achievement is not always easy to measure, either at the time it occurs or later. Thus, the public failed to recognize or appreciate the Wright brothers' achievement when they first flew in 1903. Contemporary newspapers have also been blamed for their lack of insight and interest at the time, but reporters and editors had become wary of the claims and announcements they were receiving which later proved to be unfounded. There was nothing in the modest, private, and at times almost secretive activity

Fig. 12-1. The Wright brothers' first flight at Kitty Hawk, 1903. (Courtesy of *The Smithsonian Institution*)

of the two obscure men from Dayton, Ohio, to mark them as Destiny's choice.

To be sure, Wilbur and Orville Wright were certain they had succeeded in 1903, but theirs was the private, internal knowledge of the experts, not easily communicated. Experts can become hopeful of their progress by the kinds of unanticipated mistakes they make at first and then stop making. They can be persuaded by the small solutions they propose along the way that really do work when tested; and can be convinced by the pattern of evidence that they see emerging from the trend of technical events in which they are deeply and intimately involved. Out of such private knowledge they can cry, "Eureka! I have found it!" when to the outsider the evidence remains unconvincing and the success undemonstrated.

So it was at the beginning of powered flight by heavier-than-air craft. The epochal four flights the brothers made on December 17, 1903, convinced them they had mastered the air, even though the longest flight, by Wilbur Wright, lasted only 59 seconds and covered a mere 852 feet. An outsider would have been more impressed by a flight Wilbur made on October 5, 1905, outside of Dayton, when he flew more than twenty-four miles in thirty-eight minutes, banking and turning, climbing and descending at will.

Five years after the Wrights's 1903 success, outsiders finally came to believe. In July 1908, Glenn Curtiss's public flights of his *June Bug* at Hammondsport, New York, attracted more attention than anything the Wrights had yet said or done; however, in August Wilbur Wright's flights in France convinced European crowds that he and his brother had no equal in the building and piloting of heavier-than-air craft. In September Orville Wright's demonstrations before army observers aroused the continuing interest of the United States government.

From that time onward, people enthusiastically accepted the reality of mastered flight. In 1909 Louis Blériot flew across the English Channel. In 1910 Glenn Curtiss set a world speed record of 55 miles per hour. In 1911 Lincoln Beachey set a world altitude record of 11,642 feet; that same year Calbraith P. Rodgers flew all the way across the continent, from New York to Long Beach, California, in forty-nine days, spending eighty-two hours and four minutes of this time aloft and surviving nineteen crashes en route. The "romantic period" in aviation history had begun, dominated by flamboyant adventurers who engaged in foolhardy scrapes, such as flying under the bridge at Niagara Falls, and heroic feats like flying over the North Pole.

In retrospect, the invention of the airplane was a civilian, not a military, affair. Two brilliant engineers, the Wrights, who lacked formal university training and who performed their work without government or private subsidy, accomplished the breakthrough. By the end of 1908 they had satisfied the world that their solution really worked. In the decades that followed, industrialized Europe and the United States led the rest of the world in promoting aviation progress through military research and development.

DEVELOPMENT OF THE PROPULSION UNIT

As aviation technology gathered impetus during the 20th century, conspicuous changes occurred in the shape of the airframes and in the power of the propulsion units. Behind the diversity of models produced lies an evolutionary pattern of technological progress that is measured by increases in speed and in altitude, and by improvements in operating costs and efficiency.

For all their variety, aircraft power plants have been largely restricted to one type of propulsion unit, the internal-combustion engine, because of the relatively large amount of power produced by a relatively light engine—in technical terms, a favorable weight-to-power ratio. This engine was used earliest in the form of the reciprocating piston engine and later in the alternate form of the gas turbine, or turbojet. From the far less than fifty-mile-an-hour, 12-horsepower engine and twin-propeller arrangement that Wilbur and Orville Wright used in 1903 to the faster-than-sound warplanes and the ten-miles-a-minute transports of sixty years later, the story is one of rapid, progressive evolution of power-plant design.

European engines surpassed American ones in quantity and quality during the first two decades. American involvement in World War I compelled American manufacturers to borrow from and imitate English and French engine designs in order to meet war needs. As a consequence of the European lead in both liquid-cooled and air-cooled designs, competitive American prototypes did not appear until the early 1920's.

From the late 'twenties to the middle 'forties, the dominant engine type was the radial, air-cooled engine. During World War II, liquid-cooled, in-line engines began to appear attractive because they made possible improvements in streamlining. However, the gas-turbine (jet) engine was to supersede both types as the best high-performance power plant available.

In England by 1930 and in Germany by 1935, Frank Whittle and Hans von Ohain, respectively, were working on turbojet designs. Not until August 1939, however, was the first turbojet flight made, in the German Heinkel He-178; by the end of the war the Germans had one turbojet engine—the Junkers 004—in production and one jet-powered aircraft—the Messerschmitt Me-262 fighter.

The first British jet-powered flight took place in May 1941, when Whittle's W-1 turbojet soared aloft in a Gloster E28/39 experimental airplane. By the end of the war the British, too, had one flying production model—the Rolls Royce "Welland," installed in the Gloster "Meteor I."

Just as the United States had entered the aircraft piston-engine, design-progress picture late in World War I, copying and improving upon European advances, so did it enter the World War II jet picture late, copying and improving upon British turbojet designs. In 1941 serious efforts to accomplish flight by jet propulsion were finally begun, and by mid-1943 wartime pressures narrowed the field to four models which might be ready for the later phases of the war. As affairs turned out, the day of the jet was to come after the war. Its German and British inventors had foreseen at the start that the turbojet's principal contribution should be a marked jump in aircraft speed—say, from 300 mph to 500 mph—in the near future, and travel approaching, and perhaps surpassing, the speed of sound later.

Propulsion-design progress is reflected in the rated performances of fighter aircraft in the four decades 1917-57. A World War I French Nieuport biplane, Model 28C-1 of 1625 pounds gross weight, and powered by a 160-horsepower Gnome rotary engine, could reach 120-125 miles per hour. A World War II British "Spitfire" monoplane, Model VB, weighing 6750 pounds, loaded, and equipped with a 1470-horsepower Merlin in-line piston engine, could reach a maximum speed of nearly 370 mph at 19,500 feet. German wartime research into swept-wing monoplanes and British pioneering efforts in turbojet-engine design enabled American engineers after World War II to produce the North American Aviation F-86A "Sabrejet," weighing over 16,000 pounds gross. An F-86A set a world speed record of 670 mph in September 1948. In October 1953, a North American F-100A "Supersabre" set a world record of 755 mph. The F-100 was a second-generation design descendant of the F-86,

Fig. 12-2. F-86 "Sabrejets." (*U. S. Air Force* photo)

with a rated gross weight of 34,800 pounds; it became the first operational fighter capable of supersonic speeds in level flight. In December 1957, a special McDonnell F-101C "Voodoo" set a world speed record of 1207 mph; the standard rated gross weight of the "Voodoo C" series aircraft was 47,000 pounds.

It had taken forty years for aircraft speeds to increase by a power of ten, from 120 to 1200 miles per hour, while gross weights went up twenty-nine fold. The advent of the jet engine doubled aircraft speeds in a decade and took the airplane through and beyond the speed of sound, into a physical environment in which the air no longer behaved like the compressible medium the designers had always dealt with. Aerodynamics and structural engineers, after incurring more than one mistake while invading the unknown, successfully met the airframe design challenges that the punishing, tremendous thrust of the jet engine posed.

By the end of the first sixty years of powered flight, diverse types of power plants were serving specialized functions. Slower speeds were the domain of piston engines; intermediate speeds, of the turbojets; higher speeds appeared to be in the regime of the still-undeveloped ramjet; and the highest speeds belonged to the rockets. Experimental airplanes using each of these major types of engines had already flown.

DESIGN DEVELOPMENTS

Airframe structures and contours responded, particularly in their design progress, to speed and efficiency requirements, and then to mission requirements. A one-man flyer, a mail carrier, a transport, a warplane, or a speed, temperature, and aerodynamics research craft (such as the X-1, X-2, and X-15 research airplanes) had different requirements and posed different problems to the designers who sought to make form follow both aerodynamic and utilitarian functions. The efficiency of each airplane as a flying machine; the importance of designing parts to be strong enough to be safe, while keeping the weight of all materials as low as possible; plus the insatiable demand for more speed —these requirements of aviation technology conspired to produce an exciting, vigorous, and competitive atmosphere in the aviation industry.

As designers, flying enthusiasts, and military agencies expanded the range of their needs—for example, the ability to fly under various weather conditions, or to fly heavier planes faster—technical improvements were stimulated. These improvements, in turn, prompted new expectations and requirements from designers and fliers which scientific and engineering ability increasingly accomplished. Although during the first decade of flight it was possible to fabricate an airplane without undertaking elaborate, technical engineering investigations, as the third decade of flight passed into the fourth, the state of the art had progressed so far that it was rapidly moving out of the realm of "backyard" empirical invention and into the exclusive domain of scientific technology.

After World War I the airplane became an increasingly complex machine that consisted of many smaller machines and systems—airframe, control surfaces, power plant, pilot's instrument panel, cockpit controls, and so forth. To these, during the 'thirties and after, were added more and more complicated electrical systems, surface-control systems, hydraulic systems, gunnery and bombing systems, de-icing systems, and other special-service equipment. Design progress in each of these components encouraged progress in the others; thus, more powerful engines permitted more powerful hydraulic systems, larger airframes, and greater airspeeds. Greater airspeeds encouraged (and later required) all-metal cantilever-wing monoplanes without external bracing, which were pioneered by the Junkers aircraft firm in Germany. Similarly, greater airspeeds ultimately required engineers to retract the landing gear; thus, while a Fokker or a Ford Trimotor in the airlines of the late 'twenties did not carry retractable landing gear, the Boeing 247 and Douglas DC-3 of the early 'thirties retracted the two main gears far enough to leave the bottoms of the tires awash in the airstream, and the transports of the 'forties (their arrival delayed by World War II) withdrew their tricycle landing gear behind closed doors. The tricycle gear permitted better distribution of loads and better controlled landing and takeoff runs under a wider range of wind conditions.

Some of the streamlined airplanes of the 1930's were equipped with anti-dragging cowls to reduce the turbulence and drag of the radial engines. A government research laboratory, under the National Advisory Committee for Aeronautics, was responsible for this minor yet typical advance in design. Not until the more powerful turbojets appeared did the rounded, streamlined contours yield to the pointed, swept-back-wing configuration of the subsonic, transsonic, and supersonic fighters, bombers, and transports.

EQUIPMENT PROBLEMS

Design improvements resulted in part from the attitudes of engineers, whose latest improvements suggested refinements and alternatives which they wished they *had* tried and which they *could* try on the next model; they also arose from the engineering habit of attacking practical problems that looked as though they could be solved. Many of these solutions were on a cut-and-try basis rather than on the more sophisticated theorizing and experimental research basis characteristic of the best aerodynamics progress. For example, the automotive, float-type carburetor had reached a relatively stable (even though not particularly efficient) design for aircraft during the 1920's; only when it failed to supply fuel in dive-bombing and similar sustained accelerative maneuvers—which commanded the attention of military and acrobatic pilots early in the 1930's—pressure carburetors were developed at American military request and expense. In these the supply of fuel was determined by diaphragm-actuated slide valves insensitive to sharp accelerations and maneuvers but sensitive to the pressures generated from air flowing through the intake manifold into the engine cylinders.

In general, airframe and component-system designers greedily used all the power that power-plant engineers could provide, at least during the first four or five decades of flight. Post-World War II piston- and turbojet-engine designs —especially the latter—finally began to supply enough power to give designers and flight crews some feeling that they had about as much propulsive and equipment power as they needed. Such judgments are qualitative and on a sliding scale, of course; while aircrews became enthusiastic over the performance of the DC-3 in the 1930's and over the Lockheed "Electra" in the 1950's and 1960's, the expectations that the "Electra" satisfied could no longer possibly be met by the DC-3. Aviation technology, by its very nature, promotes design progress and design obsolescence simultaneously.

Also, during the 1930's and 1940's, problems of ice formation in the fuel-air mixture under certain conditions of altitude and humidity were gradually brought under control, reducing the number of engine failures and crashes due to that cause. Carburetor icing came to be controlled partly by heating the incoming air from the warmth of the exhaust pipes (although such heating could reduce engine power under certain conditions), partly by shifting the position at which the fuel entered the airstream on its way to the cylinders, and partly by making sure that the gasoline was not too volatile, for this cooled the air (in the same way that evaporation of ether or alcohol cools one's finger), and ice crystals would collect.

Ice on windshields, obscuring visibility, and on wings, destroying lift, combined with carburetor-icing problems during those years to produce numerous crashes, as airplanes ventured to fly in worse weather. Anti-icing fluids to wash windshields, and defrosting heat applied to the glass represented typical engineering "fixes." Rubber "boots" along the leading edges of wings and tail surfaces could be distorted mechanically to crack off collecting ice, but a more permanent solution to prevent ice from forming was achieved—once powerful enough engines became available—by piping air heated by the engines along ducts strategically routed in the wing and tail surfaces.

The military advantage of flying higher than the enemy and the commercial advantage of maintaining schedules by flying over the weather whenever possible provided challenges to mechanical engineers and aeromedical experts during the 1930's that were first met, in a partial way, with oxygen masks for military crews and superchargers for the engines. Airplanes so equipped were few in number before World War II. The feasibility of providing pressurized, air-conditioned quarters for the passengers and crew was shown by the performance of the Lockheed-built, U.S. Army XC-35, which won the famous Collier Trophy in 1937 for its aeromedical demonstration and its equipment demonstration of the value of supercharged cabins in aircraft. But the approaching war emphasized military developments, and the immediate military solution was to provide engine superchargers and oxygen masks. After the war the turbojet engine, which was itself a combined gas turbine and giant-capacity supercharger, provided the air needed for pressurized crew quarters of warcraft, while the more modest priorities and financial outlays of the airlines obtained supercharged, piston-engine aircraft equipped with special cabin superchargers, heaters, and refrigeration units, deriving their power from the aircraft engines. A decade after the war, pressurized jet transports finally began to appear.

COMPONENTS SYSTEMS

The pressure-cabin solution was far more elaborate than the oxygen-mask approach, for in addition to cabin superchargers, there were required pressure-regulator valves, to control the outflow of air from the cabin; safety "pop-off" valves, in case the regulators should malfunction; and elaborate cabin-air temperature and humidity controls. The mere grouping of these components, each of which performed excellently by itself, was not enough, because the various items of equipment interacted with one another; what was needed were *inte-*

grated systems of ducting, controls, power units, valves, heaters, and refrigerating units, developed and tailored to the needs of the various models of pressurized military and civil aircraft that flew during the 1950's and the 1960's. By that time, of course, the integrated-system concept was no longer the novelty that it had been at the end of the first thirty years of flight. Its continuing development by mechanical and electrical engineers was a cornerstone of aviation-design progress toward more complex and more reliable aircraft.

The growing number of functions and uses to which the airplane came to be put with the passing years encouraged electrical and mechanical engineers to develop the more elaborate component systems and equipment that have been installed in the airframe. Especially useful were the hydraulic and the electrical systems. The former was primarily a power system dependent on a pump mounted on the power plant. Hydraulic fluid under pressure actuated pistons that retracted the landing gear, opened and closed bomb-bay and passenger compartment doors, actuated cowl flaps to control the amount of cooling air passing among the fins of air-cooled engines, extended landing flaps and dive brakes, operated subservient boosters to assist the pilot in moving the aircraft control surfaces, and generally accomplished any motions of heavy equipment or of mechanisms operating against the airstream.

During the 1940's, 1950's, and 1960's electrical systems not only became sufficiently developed to compete seriously with the hydraulic systems in such roles as referred to above, but also came into wide use wherever delicate control signals were required—as in the automatic pilot system, the cabin pressure, temperature, and humidity systems, the pilot's engine and flight instruments, gun and bomb sights and controls—and continued customary chores of engine starting and ignition, illumination and running lights, flap and landing gear position indicators, warning lights of various kinds, and last but by no means least, radar and radio communications equipment.

AERODYNAMICS RESEARCH

Another cornerstone was the correlating of fundamental and applied research with developmental work that went on in the realm of aerodynamics and airframe design. Contributions from mathematicians interested in understanding airflow phenomena and from engineers interested in controlling these phenomena resulted in faster and more efficient aircraft, although the interplay of their theoretical and experimental activities was usually too technical and difficult to evaluate and explain to attract the attention of journalists and laymen. Frederick W. Lanchester (1868-1945), Ludwig Prandtl (1875-1953), Osborne Reynolds (1842-1912), and Theodore von Kármán (1881-1963) are representative of the more important historical figures who developed theoretical descriptions and appropriate equations, suitable for designers to use, of such key phenomena as lift, drag, boundary-layer conditions, laminar and turbulent flow, skin friction, and aerodynamic stability.

As swifter airplanes were sought and airfoil-design configurations became more complex, mathematical formulations become more complicated and more intimately involved with wind-tunnel testing of precision-scaled models. By the early 1930's, for example, combined wind-tunnel and mathematical-physics analyses of the tendencies of some models and prototypes to engage in small, rapid, pitching motions (technically called "buffeting") indicated that a major cause lay with the contours of the joints where wing and fuselage met. The solution achieved by combined mathematical and wind-tunnel studies at the Guggenheim Aeronautical Laboratory of the California Institute of Technology took the form of "fillets," or fairing, so designed as to smooth out the aerodynamic turbulence encountered in the non-faired designs. The technical term for one cause of this aerodynamic phenomenon, "vortex shedding," is a good example of the descriptive scientific terms—increasingly employed in aviation-engineering circles—that caused the true nature of aviation research and development activity to become increasingly obscure to the lay public.

So complicated and theoretical-experimental had the aerodynamics of high-performance aircraft become by the early 1940's, and so successfully did the intricate, dovetailed, and massive explanations of contemporary theory seem to be answering important engineering and research questions, that many experts were unprepared to account for the unexpected behavior of airflows they encountered just below and above "Mach 1" (the speed of sound, which varies with the density of the air). Consequently, the epithet "sound barrier" enjoyed brief popularity during that decade, until engineers and mathematicians too numerous to mention made the many modifications necessary in their mathematical procedures, their experimental equipment and techniques, and ultimately in the shapes and the structural forms of the airframes. In retrospect, the sound barrier proved to be a hurdle, not an obstacle, in the progress of aviation.

As engineering and aerodynamic skills progressed during the second quarter-century of flight, the relatively simple wing with aileron and trim tab became a more protean airfoil, the shape of which could be altered by extending trailing flaps and flaps attached to flaps, by incorporating slots near the leading edge, or by detaching the leading edge and extending it forward to form slots at will. The flaps generally increased the lifting power of the wing, permitting faster aircraft to land and take off at slower speeds. The slots prevented stalling by maintaining proper airflow, and hence, lift, across the wing throughout changes in attitude of the airplane. While these devices and their actuating mechanisms added considerable weight to the airplane, they more than made up for it by the increased safety, maneuverability, and aerodynamic versatility of the higher-performance aircraft. Their proper design was made possible by the elaborate combination already mentioned of theoretical mathematical investigations and experimental testing procedures.

LIGHTER-THAN-AIR SHIPS

The passing decades thus transformed the airplane persistently, and rapidly, from its original form, of a powered glider big enough to carry a man, to a great, versatile, and increasingly self-sufficient (when airborne) ship of the air. Yet none of these ships of the air could compare in breathtaking majesty with several generations of giant lighter-than-air ships that flourished during the second, third, and fourth decades of flight, before finally disappearing from the scene. The origins of these "dirigibles," as they came to be called, are hinted at by their name, for they emerged out of the earlier state of the art of the non-directable, free balloons.

Ballooning, or "aerostation," was born when Joseph Montgolfier (1740-1810) and his brother Étienne (1745-99) developed the first freely soaring hot-air balloons in France in 1782-83, and when their countryman, J. A. C. Charles (1746-1823), later in 1783 released a rubberized-silk balloon filled with hydrogen. During the next century and a half, ballooning attracted both amateurs and scientists. The former enjoyed it as a sport, while the latter regarded it as an opportunity to study the weather and physics of the atmosphere first-hand. Desultory efforts through the years produced sufficient technological progress by 1935 to enable Army Captains A. W. Stevens and O. A. Anderson to soar aloft in a sealed, spherical gondola to a record altitude of 72,395 feet—over thirteen miles up. In 1961 Navy Commander M. D. Ross soared to 113,740 feet.

Meanwhile, the dream of powered flight with balloons had attracted isolated experimenters throughout the 19th century. By the end of the century the development of the internal-combustion engine provided the relatively lightweight and sustained power necessary to make manned, powered, lighter-than-air flights practical. Two investigators, working independently, demonstrated the practical possibilities. The first was a wealthy Brazilian sportsman who achieved popular fame for his exploits: Alberto Santos-Dumont (1873-1932). His trial-and-error efforts produced more than a dozen small, non-rigid, propeller-driven gas bags with attached gondolas, which he flew between 1893 and 1906 before turning his attention to powered gliders. Although his activities caught the popular fancy, they were technologically no match for the sustained and serious engineering enterprise taken up in 1897 by Count Ferdinand von Zeppelin (1838-1917) of Germany. Zeppelin more than any other man deserves the title "Father of the Dirigible." He developed a fabric-covered, rigid, sausage-shaped, bluntly pointed-nosed framework of light, metal girders, containing numerous gas and ballast cells and auxiliary equipment. Along the bottom of the frame was attached a roomy, passenger-carrying gondola cabin and the necessary engines and propellers. Zeppelin and his engineers preferred the practical engineering service and safety features (against disastrous leaks) of many cells, and they preferred a constant-size vessel with constant size tail fins and control surfaces, for stability and desirable propulsion and load-carrying capacity. To obtain the controlled maneuverability, structural strength, lift, size, and passenger-carrying capacity they sought, rigid airships appeared to them the optimum engineering solution.

Zeppelin's first ship flew in 1900. Ten years later his dirigibles were carrying paying passengers, and by the time World War I began, his factory had produced more than twenty-five "zeppelins." The Germans continued zeppelin development during World War I, although their raids over London were more spectacular than militarily effective. By the middle 1930's, Germans had achieved regular transatlantic flights to the United States. The Germans used hydrogen to obtain lift. Even though nonflammable helium became commercially available for special uses in the United States during the 1930's, the supply was not large at first. Later, when more helium was available, the warlike behavior of Hitler prevented the sale of the gas to Germany by the United States, which was the sole world supplier.

Although some of the German dirigibles suffered unfortunate accidents, the Germans avoided the relatively disastrous and short-lived engineering and flying programs initiated by Britain and the United States. United States Navy leaders and civilian engineers persuaded the Congress to provide funds for two enormous, helium-filled, rigid-frame dirigibles, the 785-foot *Akron* and its twin, the *Macon*. The latter carried five scouting biplanes, could launch and receive them while in flight, and played a promising part in war games. But the *Akron* was lost in a storm in 1933, and the *Macon* crashed in 1935.

It appeared that they foundered either because their crews really did not understand how to fly them or because their huge size, bulk, and lightweight structure rendered them dangerously vulnerable to strong winds and bad weather. Opponents of dirigibles argued that even though contemporary engine and propeller designs could be readily adapted for dirigible use, the small propulsive power relative to the huge size, together with the relatively delicate structure, placed these ponderous but fragile airborne "whales" at the mercy of the turbulent ocean of the air. In their opinion, the giant craft could not help but be underpowered, oversized, understressed, and undercontrolled. In spite of the relatively successful German engineering and flight-operation experience over several decades, many seriously questioned the ultimate airworthiness of the giant, rigid airships, even while admitting the impressive safety and operational record (144 transoceanic flights) of the German dirigible *Graf Zeppelin* and the demonstrated reliability and limited usefulness of the smaller, non-rigid blimps.

Meanwhile, the *Graf Zeppelin* and its successor, the 803-foot *Hindenburg*, set record after record in long-distance flights. Then, on May 6, 1937, as the *Hindenburg* was approaching her mooring mast in New Jersey after a routine transatlantic flight, flames suddenly erupted from her stern topsides, and she crashed a flaming wreck before horrified onlookers, killing 35 of the 97 people on board. No authoritative answer has ever been given to the question of what ignited the hydrogen. This disaster terminated the era of the giant dirigibles —the longest era of powered flight at that time, since the Wright Flyer had first shown heavier-than-air flight to be possible several years after Santos-Dumont and Zeppelin first flew. The Germans had been the first to build ambitiously large, rigid airships; they were also the last.

Had airplanes not proved so successful, it is reasonable to suppose that men would not have been content to remain earthbound, that in spite of the disasters they would have gone on building and flying rigid dirigibles, just as they continued to build non-rigid, small, modestly powered blimps for military surveillance, antisubmarine warfare, and kindred special functions. The state of the art would then have continued to be cultivated. Although practical experience had been generally disappointing, there were those, such as Admiral Charles Rosendahl, an experienced airship officer, who felt that sufficient time and effort had never been expended to provide for mature judgment regarding the feasibility of the giant rigid airship.

Dirigibles offered smooth, comfortable, roomy, leisurely flying conditions. Yet these advantages did not commend them to designers, financiers, or military or civilian potential users in the third of a century that followed. Hence, dirigibles were not the object of the funds, time, engineering experience, ingenuity, and persistence of purpose that have characterized the history of ocean-going vessels, railroads, or the airplane. To assert positively, however, that there is or is not a place for dirigibles in the future of aviation would be to presume to predict the very future of the research and development process that lies at the heart of modern technology.

MILITARY AVIATION

The long-range military association of aviation technology was established before the first decade of the 20th century had passed. In the United States the Wrights sold the Army its first airplane in 1909; in Europe, governments began to acquire airplanes several years before World War I began. After the war, important aspects of the technical development of the airplane in both Europe and the United States remained a military story, in which the engineering component was contributed by college-trained civilian engineers, while military officials determined how appropriate the engineers' innovations were in relation to their needs.

Generally, though not always, the engineers were more imaginative and eager than the military officials and their own industrial managers. On the one hand, the accumulation of experience before World War II in the untried reaches of aerial warfare was punctuated by the appearance of prophets, such as Generals "Billy" Mitchell and Henry H. "Hap" Arnold in the U.S. Army and Giulio Douhet in Italy, and by the trials of martyrs—Mitchell and Douhet. Both were court-martialled for their impatience at the slowness of military policy in their countries to exploit the techniques of aerial warfare and achieve the military preparedness that advancing military technology demanded.

On the other hand, to assume that the "military mind" was reluctant to have anything to do with anything aerial and untried is to ignore the relative alacrity with which the Navy converted a collier into its first aircraft carrier, the *U.S.S. Langley*, by 1922. It is also to overlook the extensive use that armed forces everywhere sought to make of aerial reconnaissance since the days of the biplanes and the stationary captive balloons of World War I. The fact is that military officials were sometimes ahead of the aviation engineers. For example, the air-cooled engine was a Navy idea, and General Arnold pushed for a giant bomber (the B-36) before engineering managers were ready with the idea.

MILITARY AIRPLANES

World War I witnessed the practical beginnings of a growing aerial military tradition, when the first pilots decided to mount carbines or machine guns on their hitherto unarmed planes, and when the Germans sent giant lighter-than-air dirigibles to bomb London. As the years passed, the battle functions of the airplane became more specialized and this brought about the emergence, during the second decade, of the classic categories: the reconnaissance, or observation, airplane; the fighter and pursuit types; and the bomber.

Aerial reconnaissance, the first military function of the warplane historically, is a century older than the airplane, for captive balloons had been used briefly by Napoleon's armies and later in the American Civil War. Reconnaissance airplane flights were carried out by Italian flyers as early as 1911-12, when Italy seized Tripoli from Turkey; and in World War I both sides used observation planes.

Specialized types continued to appear thenceforth in all major categories, but the most important military concept to emerge, which brought a third dimension to warfare, came before the airplane was two decades old; the idea was that of the warplane as a "weapons platform." World War II saw what was considered to be a culmination of this trend in its long-range bombers, but the culmination proved to be only a plateau, marked by the impressive performances of the B-17, the B-24, and the B-29. These bombers are of interest not

Fig. 12-3. The "Flying Fortress," B-17 bomber of World War II fame. (Courtesy of *The Smithsonian Institution*)

only for their demonstration of the indebtedness of aviation progress to military funds, but also for their demonstration of the rapid maturing of aerial warfare techniques.

The first of the Boeing B-17 "Flying Fortress" series made its maiden flight in 1935. It was intended to be a defensive weapon, a four-engine "flying artillery" vehicle to protect American coasts, hence its name. Subsequent versions, affected by operational and battle experience, underwent considerable refinement and redesign, most of it not readily visible to the casual eye; thus, by 1942, Model B-17G airplanes were being produced in quantity. Before the war ended, more than 12,000 B-17's were built; of these, more than 8600 were B-17G's.

An airplane of comparable size and function was the Consolidated B-24 "Liberator," which first flew in 1939. The product of a policy of military preparedness, it was brought into being as a "second source" airplane to protect the United States in the event that the Nazis' aggressive policies should involve the United States in a war. The B-24J model was the version most widely used; between August 1943 and November 1944 over 6600 were built, and many saw service in Europe and in the Pacific Theater. Like the B-17, the B-24 was a monoplane of all-aluminum, semi-monocoque construction, but it had a novel tricycle landing gear which the B-17 lacked.

The Boeing B-29 "Superfortress," the last of the big American bombers to see duty in World War II, was designed in response to specifications issued by General Arnold in January 1940. The prototype experimental model flew for the first time in September 1942, and the first B-29 went to war in the Pacific theater in April 1944. The B-29B was powered by four radial engines of 2200 horsepower each. (The B-17 and B-24 bombers had four radial engines of 1200 horsepower each.)

Hitler's staggering successes in Europe by 1941 caused military requirements to be issued for the largest United States bomber ever to see military service, the Convair B-36. The experimental prototype first flew in August 1946, and the Strategic Air Command finally retired the last B-36 from active service in February 1959, in order to become an all-jet nuclear striking force. Six 3500-horsepower piston engines pushed the B-36B through the air. After 1949, jet pods were added for additional power and speed in the B-36D and later versions. The last of the piston-engine heavy bombers, the B-36 was held in reserve as a strategic retaliatory threat; it dropped no bombs "in anger" before it was retired.

Increases in weight, size, power, carrying capacity, and range are the obvious consistent design trends in these bombers, from the B-17 to the B-36, conceived between 1934 and 1941. Less apparent, but more indicative of the true nature of scientific technological progress, was the increased *efficiency* in the power-plant and aerodynamic functions that made the improvements in performance possible. Not only were the later models bigger, not only could they carry more; they could do these things *better*. The piston-engine heavy bombers thus became obsolescent not because of internal shortcomings, but because other aviation developments in the field of jet propulsion were in the making.

This was not a technology that annihilated its past as it progressed; rather it was one that broadened its base and widened its area of application. The versatility of the airplane by 1959 is obvious when one looks back fifty years to the first Wright Flyer the Army accepted in 1909. The Model A had a wing span of thirty-six feet, four inches and a length of twenty-eight feet. Its weight empty was 740 pounds and gross weight, 1200 pounds. Its top speed was 44 miles an hour: fifty years later a fighter could fly at twice the speed of sound.

The warplane was not to reign without a peer. Although the advance of warplane designs by no means ended in 1945 (jet-powered, heavy bombers were still to be built, for example), the impact of the devastating, short-range Nazi V-2 rockets upon a defenseless London marked the dawn of the guided-missile era and the end of the unqualified supremacy of the airplane in three-dimensional warfare. As the new jets moved the piston-engine airplanes into the particular, specialized, functional niches for which they remained best suited, so did the rockets with nuclear warheads affect jet warplanes.

Table 12-1   Statistics on Heavy Bombers of the 1940's

	B-17G	B-24J	B-29B	B-36B
WING SPAN (FEET)	103	110	141	230
FUSELAGE (FEET)	74	67	99	162
WEIGHT (POUNDS)				
Empty	36,000	36,500	69,000	140,600
Gross	65,500	65,000	137,500	328,000
SPEED (MPH)				
Cruising	180	215	225	200
Top	285	290	360	380
ALTITUDE	25,000 ft.	25,000 ft.	25,000 ft.	34,500 ft.
RANGE (MILES)	2,000	2,100	4,200	8,100

Thus, missiles did not make the warplane old-fashioned and obsolete, as enthusiasts had at first argued, but they did mark the beginning of a new design phase that produced diverse, specialized airplanes to serve as airborne missile-launching platforms (whose counterpart, in the form of atomic submarines, United States Navy policy-makers reluctantly adopted at the impatient prodding of Admiral Hyman Rickover, after he obtained congressional support for his views). The new design phase also produced "spy planes," the high, stratospheric, continental-reconnaissance vehicles of the Lockheed U-2 type, and vehicles to provide the close tactical support in jungle guerilla warfare that helicopters uniquely came to perform.

THE DEVELOPMENT OF CIVIL AVIATION

Airplanes for peacetime use began to emerge during the second decade of the century. World War I affected the United States too briefly to provoke any important new American warplane designs that might be modified for peaceable use. In Europe, although the wartime Nieuports, Spads, Fokkers, SE-5's and others led to generations of faster, more powerful warcraft, there seemed but few peacetime uses for any airplane.

The novelty of flight itself was still the major feature. Barnstorming, air shows and air races, enthusiasm for faster mail service (weather and daylight permitting, of course), and the dreams of some aviators to institute passenger-carrying operations, all contributed to what was, especially in the United States, a colorful period of civil aviation. This reached its peak, measured by public enthusiasm, when a quiet, modest, determined "loner" with considerable flying

Fig. 12-4. Charles Lindbergh's *Spirit of St. Louis.* (Courtesy of *The Smithsonian Institution*)

experience, young Charles A. Lindbergh, flew nonstop from New York to Paris in May 1927, and collected the $25,000 Orteig Prize. Raymond Orteig had first offered it in 1919, a month before Captain John Alcock and Lt. Arthur W. Brown flew from Newfoundland to Ireland to become the first—yet not the most famous—to fly the Atlantic.

Lindbergh made the trip alone in a specially built Ryan monoplane, *The Spirit of St. Louis,* which was powered by a single, air-cooled, radial "Whirlwind" engine. He had selected this engine particularly for its reliability, economical performance, and high power, and the flight was as much a tribute to the engine as it was to the airplane and pilot, even though the engine never attracted the popular attention that the man and the airplane did. As the parent designer of that line of engines, Charles L. Lawrance, philosophically remarked, "Who remembers Paul Revere's horse?" It was Lindbergh's 33-hour solo feat that captured the public imagination. Mobbed by admiring throngs on his arrival in Paris, and throughout Europe and America, he became a living symbol of the glorious future of manned flight, and an international hero.

For a short time enthusiasm for airplanes and investment in the fledgling aviation business (whether building, flying, or both) knew no bounds—until the United States stock market crashed in 1929, and the worldwide Great Depression set in. The grim economic conditions that followed effectively wiped out the heady, glamorous, and exaggerated expectations that aviation had engendered but a few years earlier. Nevertheless, the building of airplanes had already become an industrial technology, for businessmen had moved into the manufacturing and air-transport fields during the 1920's, competing for mail contracts, passengers, and government subsidies from the military and the Post Office departments. In 1918 the Army began to fly scheduled mail from New York to Washington, D.C. In 1919 the Post Office added air-mail service between New York and Cleveland and initiated daytime flights along the route from New York to Chicago. In 1920 the Chicago-New York run was extended to Omaha, Nebraska, then to San Francisco, but around-the-clock mail flights across the continent had to wait until 1924.

AIRLINES

The first passenger-carrying airline in the United States, the St. Petersburg-Tampa Air Boat Line, opened for business in January 1914. In November 1919 Aeromarine-West Indies Airways began flying passengers back and forth between Miami and Cuba, ninety miles apart. While the 'twenties witnessed the steady expansion of air-mail service according to deliberate policies pursued by the Post Office, carrying passengers remained a sometime, fly-when-you-can operation that did not provide a steady or predictable income. In the summer of 1929 it became possible, weather permitting, to travel by train at night and by plane during the day, in a co-ordinated schedule, and go coast-to-coast in forty-eight hours; however, the novelty of this arrangement proved to be more significant than its convenience.

A great many airlines started, failed, merged, changed their names, merged, and changed their names once again during the late 'twenties and early 'thirties; in fact, many of the major airlines had their beginnings during this period of sometimes desperate bidding to receive the air-mail contracts that spelled the difference between business survival and death. The first passenger planes were usually those carrying mail; indeed, the Post Office Department had to force the airlines to carry passengers in their flimsy, cloth-covered biplanes. William B. Stout provided the Ford Airline with the first all-metal passenger plane; his Ford Trimotor (nicknamed "the Tin Goose") became a landmark in aviation progress. During the early 1930's the twin-engine transport monoplane appeared. Lockheed offered its ten-place "Electra"; Boeing produced its larger Model 247; and Douglas, first its DC (for Douglas Commercial)-2 and then, in 1935, the DC-3, the most famous transport airplane of the first fifty years of flight. So reliable and economical was this airplane to operate that many thousands of DC-3's were built for the government during World War II; by 1964, thirty years after the prototype, there were still more than 450 DC-3's flying on the air lanes of the world.

In 1939, just before World War II broke out in Europe, Boeing began to produce its Model 307 "Stratoliner." Five were built and taken over by the Army in 1942. The 307 was designed to fly pressurized over most bad weather at nearly 250 miles per hour. The Douglas Aircraft Company tried to match this four-engine, low-wing transport with a triple-tail DC-4, which proved to be uncompetitive and was sold to Japan, where it finally came to rest on the floor of Tokyo Bay. Lockheed was hard at work on a more successful triple-tail model of its own, the pressurized "Constellation," and although production of this airplane continued during the war at a very modest pace, all models were taken by the military services. The same fate befell the successful single-tail Douglas DC-4, which became known by its military designation, C-54. Although the fuselage was designed to be pressurized, wartime shortages caused it to be used as an unpressurized airplane.

Once the hiatus in domestic air transport caused by World War II was over, business resumed. Boeing had developed a military cargo version of its B-29, the C-97, and it offered a commercial version of this cargo plane, which it called the Model 377 "Stratocruiser." This was an interesting double-deck airplane, the fuselage cross-section of which was an inverted figure 8. Like the Lockheed "Constellation," its cabin was pressurized, but it was never economically competitive with the "Constellation" family (models 049, 749, 1049, and 1249 were among the more important versions), nor could it match the low operating costs of the DC-6 and DC-7 family.

The Lockheed and the Douglas four-engine transports were the big, long-range, propeller-driven, air-cooled-engine-powered, pressurized, and air-conditioned transports of the early 1950's. All of the knowledge and skill that the war had provided the builders went into these airplanes. DC-3's as war-surplus items were inordinately cheap, but they were relatively slow and their cabins were unpressurized. Convair produced its twin-engine pressurized "Convairliner" series (models 244, 344, and 444) for the short-haul, frequent-stop airline schedules. Its speed, operating economy, and capacity (more than forty passengers as compared with approximately half that number in the DC-3) rendered it competitive in a market in which personal comfort and quality of service increasingly spelled the difference between profit and loss among competitors.

In 1945 the first Model 049 "Constellation" appeared. In 1946 the Douglas DC-6 joined the 049, and the Convair 240 followed a year later. The Boeing "Stratocruiser" was flying in 1949, and in 1951 the last of the five basic designs, the twin-engine Martin 404, had joined the group. All were pressurized, propeller-and-piston-engine transports, designed to cruise at altitudes between 15,000 and 25,000 feet and at speeds ranging from 250 to 300 miles per hour.

A significant feature of these postwar airplanes was their "growth factor." The airframe-builders had decided that, at the rate of improvement of power plants expected in the years to come, an airframe basic design that permitted

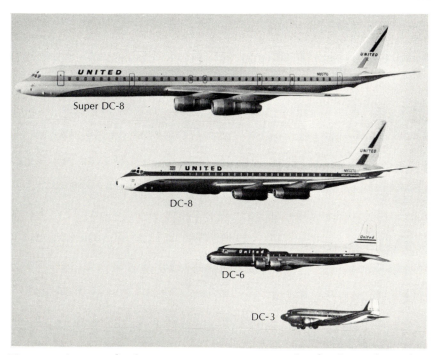

Fig. 12-5. An example of successive generations in one family of aircraft, 1936 to 1967. (Courtesy of *United Air Lines*)

newer models to have longer fuselages and longer, wider, more efficient wings would accomplish striking reductions in both development and production costs. Consequently, there appeared the Lockheed and the Douglas families of planes mentioned above, successive generations of which achieved economical increases in size and speed as one passed from the Model 049 "Constellation" to the Model 1649, or from the DC-6A to the DC-7C.

The statistics of domestic air travel after World War II reveal that the travelling public did not wait for the pressurized transports to appear before desiring to fly, and as the ocean-spanning versions of these four-engine monoplanes were put into service, worldwide air travel increased. Yet only modest numbers of new aircraft were built. Despite the military pressures generated by continuing international frictions during the 1950's, together with pressure created by the worldwide expansion of air commerce, the total number of airplanes produced per year in the United States, for example, varied between 6000 and 13,000, compared to the wartime peak, when in 1944 alone more than 95,000 airplanes were built. During a ten-year period beginning in 1956, more civil than military aircraft were produced each year, the number of the former alone varying between 6000 and 13,000 per year. A more stable, if less eventful, economic and technical scale of operations had come into being.

But although relatively modest numbers of airplanes were produced, the growth in commercial air travel was dramatic. In 1929 there were 105 million passenger-miles flown throughout the world; by 1939 the number had risen to 1260 million passenger-miles; by 1949 to 15,000 million; by 1959 to 61,000 million; and by 1965, it had reached 123,500 million passenger-miles per year. Nor was the end of this growth in air traffic in sight.

THE DEVELOPMENT OF JET PLANES

The engineering problems and the design peculiarities of the turbojet engine caused it to be mated cautiously at first with single-seat airframes. Development costs were borne by governmental military agencies in Europe and the United States, and as a natural result, the first operational jets were small warplanes. Their high initial cost and the high cost of operation would have discouraged peaceful applications—even if the military agencies had been inclined to encourage these—during the war. After World War II ended, the technical problems and the costs that lay ahead were still too formidable to encourage peaceful applications immediately, so the first new wave of postwar transports did not include a single jet. There was, however, no question as to whether there would be jet transports; the question was *when* would the jet transports become feasible.

During the 1950's the turbojet-powered transports came onto the scene. The ill-fated British DeHavilland "Comet," its fuselage too weak, appeared first. Lockheed offered its new jet-prop "Electra" for intermediate-haul service. Douglas was working on an all-jet DC-8, and Convair on its all-jet 880. But Boeing reached the transport market ahead of its American competitors, with the Model 707.

Although the Boeing management had courageously decided to develop the 707 using its own corporate funds, and had set to work earlier on the progenitor Type 367-80 transport, Boeing enjoyed a technological head start as a consequence of the military development and production contracts that produced, first the B-47 intermediate bomber and then the B-52 heavy bomber—both swept-wing, all-jet designs. The military need for jet tankers to refuel the B-47 and B-52 airplanes in flight led, after the 367-80 flew in July 1954, to the KC-135. Thus, long before Boeing had finished developing and producing its multi-engine subsonic jet bombers, it had shrewdly set to work to bring out a similar line of peacetime transports and military tankers.

As civilian air travel steadily mounted, airline profits soared because of growing demand and the economy of operation of jet planes. (Faster times allowed more flights, and the maintenance costs were lower than with piston planes because the jet engines were relatively trouble-free.) Therefore, the

Fig. 12-6. A model of the proposed British-French supersonic transport *Concorde*, 184 feet long with a wing span of 84 feet. Powered by four turbojet engines developing more than 35,000 pounds thrust each, the aircraft will travel at 1450 mph at altitudes up to 60,000 feet, and carry 136 passengers. Its maximum range will be 4000 miles. (Courtesy of *United Air Lines*)

airlines demanded larger and larger jet planes. In 1966 plans were announced for "jumbo jets," seating from 200 to 400 passengers, to fly at subsonic speeds. These were to embody no new technical innovations, but were simply to be an enlargement of existing designs; thus, their larger passenger capacity was to lower the cost of air travel, making it available to a larger market.

At the same time, the demand for greater speed was insatiable. And, as in the case of so much aviation history, military developments preceded the civilian. Military planes had long exceeded the speed of sound (Mach 1), and during the 1960's, aviation engineers began working on plans for civilian air transports which would travel at supersonic speeds. The developmental costs of such planes were so great that they could not be borne by private industry alone; only governments possessed sufficient resources to underwrite the research and development involved. Nevertheless, once again in the history of aviation technology it was a question not of whether but of when: supersonic transports were inevitable.

SUPPORT FACILITIES

Just as the airplane became an integrated system of machines, so did flying become a complicated ground-air activity. A barnstormer could take off from a grassy field, but commercial air travel required waiting rooms, ticket counters, baggage-handling, refueling, and service facilities. Furthermore, heavier air-planes and the idea of trying to maintain a flying schedule required reliably smooth, heavy-duty, wet-weather, paved runways, as well as longer and longer takeoff distances. During the 'twenties and the 'thirties these problems were at-tacked and preliminary solutions worked out by many investigators.

Difficulties were also posed by nighttime landings and takeoffs, which re-quired good visibility, runway marker lights, and ideally, bright landing lights on the airplanes themselves. Air-mail pilots needed weather reports and marker beacons to see and navigate by at night. At first the pilots depended on visual flight plans, relying upon railroads, highways, rivers, and other topographic features by day and upon city lights and marker beacons by night. As aviation developed it required more than "flying by the seat of one's pants," and the federal government became actively involved. First the Post Office, then, from the mid-1920's on, the Department of Commerce, and, from the 1930's on, spe-cial administrative agencies (for example, the Civil Aeronautics Board and, in 1958, the Federal Aviation Administration), took on the responsibility of pro-viding auxiliary navigation, communication, and airport services; of regulating flying practices among private and commercial airplanes; and of actively pro-moting flight-safety and accident-prevention investigations. The military agen-cies provided for their own airport and flying needs.

Among all the forms of transportation, flying was the first to exploit the ad-vantages of voice communication by radio, just as the railroads had seized upon the telegraph in the 19th century and ocean-going shipping had adopted wireless telegraphy earlier in the 20th cenutry. Voice-radio communication re-quired considerable development before it became reliable for weather report-ing and for airplane-to-airport and plane-to-plane communication. Weather-free, static-free transmission, together with design limitations imposed by the state-of-the-art, provided a host of problems. To single out the engineers who contributed solutions would—as in the story of airports, night flying, and later, instrument flying--only distort the characteristic process of accumulation and synthesis of inventions, concepts, and techniques that many carried out.

The increasing technological and sociological importance of aviation was a consequence of the converging, separate developments of day-and-night aerial navigation and communication; of the perfection of flight instruments, radio compasses and altimeters; of specialized flying and navigational techniques that enabled the pilot to rely solely on his instruments and fly "blind"; of the progress in weather forecasting and in availability of up-to-the-minute weather information for destinations miles ahead; and of the increasing sophistication of business management of airline and airport operations through the years.

At the end of the first fifty years of flight, commercial, military, and private flying enjoyed elaborate and invaluable airport, radio, and radar-navigation aids—and already showed signs of beginning to suffer from overcrowding of the skies. It was characteristic of the strongly empirical nature of flight operations that mid-air collisions still occurred on rare occasions with aircraft flying on scheduled routes at scheduled times, even though the *technical* means of averting such disasters through air traffic control had been devised and explored by aviation, communications, and computer experts ever since World War II had ended. The technical lessons mastered in the massive postwar defense effort and the experience of setting up continental defense systems, such as "SAGE" and "DEW," to intercept enemy aircraft and missiles were not fully applied to the domestic air-traffic-control problem, even though the basic technical elements were similar: for air defense, the military traffic-control problem was to identify and obtain collision courses for purposes of interception, while for peaceful air traffic the problem was to identify and *avoid* collision courses.

However, technical, administrative, political, economic, and military policy interests could not always be reconciled and co-ordinated in matters of air safety. Not only were there strong and sometimes conflicting interests, but the problems were complex, and policy-makers often failed to place air safety above all other considerations. Such difficulties were signs of the high social importance and the advanced technological status that aviation had achieved, but they were by no means peculiar to aviation.

AVIATION GROWS UP

As the war had earlier made the new propeller-driven transports available, so did continuing military and defense needs make possible the subsequent advent of the jet transport. And although half a century had passed since it all started, the economic and the technological circumstances shaping aviation progress had not fundamentally changed. True, the wood frames covered with cloth were gone; the novelty and the excitement of the barnstorming days also were gone. It was during the 1930's that the gallant, early adventurers faded from the scene. Airplanes became commonplace in the industrialized nations, and aviation became a business, the very sort of business the Wright brothers had once vainly hoped for.

Between the time the Wrights showed the way and the outbreak of World War I, no great scientific and professional engineering talents were needed to follow the Wrights' example. Then increasingly, engineers took over the building of airframes and engines, until the 1930's. At that time the industrial managers and financiers gradually took leadership away from the engineers and from the few, mellowed, adventurous pioneers who remained. The unprecedented performance and production demands of World War II accelerated this trend, and the glamorous "world of the air" that had captured the romantic fancy of brash young minds a generation earlier became more and more the domain of experienced older men who were still entrepreneurial but more cautious, shrewd, and committed to the goal of obtaining a financial return on an investment. In return for the loss of its early glamor, aviation became more durable and more reliable, surrendering the flaming torch that it had snatched up in its first years for the softer, steadier glow of a seasoned technology, whose social and technical worth was proven. The flaming torch itself passed on to a new enterprise: the exploration of space.

Part **IV**
Materials and Structures

13 / Man Makes His Materials
EDUARD FARBER

In the first two thirds of the 20th century, two worldwide wars destroyed millions of lives and billions of dollars' worth of property. Despite this tremendous destruction, the recovery, both in population growth and the restoration of property damage, was remarkable. World population, especially after World War II, increased at such a prodigious rate as to cause grave concern about the ability to feed the growing mass of people on the earth. At the same time, an outpouring of material goods more than overcame the losses suffered during the wars. Among the factors which made the wars so destructive and the recoveries so spectacular, chemical science and technology played a prominent role.

The development of chemical science and technology depended partly on human factors, more particularly on better education and increased research, and partly on material factors—and the two were closely interrelated. Greater knowledge of chemistry made possible the creation of new, better, and more material goods through the effective utilization of physical resources. At the same time, a society rich in material goods could allocate more of its resources, both human and material, to support scientific research and technological innovation.

The growing number of consumers made increased production in both old and new directions both necessary and possible. Not only were older resources from forests, farms, and mines expanded, but newer resources from oil and gas fields rose in importance. A whole host of "man-made" resources, produced by chemical synthesis, became of major significance in extending man's control over his environment.

The idea of producing chemicals by synthesis had first been seriously broached a little over a century ago, and its first application had been in the making of aniline dyestuffs. It made slow headway at first; then it began to receive increasing application; and since the first decade of this century, the development of synthetic (man-made) chemicals has proceeded at an exponential rate.

Nevertheless, the turn of the century did not bring with it any sudden or great change in chemical manufacturing plants. The main products remained, as they had been for some time, sulfuric acid, alkalis, coal-tar distillates, and dyestuffs. Competition continued to be strong, especially between Great Britain and Germany; they were about equally matched in the markets for sulfuric acid and alkalis, but Germany led in synthetic chemicals, producing more than 80 per cent of all the synthetic dyestuffs.

ELECTRICITY AND CATALYSIS

Two major changes in chemical technology had begun in the last two decades of the 19th century: (1) the use of electricity, and (2) the development of catalysts. Both of these developments became of increasing significance in the 20th century. Electricity was essential for the production of the new light metals. Electrolytic reduction of bauxite (the clay-like ore containing aluminum oxide), with the process found by Charles Martin Hall in 1886 or in the oven designed by Paul Louis Toussaint Héroult, furnished aluminum, "the silver made from clay." In 1900, about 3000 tons of that light metal were produced, almost half of it made at Niagara Falls, where cheap electric power was available. Magnesium, another strategic light metal, was also produced electrolytically at high temperatures. In 1915, a mere 44 short-tons were produced in the United States; by 1943 production had risen to 170,267 tons.

Alloying and annealing, arts rooted in antiquity, were carried out with aluminum and magnesium and with other new metals. In Great Britain and in Germany, alloys of iron with nickel and chromium were developed for increased hardness and resistance to corrosion. Krupp's "stainless steel" of 1914, containing 8 per cent nickel and 18 per cent chromium, was particularly successful. Almost all the relatively rare metals found applications in special alloys. For example, 2.5 per cent beryllium in copper, after an hour's reheating at only 350°, gave an alloy which doubled in strength.

The electric furnace made it possible to produce a compound of calcium with carbon at a temperature between 1050-1100°. The product, calcium carbide (CaC_2), opened the way for the transition from inorganic to organic chemistry; it still furnishes a good part of acetylene production through its reaction with water. The calcium carbide reaction with nitrogen, again at high temperature, leads to calcium cyanamide, first mainly used as a nitrogenous plant food, later for melamin as the starting material for synthetic resins.

Electrical energy was important in chemical technology in many other ways. Electrolysis of aqueous solution, particularly of sodium chloride, furnished caustic soda and chlorine. Efficient cell arrangements for this process were introduced just before the turn of the century, thereby reducing in importance the catalytic oxidation of hydrochloric acid, for which Henry Deacon had completed a successful method in 1867. Other catalytic processes spread from oxidations and reductions to hydrolyses and polymerizations.

The long-sought way of converting nitrogen and hydrogen to produce ammonia (NH_3) was finally found with the use of osmium as a catalyst by Walter Nernst and Fritz Haber. Working from theoretical principles first enunciated by the Frenchman Henri le Chatelier in 1888, these two German chemists provided a spectacular confirmation of the philosopher Immanuel Kant's dictum: There is nothing so practical as good theory. Yet more than theory was necessary: also required were many temporary working hypotheses for the selection of effective catalysts, thousands of trial-and-error experiments, and then the development of new designs and materials for construction. The search for economical catalysts in this synthesis of ammonia had begun in the summer of 1909; by February 1912 the daily production of ammonia had risen above one (metric) ton a day, and with the new method reached 200 tons per day by July 1916. Much of this synthetic ammonia was oxidized to nitric acid over a platinum catalyst, and the nitric acid went into making explosives. Thus Germany, cut off from Chilean nitrate, could manufacture the explosives which enabled her to continue the war begun in 1914.

The synthesis of ammonia shows how chemical technology can serve man for both war-like and peaceful purposes. Nitrates are useful for agricultural fertilizers, and even explosives have peaceful uses in mining and road construction.

ORGANIC SYNTHESIS: CELLULOSE AND THE BEGINNINGS OF PLASTICS

The techniques and concepts developed in searching for new catalysts were soon applied to other processes. Thus, the catalyzed combination of carbon monoxide with hydrogen led to methanol or hydrocarbons, depending upon the conditions under which the reaction took place.

Until 1923 wood distillation had been the only source of methanol, also called wood alcohol. The synthetic production of this alcohol had a pronounced effect on the economics of the ancient wood distilling industry, whose position as the supplier of acetic acid was also weakened by the synthetic product from acetylene. Instead of making new efforts to utilize wood tars, the industry relied mainly on the unique properties of charcoal, which would not be challenged by chemical synthesis. Chemical synthesis from elements thus competed successfully with chemical disintegration of wood for the production of simple compounds.

Less drastic methods for disintegrating wood were to form the basis for expanding industries. These methods had begun between 1850 and 1870, relatively late, considering other industrial developments in the 19th century. Wood had so long been considered as a material of construction, to be shaped by splitting and sawing, that the possibility of producing shaped articles from the fibrous elements came as a real discovery. Mechanical grinding and recombining of wood fibers was followed by chemical separation of the cellulose from the lignin and other accompanying wood substances through cooking with acidic sulfite or caustic soda solutions. The mechanical and the chemical pulps so produced went into paper and board products. In 1900, the per-capita consumption of these products in the United States was about 60 pounds; it had increased to 200 pounds in 1930; and it reached almost 400 in 1960.

Starting slowly in the first years of this century, a very small part of wood-pulp production was further refined for chemical derivatives of cellulose. Cellulose acetate was at first most extensively used for lacquers and films. Esters of cellulose with other organic acids were studied. The step from acetic to propionic or butyric acid was readily suggested by their close proximity in the system of chemistry, but each of these acids produced specific qualities in the compound formed with cellulose, especially of workability, strength, and stability.

The backbone of these plastic materials was furnished by the large molecule of cellulose. For other plastics, the backbone was built up from small units through the links provided by formaldehyde. Phenol or urea form compounds with formaldehyde; from this Leo Baekeland developed his Bakelites, the first of the great successes in the history of plastics, and Fritz Pollak his Pollopases from about 1914 on, but mainly after 1918.

Here the aim was to produce moulding compounds, that is, material which could be poured into a mould and which would harden while setting. For moulding purposes metals have to be brought to high temperatures to reach the fluid state, and then given the desired shape by cooling in a mould. Phenol or urea and formaldehyde resins, however, were first condensed to an intermediate stage, which flows sufficiently at relatively low heat and pressure. They can thus be formed while changing into a final, insoluble, and infusible stage. They are thermosetting. For the production of formed articles from the fibers of wood, water served as the carrier which was mechanically removed afterwards. In this respect, the technique was similar to that used in the ancient arts of pottery, where the baking of the clay removed the moisture and hardened the object. For the production of the new synthetic resins, water was chemically released by the condensation reaction between formaldehyde and its various partners.

The great demand for these synthetic resins required the manufacture of vast quantities of urea. To meet the need for urea, a new synthesis was devised which was connected with the synthesis of ammonia. In producing the pure hydrogen for this process, water vapor was reduced by carbon monoxide. In this reaction, a great quantity of carbon dioxide was produced, and its condensation with ammonia furnished urea.

Leaving out the intermediate steps, the synthetic urea-formaldehyde resins could be said to be made from water, air, and coal. The air furnished the nitrogen for the ammonia and the oxygen for converting coal into carbon monoxide; the water provided the hydrogen to be combined with CO to methanol. The oxygen for burning part of the hydrogen in methanol to produce the formaldehyde for the synthesis came from air. The phenol came from coal distillates, either directly or indirectly by way of the benzene that was partially oxidized.

The industrial development of these synthetic resins expanded mainly after 1918. In 1929, celluloid was still the dominant plastic, with a production of 55 kilo-tons against 28 kilo-tons for Galalith and Bakelite together.

DYESTUFFS

Coal-tar distillates were also the basis for the production of dyestuffs. Again, the technical and scientific foundations for the new developments in this field had been laid in the 19th century. In this, as in so many other cases, the technology was first based on accidental discoveries; then the interest of scientific chemists was drawn to the new, highly successful products, and the insights obtained by the scientific work served as the basis for later expansion. When the chemical structure of the dyestuffs became known, theories and analogies were formulated resulting in new methods of synthesis and the construction of planned molecules. Chemical technology thus enabled man to reassemble the building blocks of nature.

The synthesis of indigo is an outstanding example of many aspects of this development. For centuries natural indigo had been the most important dyestuff; plants from which it could be extracted grew in Europe, South America, in large plantations in Bengal and Java, and from colonial times, on the northeastern coast of the United States. There was no urgent need to make it by chemical synthesis. Nevertheless, chemists wanted to know its composition. Whether it would be economically feasible to manufacture it remained in doubt even after Adolf Baeyer summarized more than ten years of laboratory work with the statement, in 1883, that he knew the place of each atom in the molecule of indigo and proposed ways to its synthesis.

The known structure of the indigo molecule furnished the guide to synthesis, but the most direct way proved not to be the most advantageous one. Many preliminary steps had to be taken, producing other chemical materials on the way to producing the synthetic indigo. Primary considerations included the availability of naphthalene from coal tar and of chlorine from electrolysis. Partial oxidation of naphthalene yielded phthalic acid anhydride, from which indigo was reached in five steps. After Baeyer had completed his work it took almost 20 years before synthetic indigo came on the market and gradually made the culture of indigo-yielding plants obsolete.

Once the imitation of the natural product had succeeded, its modification began and a series of indigo derivatives was produced. For example, when the NH- groups in indigo were replaced by sulfur, a beautiful thio-indigo-red was obtained. Methylations and chlorinations led to other red and orange dyestuffs. René Bohn (1901) conceived the plan of making an analogue from anthracene by some of the newly developed steps. He obtained a beautiful dyestuff, believed to be an *indigo* from *anthracene* and, therefore, called indanthrene. Its structure turned out to be not at all indigo-like. Although the supposed analogy was proved false, it led to a series of new dyestuffs of exceptional beauty and fastness.

These successes did not cause the chemists to diminish their efforts in regard to dyestuffs. Appreciation for what had been achieved was combined with their realization that any success could only be temporary. Scientific and technological advances provided the basis for their deep conviction that further improvement was possible; competition also made it necessary.

DRUGS

Another kind of urgency was provided by the need for medicaments, often called drugs as a reminder of the time when dried herbs were the great source of materials used in the healing arts. Again, it was in the late 19th century that widely used "drugs" were produced by chemical synthesis. Antifebrine, the acetyl derivative of aniline, was converted to a new product, aceto-phenetidine (well known as phenacetin since 1887). Similarly, salicylic acid was improved (1899) by acetylation to acetyl-salicylic acid; this is aspirin, whose analgesic properties make it still the most widely used of drugs.

The beginning of the new century brought a truly dramatic event when the structure of adrenalin (also named superarenine or epinephrine, because it is present in the suprarenal glands) was found. In 1901, J. Takamine, then H. Pauly and F. Stolz, determined the chemical constitution of this hormone, and in 1904 Farbwerke Hoechst (Hoechst Dyestuffs Factory) announced its completed synthesis.

At about the same time, Paul Ehrlich found the "magic bullet" to hit the microorganism that causes syphilis. This was a triumph of chemical technology rather than the medical art. Starting with the ideas of certain affinities among chemicals and special atomic groups in organic molecules that would attach themselves to the offending germs and overwhelm them by the poisonous arsenic without killing the host, Ehrlich made over 600 tests before he found the compound, Salvarsan, which was effective against this scourge of mankind.

For the development of chemical plant nutrients, chemical factories added agricultural research stations. When the production of sera and hormones from animals began, several large factories obtained their supplies from slaughter-houses and set up their own stables in which animals served as both reactors and reagents. Biologists and veterinarians joined the staff of chemists, engineers, and physicians in chemical laboratories and factories. The growing specialization, though much deplored, had its good side in organized co-operation. Among its results was the chemical elucidation and subsequent synthesis of vitamins C and D.

INDUSTRIAL CHEMICAL PROGRESS TO 1930

During the first three decades of this century, the picture of man-made materials changed considerably. The production of the traditional heavy chemicals increased; for example, sulfuric acid production in the United States grew from 0.338 million tons in 1899 to 4.14 in 1929. A number of new products also arrived on the scene. World production of margarine, that is, hydrogenated edible oils, amounted to 1.45 million tons in 1927, and artificial silk to 200,000 tons in 1929 with about 84 per cent consisting of viscose rayon made from cellulose xanthogenate. Acetate rayon was produced in the United States beginning in 1926 with 1310 short-tons and rose to 5000 short-tons in 1930, a relatively slow start compared with the increase to 90,000 tons in 1940.

The American production of dyestuffs from coal-tar distillates rose from about 3000 tons in 1913 to 50,000 tons in 1929, thus coming close to the German figure for that year. About 10,000 different substances were comprised in this tonnage. Indigo, however, declined after its German production had reached 5700 tons in 1911; it dropped to 1400 tons in 1930 (figures calculated for 100 per cent indigo, but sold in pastes of about 20 per cent concentration). In these first three decades, the value of American production of "chemical and allied products," excluding animal and vegetable oils, increased from $62 million to $2377 million.

Progress during this period was further characterized by industrial uses of elements and compounds that had formerly been laboratory curiosities. Another general feature is the increase in purity of materials. For some of them, and especially for metals, impurities of a hundredth or even millionth of one per cent were recognized as important. Today we have instances where we are watching and controlling the parts per billion.

PETROCHEMICALS

Chemical exploitation of petroleum and natural gas has yielded so many new manufactured materials that these have been combined under a new name: petrochemicals. In this field new techniques have developed hand in hand with new scientific knowledge of atomic structure, electronic binding, spatial arrangements between the atoms of molecules, and specific forces on the interface between various states of matter.

Petrochemical products in everyday use just for automobile transportation include: materials for road construction; high-octane gasoline that burns rapidly and efficiently in the cylinders of our automobiles; heavier oils and greases for lubricating the moving parts of our cars; the synthetic "rubber" of tires; plastic upholstery and plastic dashboards for the inside; and a plastic protective coating for the outside of the car. In addition, petrochemical products are used in a host of other materials: wrappings, bottles, toys, and so forth.

The starting materials for petrochemicals are called hydrocarbons, after their composition of hydrogen and carbon. Deliberately continuing to use an old-fashioned expression, we call these compounds lipophilic to indicate their "love" for fatty substances. Sulfuric acid, to the contrary, is hydrophilic, it "loves" water. The combination of a hydrocarbon residue with a sulfuric acid residue produces a compound with one lipophilic and one hydrophilic end. Such a compound can be active for fatty and for watery materials at the same time. Detergents and emulsifiers are built on this principle. Materials of this kind were first introduced as special aids for treating textiles in 1920 and have expanded since then, partially replacing and especially amplifying the uses of soaps.

THE AGE OF PLASTICS

The period after 1930 has often been called the "age of plastics." That title is applicable, but with the same reservations that apply to the early periodization into Stone, Bronze, and Iron ages. Indeed, this new age saw the turn from natural materials to the synthetic products which the name "age of plastics" emphasizes, but it was also a period characterized by increased work on the chemistry of highly complex substances produced by plants and animals. This work in turn contributed greatly to the development of basic concepts which stimulated the growth of the plastics industry. The same period was also one of great specialization and development of instruments and automatic regulators and, at the same time, metals and special alloys had an important part in the construction of tools, utensils, and production equipment.

Plastics are usually synthetically produced from organic compounds. The natural processes of plant life build large molecules of cellulose from small molecules of carbon dioxide and water; for the giant molecules of proteins, ammonia is the main additional starting material. The new industrial processes use the small molecules of the gases acetylene and ethylene. Under selected and controlled conditions of temperature, pressure, and special catalysts, up to several hundred thousand of the small units are linked together by chemical bonds. By this means highly reactive gases are converted into the chemical equivalent of paraffins, but these synthetic resins are free from the limitations of paraffins with regard to their melting points and mechanical strength characteristics. Strength and heat stability, often also electrical resistance, transparency, film- and fiber-forming, and mouldability are among the highly valued properties of synthetic resins.

One side of the technical advance in plastics involved lowering the cost of production and materials; the other, and in some ways more important side, was increasing the quality and performance. An example of lowering the costs can be seen in the case of the fine filaments of stainless steel used to reinforce plastic materials. With a tensile strength of 300,000 psi (pounds per square inch) these filaments commanded a price of more than $1000 per pound, but new techniques reduced this to about $50 per pound, thereby considerably lowering the cost of the reinforced plastic. On the other hand, in order to increase the strength of the reinforced plastic, without reference to cost, silicon carbide "whiskers" were developed having a tensile strength of 3 million psi but costing $750 per pound.

Perhaps most startling is the increase in production. The production of polyethylene plastics started in England in 1941, and in the United States two years later. In 1958, American production was about 400,000 metric tons (mt.) and increased by 50 per cent in 1960.

Styrene, an ethylene derivative, containing one vinyl group attached to benzene, left the laboratory about 1940, when about one thousand metric tons were converted into high polymers; four years later, polystyrenes had multiplied by a factor of 146, and in 1960 production was close to 478,000 mt. In addition, 541,000 mt. of other vinyl polymers and co-polymers were made in 1960. Cellulose plastics, on the other hand, remained at a relatively modest range of about 65,000 mt.

A whole new family of plastics came into being. Of the many modifications of the ethylene molecule, chemical combination with fluorine led to a new group of resins. Paradoxically, the incorporation of fluorine, one of the most reactive of the elements, gave the most inert polymers. The special properties built into these new resins opened markets for them which the "old" resins could not fill.

Nevertheless, production of phenol- or urea-formaldehyde resins continued to expand. The industrial synthesis of urea, which had been started at the Badische Anilin-und Soda-Fabrik in 1914, utilized a basic reaction that looks very simple, almost like the photosynthetic reaction in green plants. However, like photosynthesis, it contains many complex intermediary steps. In the production of urea, problems of corrosion, conditions of equilibria, and recovery of unreacted gases taxed the ingenuity of inventors and apparatus builders. Constantly improving processes and expanding uses in plastics, fertilizers, and animal foods helped to increase the production capacity for urea; in 1963 production exceeded one million mt. in the United States, 4.8 million in all countries. For this country this was ten times; for the world, twenty-six times, the corresponding figures for 1950.

During and shortly after World War II, three new groups of plastics were developed: the nylons, in which amino residues served to connect long chains of carbon atoms; the silicones, in which the connecting link was silicon; and the urethanes, derived from isocyanates. The urethane resins can be made to decompose partially with internal evolution of gas, which blows the resin up into soft or rigid foams.

The development of synthetic resins called forth a considerable supporting industry manufacturing auxiliary materials: plasticizers, stabilizers, lubricants, anti-static and mould-release agents. In certain applications, the synthetic resins competed with glass and wood, but glass fibers were also used to reinforce plastics, and as impregnants and adhesives they expanded the uses of wood.

NEW DYES AND DRUGS

A new type of dyestuff started from an accidental and, at first, disturbing discovery during the manufacture of phthalimide from phthalic anhydride and ammonia. When small amounts of iron or copper were present, a deep blue product was obtained instead of the colorless imide. Chemists at the Scottish Dye Works turned this accident into an avenue to new dyestuffs, the phthalo-cyanines. Large-scale production of these phthalo-cyanines had to wait until after the war. In 1945, the sales value of these dyestuffs was $0.8 million, in 1953 it reached $7.5 million.

Despite the new dyes, some of the old aniline-derived dyestuffs remained in production. For example, crystal violet, discovered in 1883, and auramine, discovered in 1887, were produced at an annual rate of close to a million pounds each in 1954.

Why was so much scientific and technological effort devoted to variations on the basic theme of dyestuffs? There are several answers to this question. First, the skill and the imagination of the chemists could, and therefore did, provide these variations; in other words, their curiosity and ingenuity could not be restrained. Second, some of these dyes sold so well that the profits could provide the funds for experimenting with others, especially since even the unsuccessful dyes might point to other steps. Third, the experience gained in producing dye products for a luxury trade were indispensable for the chemically related field of medicaments.

Indeed, the inventors of sulfa drugs started from an analogy between dyeing wool and anchoring a chemical on tissue. It started with Prontosil, an azo dyestuff into which a sulfamyl group was introduced in 1932, by Fritz Domagk and his collaborators at the Farbenwerke Bayer in Germany. Soon afterward a group of French chemists in the laboratory of Ernest Fourneau at the Pasteur Institute in Paris found that para-aminobenzene-sulfonamide is active against streptococci germs.

This discovery started the idea of searching for anti-metabolites, substances that are sufficiently similar to metabolically needed materials to be attractive to microorganisms. The microorganisms could not distinguish between the proper and the lethal material; they were killed off as they assimilated the alluring drug.

An entire family of sulfa drugs was soon introduced, as variations were made in the chemical combinations. Although largely supplanted by the anti-biotics, the sulfa drugs have retained many important medical uses.

VITAMINS AND ANTIBIOTICS

Chemists and physiologists of the 19th century had shown that the heat developed (calories) on oxidation of foods afforded a measure of their energy value. Scarcely had the conclusions from this work been generally accepted when they had to be modified to an important degree. Small quantities of addition agents to foods were found essential for their nutritive effect; their value for life, though not their chemical nature, was indicated by the name vitamin.

The first of the vitamins to be chemically identified and soon also synthesized was Vitamin C (ascorbic acid), which prevents scurvy. Soon, other vitamins were found essential for growth, fertility, and other vital processes. Components with specific vitamin actions were separated from carrots (carotenes), yeast, milk (lactoflavins), and wheat germ. In secretions and excretions of animals, minute proportions of bioactive substances were identified. These acted in very small quantities, as messengers which brought the signals for initiating specific bodily processes. Substances of closely related chemical structure showed great differences in physiological effect, especially in the sex hormones. On the other hand, vitamins and hormones were chemically linked with enzymes, the catalysts in physiological processes like fermentation.

The conversion of sugar, by fermentation, into other products, such as wine, is an ancient art. Yeasts of the saccharomyces family produced alcohol or reproduced themselves, lactobacillae made lactic acid. Two new developments started during World War I: the modification of fermentations by yeast which diverted the normal course of events to yield glycerol, and the use of a different kind of microorganisms to convert carbohydrates into acetone and butanol. During World War II, alcoholic fermentation was used to obtain the raw material for butadiene, a component in synthetic rubbers. Since then, alcohol and glycerol have been produced from the hydrocarbons of natural gas. Methods of fermentation did not thereby become obsolete; on the contrary, they are used in the production of biotic and of antibiotic substances.

From an accidental discovery by Alexander Fleming, made in 1928, arose the use of certain strains of a mold (Penicillium notatum) for producing the antibiotic penicillins. Production began in 1943 with very small yields that were increased by a factor of 10,000 during the following 20 years of research. The success of penicillin led to the testing of molds from all over the earth for their ability to make antibiotic substances in their life cycles. The search was intensified after the lowly streptomyces group was found to be a source of the highly effective streptomycins. Under controlled conditions of microbial purity, of varying nutrients in the growth medium, and by differentiating methods of separation, numerous kinds of "mycins" were isolated and put to use.

By 1960 these developments resulted in American production of about 11 million pounds of vitamins and 3 million pounds of antibiotics, together valued at about $400 million.

CHEMICAL PROCESS UNITS

Connected with this new field of chemical industry was the development of a new technology. In 1915 Arthur D. Little had proposed the concept of unit operations to bring together processes that have the same function, such as heat transfer, distilling, dissolving, mixing, and crystallizing. This concept proved to be of great help in teaching and planning, for a bewildering variety of industrial processes could now be simplified as representing varieties and alternatives in a few basic flow-sheets.

Another new approach considered phase-contact as the unifying aspect in all those operations which were based on the contacts between gases, liquids, and solids, representing different phases of the same homogeneous material (as, for example, steam, water, and ice represent different phases of H_2O). Such contacts are essential in catalysis, in evaporations, and particularly in adsorptions from gases or liquids on solids. The utilization of the "weak forces" of adsorption made it possible to isolate highly sensitive substances present in states of great dilution. This constituted the counterpart to the development of highly concentrated energies during the same period.

THE PROMISE OF CHEMISTRY

It is, of course, difficult to predict the future progress of innovation in technology which may be expected from the continued application of chemical knowledge. Yet judging from the experiences of the 20th century thus far, we

Fig. 13-1. A plant for manufacturing alcohol from ethylene. The large towers are for absorbing the ethylene in sulfuric acid, adding water to form the alcohol and split off the acid, and for fractional distillation to separate the ether that is formed as a by-product, and to refine the alcohol. (Courtesy of *U. S. Industrial Chemicals Co.*)

can safely predict that the extension of the boundaries of our knowledge will result in an extension of man's mastery over his physical and material resources. Until a few years ago it was necessary for men to limit their designs to the characteristics of available materials; however, we are now approaching the time when materials can be produced at will to meet the specifications of any design. Whether we create something of non-material worth from our explorations of the chemical secrets of nature will depend upon our willingness to place human values foremost in our thoughts and designs.

14 / Building with Steel and Concrete
MELVIN M. ROTSCH

Since the beginning of civilization man has always aspired to build towers. In the remote past, high structures were expensive and were limited to load-bearing construction; that is, the walls had to carry the entire weight of the building. Such structures were therefore justified only as symbols of religion, or as means to satisfy the vanity of rulers. In the last half of the 19th century, however, the development of vertical passenger transportation elevators and the need for concentration of office space have justified the use of the high-rise structure in the commercial world, and the development of new building materials and new structural systems have made possible towers that exceed the greatest dreams of priests and potentates.

The skeleton frame, or cage construction, first developed about 1890 in the skyscrapers of Chicago (see Volume I, Chapter 37) reached maturity in New York City in the early decades of the present century. In 1898, when a 26-story office building was completed in Manhattan, many predicted that the maximum height had been attained; however, fourteen years later a building rose 55 stories, and in 1932 the 86-story Empire State Building was completed. It has remained to this day the world's highest, but the new 110-story twin towers, now contemplated in New York, will rise to a height of more than one-quarter mile, and will have ten million square feet of rental space.

This new building form evolved as a result of the sociological and technological developments that were predominant in the booming city of Chicago during the last decades of the 19th century. The phenomenal commercial expansion and population growth of the prairie metropolis gave rise to large corporate business firms; these organizations operated with new efficiency and demanded concentration of office space. Together with this came the speculative rise of land values in the central area of the city. In the 1880's new office buildings rose higher and higher, still using exterior load-bearing walls but with cast-iron interior columns; the Monadnock Building (1889) was 16 stories high, and to carry the immense loads, the exterior brick walls were more than ten feet thick. Despite this reliance on older methods, technological advances had already made possible a new system of high-rise construction. A century earlier the cost of iron production had been greatly reduced, and during the first half of the 19th century, iron achieved limited use in building construction in the

Fig. 14-1. The Monadnock Building, Chicago, 1889.
(Courtesy of *Verlag Gerd Hatje*)

form of internal columns, beams, and trusses. Then rolled wrought iron came into production (1847-55), passenger elevators came into use (1854), and there were great advances in cheaper processes of steel production (1856-68). These and other developments helped make possible the rise of the skyscraper.

THE SKYSCRAPER AT THE TURN OF THE CENTURY

The skyscraper was on its way when the architect-engineer William Le Baron Jenney designed and constructed in Chicago the twelve-story Home Insurance Building (1885), using a metal skeleton frame to support the exterior masonry curtain walls and the floor loads. Seven years later the Masonic Building rose to a height of 21 stories.

The years between 1890 and 1905 brought great advances in industrial pro-

Fig. 14-2. Louis Sullivan's Carson, Pirie, Scott Building, Chicago, 1899-1901. (*Verlag Gerd Hatje*)

duction and building techniques; almost all of the basic systems and structural
methods evolved at that time into forms not unlike those in use today. Improved foundations were devised that made use of piles driven by the double-
acting steam hammer or used the newly developed material, reinforced concrete; standard I and H steel sections were already in use, and the wide-flange
sections were soon to appear; rivets with gusset plates had replaced the earlier
threaded bolts; steel columns were spaced on standard bays (16 to 24 feet),
and interior partitions, usually of plastered building tile, were spaced independently of the structural bays; and metal lath (light sheet metal with holes,
or wire cloth to serve as groundwork for plastering or tiling) was soon to appear. Experience led to the development of improved fire and building codes;
structural members were usually faced with terracotta; fireproof floor construction of flat arches of terracotta between beams was being replaced with slabs
of reinformed concrete. To assure water pressure for the upper stories, tanks and
pumping equipment were installed; and vertical chases were provided for
plumbing, heating, electricity, and telephone service. The electrically operated

elevator, still somewhat hazardous, was soon to be improved with the direct-drive gearless system.

The "Chicago School" of architecture of the 1890's had developed a distinctive, indigenous skyscraper form that turned its back on the traditional styles of Europe. The firm of Holabird and Root in the Gage Building (1898) and Louis Sullivan in his Carson, Pirie, Scott Building (1899-1901) created a new type of aesthetic design which was no longer based on the heavy forms of traditional masonry construction; this design, with a reticulated structural pattern and large glass areas, expressed the steel frame and interior function of the high-rise office building. Their designs were to influence the development in Europe of the "International" contemporary style in the following decades. Most American designers, however, greatly influenced by the academic eclecticism of the École des Beaux-Arts in Paris, disregarded the functional simplicity of the "Chicago School"; they turned instead to classicism and medievalism for their building forms and decorative elements.

THE EARLY DECADES OF THE TWENTIETH CENTURY

New York City became the skyscraper center of America and the world at the beginning of the century. In the preceding years the architect, or men in his employ, had been in complete charge of the architectural and structural design of buildings; but as the structures increased in size and complexity, there arose a new professional group, the structural engineers. Later, after World War I, other engineers began specializing in the heating and electrical equipment of buildings. Though these specialists worked with the architect in the preparation of plans, the collaboration was often inadequate, and the early buildings showed a lack of unity of design and execution. In addition, although some mathematical studies had been made in the field of statics (the branch of mechanics that deals with forces and bodies at rest) in the early 19th century, builders before the 1890's arrived at their structural solutions strictly through empirical methods. Squire Whipple (1847) and W. J. M. Rankine (1858) contributed to the methods of truss design by their mathematical studies of stresses and strains; and Carl Culmann, Maurice Levy, and Otto Mohr made further contributions to the science of statics. Thus, at the beginning of the new century, the structural engineers of America had available practical methods and tables for the design of high-rise skeleton metal frames for building.

The Singer Building (1908), with its neoclassic tower, rose in New York to 47 stories; four years later the F. W. Woolworth Company, desiring to erect an architectural symbol, employed architect Cass Gilbert. The Woolworth Building, which is in Lower Manhattan, has a tower rising 55 stories to a height of 760 feet. The engineering firm of Gunvald Aus used various methods of solving the problem of wind-bracing in the slender tower. The column footing rests on concrete-filled caissons sunk to a depth of 100 feet. At the time, with the narrow streets already congested with traffic, the contractor faced new problems of delivery and handling of masonry materials and the necessary 24,000 tons of structural steel; night deliveries had to be arranged and special hoists devised, and systematic scheduling thus entered into the building construction field. The Woolworth tower, with its terracotta "gothic" decorations, was for twenty years the symbol of commercial America. Another prominent high-rise structure, designed as a monument to its owners and clothed in "gothic" decoration, was the 34-story Tribune Tower (1923) in Chicago, designed by architects Hood and Howells.

The form of the skyscraper of this period was frequently based on classic proportions, a reflection of the Beaux-Arts eclectic training of the leading architects in America. The lower floors, devoted to retail space, were often expressed in massive masonry; the uniformly designed office floors were the shaft; and the building was topped with a cornice or multi-story entablature. Unlike the Chicago skyscrapers of the late 1890's, those of the early 20th century had relatively small windows, using only about 25 per cent of the exterior wall surface. To the man on the street it appeared that these lofty structures were supported by the visible exterior masonry walls, not by the concealed frame of steel. These exterior walls, usually 12 inches of brick, added materially to the massiveness and cost of the structural frame; building codes were still based on traditional forms of construction, and only many decades later were they revised to permit thinner, lighter exterior curtain-wall construction (that is, where the wall serves merely to cloak or curtain the building rather than to support it structurally).

During this era cities in Europe and America began enacting zoning regulations to control the height of skyscraper structures. These laws resulted from the restriction of light in canyons between the high buildings and from the increased congestion of pedestrians and motor vehicles experienced in Lower Manhattan. Paris limited the height of buildings to 56 feet, with certain exceptions; London's maximum height for occupied structures was 80 feet, later increased to 100 feet. The only large skyscraper in Europe before World War II was the 26-story Torengebouw (1931) in Antwerp. Beginning in 1903 the city of Boston limited buildings in the central district to 125 feet, with 90-foot heights elsewhere in the city. After the San Francisco earthquake and fire of 1906, California cities limited the height of structures, and strengthened the codes regulating structural design and fireproofing.

New York City had the most advanced codes regulating the structures and fire safety of building construction. In 1916 the city enacted a zoning ordinance controlling the form and height of buildings. Its rules were based on street width and were adapted to the needs of area zones. In the central area the vertical rise from the sidewalk was limited, and above that level, setbacks were required; towers, unlimited in height, could occupy only 25 per cent of the total lot area. As a result, the New York skyscraper took on a new form; larger plots were assembled to permit larger central towers; light courts were eliminated; and large buildings took on a pyramidical form with a series of setbacks. These setbacks, when not full bay depth, created new problems in designing the structural frame. In the late 1920's the old forms, based on classic and medieval design, were abandoned in favor of cubical masses sometimes embellished with decorations of neoclassic, art nouveau, or French moderne origin. New York skyscrapers resembled large, square, tiered wedding cakes.

THE SKYSCRAPER BOOM OF THE LATE 'TWENTIES

Reflecting the post-World War I belief that the "business of America is business," the large cities of the nation showed a great surge of high-rise construction between 1925 and 1931. In that span of years the office space in New York City increased a phenomenal 92 per cent and Chicago's office space increased 74 per cent. However, except for improvements in detail, there were few structural innovations; and design form seemed to have no direction.

Then one architect, Raymond Hood, a partner of the firm which had designed the eclectic Tribune Tower, began applying a new, simplified design to building mass and the window pattern. His 36-story Daily News Building (1928-30) in New York had simple sculptural masses suggestive of the "De Stijl" movement in Europe, where Dutch artists had stressed simple, straight lines. Its vertical lines, emphasized with white glazed brick, were striking in appearance, but the aesthetic expression was deceptive since two thirds of these brick piers were false shells rather than coverings for the widely spaced steel columns; the windows were small and quite inadequate for lighting the interior spaces. Hood's later 34-story McGraw-Hill Building (1931), with its dominantly horizontal effect, foreshadowed the design trend of later skyscrapers. The vertical steel columns, fireproofed and faced with dark brick, were visible on the exterior, and the spaces between columns were filled with metal window sash that assured airy, well-lighted office interiors. This accent on the horizontal, first developed in concrete construction and emphasized by the European "International" designers, was even better expressed in the Philadelphia Savings Fund Society Building (1931-32), designed by architects Howe and Lescaze.

The tallest structure of this era was the Empire State Building (1929-32), built by architects Shreve, Lamb, and Harmon and engineers N. G. Balcom Associates. With a total height of 1239 feet it exceeded the Eiffel Tower (1889) in Paris by 245 feet. The building has 86 occupied stories with an observation tower rising an additional 189 feet, and this is now topped with a 233 foot television tower. With over two million square feet of office space it houses

Fig. 14-3. The Philadelphia Savings Fund Society
Building, 1931-32. (*Verlag Gerd Hatje*)

twenty thousand employees; each day thirty-five thousand others enter the
building. Completed in the early Depression years, it could not be completely
rented, and portions of the upper tower remained unfinished for several years,
but in recent decades it has been financially successful. The site of the old Wal-
dorf-Astoria Hotel was purchased for $14 million, and the building was erected
at a cost exceeding $35 million. No structural innovations were introduced; the
tower form, with few setbacks, permitted a simple design with continuous column lines. It was erected with remarkable speed; steel girders were put in place
80 hours after they were fabricated in the shops in Pittsburgh. The structural
frame, using 57,000 tons of steel, was completed in a six-month period in 1931.

The technically sound design of such buildings was dramatically proved one foggy morning in July 1945, when a ten-ton U.S. Air Force B-25 bomber, flying at 250 mph, struck the 79th floor of the building. The body of the plane hit a structural column and the two motors passed on either side; one motor struck an elevator shaft, snapping the cables and destroying the automatic braking device. The cab with its operator dropped 80 floors. Three crewmen of the plane and ten occupants of the building died, and twenty-six others were injured. A thorough inspection of the building revealed local damage to the floor structure, the exterior spandrel beams, and the elevator shafts, but there was no mis-alignment of the major structural frame, and repairs were made. Although the cost of repairs was three quarters of a million dollars, the accident demonstrated that a major impact to a local area of a skyscraper would not impair the whole structure.

During these years there were some improvements in construction methods and equipment. Riveting remained the standard system of field assembly (that is, the steel beams were riveted together at the building site), but there were experiments in the use of electric welding. Industrial buildings were welded in 1920, and the first high-rise welded structure was erected in 1931; however, it is still difficult to test the real effectiveness of field-welded joints.

The passenger elevator, first perfected by Elisha Graves Otis in the 1850's, went through a series of basic changes. The early steam-powered, suspended cab was replaced by the hydraulic elevator; then about 1890 the electric-powered system came into use, but accidents were frequent. In 1904 a direct-drive gearless unit was perfected that could be operated at greater speeds. Automatic signal controls came into use in 1924, and passenger-operated controls were installed in apartment buildings in the late 1920's. These and other improved systems made possible the safe operation of elevators up to a speed of about 1400 feet per minute.

During the years 1929-30 the economist W. C. Clark and architect J. L. Kingston prepared a "Study in the Economic Height of Modern Office Buildings," based on the costs of financing, constructing, and maintaining structures, on real estate values, taxes, and rental income. Their conclusion, published in 1930 in the book, *The Skyscraper*, was that in New York the economic requirements could best be met by constructing office buildings to a height of 63 stories. However, the Depression was already under way when the book was published, and for the next eighteen years few skyscrapers were erected in New York or elsewhere. Vacancies of office space were 5 per cent in 1925; in 1931 they rose to 17 per cent, and rental incomes obviously declined.

The application of the steel frame came slowly in Europe. Structural steel sections were rolled in England in 1885, and limited production began in France about the same time; yet when Gustave Eiffel built his 984-foot tower (1889) in Paris, he used structural members of wrought iron. The rectilinear column-and-beam system reached its greatest development in America, but the spanning of large spaces advanced in Europe. Dutert and Contamin built the great Machinery Hall (1889) in Paris with three-hinged arch trusses spanning 375 feet. About the turn of the century the rigid frame came into use in Germany. At the same time the development of yet another building material was being proposed in Europe.

REINFORCED CONCRETE—THE FIRST THREE DECADES

While steel construction and the skeleton frame reached maturity early in the 20th century, the development of reinforced concrete was still in its infancy. The Romans had used a crude mass (unreinforced) concrete; the use of Portland (hydraulic) cement began in England in the early 19th century; and the first application of reinforcement began with Joseph Monier in France (1867), and was developed for building construction by G. A. Wayss in Germany in 1885. Meanwhile in America some practical applications of reinforced concrete were developing. Portland cement production began in 1876, and ten years later E. L. Ransome built a rotary kiln in California. To secure better bonding he used twisted square bars, and then developed the T-section for the construction of his Borax Factory (1892) at Alameda. At the turn of the century reinforced concrete was being used in many sections of the United States, but design was largely empirical, and reinforcing systems were not standardized.

The major development of the theory of reinforced concrete design came in Europe. In 1892 François Hennibique of Belgium and France patented a system reinforcing structural beams with stirrups and longitudinal bars bent to resist the tensile and shear stresses. Six years later he had developed a complete system for the reinforcing of columns, beams, and floors that was not unlike that in use today, and his firm built many industrial structures throughout Europe. Experiments were continued in Germany by the firm of Wayss and Freitag, and in 1902 their data were published by E. Mörsch in the book *Der Eisenbeton*. Turner in America and Maillart in Switzerland developed independently the flat-slab system of floor construction in the years 1908 to 1910. Soon regulations were being established by the Prussian government to control the design and construction of reinforced concrete. In France, A. G. Considière devised the system for spiral reinforcement of columns, and in 1905 he assisted in drawing up regulations for the use of reinforced concrete in the city of Paris.

Organizations for the improvement and control of reinforced-concrete design came into existence in America: the American Society of Testing Materials (1902), the American Concrete Institute (1905), and the Portland Cement Association (1916). And though by the mid 'twenties standards had been adopted for design and testing, there were still cases of structural failure. In 1924 the eight-story reinforced-concrete frame of the Hotel Vincent, Benton

Harbor, Michigan, collapsed during construction due to inadequate protection against freezing temperatures; but from such experiences came improved design and construction practices. Eventually the building codes of the United States became quite rigid and more conservative than those of Europe and Latin America.

Improved systems of foundations were developed to replace those of traditional masonry construction. Reinforced floating slabs were used in Chicago in the 1890's, and precast concrete pilings were developed in Europe about the same time. Cast-in-place piling was invented by A. A. Raymond in 1901. The reinforced concrete frame, apparently patterned after the steel frame, came into use in high-rise construction. An outstanding early skyscraper of this type is the 16-story Ingalls (Transit) Building (1902-03), built in Cincinnati by architects Elxner and Anderson and engineer Hunter Handley. Although a successful building and still standing, its structural details indicate that the designers lacked complete knowledge of the theory of reinforcement. During the 1920's concrete frames were built to 21-story heights, and in many areas, particularly in Latin America, this type of construction was more economical than the steel frame.

The pioneers of the "International school" of architecture—Gropius, Le Corbusier, and Mies van der Rohe—found reinforced concrete a suitable medium for executing their theories of rationalistic design. In 1914 Le Corbusier (Charles Édouard Jeanneret-Gris) produced his Dom-Ino system of construction, exploiting the possibilities of cantilevered floor construction, and began the break from the traditional bay system with its regularly spaced exterior window openings. Ludwig Mies van der Rohe, in his project (1922) for a concrete office building, foreshadowed the trend for horizontal ribbon windows. Walter Gropius's buildings for the Bauhaus (1926) at Dessau and the teachings of that school had significant influence on the shaping of architectural form and the related concrete structure in all parts of the world for the next three decades.

While American structural engineers were perfecting the rectilinear column-and-beam building frame in concrete and the European "International school" was building an ideology based on this system, there were others who saw greater possibilities in this new plastic material, concrete. Up to that time the predominant feeling was that of the architects of eclecticism, who viewed concrete as a crude, contemptible structural material that needed to be covered or veneered with brick or stone. However, some advanced designers began to recognize concrete as a respectable architectural material that could be employed advantageously utilizing its structural or plastic nature, or that could be moulded or finished in a sculptural manner. Auguste Perret, the pioneer architect-engineer of France, made significant contributions to the technical-aesthetic development of exposed concrete in buildings in Paris (1903-5); Frank Lloyd Wright used exposed monolithic concrete walls and moulded decorative forms

Fig. 14-4. Gropius's Bauhaus at Dessau, Germany, 1926. (*Verlag Gerd Hatje*)

in his Unity Church (1906) at Oak Park, Illinois, and in 1922 he pioneered in the development of patterned concrete blocks. In the first decade of the century, architect Antonio Gaudi of Barcelona was creating new, imaginative, curvilinear sculptural forms in architectural concrete, and in Germany architect Erich Mendelsohn explored the possibilities of the use of concrete as a plastic, sculptural building material in his expressionist design for the Einstein Observatory (1920-21) near Potsdam. However, imaginative sculptural use of concrete was not truly developed until the late 1930's.

ADVANCES IN REINFORCED CONCRETE IN RECENT DECADES

The use of reinforced concrete in the building industry rose continuously decade by decade from the beginning of this century; its use in building construction apparently roughly parallels the total consumption of Portland cement in the United States as indicated in the following table.

Table 14-1   Production and use of Portland cement in the United States in millions of barrels (1 barrel now equals 376#; 380# before 1920)

DATE	PRODUCTION USA	IMPORTS	EXPORTS	APPARENT USE USA
1890	not available	1.9	0.1	—
1900	8.4	2.3	0.1	10.6
1910	76.5	0.2	2.4	74.3
1924	149.3	1.5	0.9	149.9
1933	63.5	0.3	0.7	63.1
1941	163.5	0.001	2.5	161.0
1950	222.8	1.4	2.4	221.8
1963	346.0	3.4	0.4	349.0

Throughout the early decades of this century continued improvements were made in the mixing, handling, and methods of pouring concrete. In 1908 concrete-chuting plants were developed for use on large building sites and these continued in use for two decades but were eventually replaced with more efficient equipment of portable nature. The transit-mixer, initially developed in 1916, did not come into use until 1926; once in production, these truck-mounted concrete mixers were greatly improved in capacity and efficiency during the 1930's. In the United States today there are 6000 ready-mix concrete plants which produce each year 135 million cubic yards of concrete; about two thirds of this material is delivered by transit-mix trucks for use in building construction.

In the past three decades there have been great advances in the manufacture of Portland cement and the design of reinforced concrete which have led to new, imaginative structural forms and new concepts in architectural design and form. The Portland Cement Association, established in 1916, opened its first laboratory in Chicago, and in 1950 built its research and development laboratories in Skokie, Illinois. Here, and in many engineering laboratories in universities, research is carried on in basic theory, manufacturing processes, precasting and prestressing, and many other aspects of concrete building construction. Improved methods of proportioning concrete mixes by the water-cement ratio came into use in dam construction in 1924, and were soon adapted by the building industry. Concrete hardens with its initial set in a few hours, and attains its major strength in one month (28 days), but it continues to gain strength for a period of five years or more. Table 14-2 gives the compressive strengths, which indicate the relative quality of concrete, from 1919 to 1937.

Table 14-2   Typical compressive tests of concrete in psi
(pounds per square inch)

DATE	28 DAYS	5 YEARS
1910	1,920	4,250
1923	3,005	6,215
1937	5,145	7,640

There have been only minor improvements in recent decades in the strength of normal Portland cement commonly used in construction; however, high-strength Portland cement and other special cements now produce concrete that tests up to 10,000 psi (28-day test). Early codes required that reinforcing steel test to 16,000 psi in tension; this was later raised to 18,000 and now stands at 20,000 psi for the design of typical poured-in-place concrete structures; and some steel tests to 30,000 psi. The ACI (American Concrete Institute) codes of 1956 included the ultimate-strength method of design and under this method reinforcing steel with a yield point stress to 60,000 to 75,000 psi is now being used in America, and has long been in use in Europe. Cold-twisted bars, with higher ultimate strength, are coming back into use; and high-strength piano-wire reinforcement, with greater bonding surface, is used in prestressed precast units.

Improved cements and aggregates have made possible special concretes with high strength, high density, or lightweight qualities. The greatest structural achievement was in the development of precast units using prestressing and post-stressing. The theory of prestressed concrete had been proposed in the last decades of the 19th century but was not practical due to the lack of high-tensile steel. Franz Dischinger used prestressing in bridge construction in Germany in 1928, and in the same year Eugene Freyssinet, the French pioneer of concrete theory, developed the modern conception of this system. By the mechanical stretching of the high-tension reinforcing material, often piano wires, stresses are introduced into the concrete member to resist those of the external loading; lighter yet stronger beams are produced by this system, which is now extensively used in the building construction industry. The production of precast, prestressed systems has long been used in Europe, and came into production in America in the 1940's, in the form of I-beams, T-sections, and floor channels and spandrel units.

In custom-built concrete-frame structures, the forms into which the concrete is poured are of lumber and plywood and are built by skilled hand labor. This labor is a major cost item, and much of the forming material is wasted. Several systems have been devised to reduce the labor and to avoid expendable-form materials; the simplest of these is the tilt-up method, in which the walls of one-story buildings are cast horizontally on the floor slab, and then tilted into vertical position. This system, invented in 1907 by R. N. Aiken, was used in 1917 in the construction of United States Army barracks. The lift-slab system, first developed in 1948 by Philip N. Yountz and Thomas B. Slick, was applied two years later to building construction. By this system successive floor slabs, with reinforcing and wiring conduits in place, are poured on top of the ground floor slab; these upper floor slabs are then elevated into place by means of a system of carefully controlled hydraulic jacks on the columns. A 15-story apartment building (1963) in Ann Arbor, Michigan, was constructed by this method. In England, building units of floor and walls are constructed at ground level and then raised to upper levels by the jack-block system.

Another method, known as the slip-form system, is being applied to vertical elements of high-rise buildings, and is also beginning to be used for horizontal forming; the builders of cylindrical grain elevators developed this system in the early decades of this century and it is now being used on more complex building forms, such as the 25-story Bay View Terrace Apartments (1963) in Milwaukee, Wisconsin. For buildings with standard floor plans, the exterior walls, elevator shafts, stair enclosures, and other vertical elements are so designed that the framework can be raised as soon as the concrete has taken its initial set; in a twenty-four-hour day the forms can be raised 12 to 16 feet.

The prefabrication of building units began in the mid-19th century, at first making use of wood and cast iron. Grosvenor Atterbury, a pioneer in standard housing, produced in 1907 experimental cavity-concrete panels for walls and floors; and between 1913 and 1921 such houses were built in Forest Hills, New York, but after that production ceased. Numerous experiments were attempted in the 1930's, but no large-scale production in America has ever been developed. However, in Europe, after many experiments dating back to 1920, prefabrication systems are extensively used in the construction of large-scale housing projects. While in the United States the skeleton frame column-and-beam system in concrete is used almost universally, the box-frame system is widely used in Europe in prefabricated housing structures, some up to 25 stories in height. With uniform floor plans, the reinforced concrete partition walls carry the loads without the use of columns.

One of the earliest successful developers of precast housing units was the firm of Larsen and Nielsen of Denmark. The Jesperson system, developed in Denmark and now used in Britain, makes use of factory-produced floor and wall units; these are medium-sized units weighing a maximum of two and a half tons, and which can be varied in width to permit some flexibility of design. The newly developed Tersons system of Britain produces floor and wall units at the building site. The Camus and Coignet systems, long used in France and elsewhere in Europe, make use of panel units for multi-story housing construction. The recently developed Sectra system in France has standard reusable formwork in units which permit the pouring of concrete partition walls and floors in place; steam heat speeds up the curing time.

In the Soviet Union, too, various prefabrication systems have been successfully used in housing construction. One type produces room-sized concrete boxes weighing up to 25 tons; these are hoisted into place with a specially designed gantry crane. The Koslov system consists of a moving production belt on which a room-height, waffle-patterned, continuous wall slab is poured, heat cured, and then cut to required sizes for delivery by truck to the building site. This is one of the most promising techniques, though little used at present. While a great amount of prefabricated housing construction is being done, particularly in Moscow, many difficulties have been encountered in scheduling, transporting, erecting, and hand finishing, and the resulting structures are therefore usually inferior in space planning and livability to those produced in Western Europe.

These prefabricated building systems have been successful only on large-scale projects in which there is a certain amount of standardization of building shapes. It appears that in most sections of America, families prefer to live in suburban, wood-frame, detached houses which, though not fireproof, express a degree of individuality.

SHELL STRUCTURES IN CONCRETE

Probably the most spectacular advance in building construction in this century is the development of the thin-shell concrete structure. It has resulted in new concepts of architectural form, and the shape of things to come is without limits. Since the earliest development of vaults and domes in Mesopotamia, man has used heavy masonry units in arch forms that required massive haunches to resist the outward thrust. In the thin, monolithic shell structure, with a network of steel reinforcement, stresses are not all in a single direction and the whole shell acts as a structural unit that can be supported with vertical columns at various points. The ideal shell form has neither bending nor shear stresses. Concrete shells properly designed, are remarkable for their thinness and strength. For example, the 138-foot dome of St. Peter's Basilica (1570) in Rome, built of masonry blocks, has a ratio of dome thickness to diameter of 1 to 13; the shell of a hen's egg has a ratio of 1 to 100; the earliest true shell of concrete, 130 feet in diameter, had a ratio of 1 to 666, and more recent shells are proportionately even thinner.

The great variety of shell roof shapes that have been developed since 1924 are too numerous to discuss in detail, but they may be classified as follows: (1) domes (shells of revolution) of semi-circular, elliptical, or parabolic section; (2) cylindrical (singly curved) forms, including barrel vaults of semi-circular, elliptical, inverted catenary, and parabolic sections; (3) conoidal shapes; (4) shapes based on hyperboloids, paraboloids, and hyperbolic-paraboloids (known as *hypar* in Britain), many of which have straight-line generatrices. Other related shapes are the monkey saddle, the hyperbolic inverted umbrella, domes and barrels using sections of undulating or folded plate forms, and free forms.

The history of the shell can probably best be expressed by discussing the figures and projects that were significant in its development. The early shells were empirical in their conception; Edmond Coignet built elliptical barrel vaults of concrete in 1892 to replace the massive masonry sewer structures of Paris. In 1896 August Föppl of Germany investigated the deformation of cylindrical networks of bars. Thin-shell, barrel vaults were built in France in 1910, and Eugene Freyssinet built two huge hangars (1916) at Orly Airport near Paris using parabolic barrel vaults with a section consisting of thin, rib-like folded plates.

The major advance in the scientific analysis of shell forms was begun in Germany in 1922 by Dr. Walter Bauersfeld; his design of the 130-foot hemispherical dome of the Zeiss Planetarium at Jena was built in 1924-25 by Dyckerhoff

Fig. 14-5. Airship hangar at Orly, France, 1916. (*Verlag Gerd Hatje*)

and Widmann. Martin Elsässer, of the same construction firm, built the market hall (1926-27) at Frankfurt am Main using a series of transverse barrels, spanning 150 feet, and supported on the ends. For the repair shops (1928-29) at Bagneux, France, Freyssinet made use of conoidal shapes. Between 1929 and 1933 Bernard Laffaile of France experimented with tension structures of *hypar* (straight-line) shapes and built the first roof of this type. Eduardo Torroja and Ricardo Barredo built the market hall (1934) at Algeciras, Spain, with a low, spherical dome, 156 feet in diameter, supported at eight points. Torroja also built the roof of the Zarzuella racecourse grandstand (1935), using a series of hyperboloid barrel shapes in a spectacular cantilevered design. The first significant shell dome in the United States was the Hayden Planetarium (1935) in New York City by Roberts and Schafer, engineers; it was designed in the manner of the Zeiss Planetarium at Jena.

In 1936 F. Almond developed a precise method for calculating stresses in *hypar* shells. For spanning large spaces in various types of industrial buildings, the shell became an economical structural form. Low spherical domes were used over nine square bays of the rubber factory (1945) at Brynmawr, Wales; and an area of 1.8 million square feet of the Volkswagen plant at Wolfsberg, Germany, is roofed with shells. The *hypar* structures of Felix Candela of Mexico are significant and imaginative design forms; these include the cosmic ray laboratory (1952) at the University of Mexico, the San Antonio de las Huertas Church (1957) at Tacuba, and the Los Manantiales restaurant (1958) at

Fig. 14-6. TWA air terminal at Kennedy International Airport, New York, 1962. (*Verlag Gerd Hatje*)

Xochimilco. Recently some significant shell structures have been constructed in the United States. Eero Saarinen with Anderson Associates, engineers, built the Kresge Auditorium (1954-55) at M.I.T., Cambridge, Massachusetts, using a low, spherical shell dome with three supports spaced 156 feet apart; with Ammann and Whitney, engineers, Saarinen also built the TWA terminal (1962) at Kennedy Airport in New York with an imaginative expressionistic design in shell construction. Perhaps the most outstanding large shell structure in the world is the C.N.I.T. Hall (1963) in Paris, by engineers Nervi and Prouve. It is a groined structure, triangular in plan, with its three supports 655 feet apart. Cylindrically arched segments fan out from the supports, and are built of double shells, each only two and a half inches in thickness; the two shells, 5 feet, ten inches apart, are connected with diaphragms.

While the basic cost of cement materials and steel for shell construction is remarkably low, the cost of building formwork is quite expensive, particularly in America, where labor costs are high. Sometimes the traditional systems of shoring or trusswork can be used repeatedly; however, some new ingenious systems have been introduced which measurably reduce construction costs. Architects Gordon B. Ferguson and Donald P. Stephens, with engineer Frederick J. Fricke, built the civic auditorium (1955) at Albuquerque, New Mexico, by pouring the 215-foot diameter, low spherical concrete dome over a prepared earth mound; the earthwork was subsequently removed. The Zeiss Planetarium (1924-25) was constructed with a triangulated network of thin, steel rods to which metal lath was attached, and over which sprayed concrete ("Gunite") was applied to form a two-and-a-half-inch-thick concrete shell.

James Marsh at Texas A & M University developed the "lift shape" system by which the 80-foot dome of the Eastman Kodak Pavilion at the New York World's Fair (1964), was built. In this method of construction, the flexible steel reinforcing rods are laid out on the site in a radial pattern; they are wired together and metal lath is attached. Then with a crane, the central portion is lifted and the outer "legs" are pulled inward and attached to ground supports. The resulting domical network is sprayed with "Gunite" and plastered to form a thin, rigid concrete shell. Another system, the "inflated balloon" process, was developed by Wallace Neff in 1940; in this method, sprayed concrete is applied over the inflated balloon forms.

STEEL STRUCTURES IN RECENT DECADES

As fabrication methods in the steel industry have progressed, new developments in standardized units for building construction have followed. For small structures, steel pipe columns were introduced in the 1930's, and later rectangular tubing was used. Factory-fabricated open-web steel joists were first produced in 1923; originally standardized at 32 feet in length, they are now manufactured in lengths over 100 feet, and are used in one-story frame buildings and in skyscrapers. The space frame is another recent development in steel structures; this three-dimensional truss-like system can be used effectively to roof large areas with minimum column supports. In 1944 Konrad Wachsmann began research on this type of structure at the Illinois Institute of Technology, and two years later produced a roof structure for a spacious aircraft hangar.

Another recently developed space structure takes the form of the dome. In 1947 R. Buckminster Fuller began experiments with his "geodesic" principles, using polyhedral elements to form lightweight dome structures. Fuller built a dome of paperboard at Yale University in 1952 and a year later he built the steel dome structure of the Ford Rotunda Building at Dearborn, Michigan. The same year he produced a dome, 140 feet in diameter, of aluminum framework that could be transported in assembled form by helicopter, and covered with nylon plastic in one and a half hours. The architects Battey and Childs assisted him in building his largest structure, the Union Tank Car dome (1958) at Baton Rouge, Louisiana; this 384-foot diameter structure is built of hexagonal-folded sheet-steel panels which are braced with tubular framework.

Another form long used in bridge construction, is now being applied to building structures: the suspension system. A theoretical proposal was made in France in the 1920's, but one of the earliest successful buildings was the Travel and Transportation Building (1933) at the Chicago Century of Progress Exposition. The engineers, Thorud and Moisseiff, hung the 200-foot diameter metal roof from cables that were supported by twelve masts around the perimeter of the building. A spectacular design was the State Fair Arena (1954-55) at Raleigh, North Carolina, designed by the architects Nowicki and Dietrick with engineers Severud, Elstad, and Kruger. Prestressed steel cables stretched between two low-angle, intersecting parabolic concrete arches supported the

Fig. 14-7. State Fair Arena, Raleigh, North Carolina, 1954. (*Verlag Gerd Hatje*)

saddle-shaped steel roof deck. Other significant suspension-type roofs are the Ingalls Hockey Rink (1958) at Yale University, New Haven, the circular Municipal Auditorium (1959) at Utica, New York, and Dulles International Airport (1962) at Chantilly, Virginia.

RECENT HIGH-RISE STRUCTURES

For seventeen years following the Depression of 1931 few skyscrapers were built in New York or elsewhere. But following World War II the high-rise again became an advertising symbol for business corporations, and the skylines of the cities of America and of the world began to change. At that time New York City changed its height zoning law so that a tower was permitted to rise to unlimited height adjacent to the sidewalk, providing the tower occupied only a limited percentage of the total lot area. This action encouraged the development of small, open plazas in the crowded skyscraper areas. Cities throughout the world enacted new zoning laws permitting the erection of high-rise structures. Skyscrapers, usually 20 to 30 stories in height, began to rise in many areas of Europe, Latin America, and East Asia.

In 1920-21 Ludwig Mies van der Rohe had proposed that the skyscraper be sheathed in glass walls. His Lake Shore Drive Apartments (1950-51) seemed the epitome of skeleton-frame design: with its bold reticulated pattern of exterior steel columns and spandrel beams it appears to express the ultimate of simplicity in architectural form; the exposed exterior steel shapes are, however, merely decorative since the load of the structure is carried by fireproofed columns behind the façade. The architectural firm of Skidmore, Owings, and Merrill became the style leaders with their all-glass façade of the 21-story Lever House (1951-52) in New York, and the First City National Bank (1959-61) in Houston, Texas, with its reticulated exterior pattern recalling the designs of Sullivan and Mies van der Rohe. Structures in concrete are reaching new heights; the 54-story Place Victoria Building (1964) in Montreal was constructed with a frame of high-strength reinforced concrete.

Building codes in many cities of America have been modified to permit thinner and lighter exterior curtain walls in multi-story frame construction. In many of the recent high-rise buildings, prefabricated metal spandrels are backed up with four- to six-inch lightweight concrete or other insulation material. The Alcoa Building (1953) in Pittsburgh has floor-to-floor, exterior aluminum panels

Fig. 14-8. Lake Shore Drive Apartments, Chicago, 1950. (*Verlag Gerd Hatje*)

Fig. 14-9. World Trade Center Towers, New York.
The 110-story twin towers will be 1350 feet in
height, making them the highest buildings in the
world. (Courtesy of *Balthazar Korab*)

which include the windows with the insulated spandrels. There is also a trend
toward structures with larger inside spaces which will be free of obstructing
columns. Using 57.5-foot girders, the 19-story Inland Steel Building (1957) in
Chicago provides 10,200 square feet of space per floor; an attached tower, with
elevators and stairs, was heavily braced to provide rigidity for the entire structure.

There is planned for Lower Manhattan twin 110-story towers rising 1350 feet
in height. The World Trade Center Towers, designed by the architects Yamasaki
and Roth, with the engineers Skilling and Robertson, will have a total rentable
floor space of 10 million square feet. An improved system has been devised for
vertical transportation; express elevators will carry the passengers to "sky lobbies" where they will transfer to locals. There is also a new approach to the
design of the structural frame; instead of the usual bay spacing of columns, the
vertical loads are carried by the heavily braced structure of the central core and
closely spaced columns (about three feet apart) around the perimeter of the
square tower. The large areas of column-free space around the central core are

spanned with 60-foot open-web joists. To speed up the time of erection large units of floor structure are shop-welded to be assembled with bolts on the job. Although the building technology continues to advance, the occupancy of these new towers will greatly increase traffic congestion on the streets below, thus complicating another technological problem that remains unsolved.

While the manufacture of automobiles and many other complex products is accomplished by the automated production of standardized parts, and the assembly by highly mechanized methods, the building industry continues to make use of custom-designed materials erected, in part, by hand craftsmen. This is apparently due to the very nature of the product, the industry, and the client. The buildings in which man lives and works are spaces designed for a particular use and must be erected on a given site, and to meet the variety of present needs with complete standardization of space use and form is not possible. The past decades have brought about more and more standardization of materials and mechanical equipment, but the need for flexibility of space design and aesthetic design of most buildings will continue, and is possible only through custom manufacture and specialized, field erection. Nevertheless, no one can predict the future rate or direction of innovation in the construction industry, especially if, as seems likely, it is soon to be the object of increased research and development.

15 / The Home Environment
MELVIN M. ROTSCH

Since the earliest establishment of towns and cities, man has struggled to provide better shelter and an improved living environment for his family. Although the Industrial Revolution brought technical progress in building construction and in many other fields, the facilities in the home for sanitation, lighting, and heating were slow to develop. One of the major problems was, of course, that to a large degree the amenities within the home (running water, flush toilets, gas or electric illumination) were dependent upon the general availability of utilities within the municipality. And because the cities were developing so rapidly, utility services almost inevitably lagged behind urban growth.

THE MID-NINETEENTH-CENTURY HOME FACILITIES

London in 1840 had a population of two and a quarter million when New York's was 400,000. In those cities the building structures of middle-class apartments or detached houses were not greatly dissimilar or inferior to those of today; the great difference was in the facilities available. The larger cities pumped unfiltered water from rivers that were polluted with sewage; in the suburbs and smaller cities water was obtained from shallow wells that were also often polluted. In the better homes in the city, water was piped into the house, usually only to the kitchen; the tenement-dwellers carried water for the household from hydrants on the streets. At that time metal-lined wood bathtubs, without running hot water, were a luxury of the very wealthy. Although the cities still lacked adequate sewer lines, primitive water closets were installed in a few of the better homes. The residue of the brick-lined cesspools of London flats had to be removed at frequent intervals. In the smaller cities and towns of Europe and America, pit privies were dominant.

Lighting and heating were also quite primitive by modern standards. Although gas lighting was being introduced, it was principally for street lamps; most homes were lighted with flickering whale-oil lamps or candles. Men worked long hours, but most factories had to be closed at night due to inadequate illumination. Central-heating systems for larger buildings were experimental and quite rare, while homes still depended on the fireplace or the primitive cast-iron stove for both heating and food preparation.

WATER SOURCES AND DISTRIBUTION SYSTEMS

Even before the Christian era the Romans had recognized the need for clean, pure water and had secured their supply by aqueducts from distant mountain streams rather than from the murky Tiber River. Yet it was not until 1721 that the first London company began pumping water through wooden mains. Throughout the 19th century increased quantities were pumped from the Thames and Lea rivers, and as the metropolitan area grew, these sources became more and more polluted. In America it was not until a cholera epidemic struck Philadelphia in 1793 that the first major water system in America was constructed there a few years later. New York City, scourged by a cholera epidemic in 1832, completed its first major supply system from the Croton River ten years later. As the city grew, a larger Croton aqueduct was built in 1890, and in this century even greater supplies were brought from the Catskill Mountains and the Delaware River. The city now uses one and a half billion gallons per day; this amounts to 180 gallons per person. Other cities of America consume up to 300 gallons per person daily.

Although impure water had been identified as a source of disease at the beginning of the 19th century, means of purification came slowly. With the major aim to remove sediment and discoloration, systems of charcoal and sand filtration came into use in Europe. Stein installed one of the first slow sand filters in America at Richmond, Virginia, in 1832. The improved filtration system with forced flow and reverse-flow cleaning was developed by Kirkwood forty years later at Poughkeepsie, New York, and has since been adopted by cities throughout the world. But sand filters did not remove all of the dangerous bacteria, of whose existence they were unaware at that time. Finally, the new science of bacteriology, first developed in the 1860's by Pasteur and Koch, provided the key to this problem. As soon as the typhoid bacillus and cholera vibrio were isolated (1880 to 1883), laboratory techniques were developed, and application to analysis of water supply soon followed. Tests indicated that dangerous human pollution could be reduced 98 per cent. The use of chlorine was patented in England (1887) and America (1888), and in the 1890's electrolysis, aeration, and water softening came into use.

At the turn of the century most large cities of the Western world had an adequate water supply that was filtered and chlorine-treated. The reduction of diseases caused by waterborne bacteria testifies to the effectiveness of water treatment. Yet even today the water supplies of many cities in the underdeveloped lands remain possible sources of typhoid fever and cholera.

SEWAGE DISPOSAL

Although the Aegean peoples and the Romans had developed limited use of underground sanitary sewers, medieval and Renaissance towns were notorious for their filth and lack of sanitary facilities. Storm sewers were developed in London and Paris, but these drains were not used for disposal of sanitary wastes until about the middle of the 19th century. Pit privies and septic tanks, along with nearby shallow wells, were still in use in crowded London. In the mid-19th century, when the house drains were attached to the sewer mains, the raw sewage was dumped into the Thames; then downstream the untreated water was pumped into the water mains. Boston built sanitary sewer lines in 1833, but in New York it was not legal to connect building drains to the public sewer system until 1845. As late as the 1880's there were pit privies in the back yards of most tenements, and some still existed into the present century.

The earliest water closets were developed in England in the last decades of the 18th century. The cast-iron bowls, with a flap valve emptying directly into the drains, were difficult to clean. Later the P-trap was used, but, due to back pressure in the drains, these traps were ineffective; also sewer gases penetrated the house. There were improvements in form, and the English pottery-makers began producing better bowls by mid-century. Pottery closet bowls were first produced in America at Trenton, New Jersey, about 1875.

When the owner of a large, new mansion in New York complained to the plumbing contractors in 1874 that the stench due to sewer gas was unbearable, it was proposed that all traps be vented; this measure, solving the problem of sewer-gas odors, was soon adopted universally. In 1890 the washdown closet came on the market and since that date there have been only minor improvements in form, action, and materials. The flush valve, which came into use at the turn of the century, is now standard equipment in public toilets. The supply tank for domestic water closets remained elevated until about 1915 when it was replaced by the low tank.

BATHING FACILITIES IN THE HOME

Bathing in ancient Rome had been an accepted practice, but in medieval and Renaissance Europe neither the desire nor the facilities existed. Even in the early 19th century medical controversies arose about the desirability of bathing. At first there was limited use of portable, sheet-metal tubs for bathing in the home, but at mid-century better homes were equipped with boxed-in tubs that were lined with lead, zinc, or copper. The Tremont House (1828) in Boston was among the first hotels to provide central bathrooms along with water closets, although patrons continued to use the ewer and basin on the marble-topped washstands. It was another half-century before running water (in basins) was provided in every room. In the 1880's a few hotels provided the first private bathrooms in luxury suites.

The well-to-do home of the 1890's in England and America had a very spacious bathroom fitted with a free-standing tub and a manually operated water heater of grotesque design; plumbing pipes continued to be exposed. The bidet, developed in France before 1770 and still widely used in Europe, has not been adapted for most bathrooms in this country.

The Romans had piped hot water from central boilers to the various rooms of the thermae (public baths), but during the fourteen centuries that followed, no systems for hot water existed in the Western world. In the early 19th century water pipes were sometimes coiled in the chimney flues to provide flowing hot water; near the end of the century the manually operated gas water heater came into use.

Not until the 20th century was the automatic heater developed in America. A patent was granted for the built-in bathtub in 1913, and following World War I there were refinements in space use, efficiency, and appearance of the American bathroom. The sale of enamelled bathtubs and basins rose from 2.4 million in 1921 to 4.8 million pieces in 1923; well-equipped baths were being installed in millions of homes. However, the housing census of 1940 indicated that many homes still had no bathtubs and used the outdoor privy.

FACILITIES	URBAN DWELLINGS PER CENT	RURAL FARM DWELLINGS PER CENT
with running water	93.5	17.8
with indoor private toilet	83.0	11.2
with private bathing facilities	77.5	11.2

For the above, the percentages were higher in the West, slightly higher in the East, and much lower in the South.

Fig. 15-1. An American bathroom, early 1900's.
(Courtesy of *Kohler Company*, Kohler, Wisconsin)

APPLIANCES FOR THE KITCHEN

In the *American Woman's Magazine* of 1869, Catherine E. Beecher urged the replanning and modernization of kitchens into compact, labor-saving spaces. But progress was not rapid; kitchen appliances were slow to develop in America and lagged even more in Europe.

The gas range was first demonstrated at the London Exhibition in 1851. In the next decades it came into use in restaurant kitchens, but was not adapted for domestic use until after the turn of the century. With the expansion of the gas pipelines in the third and fourth decades, the gas range became widely used in all parts of the country.

An electric range with oven and broiler was on exhibit at the World's Columbian Exposition in 1893, but its adoption was slow, probably due to high electric rates. The gradual application of power to many kitchen appliances came with the improvement of the small electric motor. In the early decades of the century the powered domestic washing machine was in a developmental stage, and it was not until the later 1930's that the automatic washing machine

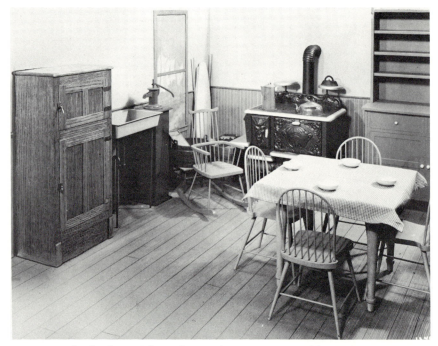

Fig. 15-2. This kitchen of the early 1900's contains a wood-burning range, an icebox with drain pan, and a pump at the sink. (Courtesy of Frigidaire Division, *General Motors Corporation*)

was perfected. The garbage disposal unit and the automatic dishwasher came into limited use about the same time. The domestic electric refrigerator was produced in an experimental model in 1917; five years later the compact, heremetically sealed absorption unit was developed, and in the mid-1920's the successful refrigerator came on the market.

LIGHTING

Man in his earliest cultures sought to extend the daylight hours by illuminating his dwelling with torches or oil lamps, but the development of good lighting had to await the age of electricity. The sources of artificial light may be classified as: *combustion*, including candles, oil lamps, and gas lighting; *incandescent* (glowing with heat), represented by the filament-type electrical lamp; and *electric discharge* (through a gas or vapor), including mercury vapor, neon tube, sodium vapor, and fluorescent lamps.

In the early 19th century, oil lamps had been improved with better burners and the addition of the glass chimney. Whale oil was used extensively, but when petroleum came into production about 1860, kerosene (coal oil, as it was called, because it was first distilled from coal) became the major fuel for lighting during the next decades. The "coal-oil" lamp remained in use in most rural homes as late as the 1930's.

London began lighting its streets with manufactured gas in 1813, and this improved lighting was extended to other cities of Europe. Baltimore installed this type of street lighting (1816 to 1820), but homes were slow to adapt the gas light. Gas lighting was installed in the national Capitol in 1840 to 1847. Natural gas came into production during the Civil War era, but for more than half a century it was piped only to cities near the gas fields. In 1886 Welsbach de-

Fig. 15-3. A table with thirty switches and plugs constituted General Electric's first electric range in 1906. There were thirteen appliances including a fry pan, oven, several double boilers, several skillets, a coffee-maker, toaster, waffle iron, and other utensils —all equipped with a connection for plugging into the simple wooden table. (Courtesy of *General Electric Company*)

Fig. 15-4. The old Guardian refrigerator, *c.* 1917, forerunner of the modern refrigerator. (Courtesy of Frigidaire Division, *General Motors Corporation*)

veloped the incandescent mantle for the gas burner, and this improved brilliant white light became more widely used than the newly introduced electric lamp. During the 1890's streets, public buildings, and fine homes were ablaze with gas lighting, but with the beginning of the new century improved lighting with electricity began to replace it.

One of the first large electric light installations was made in 1878 in the Philadelphia store of John Wanamaker using the arc-lamp system developed by Charles F. Brush of Cleveland, Ohio. In that same year the Avenue de l'Opera in Paris was lighted with Jablockhoff candles (arc lamps). Electric-arc street lighting soon followed in America—Cleveland (1879), portions of Broadway in New York (1880), and a few streets in Washington (1882-90). Portions of the Capitol Building were lighted in 1888, and the entire building was wired in 1897. The effect of the "Great White Way" of the Chicago World's Columbian Exposition of 1893 greatly stimulated the use of electrical lighting in America.

In 1882 the Edison Electric Company constructed in New York the first steam-powered central generating plant, and within one year it was furnishing direct current power to over 500 customers. In the same year a hydroelectric plant was opened at Appleton, Wisconsin. Cheaper electricity soon brought electric lighting into most American homes in urban areas. In the 1930's the formation of the Rural Electrification Administration helped to bring electric power into most American farmhouses.

The traditional measurement of light is the international foot-candle (the amount of direct light thrown by an international candle on a surface one foot away). This measures the intensity of a given light source, but it is not an adequate measurement for the design of interior illumination. More generally used is the lumen method, based on the percentage of light generated by the lamp which eventually reaches the work plane. During the early part of this century most interiors were inadequately lighted with bare incandescent bulbs that

Fig. 15-5. Brush single-arc lamp. (Courtesy of *Consolidated Edison Company*)

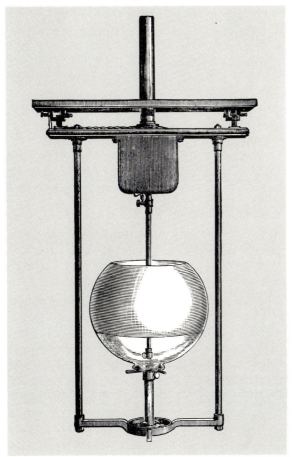

caused eyestrain due to low intensity and glare. New and better types of lamps continue to be developed during the 20th century.

TYPES OF LAMP	WHERE DEVELOPED	DATE	LUMENS PER WATT
Incandescent filament lamp	England & USA	1800	4-7
Improved incandescent lamp	USA	1934	12
Mercury-vapor arc lamp	England	1901-03	22
Neon tube	France	1910-23	9
Sodium-vapor lamp	England	1932-33	55-75
High-pressure mercury vapor	England	1932-34	28-37
Fluorescent lamp (pat. 1896)	USA	1938	38
Improved fluorescent lamp	USA	1960	75

The fluorescent lamp, now widely used for lighting commercial and industrial interiors, develops less heat, has greater range in the color spectrum, and is more economical to operate than the incandescent type. In recent decades engineering specialists have devised improved lamps, better fixtures, and architectural forms that minimize glare and shadows, and give a uniform level of illumination for the task at hand. During the 1930's it was predicted that the windowless factory, office, and home would be the ultimate ideal. Today many large industrial plants are windowless, but there is a public reaction against the elimination of natural light and view from most types of buildings.

CONTROL OF INTERIOR CLIMATE

Heat may be distributed to various parts of a room or space by *convection, forced-air circulation,* or *radiation;* some systems use more than one of these principles. Examples of the convection of heated air are open fireplaces, stoves, floor furnaces, gravity warm-air systems, and "radiator" systems using hot water or steam. Forced-air circulation, made possible by the development of fans and blowers, includes unit-space heaters, central warm-air systems, and year-round conditioning systems. Radiation, used in the Roman hypocaust, has recently been applied to modern buildings.

The early civilizations arose in warm climates where protection against the cold was not a major problem. The Romans developed the hypocaust (radiant) system which heated a room by warm air piped into a space below the floor, but this disappeared with the decline of Rome. Heating was again quite primitive in the medieval period before the development of the fireplace in Western Europe and the *kochelofen* in Central and Eastern Europe. However, the fireplace, still a picturesque feature of our homes, was never an efficient method for heating.

Sheet-iron stoves were used in Germany in the 16th century, and in 1742 Benjamin Franklin developed the metal-box "Franklin stove," probably derived from the earlier stoves of the Pennsylvania Dutch; this allowed for better circulation of the heated air. Iron stoves were sometimes enclosed in a brick chamber to effect better circulation of the warm air. A primitive gravity warm-air furnace was installed in 1792 for heating Darby Hospital in England, and in the 1820's wood-burning warm-air furnaces were installed in the Capitol in Washington, D.C. Gravity warm-air systems are still extensively used today because of their effectiveness and economy in heating small buildings.

Heating with hot-water pipes began with the horticultural greenhouses of Europe in the 18th century. Water circulated in large cast-iron pipes was used to heat buildings in England in 1816, and coils of tubing were used in Westminster Hospital in 1830. The national Capitol was equipped with a hot-water heating system, 1857 to 1867. Parallel to this development, steam systems were also being used—in 1824 in a silk mill at Watford, England, and in 1870 in several schools in the city of Chicago.

There were several improvements in radiators between 1858 and 1877, and the sectional cast-iron radiator, much like present models, was on the market in the 1880's. The early skyscrapers of Chicago were equipped with effective central-heating systems, some using hot water, others steam. There has been little change in basic "radiator" heating in the present century.

The central-heating systems used coal for fuel; furnaces were stoked by hand, but in 1903 the under-feed automatic coal stoker was marketed. Manufactured gas, used extensively for lighting, was little used in the 19th century for heating; with cheaper natural gas and the expansion of the pipelines, however, the use of coal began to decline. In 1940, 55 per cent of the central-heating systems of this country were fired with coal; in the decade that followed, heating with gas tripled, and in 1950 only 34 per cent used coal. According to the census of that year 50 per cent of the homes of America were heated with central systems, but even now a great number of modest homes are heated with open-flame gas heaters. Today 25 billion cubic feet of natural gas is pumped daily through a 710-million-mile pipeline system to every major urban area in this country to be used for heating or industrial purposes.

The mechanical system of heating by forced-air circulation was slowly developed after the improvement of fans and blowers in the late 19th century. At the turn of the century a forced warm-air system with a plenum space under the floors was installed in the Senate and Representative halls of the national Capitol; theaters and assembly halls began using similar forced-air systems. When heating was not required, fresh air was circulated. The unit-space heater was first marketed in 1918; this unit, though not highly efficient, is extensively used to heat large industrial spaces.

Custom-built warm-air systems were developed in the 1920's for use in homes and small buildings. The basement was considered essential in residences to house the central furnace, but soon standard units were produced for the one-story "ranch-type" house. The thermostatically controlled, gas-fired furnace was placed in a central closet and heat was distributed through ducts in the attic; in the past decade the horizontal furnace, for attic spaces, has been developed. In many large buildings hot water is piped from the basement furnace to air-handling units on each floor or section of the structure, and the heated air is distributed through metal ducts to the various rooms of the building.

About two centuries ago some portions of the Houses of Parliament were heated by circulating warm air under the floors, but during the last century no similar attempts were made to use radiant heating. In 1908 A. H. Baker wrote on the theory of the application of radiant heating to buildings; in the same year Arthur Blake installed a successful system in Liverpool Cathedral by circulating warm air under the floor quite in the manner of the hypocausts of the Romans. Following World War I there were numerous applications in England, using heated pipes for floors, walls, or ceilings. It was rarely applied in this country before World War II, but it has been more generally used in recent decades. It provides a clean, comfortable, efficient warmth for the occupants without heating the entire room. It has also been ingeniously applied to snow removal from sidewalks and driveways, and to the warming of outdoor terraces. This kind of radiant heating is usually done by electricity; wires of high electrical resistance, thereby producing much heat, are imbedded in the concrete sidewalk or in the walls of homes to provide heat.

AIR CONDITIONING

Throughout history the oppressive heat and humidity of warm climates have had a debilitating effect on man. Ancient rulers in sub-tropical lands devised fans that were operated by slaves. In the southern states of America during the last century there was limited use of ice for cooling rooms. The development of the refrigerating ice machine and fan-driven, forced-air cooling-heating systems were steps toward the production of machines for room cooling. The term air conditioning was coined in 1906 by a textile engineer, Steward W. Crane.

One of the earliest refrigerating machines for ice production was manufactured in 1849 by John Gorrie, a physician of Charleston, South Carolina. Power-driven fans were improved with the development of the multi-blade, high-efficiency centrifugal blower in 1892 by C. E. A. Rateau of France. Two years later Herman Reitschel published a "Guide for the Calculation and Design of Ventilating and Heating Installations" which set forth many basic principles of air conditioning. Theaters in Europe and America began making use of forced-air ventilating systems, and the filtering and washing of air was introduced before the turn of the century.

A major breakthrough came in 1902 when Willis H. Carrier devised the principle of the air washer method for dew-point control. That year he developed a fan-coil-type dehumidifying unit that controlled the moisture in the air, and installed a successful 30-ton unit in a printing plant in Brooklyn, New York. This system was applied to many industrial plants where moisture control was essential for manufacturing processes: a cotton mill (1906), a silk mill (1907), and a meat-packing plant (1908). Stuart W. Cramer in 1906 developed a modified system for controlling humidity in the air; it depended upon the relation between wet and dry bulb temperatures. In 1913 Shepherd and Hill demonstrated by tests the relation between temperature and humidity necessary for human comfort.

One of the first large installations of air conditioning for comfort control of office spaces was the 300-ton unit installed in 1904 in the New York Stock Exchange. Three years later Alfred R. Wolf designed a year-round system for the galleries of the Metropolitan Museum of Art. Before 1920 most systems were used in industrial plants, but in 1924 Hudson's Department Store in Detroit air-cooled its basement and found that more customers were attracted. A few restaurants and other commercial establishments installed comfort-control systems, but the greatest expansion was in the construction of new motion-picture theaters. A plant was installed in 1917 in the Empire Theater in Montgomery, Alabama, and five years later Grauman's Metropolitan Theater of Hollywood developed an advanced system in which conditioned air entered at the ceiling and was removed at the floor under the seating. This became the prototype for theater installations throughout America.

In the development of cooling systems for buildings new problems arose: ammonia, the standard refrigerant for ice-making machines, proved hazardous in air-conditioning plants; and the old type reciprocating compressors were not adaptable for the flexible use of air conditioning. Carbon dioxide was safe but ineffective, and could not be used in the improved centrifugal compressors that came into production in this country in 1922. Other refrigerants, diolene and methyl chloride, were tried but were not totally successful. Finally, in 1931 Midgley and Henne of the Du Pont Company developed Freon 12, which became the standard refrigerant for use in air-conditioning plants and home refrigerators. In 1934 the Servel Company came on the market with the gas-operated absorption-cycle unit, a system now used extensively, and particularly efficient where process heat is available for use in the cooling equipment.

The first completely air-conditioned high-rise structure was the 21-story Milam Building in San Antonio, Texas, built in 1929. Equipment continued to improve, but in large buildings excessive ceiling space was required for duct work on each floor. In the late 1930's the Carrier Corporation developed a new, improved system with small high-velocity ducts supplying air to room units which cooled or heated and then diffused the air throughout the room.

This was first installed in 1940 in the Bankers' Life Building, Macon, Georgia, and is now a widely used system for larger installations.

The beginning of the theory of reverse-cycle heating and cooling dates from the early 19th century, but its application was advanced by the publications of T. B. Morley in 1922 and A. R. Stevenson in 1926. In the conventional cooling system heat is removed from the building and is dissipated into the outside atmosphere; by reversing the process, the building can likewise be heated. The air-to-air system is most effective in mild climates where the temperature differential is not too great. In colder areas use is made of the earth-to-air method in which the relatively stable temperature of water from wells is utilized. The first experimental installation of the air-to-air system was made in Los Angeles in 1931, but for the next decade there were few plants in use. Following World War II standard units were produced for use in residences, and this system is now quite competitive with other types. Electrical power in a single unit furnishes heated or cooled air without dust, smoke, and fire hazards of normal heating systems.

The development of central systems for air conditioning continued to advance, but these larger plants could not meet the need for a low-cost room-cooling unit. The "ILG Airator" evaporative cooler was developed in 1928; this small box unit cooled the air by moving it through water-saturated pads, and was quite effective in the arid western portions of the country. This led to the development of the refrigerated type unit that could be used in any area. Experimental production began in 1930, and two years later Galson and Neeson perfected the self-contained, air-cooled "Freon 12" unit for room coolers. The development and sale of these during the next two decades was limited, but the market expanded greatly and today a large portion of the dwellings in southern cities use these compact room air-conditioning units.

The central plant has long been in use for heating of groups of buildings of institutions or business districts; during the past decade large hospitals, colleges, and so on, of the South and West have installed efficient central plants which produce chilled water for the cooling of outlying buildings. The large shopping centers being built throughout the land are a big market for comfort-control systems; The Rochester (New York) Midtown Plaza has 1.3 million square feet of enclosed mall and shopping space, all air-conditioned. Planners see in the near future the probability that central pedestrian malls of entire business districts will be roofed over and completely comfort-controlled.

The design of the system for the 650-foot span, $32-million Astrodome sports arena in Houston, Texas, presented special problems. On various sides of the building there are radio-controlled thermostats which register the temperature and humidity; a pyroheliometer on the roof records the angle and intensity of the sunlight, and an anemometer registers the direction and velocity of the wind. In different areas of the vast interior the temperature and humidity are

Fig. 15-6. This 1929 room air conditioner was available in either air- or water-cooled models. The cabinet, about four feet high, weighed about 215 pounds, and the remote compressor, usually located in the basement, weighed another 425 pounds. The air was circulated by a 12-inch propellor-type fan. The price, including compressor and cabinet, ranged from $565 to $613, depending on electric current requirements. (Courtesy of Frigidaire Division, *General Motors Corporation*)

recorded; and an ultraviolet sensor checks the density of smoke and dust in the air. All of these recordings are automatically transmitted to a control center where a computer makes constant corrections for the distribution of the conditioned air. Variations in any part of the arena from the normal visibility, humidity, or temperature (78° F in summer) are corrected immediately; to maintain this, the air-conditioning system must run almost continuously. Brilliant lighting (200 footcandles) is maintained for night games, but difficulty was encountered immediately after opening the arena in April 1965. While intense sunlight through the steel-supported, clear plastic shell made it possible to grow a turf for the diamond, the glare blinded the players in left field. To overcome the glare, the plastic was painted over; with the limited sunlight thus available, natural grass refused to grow, and an artificial "grass carpet" had to be devised for installation on the playing field.

THE DESIGN OF BUILDINGS FOR ACOUSTICAL CONTROL

The ancient Greeks were the first people to devise open-air theaters for seating large audiences; they were also the first to become aware of the problem of acoustics. Their actors used megaphones to magnify their voices, and they built their rounded theaters into hillsides so that the sound could be heard throughout. The Roman engineer Vitruvius made a remarkable analysis of theater acoustics, explaining and defining the terms *interference, reverberation,* and *echo.*

During the Renaissance the form of the enclosed theater was established, and even though many that followed were acoustically faulty, no scientific analysis of acoustics was made until the 19th century. Among the first to advance an hypothesis and investigate the application of sound control was Dr. J. B. Upham, who in 1853 conducted experiments in the Boston Music Hall, measuring the time of reverberations, and observing the effect of carpets, draperies, and upholstered seating on the sound. In 1854 and 1856 Joseph Henry, the noted American physicist, read papers which gave scholarly discussions of echoes, reverberations, resonance, and the effect of the shape of interiors. Yet even without adequate scientific theory, such marvels as the Mormon Tabernacle in Salt Lake City could sometimes be built with nearly perfect acoustical qualities.

Professor Wallace C. Sabine, Harvard University physicist and the "father of architectural acoustics," began his studies in 1895. Between 1900 and 1915 he published a series of papers which set forth exact methods for the analysis of the acoustic properties of buildings. *Sabine's equation* for calculating reverberation time is still used today. This reverberation time, variable for different frequencies, determines the acoustic quality of an audience hall; for a large opera house it can be up to 2.0 seconds; for a piano recital hall 1.1 is the optimum; for spaces used for speaking it should be somewhat lower. Through the work of Professor Sabine and others that followed, a new science of architectural acoustics was developed, and specialists began to aid the architects in designing and testing the acoustic qualities before construction began.

The introduction of electronic amplifying equipment has intensified acoustical problems. With experience in designing studios for radio, sound pictures, and television, highly specialized techniques and materials have been developed by acoustical engineers.

CONCLUSION

In less than two centuries remarkable changes have been made in man's living environment through the improvement of the mechanical equipment of buildings. Today, members of a middle-class home take for granted many material things that were quite unknown to their ancestors. In warm seasons they awake refreshed in an air-conditioned house; the father shaves and bathes in a fully equipped bathroom while his wife prepares breakfast with the benefit of automatic gas and electric kitchen appliances. The children may depart in an air-conditioned bus to attend classes in a comfort-conditioned building, and the father drives his air-conditioned car to his place of employment, an air-conditioned office or plant. In the evening the family has the choice of visiting an air-conditioned movie or a sports arena, or they may watch a television show in their living room. All of this in air-conditioned comfort and aided by technological devices and appliances that make life easier, pleasanter, and more comfortable.

There are many problems still with us, however, and new ones are arising. Man is becoming highly dependent on the machine; the cost of mechanical equipment in his home, once negligible, is now consuming an alarmingly large portion of his income; and the power supplies for the machines (electricity and gas) are highly vulnerable to malfunction or destruction by war, natural catastrophe, or technical failure. The massive power blackout in the northeastern United States late in 1965 dramatized the growing dependence on artificial environment which has characterized our age.

At the same time, man's aesthetic senses are apparently being dulled by the propaganda agencies of progress and the machine. The natural beauty of the seashore, the countryside, and the city are being sacrificed; unsightly utility poles and neon signs, products of the electrical age, dominate the cityscape. The intense noise of industry, city traffic, and jet aircraft are on the increase; the smoke and smog of the urban center threaten public health. In short, there are still technological and sociological problems to solve, for as our artificial environment has been improved our natural environment has seriously deteriorated. The solutions to these environmental problems will require political wisdom and the exercise of both technical and social ingenuity.

Part **V**
Energy Resources

16 / Developing the Energy Inheritance
BRUCE C. NETSCHERT

At the beginning of the 20th century coal, which had risen to dominance in the 19th century, was still king in the energy field. Its place in the United States was typical of its place throughout the industrialized countries: coal accounted for almost three quarters of the total energy consumed. Wood was still a significant energy source, however, totalling roughly one fifth of all energy consumption. The remainder was divided about equally among crude oil, natural gas, and hydroelectricity. Crude oil was important chiefly as a source of illuminating oil; and its future was largely discounted in expert opinion because of its expected exhaustion within a decade or so. Natural gas was looked on as a nuisance and waste product, being used only near its places of occurrence. Manufactured gas, as a by-product or co-product of coking operations, was used in some cities for street lighting and in urban homes for illumination and cooking. Electric power, a late innovation of the 19th century, was no longer a novelty, but its use was still chiefly in industry. It was available in cities and towns for use in the home, mostly for lighting. Total electricity consumption was less than 10 per cent of all energy consumption.

Although one can think of "energy" as a single input into man's economic activity, it is obvious that the pace and degree of technological progress are not the same in each of the several industries that make energy available for general use. This chapter, therefore, considers separately each of the fuels: coal, crude oil, natural gas, and electric power.

COAL MINING

Coal mining in 1900 was essentially the same procedure that had been used since the beginning of the industry. Men tunnelled laboriously underground with pick and shovel, loading the coal, after it had been blasted out of place, into small rail cars hauled by mule. At the surface the coal was dumped in front of corps of small boys who picked out by hand the pieces of rock and impure coal. In economic terms, the procedure was highly labor intensive and highly inefficient. The average coal miner in the United States in 1900 produced only three tons in a day's work.

Changes had, however, already begun to take place. Machines for cutting into the bottom and sides of the coal face so as to improve the results of blasting had been introduced a decade or so earlier, and in 1900 accounted for one quarter of mine output. Both compressed air and electricity to power locomotives for hauling and augers for drilling blasting holes were already in some mines by 1900. In this century, however, the pace of development has gradually quickened. Electric locomotive haulage became predominant in 1924; mechanical loading, after several false starts, became a commercial reality in 1922. As mechanization spread to other operations and to more and more mines, labor efficiency improved greatly. Productivity rose to 4.5 tons per man day in 1925 and reached 6.3 tons at the close of World War II.

The mechanization of loading and haulage also led to a great increase in overall efficiency. Haulage was the pace setter and stabilizer of mining operations, and the ability to dovetail and integrate all operations to it was in itself a vast improvement in efficiency.

In the post-World War II era the mechanization of the mining operation became complete with the introduction of the continuous-mining machine in 1948. This machine chews its way along the coal seam, at the same time passing the coal back to a conveyor belt or shuttle car behind it. By converting all main haulage within the mine to conveyor belts and putting the hoist to the surface under automatic control, mechanization brought a constant flow of coal to the surface. It brought a huge step forward in efficiency. The use of continuous-mining machines in American mines spread rapidly, to 39 per cent of total underground production by 1964, and productivity reached the high level of 13.7 tons per man day.

In Europe the broken and steeply pitching attitude of the coal seams made progress along American lines impossible. The mining technique commonly employed there was the "longwall" method, in which a long face of the coal seam is mined at once, allowing the roof to cave in on the area from which the coal has been removed. This is in contrast to the "room and pillar" method commonly employed in this country, in which large blocks, or pillars of coal are allowed to stand between the narrow passageways from which the coal is removed. The pillars may or may not be removed after the passageways have been mined. Most recently there has been introduced into longwall mining an arrangement of roof supports that can move itself, keeping pace with the progress of mining along the seam, and allowing the roof to cave almost up to the working face itself.

In Russia in 1936 a scheme of hydraulic mining was developed in which powerful jets of water erode the coal face, the fine particles of coal being carried by the water to collecting points in the mine. This has proved advantageous in the steeply pitching seams of that country.

In addition to underground mining, coal can be mined by surface methods. The original method, known as "strip mining" because the overlying dirt and rock are stripped away to expose the coal seam, was introduced early in the century. It was not until 1941, however, that strip mining accounted for as much as 10 per cent of the total. The depth to which strip mining can work depends on the size of the shovel used for the stripping. With time, the shovel size gradually increased until, in the 1950's, shovels of gigantic size were built. The more recent machines are capable of digging away a cliff 120 feet tall and moving 140 cubic yards in each shovelful. Costing millions of dollars, these machines are kept working continuously day and night, reaching high levels of efficiency. In 1964 strip mining accounted for 31 per cent of total coal production in the United States; productivity by this method was 29.3 tons per man day.

The latest innovation in surface mining was created in 1945 to deal with the coal still exposed in the cliff face where strip mining has reached its limit. Large, self-contained auger machines drill into the exposed coal seam and convey the coal back to the surface. The productivity in this method is highest of all, exceeding 40 tons per man day. In 1964, 3 per cent of United States coal output was by this method.

Strip mining in this country has also benefitted from the huge machines developed to work the softer, brown-coal deposits such as occur in Germany and Australia. Giant self-propelled machines have been developed in those countries, featuring bucket wheels as the cutting device and conveyor belts extending on long booms to take the coal or spoil to the desired point.

PREPARATION OF COAL

The treatment or "preparation" of coal at the surface has also undergone dramatic improvements. Hand sorting gave way to washing of the coal, and this in turn evolved into complex cleaning and separation processes which removed the impurities and upgraded the product. From less than 10 per cent of United States production in 1932, "prepared" coal has risen to over 60 per cent.

The stimulus for the preparation of coal had a triple origin. As mechanization increased, the product brought to the surface came to contain an increased proportion of impurities; at the same time, the progressive exhaustion of the seams lowest in ash and sulfur, the principal impurities, forced the industry to turn to ever lower quality seams. And in the markets, as coal lost its place as a fuel for heating, railroads, and shipping, power plants became increasingly the most important single market. Intent themselves in maximizing efficiency, they began to buy coal in terms of its contained heat rather than by weight. Finally, since half or more of the delivered price of coal is accounted for by transportation costs, the industry began to appreciate that, as had been stated in one pungent description, "It didn't make sense to haul a lot of dirt around the country." As a result, the coal industry of today no longer merely moves coal from its place in the earth's crust to the transportation facility, but offers for sale a prepared product whose energy content has been concentrated. It has become less a materials handler and more a processor.

COKE

A discussion of the coal industry would not be complete without mention of coke. The coke industry arose to supply steel-makers with the ingredient needed to reduce iron from its ore. To produce coke thousands of beehive ovens, so called because of their shape, were built. In these ovens the volatile constituents of coal were driven off to the atmosphere, in the process wasting the gas and chemical compounds of which they were composed.

In the 1890's by-product furnaces to produce coke and at the same time recover the gas and chemicals had already been built, but progress in the early part of the century was slow as the demand for the by-products grew only slowly. World War I provided the great impetus, with its demand for the by-product chemicals for munitions; as a result, by-product coke production exceeded beehive coke production for the first time in 1919. The ease with which the beehive ovens could be put into and out of production, however, caused them to linger even into World War II, and it was not until after the war that they went into a terminal decline. Nevertheless, even in 1964, almost 2 per cent of coke production still came from beehive ovens.

EXPLORATION AND PRODUCTION OF PETROLEUM

In contrast to coal deposits, most of which had been identified early in the industrial development of a region or country, oil and gas deposits are discovered only through constant search. Discovery is therefore a crucial aspect in the ongoing activity of the oil industry. Although scientific theories of the basis of oil occurrence had been suggested in the 19th century, the search was still conducted on the basis of either visible surface indications of oil or purely at random. Not until 1912 was geologic knowledge applied to the determination of drilling sites. The success of this approach led quickly to its widespread adoption.

In the early 1920's attention shifted from surface to subsurface geology through the use of drill core samples and the application of the sciences of paleontology and mineralogy. In the middle 1920's these were supplemented by the revolutionary application of geophysical techniques employing seismol-

Fig. 16-1. Oil drilling rig, *c.* 1890. (Courtesy of *Standard Oil Company of New Jersey*)

ogy (the study of the transmission of shock waves through the earth), gravimetry, and magnetometry (the studies of minute variations in the force of gravity and the earth's magnetic field, respectively). With these techniques it became possible to identify the large-scale features of the subsurface geology and to indicate the most promising sites to drill.

Since then the record has been one of constant gradual improvement in the use of geophysical techniques, most recently through the application of electronic equipment and computers to process the data obtained thereby, together with an improved ability to detect the presence of hydrocarbons in the rocks penetrated by the drill by lowering specialized instruments down the drill hole.

Nevertheless, the only way of determining for certain whether or not oil or gas occurs beneath a particular spot on the surface remains what it always has been—drilling a hole. The wells of the 19th century were drilled with the cable tool apparatus originally developed for water-well drilling. A heavy bit was repeatedly lifted and dropped, breaking up the rock; periodically the pieces were scooped up and lifted to the surface. This procedure is inefficient, slow, and generally feasible only to depths of a few thousand feet. Yet cable-tool drilling is still used, although it is limited to areas of shallow drilling and suitable rocks.

Around the turn of the century a new method, hydraulic rotary drilling, was introduced and quickly became common. In this method the drill bit is attached to the end of a pipe which is rotated at the surface. Fluid circulates through the pipe and out the bit, returns to the surface in the space around the pipe, carrying the cuttings with it. Since additional lengths of pipe can be added indefinitely, the only limitation on drilling depth is the strength of the pipe and bit and the power that is available.

With the depth limitation removed, the oil industry has probed ever deeper over the years. In 1900 a well of 2000-3000 feet was considered deep, and its drilling was difficult. By 1925 the deepest well drilled was over 7000 feet, and today the record depth is over 25,000 feet. Hundreds of wells are drilled each year below 15,000 feet. This increased capability has been achieved by improvement in every phase of drilling and in all types of equipment involved in it. Stronger steels, greater power, larger derricks, and scientific control of the drilling fluid are all utilized. As a result, the portion of the subsurface environment that can be searched for oil and gas has constantly increased. The export of this technology to the rest of the world has been responsible for the discovery of very large reserves elsewhere.

Along with this has gone the creation of a science of reservoir management. Until the 1930's the industry produced oil and gas in almost total ignorance of the natural forces involved and of their effect on both rate of recovery and total recovery; in the process enormous waste occurred. The famous "gushers" produced oil faster than it could be handled and dissipated the natural reservoir energy before it could produce but a small fraction of the total oil present.

With the increased knowledge of reservoir engineering, the industry subsequent to the 1930's was able to control the rate of production, increase the total recovery, and prevent the waste of both gas and oil. Along with such practices there developed, especially in the period since World War II, the practice of "secondary recovery," in which water or gas is injected into the reservoir to force out oil which previously was unrecoverable. In the past few years this has been supplemented in certain areas by the techniques of steam injection and controlled burning of a portion of the oil in the reservoir, to recover oil too viscous to bring up by conventional means. The secondary recovery techniques have themselves been responsible for the creation of billions of barrels of reserves, and secondary production constitutes an increasing portion of total annual output in the United States.

The improved production techniques have been aided by laws and regulations to prevent the drilling of unnecessary wells and the wasteful production of oil and gas. Unfortunately, the legal provisions have tended to lag behind the ability of the industry to avoid waste, but in the last decade efforts have been made to catch up.

OIL REFINING

As stated earlier, crude oil at the beginning of the century was processed principally for its yield of kerosene for lighting and stove use, although almost as much crude was burned directly as fuel oil as was put through refineries. Kerosene accounted for roughly half the refinery output, gasoline and lubricating oils about 10 per cent each, fuel oils a little more than 10 per cent, and losses 10 per cent or more.

The refining process, done by the batch rather than in a continuous operation, consisted of simple distillation, in which the oil was heated and the various vaporized fractions separately condensed. Refining was thus mere separation rather than conversion, with little flexibility in tailoring the output either to demand or to the highest value products. An important goal of refining was the production of lubricating oils, essential for the new high-speed machinery being adopted by industry.

Although the first decade of the century was marked by the beginnings of continuous processing and improvements in the stills, the first momentous advance occurred with the commercial introduction of thermal "cracking" in 1913. In this process, selected straight-run distillation fractions were further heated under pressure of 75 pounds to "crack" heavy molecules into the lighter molecules of gasoline components. The result not only greatly increased the yield of gasoline but lowered its cost at the very time that the age of the automobile arrived in earnest. By 1920 gasoline accounted for one quarter of refinery output, kerosene only one eighth. Without thermal cracking, the consumption of crude oil would have been one fifth greater for that year.

One of the advantages of cracked gasoline is its superior anti-knock performance, but the limitation on engine performance brought about by even occasional knocking spurred the search for a specific anti-knock agent. The result of this search, which lasted from 1916 until success was achieved by Thomas Midgley in 1921, was the now standard tetraethyl lead anti-knock compound, and "premium" gasoline was born.

Although no other refining advances were as spectacular as the solution of the knocking problem, there was general progress on all fronts. Fractionation became better, yielding finer and cleaner separation of the products of distillation, and thermal cracking improved. Refining was changing in the direction of a chemical process undertaken by trained professionals rather than a manufacturing process managed by rule of thumb. At the same time, the growth of cracking and the use of petroleum products as the raw materials for the chemicals of World War I munitions generated the realization that crude oil could also constitute the basis for what is now called the petrochemical industry. The beginnings of that industry can be said to date from World War I.

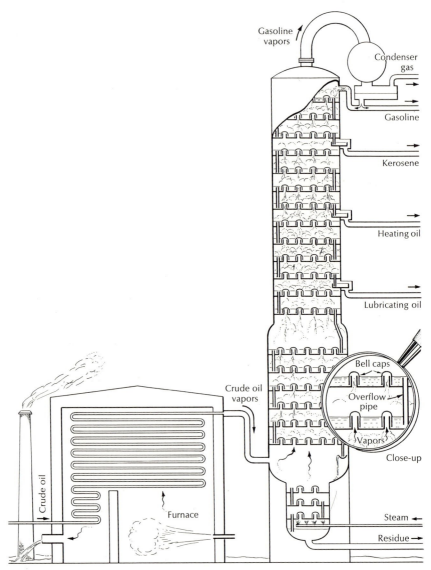

Fig. 16-2. Initial petroleum distillation takes place in tall fractionating towers. The crude oil, heated to about 800° F, is largely vapor when it enters the tower and it thus rises through holes in horizontal trays. These vapors are cooled as they rise, making various fractions condense, which are withdrawn from the trays as liquids. Because some liquid from each tray drops to the tray below through overflow pipes, parts of it may be revaporized to rise again. The bell caps over the openings in the trays aid condensation. The heaviest fractions collect in the bottom of the tower and, depending on the crude, become

By the mid-1930's the art of thermal cracking had reached its greatest height but the inexorable demands for higher octane fuel in the horsepower race in automotive engines called forth a new important advance: catalytic cracking. Not only did the use of a catalyst permit the cracking of much heavier fractions, but the yield was a much higher octane gasoline. Eugene Houdry developed (1930-35) the first commercially practicable catalytic cracking system for petroleum. Introduced in 1937, catalytic cracking was quickly improved to a continuous process. The use of catalysts was investigated on a wide front, and it became apparent that the refining industry was creating the ability to break apart, recombine, and manipulate hydrocarbon molecules at will. The realization of this ability was accelerated by the demands of World War II for 100-octane gasoline and a host of petrochemical products, including a spectacular new one, synthetic rubber.

At the close of World War II the refining industry was already what it is to-day—a chemical industry using petroleum hydrocarbons as its raw material and producing to tailored specifications not only the traditional fuels and petroleum products but a wide range of petrochemicals from plants closely integrated with the refineries. In 1964 the composition of refinery output was as follows:

Gasoline	44 per cent	Petrochemical	3 per cent
Kerosene	5 per cent	feedstocks	
Fuel oils	36 per cent	Other	12 per cent

Volume losses had largely been eliminated, and because of the supplementation of crude oil with other hydrocarbons and hydrogen, the refineries produced about 2 per cent over a barrel of products for every barrel of crude oil processed. Residual oil, the untreatable bugaboo of the early refiner, had disappeared at most refineries; the refiner was like the meat-packer, who had learned to use everything but the squeal.

It should be noted that the story of refining technology elsewhere in the world is not, like that of exploration and production technology, nearly identical with that in the United States. Refinery operation is tailored to the demand pattern for petroleum products and, since the major demand elsewhere has traditionally been for heating oils, the emphasis on ever higher gasoline yields and ever higher octane ratings was not present. As a consequence, refiners elsewhere have adopted whatever advances were profitable, but their product mix has continued to be more like that of the United States in earlier decades of this century. Only in the past few years, with the rise of the automotive population in Europe, has there been a trend toward paralleling current United

---

asphalt, heavy fuel oil, or heavy lubricating oil. Other fractions will become lubricating oil, heating oil, kerosene, and gasoline. These fractions, in turn, are further processed and refined. (*Standard Oil Company of New Jersey*)

States patterns. Nevertheless, residual oil still remains an important product of most foreign refineries.

NATURAL GAS

The story of natural gas technology is really the story of a specialized transportation technology—the development of long-distance, large-diameter, high-pressure pipelines. Until the late 1920's the transportation of natural gas was by means of small-diameter pipe joined together with screw couplings. The high cost of the great construction effort involved in laying a pipeline, together with the limited capacity of the pipeline itself, limited the distance over which gas could be economically transported to 250-300 miles. As a result, enormous quantities of natural gas discovered over the years remained largely unused except for such low-value use as burning to make carbon black. Other large quantities of gas associated with oil were wholly wasted by being blown to the air or burned in flares.

About the time of the Great Depression, however, the art of welding was applied to pipeline joints, and seamless pipes of large diameter and high strength began to be manufactured. At the same time, the work of digging the trench for the pipeline and handling the pipe itself began to be mechanized. By the mid-1930's it was possible to transport gas economically for 1000 miles. Although some longer lines were laid, it remained for the "Big Inch" and "Little Big Inch" of World War II to demonstrate unequivocally the practicability of long-distance, large-scale pipeline transmission. These lines, 24 and 20 inches in diameter, respectively, were laid by the government from the southwestern oil fields to the northeast as a defense measure to relieve the burden on tanker transport of petroleum.

At the close of the war these lines were purchased for natural gas transmission, and the great gas boom began. In 1945 there were 77,000 miles of main line transmission pipeline; by 1963 there were 200,000 miles. Along with this expansion came an explosive growth in construction technology that completely mechanized the laying of the pipeline and greatly reduced costs. At present lines of 40-inch diameter can be constructed, and pressures above 1000 pounds are used to move the gas.

The pipeline boom also revolutionized gas consumption. By 1955 all but two states were served by natural gas. Offered a heat content twice that of manufactured gas at a much lower price, most of the great urban population centers converted *en masse* from the use of gas for cooking only to gas for house heating as well. Gas was also fed to power stations and found industrial applications on a large scale. The gas industry then changed from local production of an expensive product for a limited market to mass marketing of a cheap and abundant fuel.

Since pipeline technology could not cope with the problems of long-distance transmission across large bodies of water, the development of a natural gas industry was confined to those countries with both large gas deposits and large centers of demand—the United States, Canada, and the Soviet Union. Elsewhere gas continued to be unused or wasted. In 1959, however, a new revolutionary technique appeared—the transportation of liquefied gas by tanker. Through cooling of the gas to a temperature of $-260°F$ it becomes liquid at atmospheric pressure, with a volume reduction by a factor of 600. The technique was first applied to transport gas from Algeria to England in 1964; and it is possible that eventually gas will be transported all over the world, much as is oil. In the United States the liquefied-gas technique is being applied to underground storage as a solution to the problem of storing a product which takes up so much space.

ELECTRIC POWER

At the beginning of the 20th century electric power, with two decades of commercial existence behind it, already exhibited the essentials of the modern power system. The direct current system had become limited to the central business district of cities. Elsewhere the alternating current system was established, together with the necessary transformers and switching gear. Suitable motors had been developed for a wide variety of uses, so that almost 200,000 horsepower of electric power capacity could be installed in factories. In homes with electricity the dominant use was still for lighting, but it had limited use in such appliances as hot plates, irons, and fans, and occasionally even in heating.

There were, nevertheless, still large obstacles to overcome. Home use was largely confined to the towns and cities; the great rural hinterland was still without electricity because of the very high distribution costs associated with low population density, and was to remain that way until the federal government's Rural Electrification Administration program of the 1930's. In the factory there was little reason to electrify, so that only five per cent of total factory horsepower was in the form of electric motors. After all, factories had their own mechanical power plants, and the use of mechanical power had been developed to a high art. Thus, paradoxically, the small factories, who could not generate mechanical power as efficiently as the larger ones, first found the small electric motor attractive.

GENERATION OF ELECTRICITY

Electricity generation was no model of efficiency, however. In most cases steam engines merely ran dynamos rather than machines directly. Boilers were the same as those used for supplying other steam engines (although automatic

Fig. 16-3. Steam turbines in an electrical generating plant. (Courtesy of *Westinghouse Electric Corporation*)

stokers were developed early in the century), and the engines themselves were the same as those used elsewhere for mechanical power. Then, about 1900, a major advance in electrical generation occurred with the introduction of the steam turbine, a high-speed machine immensely more efficient and less bulky than the conventional reciprocating steam engine.

Almost at once the turbine began to demonstrate the outstanding economic characteristic of electrical power generation and transmission, the reduction of unit cost with larger size, known to economists as "economies of scale." It was the greater economy of the larger turbines that eroded the original cost advantage to the manufacturer of generating his own electricity.

Along with the opportunities for greater economic efficiency through larger size were those for greater physical efficiency through higher steam temperature and pressures, as established in the laws of thermodynamics. The history of generation technology in this century is thus a history of progress on the two fronts of size and pressure-temperature conditions. Unit and station size, temperature and pressure all increased with the accumulation of experience, the development of improved materials and techniques, and the growth in power consumption within the separate power systems. In the first decade of the century a generating unit of 25,000-kw capacity was large, and pressures and temperatures up to 200-300 pounds and 400-500°F, respectively, were employed. In the 1920's units over 100,000 kw in size were being introduced, and by 1930 the largest unit was 208,000 kw, and the highest pressure in use was 1200 pounds, with a temperature of 725°F.

In the 1930's there was a brief period of experimentation using mercury in place of steam, but the increased efficiency was not sufficient to offset the higher capital costs. Conventional steam technology continued to advance, on the other hand, and in the post-World War II period the new levels of power consumption contributed to an acceleration of the advance in size and pressure-temperature conditions. The 208,000-kw maximum size was finally exceeded by a 260,000-kw unit in 1956. In 1957 an especially significant breakthrough occurred in the "supercritical" range of temperature and pressure, making possible new efficiency gains. By 1963 the largest unit on order was over one million kw, and the most advanced pressure-temperature conditions in use were 5000 pounds and 1200°F.

The course of this constant improvement was reflected dramatically in the measure of the efficiency—the pounds of coal needed to produce a kilowatt-hour of electricity—and in the price per kwh, as rates were reduced to keep pace with declining unit costs. From 7 pounds per kwh in 1902 the coal requirement declined to 0.86 pounds in the United States in 1964. The average price for all residential use in 1902 was 16.2¢ per kwh, compared with 2.31¢ in 1964, and this despite the cumulative effect of inflation over the period.

TRANSMISSION OF ELECTRIC POWER

The economies of scale in power transmission operate through both the quantity of energy and the distance over which it is transmitted. The capacity of a line varies roughly with the square of the voltage and decreases proportionately with distance. At a given distance, doubling the voltage increases capacity roughly four times; transmission efficiency also increases. In the early years of the century, with power stations situated near load centers and loads themselves small, there was little incentive to go to very high voltages, although a 155-mile line at 110,000 volts was put in operation in California in 1908.

As loads grew, transmission voltages settled at several established levels between 100,000 and 230,000 volts. This upper limit held until the Hoover Dam project of the 1930's, which utilized 287,000 volts on a 300-mile line. A level of 345,000 volts was reached in 1954 and has since become established as the "standard" high voltage, with higher voltages termed "extra high voltage" (EHV). At this level the economic distance limit under most conditions is 300-350 miles.

In the 1950's a new wave of technical advance began with the installation of a 400,000-volt, 600-mile line in Sweden in 1952, made necessary by the

Fig. 16-4. View of substation for a 750,000-volt test project. (Courtesy of *Westinghouse Electric Corporation*)

long distances between the load centers and the good power sites. This was fol-lowed in 1961 by the use of 500,000 volts in the USSR. Not until 1965 was this voltage put into use in the United States, but this new "standard" EHV for large projects will undoubtedly be surpassed shortly. Indeed, even higher volt-ages of 700,000 to one million volts are called for on lines scheduled for com-pletion in the late 1960's.

At distances over 450 miles or so direct current becomes an economic alter-native to the traditional alternating current mode of transmission. The USSR began experimental use of a high-voltage d.c. transmission line in 1962 and has scheduled it for eventual operation at 800,000 volts. In the United States two direct current, 750,000-volt lines over 800 miles long are scheduled to tie the Pacific Northwest with the Pacific Southwest by 1971.

HYDROPOWER

No account of power technology would be complete without mention of the use of falling water for electricity generation. The mechanical use of water power was, of course, centuries old by the time electric power appeared. The logic of applying a water wheel to turning a dynamo was readily apparent and, depending on the relative availability and cost of fuels, hydropower has since accounted for varying proportions of total electricity production in different countries. Even in this country, with its abundant endowment of fossil-fuel resources (coal, petroleum, and gas), hydropower has averaged some 30 per cent of our total annual *electricity* production throughout most of this century.

The history of technological advance in hydropower has been one of constant improvement in water-wheel design, to attain the present incredible efficiencies of better than 90 per cent; advances in the design of the large structures—especially the dams—that are involved; and progress in construction techniques. The result has been a progressive lowering of construction and operating costs and the increased ability to develop hydropower sites previously uneconomical. Since World War II a tendency has developed to regard hydropower installations less as "base-load" plants available for steady generation and more as "peaking" plants operated intermittently to meet daily and seasonal peaks in power demand. Thus, in this country the proportion of total power supplied from hydropower has declined to about 20 per cent. This tendency was greatly stimulated in 1950 by the introduction of the reversible pump-turbine and motor-generation on a single shaft, which led to rapid adoption of the technique of "pumped storage."

Fig. 16-5. A hydroelectric generator at Grand Coulee Dam. (Courtesy of *Westinghouse Electric Corporation*)

This new technique employs two reservoirs at different elevations. During periods of low demand the surplus thermal power capacity of a system is used to pump water to the higher reservoir; during peak demand the water is released to generate power, as in a conventional hydro installation. Despite the fact that only 2 kwh are produced for every 3 kwh used in pumping, pumped storage can offer an economical means of providing peak generating capacity. Although several score pumped-storage units had been installed in Europe in earlier decades, the technique suffered from the need to provide separate pumps and turbines. The 1950 innovation consisted of making the blades on the water wheel reversible so that, with the generator acting as a motor, the unit could be used to pump. The cost saving this provided opened entirely new opportunities for pumped storage, and the technique has spread rapidly. The special significance of pumped storage is that both reservoirs can be entirely artificial, enabling it to be installed even where there is no existing stream. This siting flexibility has also contributed to its rapid adoption.

ELECTRICAL SYSTEM OPERATION

Along with the aforementioned progress in power technology there has been improvement in the technique of electrical system planning and operation. The size of the system limits the size of the individual units and stations that can be introduced because of the need to maintain maximum reliability of service. As the number of systems grew it became the practice to provide interconnections for emergency use; these connections also came to be used for the interchange of surplus "economy" power between systems. At the close of World War II, however, the power industry of the United States still consisted, for the most part, of many relatively small, independent systems.

It is no coincidence that in the postwar period acceleration in the growth of the unit and station size and in voltage has occurred to match the growth in demand. Not only have the number of interconnections greatly increased, their manner of use also changed. Increasingly, interconnections have been used to form "power pools" in which two or more systems plan the joint installation of new generating facilities, the output to be shared via the interconnections. The greater capacity of the pooled systems thus enables the new facilities to be larger than any single system could justify. Most recently there has also been a trend toward the widespread adoption of the fullest use of such pooling in which the daily operation makes use of the pool as a whole, permitting the generating, at any one time, of power from the lowest cost facilities in the pool.

This trend is continuing, as more and more pools are being considered in terms of integration rather than mere interconnection. Inter-pool ties are now being constructed (namely, the Pacific Northwest-Southwest inter-ties referred to above). It is now probable that sometime in the 1970's the United States will have complete interconnection of its major geographical regions, leading to still larger amounts of power interchange, higher voltages, and larger new facilities—all with consequent economies. Finally, the complexities of these pools and supersystems and their operations, which already require the use of computers, are also leading to the eventual use of computer control of daily operation, again with new economies. The dangers of pooling were, however, dramatically demonstrated in the fall of 1965 when a considerable part of the northeastern section of the United States, as well as a part of Canada, was blacked out by a failure in one part of the system.

The preceding pages have traced the course of developments in the technologies of fuels and electricity in this century, with emphasis limited, by and large, to a description of those developments. It remains to consider the implications and significance of the changes described, not merely within each subject area, but for society and the economy as a whole.

Consider first the current consumption pattern of energy in contrast to that of 1900. In the United States in 1960 crude oil accounted for 39 per cent of total energy consumption; natural gas and natural gas liquids, another 33 per cent. Petroleum hydrocarbons have thus replaced coal as the dominant energy source, accounting for almost three quarters of the total. Coal consumption has been cut to a quarter of the total, with hydroelectricity still a minor percentage. The contribution of wood was insignificant. Of total energy consumption, 20 per cent was for the generation of electricity. Elsewhere in the world, coal has remained predominant—although it is increasingly being replaced by oil—and gas is still a minor component.

These shifts in the consumption pattern in this country occurred at the same time that total energy consumption increased four and three-quarters times. This increase so far exceeded population growth that energy consumption per head doubled. The growth in energy consumption, in other words, was not due merely to national growth but also to the more intensive use of energy. Thus it can be said that the changes in both the level and pattern of energy consumption were made possible by the technological progress described above.

Specifically, the relation between technological advance and energy use can be identified as follows: (1) with respect to oil and gas, the first effect was on discovery. The resources which currently supply our needs were unknown and, indeed, unsuspected half a century ago. As previous discoveries were consumed, advances in the art of discovery more than kept pace with the need for additional resources; also (2) as the environment was searched to ever greater depth, improved drilling and production techniques (including higher recovery efficiency) enabled these deeper resources to be made available at no higher cost. Finally (3) advances in petroleum processing provided the liquid fuels and lubricants for the age of internal combustion in land, sea, and air transportation. The change in crude oil from an illuminant to a liquid fuel resource constitutes the most dramatic example in history of the adaptation of a resource to a totally different use.

With respect to gas the implications of discovery and production improvements noted above are equally applicable. In addition, the development of the art of long-distance pipeline transportation brought the householder throughout the United States the ideal fuel for home use at competitive prices and brought industry a new fuel in competition with the others.

In the coal industry, after economic vicissitudes that included a severe loss of markets and a large increase in labor costs, technological progress brought about a delayed but eventual triumph over the latter and an adjustment to a wholly new market situation. In 1964 the bituminous coal industry in the United States produced twice as much coal as in 1900 with fewer than half as many men. In addition, technology also managed to overcome a decline in resource quality to yield a product that is in some respects superior.

The uninterrupted record of progress in the power industry constitutes another triumph of greater efficiency, and the introduction of electricity into industry led, in turn, to the most far-reaching efficiency gains of all. With the use of the electric motor the efficiency of power use in manufacturing rose sevenfold or more. Still further, the change from central mechanical power transmitted by belts and shafting to electric motors mounted on each individual machine, together with electrical control equipment, brought to manufacturing new flexibility in plant layout and operations and made possible the adoption of modern techniques of industrial and business management.

At the resource level, the evolution of technology in the energy industries created energy resources that were previously either unknown or unusable. At the same time, improved efficiency in recovery, processing, and use in effect created other new resources by reducing resource needs below what they otherwise would have been. In this respect technology has been called "the great multiplier."

The other side of the coin is the development of the tendency to use energy in secondary (for example, gasoline or kerosene) and tertiary (as electricity) forms. Because of the inevitable loss of energy in converting from one form to another this consumption requires a greater total energy. In terms of raw energy needs the system is less efficient, but overall efficiency of energy utilization is greater than it used to be because of the high levels of conversion and use efficiency that have been achieved.

FUTURE SOURCES OF ENERGY

Although continued further progress along the lines of past advance sketched here can be expected in the future, possible revolutionary changes also appear in the offing. There is, for one thing, nuclear power, discussed in the next chapter. In addition, there are other potentials for producing electricity directly that can be given only brief mention. One is the fuel cell, in which a gaseous or liquid fuel is consumed without a flame, thereby producing electricity; another is thermoelectricity, a process by which heat applied to a semi-conductor material (such as transistors are made of) yields electricity directly. Still a third is magnetohydrodynamics (MHD), a process which yields electricity by the movement of ionized gas through a magnetic field.

These three devices or processes directly produce direct current electricity using no moving parts or any mechanical energy. Partly because of this, MHD and the fuel cell offer much higher possible efficiencies than can be attained with conventional generating methods. Although research continues on all three, there have been some isolated semi-commercial applications of the fuel cell and thermoelectricity. And while it is too early to say what their future will be, the following opportunities exist: for the fuel cell, powering lift trucks, tractors, and perhaps even automobiles; for thermoelectricity, auxiliary generating units on furnaces, perhaps even home furnaces; for MHD, auxiliary generating units in large power plants as a means of greatly increasing overall power generation efficiency.

Mention should also be made of unconventional energy resources that may be on the verge of exploitation. One such is shale oil, derived from rocks that occur in immense quantity in western Colorado and adjacent states. The hydrocarbon content of these rocks, present in solid form, can be freed from the rock as a liquid, reduced in viscosity, and then processed in a conventional oil refinery to produce the whole range of petroleum products. The shale-oil resources of this country are several times the known crude-oil reserves of the entire world. Pilot-plant production is scheduled to begin within the next few years, and it is likely that in the decades to come this resource will eventually become an important supplement to crude oil.

A second resource is "tar sand," a rock containing a tar-like bituminous substance that can be extracted and processed in a conventional oil refinery to yield petroleum products. Extensive deposits occur in Saskatchewan, Canada, and commercial exploitation is about to be attempted. Again, these resources are the equivalent of several times the known world oil reserves. Both resources, incidentally, as well as coal, can also be processed to yield synthetic gas of the same composition as natural gas, although at present such an operation would be wholly uneconomic.

The development of these new sources for energy and the increasing exploitation and more efficient utilization of older sources indicate how greatly the energy picture has changed during the first two thirds of the 20th century. Coal was dominant at the beginning of the century, and there seemed to be but a limited amount of it which could be used without increasing costs. Indeed, some "viewers with alarm" calculated that the supply of easily mineable coal would run out during the century, and the world would be depleted of its low-cost energy resources. At the beginning of the final third of the century, however, there is every confidence that man can continue to meet his energy requirements indefinitely.

17 / Man Harnesses the Atom
RICHARD G. HEWLETT

Among the several potential supplements to fossil and hydroelectric power sources, nuclear energy is among the most attractive. The development of nuclear energy illustrates several trends in the history of technology: the shrinking interval between a discovery in theoretical science and its practical application; the blurring of traditional distinctions between scientific and technological disciplines; and the increasingly important role of the federal government in fostering scientific and technological advance. It also demonstrates the age-old way in which scientific ideas, conceived in peace, are quickly applied to military purposes under the impetus of war, and then find new civilian uses in peacetime.

Atomic energy, first harnessed in the open conflict of World War II and further exploited in the ensuing Cold War, has yet to fulfill its larger promise. Yet, within the brief span of thirty years, much has been accomplished.

Early in 1947 Enrico Fermi, the renowned nuclear physicist, spoke before a group of American college students about the revolution which had occurred in the physical sciences during World War II. Fermi recalled with some nostalgia those exciting days in Europe during the mid-1930's when the few dozen men and women who made up the international community of physicists freely exchanged experimental data with no concern about the impact of such information on politics or human affairs. By 1947 the devastation suffered by Hiroshima and Nagasaki made it unnecessary for Fermi to convince his listeners that the fate of mankind might well lie in the hands of scientists and engineers rather than statesmen or soldiers; the story of the atom during World War II (1939-45) made it seem so.

FISSION AND THE CHAIN REACTION

One of the first steps in this technological and military revolution was the stunning news from Berlin late in 1938 that two German scientists, Otto Hahn and

Fritz Strassman, had discovered a radioactive barium isotope among the products resulting from their bombardment of uranium with neutrons. The appearance of barium, a relatively light element in the middle range of the periodic table, suggested that the impinging neutrons had not just dislodged a few particles from the uranium nucleus but had in fact split it almost in two. Since the total mass of the resulting fragments was significantly less than that of the original uranium nucleus, anyone acquainted with the work of Albert Einstein could conclude that the process released a large amount of energy. Furthermore, experiments in several countries soon demonstrated that each fissioning uranium nucleus, in turn, emitted an average of two or more neutrons which theoretically were capable of splitting other uranium nuclei, thus initiating a chain reaction of fissions which might produce energy.

No one, however, understood better than the nuclear physicists the distance that separated the theory from practical demonstration. For a time it seemed that the more physicists learned about fission, the less promising were the hopes of harnessing the energy of the atom. Fermi soon discovered that unless the neutrons emitted by the fissioning uranium nuclei were slowed down or "moderated" by inelastic collisions with very light atoms, most of them would be absorbed by uranium nuclei or other elements without causing fission. Fermi and Leo Szilard at Columbia University decided to use high-purity graphite as a moderator while Hans von Halban and Lew Kowarski, two scientists who had fled from France to England, were planning to use the heavy-hydrogen isotope, deuterium, a quantity of which they had smuggled from occupied France in the form of "heavy" water (so called because it contained more of the heavy hydrogen isotope, deuterium, than ordinary water).

URANIUM 235 AND PLUTONIUM

Even had the physicists possessed sufficient quantities of uranium and a moderator (which they did not before the end of 1942), they were not certain that they could at that time establish the chain reaction. For example, like many elements found in nature, uranium exists as a mixture of several isotopes, and they did not know which of the isotopes would best lend itself to the fission process. Not until March 1940 did John R. Dunning and his associates at Columbia University demonstrate that the uranium-235 isotope, which constitutes less than one per cent of natural uranium, and not the relatively plentiful 238 isotope, was readily fissionable with slow neutrons. With luck, the scientists thought, it might be possible by assembling sufficiently large stocks of uranium and a moderator to sustain a chain reaction with the uranium 235 present in natural uranium. Fermi, for one, feared that it might first be necessary to separate the uranium isotopes, a difficult task not ordinarily possible using chemical means, but to be done rather by a physical process that would be sensitive to the relatively small difference in the atomic weights of the two isotopes. Thinking in these terms, American physicists conceded in the summer of 1940 that it might be possible to build a "pile" of graphite interspersed with lumps of uranium metal that might produce thermal energy. However, the idea of using such an assembly, weighing hundreds of tons, as a military weapon seemed too remote for serious consideration.

Yet within a year prospects improved, both for the chain reaction and the weapon. In Great Britain, Rudolph Peierls and his associates concluded that the uranium-235 isotope would fission with fast as well as slow neutrons. Thus it was thought possible to produce a chain reaction in a small mass of reasonably pure uranium 235 without incorporating the additional weight of uranium 238 or a moderator, and to produce a device that would fall within the dimensions of a practical weapon with extraordinary destructive power. Furthermore, the British scientists became convinced by laboratory experiments that they could separate the isotopes on a large scale by diffusing a gaseous compound of uranium through a series of porous membranes or barriers. Since the lighter uranium-235 atoms tended to pass through the barrier more easily than the 238, relatively pure 235 could be isolated by pumping the gas through a very large number of barriers.

In the United States, an entirely different approach offered a means of avoiding the difficult problem of isotope separation. In February 1941, Glenn T. Seaborg and others at the University of California, Berkeley, succeeded in identifying a new man-made element of atomic number 94, which was named "plutonium." In May 1941, Seaborg reported that plutonium was even more readily fissionable than uranium 235 by slow neutrons. Plutonium could be created by the non-fission absorption of neutrons in uranium 238. It was thus conceivable that the uranium 235 in a pile of natural uranium might be used to sustain the chain reaction while the uranium 238 was transmuted into plutonium, which could be isolated by chemical means for use in an atomic weapon.

NUCLEAR WEAPONS

Ironically, the secrecy restrictions invoked as the military implications of atomic energy became more obvious prevented both the Americans and the British from learning for many months what the other nation had accomplished. Not until late in 1941 did scientists in both nations understand the significance of the fast-neutron reaction and the possibility of creating plutonium in a chain-reacting pile. This realization, plus the United States entry into World War II on December 7, 1941, spurred a series of decisions which resulted in a large-scale effort in the United States to explore, with British help, both the uranium-235 and the plutonium routes to an atomic weapon.

In what the Anglo-American alliance conceived to be a desperate race against the Germans for the atomic bomb, most of the initial speculation about peaceful uses of atomic power had been laid aside for the duration of the war. The promising early accomplishments of the French had been negated by the fall of France and the dispersal of most of the French team to England and then to Canada. Little was known of the Soviet atomic energy program, but there were indications that an effective and energetic team of scientists under Igor V. Kurchatov had made great strides in exploring the fission reaction and in investigating the gaseous diffusion process before the pressures of war diverted their talents to more immediate scientific problems in the summer of 1941.

Although World War II obliterated all research directly related to the development of nuclear power, the accomplishments in the United States during the war years constituted a substantial advance in nuclear technology. The army's Manhattan Project, with the help of scientists at Columbia University, the University of California at Berkeley, and other institutions, successfully transformed not merely one, but three different principles of isotope separation into production plants at Oak Ridge, Tennessee. All three contributed uranium 235 to the weapon dropped on Hiroshima in August 1945. The gaseous diffusion plant, once the technology of fabricating the barrier had been mastered, operated far better than its designers dared to hope. As a result, isotope separation no longer posed a limitation on postwar plans for using the uranium-235 isotope for nuclear power production.

THE FERMI PILE

The heart of any nuclear power effort is the atomic "pile," or reactor, as it came to be called by the end of the war. The reactor was a cardinal achievement of the Manhattan Project. Beginning in early 1942 with small stacks of uranium oxide and commercial-grade graphite, Fermi studied neutron multiplication from an independent neutron source, first at Columbia University and later at the University of Chicago. Not until late in November did Fermi and his team have enough metallic uranium and pure graphite to attempt a truly self-sustaining chain reaction. Finally, however, on December 2, 1942, in the presence of members of a review committee appointed to determine the fate of the plutonium project, Fermi succeeded in producing the world's first nuclear chain reaction.

This first nuclear reactor, built under the football stadium (Stagg Field) at the University of Chicago, was little more than a laboratory demonstration of the theory of the fission chain reaction; but though the reactor had no practical significance for the production of either bombs or nuclear power, it did provide basic information for the design of six other reactors, all graphite-moderated, built during World War II. Three of these large plutonium-production reactors, located at Hanford, Washington, were central to the war effort and to postwar

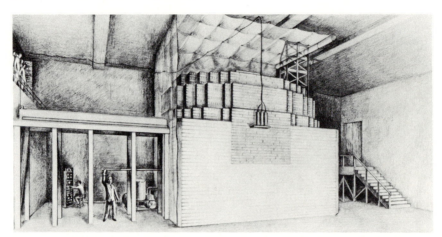

Fig. 17-1. Sketch of the world's first nuclear reactor built at Stagg Field, University of Chicago. The reactor was composed of layers of graphite interspersed with uranium, and achieved a self-sustained chain reaction on December 2, 1942, when the 57th layer was added. This gave rise to the early name for the reactor: "pile," because of piling one layer on another. (Courtesy of *Argonne National Laboratory*)

developments. The Hanford reactors not only produced the plutonium for the first weapon device tested at Alamogordo, New Mexico, on July 16, 1945, and for the weapon dropped on Nagasaki, but they also provided valuable experience in the continuous operation of relatively large reactors. Even so, this experience contributed little toward the peacetime uses of nuclear power. Although the Hanford reactors, with their huge water-cooling systems, were designed to operate at 250,000 kilowatts, the operating temperature was too low to make power generation attractive, and the emphasis remained on plutonium production until the war was won. At that time the technical feasibility of producing power through nuclear energy could be seriously explored.

PROSPECTS FOR NUCLEAR POWER

The first use of atomic weapons in the summer of 1945 brought four years of global warfare to a dramatic end for the United States. American scientists, already impatient with military security restrictions and the regimentation of government laboratories, turned to plans for controlling the use of this dismaying new force they had helped to create. They provided leadership in efforts to achieve realistic international controls of atomic energy and, through a variety of committees, offered the government helpful advice on the postwar development of atomic power. Foremost in their thinking was the idea that the worldwide image of atomic energy as an instrument of war could be transformed into a symbol of peace by harnessing the atom for civilian purposes.

Although the possibility of using heat energy from the nuclear reactor to drive electrical generators was evident in the water-cooled systems at Hanford, the translation of that concept into hardware proved much more difficult than many had expected. Sensational newspaper accounts hastily written during the exciting summer of 1945 gave the general public reason to believe that free electric power and automobiles operated with an atomic pill in the fuel tank would be realities within a few years. Responsible advisers to the government, on the other hand, saw economic nuclear power at least twenty-five years in the future, but there were scientists and engineers associated with the Manhattan Project who thought they saw in certain reactor designs a short-cut to a convincing demonstration of the feasibility of nuclear power.

THE ATOMIC ENERGY COMMISSION

Many of the obstacles, as it turned out, were administrative. The Manhattan Project had been organized to produce fissionable materials and nuclear weapons; it possessed no legal or practical means for fostering power reactor projects. Although there seemed to be general agreement within the United States that the government would have to control all aspects of atomic energy activity, at least until effective international controls were established, the main outlines of a national policy emerged only after a year of congressional debate, which culminated in the Atomic Energy Act adopted on August 1, 1946.

The act created an Atomic Energy Commission of five members, with absolute authority over all source materials, fissionable materials, equipment for utilizing these materials (including weapons and reactors), and all related technical information. Until the Commission could formulate its own policy and develop new programs, there could be little progress in developing nuclear power systems. That initial process took almost two years. In the meantime, several projects organized in the Manhattan laboratories to explore possible power reactor systems foundered and died.

SHORTAGE OF SOURCE MATERIALS

There was an element of truth in the complaints from the laboratories that the lack of policy direction from Washington crippled the modest power reactor projects which had developed in the laboratories in 1945 and 1946. But from the Commission's point of view, there was reason for delay and even for inaction. To be sure, the Commission shared with the scientists the desire to demonstrate the peaceful side of the atom in a power reactor; at the same time there were convincing arguments against hasty action. Most important was the extreme shortage of source materials for atomic energy projects. The war effort had depended almost entirely on uranium ores from the Belgian Congo and northern Canada. Since there were no known high-grade reserves in the United States, existing production facilities would have to rely on these foreign sources of supply. Even if these foreign sources could be assured for the immediate future, they could not be expected to furnish more than the minimal needs of the existing plants.

In light of the worsening international situation in late 1947 and the emergence of the Cold War in 1948, the Commission found it impossible to divert its slender stocks of fissionable material from weapons to power reactors. The Commission's General Advisory Committee, which included among its members such distinguished scientists as Fermi, J. Robert Oppenheimer, James B. Conant, and Isidore I. Rabi, concurred in this opinion. In a public statement early in 1948 urging a cautious approach to nuclear power, the committee noted that "the first instances of the generation and uses of heat or power are likely to be on a small scale and be uneconomical. Further development may increase the scale without substantially improving the economy, and many steps surely lie between the present and the ultimate future in which atomic power is possible, economical, practical, and abundant." Nothing would be gained by demonstrating the simple fact that heat from an atomic reactor could be used to turn an electrical generator. Achieving economical, practical, and abundant nuclear power would depend upon a sound technological base, which had been neither the objective nor the result of the war program.

THE 1948 POWER REACTOR PLAN

The Commission's first reactor development plan, formulated in 1948, reflected this kind of reasoning. First, the emphasis would be on technical feasibility rather than a simple demonstration of nuclear power generation. Second, in recognition of the severe shortage of fissionable material, the Commission would give priority to power-breeder designs.

The theoretical possibility of breeding had been evident in Fermi's earliest studies of the fission chain reaction. If, on the average, slightly more than two neutrons were emitted from each fissioning uranium nucleus, one neutron could be used to continue the chain reaction. A second could be captured by a uranium-238 nucleus to produce an atom of plutonium, thus replacing the original atom of fissionable uranium 235. The occasional third neutron by the same process could produce an additional atom of plutonium. If a reactor could be built to achieve this kind of neutron economy, it might be possible to use the chain reaction to generate power and at the same time to produce more fissionable material than was consumed.

It was not surprising, then, that the Commission's 1948 plan authorized the development of two breeder reactors, one operating with very high-energy or "fast" neutrons, the other with neutrons at energies intermediate between "fast" and "slow." The fast-breeder concept was primarily the creation of Walter H. Zinn, one of Fermi's wartime assistants who became director of the Commission's Argonne National Laboratory near Chicago in 1946. The intermediate power breeder was originally conceived by a group of scientists led by Harvey Brooks at the General Electric Company's laboratories in Schenectady, New York.

To broaden the base of reactor technology, the Commission also authorized the development of a Materials Testing Reactor. This facility was to be designed to produce a very high flux of neutrons in the reactor core, which would be accessible by means of numerous ports and channels for the insertion of test materials. Irradiation in this intense flux for short periods would subject proposed reactor materials and components to the equivalent of years of neutron bombardment in power reactors.

The difficulties encountered in building these first experimental reactors in the years following 1948 amply demonstrated the obstacles in the path of successful power reactor development. To be sure, such sophisticated research as measuring the fission or capture probabilities in uranium for neutrons at various energies was necessary to prove that optimum breeding ratios would be obtained with fast rather than intermediate-energy neutrons, but most of the questions had little to do with nuclear physics. The realization that reactors of the type contemplated in these experiments could not be built at existing Commission installations delayed the start of construction for almost a year until a site had been selected for the National Reactor Testing Station in central Idaho in 1949.

Just as prosaic were the problems Zinn's team encountered in developing the components for the fast breeder. Because many commercial manufacturers were unwilling or unable to fabricate components to the specifications required for reactor use, the Argonne staff itself designed and built many of the fast-breeder components or endured long delays in procurement. Partly as a result of such difficulties the Experimental Breeder Reactor No. 1 (as the fast breeder was called) did not begin operation until August 24, 1951. Four months later, on December 20, 1951, EBR-1 became the first nuclear reactor to produce a significant amount of electric power. Later, careful analysis of uranium 235 from the reactor core and uranium 238 from the surrounding "blanket," in which plutonium was formed, convinced Zinn and his associates that EBR-1 had verified the principle of breeding. The Intermediate Power Breeder Reactor, a victim of more detailed studies of the neutron spectrum in uranium, was never built.

Like the fast breeder, the design of the Materials Testing Reactor had been conceived during the closing years of World War II. Eugene P. Wigner, the

Fig. 17-2. A view of the Experimental Breeder Reactor at the National Reactor Testing Station, Idaho. (Courtesy of *Lookout Mountain Laboratory*)

renowned theoretical physicist, and Alvin M. Weinberg, his young protégé, saw the MTR not only as a necessary research device for testing the components for new types of reactors, but also as a promising reactor design in itself. By using fully enriched uranium 235 as fuel, Weinberg planned to employ ordinary water (rather than the much more expensive "heavy" water) as both moderator and coolant. Conflicting and changing objectives in the Commission's reactor program hampered development of the MTR both at Oak Ridge and Argonne. When the MTR was finally placed in operation at the Idaho testing station in March 1952, its main purpose was only the testing of reactor materials, but its use of water as both moderator and coolant was to set the course for power reactor development for more than a decade.

Another long-range approach to nuclear power was the homogeneous reactor, conceived by Weinberg and his associates at Oak Ridge. In addition to the possibility of breeding, the homogeneous reactor would have the advantage of using a fluid slurry of fuel, moderator, and coolant. The slurry, which would achieve a critical configuration only in the reactor vessel, could be pumped continuously through auxiliary systems to extract the heat energy and even to reprocess the fuel. This design would eliminate the costs of fabricating and reprocessing metallic uranium fuel elements, which would be a substantial factor in the price of nuclear power in heterogeneous systems. Like the EBR, however, the homogeneous reactor involved technical problems for which solutions were not clearly apparent and which required intensive research before they were successfully resolved.

Although ostensibly designed for other purposes, nuclear propulsion systems for submarines seemed by the early 1950's to offer more immediate promise for nuclear power development than did breeder or homogeneous reactors. In the summer of 1946 the U.S. Navy had assigned a small group of officers under Captain Hyman G. Rickover to the Oak Ridge laboratory to study reactor technology. Rickover soon discovered the advantages of the water reactor system advocated for the MTR; he was also impressed by the thermal efficiencies of sodium-cooled systems, such as those being planned for breeder reactors. By the time Rickover became the director of a joint Navy-Commission project in 1948, the design work for the submarine reactor had been centralized at Argonne National Laboratory and strong development programs had been established by the Westinghouse Corporation in Pittsburgh and the General Electric Company in Schenectady. The Westinghouse approach was to employ a pressurized-water system to remove heat from the reactor at temperatures high enough for efficient steam generation; the General Electric system was to use liquid sodium.

Acceptance of these proposals reflected changing conditions not directly related to reactor technology. Rapid improvement in the prospects for uranium-ore procurement in the late 1940's made it possible to plan for power generation without breeding. At the same time, mounting international tensions seemed to justify the use of fissionable materials for submarine propulsion. Also significant was the fact that, to save time, Rickover was willing to accept a design based on existing technology rather than striving for a more advanced concept which might offer cheaper power or more efficient use of fissionable material. This more practical (but perhaps less imaginative) approach to reactor design would come to dominate the United States power program in the 1950's.

EUROPEAN PROGRAMS

If the United States in the years 1947-53 did not advance much beyond its substantial base of wartime technology to studies of feasibility, other nations could hardly have been expected to do more. Wartime co-operation with the United States and Britain did give Canada an especially valuable research reactor in the summer of 1947, but there were no immediate plans for a power reactor.

However, with experience in the Canadian project, British scientists by the summer of 1947 had built a low-power reactor at the new research center at Harwell, England, and had designed Britain's first major experimental reactor, BEPO, which served as the prototype for several gas-cooled power reactors. The French, whose early nuclear research effort had been scattered by the war, did not operate their first experimental reactor until 1948 and did not begin to plan larger reactors until 1952. The first experimental chain reaction in the Soviet Union probably occurred in the summer of 1947. Presumably most of the Soviet effort was directed to plutonium-production reactors, but in 1949 the Russians did begin development of a small power demonstration reactor at their new research center at Obninsk.

ATOMS FOR PEACE

On December 8, 1953, before the United Nations General Assembly in New York, President Eisenhower offered a proposal for developing the peaceful uses of atomic energy. "Peaceful power from atomic energy is no dream of the future," the President declared. "That capability, already proved, is here—now—today." The imagination and idealism of the President's words rekindled an interest in nuclear power not only in America but abroad also.

Changes in law and policy offered new impetus to atomic power in the United States during 1954. A major revision in the Atomic Energy Act permitted private industry for the first time to own reactors (but not nuclear fuel) and gave the Commission new authority to provide financial and technical assistance to non-government reactor projects. The new law also freed the Commission to exchange certain technical data with foreign countries and to negotiate co-operative agreements for reactor development. Both the domestic and international provisions were designed to promote the development of a private atomic energy industry in the United States. For the next five years, the major thrust was to be in the direction of building prototype reactors for power purposes.

THE FIVE-YEAR PROGRAM FOR POWER REACTOR PROTOTYPES

The Commission responded early in 1954 to President Eisenhower's call for peaceful atomic development with a new program for power reactor development. The objective was to build, in the next five years, five experimental reactors which would test the basic reactor designs then under study. The plants would cost $200 million and would require annually about $8.5 million for research and development.

The first project, based on Rickover's practical approach and the technology developed for submarine-propulsion reactors, promised a short-term demonstration of the commercial use of nuclear power. The Pressurized Water Reactor, to be built at Shippingport, Pennsylvania, was planned to provide 60,000 kilo-

Fig. 17-3. The heart of the nation's first full-scale atomic electric generating station—the 58-ton nuclear core—is shown as it is slowly lowered into position at the plant in Shippingport, Pennsylvania. The core contains 14 tons of natural uranium and 165 pounds of highly enriched uranium. This nuclear furnace heats high-pressure water, which converts a second supply of water into steam for a turbine generator that produces electricity. (Courtesy of *Westinghouse Electric Corporation*)

watts of electricity for the Pittsburgh area by the end of 1957. The co-operative agreement with the Duquesne Light Company provided for Commission ownership of the reactor and company ownership of the generating facilities.

The Commission also placed in the short-term category the Sodium Reactor Experiment (SRE), to be built by North American Aviation, Inc., a Commission contractor in southern California. The SRE, taking advantage of extensive United States experience with graphite reactors, was planned to produce efficient steam-generation temperatures through the excellent heat-transfer properties of a liquid-sodium coolant.

Of somewhat longer range promise was the Experimental Boiling Water Reactor (EBWR), to be constructed at the Commission's Argonne Laboratory. Argonne research at the National Reactor Testing Station in Idaho had indicated that stable operation of a power reactor might be achieved even if the water coolant were permitted to boil in the reactor. The EBWR, if successful, would eliminate the need for high-pressure equipment required in pressurized-water reactors. Plans called for the EBWR to be generating 5000 kilowatts of electricity by the end of 1956.

The final two reactors in the Commission's five-year program were to be new models of the fast breeder and homogeneous experiments which had been built at the beginning of the decade at the Idaho test station and at Oak Ridge. The Experimental Breeder Reactor No. 2, using a sodium coolant, was expected to be in operation in 1958 and to produce about 15,000 kilowatts of electricity. The Homogeneous Reactor Experiment No. 2, a greatly improved version of the original reactor at Oak Ridge, was scheduled to be operating at thermal power levels approaching 10,000 kilowatts in 1956.

To supplement its own effort in prototype development, the Commission launched a new co-operative program with American industry. Largely because of the strictures in the original Atomic Energy Act, industrial participation had been limited to technical study and training programs. Now, thanks to new legislation, private industry could be invited to build its own nuclear power plants using fissionable material leased from the Commission. Echoing the President's note of optimism about the imminence of nuclear power, the Commission in January 1955 invited private companies "to assume the risk of construction, ownership, and operation of reactors designed to demonstrate the practical value of such facilities for commercial or industrial purposes." In return, the Commission offered to waive use charges on inventories of fissionable material in the private projects, to perform certain research and development work in Commission laboratories at no cost to the company, and to enter into research and development contracts, which in effect would help to underwrite development costs.

Response to the Commission's invitation was encouraging; it received four proposals which would mean large-scale prototypes for all but one of the five reactor types in the Commission's experimental program. The Yankee Atomic Electric Company, comprised of eleven power companies in New England, planned to build a 134,000-kilowatt pressurized-water reactor in northwestern Massachusetts. The Commonwealth Edison Company proposed a 180,000-kilowatt boiling-water reactor to be built at Dresden, near Joliet, Illinois. The Consumers Public Power District of Nebraska offered to build a 75,000-kilowatt sodium-cooled, graphite-moderated reactor at Hallam, Nebraska. And a 100,000-kilowatt sodium-cooled fast breeder named after Enrico Fermi was the goal of the Power Reactor Development Company, representing Detroit Edison and twenty other companies in the Northeast. Subsequent invitations elicited a

Fig. 17-4. The Yankee Atomic Electric Company's plant at Rowe, Massachusetts. (*Westinghouse Electric Corporation*)

dozen additional proposals, four of which were eventually completed. These included two small boiling-water reactors at Elk River, Minnesota, and Sioux Falls, South Dakota; a small reactor using an organic material as a moderator at Piqua, Ohio; and a pressurized heavy-water reactor at Parr, South Carolina.

The Commission's new emphasis on building reactor plants encouraged some companies to undertake projects independent of government support. The Commonwealth Edison Company's Dresden plant, originally proposed under the co-operative program, proceeded as a project of private industry. Another independent enterprise, proposed in February 1957 by the Consolidated Edison Company of New York, was a 163,000-kilowatt pressurized-water reactor on the Hudson River at Indian Point, New York. Also without government support, the General Electric Company built a 5000-kilowatt experimental boiling-water reactor at its Vallecitos, California, laboratory to develop technical data for the Dresden power station.

AMERICAN ACCOMPLISHMENTS

In the meantime, the Commission's experimental program was gaining momentum. Construction started in April 1955 on the pressurized-water reactor plant at Shippingport, Pennsylvania. Despite major engineering innovations, including the use of zirconium-aluminum alloys in fuel elements and the fabrication of the largest pressure vessel built up to that time, the PWR was completed on schedule and was generating electric power before the end of 1957. Argonne National Laboratory, specializing in boiling-water reactors, completed the Experimental Boiling Water Reactor on schedule in 1956 and the fourth of a series of boiling reactor experiments at the Idaho test station in 1957. The Experimental Breeder Reactor No. 1 continued to test the fast-breeder idea until April 1956, when a power surge destroyed the reactor core and stopped operation until November 1957. Construction of the Homogeneous Reactor Experiment No. 2 was completed at Oak Ridge in May 1956, but a series of difficulties, including stress-corrosion leaks, delayed initial power operation until late in 1957. The Commission supplemented these original projects with studies of more advanced high-temperature systems, including the use of organic moderators and liquid-metal and molten-salt fuels.

By the end of 1957 the Commission had reason to be enthusiastic about progress toward nuclear power in the United States. The Commission itself had seven experimental reactors in operation investigating the most promising power reactor designs. Supplementing these were nine independent or co-operative projects capable of producing almost 800,000 kilowatts of electricity by the mid-1960's. Furthermore, there was a possibility of cutting costs through improving plant performance, building larger plants, simplifying design, and using conventional components and commercial specifications.

EUROPEAN EFFORTS

In contrast to the American emphasis on water-cooled reactors, both the United Kingdom and France chose to rely on gas-cooled systems. The course adopted by these two nations was to some extent dictated by the need for reactors to produce not only power but also plutonium for weapons. Although conflicting parameters made it impossible to optimize the production of both power and weapon-grade plutonium in the same reactor, the British and French believed that a practical compromise could be developed, particularly in view of the high cost of conventional fuel in postwar Europe and the possibility of crediting plutonium production against the cost of power.

In August 1953, the British began building the first of four plutonium power reactors at Calder Hall in Cumberland, England. They were designed to use natural uranium as fuel, graphite as the moderator, and carbon dioxide gas as the coolant. The designed electrical capacity of each reactor was 41,000 kilowatts. The first reactor at Calder Hall was completed in May 1956, and in October began delivering power for commercial use. In August 1955, the British broke ground for the first of four reactors of the Calder Hall type at Chapel

Cross in Scotland. For power production only, the British in 1957 started four additional gas-cooled reactors with a total capacity of more than 685,000 kilowatts, which with the eight reactors at Calder Hall and Chapel Cross would provide generating facilities in excess of one million kilowatts. The British also built several experimental power reactors other than gas-cooled types, the largest being the 15,000-kilowatt fast breeder at Dounreay, Scotland.

Following a similar course, the French began construction of the first of three natural uranium, graphite-moderated, gas-cooled reactors at Marcoule in May 1954. Although the first reactor had power generating equipment, it was optimized for plutonium production and consumed more electricity than it produced. The second and third Marcoule reactors, started in 1956, were each planned to produce 28,000 kilowatts of electricity. For power production alone, the French in March 1957 began to build near Chinon a 68,000-kilowatt reactor cooled with carbon dioxide. A second reactor with a capacity of about 200,000 kilowatts was in the planning stage.

Few details of nuclear power development in the Soviet Union were published in the late 1950's, but the Russians, like the Americans, appeared to be emphasizing enriched-uranium, water-cooled systems. In 1954 the Russians began operating a small reactor experiment at Obninsk as a pressurized-water system. This unit, converted to boiling-water operation in 1957, provided data for a 200,000-kilowatt pressurized-water reactor plant at Novovoronezh and for two smaller boiling-water reactors at Ulyanovsk and Beloyarsk. The Russians were also experimenting with a small plutonium-fueled fast reactor at Obninsk.

MOVING TOWARD MATURITY, 1958-62

Despite the enthusiasm and widespread activity in building power reactor prototypes in the mid-1950's, the goals outlined by President Eisenhower were not reached by the end of the decade. The glowing reports of achievements presented at the Second Geneva Conference on the Peaceful Uses of Atomic Energy in the summer of 1958 could not disguise the growing skepticism within private industry. Although the long-range outlook was promising, equipment manufacturers could not anticipate a reliable market until the costs of nuclear power began to approach those of conventional fuels.

In the United States, there was momentary hope that the bilateral agreements which the government had negotiated with 40 nations and with the European atomic energy community (Euratom) would provide new contracts, but these hopes were dashed in 1959 by the discovery of new oil reserves in North Africa. The bilateral agreements resulted in only six power reactor contracts in five countries: West Germany, Belgium, Italy, Japan, and France. The Euratom program announced in 1958 contemplated the construction of five or six reactors between 1963 and 1965 with a total installed electrical capacity of

Fig. 17-5. Aerial view of the Dresden Nuclear Power Station, located about fifty miles southwest of Chicago. (Courtesy of *Commonwealth Edison Company*)

about one million kilowatts. But by mid-1962 only one project had been started and one other approved. The British announced a cutback in nuclear power goals, while the Russians indicated a more conservative approach also. This sombre outlook for nuclear power at the end of the 1950's forced government officials and engineers in many countries to concentrate on the technical problems of the present rather than the glowing promise of the future.

For the United States, prospects for 1959 seemed particularly bleak at the beginning of the year. Although the Pressurized Water Reactor was operating well, construction of other large-scale power reactors had been delayed. Not until late in the year was the new 180,000-kilowatt boiling-water reactor placed in operation at Dresden, Illinois. The Atomic Energy Commission announced that it would concentrate on reactor prototypes and a variety of experimental programs to improve the efficiency of existing systems. Most important were experiments to produce superheated steam in water reactors. In May 1959, saturated steam produced in the Vallecitos experimental reactor was fed back into the reactor to produce dry steam at very much higher temperatures for turbine operation. Before the end of the year, ground had been broken for the Pathfinder plant at Sioux Falls, South Dakota, and studies had been completed for the Boiling Water Superheat reactor (BONUS) in Puerto Rico.

By 1961 the outlook was brighter. The Yankee Company's reactor had joined Dresden and the PWR in full-power commercial operation which produced more than two billion kilowatt-hours of electricity during the year. Furthermore, Yankee had been built for 20 per cent less than the original cost estimates and gave evidence of producing power at less than the estimated operating cost.

There were also signs of renewed interest in nuclear power among private utility companies. Boiling-water reactors in the range of 48,000 kilowatts were under construction by the Consumers Power Company of Michigan at Big Rock Point and by the Pacific Gas and Electric Company at Humboldt Bay, California. The Pennsylvania Electric Company broke ground for a small pressurized-water reactor at Saxton. All three plants were operating at designed power levels by 1963.

The emphasis on boiling-water reactors and superheated systems was not the only evidence of the determination in the United States to concentrate on power reactor designs with immediate promise; the more ambitious long-range projects were receiving less attention than they had in the 1950's. Continuing difficulties with corrosion in the homogeneous reactor experiments led to termination of that approach in 1961. The meltdown of the core of the Experimental Breeder Reactor and the continuing delays in completion of the Enrico Fermi fast-breeder plant dampened interest in breeder reactors. At the same time, Americans reconsidered the advantages of gas-cooled reactors, which were being developed with some success in Europe, and in the spring of 1962, the Philadelphia Electric Company began construction of a prototype high-temperature, gas-cooled reactor at Peach Bottom, Pennsylvania.

THE BEGINNING OF THE AGE OF ATOMIC POWER

At the close of 1962, the Atomic Energy Commission surveyed the accomplishments of a decade of effort to develop economic nuclear power in a special report to President John F. Kennedy. It had cost the federal government over one billion dollars and private industry a half-billion. But the results were impressive. Operating costs had dropped from about 50 mills per kilowatt-hour for the initial operation of the Shippingport reactor to about 10 mills for reactors then in operation. The Commission expected that plants then under construction could reduce the cost to about 5 mills. These figures, based on the nuclear generation of more than five billion kilowatt-hours of electricity, compared favorably with a cost range of 4.1 to 6.2 mills per kilowatt-hour for conventional power plants in the United States. The Commission could only conclude that "nuclear power is on the threshold of economic competitiveness and can soon be made competitive in areas consuming a significant fraction of the nation's electrical energy." Once the economic battle was won, the United States could turn to the development of converter or breeder reactors, which would conserve the natural supply of fissionable materials.

Although it would take years before the accuracy of the Commission's prediction could be fully known, there were signs as early as 1964 that the world was about to enter the age of atomic power. In the spring of that year the Jersey Central Power and Light Company announced that, after an exhaustive study of the economics involved, the company had decided that nuclear power would be cheaper than conventional fuels in a new plant at Oyster Creek, New Jersey. Until the reactor could be completed, the cost estimates would be subject to debate; but it was perhaps significant that the Atomic Energy Commission soon received not only several proposals for additional large-scale nuclear plants but also demands that it announce, in accordance with the Atomic Energy Act, that a "type of utilization or production facility has been sufficiently developed to be of practical value for industrial or commercial purposes."

Bright prospects for nuclear power were not limited in 1964 to the United States. When the Third Geneva Conference on the Peaceful Uses of Atomic Energy assembled in August, delegates from the industrially developed nations presented impressive reports of the progress made in reactor technology and in constructing nuclear power plants since 1958.

Great Britain announced that three of eight twin-reactor plants were already producing commercial power, one plant of advanced design was operating in Scotland, and two were being planned in England. Gas-cooled reactors also continued to be favored in France, where one experimental power station was in operation and four larger plants were in the construction or design stage. In the Soviet Union, where uranium 235 was available as a fuel, the emphasis was on enriched reactors using ordinary water as moderator. The Russians reported that their 210,000-kilowatt pressurized-water reactor had begun operation; announced plans for constructing a much larger reactor of the same type in the 1960's at the Novovoronezh power station; reported great improvements in the use of superheat in the second boiling-water reactor at the Beloyarsk station; and told of a sharp reduction in fuel costs in the BR-5 5000-kilowatt fast reactor at Obninsk. Canada, taking advantage of large stocks of high-grade uranium ore, was operating a demonstration power plant and building a larger station, both using natural-uranium, heavy-water-moderated reactors. West Germany was planning four power stations using reactors of several types; and both Italy and Japan were operating commercial nuclear plants built by American or British companies.

Summing up the Geneva Conference, Glenn T. Seaborg, chairman of the United States Atomic Energy Commission, concluded that it marked the beginning of the age of nuclear power. Economic nuclear power was already available in limited but important geographical areas. Before the end of the century, he predicted, the atom would be a leading energy source in most areas of the world.

18 / Energy Resources for the Future
J. A. DUFFIE

A consideration of the history of technology makes it clear that the availability of energy resources upon which to "feed" our present energy-hungry society, and on which to base future technological development, is a matter of serious concern. The seriousness of this question is emphasized by three factors.

First, the world's population is increasing at a tremendous rate as mankind learns to control disease, increases life spans, and generally develops a higher standard of living. This increased population must be fed, clothed, housed, and occupied in useful pursuits, all of which require the expenditure of energy. The alternatives to meeting the needs of increased population are to be satisfied with a decreasing standard of living for a substantial part of the world's population, or to influence in some way the growth of the population.

Second, even at present population levels, the per-capita demand for energy is increasing. Each member of the world's population is increasing his annual use of energy by, on the average, about three per cent. This increase is significant, for though it is relatively small in the United States (where energy use per person is about six times that of the world average), it is much larger in areas where consumption is now at a comparatively low level. This increase must be met if mankind is to continue progressing toward what we now view as a better material way of life.

Third, the pattern of energy resource availability is variable with time. *Capital resources* of energy (coal, oil, natural gas, and so on, the stored energy sources) are discovered, exploited to varying degrees, and eventually depleted to the extent that further extraction is economically impractical. *Income resources* are developed (the principal example now being hydroelectric resources), and continuing use is made of them for long periods of time. Research and development are also carried on with varying intensity to develop new energy resources. The result is a time-dependent pattern of energy availability for the world.

Any study of energy resources for the future must take into account these and many other aspects of a changing society, both at international and local levels. A consideration of recent history and a study of the many factors that affect energy requirements, however, lead to the inescapable conclusion that somehow mankind must continue to expand his energy resources, and ultimately come to depend heavily on resources which are not now major contributors to the energy economy. Success in these ventures, on the local, national, or international level, is necessary if we are to maintain and continually improve the world's standards of living. At the same time, success or failure in these ventures will have far-reaching economic and political implications.

ENERGY ECONOMICS AND SUPPLIES

The development and use of energy resources are influenced markedly by a complex and interrelated set of economic, political, and social factors. Of primary importance is the cost of delivered energy. This cost includes a number of elements—mainly exploration, plus the different costs of production, distribution, and conversion. Exploring for energy resources, developing processes for their exploitation, and bringing an energy resource to a productive level all involve costs which are ultimately assigned to the energy consumer, or to the community at large. These costs can be tremendous, as in the case of developing nuclear energy for electrical power generation, or relatively small scale, as in the exploration and development of a new oil field or hydroelectric plant. Production costs include the expenses of mining and pumping, plus the costs of operating and maintaining equipment for recovery, and the like. The world's energy resources and means of conversion of energy do not coincide geographically with the location of energy consumers. Therefore, the payment of capital and operating costs to transport energy in raw or converted form from its source to the user is, in most cases, a significant element of energy cost to the user.

Energy costs vary with time. The most easily discovered and extracted energy resources are exploited first, and they are cheapest for these reasons. As consumption continues, the easily recovered reserves are depleted, the mines get deeper, the coal seams thinner, the oil wells deeper, and the hydroelectric sites less accessible. Thus, there is a tendency for energy costs from conventional sources to rise with time. This tendency is modified in relatively short time periods (decades perhaps) by technological development and discovery of new resources. The point, however, is that the pattern of use of energy resources is variable over the decades. We will never "run out of" a given capital resource, such as oil, but at a future date it may become uneconomic further to exploit the resource.

The value of energy depends upon *when* it is available, as well as *where* it is available. The income energy resources may be available only at particular times of day or year (as, for example, solar or wind energy); unless the demands for energy coincide with availability of energy from the resource, some form of storage must be provided (at additional expense), or combinations of sources used. If the problems of energy storage cannot be solved, energy from sources which are intermittent may be of less value than that from sources with a higher degree of availability.

An interesting theoretical picture of the changing quantities of energy available from capital resources has been worked out for oil, and it provides a ready means of visualizing the changing supply of this type of resource. Several definitions will help to clarify this analysis:

> *Proved Reserves*, Q_R, are the quantities of crude oil (or other raw fuel) which geological and engineering information indicate are recoverable under existing economic and operating conditions.
>
> *Cumulative Production*, Q_P, is the total accumulated quantity of the resource removed from the ground up to any time.
>
> *Cumulative Discoveries*, Q_D, are all of the quantities of fuel removed from the ground, plus the recoverable quantities of the fuel remaining in the ground.

From these definitions:

$$Q_D = Q_P + Q_R.$$

Fig. 18-1. Cumulative discoveries and production and proved reserves. (Adapted from *Energy Resources: A Report to the Committee on National Resources*, National Academy of Sciences, 1962)

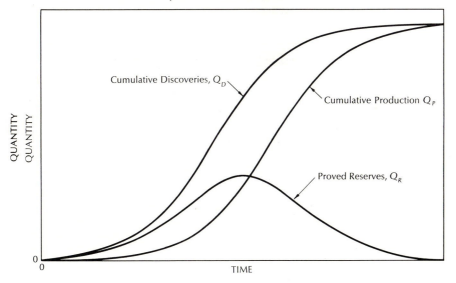

Figure 18-1 shows the approximate history, over the total time of its exploitation, of a capital energy resource. The three energy quantities Q_D, Q_P, and Q_R, are plotted against time. The cumulative discoveries curve increases from 0 (before the initial development) to a steady value representing the total of the energy resource that can be economically extracted. The cumulative production curve also starts at zero, is always less than discoveries by an amount equal to the proved reserves at any time, and ultimately approaches the same level as the Q_D curve when most of the reserves have been extracted.

This figure represents an idealized and simplified picture of complex changes that occur in various parts of the world at various times. As the need for more energy develops, the rate of discovery increases (due to increased exploration and intensified technological development), and production also increases. Thus, the time span of the use of the resource must be shortened, because the total energy derivable from the resource is essentially fixed. It is to be noted that costs differ from one coal, oil, or natural gas field to another. The picture is changed by the utility of the fossil-fuel resources as sources of chemical materials, which modifies the value of the resources. However, the trends illustrated by Figure 18-1 must ultimately be considered in assessing future energy resources.

The time span of the figure varies depending on the resource, and might be thought of as being of the order of a hundred years or so for natural gas, with longer periods for crude oil, coal, oil shale, and tar sands (with the latter two not yet exploited to a significant degree). Nuclear energy, from the point of view of energy availability, may perhaps have a time scale of even greater magnitude than the fossil-fuel resources. The questions of extent of energy available from these sources will be discussed below in more detail.

The situation for income energy resources is different. The cumulative production of energy from a specific source, such as a hydroelectric station, continually rises with time. Production rates may have highs and lows due to seasonal nature of rainfall, or variation of availability of solar or tidal energy, yet the total extent of this type of resource is perhaps easier to estimate than are the "ultimate reserves" of capital resources, and the picture of the total income energy available is thus less subject to upward revision. For these reasons, the total rate of availability of income energy, from all income resources, is essentially fixed and reasonably well established.

In contrasting capital and income energy resources, one should remember that the state of development determines what man can derive from the income energy sources within any time period, while a total and essentially fixed quantity of energy from capital energy sources is available to mankind to use over any time period he may decide. Up to about the middle of the 19th century, man depended almost entirely on income energy, most of which was derived directly, or indirectly (through animals), from solar energy stored in plants by photosynthesis. At the present time, most of the world's energy comes from capital resources, such as coal or petroleum, but significant contributions are still made from income sources, such as hydroelectric. The present situation will probably continue for several generations, with increasing use of both capital and income sources, but with capital resources supplying most of the energy on a worldwide basis. Farther in the future, man can expect to fall back on more intensive use of income resources.

ENERGY CONVERSION

The conversion of energy from its "raw" form to that suited for transport or use is significant in the energy picture, for the overall product of efficiencies in the processes determines how much of a raw energy resource must be used to accomplish a desired end. For example, an output of useful work of one kilowatt-hour (kwh)—lifting a 10,000-pound elevator a distance of 265 feet, for example—might require that 10 kwh of energy in the form of chemical energy in coal be mined from the ground; this overall efficiency of one tenth is due to the efficiencies of mining, transportation, conversion in an electrical generation plant, transmission, voltage changes in transformers, and in the motor and mechanical system of the elevator. This is an example of a relatively good conversion system, and many are less efficient than this.

One of the more significant aspects in this developing technology is that the efficiency of conversion has improved with time. Thus, while the early steam engines were less than one per cent efficient, modern large-scale steam power plants can be 40 per cent efficient in converting chemical energy in coal to electrical energy. This development has meant that less of our energy resources have been used to meet energy needs, and future improvements in the process for energy conversion will further conserve energy resources.

ENERGY RESOURCES

With the preceding background information, we can now examine briefly the nature and extent of specific energy resources, their distribution, and their utility in meeting the world's energy needs.

A recent overall picture of the estimated ultimate reserves of fossil fuels, for the world and for the United States, compiled by M. K. Hubbert, is summarized here. The estimates are in terms of energy content of the fossil fuels, that is, their heats of combustion are expressed in equivalent electrical energy units, kilowatt-hours, and for convenience a large energy unit of 10^{15} kilowatt-hours is used.

Figure 18-2 shows 1962 estimates of the ultimate world reserves of various fossil fuels, and the percentages of these that had been used up to that time. It

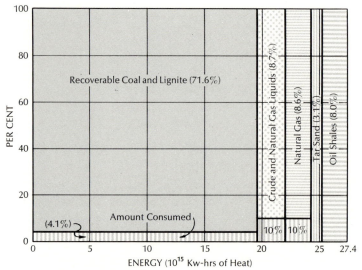

PER CENT

ENERGY (10^15 Kw-hrs of Heat)

Recoverable Coal and Lignite (71.6%)

Crude and Natural Gas Liquids (8.7%)

Natural Gas (8.6%)

Tar Sand (3.1%)

Oil Shales (8.0%)

(4.1%)

Amount Consumed

10% 10%

Fig. 18-2. Total world energy of fossil fuels. (Adapted from *Energy Resources, National Academy of Sciences*)

can be seen that coal and lignite constitute 71.6 per cent of the total energy, and that only four per cent of this had yet been used. Crude oil, liquid fuels associated with natural gas, and natural gas, each constitutes a little less than 9 per cent of the energy, with a tenth of each used. Tar sands and oil shales together provide about 11 per cent of the total energy, and these have not been used to any significant extent.

The equivalent picture for the United States is shown in Figure 18-3. The total energy is about one third of the world total, and coal represents an even larger fraction of the total energy here than for the world as a whole. Although oil shale represents 16 per cent of the energy, it has not yet been utilized to a significant extent. Natural gas and petroleum each represent about 3 per cent of the total energy, but here the use picture is different; as of 1962 about 22 per cent of the ultimate reserves of natural gas in the United States had been used and about 38 per cent of the petroleum.

COAL

Coal historically has been the most significant of the fossil fuels. It was first mined and used in the 13th century, and still provides more than half of the world's production of energy. It has been used on both large and small scale for a wide variety of purposes. The chief limitation of coal in the transport field has been due to its solid form, and much of the energy needs of transportation are now being met by liquid fuels. It can be readily handled, however, in large power plants where its chemical energy is converted to electrical energy. Coal has widespread industrial use, particularly in metallurgical industries, and attention is being given to its liquefaction or gasification to increase the convenience of its use. It is also a significant source of chemical raw materials.

Estimates of the distribution of recoverable coal reserves ("reserves in the ground. . .that past experience suggests can actually be produced in the future") as of 1961 are shown in Figure 18-4. The quantities of coal are shown in United States tons. The per-cent scale is that part of the recoverable energy which is available in the individual countries shown, arranged by geographical areas. It is clear that the distribution of coal is not uniform to the world's population; the United States, Russia, and China have the bulk of the resources, while Australasia, Africa, and South America have relatively little. It is estimated that on a worldwide basis, only four per cent of the recoverable reserves of coal have been used. Coal resources thus represent a very large block of energy available in the future.

OIL

Petroleum has, during the present century, become increasingly important as a source of energy. On a worldwide basis, it contributes about 30 per cent of the energy requirements. In the United States, the energy derived from petroleum

Fig. 18-3. Total United States energy of fossil fuels. (Adapted from *Energy Resources*, National Academy of Sciences)

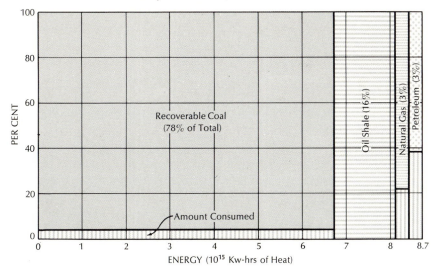

and natural gas is three times that of coal, the other chief contributor, and petroleum is now the single most important energy resource in the United States. Petroleum is available in amounts which are only a little more than a tenth that of coal (on an energy basis), and we have already used a considerable portion of this resource (about 10 per cent on a worldwide basis, and about 38 per cent for the United States). For these reasons, study of petroleum resources has received very great attention, although widely varying estimates have been made of the extent of petroleum reserves.

A picture of the world's ultimate potential petroleum reserves (cumulative total resources) is summarized in Figure 18-5, in terms of billions of barrels of reserves. The resources are shown by country. It is apparent that the United States has used a significant part of its crude oil, that South America has produced about one fifth of its petroleum, and that production has reached significant proportions of the total reserves (as we now visualize them) in all but the offshore areas of the world where relatively little exploration has been carried out.

Fig. 18-4. Recoverable world coal reserves. (Adapted from *Energy Resources*, National Academy of Sciences)

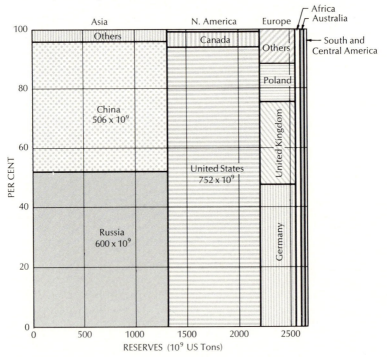

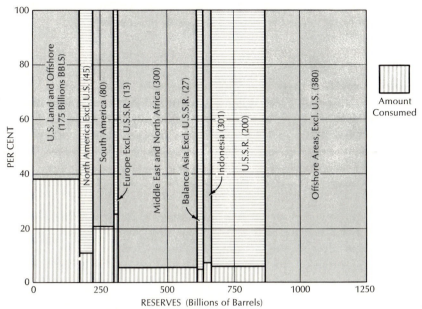

Fig. 18-5. World ultimate potential petroleum reserves. (Adapted from *Energy Resources*, National Academy of Sciences)

It has been estimated that the peak of world oil production will occur about the year 2000. It does appear evident that within a generation or two, at least in certain local areas, petroleum resources may have to be conserved for uses to which they are uniquely and particularly well adapted, namely for transportation and as sources of chemicals.

NATURAL GAS

Natural gas, which is generally associated with petroleum and chemically related to it, has come into greatly increased use. This is particularly true in the United States where, in the years since World War II, extensive pipeline systems have been developed for its distribution.

The picture of reserves and consumption of natural gas is similar to that of petroleum. Each constitutes between 8 and 9 per cent of the world's fossil-fuel energy resources, and about one tenth of what is now considered the ultimate recoverable amount of each has been exhausted. In the United States, it is estimated that 22 per cent of the natural gas supply has been used. The use of natural gas has been, in the past, largely confined to areas to which the gas could be economically distributed by pipeline. This situation is now changing, as methods of tanker transport are developed, and natural gas from North Africa is now being shipped to southern Europe by this method.

Reserves of energy in large quantities are known to exist in the form of organic materials associated with shales and sands, and their total energy content is estimated to be three fourths that of the total of petroleum crudes and natural gas. The best known of these reserves are in North America, where it is estimated that there is a reserve of 850×10^9 barrels of shale oil, largely in the United States, and possibly 600×10^9 barrels of crude-oil equivalent in tar sands (largely in Canada). There are other known reserves of oil shale in Brazil and elsewhere.

These energy resources are not now being exploited to any significant extent. One explanation is that the costs of recovering fuels (hydrocarbons) and other chemicals from these sources is higher than that of fuels from other sources. The recovery process as now envisaged consists of mining the rocks or sands, heating them in retorts to drive off the volatile hydrocarbons, and condensing the hydrocarbons for further processing. Pilot-scale operations of this type have been carried out for oil shales, and may soon be economically competitive, at least in some areas. Experiments are also being done on the recovery of fuels from tar sands.

The known presence of large reserves of oil shales and tar sands, which can be made to yield fuels at costs higher than those of present conventionally derived fuels, but not so high as to rule out consideration of their use, is an indication that present patterns of energy resource use will not drastically change in the next few decades in North America.

WATER POWER

In past years, water power was used directly to "turn the wheels" of industry. Today, hydroelectric stations convert the energy of falling water into electrical energy which is then distributed to users.

Water power, as an income resource, is measured in terms of the rate at which energy is available, that is, in available power. The units are megawatts of capacity or kilowatt-hours of generated power per year. Table 18-1 shows an estimate of water-power potential for various parts of the world, and the percentage of the capacity in each area which was developed as of 1961. Major power schemes, such as the Snowy Mountains plan in Australia, major dam construction in India and on the Nile, and others, are being developed. The present world development of water power is only about five per cent of the total potential.

The world's total water-power *potential* is several times the total present electrical power *consumption* from all generating sources. However, much of the potential is in areas which are not now highly industrialized (such as Africa) and therefore not now in need of large quantities of electrical energy.

Table 18-1.   World Water-Power Capacity

REGION	POTENTIAL (10^3 MEGAWATTS)	PER CENT OF TOTAL	DEVELOPMENT (10^3 MEGAWATTS)	PER CENT DEVELOPED
North America	313	11	59	19
South America	577	20	5	
Western Europe	158	6	47	30
Africa	780	27	2	
Middle East	21	1	—	
Southeast Asia	455	16	2	
Far East	42	1	19	
Australasia	45	2	2	
USSR, China, and Satellites	466	16	16	3
TOTAL	2,857	100	152	

(Computed from data given by Adams, Francis, L., 1961, Statement on Water Power: at Conference on Energy Resources, Committee on Natural Resources, National Academy of Sciences, Rockefeller Institute, New York, N. Y., July 19, Chart I.)
Source: M. K. Hubbert, "Energy Resources," Publication 1000-D, National Academy of Sciences—National Research Council, Washington, D.C. (1962), p. 99.

TIDAL POWER

The rise and fall of the tides provides intriguing prospects for electrical power generation in a few selected locations where tides are high and the land forms are such as to admit the possibility of damming of bays or other inlets. The number of such sites is limited, and includes locations on the Bay of Fundy in Canada, in Argentina, England, France, and on the northwest coast of Australia. The total proposed development of these various sites would be very large (a total of about 9000 megawatts). The first large-scale tidal power experimental installation is now being built in Northern France.

WIND POWER

Wind has traditionally been used to propel ships and provide mechanical energy in small quantities for special purposes such as pumping water. In recent years, attention has been given to wind generation of electrical energy, and several experimental plants of large capacity have been built and operated.

Wind energy is, in most locations, not a highly reliable source of energy, for as wind direction and speed vary, so will the power output of wind generators.

Surveys have been made of potential sites where wind velocities over extended periods of time are high enough to warrant attention. The conclusion drawn from these surveys is that the world's total potential capacity is very large; however, at the present time, a negligible portion of this available energy is being used, and energy from wind makes very small contributions to the energy economy.

SOLAR ENERGY

Among several non-conventional sources of energy, solar energy is perhaps the most intriguing. The radiation received from the sun over the total surface of the earth is many times larger than the present world's energy needs. Offsetting this large total supply are the problems of low energy density and variability of the supply. The intensity of solar radiation at the earth's surface is, at best, a little over one kilowatt per square meter, and large energy demands can be met only by correspondingly large solar-energy collecting areas. The energy supply is variable in a predictable manner, due to time of day and declination of the sun (seasons); superimposed on these regular variations are less predictable changes caused by weather. Thus any process for using solar energy will have an intermittent output, unless a means of storing energy (or other products of the solar process) can be provided for periods of no radiation.

Solar energy is, in a real sense, already distributed to potential users. This fact, coupled with the characteristics noted above, indicates that its most probable uses are in relatively small-scale, low-temperature operations. Applications under study include use for domestic heating or operation of air conditioners and water heaters, and in stills for desalinization of salt water. Solar evaporation and drying have been carried out on an industrial scale for centuries. In comparison to other energy resources, very little research has been directed toward this energy resource and the processes for its use. In areas of low population density and relatively high cost of conventional energy, however, solar processes are now, or have the prospect of soon becoming, competitive with conventional fuels. Thus, solar energy can be viewed as an energy resource which now makes a very small contribution to the world's energy economy, but one which is significant in meeting certain kinds of local energy needs. As efforts at solar-process development go on, the scope of these applications will increase.

BIOLOGICAL ENERGY

A special case of solar-energy utilization is the biological process of photosynthesis by growing plants. In this process, carbon dioxide and water are combined to form carbohydrates, the major constituents of plants, and oxygen. These materials can be stored, and on recombination with oxygen, that is, on burning, stored energy is released as heat. Plant materials are used as an energy supply to a limited extent, particularly in some rural areas of low population density. Still the products of photosynthesis are more valuable as food for animals or humans, or as chemical raw materials, than as fuels.

From the point of view of energy conversion, photosynthesis is an inefficient process, converting, at best, less than one per cent of incident solar radiation (on, for example, a farm field) to stored chemical energy. Efforts have been made to improve this energy-conversion process by growing algae or other plants in water, or in raw or treated sewage. As yet there is little expectation that such processes can be economically competitive with fuels from conventional sources, although they may in the future be used to provide foods and chemicals.

GEOTHERMAL ENERGY

In certain locations in the world, there exist such combinations of geologic structure, volcanic heat close to the surface, and supply of ground water, that steam or hot water can be obtained from wells. Notable among the locations where this energy source is being used are Lardarello (Northern Italy), New Zealand, Iceland, and California. The Lardarello and New Zealand plants each have capacities of 400 megawatts. Other possible locations are being surveyed. In geothermal plants, the heat supply from the wells is the source of steam which is used either in the operation of steam turbines which, in turn, operate electrical generators, or is used directly for heating purposes.

Geothermal energy is "firm" energy (continuously available), in contrast to the other non-conventional sources. The lifetime of a geothermal field is open to some question but is believed to be finite for it is thought that the quantity of heat in the rock structure in the neighborhood of the wells is essentially fixed.

NUCLEAR ENERGY

Since the subject of nuclear energy has been covered in Chapter 17, it will only be noted here that it holds tremendous promise of yielding many times more energy than fossil fuels once the problems of radioactive-waste disposal and the development of breeder reactors can be successfully solved. The original hopes about the economics of nuclear plants have not yet been realized; the costs of power from most nuclear sources have been higher than those of conventional plants. It appears, however, that large blocks of power from nuclear power plants are now becoming available at costs which are competitive with those of conventional sources. Once this situation spreads, nuclear energy will start to make a significant contribution to the world's energy economy.

CONCLUSION

The foregoing summary of energy resources must be interpreted in the light of political and social conditions in a given locality. *Political* problems include the presence of tariff barriers which inhibit free transport of fuel, or a national economic policy which dictates that one fuel, available within a country, shall be used in preference to a more economical (or otherwise superior) energy resource that must be imported. A typical *social* problem is the possible reluctance of a people to change established customs and accept the benefits that a new energy resource might bring.

Thus, many factors go into determination of the use patterns of energy, or the matching up of energy supply with consumption. Included are the availability of various energy resources; their distribution to the potential user; their adaptability to the particular needs of the user; the political and social problems which may be incurred in use of a resource; and the attraction of energy users to the neighborhood of a particular energy resource.

The result of the increase in population and in men's appetite for energy has been a very sharp increase in the world's rate of energy use during the past several decades. Industrial and mechanized agricultural societies depend on the availability of large quantities of energy. Man's further development, particularly in those parts of the world where energy consumption is not now high and where material standards of living are low, depends upon his ability to develop and use energy resources.

Since the beginning of the Industrial Revolution, most energy has come from fossil fuels, and today about 85 per cent of our total energy comes from burning coal, oil, and natural gas. Only about two per cent comes from hydropower, and the remainder is from the burning of agricultural wastes and wood. Liquid fuels now provide almost one third of the world's energy, and solid fuels provide about half. Perhaps the most marked feature of the patterns of energy use in recent years has been the rapid expansion of the use of oil, largely at the expense of coal, and despite the fact that the anticipated total supply of oil is only one tenth that of coal. Oil and natural gas are the only two energy resources of which a significant fraction of the world's expected reserves have been used up. On the other hand, relatively little use has been made of income energy sources.

In view of these facts, we can anticipate that within two or three generations, significant changes can be expected in the world's energy economy. The expanding position of crude oil as a supplier of world energy must be reversed by an increasing reliance on coal and other energy resources which are not now used to any great extent. Chief among these, we can expect, will be nuclear energy. Solar, geothermal, and possibly tidal and wind energy will make contributions which may be small in the overall energy economy, but which are and will be very important to local energy economies. In the future, there will be greater dependence on shale oils and products from tar sands, until, ultimately, the world must base its material existence on what we now consider "non-conventional" resources, particularly solar energy.

Thus it is that energy economy, at the world, national, or local level, is dynamic, and significant changes occur over periods ranging from a few to hundreds of years. These changes are brought about by discovery and development of new energy resources, by the results of research and development on processes for extracting and using energy resources now known, and by changing political, economic, and social factors. There is vigorous activity in the field of energy resource development, and it is appropriate that man should look to the future in this critical area.

In the foreseeable future, we do not appear to be facing any critical energy shortages. As specific resources dwindle and their costs rise, or their uses for purposes other than energy become more important, developments are occurring to provide alternatives. Solutions to problems of future energy supplies are in sight, and no doubt will be obtained by sustained scientific and technological effort. It is to be hoped that men can anticipate equal success in coping with the equally important problems of population, food supply, and world peace.

Part **VI**
Electronics and Communications

19 / Electronic Communications

BERNARD S. FINN

No technical developments of the 20th century have been more startling than those in communications. In the late 19th-century, governments, business firms, and other institutions of modern society had access to nearly instantaneous communication through the network of telegraph lines and cables which knit together virtually the entire world. This system, however, was suitable only for point-to-point communication. In the 20th century all this was changed within a few decades, a remarkably short time. Radio broadcasting, and then television, made communication immediate, flexible, personal, and, with the tiny transistor radio, ubiquitous.

Radio depends upon the movement of electrons, but in a manner quite different from telegraphy, where the net shift of electrons in a wire produces a current. In radio use is made of the fact that when electrons vibrate back and forth, they set up electromagnetic waves which can move through space without wires, and which will make electrons some distance away pulse back and forth at the same frequency. Early wireless transmission was by code, in which dots and dashes were produced merely by interruption of the signal frequency. By contrast, a pattern of electric pulses, such as that produced when speaking into a microphone, can be superimposed on a regularly oscillating wave (carrier wave) sent out by a transmitter; and a receiver tuned to the same regular oscillation (frequency) can then detect the carrier wave, separate the audio component which has been superimposed on it, and amplify and deliver only the audible or message portion into earphones or a loudspeaker. Radio transmission and reception thus enable electrons to provide communication without a wire connection.

THE PREHISTORY OF RADIO

One of the remarkable things about the prehistory of radio communication is the storybook progression from Michael Faraday (1791-1867) to James Clark

Maxwell (1831-79) to Heinrich Hertz (1857-94) to Guglielmo Marconi (1874-1937)—a progression that remains historically intact in the face of considerable research. It still appears that each man stood squarely upon the shoulders of his predecessor; none followed up his own work into the next development. Indeed, each died before that development took place. Thus we have a classic history of spatial concepts (Faraday's lines of force), yielding to mathematical expression (Maxwell), followed by experimental confirmation (Hertz), and practical application (Marconi).

Heinrich Hertz, in a series of brilliant experiments performed in Karlsruhe during 1887-88, determined that it was possible to produce in the laboratory electromagnetic radiation at a lower frequency than light, as Maxwell had predicted. As a transmitter he used an electric spark, whose oscillatory character had long since been investigated by Joseph Henry, Wilhelm Feddersen, and others. As a receiver he used a wire loop with a small gap; when the electromagnetic waves generated by the spark reached the wire there was a spark across the gap between the two brass nobs at the ends of the wire loop. With a metallic reflector he could set up standing waves, and he found that he had produced wavelengths from a few meters down to 30 centimeters.

MARCONI'S WIRELESS

Although others—notably Oliver Lodge—followed Hertz in laboratory studies of this remarkable new phenomenon, it was Guglielmo Marconi who demonstrated conclusively that these curious waves could be used for practical communications purposes. Young Marconi received most of his formal education through private tutors, although he did take some college courses, primarily in chemistry. While on a summer vacation in the Alps in 1894, he was inspired by reading an account of the work of the recently deceased Hertz, and in a series of experiments performed on his father's estate from 1894 to 1896, he succeeded in transmitting signals up to one and three-quarter miles. For this he used a spark transmitter with a key in the circuit. As a receiver he used a coherer—a device, invented by Eduard Branly and developed by Oliver Lodge, which commonly consisted of metallic filings in a glass tube. Such a tube of metallic powder would not normally pass a current; however, electromagnetic waves caused the filings to "cohere" (Lodge's word), allowing current from a local battery to be conducted through the coherer to operate an ordinary telegraph receiver or earphones. A "tapper," which mechanically tapped loose the iron filings by an electric bell mechanism in the battery circuit, was necessary to cause the filings to decohere.

Marconi improved upon these several devices for his specific purposes and also introduced something new—the grounded aerial. This grounded antenna enabled him to send and receive electromagnetic signals over longer distances.

Fig. 19-1. Marconi and his early apparatus for telegraphing without wires. From a photograph taken by Russell & Sons, London, expressly for *McClure's Magazine*. (Courtesy of *American Telephone and Telegraph Company*)

His first successful transmission in December 1894 extended only thirty feet. By February 1896 he had bridged the longer distance of almost two miles mentioned above, was confident that there was no limit to the ultimate range, and set out for England, where he expected to find a customer in the world's largest navy.

Marconi applied for his basic British patent on June 2, 1896, and performed a series of demonstrations with his equipment. By 1897 he was transmitting over distances of 18 miles; he increased this to 25 miles in 1898, and to 150 miles before the end of the century. In Newfoundland on December 12, 1901, he received the historical signal " · · · (S)" from Poldhu, in Cornwall, some 1700 miles away.

RADIO RECEIVERS

The excitement generated by Marconi's work was great, and as the 20th century opened many were dabbling in the new field. For some it was just for fun —the thrill of communicating in a new and exotic way. For others it held the possibility of developing a unique and perhaps crucial device that might bring them a valuable patent. It is noteworthy that most of the important improvements made up to 1912 were basically engineering feats; they were made by wireless engineers in the field, based on known—or sometimes *no*—principles. Contributions by laboratory scientists were minor.

One obvious place for a man to start was with the receiver (detector), and there soon were almost as many variations of the coherer as there were experimenters. In addition, Marconi, Branly, and Lodge continued to make improvements, as did Slaby and Arco in Germany, and Popov in Russia. However, the coherer—whatever its form—proved to be a temperamental device, and other methods were investigated.

One of the most successful receivers was Marconi's magnetic detector of 1902, which was based on earlier work by Ernest Rutherford. In it a continuous iron-wire loop was magnetized by permanent magnets and fed through the core of a coil linked with the antenna. The radio-frequency signal current altered magnetic conditions in the coil, causing a noise in the earphones, which were connected to a secondary coil wound around the first. In 1903 Reginald Fessenden and Lee de Forest patented successful receivers functioning on electrolytic action. Crystal detectors were introduced in 1906 by G. W. Pickard and H. H. C. Dunwoody, but many others had their own variations, and with the subject so much in the air, and the impetus to invent so great, it is senseless—if not impossible—to establish priorities in the matter. Noteworthy are both the variety of devices proposed and the variety of theories put forward to explain their action. Electrolytic and crystal detectors, for instance, were described by their inventors for a number of years in terms of thermal action. As late as 1915, as described in an article published in the March 1923 issue of *Popular Radio*, J. A. Fleming could conclude with respect to crystal detectors: "It is possible that the cause may be thermoelectric." This emphasizes the point that these were, in the main, engineering and not scientifically based developments.

The same can be said of the invention of the vacuum tube. When his attention was drawn by a black deposit etched with the image of the filament in his incandescent lamp, Thomas A. Edison introduced a second electrode in the bulb and performed a series of experiments in 1883-84. He even patented the device for use as a regulator; but unknowingly, Edison had taken the first steps that were to lead to the vacuum tube. John Ambrose Fleming (1849-1945), a consultant to the Edison Electric Light Company at the time, claimed independent notice of what came to be called the "Edison effect" after he performed similar experiments. Then Fleming, like Edison, let the matter drop. Twenty years afterward, as a consultant to Marconi, Fleming was instrumental in setting up the Poldhu station that transmitted the first transatlantic signal.

In the universal search for better detectors it occurred to Fleming to try the two-electrode bulb. In 1904 he patented it as a "thermionic valve" for use as a radio-signal detector. The incoming radio-frequency signal was impressed between the hot filament and the second electrode, producing a rectified direct current in the circuit which could activate earphones. Fleming had invented the diode, that is, a vacuum tube with a plate that would collect electrons from the hot filament as long as it was positive with respect to the filament. Fleming's annoyance that this invention automatically became the property of the Marconi company was later overshadowed by his bitter realization of what he had missed when De Forest's invention of the triode turned out to be so important. These events led to endless litigation and sharp words from both sides, in which each man claimed much more for himself than he should have.

De Forest always maintained that he came to his invention without knowledge of what Fleming had done. Although there are sufficient reasons for believing otherwise, this may indeed have been the case. Lee de Forest (1873-1961) left Yale in 1899 with a Ph.D. and plunged into the tumultuous radio field. In the search for a new detector he received a number of patents for devices consisting of two electrodes in a gas flame. In all of these a local battery in series with the telephone receiver kept the electrodes at different potentials. The radio signal, also applied across the gap, caused a change in the local current. He then experimented with two electrodes enclosed in a glass bulb. In November 1904 he applied for his first patent using the lamp form with a filament and plate (actually two plates); it differed from the Fleming valve mainly in the use of a local battery to keep the plates at a potential above that of the filament. In further designs he attempted to control the activity within the bulb by various external electrodes and magnets. In January 1907 De Forest applied for a patent on a three-electrode tube in which a zigzag wire, or grid, had been introduced between the filament and plate. The patent was issued as No. 879,532 on February 18, 1908.

The importance of the three-electrode tube (or "audion" as De Forest called it) and its mode of operation were little understood for a number of years by anyone, including its inventor. Even as detectors the soft, gassy tubes of De Forest and Fleming were not very popular and were never widely used. Yet De Forest's triode (an electron tube consisting of three electrodes—anode, cathode, and control grid) was to become basic to all subsequent radio developments because it could be used to produce, detect, or amplify radio waves depending on the variations in the electric potentials applied to its components and its position within the radio system.

TRANSMITTERS

Transmitters prior to World War I were primarily spark devices. Again, there was a wide variety of designs. Generally the purpose was to get as many sparks per second as possible and a number of rotating and quenching devices were

Fig. 19-2. Lee de Forest's "audion" (triode) of 1912 (left) and the high-vacuum tube developed in 1913 for the first telephone repeater. (Courtesy of *American Telephone and Telegraph Company*)

used. In retrospect, however, the most interesting developments were those leading to continuous-wave production. This would be essential to wireless telephony, though in those early days it took someone with considerable fore-sight to realize how important this would be.

An early and obvious problem with sparks, which continuous-wave trans-mitters were, in part, designed to solve, was the lack of frequency selectivity. A famous example of this occurred in 1901 at the international yacht races in New York when Marconi and De Forest interests both tried to report the event from tugs following the yachts. The interference was so great that the shore stations could make out neither broadcast. Although the basic understanding of tuning dates back to Oliver Lodge in the late 1880's and could have been used to advantage in the 1901 event, real achievement in the area was severely lim-ited by the capricious nature of the spark discharge.

In 1903 Valdemar Poulsen, a Dane, developed an arc discharge burning in hydrogen in a strong transverse magnetic field. The arc was a continuous source of electromagnetic radiation which he used successfully to transmit voice sig-nals. The Poulsen arc achieved some renown in the field, and by 1920 there were over 800 stations using it; most were for power under 25 kilowatts, but eleven were for powers of 200 and 400 kw.

Reginald Fessenden (1866-1932), born and educated in Canada, was an-other who found practical training with Edison in the 1880's. His approach to continuous-wave generation was to develop a very high-speed alternator. Models were built for Fessenden at the General Electric works under the direction of Charles P. Steinmetz and E. F. W. Alexanderson. A 75,000-cycle one-half-kw machine was installed by Fessenden at his Brant Rock, Massachusetts, station in 1906; and wireless operators on ships in the Atlantic for several hundred miles were startled that Christmas to hear speech and music coming in over their receivers. During this same period work on high-frequency alternators was also being carried out in Germany, notably by Rudolph Goldschmidt. In the United States, Alexanderson went on to make important improvements after Fessenden's National Electric Signaling Company went out of business. Further continuous-wave transmission experiments were made in the prewar period, but the results were not completely satisfactory, and it was the oscillating properties of the triode that were, in the end, to make radio telephony a commercially successful reality.

For those who tried to capitalize on their inventions in this early period there were manifold difficulties. For it is as true here as elsewhere that the inventive spirit is not necessarily good at the business of promoting and finance. Thus De Forest and Fessenden and several others were—sometimes on numerous occasions—on the edge of the business success they sought, based upon their inventions, only to have their positions collapse under one form or another of poor judgment. In addition, there was the imposing lead that Marconi's comparatively well-run enterprises held in the field; they obtained exclusive arrangements with the British, Italian, and other navies, and had the advantage of controlling British shore stations throughout the world. Even so, it is important to note that the Marconi companies were not financially successful until 1910, and substantial profits did not come for another half a dozen years.

There were several reasons why radio did not develop more rapidly as a profitable enterprise. These included the lack of radiotelephony prior to World War I, the emphasis on point-to-point communications before the advent of broadcasting in 1920, and a confused and conflicting patent situation. The important technical advances connected with the emergence of radio as a potent economic force were to occur in the second decade of the century.

THE CRUCIAL YEARS, 1912-20

The period 1912-20 embraces the emergence of radio as an applied technology and a commercial success. The former date marks the discovery of the oscillating character of the audion, the latter marks the "discovery" of broadcasting.

As mentioned above, De Forest was not the only one who failed to understand the operation of the audion or appreciate its potential. In large part this was due to the poor vacuum used—which in turn was partly due to the audion's origins as a gas-flame detector. For De Forest, ions were the important carriers of charge. But understanding of and interest in the operation of electron emission in a vacuum increased markedly with the studies of O. W. Richardson and others. Convinced that the operation of the triode was fundamentally a property of primary emission of charged particles (ions) from the filament, and not a secondary effect due to the gas, Irving Langmuir of General Electric and Harold D. Arnold of American Telephone and Telegraph developed high-vacuum tubes in the years 1912-13. Arnold also used the high-emissivity oxide cathode (that is, one which would emit large numbers of ions), introduced earlier by Arthur Wehnelt. At the same time, systematic studies were being made of the electronic properties of the triode, most notably by E. H. Armstrong.

Edwin Howard Armstrong (1890-1954) was, in 1912. a student of electrical engineering at Columbia University with an attic full of radio equipment at his home in Yonkers. Using Langmuir's techniques to produce high-vacuum tubes, Armstrong embarked upon a series of experiments to explain their operation in terms of their static characteristics. He reported his work in a still-intriguing article entitled "Operating Features of the Audion," published in the journal *Electrical World* in 1914. Sometime in the summer of 1912 Armstrong discovered that he could feed back part of the amplified signal from the plate to the grid circuit, producing "regeneration"—and a much amplified signal. Not having funds to patent this discovery, he had a circuit diagram notarized in January 1913, and finally filed for a patent in October. Implicit in regeneration was the principle of the oscillating triode, which Armstrong realized but saw fit to patent separately.

Armstrong presented his discoveries to the Institute of Radio Engineers in March 1915 in a paper (later published in the IRE *Proceedings*) that provoked sharp reply from De Forest. This was merely the opening skirmish in a long and bitter fight over priority for these discoveries, a fight that the Supreme Court settled in favor of De Forest in 1934 on the basis of experiments he had performed in 1912. Professionally, however, the decision went the other way, since it was Armstrong who consistently received society medals and other forms of recognition and honor for this invention. Interestingly enough, the oscillating features of the triode were discovered independently in Austria, by Siegmund Strauss in 1912; in Germany, by A. Meissner in 1913; and in America, by Fritz Löwenstein in 1912. Coincidence of this sort is, of course, common in the history of technology. Armstrong's real significance is that he, more than anyone else, was responsible for injecting the information into the radio field, thus inaugurating an era in which the vacuum tube would be dominant.

One of the first practical uses for the new high-vacuum tubes was in landline telephony. The increased amplifying power allowed the American Telephone and Telegraph Company (AT&T) to open a transcontinental line for the first time in January 1915. That same year AT&T used the triode as an oscillator at the navy's experimental station at Arlington, Virginia, and achieved voice transmission to Paris. Another dozen years would pass, however, before commercial transatlantic radiotelephony would begin.

Static was a much-investigated phenomenon in this period. Roy Weagant, who had worked for a time for his fellow Canadian, Fessenden, joined the American Marconi Company in 1912 and proceeded to make systematic and extensive investigations of these annoying, naturally occurring electromagnetic waves. But, as he and others were to find out, this was not a problem that would yield to a simple solution; static was too similar to the desired transmitted signals to be easily discriminated against.

With the vacuum triode available for transmitting, problems of amplification, modulation, static elimination, and general refinements in design became important; and the lessons that had been learned about tuning could be applied to relatively pure signals. Under the stimulus of World War I these problems were attacked on many fronts with considerable success.

Successful systems of amplitude modulation (AM) were achieved in these early years by the South African H. J. van der Bijl and by R. A. Heising, both working at Western Electric. Van der Bijl's circuit was used in the 1915 Arlington tests; Heising's, being less complex, was especially suitable for airplane sets and other portable transmitters used in the First World War.

During the war the particular problem of detecting high-frequency signals (in millions of cycles) which were emitted by the sparks in German aircraft engines was tackled by Armstrong when he arrived in France with the United States Army Signal Corps. Although British development was considerably ahead of American, there were still no tubes that could respond to these frequencies. In the closing days of the war Armstrong conceived of a circuit that would do the trick with available tubes. The incoming high-frequency signal was beat against a lower frequency from a local oscillator to produce another super-audible frequency which was now low enough to be treated in more ordinary fashion.

Use of a second, "heterodyne," signal in the receiver was not new; Fessenden had patented a receiver based on the same technique in 1902. But Fessenden had produced his audio signal directly from two low-frequency radio waves; furthermore, he had had to use an alternator as his source of the heterodyne wave, since the oscillating triode was still a decade away. There were others interested in the higher frequencies during these war years: Walter Schottky in Germany, Lucien Lévy in France, Henry Round in England. Lévy was apparently the first to describe the essentials of the superheterodyne receiver. But again it was Armstrong who did the crucial development work, which required several years to complete.

In 1919 Alan Hazeltine, a professor of electrical engineering at Stevens Institute in Hoboken, found a way to neutralize the inherent capacity between grid and plate of radio-frequency amplifier tubes. Without careful adjustment this capacity otherwise caused the tubes to go into oscillation and act as transmitters by emitting radio waves at the frequency of the oscillation. The Hazeltine neutrodyne receiver was marketed in 1923—a year before the superheterodyne—and was immensely popular.

World War I thus acted as a great stimulus to the development of radio. Coming on the heels of the discovery of the triode, it directed the minds of a number of the then-available professional radio engineers toward specific problems of the field. And as quantities of high-vacuum tubes were turned out— first by the French and British, then by the Americans—the mystery of their operation, and of the problems of consistent manufacturing techniques, disappeared. The triode became understood and reliable.

As the power of transmitting tubes increased—from 25 watts in 1915, to 250 watts three years later, and 10 kilowatts three years after that—and as good receivers became available, the stage was set for the unanticipated events of 1920. In that year Westinghouse offhandedly scheduled regular broadcasts from KDKA in Pittsburgh and discovered an eager public ready to purchase receivers, matched by merchants willing to purchase advertising: radio broadcasting was born.

DEVELOPMENT OF BROADCASTING, 1920-40

The period 1920-40 was dominated by commercial development of radio broadcasting. In the United States this development took the form of a considerable amount of shuffling of patents and shifting of corporate positions. In a manner reminiscent of the electrical power industry 40 years earlier, commercialization was based upon a large number of interdependent technical innovations, many of them patented. It was essential, therefore, for the rival concerns to reach some sort of agreement; and in this case they made a series of inter-licensing settlements.

The first step had already been taken—the purchase of the British-owned American Marconi Company by General Electric in 1919, forming the Radio Corporation of America. Strong support had been given this move by the United States government—particularly by the navy—which was anxious to prevent foreign control of such an important industry. In 1920 a cross-licensing agreement was signed between RCA and AT&T: all current and future radio patents belonging to the two companies would be mutually available for ten years. Further agreements with the British Marconi Company, the Compagnie Générale de Télégraphie sans Fils, and the Telefunken Corporation gave the young enterprise the necessary international connections and patent rights from Britain, France, and Germany. Westinghouse, which had purchased Fessenden and Armstrong patents, attempted to rival RCA for about a year, then joined the group in June 1921. Final agreements had RCA, which was not designed as a manufacturing concern, purchasing its radio apparatus from GE and Westinghouse on a 60-40 split.

With consolidation also came an emphasis on the establishment or enlargement of research laboratories, which led to a number of improvements. The problem of spurious oscillations in receiving tubes, which had been investigated by W. Schottky in Germany during the war, was taken up by A. W. Hull at the General Electric laboratory in 1923. In response to the problem Hull successfully introduced a fourth electrode, screening the grid from the cathode. Improvements were made by H. J. Round of the British Marconi Company, which marketed a commercial tube in 1926. (A fifth electrode—to prevent charge from accumulating on the screen grid—was introduced about 1930.) Work at the Bell Laboratories, the United States Bureau of Standards, and Westinghouse eliminated the need for batteries in receiving sets in the 'twenties. These and other laboratories were also making significant advances in loud-speaker design, automatic gain control, and a multitude of other elements associated with radio transmission and reception.

The centralization of commercial radio interests had important effects on developments that took place in the 'thirties in television and frequency modulation, largely because both of these technical advances proposed to make fundamental changes in the industry. The response of the industry—especially in the United States—was different in each case.

TV AND FM

The first television patent, based on a mechanical scanner, was obtained by Paul Nipkow in Germany in 1884. His receiver used an ingenious arrangement depending on the rotation of polarized light in a magnetic field. The sensing element in the transmitter was, unfortunately, a selenium resistance whose photo-response is, in fact, too slow to make the system practical.

Using neon lamps in their receivers and photoelectric cells in their transmitters, John L. Baird in London, Charles Francis Jenkins in Washington, and D. Mihaly, a Hungarian in Munich, developed operational television systems in the 1920's. But even with improvements in all the basic components, the resolution and sensitivity of these mechanical-optical devices were not completely satisfactory. It became obvious that the electron-scanning tube developed by Karl Ferdinand Braun in 1897 would provide a better receiver, making necessary, however, a sufficiently sensitive transmitter to go with it.

In 1919 Vladimir K. Zworykin left the St. Petersburg laboratory of Boris Rosing with the germ of an idea growing out of Rosing's development of a television system using a mechanical-optical transmitter with a Braun tube receiver. Zworykin subsequently joined the Westinghouse laboratories and by

1928 had developed a practical "iconoscope" camera tube with great sensitivity, owing to the temporary discharge of its photocells when the scanning beam struck them. Contemporary with this work, Philo Farnsworth produced an "image dissector" tube in which the entire image was impressed on a photoelectric surface; the resulting electron streams were then focused and moved across a scanning aperture.

Public electronic television was inaugurated in London in 1936, with the help of a Zworykin-type tube. General commercialization, however, was delayed until after World War II.

In refreshing contrast to the domination of the radio field by large corporations during this period, E. H. Armstrong almost single-handedly brought FM (frequency modulation) into commercial existence. Armstrong had become a millionaire through the sale and licensing of his early radio patents. Then, in 1933, during the closing period of his bitter and protracted dispute over the regenerative circuit, he received four patents covering a system of frequency modulation. From this there developed a fight between Armstrong and the industry—particularly RCA—which was reluctant to supplant an existing and profitable system of AM radio and to give up both the research money and the frequency space on the band of wavelengths badly needed for television. The corporate stubbornness was more than matched by Armstrong, however.

By the time World War II came, over forty FM transmitters had been licensed, and some important concessions had been obtained. Yet after the war FM suffered a severe setback when it was forced to a higher frequency range by the Federal Communications Commission. Armstrong exhausted himself in one final battle with RCA over his FM patents and committed suicide in 1954. FM continued to undergo a precarious development in the United States in radio broadcasting, but it has found wide use in mobile communications, TV audio signals, and various special services. Europeans, however, taking some clues from the American experience, created successful and extensive FM broadcast networks.

SHORTWAVE AND MICROWAVE DEVELOPMENTS

In the period between the wars there were a number of improvements stimulated by the needs of broadcasting, some of which have been mentioned above. Of particular importance were those that were encouraged by and allowed for the much-needed expansion of the usable wave spectrum through higher and higher frequencies. American amateur operators pioneered this exploration in the early 1920's after they had been outlawed into the "comparatively useless" region beyond 1500 kilocycles (wavelengths shorter than 200 meters). But the voracious needs of telephony, radio broadcasting, and eventually television, meant that commercial interests quickly followed.

By 1925 tests were being made with waves down to about one meter. And in 1931 a leap was taken into the "microwave" region when André Clavier of Le Matériel Téléphonique laboratories in Paris demonstrated transmission across the English Channel using 18-cm. waves (1700 megacycles) with a Barkhausen positive-grid oscillator he had developed. Two years later Clavier set up a commercial microwave link between two stations across the Channel. The power used was about one-half watt, possible because the short waves could be focused with a dispersion of only four degrees.

Along with the improvement of the triode oscillator came techniques for handling the higher frequency waves. Notable were the experiments of G. C. Southworth in developing the hollow-pipe wave guide in the late 1920's. This not only meant that these waves could be manipulated in transmitter and receiver circuits, but they could even be conducted over long distances instead of being radiated into space. The first significant commercial application was the opening of the coaxial cable between New York and Philadelphia in 1936. These advances were, of course, very important to the development of FM and TV. Both require the wide band-widths of frequency space which are available in the upper reaches of the spectrum.

Soon even higher frequencies would be available, but only through the introduction of a different method of modulation. At high frequencies the time of flight of the electrons in the vacuum tube becomes an important, and eventually a limiting, factor. In the klystron, developed by R. H. and S. A. Varian in the United States, and in the cavity magnetron, produced by H. K. H. Boot and J. T. Randall in England, this restriction was eliminated by modulating the velocity of the electron stream. Working tubes of both types were available in the late 1930's. In the beginning, frequencies were of the order of a few thousand megacycles; eventually they were to go much higher.

RADAR

The immediate application of these high frequencies was in Radio Detection and Ranging—RADAR. Early in the 'thirties, independent work was being performed in Britain, Canada, the United States, France, and Germany toward a detection system that would use the echoes from powerful radio beams. The detection is based upon certain properties of very short radio waves, namely, the fact that they are reflected by solid objects and that they travel at a constant speed; hence one can measure the distance to an object by measuring the time it takes for radio waves to travel from a transmitter to an object and be bounced back again.

Partly because of the development of the magnetron (which at that time could transmit considerably more peak power than the klystron), and partly because of an overwhelming need, the British led in this field. With the help of

Fig. 19-3. A modern mobile radar installation. This portable early-warning search unit operates at low frequency and can be field-assembled in six hours. The inflatable nylon shelter (left) houses the radar transmitter, receiver, and monitoring equipment. The 61-foot outer balloon-shaped dome (right) protects the "Paraballoon" antenna inside. This interior sphere is made of metallized fabric, and both it and the dome are inflated. (Courtesy of *Westinghouse Electric Corporation*)

the Americans this advantage over the Germans was maintained throughout World War II.

Radar was a crucial defensive factor against German air raids in 1940 and against the V-1's of 1943. It was also a key factor in the antisubmarine campaign. Later, German antiaircraft radar was rendered almost ineffective by various radar-confusion devices. There is good reason to consider these margins of radar accomplishment equivalent to the margin of eventual victory.

POSTWAR DEVELOPMENTS

After the war the earlier trends were continued, but with additional emphasis on the scientific base. New laboratories were established with extensive funds at their disposal, and the payoff was impressive. The transistor, produced at the

Bell Telephone Laboratories by the theoretical-experimental team of William Shockley, John Bardeen, and Walter H. Brattain in 1947, was quickly developed to the point where it could perform many of the functions of the electron vacuum tube—in much smaller space and with much less power.

Meanwhile, the vacuum tube itself was continually being improved, especially in the terms of smaller size and better reliability. As a result, the first Atlantic telephone cable, with vacuum-tube repeaters, was laid in 1956. Klystrons were made for higher frequencies and higher powers, primarily for radar defense purposes, but also for communications, by microwave links that began to crisscross the American continent in the 1950's, by scatter from the troposphere (the stratum of the atmosphere below the stratosphere) in northern Canada and Alaska, and by satellite. The travelling wave tube, which also acts on the principle of velocity modulation but with exceptionally wide band-width characteristics, had been produced during the war by Rudolf Kompfner at the Clarendon Laboratory, Oxford, England. Through further development, especially at the Bell Laboratories, it found special use as a low-power, broad band amplifier in television-relay satellites.

In 1953 another leap was made in the frequency spectrum when C. H. Townes and his student J. P. Gordon at Columbia University found that they could produce coherent beams of a single frequency by stimulating excited ammonia atoms to release energy. This produced the maser. Further work on other materials in succeeding years by many investigators extended the frequencies throughout the visible spectrum. The low-noise characteristics of the maser make it an excellent amplifier. At prewar frequencies the background sky noise was so great that contemporary receiver amplifiers were quite adequate. But at frequencies much above 1000 megacycles, the sky noise becomes negligible, making amplifier design and other circuit characteristics crucial.

With the development of rocketry in the 1950's artificial satellite relays became possible. The first experimental communications device, Score, was launched by the United States Army in December 1958. Contact was made between ground stations 3000 miles apart until the batteries failed after 13 days. A much more sophisticated package, powered by solar cells, was sent aloft by the army in 1960 and performed well until it inexplicably failed after three weeks. The availability of maser amplifiers and powerful klystron transmitters made possible successful reflection experiments from a silvered balloon (Echo) in 1962 and scatter experiments from a thin belt of copper dipoles (West Ford) in 1963. Here the Bell Telephone Laboratories and the Lincoln Laboratories of M.I.T. performed the crucial developmental work. Telstar, also built at the Bell Laboratories, demonstrated the full potential of satellite relay after its launch in July 1962, although it suffered some radiation damage, was inoperable for several months, and finally failed the following February. The inclusion of a travelling wave tube in the satellite gave it television capabilities,

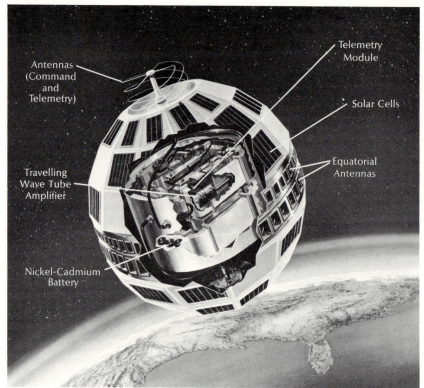

Fig. 19-4. A cutaway drawing of the Bell System's experimental Telstar communications satellite. (Courtesy of *American Telephone and Telegraph Company*)

and overseas television transmission via such satellites has now become commonplace.

CONCLUSION

The history of electrical communications in the 20th century is fairly typical of modern technology in a new field. An available scientific and technical base was sufficient to support a considerable amount of early activity. And when the practicality of the work had been demonstrated, commercial, university, and government funds were made available for further research. Most of this was applied to immediate problems, but some had more long-range, fundamental results.

There remain unanswered some very important questions about the relationship between a developing technology and the forces acting upon it, questions that apply to other areas of technology as well as electronics. Does the patent system, for instance, protect the inventor or force him to pay the cost of protecting himself? W. R. Maclaurin (*Invention and Innovation in the Radio Industry*) quotes Armstrong as saying that he sold his regenerative circuit patents because he "was in danger of being litigated to death." Not only is the expense great, but the competence of the courts to judge these technical matters is often questionable. And to what extent is monopoly desirable so that a company can make a return on its investment, or is competition beneficial in spurring further inventiveness? The creation of RCA may have been invaluable to the commercial development of broadcasting in the United States, but there is evidence that the retirement of other companies from the field slowed down technical progress. Finally, how important are the massive amounts of money being poured into "research and development" efforts? Some of the results are very impressive, but they are also very expensive, both in money and in professional talent.

The nature of these questions and their obvious importance indicate that the history presented in this chapter must necessarily be incomplete even if it chronicled all of the detailed technical accomplishments. The forces affecting these problems pervade our whole society; the studies necessary for their interpretation have only been started.

20 / Origins of the Computer
THOMAS M. SMITH

One of the dreams that the rise of modern technology has encouraged is that some day soon useful, *intelligent* machines might be developed to serve mankind. They would be more than automatic machines, examples of which have existed ever since Greco-Roman antiquity; they would "think," discriminate, make decisions, exercise judgment. Properly designed, they would never go mad, never turn into a Frankenstein's monster or enslave mankind. They would be faithful servants, docile robots; would relieve men of all sorts of dull, routine operations and otherwise inescapable drudgery; and would perform these jobs better than men.

Many have concluded that the first generation of thinking machines has already been invented and that the electronic computer, as a "mechanical brain," represents the first real step toward fulfillment of the robot dream. Such machines can carry out swiftly a multitude of mathematical and logical operations that would require teams of men years to accomplish without achieving correspondingly accurate results. Such machines already keep track of the complex inventories of enormous warehouses or industrial supply houses with ease, indicating when stocks are depleted and keeping the supply lines filled. They keep track of, and on command will write, intricate payrolls including any deductions or bonuses month after month without error. They locate unsold seats on airline flights. They calculate complicated orbits and direct satellites and spacecraft to almost any rendezvous or destination. They process all sorts of detailed census data on hundreds of millions of people, keep track of what employers pay out and what taxpayers pay in, and detect discrepancies and tax fraud. They store entire libraries full of information and produce the smallest fact on demand—or if they are not quite doing that yet, they are fully capable of doing it. The day of the thinking machine appears to have arrived.

SOURCES OF THE COMPUTER

The computer is not a wholly new machine but rather a culmination and a joining together of several machine traditions that have mutually influenced each other's progress in design for centuries. One of these traditions is that of producing machinery designed to transmit and multiply or reduce power and speed. A water wheel, a block and tackle, a train of gear wheels in a mine hoist are all examples of devices produced within this age-old tradition.

Another tradition is that of machinery designed to transmit motion with special emphasis upon the control and precision of that motion. An important example is the precision chronometer, descended from the clockwork tradition. An older device is the odometer, or mileage meter, described either by Heron of Alexandria not long after the birth of Christ, or by a later writer in ancient times who may have inserted it in a copy of Heron's writings. This mechanism consisted of a train of wheel-and-worm-gears boxed and mounted on a carriage. It is significant to the story of the computer because it embodies the principle of the pegged counter wheel as well as the scheme of using several dials in the same manner employed today in gas and electricity meters. This machine, along with a similar mechanism described by the Roman writer Vitruvius for use on ships, is part of the mechanical tradition that produced mathematical counting and calculating devices, the latest generation of which is the computer.

MATHEMATICAL CALCULATORS

Mathematical calculators are older than the pegged-wheel counter, however. One device that has taken several forms and which can be traced back to at least the first millennium before Christ is the abacus. It is quite different from the odometer we have just mentioned.

The abacus utilizes two ideas that appear to have emerged before the dawn

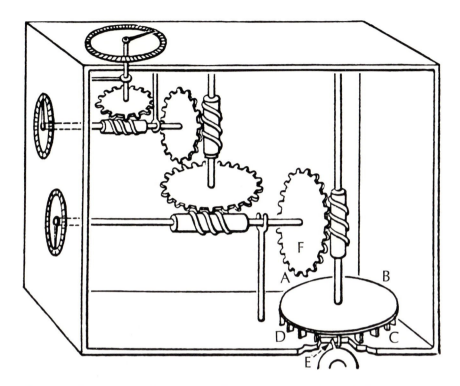

Fig. 20-1. The ancient odometer described in Heron of Alexandria's writings. "Cut an opening in the base of the framework," reads the treatise, "and through this opening let a pin [E] attached to the hub of one of the carriage wheels protrude at each revolution of the wheel." This pin engages the first of the wheels of the gear train and sets the whole in motion. The first of the gear wheels is a bronze disc [ABCD] fitted with eight pegs so as to let "this pin at each revolution push one of the pegs of the disc in such a way that the next following peg takes the position of the one before, and so on indefinitely. Consequently, when the carriage wheel has made eight revolutions, the disc with the pegs will have made a single revolution."

The shafts of appropriate gear wheels in the train protruded through one side of the case and are fitted with pointers. "Now if motion to the extent of 30 cogs [in cogwheel F] indicates a journey of 1600 cubits, the motion of one cog's distance in this wheel [F] will measure 53⅓ cubits of the journey." (A carriage wheel ten cubits in circumference was a customary size.) The pointer on the shaft of cogwheel F accordingly passes as many marks on the dial as there are cogs in the wheel, each mark designating another 53⅓ cubits. A practical limitation on the number of cogwheels, worm gears, and dials required was the length of a long day's journey. Each morning the odometer could be reset to zero. (From M. R. Cohen and E. I. Drabkin, *A Source Book in Greek Science*, Harvard University Press, 1958)

of written history: first, the idea of using physical objects, such as fingers or pebbles or knots or notches, to represent abstract notions of quantity in terms of numbers; and second, the idea of using the place and position of the physical objects to store and keep track of certain numbers while counting other numbers. By shifting the positions of the physical objects that have been systematically arranged (as in the later abacus, or *suan-pan*), one automatically erases and stores new numbers while "reckoning" or calculating.

The "little pebbles" (*calculi*) and the ancient abacus, whether Roman or Chinese, originally consisted of a board covered with dust or wax on which numerals could be traced; later a lined board or table on which counters could be arranged; and still later, after the first millennium A.D., beads strung on wires in a frame. These were employed to carry out simple and sometimes not so simple arithmetic operations. They gave useful, arithmetical, abstract meanings to the symbols or counters so employed, and the manipulation of these revealed new, abstract, arithmetical meanings in terms of the calculated results obtained. Such matters were of particular interest to mathematicians. When commercial transactions called for the use of these primitive hand calculators, their manipulation revealed concrete economic consequences, in terms of profit or loss. It is not surprising, therefore, to find that these mathematical machines came to be highly valued, too, by practical men.

Always, of course, there were a few men who enjoyed calculation and numerology and things mathematical for their own sake, apart from their practical value. Their activities produced a variety of mathematical calculators, some of which counted and manipulated numbers and some of which converted numerical quantities into physical, dimensional magnitudes according to the same principle that permits us to convert, say, thirty-six discrete numerical units into the continuous linear length we call a "yard."

John Napier (1550-1617) of Scotland was one of those who took advantage of the interchangeability and equivalence of numerical and linear magnitudes to demonstrate an aid to calculating that he invented and named the "logarithm" (literally, "ratio number"). His logarithm was based on a novel conceptual technique establishing the correspondence between two series of numbers, one series of which progresses arithmetically (1, 2, 3, 4, etc.) and the other geometrically (as, 2, 4, 8, 16, etc. or 2, 6, 18, 54, etc.). Tables of logarithms of various types were subsequently to prove of great assistance in carrying out otherwise elaborate and tedious astronomical and engineering computations.

Another calculating technique developed by Napier made use of what came to be called "Napier's bones," or "Napier's rods." They provided a mechanical multiplication table: by laying selected rods side by side, each bearing the appropriate column of numbers, one could construct mechanically a table of the multiples of any selected number without performing any computations in his head. This device, like the original "dust board" (*abax*), was a versatile, ready-reference instrument that took advantage of the principle of relative place and position to store and indicate numbers.

Napier first published word of his logarithms in 1614 and first described his rods publicly in 1617. The rods became mathematical curios, while the concept of the logarithm brought Napier undying fame for its value in shortening important processes of computation.

In his presentation of the logarithm concept, Napier had followed an ancient Greek geometrical tradition, continuous since at least the 13th century in Western Europe, of depicting motion abstractly in terms of a point moving along a line. Within six years Edmund Gunter had marked off a straight line in Napier's ratios and applied a pair of dividers to accomplish multiplication and division by adding and subtracting measured lengths. The following year William Oughtred eliminated the dividers by sliding one of the Gunter-Napier lines past another, and thereby received credit from later writers as being the inventor of the slide rule. In 1654 Robert Bissaker placed the lines on sliding strips of wood and thus produced the prototype of the modern slide rule, except for the sliding glass window with the single hairline, which was added to commercially manufactured slide rules about the middle of the 19th century.

Two classes of mathematical calculators were thus in existence before the end of the 17th century—the numerical, *digital* calculator of the abacus tradition and the *analog* computer of the logarithm, slide-rule tradition. The human operator of the former computed quantities in the form of numbers, while the operator of the latter computed quantities in the form of physical magnitudes. Both of these classes of calculators have persisted, with improvements, down to the present, the abacus especially in the East, and the slide rule primarily in the Western world.

Also in the 17th century there appeared a third kind of calculator, the mechanical adder. Since it is numerical and digital, one might place it under the first class, except that it operates under different principles. Like the abacus, this adder was a passive storer of numerical information and, like the abacus, it required a human hand to manipulate its elements. Unlike the abacus, however, it performed its mathematical operations through the carefully controlled transmission of motion through a gear train. It was, in effect and in considerable detail, Heron's odometer without the pointers and dials and with the numbers printed on the edges of gear wheels so that they could be viewed through tiny windows. In its first form it was not intended to reckon the distances a carriage was passing over but the sums of French coins in the denominations of *livres, sous,* and *deniers.*

Just as one revolution of Heron's carriage wheel caused a partial rotation of the first disc, so one revolution of the "units" wheel in the adder caused partial rotation of the adjacent wheel. In the mechanical adder this single-pin feature became a "carrying" device: every time the first wheel rotated once, the visible number on the next wheel changed by a value of 1, just as happens when a modern automobile mileage meter goes through ten tenths of a mile and "carries" or adds 1 from the "tenths-of-a-mile" number wheel to the adjacent "miles" number wheel.

The inventor of the adder was Blaise Pascal (1623-62). Between 1642 and 1645 the young Frenchman, then on the edge of an impressive career as a mathematician, philosopher, and theologian, sought relief from the computational drudgery that went on in his father's tax office. He put together a gadget, equipped with a series of pegged wheels, that would add and subtract. This ingenious predecessor of the "pocket adder" could mechanically accomplish the same results achieved by simple, mental addition and subtraction exercises. The first models were not carefully made, however, and as a result they committed occasional errors.

The mechanical adder was followed within thirty years by the mechanical multiplier. Another 17th-century philosopher and mathematician, Gottfried Wilhelm von Leibniz (1646-1716), famous for his invention of calculus independently and coincidentally with Isaac Newton, proposed a modification and improvement upon the gear-train, controlled-movement tradition of Heron and Pascal as early as 1671. His improvement was the stepped-cylinder multiplier, finally constructed in 1694. It made use of the only kind of multiplication principle practised by ancient Egyptian scribes, that of embarking on repeated additions to obtain the product. (To find the product of 5 x 7, add 7 to itself five times over.) Like Pascal's adder, Leibniz's multiplier was a passive storer of numerical information under the fingers of its human manipulator. It, too, was a mathematical machine, transmitting carefully controlled mechanical movements, and it was also not made carefully enough to avoid computational errors. The mathematical and scientific principles were soundly applied by Pascal and by Leibniz, but the engineering was faulty, a matter of little surprise since these inventors were not engineers.

The design history of calculators presented thus far reveals that a significant convergence of traditions occurred in the creative-design activities of Pascal and Leibniz. They were not wholly original, but were evolutionary contributors who brought together briefly, in a very special way, features of the gear-train design tradition descended from antiquity and features of the numerical calculating tradition, also separately descended from antiquity. In both Heron's odometer and the 17th-century mechanical calculating machines, the arithmetic tradition of counting made use of the gear-train tradition and obtained *mechanical* answers with gear teeth that agreed with the *logical* answers the human brain obtains through logical thought processes involving the addition of integers. These machines, in short, would "add" automatically as a function of their rotational motions, but in no accurate sense of the word did any of the calculators "think" or exhibit intelligence.

Furthermore, Pascal's and Leibniz's machines were the products of men who were not engineers, and their machines were subject to mechanical errors that prevented them from computing reliably. Subsequent engineering progress was necessary, over a span of two centuries, before mechanical calculators became reliable and useful enough—and inexpensive enough—to come into wide use late in the 19th century.

INTRODUCTION OF MECHANICAL PRECISION

A key to the engineering progress that occurred and led to the first information-processing computer is to be found in the separate tradition of precision machine tools. Practical mechanical calculators required the carefully controlled motions that come only from precision parts, and precision parts required pre-existing machine tools and techniques to produce them.

The machine-tool tradition itself grew, in significant measure, out of experience with watch and clockwork design, another tradition continuous in Europe since the late Middle Ages and heavily influenced by mathematics in the design of gear wheels and gear teeth after the 17th century. The clockwork tradition then, to a considerable degree, contributed the state-of-the-art knowledge of gear-train mechanisms which made possible the 17th-century contributions of Pascal and Leibniz. All together there was the gear-train tradition and the calculating-board tradition from ancient times, the clockwork tradition since the Middle Ages, and the machine-tool tradition of the 18th and 19th centuries. The convergence and interaction of these produced a thriving mechanical desk-calculator tradition by the 20th century and, as it turned out, set the stage for the electronic computer tradition that followed.

Although the electronic computer was not a direct descendant of the mechanical calculator, the successes of the latter tradition provided a powerful spur to the pioneering efforts in the computing field. Furthermore, it helped to suggest the idea of a system of integrated tasks in the form of automatic sequences of operations.

CHARLES BABBAGE

Mechanical calculators had become significant tools in commerce and science during the 19th and early 20th centuries as a result of the inventive engineering achievements and the enterprising manufacturing and merchandising talents of a host of men. Among these were Philipp Mattheaus Hahn (working about 1770), Charles Babbage (about 1821), William S. Burroughs (about 1885), Dorr E. Felt (about 1885), Herman Hollerith (about 1890), Oscar Sundstrand (about 1910), Jay R. Munroe (about 1911), Edwin Jahnz (about 1914), and Torres y Quevado (about 1920).

Experts in the engineering history of mechanical calculators have characterized the contributions of these men and others by such technical terms as automatic multipliers, monophase or polyphase rotary calculators, partial-product multipliers, electrical and mechanical comparison dividers, automatic sequence-control machines, and many other names. Of these, the one that is frequently spoken of as the progenitor of the information-processing computers was conceived, developed, and refined by the 19th-century British mathematician Charles Babbage (1792-1871).

As a consequence of ideas he worked on between 1812 and 1823, Babbage set about building a "Difference Engine." This machine, he explained, would carry out certain tedious calculations with relative speed and great labor-saving accuracy, then print out the useful mathematical tables its operations had generated. Full of enthusiasm, he contracted to build a prototype for the British government. The prototype was never finished, however, because Babbage was temperamentally incapable of accepting the engineering compromises involved in reducing his brilliant conception to practical, mechanical, working form, in spite of the fact that its principles were sound.

The Difference Engine is less important historically than a second engine he devised, his "Analytical Engine." Work on the former stimulated Babbage to intellectual activity that created this, and he mulled over the design of the Analytical Engine for the remainder of his life, from 1833 until his death in 1871. It was the first of the information-processing computers except that it, too, was never completed. Instead, it and its principles were forgotten, and when their significance was rediscovered and reappraised by Howard Aiken, the first man to reduce such an invention to practice, more than a century had passed since Babbage's first conception.

Aiken, an instructor in applied mathematics with a doctorate in physics, had already worked his way independently over much of the ground Babbage had covered before he became aware of Babbage's work three years after he began to work on the problem. It is one of the ironies of history that Babbage, who was first and who tried so hard and understood so keenly the significance of his invention, was not essential to the birth of the computer. Had he never existed, the computers of the 20th century would still have emerged and in the same form.

The machines that Babbage dreamed of and Aiken built were different— Babbage's were mechanical and Aiken's, electromechanical—but the principles they embodied were the same, except for internal storage. Both were designed to perform mathematical calculations using integers, or numbers (unlike the slide rule, the differential analyzer, and the analog computer, all of which used measured physical magnitudes or dimensions); they would compare and select alternative courses of action (later called "branching" by computer experts), and would alter the instructions in their programs as they proceeded.

Each would possess a "memory," or storage facilities, and they would print out intermediate as well as final results. In sum, they were different from all previous types of calculators because they would be able to carry out long, complicated sequences of arithmetical operations without requiring the assistance of a human operator: they were automatic sequence-controlled calculators.

These complicated machines, as Babbage envisioned them, consist of groups of smaller machines so arranged that all work together harmoniously; the smaller ones, often called components or mechanisms, are designed to carry out certain functions necessary to the successful operation of the entire assembly. Babbage's proposed Analytical Engine had the following major components: a "mill" (as he called it) to carry out arithmetical operations; a mechanism to receive information in proper coded form from punched cards; a mechanism to print out or punch out on cards the results, both intermediate and final; a component to effect the orderly transfer of numbers from one mechanism to another (for example, from the input mechanism to the arithmetic mill); and most important of all, a "store" to hold various numbers the Engine might need or generate and might use later on in its operations. The Engine would have not only this internal storage, or "memory," but would have, also, the external storage available to it from punched cards. Other punched cards, containing operational instructions, would be fed to the specific mechanism that was responsible for both the orderly transfer of numbers among the components of the Engine and for telling the mill what arithmetical operations to perform. Rods, cylinders, gear racks, geared wheels bearing the ten digits of the decimal system, and similar mechanical elements would perform the physical movements in the Engine. The Engine would be equipped with bells and numbered windows to instruct attendants what to do from time to time (as, for example, "feed in card such-and-such"), and louder bells to tell the attendant he had inserted the wrong card.

The complexity of the Engine's mechanical and logical operations persuade the observer to conclude that it could "think" with a limited intelligence and "remember"—that is, remember whether it had a certain number and where that number was stored. However, the machine could follow only the detailed instructions composed for it by a human programmer. Its storage, mill, input, output, and control components were limited to routines only, and to those routines laid out in advance by the programmer. It was incapable of constructive thought and creative recourse to its "memory." It had only a *mechanized* memory. Babbage's Engine was, after all is said and done, an automatic computer, one proposed as an ideal design but one never built and finished and never tested in practice. Computer experts point out that it should and would have worked. But in engineering history Babbage's Analytical Engine was a dead end, the principles of which were independently rediscovered without recourse to Babbage's excellent groundwork at the start.

HOWARD AIKEN

During the 1930's Aiken became well acquainted with the state of the art of desk calculators and of punched-card machinery of the type that had been developed by Herman Hollerith and his firm in the days before it became the International Business Machines Corporation. The idea of using holes punched in rolls, tapes, cylinders, or cards to determine patterns woven into cloth had been in use since the 18th century. The culmination of this technique was reached early in the 19th-century in the Jacquard loom, which made use of "yes-no" type information to move certain threads, attached to hooked wires, into position. A punched hole ("yes") allowed the hooked wire to move into position, while the lack of a punched hole ("no") prevented the wire from moving into position, during each cycle of the loom's operation. Since the selection of the threads determined the pattern, the stack of punched cards "told" the loom what pattern to weave.

Hollerith, at the end of the 19th century, had adapted the punched-hole

Fig. 20-2. Hollerith punched-card equipment similar to that used in the 1890 Census. (Courtesy of *International Business Machines Corporation*)

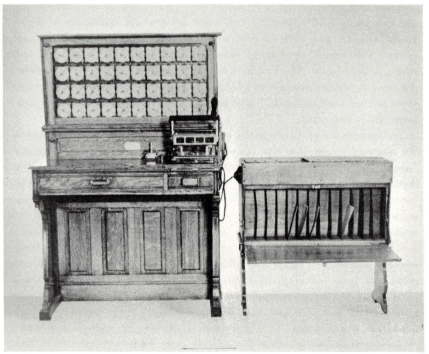

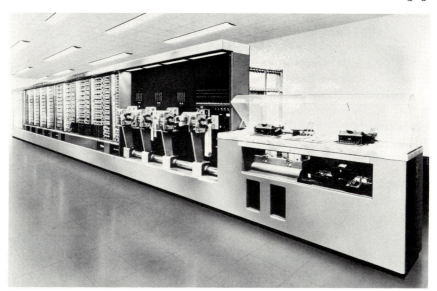

Fig. 20-3. The Mark I computer, 1944. (Courtesy of *International Business Machines Corporation*)

technique to the analysis of census data. Babbage earlier had proposed to use punched cards; and Aiken used punched tape as a source of data and a source of instructions. In addition to the examples set by Jacquard's loom, Babbage's scheme, and Hollerith's machines, existing mechanical calculators suggested to Aiken various sorts of mathematical operations and solutions that might be worked out by the arithmetical procedures of appropriate mechanisms operating in controlled sequences. The assistance to science that such a machine might provide, while at the same time performing automatic calculations rapidly and without error, offered a prospect and a goal Aiken could not resist.

By 1937 he had organized in his mind in a general way, together with many particular details, the arrangement of the mechanisms and components he wanted. He made arrangements with the authorities at Harvard University and with the management of the International Business Machines Corporation to set up the project he had in mind. He worked with J. W. Bryce, B. M. Durfee, F. E. Hamilton, and C. D. Lake of IBM and constructed a machine that IBM formally presented to Harvard in August 1944—the "IBM Automatic Sequence Controlled Calculator," commonly known as the Harvard Mark I computer—the first of the computers. Although by later standards of computer technology it was impossibly slow in its operations and was not electronic, the Mark I was the first computer that really worked and was the first of the information-processing devices.

The Mark I was regarded from the first as a mathematical machine designed to assist scientific and engineering research. It could handle decimal numbers up to 23 places, multiply two eleven-place numbers in three seconds, and make use of electrically operated mechanical components in the elaborate ways intimated by the formal title of the machine. Although punched paper tape provided the instructions and the data, certain switches could be set by hand to lock in numbers that the machine could use but not alter. Electrically driven and electrically clutched number wheels performed mechanical arithmetical operations and presented the numerical solutions. After it went into operation the Mark I underwent subsequent design modifications and improvements.

ELECTRONIC DIGITAL COMPUTERS

Electronic digital computers were the next generation, and they came hard on the heels of the Mark I. The first true electronic computer was the Electronic Numerical Integrator and Computer, better known by its acronym, ENIAC, designed and built under the direction of J. Presper Eckert and John W. Mauchly at the Moore School of Electrical Engineering, University of Pennsylvania, for the United States Army. It went into operation in 1946 and was put to work on ballistics calculations. It could multiply two 10-decimal numbers in less than three *thousandths* of a second, compared to the three-second interval the Mark I required.

The ENIAC was deliberately designed to be of limited use and was not intended to be a general-purpose computer, for its designers had enough engineering problems to solve without ambitiously extending the capacities and therefore problems of their projected machine. In this respect they successfully resisted the temptations to enlarge and improve which had caused Babbage to fail.

Aiken's Mark I occupied a wall fifty-one feet long and eight feet high. The ENIAC was also large, occupying the walls of a room approximately forty feet by twenty feet in size and including racks of assemblies on wheels in the center of the room. Eighteen thousand radio tubes and 1500 electrical relays went into its construction, together with plug boards, wiring, power units, and related equipment. Its internal storage was kept small, consonant with the mathematical chores it was expected to perform. The size of this and other pioneer computers was not an important consideration to the designers. They were interested in access to the components, so that unanticipated repairs and improvements might be made easily.

While digital computer development was proceeding, the analog-computer tradition, represented by the slide rule in the 17th century, also produced analog machines, including the famous designs of Lord Kelvin in the 19th century and the accomplished Differential Analyzer of Vannevar Bush in the 1930's. Employing physical magnitudes instead of digits (numbers), the analog-computer tradition shifted, as did the digital tradition, from instruments to machines, mechanical at first, then electronic, producing a proliferation of analog servo-mechanisms to assist the weapons technology of World War II. This tradition continues to have its important applications, even though the digital tradition became more thoroughly exploited following the ENIAC's modest but provocative success.

The ENIAC, being electronic, was not an engineering descendant of the Mark I mechanical machine. Its ancestry can be traced back to the complex history of electronics in radio and telephony. The electronic computer tradition goes back to wartime developments in the pulsed circuitry of radar, to the well-developed state of the art in radio tubes and circuitry, and to the logical abstractions of a mathematical tradition that included such names as Babbage, Edward Boole, and John von Neumann. The new computer tradition arose out of the accumulation and synthesis of many strands of endeavor associated previously with other traditions, as had been the case with the mechanical calculator.

Even before the ENIAC could demonstrate to everyone's satisfaction what the incredibly high-speed, electronic, digital computer could do, development of the components—the mill, the store, the input and output devices, and the control mechanism (that had all been identified as functional units by Babbage) —had proceeded in several directions. Of particular concern was the internal store, or mechanized memory. How big should it be? How should it operate in order to "remember"? How fast should any piece of information in the storage be retrievable, and how long should it take to return it to storage in either its original or modified form? Various arrangements were suggested. Special circuits, acoustic-delay lines, magnetic drums, large electrostatic tubes, and tiny magnetic rings called "cores" were among the most prominent inventions. By the end of the 1950's, magnetic-core storage was the most widely used because of its compact size, reliability, and speed of access to its information.

The history of computers in the twenty years after 1946 witnessed the substitution of transistors for radio tubes and printed circuits for wired circuits. The trend toward miniaturization of radio and radar components produced dramatic reductions in the physical size of computers even as their versatility and capacity to handle information increased.

Electronic and logical considerations moved the binary-digit mode of calculation to the forefront. Serving as both the electronic "building block" around which the circuitry was built and the basic logical form of the information handled, the binary system did all that the decimal system of Babbage and Aiken had done and more. The logical implications of the binary system's two-valued logic caused mathematicians to specialize in constructing ever more complex and useful "programs" to guide the information-processing operations of the computers. Especially brilliant was John von Neumann's demonstration, about the time the ENIAC was finished, that one could encode instructions to the machine in the same language as the data the machine was expected to

Fig. 20-4. A modern electronic computer installation. (Courtesy of *International Business Machines Corporation*)

use, and therefore instructions and data could be coherently intermixed in the program the machine was to follow and in the information the machine could store.

Progress in the theory of machine logic and in engineering-design theory led to widespread application of the economical "module" principle of design, construction, and operation, whereby relatively few basic types of electronic circuits and elements could be systematically arrayed in as massive and repetitive an organization as one wished, depending upon the intentions of the builders. Auxiliary devices, such as magnetic tapes, printers, and typewriters, extended the capacities and the applications of the computers. Computer systems draw upon other communications systems, their input and output components often being connected by regular telephone lines to a central computer. This allows many separate offices to share the use of a large and complex computer at relatively low individual cost.

MACHINES AS THINKERS

The engineering, mathematical, and logical traditions of the computer combined to initiate a revolution in the processing of information by machines. So spectacular were the advances that the myth readily grew that computers could "think." But, like Heron's odometer, computers perform only the tasks laid out for them. They may follow logical operations to logical conclusions, but they do not originate new tasks for themselves, do not think creatively, and do not innovate except in that restricted manner by which the concept "two," when added to the concept "three" produces the "new" concept "five."

Although machines are sometimes made to simulate creative imagination by being programmed in advance, they do not actually possess it; nor do they experience emotional tension; consequently, in this most important and funda- mental sense, they do not think. In an age of information explosion, they aid man's memory. They are mechanical zombies that are proving of inestimable assistance—like the airplane, the telephone, and the electric power grid—in the conduct of human affairs. Whether later generations of computers will actu- ally "think" is a matter for conjecture that in the end hinges upon how we will choose to define "computer" and "thinking."

21 / The Impact of Mass Communication
ROBERT C. DAVIS

Mass communication involves the transmission of messages by various mechani- cal means to a large proportion of the population. It is the technological exten- sion of man as a communicating animal, a millionfold magnification of his ability to use language.

For more than a million years speech and gesture were the sole means of communication among men; then, approximately six thousand years ago, writ- ing was developed; and five hundred years ago printing began to spread through Europe. The most recent development, mass communication, appeared little more than a century ago, in the 1830's, as the result of the convergence of the requisite technological developments and the capability of the audience under the proper social conditions. Like all of man's accomplishments, it reflects his unique ability to operate as a tool-maker, a society-builder, and symbol-user. And, like many of man's creations, mass communication is an aspect of his self- made environment which poses problems for him.

This chapter is concerned with the reciprocal effects of technology, commu- nications, and social conditions. First, we will examine briefly the social and technical prerequisites of mass communication; then we will focus on the impact of mass communication on society.

EARLY COMMUNICATION

For most of human history, spoken language was the medium for the transmission of information from one man to another. Person-to-person communication by speech served well enough to bind simple societies together and to bridge generations through oral transmission of the social heritage. The invention of writing made possible an even greater extension of communication through space and across time. And the development of phonetic alphabets and abstract mathematical notation extended communications across cultural boundaries as well.

This early revolution in the communicative arts was a necessary condition for the development of mass communication, though not sufficient in itself, for the skills of reading and writing were for the most part restricted to a small segment of society: a priestly caste, an educated nobility, and an intellectual elite. It required the conjunction of a social and a technological revolution to move man into the era of mass communication. Both the audience and the media for communication had to be developed.

PRINTING

The technological threshold was passed first. By 1447 Gutenberg's printing shop was in operation in Maintz. Skills in type founding, paper-making, and ink production were joined to serve the new printing process. By the end of the 15th century, about eight million books had been printed in Europe; but the number belies the size of the audience, which must have been a relatively small one of scholars, nobles, and clerics.

The intellectual ferment of the Renaissance, and later the Reformation, which marked the disruption of the medieval world, found expression in the books and pamphlets which poured forth. The extension of literacy and education beyond a small elite was given impetus by the religious, intellectual, and political changes of the 16th and 17th centuries. A literate, city-dwelling, commercial middle class, with an insatiable desire for newspapers and novels, began to emerge in the 17th century and grew strikingly in the next century. This bourgeois audience, supplementing the small audiences of clerics and nobles, began to show the style of consumption that would mark the era of mass communication: the desire for current news and the demand for entertainment in print.

NEWSPAPERS

The daily newspaper was the first medium of mass communication. In the years following the first abortive daily established in Leipzig (1660), the daily newspaper gradually spread through northern Europe: London (1702), Augsburg (1718), Paris (1777). American cities were not far behind. Philadelphia, which had the first American daily newspaper in 1784, had six by the end of the 18th century; New York had five, Baltimore had three, and Charleston, two. Only Boston had faltered, for two attempts to sustain daily circulation failed.

At the end of the 18th century, most American dailies, semi-weeklies, and weeklies had small circulations (600-700) but large readerships, due to the high rate of literacy in the new country and the habit of making copies available in public places where many people could read the same copy. By 1793, Noah Webster could proudly write, "In no other country on earth, not even in Great Britain, are Newspapers so generally circulated among the body of the people, as in America." Stimulated by politics and encouraged by the Post Office Act of 1792, which provided for cheap mailing of journals, the newspaper had become a permanent and important part of American life as the 19th century dawned.

But the establishment of large-scale circulation, the earmark of true mass communication, had to wait for certain technological improvements, which culminated in the communications revolution of the 1830's. The steam-driven press, first used in New York in 1825, was improved by Hoe in 1832 in his two-cylinder press which could produce 4000 papers an hour. Machines for making paper in large quantities on continuous rolls had been used in America since 1817. Ink-manufacturing and type-founding processes, already established, were improved markedly. The joint impact of these elements of newsprinting technology, plus violent partisan political battles, plus the fact that nine out of ten white adults were literate, increased the number of newspapers to 1200, of which more than 65 were dailies. By 1833 there were three times as many newspapers in the United States as in France or England, and America was far on the road to becoming the leader in mass communication.

The application of steam power to ships and railroads speeded the transmission of news until the telegraph took over. Within three years of the first news dispatch by the new electric invention (1844), the major cities from Portland, Maine, south to Charleston and west to St. Louis were linked by the telegraph.

Co-operation in news gathering quickly followed with the establishment in 1848 of the New York Associated Press. Only the linkage of the New World to Europe by the Atlantic Cable, first laid in 1858, remained to be accomplished to take the news-gathering speed of newspapers to its peak. Mass production of daily papers was speeded by technical refinements in printing, notably the stereotyping process introduced in 1861 and the web-perfecting press (1863), which printed both sides of a continuously unrolling sheet of paper.

The reign of the daily newspaper as the dominant means of mass communication is shown in these figures: from 1850, when about 250 dailies were printed, until the peak of 2600 dailies in 1909, the burst of mass circulation made possible by the technological developments of the 1830's increased unabated. Although the number of dailies has declined in the 20th century, in 1962 the 1760 extant daily papers reported a total circulation of about sixty million copies. A newspaper is read daily by nine out of ten American adults, a coverage undiminished by the rise of other media of mass communication.

Books, the oldest of the printed media, reached the status of mass media of communication with the phenomenal expansion of paperback editions in the mid-20th century. By 1964 paperbacks were selling at the rate of 350 million a year, and by 1966 about 36,000 titles were available in this inexpensive format. The availability of inexpensive paperbound books has influenced the pattern of leisure reading and given new depth and flexibility to formal education.

NEW MEDIA

Printed media commanded a mass audience for three quarters of a century, but shortly after the 20th century opened three audio-visual media in quick succession swept the communications field. By mid-century the motion picture, radio, and television rivalled or surpassed the ability of the written word to reach large portions of the population. Each of these new media has increased the experience of immediacy in communications; and each relies upon oral communication and makes few demands on literacy. Ironically, the technological ability to communicate with non-literate populations was reached only after the level of literacy had reached widespread proportions. However, the possibility of using these media in non-literate, developing countries has only partially succeeded in solving the problem of communication, for in these underdeveloped areas, where face-to-face interaction is the norm, the credibility of non-personal communication is weakened by tribal customs and assumptions which characterize the traditional society.

In America the motion picture made its commercial debut in 1896; within ten years the nickelodeon had swept the country, between 8000 and 10,000 of them having been established by 1908. The expansion of the motion-picture industry may be shown by the increase in the number of films copyrighted, from 953 in 1913 to 4216 fifty years later. The size of the audience for motion pictures grew phenomenally until the advent of television. From an estimated weekly attendance of 40 million in 1922, the audience grew to a peak in the late 1940's of 90 to 98 million, then slumped sharply after 1948. Since then the theater audience has not been recaptured, although it remains a mass audience, especially among the younger population. Meanwhile the movie industry has shifted a large portion of its efforts to the medium of television.

Radio's commercial history begins in 1920, after three decades of research and development. Three stations went on the air that year, and by the end of

1923 there were 600; forty years later there were 5305 commercial stations broadcasting. In 1922, an estimated 60,000 families had radio sets; in 1930 the Census found that 12 million families owned sets, and by 1940 the figure had risen to over 28 million families, which comprised 82.8 per cent of the occupied housing units. Although this rapid extension of a mass-media audience is phenomenal, it was soon to be surpassed by the growth of television.

The experimental phase of television began in 1925, but not until 1941 was commercial television begun on a limited scale. Interrupted by war, television's large-scale commercial phase began only in 1948, when one million sets were in operation. In slightly over ten years television swept the country with almost total coverage. In 1950 the Census found that only 12 per cent of occupied dwelling units had sets, but by 1960 the figure had risen to 87.3 per cent. Radio had taken three decades to reach more than 90 per cent of American households; television accomplished that level of saturation in little more than one third the time. With the orbiting of the Telstar satellite (1963), the possibility of intercontinental television networks became a reality, and television could rival radio communication in its global scope.

The audio-visual media of the 20th century affected one another more than they did the printed media. Films, at first a filler between live performances in theaters, eventually destroyed vaudeville and seriously curtailed live theater and lecturing; but they have had little measurable effect on newspapers. Similarly, radio seems not to have seriously competed with the circulation of printed media. Movies and radio thus did not pre-empt other media; rather they overlapped with them by serving another set of needs, primarily in the entertainment areas of drama, music, and sports.

The introduction of television, however, seriously affected both radio and the movies, for it brought together the appeals of both films and radio, the immediacy of visual presentation combined with the convenience of the in-the-home setting. The crisis was greatest for the movie theaters; between 1948 and 1953 paid admissions dropped 36.7 per cent. "Free" movies at home via television created an irresistible appeal. The motion picture industry switched a large part of its effort to television film production, and counted on expanded international markets to help pay for feature films.

Radio, on the other hand, reacted by changing its programming: the traditional "soap operas" and evening dramatic shows disappeared, and music, sports, and news dominated the air time. This type of programming was well adapted for the growing number of car radios and the new, easily portable transistor radios. In the long run, radio retained a grip on a mass audience, although, like the feature films, it is at present heavily oriented to the younger part of the population.

Some observers, such as Marshall McLuhan, assert that the very form of the new media has transformed the entire communication experience; in McLuhan's words, "The medium is the message." He contrasts the linear and sequential printed media with the multi-dimensional and simultaneous electronic media and believes the transition marks a major revolution in man's history.

THE AUDIENCE

The dire predictions that Americans would stop reading as a result of television did not come true. Instead, the circulation of newspapers, magazines, and books continues, and in the case of paperback books, has broken through to new heights. The media are differentiated in the functions they serve. According to a study by the University of Michigan Survey Research Center, in 1957, by which time television had become widely diffused, 74 per cent of American adults named it as their primary source of entertainment; newspapers remained the primary source of news for 57 per cent of the adults, although television claimed 22 per cent.

Despite this differentiation of function, the media audiences are large and overlapping. In 1957, 86 per cent of American adults watched television regularly, 81 per cent watched at least one hour a day, and 60 per cent watched two to six hours a day. In the same year, 91 per cent of adults read a newspaper regularly, 77 per cent read at least one paper a day, and 27 per cent read more than one paper a day. Magazines were read by 66 per cent, and radio was listened to by 81 per cent daily.

The pattern of consumption of newspapers, magazines, radio, and television in 1957 showed that 49 per cent of the adults in the United States were regular users of all four of these media. Another 34 per cent regularly used three media, 12 per cent used two, 4 per cent used one, and only 1 per cent used none. The conclusion to be drawn from these figures is clear: the media do not pre-empt audiences; they share them. Americans are avid consumers of many communications media.

The social characteristics of multiple-media consumers are determined largely by formal education and socio-economic status. Men and women differ little, and age shows a rather erratic relationship to volume of media consumption, except that there is a decline after the age of 60. Regional and residential location differences reflect education and wealth to a large degree: the South is a low consumer of multiple media, and the same is true of rural regions. The largest percentage of four-media consumers is found in metropolitan suburbs, where 61 per cent of adults fall into the category of high consumption. Adults with elementary school educations are low (30 per cent) and college-educated adults are high (70 per cent) with regard to four-media consumption. Income shows the same pattern: in the very low income group (less than $1000 a year) only 19 per cent use all four media, while in the income bracket of $7500 a year or more the figure stands at 69 per cent.

That Americans should be avid mass-media consumers is hardly surprising when one examines the early age at which the communications media become part of the American child's life. More than half the children become regular users of television by age four; comic books and movies by age 6; magazines, radio, and books by age 7; and newspapers by age 8.

CRITICISMS

The pervasiveness of mass communication is easier to establish than to evaluate. Critics of the mass media either decry their allegedly undesirable consequences or lament their unused educational potential. The indictment of the mass media usually includes charges that they (1) create a passive, escapist, manipulated audience, or (2) encourage behavior (crime or violence) which is undesirable.

Underlying these assertions is the assumption that mass communication helps to create mass society. A mass society may be defined as a fragmented society, in which traditional social groups, with their strong personal ties, give way to impersonal and transitory social relations. The close-knit community is replaced by an unfeeling marketplace, and intimate social groups, by complex formal organizations. In such a social environment the individual becomes alienated from others and from himself. The mass media, the argument goes, provide the pseudo-community of the mass audience, so that people do not interact with one another, but react to a common stimulus. Having no social anchorage, they cannot adequately resist manipulation and they become the creatures of the mass media.

How adequate is this description? First of all, large-scale, industrial, urban society has replaced the small, rural, village community. But urban life is by no means a matter of isolated individuals bouncing around like marbles in a bag. Studies of urban life show that great cities are, in fact, composed in large measure of neighborhoods which have some of the elements of stable, traditional communities. However, it is equally clear that not everyone is integrated into these communities. A range and variety of voluntary associations, based on interests and tastes, is characteristic of urban life as well. And, finally, there are a large number of individuals who are not tied into groups of any sort, whether neighborhoods or voluntary associations.

The main point is this: although urban life is not qualitatively or quantitatively the same as life in a small community, it comprises many membership groups which serve as reference points for ideas and standards and which act as channels or filters in the communication process.

THE COMMUNICATION PROCESS

Attention to communication is always *selective*. That is, people tend to see and hear communications which fit in with their attitudes and beliefs and to reject those which are opposed. Selectivity may be a conscious or an unconscious process. The stronger one feels about a topic, the more selective one is in communicating. There is thus a strong tendency to communicate with those of like persuasion, producing a mutual confirmation of the shared point of view.

However, there is seldom a situation of complete self-selection of communication and rarely a complete monopoly of communications. Even in totalitarian countries, where there is complete political control of the mass media, not all members of the population can be convinced. The power of continual propaganda is weakened by overexposure, skepticism, and the informal word-of-mouth counter-current of everyday interaction. This is not to underrate the power of the totalitarian state to create conditions of behavioral conformity by monopolizing the communications media; rather it is to stress the difficulty of the conquest of attitudes and beliefs.

Selective perception is supplemented by active distortion. An uncongenial fact or evaluation may be distorted or evaded consciously or unconsciously. The "misperception" of communications takes many forms: the manifest message may be denied completely, or even reversed; incongruities may be "explained" away; conflicting ideas may be kept psychologically compartmentalized; statements by well-liked persons may be seen as congenial, while the opposite may be true for persons who are disliked, and so forth.

It is easier to reinforce an existing opinion than to change it. Most successful mass-communication efforts, therefore, take the audience's beliefs and attitudes and build on them, rather than try to change them radically. Study after study of presidential election campaigns show that the massive efforts to "convert" voters are wasted. Political campaigns are effective mainly in consolidating the attitudes of party faithfuls, in keeping up involvement in the election to insure a good turnout at the polls, and perhaps in snaring a few non-committed voters. What may seem to be "conversion" is usually a matter of a temporary switch by those who are caught in cross-pressures of conflicts among candidates, issues, and interests.

Americans are fond of appealing to "facts." Yet factual presentations have been shown to be ineffective in promoting attitude change, especially in the face of strong predispositions. Even so, communications which are "factual" and seemingly "neutral" are more easily accepted than provocative evaluations. And there is some evidence that "facts" can influence behavior—by indicating specific issues or choices, for instance—without changing previous attitudes. A health program for the aged, for example, may be espoused by those opposed to "big government." If attitudes are changed, they must be buttressed by continuing communication or group support or they tend to swing back.

In brief, the research on the impact of the mass media shows that the same communication does not have uniform and universal impact. And while persuasive influence is a documentable fact, built-in social and psychological barriers refract, deflect, and mask, in varying degrees, communications.

MEDIA CONTENT

When the critics of the mass media point to *content,* their comments often hinge on the commercial nature of the media. Here the cogency of their criticism is illustrated by many studies. Mass audiences are paid for by mass marketing, and the tyranny of numbers influences television and radio content directly, while it affects the printed media somewhat more indirectly.

Because the bulk of the money for all media comes from advertising, there is built into the media the tension among the advertiser-financier, the communicator-producer, and the public consumer. Each party in this three-way struggle affects the others. The variety that does exist in media content, limited as it is by the quest for mass audiences, is attributable to external regulatory agencies to some extent, but largely to the shifting demands of a complex society and the professional needs and skills of the media producers.

No concern about media content has aroused more discussion than the alleged influence of television violence and crime upon children. There are few good studies of the topic, but the more carefully conducted research does not support the common fears.

Those who believe comic books and television "cause" juvenile delinquency tend to forget that the same charges had been made earlier about movies and radio. Earlier research showed that consumption of the older media did not have a causal relationship to crime; at the most it could be said that delinquents consumed the stories of violence and crime. In other words, children whose problems led them to delinquency were also led to media dealing with crime. Children who had no delinquency-producing life experiences witnessed crime movies with little discernible effect on their behavior.

Delinquency and crime are evidently the behavioral result of much more powerful social and psychological factors than the mass media. The first-hand human influences of everyday life have much more impact than secondary influences, such as those provided by the media.

Research on television parallels the earlier research done on the effect of movies on the viewer. Children who have fewer "internal" resources, a lower sense of achievement, or a lower degree of emotional security are likely to depend on television entertainment more than those of the opposite type. One very thorough study found that a minority of children were frightened by violence on television. However, conventional violence, expected as part of the story, was not upsetting, and fist-fighting and shooting were found to be less disturbing than stabbing. Perhaps this is a reflection of the Westerns. These conventionalized modern morality plays appeal to children by virtue of the black-and-white nature of the plots. And it is interesting to note that the tension produced by these plots is released at the end of the program. It is equally interesting that verbal aggression, anger, and emotional scenes which indicated tension or rupture of social relations disturbed the children more than physical aggression.

As far as actual criminal behavior is concerned, several major studies have indicated that those who read or watched many crime stories were no more likely to be delinquent than those who read or viewed less avidly or not at all. The research in this area may be summarized by quoting Joseph Klapper, who states that the "various findings strongly suggest that crime and violence in the media are not likely to be prime movers toward delinquency, but that such fare is likely instead to reinforce the existing behavioral tendencies, *good or ill,* of individual audience members." As in other areas of life, media audiences tend to seek those themes which fit their already established tastes, beliefs, attitudes, and behavior.

MEDIA AND EDUCATION

When discussion swings to the positive contributions of the mass media it generally focuses on the topic of education. Critics stress the enormous gap between the potential of the media and the actual performance. They point to the fact that three quarters of the television programming is entertainment and that cultural programs are sparse. Certainly the educational impact of television has been minor compared to its use as a "selling machine." And the same is true of the other media to varying degrees.

Yet defenders of the mass media can point to notable journalism, good documentary series, and occasional presentations of "high culture." According to TV publicists, more people witnessed one television presentation of Shakespeare's "Macbeth" than had been in all the audiences of all the Shakespeare plays since they were first presented.

But these discussions remain anecdotal if we do not make an attempt to research the presentation of serious topics in the mass media. As an example, one such study focused on the public's use of the mass media as the source of information about science. A representative sample of American adults was interviewed by the Survey Research Center regarding media consumption to ascertain their attention to science and medical news. When asked to recall science or medical news recently seen or heard, 76 per cent of the American adults recalled at least one such item. About half recalled science stories, while seven out of ten recalled medical items.

Of the audiences of the respective media the percentage recalling both science and medical items was: newspapers, 36 per cent; magazines, 8 per cent; television, 7 per cent; and radio, 3 per cent. Newspapers are the most important source of science news, radio the least important. Newspapers and television are mutually supplementary as sources of science news, but radio is weak both as a primary and a secondary source.

The content of the science news is mainly applied science, while the medical stories deal with major, well-publicized diseases. The style of the presentation— attempts to draw the audience by dramatic or "popular" treatment—affects the attention paid to science news, although it largely attracts the members of the audience for whom science is already salient. The principle of selection thus plays its role in science news as it does in other communications.

The skills with which members of the audience confront the media determine, in part, the decision to read or hear science news. When a science information test was constructed to explore the problem, it was found that the information test scores were strongly related to formal education and to science education, thus underscoring the importance of prior intellectual preparation. The better informed persons tended to be multiple-media users. A high degree of science information was associated with a high degree of consumption of printed media, but was unrelated to the degree to which television and radio were used. The level of current science information, the degree of formal education, and the amount of science education were all correlated with science news consumption. Of those who have had science in high school and college, 99 per cent recalled either science or medical items from the media.

Motivation also plays a part in directing attention to news. Research findings clearly demonstrate that there is a widespread positive and receptive attitude toward science and medical news among the American public. Over half the adult population is actively oriented toward science and only three out of twenty are apathetic. The "hard core" of science enthusiasts is estimated to be about one fourth of the adult population. The motivations for science news consumption are both intellectual and practical. "Keeping up with things," awareness of the relationship of science to human survival, and interest in specific applications in daily life stand out as major motivations.

Nevertheless, science news in the mass media is skimpy, despite the prominent roles of science, technology, and medicine in the mid-20th century. An information vacuum exists. An expression of this is the fact that of the newspaper audience, 30 per cent want more science news, and 46 per cent want more medical news in the papers.

All in all, the attitudes regarding science and medical news in the mass media illustrate both the strengths and weaknesses of the media. In their attempt to reach everyone they often ignore the many special-interest groups that compose a mass audience. In their attempt to communicate to everyone they often fail to present material at a level appropriate to the educational background of these special publics. The better newspapers have, thus far, done the best job in serving the multi-group public, but even there commercial needs have limited the medium.

In summary, one can see in the rise of the mass media all the social, economic, political, and intellectual problems that attend a major technological innovation. The purely technical problems are frequently solved in short order, but the values of the society direct and limit the social uses to which the innovation is put. At present, the media of mass communication are more reflections of the status quo than vehicles of social evaluation or public enlightenment.

Part **VII**
The Food Revolution

22 / Scientific Agriculture
WAYNE D. RASMUSSEN

Since the beginning of time, except for a favored few in near-utopian surroundings, mankind has had to live with the fear of starvation. Behind whatever
iniquities of distribution may have existed has stood the brute fact that enough
to eat has been hard to win and never certain. Today, even though most of the
world still lives close to this margin, the fabulous agricultural productivity of
the United States is already feeding populations far beyond its shores and holds
out the promise, at last, of plenty. This is because, in the first two decades after
World War II, American agriculture experienced a second technological revolution, even more far-reaching than the first, which followed the Civil War. One
simple measure of this change is that in 1946 one farm worker supplied all the
farm products needed by 14 people; in 1966, he supplied the needs of 37
people. Farm output per man-hour, using 1957-58 as 100, increased from an
index of 49 in 1946 to 153 in 1965.

The first American agricultural revolution, in the 19th century, was marked
by the change from hand power to animal power. This was made possible by
inventions dating back several years and even decades. The second, which included the change from animals to mechanical power (discussed in Chapter
23), contained more. Its most fundamental characteristic was the application
of scientific agriculture in a more complete sense than ever before—both in
discoveries and in adoption by farmers of these discoveries, not singly but as
a complex.

The adoption of the technology which brought about the sharp and dramatic
rise in productivity was a result of World War II. Higher prices and a seemingly unlimited wartime demand for farm products, combined with a shortage
of farm labor and appeals from the government to increase production, led
farmers to make use of new devices and processes. These technological advances, whose adoption had been delayed by the Depression of the 1930's,
included: widespread progress in mechanization, greater use of lime and fer-

tilizer, widespread use of cover crops and other conservation practices, use of improved varieties of both plants and animals, the adoption of hybrid corn, the better balanced feeding of livestock, the more effective control of insects and disease, and the use of chemicals for such purposes as weed-killers and defoliants.

Similar changes also took place during these years in most of Western Europe, also Canada, Australia, New Zealand, Japan, and other countries. Yet the agricultural potentiality of many nations is still underdeveloped.

GENETICS

Productivity usually increases most rapidly when several technological advances are adopted together. However, the advances based upon genetics, such as hybrid corn and other improved crops and animals, or upon the more intensive use of fertilizer, by themselves accounted for two thirds of the rise in crop production per acre in the United States from 1940 to 1955.

The application of the science of genetics to the technical problems of producing improved crop and livestock is a recent achievement. Organized study of genetics, the mechanism of heredity and evolution, began only in the 20th century. Plant- and animal-breeders of earlier centuries achieved many important advances by utilizing, unknowingly, some of the principles of genetics; but only in recent years has that science, through research into basic biological laws, made available the theoretical basis for major changes in plant- and animal-breeding.

The modern science of genetics has a complicated background, built up from the work of many men. Nevertheless, Gregor Johann Mendel (1822-84) is generally credited with its founding. Mendel was a monk who purposefully crossed garden peas in his monastery garden in Brunn, Austria (now Brno, Czechoslovakia). Working in 1865, Mendel did a simple but revolutionary thing. He carefully sorted the progeny of his parent plants according to their characteristics and counted the number that had inherited each quality. He discovered that when the qualities he was studying, including flower color and shape of seeds, were handed on by the parent plants, they were distributed among the offspring in definite mathematical ratios, and in no case was there a significant variation from these ratios. Definite laws of inheritance were thus established for the first time.

Mendel reported his discoveries in an obscure Austrian journal in 1866, but his work was not followed up for a third of a century. Then in 1900, Hugo de Vries in Holland, Karl Correns in Germany, and E. von Tschermark in Austria, all working on inheritance, independently rediscovered Mendel's paper and brought it to the attention of the scientific world. By that time scientists were ready to appreciate the significance of Mendel's work and to go forward with the study of heredity.

The word "genetics" comes from "genes," the name given to the minute quantities of living matter which transmit characteristics from parent to off-spring. By 1903, W. S. Sutton of Columbia University and Theodore Boveri of Germany had concluded that the genes are carried in the chromosomes, nuclear structures visible under the microscope. In 1911, Thomas Hunt Morgan (1866-1945), then at Columbia University, developed the theory that the genes are arranged in a linear file on the chromosomes, and that changes in this confor-mation are reflected in changes in heredity.

Genes are highly stable. However, during the processes of sexual reproduc-tion, means are present for assortment, segregation, and recombination of genetic factors. Tremendous genetic variability is thereby provided within a species. This variability provides the basis for the potential improvements that man can make within a species to adapt it to his specific uses. Occasional mutations of genes also contribute to variability. One hundred years after Mendel's discoveries, no scientist has yet been able to examine a single whole chromosome. Experiments with deoxyribonucleic acid (DNA), of which genes may be mainly composed, however, are perhaps getting at the very foundations of the continuity of life.

Genetics has provided the theoretical scientific basis for the great strides in plant- and animal-breeding which have helped make up America's second agricultural revolution. However, experiments in plant- and animal-breeding were going on long before the science of genetics had developed, and, indeed, progress was still made by empirical methods even after the application of genetic science to agriculture. For example, the American Luther Burbank (1849-1926) developed the Burbank potato as early as 1873 and continued his plant-breeding experiments, which produced numerous new varieties of fruits and vegetables, without any thorough knowledge of genetic principles.

Some of the early and very practical experiments contributed to major tech-nological achievements, just as had the theories and experiments in "pure" science. This is well illustrated by the development of hybrid corn.

HYBRID CORN

The corn that the first English settlers in colonial America adopted from the Indians was probably the long, slender-stalked, northern flint variety. It kept well and was prized as food by the Indians, but its yield was low. Indians in the south-central part of what is now the United States grew white, southern dent corn. This was late-maturing, heavy-stalked, and soft-kerneled, but gave a higher yield than the flint.

Haphazard mixtures of the flint and dent varieties doubtless occurred many times. However, the first definite record of the conscious mixing of the two came in 1812. John Lorain, a farmer living near Philipsburg, Pennsylvania, had an experimental turn of mind. He demonstrated that certain mixtures of flint and dent corn would result in a yield much greater than that of the flint, yet with many of the flint's desirable qualities.

Other farmers and breeders followed Lorain's example, some aware of his pioneer work, others not. One famous variety, Reid's Yellow Dent, originated in 1846 when Robert Reid took a late, rather light reddish-colored variety from Ohio to Illinois. Because of a poor stand the next year, a small, early yellow variety, probably a flint, was used in replanting the missing hills. The resulting mixture was grown by the family. This new variety eventually became the most widely grown in the corn belt. Reid's Yellow Dent was also to contribute valuable characteristics to modern hybrid corn.

Even as the common maize of the corn belt was being developed in the 19th century by practical technologists—farmers and seedsmen—scientists in addition to Mendel were carrying out experiments and making observations which were to lead directly to hybrid corn. In 1876, Charles Darwin (1809-82) published the results of experiments on cross- and self-fertilization in plants. Carrying out his work in a small greenhouse in his native England, the man who originated the theory of evolution found that inbreeding usually reduced plant vigor and that crossbreeding restored it.

William James Beal, a young botanist born on a farm and educated at the University of Michigan, heard of Charles Darwin when he went to Harvard College for graduate work. He studied with Louis Agassiz (1807-73), the Swiss-born zoologist who vigorously opposed Darwin and his theory of evolution, and with Asa Gray (1810-88), the great botanist who enthusiastically accepted Darwin's views. Beal graduated from Harvard in 1865. After teaching at other institutions, he became professor of botany and horticulture at Michigan Agricultural College (now Michigan State University) in 1870. There he followed the work of Darwin, Gray, and others, and began his own experiments with crossbreeding corn, with emphasis upon the necessity of parent control. Beal reported later that yields of the crosses on the average exceeded those of the parent varieties by almost 25 per cent. Beal probably made the first controlled crosses between varieties of corn for the sole purpose of increasing yields through hybrid vigor.

Controlled crossing was of great practical value to seedsmen and farmers and was a necessary step to the development of hybrids. However, understanding of the genetic principle involved in hybrid vigor is very recent, dating from 1908, when George Harrison Shull published a short paper, "The Composition of a Field of Maize," and Edward M. East published "Inbreeding in Corn." Shull's greatest contribution to both genetics and the development of hybrid corn was the conclusion that self-fertilization tended to separate and purify strains while weakening the plants, but that vigor could be restored by crossbreeding the inbred strains. At about the same time that Shull was developing his theories, Edward Murray East was also experimenting, first at the

University of Illinois, then at the Connecticut Experiment Station. He found that inbreeding could increase the protein content in corn, but with a marked decline in yield. Working with both inbreeding and outbreeding, East reached conclusions similar to those of Shull. When East went to Harvard University in 1910, his corn work was taken over in Connecticut by Herbert Kendall Hayes. In 1915, Hayes went to Minnesota, where he brought the technical knowledge gained in Connecticut to the attention of practical corn-breeders. Later, he won world renown for his work in breeding Thatcher wheat.

An important advance was made by Donald F. Jones, who succeeded Hayes at Connecticut. Although much had been done at Connecticut on both inbreeding and hybridizing corn, there was yet to be developed a technique whereby hybrid corn with the desired characteristics of the inbred lines and hybrid vigor could be combined in a practical manner. Within three years, Jones had the answer, the "double cross."

The double cross was the basic technique used in developing modern hybrid seed corn and has been used by commercial firms since. Jones's invention was to use four inbred lines instead of two in crossing. Simply, inbred lines A and B make one cross, lines C and D another. Then AB and CD are crossed and a double-cross hybrid, ABCD, is the result. This hybrid is the seed which has changed much of American agriculture. Each inbred line is constant for certain desirable traits. The technologist will also recognize that each line is also constant for certain undesirable traits. Thus the practical breeder must balance his four or more inbred lines in such a way that the desirable traits outweigh the undesirable. Too, foundation inbred lines must be developed to meet the needs of varying climates, soils, growing seasons, and other factors. All of the large hybrid seed-corn companies now maintain complex applied-research programs, while state experiment stations and the United States Department of Agriculture tend to concentrate on basic research.

The first hybrid corn involving inbred lines to be produced commercially was the Burr-Leaming double cross developed by the Connecticut Agricultural Experiment Station. In the spring of 1921, about 10 bushels of this seed was sold at $8 a bushel. The second hybrid to be produced and sold commercially was a single cross between one of the inbred Leaming strains and an inbred line developed by Henry A. Wallace (1888-1965) of Des Moines, Iowa, a future Secretary of Agriculture and Vice President of the United States (1941-45). Wallace sold a small quantity of the hybrid seed in the spring of 1924 under the name of "Copper Cross."

Wallace joined with a few others in 1926 in organizing the first seed company for the commercial production of hybrid corn. About 1932 hybrid-seed production was taken up by several other companies; later, because of the expense of developing foundation inbred lines, production was mainly concentrated in a half dozen firms. While many midwestern farmers began growing hybrid corn

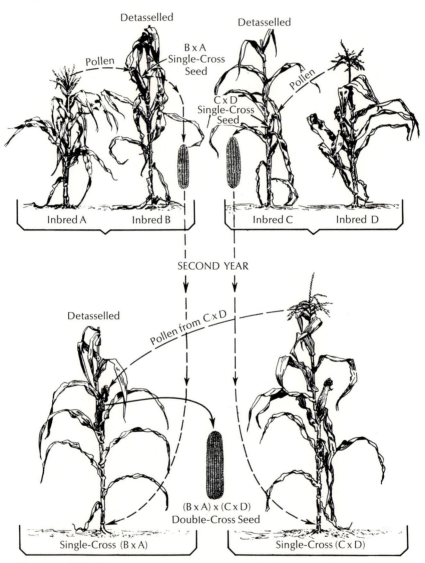

FIRST YEAR

Detasselled

Pollen

B x A
Single-Cross
Seed

Detasselled

Pollen

C x D
Single-Cross
Seed

Inbred A   Inbred B   Inbred C   Inbred D

SECOND YEAR

Detasselled

Pollen from C x D

(B x A) x (C x D)
Double-Cross Seed

Single-Cross (B x A)   Single-Cross (C x D)

Fig. 22-1. Hybrid Corn. Diagram of the method of crossing inbred plants and the resulting single crosses to produce double-cross hybrid seed for commercial planting. (United States Department of Agriculture *Yearbook,* 1937)

in the late 1920's and the 1930's, its dominance throughout the United States awaited the economic impetus of World War II and the second American agricultural revolution. In 1933, one per cent of the total corn acreage was planted with hybrid seed; the figure was 15 per cent in 1938, the year before the outbreak of World War II in Europe. In 1946, the percentage rose to 69, and in 1960 to 96. The average per-acre yield of corn rose from 23 bushels in 1933 to 62 bushels in 1964. Furthermore, hybrid corn has roots and stalks that resist wind damage and make machine harvesting both practical and efficient.

The techniques used in breeding hybrid corn were also successfully applied to sorghum grain. In 1958, about half the acreage devoted to this feed grain was planted with hybrid seed. Yields increased from 19 bushels per acre in 1951 to 41 bushels per acre in 1964.

Hybrid seed is also available for cabbage, cantaloupe, castor bean, cucumber, eggplant, onion, pearl millet, spinach, squash, sugar beet, tomato, and watermelon. One type of hybrid seed even promises seedless watermelons in the near future.

NEW VARIETIES OF WHEAT

Advances in wheat production during the 20th century have seen improvements through: the introduction of new varieties and strains from abroad; careful selection by farmers and seedsmen, as well as by scientists; crossbreeding to combine desirable characteristics; and finally, the application of the techniques of hybridization. Since World War II, planned breeding by scientific methods has become almost universal. In 1959 varieties produced by the experiment stations accounted for 99 per cent of the acreage in hard red spring wheat, 100 per cent of the durum, 77 per cent of the hard red winter, 93 per cent of the soft red winter, and 99 per cent of the white wheat acreage.

Wheat-breeders have had various goals. These have included varieties with higher or lower protein contents, earlier maturing varieties, drought-resistant varieties, disease (particularly smut) resistant varieties, and other particular characteristics.

New varieties have been introduced by immigrants from all over the world. For example, in 1873 a small group of Mennonites who emigrated from southern Russia to central Kansas first introduced hard red winter wheat, an innovation which led to a revolution in flour milling. Club wheat was introduced repeatedly, the first recorded time being in 1818 when Theodorick Bland, a member of the South American Commission of 1817-18, brought some back to Maryland from Chile.

The 20th century saw the application of science to wheat-breeding. W. J. Spillman, then at the Washington State Agricultural Experiment Station, led the way in hybridization from 1894 to 1901. His work resulted in the development of four commercial hybrid club wheats, and demonstrated that by hybridization predictable recombinations of parental traits could be bred.

The development of world-famous Marquis wheat, released to farmers in 1908, came about through sustained scientific endeavor. Sir Charles Saunders, its discoverer, followed five principles of plant-breeding: (1) the use of plant introductions; (2) a planned hybridization program; (3) the rigid selection of material; (4) evaluation of all characteristics in replicated trials; and (5) testing varieties for local or national use. Marquis was the result of a cross of Red Fife wheat with a variety introduced from India, Hard Red Calcutta. The cross was made in 1892, but continued selection, evaluation, and testing was necessary before the wheat was released to the wheat-growers of western Canada. For 50 years, Marquis and varieties crossbred from Marquis dominated hard red spring wheat growing in the high plains of Canada and the United States.

During the 1960's, the development of semi-dwarf winter wheat in the Pacific Northwest brought to the fore varieties which had stiff straw, and which gave much higher yields with fertilizer and irrigation than any other known wheat. Gaines was an outstanding variety among the semi-dwarfs. It originated from a cross made in 1949 at Pullman, Washington, of an imported Japanese semi-dwarf wheat and a wheat grown in the Northwest, called Brevor. This basic cross was then crossed with two additional crosses. The new variety was selected in 1956, and after five years of further evaluation and testing, was released to farmers. In 1964, a Washington wheat farmer produced 169 bushels per acre of Gaines wheat on irrigated land. Yields of 120 bushels on irrigated land were not uncommon, while occasional fields without irrigation yielded over 100 bushels.

SOYBEANS

Soybeans are of interest because, while they were introduced into the United States by Benjamin Franklin as early as the 1790's, they were not widely grown until 20th-century technological developments made their use as an oilseed crop profitable. Three varieties useful as forage were brought from Japan in 1900. The Department of Agriculture secured 300 varieties from China, Japan, and India in 1909. Mills for extracting the oil from the soybeans were built beginning about 1920, and by the end of that decade soybean oil was in considerable demand.

Extensive searches of the soybean regions of the Far East were made by the Department of Agriculture, and about 3000 varieties were collected. However, it became apparent that various combinations of the desired attributes could not be readily obtained by direct selection. Between 1930 and 1940, hybridization became the breeding procedure. Breeding of soybeans was effective in isolating types superior in yielding ability, resistance to lodging and shattering, adaptation to suit various requirements as to maturity, and resistance to disease.

Other major crops, such as cotton, tobacco, fruits, vegetables, and grain have been improved through plant introductions, crossbreeding, and selection. Such characteristics as adaptability to climate, resistance to disease, and productivity have been stressed by the breeders.

LIVESTOCK

Gains in livestock-breeding have not been as spectacular as those for many crops, but they are, nonetheless, very real. Part of the difference lies in the fact that it takes nearly all animals, with the possible exception of poultry, longer to mature than plants. Thus, breeding experiments must extend over longer periods of time.

In 1936, the Secretary of Agriculture's Committee on Genetics, which did much to define the scope of the science, reported many advances in plant-breeding following the genetic laws mentioned earlier. But, according to the committee, livestock-breeding was at the crossroads. Emphasis upon purebred livestock had broken the hold of the nondescript livestock of an earlier America; yet while those methods and practices had accomplished a great deal, giving us fine breeds of livestock, they had taken us about as far as they could. It was time to question the value of purebreds and the insistence upon artificial show standards, especially when these interfered with possible genetic advances.

The move to develop meat-type hogs illustrates some of the problems—economic as well as genetic—involved in improving livestock. The traditional American breeds of swine—Duroc, Poland China, Spotted, Chester White, and others less numerous—had become fixed after the Civil War by crossbreeding and selection. Much emphasis had then been given to weight, and breeders consequently developed notable lard-type strains. During the 1920's, however, lard became less important as a source of fat because of the greater use of cheaper vegetable oils. Meat-packers then called for a hog that would yield more lean meat and less fat, and thus more nearly meet consumer demands, even though the market had only slowly moved to making it profitable to produce such hogs.

Scientists in the state experiment stations and the Department of Agriculture turned to the experience of the Danes, Poles, and other Europeans who were then crossbreeding swine to obtain lean meat and vigorous animals. The Department of Agriculture and the Iowa Agricultural Experiment Station in 1934 imported a number of Danish Landrace hogs, one of the most outstanding European breeds in terms of the production of high-quality bacon carcasses. Crosses of American breeds with the Landrace and subsequent intermating of the cross-progeny gave rise to several new, mildly inbred lines. These lines produced more lean meat and less fat, as well as larger litters and bigger pigs.

Similar crossbreeding, followed by intermating and selection within the cross-breds, effected major changes in the sheep industry in the western United States as well. The traditional fine wool breeds, the Rambouillet and Merino, were deficient in size and in quality of meat. The British meat breeds, on the other hand, tended to be deficient in the fleece characteristics in which the fine-wool breeds excelled. Animal-breeders in the Department of Agriculture in 1912 made initial crosses between the long-wool mutton breed, the Lincoln, and fine-wool Rambouillets. Subsequent intermating and selection within the crossbreds led to a new breed, the Columbia. Both the Columbia and the Targhee, another breed developed in the same way as the Columbia, have been widely used. Another breed, the Corridale, imported from New Zealand by American breeders, was developed in the 19th century from crosses of the fine-wool Merino and the Lincoln and Leicester long-wool breeds.

Changes have taken place in the beef cattle and dairy cattle industries, also. The beef cattle industry had long been dominated by breeds that were imported in the 19th century from the British Isles. More than 95 per cent of the registered purebreds were of these breeds. However, these were not satisfactory in parts of the South because they lacked resistance to heat and insects and did not thrive on the native grasses. Zebu cattle were introduced into the American South from India, but did not meet all needs. The American Brahman was finally developed by crossing several of the Indian Zebu breeds. When the King Ranch of Texas then crossed the Brahmans with British shorthorns, this culminated in the establishment of a new breed, the Santa Gertrudis, which has been popular in the South and in several foreign countries. Other new breeds developed by various crossbred foundations include the Brangus, Beefmaster, and Charbray. The major gains in productivity in American beef cattle during the 20th century have resulted primarily from improvements in nutrition. The conquest or control of many diseases and insect pests has also been an important factor in improving the production of beef.

America's dairy cattle originated in Great Britain (particularly the Channel Islands of Jersey and Guernsey), the Netherlands, and Switzerland. Breed associations have been in existence in the United States for less than a century, but even before such groups were established, breeders individually initiated practices for measuring producing ability by weighing the milk and the butter for a given period. After the establishment of the breed associations, even greater emphasis was given to measuring productivity. Yet in 1936, the Department of Agriculture reported: "It has been estimated that in our dairy-herd improvement associations only about one-third of the cows produced enough to be profitable to their owners, another third just about break even, and the last third are such low producers as to lose money each year for their owners."

Fig. 22-2. Cattle shown with a combination scratcher and insecticide applicator. The animals walk under the insecticide applicator at the end of the beam to scratch their backs and in so doing apply insecticide to themselves. (*United States Department of Agriculture* photo)

In the years since that report, greater attention has been paid to measuring productivity and eliminating uneconomic animals. As herd associations accumulated data and published some of them, students noted that the daughters of certain sires would regularly excel in productivity. This led to building up superior inheritance in dairy cows through successive crosses of sires of proven merit, uninterrupted by crosses with unproven or poor sires. Several formulas were devised for measuring a sire's ability to transmit desirable qualities.

The emphasis upon proven sires led directly to the widespread adoption of artificial insemination. A bull could normally service 30 to 50 cows a year; using artificial insemination, 2000 cows a year could be impregnated by the same bull. Although an Italian scientist experimented successfully with artificial insemination as early as 1780, its practical usefulness was first demonstrated in the Soviet Union in the 1920's, where by 1936, more than six million cattle and sheep had been artificially inseminated. Scientists in many nations, including the United States, experimented with artificial insemination after the Russians reported their successes. Denmark established such work on a co-operative basis in the 1930's. Impressed with the Danish program, E. J. Perry organized an artificial breeding co-operative in New Jersey in 1938 which included about 125 co-operators who entered 1050 cows in the project. This program spread rapidly; by January 1, 1939, seven local co-operative artificial breeding associations were serving 646 herds totaling 7539 cows, and by 1962, over 7.7 million cows in 862,000 herds were bred artificially.

The Department of Agriculture began collecting statistics in 1943 through the artificial breeding associations to show the milk and butterfat production of proven sires' daughters. In 1943 such cows produced an average of 10,155 pounds of milk and 419 pounds of butterfat; and in 1964, 11,685 and 447 respectively. These data should be compared with the average productivity of all dairy cows. In 1943, the average cow produced 4598 pounds of milk and 183 pounds of butterfat; and in 1964, 7880 and 291. The noteworthy increase in productivity both in the average cow and of proven sires' daughters was due not only to the use of proven sires, but also to the influence of markets, prices of milks and feeds, better knowledge of feeding, and better herd management.

FERTILIZERS

At the beginning of the 20th century, most agricultural reformers and farm management specialists urged farmers to diversify, that is, to raise both crops and livestock. The manure produced by the livestock, when applied to the cropland, increased the fertility and productivity of the soil. The addition of lime to make manure more readily available for plant nutrition by reducing soil acidity had been urged by agricultural reformers, such as Edmund Ruffin (in 1821), since early in the 19th century, and it had been widely adopted in the eastern part of the United States by 1900. On the other hand, the use of mixed chemical fertilizers was regarded by many midwestern farmers as proof of poor management. The widespread and intensive use of commercial fertilizer developed only after World War II and was one aspect of the second American agricultural revolution.

The first mixed chemical fertilizers manufactured commercially in the United States were sold in Baltimore in 1849. By 1860 there were seven factories in the United States. After the end of the Civil War, commercial fertilizers were widely used in the Old South.

The theoretical basis for the use of mixed fertilizers, like the theoretical basis for hybrid corn, came from Europe. In 1840 the noted German chemist Justus von Liebig (1803-73), published his *Chemistry in Its Application to Agriculture and Physiology*, wherein he identified the mineral nutrients that plants require. This discovery has been described as one of the most spectacular advances in agriculture, exceeded only by the development of hybrid corn. Liebig discussed the importance of ammonia (nitrogen) and other substances. He demonstrated the essential nature of potassium in 1845, and within a few years was emphasizing the necessity of supplying plants with both phosphorus and potassium.

Many substances were used to supply some of the needed elements. Ground bones from slaughter houses, for example, were first used in the United States in 1825. Liebig demonstrated 15 years later that the fertilizing value of bone could be increased by treatment with sulfuric or hydrochloric acid, and in 1842, Sir John B. Lawes patented a similar treatment for ground phosphate rock. Peruvian guano (bird dung) was widely used in England and the United States beginning in the 1830's. At about the same time, the exploitation of Peruvian (later Chilean) deposits of sodium nitrate began. Germany began using her deposits of potassium salts for fertilizing purposes in the 1860's, and exported quantities to the United States. The mining of phosphate rock began in the United States in 1868 and in North Africa about 1899. Thus, by the beginning of the 20th century, theories of plant nutrition had been supported by the discovery and exploitation of supplies of basic materials which could be made available for plant nutrition.

In the United States, the annual production of mixed fertilizers grew to about 1,150,000 tons in 1880 and to 2,000,000 tons in 1900. Mixed fertilizers had proved their worth, particularly in the prevailing row-crop systems of agriculture in the southeastern states. At the same time, unscrupulous dealers often sold so-called mixed fertilizers that were practically worthless. During the 1870's and 1880's, therefore, legislatures in the South Atlantic states passed laws requiring that each bag of fertilizer sold bear a tag carrying the name of the manufacturer and a true analysis of the contents. All the states employed chemists to analyze fertilizers and chemicals offered for sale. Worthless or knowingly misbranded fertilizer could be seized or ordered from the market; however, even if a fertilizer was what it claimed to be, the ordinary farmer did not know just what combination was needed by his soil. Thus, many of the state chemists also tested soils. The most common mixed fertilizers sold in the South by the end of the century contained two-and-a-half to three per cent ammonia, 9 to 10 per cent phosphoric acid, one-and-a-half to two per cent potash in a filler of sand, cinders, or similar material.

Phosphate was the first mineral fertilizer discovered and mined in the United States. In 1868 mining began in South Carolina, which furnished 90 per cent of the world's consumption of phosphate rock until 1888. Later, Florida, Tennessee, and some of the western states displaced South Carolina as a producer.

Since ground phosphate rock generally has been found to be too slow in its action for the most profitable production of the common farm crops, most of the ground rock is converted into superphosphate, which makes the phosphorus more readily available to plants. As mentioned earlier, an Englishman, Sir John B. Lawes, patented (1842) a process for converting the ground rock into superphosphate by mixing it with an approximately equal amount of sulfuric acid, and made a fortune from its manufacture. After its establishment in 1933, the Tennessee Valley Authority (TVA), using electric furnaces to reduce rock from deposits it owned, began the manufacture of concentrated superphosphate, calcium metaphosphate, and fused tricalcium phosphate. These phosphates provided economies in handling and shipping, and demonstrations over a period of years in the TVA area proved their value as fertilizers.

Potash was one of colonial America's first exports. It was extracted from wood ashes and shipped to England by the first settlers in Jamestown, Virginia, as early as 1608. Later, a partly refined product was sold as pearl ash. Since the settlers had to dispose of the forests before they could farm, and potash, in demand by English industry, was a ready source of cash, the production of the chemical became an important element in American commerce. The peak in the value of exports was reached in 1825, when the total reached $2 million.

Tremendous deposits of soluble potassium salts were discovered in Germany in 1839, and were being exploited by 1860. The European potash industry dominated the American market until World War I. At that time, when German imports were not available, the United States took steps to develop a new industry, but these efforts declined after the war, when European imports again became available. However, Congress appropriated funds for exploration and investigation of potassium deposits within the United States by the Bureau of Mines and the Geological Survey. This work resulted in the discovery of commercially usable salt beds containing potash in several areas in the Southwest. Mining began at Carlsbad, New Mexico, in 1931. World War II gave impetus to the American industry, and after 1942, nearly the entire American consumption of potassium fertilizers was supplied by American industry. About 85 per cent of the production in 1955 came from the Carlsbad region in New Mexico, with a great deal of the remainder coming from the natural brines or salt lakes of California and Utah.

Nitrogen is the third major element in mixed commercial fertilizers. Although Justus von Liebig wrote of nitrogen, using the term ammonia, the necessity for supplying plants with it was not recognized until 1857, when Sir John B. Lawes and others working with him at the Rothamsted Experiment Station established its essential nature. Organic materials, including guano, animal manures, by-products of the slaughterhouses, and seed meals, were the main sources of nitrogen for fertilizers during the 19th century. Inorganic sources were relatively unimportant until about 1900, but by 1960 they supplied virtually all nitrogen used in commercial mixed fertilizers.

Sodium nitrate was the first widely used inorganic nitrogenous fertilizer. Natural deposits in Chile, the origin of which is a scientific mystery, supplied nearly all of the world's consumption for nearly a century after the first exports of record were made in 1830. These deposits, called caliche, must be refined in order to extract the sodium nitrate. The Shanks process was introduced about 1884 by J. T. Humberstone, and the more efficient Guggenheim process was developed in 1926, permitting modern mechanical methods to be applied to the industry. Costs were reduced, particularly when mechanical mining was also used, and the utilization of lower-grade caliche deposits became profitable. Competition from synthetic sodium nitrate, trade barriers, and other problems led to a reorganization of the Chilean industry with government help in 1930. After that, world consumption of the Chilean product again rose. Beginning in 1929, synthetic sodium nitrate was manufactured and sold in the United States at a price competitive with Chilean sodium nitrate.

By 1950, another product, ammonium sulfate, was more widely used as fertilizer nitrogen than sodium nitrate. Much of the ammonium sulfate is a by-product of the destructive distillation of coal, bituminous shales, and bones. However, beginning in 1950 the tonnage of ammonium sulfate made from synthetic ammonia surpassed that from the coke oven industry.

Still another synthetic nitrogenous fertilizer, ammonium nitrate, also based upon synthetic ammonia, supplied in 1953 about one third of the total consumption of nitrogen fertilizer in the United States. Ammonium nitrate is manufactured for both explosives and fertilizer by passing ammonia gas into nitric acid. During World War II, the federal government built several plants for manufacturing anhydrous ammonia to insure an adequate supply of explosives. After the war, several of these plants were sold or leased at a fraction of their cost to private industry for the production of ammonium nitrate for fertilizer. The Tennessee Valley Authority began making ammonium nitrate in 1942 at Wilson Dam, Alabama. It constructed a new synthetic ammonia plant and modernized one of the World War I nitrate plants at that site, and began an effective operation.

During the 1950's and 1960's, there has been experimentation with and discussion of the value of urea as a nitrogenous fertilizer. It is usually manufactured by combining pure ammonia with pure carbon dioxide gas under high pressure. Its high nitrogen content, obtained at low cost, and its complete availability to crops may lead to wide adoption. There has also been some use of anhydrous ammonia applied in liquid form directly to the soil.

The manufacture of synthetic nitrogenous fertilizers is, in itself, an interesting chapter in technological development. There have been three nitrogen-fixing processes of interest to the fertilizer industry—the arc, the cyanamide, and the direct synthetic ammonia—all developed during the 20th century. The basic reaction of the arc process involves the union of nitrogen and oxygen gases by means of an electric arc. It may be compared to the fixing of nitrogen in the atmosphere through the lightning discharge of electrical storms. The high power requirement of the process has largely limited its use to Scandinavia, where cheap water power is available. The cyanamide process was developed in Germany in the early 1900's. Using coal and limestone as raw materials, it required less than one fourth of the electric energy required by the arc process.

Fig. 22-3. This self-propelled spray rig with 100-foot boom span covers ground rapidly and applies liquid fertilizers or chemicals in precise amounts. (*Agricultural Research Magazine*, June 1964. *United States Department of Agriculture* photo)

The first cyanamide plant in North America was built at Niagara Falls, Canada, in 1909, and was still in production during the 1950's. As of 1955, there were no such plants in operation in the United States.

The direct synthetic ammonia process has largely displaced the arc and cyanamide processes. Known as the Haber process, after Fritz Haber (1868-1934), who developed it in Germany in the early 1900's, it involves the combination of nitrogen and hydrogen gases at high pressure in the presence of an iron or other catalyst at a high temperature. The resulting product is anhydrous ammonia. Costs of direct synthetic ammonia plants are high. As mentioned earlier, World War II led the United States government to finance several such plants, while the Korean War saw the capacity of the industry further increased by direct and indirect government subsidy. The result has been the development of a major industry supplying synthetic nitrogenous fertilizers at reasonable cost to American agriculture.

The growth of the worldwide chemical fertilizer industry, with ability to supply farmers with the elements needed for more effective production at reasonable cost has helped bring about major changes in agriculture in many nations. The Department of Agriculture has estimated that the increased use of fertilizers was responsible for 55 per cent of the increase in productivity per crop acre from 1940 to 1955—a period of increase unparalleled in American history. During this same period, hybrid corn accounted for 12 per cent of the increase in productivity per crop acre.

INTERRELATEDNESS OF FACTORS

It should be emphasized that the effectiveness of one factor or practice in producing agricultural abundance frequently has been enhanced because of its use in conjunction with other improved practices. At the same time, one improvement has often made another possible. Hybrid corn, bred for a stronger root system and stalk, could better utilize fertilizer and was more suited for mechanical harvesting than earlier types. The semi-dwarf wheat in the Pacific Northwest made spectacular gains from irrigation and fertilization as a result of being selected for those characteristics. More abundant and better quality livestock are a result, at least partly, of more abundant feed grains, as well as of better feeding and breeding practices and the control of insect pests and diseases.

There is, in the mid-1960's, virtually no theoretical limit to possible increases in agricultural productivity over the next several years, although gains in productivity will tend to level off by the 1970's unless there is an additional economic stimulus to the development and, especially, to the adoption of more advanced technology. Some scientists believe that we have nearly reached the outer limits in exploiting, for agriculture, some of our technological knowledge. Nevertheless, two influences alone, the potentialities of hybridization, especially in livestock, and the possibilities of the more intensive use of chemical fertilizers are such that the age of agricultural abundance should remain a permanent feature of American life.

23 / Mechanization of the American Farm
REYNOLD M. WIK

Science and technology have provided the machines which have made obsolete the "Man with the Hoe." And while the mechanized farm removed most of the drudgery in farm labor and brought the luxuries of city life to rural America, so also has technology helped increase the productivity of the nation's agriculture.

INCREASED PRODUCTIVITY

A farmer in 1800 needed 344 man-hours to raise 100 bushels of corn; in 1910 he required 147 hours to raise this amount; while in 1960 he could achieve the same result in four hours. This increased efficiency aided the transformation of an essentially agrarian society into an industrialized urban society. A century ago one farm worker produced the food and fiber to care for the needs of five townspeople; in 1900 he could support seven; while today he can provide for the needs of over thirty. Today only 7 per cent of the total labor force is employed on farms as compared with 70 per cent 150 years ago. In fact, an hour of farm labor now produces four times as much as it did in 1920. From 1937 to 1957 the net agricultural output per man-hour increased 60 per cent compared with 28 per cent in the industrial economy. Secretary of Agriculture Henry Wallace affirmed this trend in 1938, saying that the efficiency of farm workers had increased more rapidly than that of factory workers, and today farmers operating tractors are among the most efficient workers in the nation. According to the *United States Census Report* of 1960, seven million farm workers did virtually all the major farm work in the country. They farmed 400 million acres, earned a gross income of 38 billion dollars, produced enough food for domestic consumption, and piled up large enough surpluses to discredit the grim predictions of Malthus.

Since the cost of food decreases as the proportion of farmers within the total labor force decreases, food costs are relatively low for the average family in the United States. Here 20 per cent of the family budget goes for food, while it soars to 35 per cent in most Western European countries, and 55 per cent in the Soviet Union; and in parts of Asia and Africa some people pay almost everything they earn for food, and even then they often rise little above the level of starvation.

EARLY MECHANIZATION

The mechanization of American agriculture did not occur overnight; it emerged from the technical discoveries of the preceding centuries. The first cycle of progress shifted the burden of farm work from the backs of people to draft animals; the second transferred work from animals to machines powered by steam, gasoline, or electricity. The more recent transition from animal to mechanical power has been so complete that the Statistical Reporting Service of the United States Department of Agriculture in 1962 discontinued listing the number of horses and mules on farms because they were no longer of significance to farm production.

During the 19th century, improved farm implements facilitated the production of grain crops. Better plows were designed by Thomas Jefferson, who used mathematical principles in making mouldboards, while Charles Newbold patented a cast-iron plow in 1797 which permitted their mass production. However, farmers in the Midwest found that cast-iron plows failed to scour (clean themselves) in the rich, black soil of the prairies. To meet this problem, John Lane, an Illinois blacksmith, in 1833 began using strips of saw steel fastened over wooden mouldboard plows. John Deere, another blacksmith, in 1837 designed plows with highly polished wrought-iron mouldboards and steel shares. These plows scoured in the sticky prairie soil and required about one third less power to pull them. During the Civil War a two-wheeled sulky plow appeared on the market which permitted plowmen to ride across the field instead of plodding down the furrow on foot.

Because the new horse-drawn plows, harrows, and grain drills cut the time necessary for planting grain, farmers discovered they could plant more acres than they could harvest in a season. Aside from the sickle, scythe, and cradle, there had been little improvement in harvesting since the days of Pliny (23-79 A.D.), who described ancient Roman techniques of agriculture in his encyclopedic writings. The first practical, mechanical reapers were built by Obed Hussey in 1833 and Cyrus H. McCormick in 1834. McCormick's machine incorporated the essential elements of a successful reaper, namely, (1) the cutter at one side and behind the horses; (2) a heavy main traction wheel; (3) knife-teeth with serrated edges bolted to a horizontal cutting bar; (4) double fingers with a slot through which the sickle vibrated; (5) a divider to separate the swath to be cut from the rest of the standing grain; (6) a reel to bend the grain toward the knife; and (7) a platform to carry the grain from the knife and lay it in a swath on the stubble side of the machine.

The reaper was probably the most significant single invention made in agriculture prior to the Civil War, for it reduced the harvesting labor by one half at the critical point when work had to be completed quickly to save the crop. The McCormick factory in Chicago manufactured 1000 reapers in 1851 and 50,000 in 1884. By 1872 a successful wire binder was in production, and in 1878 the twine binder appeared on the market, speeding up the harvesting still further.

Meanwhile, the harvested grain still had to be threshed, and this was done by the ancient and traditional methods of beating the grains out of the husks by whacking with a flail or by having the farm animals trample on them. The flail method produced only eight bushels of wheat in a day, and treading by animals was both unsanitary and inefficient. As a result, scores of inventors worked on this problem before Andrew Meikle of Scotland in the late 1780's built a threshing machine worthy of the name. His machine, which featured a beater revolving inside a set of concaves to thresh out the grain, became the standard design.

The grain, chaff, and straw still needed to be separated, so Hiram and John Pitts of Winthrop, Maine, built a machine in 1834 which combined the threshing and separating processes. Their design was copied by all the prominent threshing-machine manufacturers in the United States. In the 1850's the vibrator or shaker principle was employed to separate the grain from the straw. Later, refinements such as steel cylinder teeth, grain elevators, stackers, weighers, self-feeders, band-cutters, wind-stackers, and all-steel construction helped to improve agricultural efficiency and increase production.

STEAM POWER ON THE FARM

The history of rural technology shows that farm machines depend on an adequate source of power. To provide power for belt work, horse-power machines were built as early as 1820. Treadmills carried two or three horses whose weight turned a revolving inclined platform. Sweep powers accommodated four to seven teams of horses hitched to sweep poles which revolved like a ship's capstan and transmitted power through a set of gears to provide rotary power for belt work. Since these horse powers failed to provide enough power to meet the increasing demands of an expanding agriculture, farmers turned to steam engines for the first practical application of mechanical power to American agriculture. Stationary steam engines were, in fact, used on this nation's farms before steam locomotives appeared on railroads. Many farm engines were installed on southern plantations from 1807 to 1812, long before the *Stourbridge Lion* made its first successful run in 1829. By 1838, 585 farm steam engines were in use for driving saw mills, sugar mills, grist mills, threshing machines, and cotton gins.

By 1849 portable steam engines mounted on wheels and moved by horses had been introduced on the farms in both the southern and northern states. These engines, developing 10 to 20 horsepower and costing about $1000, encouraged large-scale farming by providing twice as much belt power for threshing as furnished by the obsolete sweep horse powers. During the 1870's these engines were equipped with self-propelled attachments, and they were improved in the 1890's to the point where they could be used for plowing. After 1900, steam traction engines, pulling 10 to 14 breaker bottoms, ripped up much of the virgin sod lying between the Canadian provinces and Texas.

Because steam remained the only practical and available source of mechanical power for general farm use, farmers increased their purchase of steam engines. In 1880 a total of 1,200,000 steam horsepower served American farmers; in 1910 the figure reached 3,600,000 horsepower, an amount equal to the strength of seven million horses. At that time, also, the Department of Agriculture estimated that approximately 100,000 farm engineers were operating self-propelled steam engines for plowing, grading roads, grinding feed, hauling

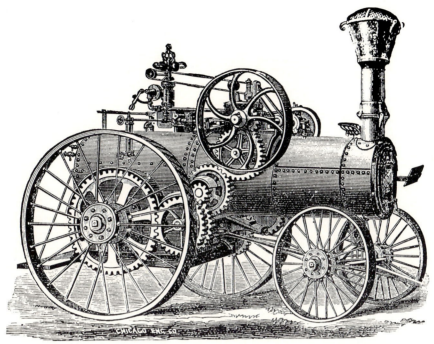

Fig. 23-1. A self-propelled steam engine, built about 1880. (Courtesy of *J. I. Case Company*)

freight, moving buildings, and threshing. Some of these leviathans weighed 20 tons, carried 200 pounds of steam pressure per square inch of the boiler, and developed 110 horsepower. Such machines cost $6000. On the Pacific Coast the Best and Holt traction engines could outpull 40 mules, and when attached to combines, could harvest 100 acres a day.

Experience with steam engines made the farm engineers familiar with the mechanical features of slide valves, injectors, steam boilers, governors, gear ratios, and lubricants. They encouraged the building of better roads to move the giant engines from one farm to another and the introduction of mechanics courses in state agricultural colleges, thus paving the way for the later introduction of the gasoline tractor.

GASOLINE TRACTORS

After 1900, the mechanization of agriculture continued with the advent of the internal-combustion engine and the electrical motor. The tractor, truck, automobile, and dynamo led to an era of power farming, and the subsequent re-

Fig. 23-2. A 1906 model tractor. (Courtesy of *International Harvester Company*)

finement of these new sources of power reduced the number of horses and mules in the nation from 28 million in 1917 to less than 2 million in 1965, thereby completing the transition from muscles to motors. However, it is well to remember that these technological achievements grew out of the discoveries of the preceding century. The gasoline motor arrived so late on the scene because its inventors had to wait for the discovery in 1859 of oil which could provide fuel and engine lubricants. Then too, electrical currents for ignition systems from batteries and generators came later in the same century.

Dr. Nicolaus A. Otto of Germany is credited with the invention of the first economical and commercially successful gasoline engine (see Volume I, Chapter 40). In the 1860's he built gas engines with four-stroke cycles, an ingenious principle which has remained basic in the design of gasoline motors until the present time. In this sense, the Otto engine was the father of the tractor, automobile, truck, and airplane. Since Otto's company, Gasmotorenfabrik Deutz, held a monopoly on this engine design, very little effort was made in the United States to manufacture the motor until the patents expired in 1890.

During the 1890's the American tractor remained in the experimental stage. Probably the first gasoline tractor to be used successfully on an American farm was one built by John Froelich of Iowa. He mounted a single-cylinder Van

Duzen gas engine made in Cincinnati on a Robinson steam-engine running gear equipped with a traction arrangement of his own design. This tractor completed a 50-day threshing run in 1892 and later became the forerunner of the John Deere tractors. In the same year, William Patterson built a two-cylinder tractor in the shops of the J. I. Case Threshing Machine Company of Racine, Wisconsin. Other early tractors included the Morton (1899), which became the father of the International Harvester tractors of 1905.

The Hart-Parr engines were the first successful gasoline tractors manufactured in the United States. Charles W. Hart and Charles H. Parr met as engineering students at the University of Wisconsin in 1892; the following year they manufactured 15 air-cooled, valve-in-hand, slow-speed, two-cylinder engines developing 20-45 horsepower. These were crude, cumbersome machines quite similar to the ordinary steam traction engines of the day, yet they performed well. The first Hart-Parr tractor ran for 17 years, while five of the fifteen built in 1903 were still in operation in 1930. In 1906 the Hart-Parrs were used for plowing, and in the following year, in order to distinguish them from steam engines, the company adopted the name "tractor," a term used by George H. Edwards of Chicago on patent No. 425,000 issued in 1890. In 1907 there were about 600 tractors in use in the United States; one third of them were Hart-Parrs with the rest divided among Kinnard Haines, International Harvester, and several smaller firms. E. W. Hamilton, after viewing the Winni-

Fig. 23-3. A 1911 tractor. (Courtesy of *J. I. Case Company*)

peg plowing contests of 1908, stated, "Five years ago there were but two oil motors on the American market; today there are in the neighborhood of thirty [models] good, bad and indifferent. We are in a swift race. We are attempting to do ten years' work in one." W. C. Allen, editor of the *Dakota Farmer,* stated in 1909 that the gasoline tractor was becoming more popular than the steam engine.

Most of the tractors before 1910 had automatic intake valves, hit-and-miss governors, and make-and-break ignition systems. For starting the engine, electric current was supplied by dry batteries, while a low-voltage, direct current magneto furnished the current for running the motor. Frames were of channel iron, selective-type transmissions were provided, and the large drive wheels turned on a "dead" or floating axle. Unfortunately, the tractor industry went through severe growing pains. Since the machines were modelled after their steam predecessors, many appeared on the market weighing 20,000-50,000 pounds. Some of these monsters had fly-wheels weighing over a ton, with drive wheels eight feet in diameter and tanks holding 110 gallons of water, 70 gallons of gasoline, and 5 gallons of oil. Some were so hard to start that engineers let them run all night rather than face this baffling problem in the morning. Farmers complained that their tractors had broken crankshafts, warped clutches, bent axles, cracked gears, and burned-out connecting rods; some spent as much as $1500 a year for repairs. As a result, many of the manufacturers of the early tractors had gone bankrupt by 1912.

After a series of reversals, the tractor industry switched to the manufacture of smaller machines. The Bull Traction Machine Company of Minneapolis in 1913 introduced a small tractor, advertised as "The Bull with a Pull," which set the new trend in tractor design. In 1915, Henry Ford entered the tractor business with the automotive system of mass production. Most of the lighter tractors sold for under one thousand dollars, and tractor sales jumped to 14,500 in 1914, and to 35,000 in 1916, while the total number in use in 1917 was nearly 90,000. The increased popularity of the small tractor convinced the manufacturers that the future would be an age of gasoline power rather than steam power. In 1925, the Case, Huber, Aultman-Taylor, Geiser, and Minneapolis companies combined built only five steam traction engines. During the 1920's the steam engines were slowly pushed aside to accumulate in junk yards to rust out in solitude.

Over the years significant engineering improvements were made in tractor design, including the frameless, or unit, design of 1913 and the three-wheeled motor cultivator of 1915. The power takeoff of 1919 opened the way to an entirely new phase of tractor use; the operation of power-driven machines such as binders, corn pickers, balers, forage harvesters, combines, sprayers, and many others. Starters and lights were available on some tractors as early as 1920.

Two of the technological milestones that laid the foundation of modern tractor farming were the all-purpose, or tricycle-type, tractor in 1924 and rubber tires in 1932. The tricycle-type tractor combined drawbar usefulness for the first time with the ability to do row-crop work. It also served as an ideal carrier for many types of mounted and semi-mounted implements, such as cultivators, planters, mowers, listers, and lift plows. This versatility led to the final demise of the horse in farm work. The low-pressure rubber tires increased the power on the drawbar by about 25 per cent, with an equal amount of saving in fuel. The tricycle-type tractor on rubber wheels increased the speed of most field operations from 25 to 50 per cent.

During the 1930's, various power hydraulic lifting attachments were available which could manipulate loaders, control tillage implements, activate power steering, regulate the cutting height of harvesters, and operate earth-removal scoops. An improved three-point hydraulic hitch developed by Harry Ferguson in Ireland and brought to this country in 1939 strongly influenced the design of tractor hitches. These hydraulic systems include an oil receptacle, pump, valves, and a control lever within reach of the driver, connected by means of a high-pressure hose to a power cylinder which can be located on any part of the tractor or trailed equipment where the control is desired. Another adaptation of hydraulic control came in 1947 when an Allis Chalmers tractor was fitted with a device for power adjustment of the rear wheel tread. It permitted the driver to use engine power for spacing of the rear wheels while sitting on the tractor seat.

Since 1954 more versatile transmissions have permitted the operator to shift gears on the move. An International Harvester "Farmall" can be reduced 33 per cent in speed without stopping, shifting, or declutching, and without touching the throttle. A J. I. Case model has a torque converter which gives the driver the option of using a hydraulic torque converter or mechanical direct drive. The Ford tractor in 1959 had a 10-speed fully selective power-shift unit; it was without a clutch pedal but the driver could shift gears with a small hand lever while the tractor was in motion.

In recent years there has been an increase in the use of self-propelled tractors, wherein the motive power and the machine for performing a given task form one unit. These are easier to operate and have faster working speeds than trailed machines. Depending on the type of agricultural device which forms part of the unit, these self-propelled tractors can be used as grain windrowers, hay balers, forage harvesters, corn pickers, sugar beet harvesters, and cotton pickers, but their most significant use has been in harvester combines. By 1956, 200,000 self-propelled combines were in use. Since the tractor and harvesting combine machinery comprise one unit, the machines lose less time in opening fields and moving between jobs. These tractor combines were so important to harvesting efforts during the Second World War that the United

Fig. 23-4. A modern combine for harvesting grain. (Courtesy of *J. I. Case Company*)

States Department of Commerce stated that without them bread rationing would have been inevitable.

The efficiency of tractors has also increased. In 1920 the average wheel tractor delivered five drawbar horsepower-hours per gallon of gasoline or distillate, while today these tractors deliver 13 horsepower-hours per gallon of fuel. Some of this efficiency comes from higher-compression engines. The compression ratio ranged from 4 to 6 in 1941, and from 4 to 8.7 in 1960. Moreover, farmers today have access to more power and a wider choice of tractors than ever before. There are approximately 5 million tractors in use on American farms, not counting the 401,000 garden tractors. On the average, there are fifteen tractors used on every 1000 acres of farmland under cultivation. While in 1850 each farmer had access to 1.5 horsepower, in 1930 the figure was 6.7 horsepower, and in 1960, 12.4 horsepower. The 1960 Directory of American Manufacturers lists 13 manufacturers of crawler tractors and 35 builders of wheel-type tractors.

Today's tractor provides more comfort for the driver, with power steering, foam rubber seats, umbrellas, air-conditioned cabs, windshield wipers, and radios. There is even a possibility that the driver himself will not be needed; over a decade ago at the University of Nebraska a tractor was driven by remote control. A radio device started the motor, stopped it, shifted gears and guided the machine across the field by means of an automatic pilot, activated by feelers which sensed the position of the rows being cultivated.

HARVESTING OF CROPS

With access to tractor power, farmers have mechanized the harvesting of many crops. Approximately 24,000 cotton-picking machines harvested one third of the cotton planted in the country in 1959. In the western states more of the cotton crop is mechanized because of larger fields, higher yields, fewer insect problems, and better weather for harvesting. In California, 94 per cent of the cotton was picked by machine in 1964.

The cotton pickers are either single-row machines which are tractor mounted or two-row, self-propelled machines. Because the cotton bolls do not mature uniformly, the machines usually go through the field two or three times in order to pick all the available cotton. The cotton pickers usually have a spindle-drum arrangement, that is, the spindles are mounted on vertical bars arranged in a cylindrical manner somewhat like a drum set on its end. The spindles are 1½ inches apart and revolve on each side of the row being picked to remove the lint from the burs, after which the cotton is unwound from the spindles by a

Fig. 23-5. A modern two-row cotton picker.
(Courtesy of *International Harvester Company*)

Fig. 23-6. A modern corn picker. (Courtesy of *International Harvester Company*)

rotating mechanism turning in the same direction but at a faster speed. The cotton is then picked up by air suction and blown into a large basket.

Mechanization has reduced the labor required to grow an acre of cotton from 150 hours with horse-drawn equipment to as low as 6 hours in the Southwest, where the conditions are most nearly ideal. A modern two-row cotton picker, costing about $22,000, is capable of producing four 500-pound bales an hour.

Machines cut the entire plants of spinach and green peas and load them into trucks that carry them to processing plants. Sweet corn and green beans are harvested by two-row harvesters that hold the leaves and stems of the plants between rollers which strip the vegetables from the stalk and drop the refuse on the ground; these harvesters are also used for celery and cabbage. As the machine moves slowly through the field the vegetables are cut and placed on conveyor belts which radiate from each side of the harvester. A mechanical cucumber machine can harvest two acres an hour—equal to the work of forty harvest hands. And a radish attachment for a tractor can pick six rows simultaneously, reducing the cost of harvesting by 60 per cent.

In the 1960's the first self-propelled lettuce pickers appeared; these cost $20,000 each and packed 600 boxes of lettuce per hour in the field. These mobile factories carry ten girls and a packing crew. The girls wrap and seal each head of lettuce in a plastic cover while the rest of the crew pack them in boxes for trucks that follow. The trucks carry the cartons to cooling plants at rail sidings, and within a few hours of picking the chilled lettuce is on its way across the continent.

In addition there are many mechanical operations in modern orchards. There the trees look like giant hedgerows after being trimmed by buzz saws carried by tractors. However, it is in the harvesting of the fruit crops that the greatest ingenuity is shown. Some machines shake the trees, and the fallen fruit is gathered in nets to prevent bruises. Fruitgrowers have reduced field labor at harvest to one tenth of former requirements by using these mechanical tree shakers.

AUTOMOBILES ON THE FARM

During the 20th century, the internal-combustion motor provided additional farm power in automobiles and trucks. Early autos had been purchased by wealthy people living in the cities, but by 1904 farmers were beginning to buy them for both business and pleasure. The United States Census of 1910 reported 3723 automobiles manufactured in the United States in 1899 and 127,289 in 1909. As total car production soared, so did the automobile purchases by farmers. The *Northwest Farmstead* estimated that farmers had bought 100,000 cars in 1913, and by 1916 one million owned them.

In October 1908, Henry Ford introduced the Model T which became popular with farmers because of its low cost, its stamina, and its ease of repair. Farmers frequently took them apart in the barnyard, cleaned the spark plugs, ground the valves, tightened up the connecting rods, and changed the transmission bands. These "Tin Lizzies," featuring a 20-horsepower motor on a light chassis, were adept at traversing rough roads and muddy terrain, but they could be used for purposes besides transportation. At times farmers attached pulleys to the crankshaft or rear wheels to use the motor for grinding grain, sawing wood, churning butter, shearing sheep, washing clothes, or pumping water. They hauled cream cans and egg crates in the back seat and tied boxes on the running boards.

The Ford Motor Company manufactured 15 million of these Model T's from 1908 to 1927. However, the other 1400 auto manufacturers also helped replace the horse for transport on the farms of the nation. In 1960, the farm population owned 3,000,000 trucks and 4,260,000 automobiles. This means that today the nation's entire labor force of 7,000,000 farm workers is mobile, with an auto or truck for each person.

ELECTRIFICATION

Electrical power became one of the most versatile aids for rural Americans during the 20th century. Farmers had talked about using electricity as early as 1830, and in 1849, the United States Commissioner of Patents believed electrical power would revolutionize human affairs because it could propel machines and lighten the burden of farm labor. It remained, however, for Europeans rather than Americans to pioneer in the application of electrical power to agriculture. During the 1880's, the French, Germans, and Italians were using electricity for illumination and for plowing. By 1918 there were 1600 electrical plowing outfits in Germany.

In the United States some of the earliest experimentation included the use of electricity to light a dairy barn in Pennsylvania in 1892; an electric motor to drive a threshing machine in Louisiana in the same year; and an electric tractor used for plowing in Illinois in 1896. On the other hand, efforts to pick cotton with electrified belts were unsuccessful. In 1918, fifteen Kansan farmers were threshing with electricity, and Californians were using 200,000 horsepower for driving irrigation pumps.

Yet rural electrification in this country is a more recent phenomenon. In 1900 a farmer needed $7000 to install his own electric plant powered by steam or a water wheel. This cost was reduced after 1904 when small gasoline engines were belted to generators. The Delco electric light plants appeared in 1912 and became popular with some of the wealthy farmers. In the meantime, most farmers were without electricity because the private utility companies failed to provide electric current to rural people at reasonable rates, believing that the farm market was too limited to warrant the investment needed to build rural power lines. When these companies did provide electricity for farmers they often set rates which gave a 20 per cent profit. As a result, only 100,000 farmers were supplied with electricity from private lines in 1919. When the companies were told that they had a social responsibility to bring electricity to the farmer, power company spokesmen retorted tartly that the utility industry was not a charitable institution. Even as late as 1935 only 10 per cent of the farms in the United States had electricity, while the figures were 90 per cent in Japan, 95 per cent in France, and almost 100 per cent in Holland.

The real expansion of rural electrification occurred during the days of the New Deal when Franklin D. Roosevelt on May 11, 1935, created the Rural Electrification Administration. Given statutory authority a year later and made an agency of the Department of Agriculture in 1939, this agency made loans to local organizations for financing the generation, transmission, and distribution of electricity to rural people. Half the farms in the United States received REA electrical power in 1960 when almost 2 million miles of line served 5 million customers. The REA loaned four billion dollars by 1962, of which one billion has been repaid with interest. Today 98 per cent of all farms have electricity furnished either by REA or private utility companies.

To provide electricity at lower cost, the REA adopted a standard of 7200 volts instead of the 2400 commonly used in industry. Increased voltage meant that the same power could be transmitted nine times farther. The neutral, or return, wire of the circuit was grounded every 1200 feet and a transformer and lightning arrester installed at every farm. Improved materials and methods helped reduce the cost of electric wiring from $2000 to $500 a mile.

With electric lights farmers could discard their smoky kerosene lanterns and save an hour a day in doing chores. Incandescent bulbs could be used to accelerate the flowering of various plants and promote a more rapid growth of herbaceous plants started from seedlings. Electricity also helped control insects by creating ultraviolet rays to lure corn borers and earthworms into traps. In addition, the electric motor permitted the farmer to apply a small amount of power to a task for a long period of time instead of using a large amount of power for a short time. A one-horsepower motor can do as much work in an hour as the average man can do in one day and at a small cost. For five cents a farmer can pump a thousand gallons of water from the well, milk thirty cows, heat fifty gallons of water, shell thirty bushels of corn, cool ten gallons of milk, or cut a ton of silage and raise it thirty feet into a silo.

Today there are over 200 different uses of electricity on the farm. Besides standard household appliances there are electric motors, power grain elevators, air compressors, milking machines, hay driers, power saws, drills, welders, and other power tools. In addition, 156,000 electric irrigation pumps are to be found in nineteen western states.

Similarly, electricity has introduced automation to many farm jobs, also. For example, some farm pigs are kept warm in winter by automatic radiant-heat lamps. Feeding troughs are filled automatically by electrically controlled augers, while the pens are cleaned twice a day by a time clock that activates two water nozzles which wash the refuse into septic tanks where it is carried off by a pumping system. Thus the new "hogomatic" systems remove virtually all the manual labor in raising hogs. It has been estimated that electric pig brooders save half the litters at birth.

Egg production also features artificial lighting, automatic feeders, egg collectors, egg graders, egg coolers, and water systems. Some farmers insist that cows give more milk when listening to a radio, thus suggesting that the uses of electricity are almost unlimited.

AIRPLANES

Another mechanized feature of modern agriculture is the use of aircraft for numerous farm jobs. Airplanes were first used for agricultural purposes near Dayton, Ohio, in 1921 to spray fruit trees infested with the larvae of the catalpa sphinx which defoliated the trees. The following year airplanes were used to spray calcium arsenate on cotton fields to control the boll weevil. In 1960 over five thousand planes were used to spray 61 million acres of crop land with DDT; this insecticide, developed during World War II, was ten times more potent than the sprays previously used.

Aircraft have proved to be efficient spreaders of fertilizers and pesticides where large acreages require quick, uniform treatment. At times planes are employed to seed lakes with fish, to fight forest fires, to control mosquitoes, and reseed forest terrain. In addition, because rice fields are often flooded, farmers hire planes to seed, fertilize, and spray pesticides; and when the crop is about to ripen, they hasten maturity by spraying hormones from the air. Rice growers have also learned that planes are more effective than scarecrows at dispersing blackbirds. When the birds become a problem, the farmer calls an air service to send a pilot to buzz the field.

After severe blizzards on the western plains, aircraft have flown hay lifts to drop baled hay to the cattle stranded in the snow. At times cattlemen have carried stranded cattle to safety with helicopters. Today there are thousands of flying farmers who own their own airplanes for business and recreation. Ohio State University offers a course in aerial application to instruct flyers in the use of airplanes for agricultural purposes.

AGRICULTURAL TECHNOLOGY AND THE ABUNDANT SOCIETY

There can be no doubt that the application of technology to agriculture has contributed to the abundance of American life. As in other sectors of the economy, the impact of technology was enlarged by developments in other and related fields, such as hybrid seed, better livestock, more effective control of insects, greater knowledge of diseases, improved roads, and advances in all scientific fields including the chemical, biological, botanical, and entomological. In addition, the nation has benefitted from a large amount of good land, a stable national government, an energetic population, and a cultural background which has encouraged innovation in a community life which accommodates both competition and co-operation. The result of this happy combination of technological, scientific, economic, political, and social factors has been an agricultural productivity which makes America "the promised land of milk and honey." Today the problem is not the country's ability to produce food, but rather its ability to distribute the surpluses to the hungry people of the world.

24 / Pest and Disease Controls

AARON J. IHDE

PEST AND DISEASE PROBLEMS

Since antiquity farmers have sought to control insect pests and plant and animal diseases, but it was not until the 19th century that such problems became sufficiently troublesome to stimulate a search for major counter measures. As long as agriculture was diversified and small in scale, pests and diseases were a constant problem but only occasionally an acute threat. The increase in pest-control problems was associated with the increased mobility of human beings and the development of specialized agriculture.

In the 19th century there was both expansion and intensification of agriculture. Plant- and animal-breeders developed varieties capable of faster growth, higher production, and adaptation to unfavorable environments. There was a conscious effort to seek new plant varieties in exotic parts of the world and transplant them to agricultural regions. At the same time, there was a marked tendency toward production of a single crop particularly suited to climate, soil type, and economic conditions. Thus, grape culture became intensive in France and other parts of southern Europe, cotton in the southern United States, fruit-growing in southern California. Vegetable-raising was developed on the muck soils near large cities, and cattle- and sheep-raising flourished in the prairie and mountain areas of the United States, on the pampas of Argentina, and in the open spaces of Australia and New Zealand.

Such agricultural "division of labor" was aided by many technological advances. The development of refrigeration made it possible to ship perishable foods great distances, thereby making large-scale production practical. Similarly, the growth of commercial canning stimulated mass production. The invention of agricultural machinery further intensified agriculture, as for example, when planting, cultivating, harvesting, and threshing machinery stimulated the culture of wheat on the American prairies.

While the intensification of agriculture led to more efficient production, it also created an environment favorable to the explosive spread of pests and diseases. As long as agriculture is diversified, farmers are apt to have the yield of a certain crop seriously reduced by insect ravages from time to time, but they will have successful yields of other crops. On the other hand when farmers restrict their efforts to monoculture, that is, the cultivation of a single crop, they create favorable conditions for the spread of a particular pest; not only do they sometimes eliminate natural predators which hold the pest in check, but they become wholly dependent on the success of a single crop.

The search for plant varieties that could be introduced into other parts of the world also led to problems. On a number of occasions, foreign pests were introduced and since they were no longer struggling for survival among natural predators, they proved an explosive menace. Phylloxera, a type of plant louse, began to infest French grapevines about 1859 and caused serious deterioration of viticulture in that country during the next two decades. It ultimately appeared in all grape-raising parts of the world. The insect, which is present in two forms infesting roots and leaf galls, was a native of the eastern United States whence it entered France with imported rootstocks.

The cotton bollworm was a Mexican insect first described by a Swedish entomologist in 1843. In 1880 the insect was reported to be damaging cotton near Monclava in northern Mexico; by 1894 it had become established near Corpus Christi, Texas; it entered Louisiana in 1903, Mississippi in 1907, and within 31 years after crossing the Rio Grande River, the bollworm had spread throughout the cotton-growing lands of the United States where it wrought enormous damage.

San Jose scale, a scale insect which attacks bark, leaves, and fruit of most deciduous fruit trees, was reported in the Santa Clara Valley of California by John H. Comstock in 1880. It was brought into the country on fruit trees imported from China by James Lick (better known as the businessman-philanthropist who founded the Lick Observatory). By 1893 the insect was established in the eastern states as the result of New Jersey nursery dealers' bringing infested trees from California.

The gypsy moth was introduced into Massachusetts by a French astronomer, Leopold Trouvelot, when he was working at Harvard. Trouvelot was carrying on experiments in which he sought to cross the gypsy moth, brought from Europe in the egg stage, with silkworm moths in an effort to produce a worm resistant to pebrine disease, which was destroying the French silk-producing business. Some of the insects accidentally escaped in 1869. They slowly increased in numbers and, in 1889, a severe plague of caterpillars appeared in Medford. The insect, which feeds on the foliage of oaks and other hardwoods, has been a nuisance ever since and has spread over the whole northeastern United States.

Dutch elm disease, caused by a fungus which clogs the sap vessels of the tree, was first found in America about 1930. Although transmission of the fungus from tree to tree is normally slow, in America it was speeded up by the presence of an elm bark beetle which had been introduced from Europe somewhat earlier. The bark beetles, in feeding on dead and diseased elm trees, readily transmit the fungus to healthy trees. First observed in the elm trees of New

England, Dutch elm disease soon spread into Canada and the Middle Atlantic states, seriously depleting mighty trees prized in American cities for their ornamental value. The disease has now spread through the North Central states and has been reported as far west as Kansas.

Various other examples could be given. Transplantation of an insect pest frequently leads to explosive increase if food supplies are adequate, since natural enemies are seldom present to hold the insect in check as is the case in its native habitat. Furthermore, the plants in the new habitat frequently are without inherent resistance to the transplanted insect.

NATURAL ORGANIC PRODUCTS AS INSECTICIDES

Efforts to control insect pests have been made from early times. The methods include mechanical destruction of insects, proper cultivating practices, and the use of poisons. The early poisons were usually derived from plants observed to be avoided by insects. Such plant poisons were normally regional in their use until the past two centuries, when increased trade brought them to general attention.

Pyrethrum, a chemical substance present in the daisy-like flowers of certain plants of the chrysanthemum genus, came into early use as an insecticide in Yugoslavia, Iran, and the Urals. The plant was ultimately transplanted to Japan and East Africa, where production was encouraged for the world market. Originally it was used in the form of ground flowers, but this was ultimately supplanted by kerosene extracts. Pyrethrum was employed in the United States from 1858 and gradually became an important household insecticide because of its low toxicity to warm-blooded animals; however, its high price prevented its ever achieving large-scale field use.

The active principle of pyrethrum was shown to be an ester (an organic compound formed by the reaction of an acid and an alcohol) when it was studied by J. Fujitani in 1909, and in 1924 Hermann Staudinger and Leopold Ruzicka isolated pyrethrin I and II, two esters within pyrethrum. Later investigations, particularly those of F. B. La Forge and his group at the United States Department of Agriculture, showed the presence of two additional esters, cinerin I and II. Studies revealed these compounds to be toxic as esters, but the free acids and alcohols derived from the compounds had little toxic effect. Hence, they function as contact insecticides. The hydrolytic effect of digestive juices causes them to lose their toxicity when ingested by higher animals. La Forge's group was successful in the synthesis of pyrethrin-like compounds with insecticidal properties, but again the relatively high cost of natural and synthetic pyrethrins has prevented widespread general use.

In the Amazon region and in the East Indies, rotenone and allied compounds were originally used as fish poisons. These compounds occur in certain species of leguminous plants, and in 1848 a preparation of the rotenone type was used against leaf-eating caterpillars in British Malaya. The name rotenone was given to an active compound isolated from derris by K. Nagai in 1902; it was identical with a compound that had been isolated by E. Geoffroy in 1892, but its chemical structure was not established until 1933. La Forge and his associates studied six naturally occurring compounds and showed rotenone and its associated compounds to have a complex organic structure. The rotenoids are both contact and stomach poisons but are sensitive to light and oxidation. Since they decompose rapidly as a result of weathering, there is comparatively little residue hazard to higher animals and human beings.

Tobacco was used in France in 1690 for control of the pear lacebug. During the next century its pesticidal use increased, both as smoke and as an extract. Much later, nicotine was found to be the insecticidal component in tobacco, and preparations of the alkaloid began to appear on the market. Nicotinic alkaloid is a highly toxic contact poison both to insects and to warm-blooded animals. It has had extensive use for specialized purposes in homes and greenhouses, but its scarcity and the danger to the man who applied it have limited its use on field crops.

Many other plant products have been used for insecticidal purposes—for example, sapodilla, rhododendron, and croton oil—but none of these products has become widely used, in part because of high cost, and in part because the availability of synthetic chemicals has discouraged a search for naturally occurring sources of insecticides.

Besides the above plant substances, many organic materials derived from animals and minerals have been used as insecticides. Particularly important have been petroleum products, soaps, and tars in varying degrees of refinement. Mineral oils and tars were used as pesticides before Pliny (A.D. 23-79), but they were also known to be injurious to plants. Marco Polo reported the use of mineral oil in the treatment of mange in camels.

Kerosene was applied to scale insects on orange trees in California in 1865. The practice of emulsifying it with water by use of soap became widespread in the years that followed. Between 1880 and 1900, kerosene-soap emulsions were the favorite insecticide for control of such insects as San Jose scale. Because scale insects feed by sucking plant juices, they are not easily killed by the stomach poisons suitable for chewing insects; hence, contact insecticides, which kill upon absorption into the body, need to be used.

The mechanism by which contact poisons kill has been the subject of extensive debate. Unquestionably some substances are introduced into the breathing tubules of the insect and cause suffocation. This is partially the case with kerosene and other petroleum oils but there are other factors as well. Soap was long believed to act mechanically in the breathing mechanism and through the irritant action of the alkali always present in a soap solution. It is now known that the fatty acids themselves exert a toxic action, an action that varies with chain length and structure of the chemical molecule. Wetting and film-forming properties of soaps are also involved.

INORGANIC INSECTICIDES

The use of inorganic poisons came into prominence in the 19th century and grew to major proportions by the time of World War II. Paris green, a complex of copper meta-arsenite and copper acetate [$Cu(CH_3CO_2)_2 \cdot 3Cu(AsO_2)_2$], so called because of its bright green color and from the fact that it had once been manufactured in Paris, was introduced in America in the 1860's for control of the Colorado potato beetle. This insect had originally been an unspectacular part of the Rocky Mountain ecology, where it fed on native solanaceous plants (those of the nightshade family). When settlers introduced the Irish potato into that region the insect developed a voracious appetite for the plant and began moving eastward into more highly cultivated areas. In 1859 it was reported 100 miles west of Omaha, Nebraska; by 1868 it had reached Illinois; and in 1874 it was found on the Atlantic seaboard, the species having moved two thousand miles in 15 years.

It is not known who first used Paris green for potato beetle control, but by 1868 its value was well known. Application was made by shaking a water suspension on the plants with brooms, for spraying equipment was still to be developed. The use of Paris green was soon extended to control of the cankerworm and the codling moth. Between 1880 and 1900 it was the most popular insecticide, although other substances were coming into use.

London purple, a by-product in the manufacture of such dyes as magenta, was suggested to C. E. Bessey of Nebraska by the English firm of Hemenway and Co. It became a popular insecticide despite the variable composition of the commercial product, which contained calcium arsenites and arsenates as the active ingredients. Its uncertain effectiveness, coupled with frequent damage to foliage, led to experimentation with arsenic compounds of controllable composition. White arsenic (As_2O_3) had been used for many centuries as a poison for lower as well as higher animals. It is a by-product in the roasting of metal ores, where it accumulates in the flues as a dust which is easily collected and purified by sublimation. Although it causes damage to plants when used directly, it is valuable as a starting material for the manufacture of various arsenites and arsenates.

F. C. Moulton, a chemist with the Gypsy Moth Commission in Massachusetts, suggested the use of lead acetate and sodium arsenate in the campaign against the insect in 1892. Trials indicated the superiority of this form of arsenic, leading to production of lead arsenate (chiefly $PbHAsO_4$) and the ascendency of this insecticide until the introduction of chlorinated hydrocarbons half a century later. Lead arsenate was easily produced, easily handled, tenacious in its adherence to vegetation, and chemically stable. These advantages readily outweighed its lower arsenic content and the greater cost attributable to the presence of lead, which served as a second toxic element. Of the various arsenic compounds tested, none proved more universally useful, and only calcium arsenate proved an important competitor. The calcium form came into widespread use after 1906, particularly in control of the boll weevil in cotton fields.

Another extensively used insecticide was lime-sulfur. Cato the Censor (95-46 B.C.) in ancient Rome mentioned the fumigant power of sulfur fumes in controlling the vine fretter, which nibbled away vine leaves. In 1800 Erasmus Darwin referred to the insecticidal value of a lime and sulfur preparation, and during the subsequent century such sprays came into extensive use. As *Eau Grison*, named after the head gardener at Versailles in 1851, lime-sulfur became popular as a fungicide in the treatment of mildew on grapevines and other fruit-producing plants. In Australia it was used as a sheep dip, and as "Victoria lime-sulfur dip," was introduced into California about 1881 in an attack on San Jose scale. Prepared by boiling freshly slaked lime with sulfur, this pesticide contains calcium polysulfides; on contact with organic material, sulfur vapor is slowly released and reduced to toxic hydrogen sulfide.

As infestation became more troublesome other toxic substances were examined for insecticide potentiality. In 1896 a British patent was issued to C. H. Higbee for sodium fluoride and various other fluorine compounds such as the fluosilicates. These latter were extensively developed by S. Marcovitch in Tennessee. They had some use in mothproofing, ant and roach dust, baits, and wood preservatives, but never became serious competitors of the arsenates for field use. Other inorganics which had some use include mercury, selenium, and thallium compounds. Compounds of many other elements were tested but none achieved great significance.

SYNTHETIC ORGANIC POISONS

Numerous efforts have been made during the past half century to synthesize organic compounds of insecticidal value and to examine known compounds for such properties. During the decade following World War I extensive toxicity surveys were made by William Moore at the University of Minnesota, F. Tattersfield of the Rothamsted Experiment Station in England, and C. H. Richardson, R. C. Roark, and R. T. Cotton of the United States Department of Agriculture. Although their studies gave information regarding toxic groups and chemical structures, they were more productive of knowledge regarding fumigants of stored foodstuffs and fruit trees than of field insecticides.

Moore's boiling-point theory of toxicity stimulated a great deal of research, although it ultimately proved too full of exceptions to be really valuable. The theory, published in 1917, grew out of Moore's studies of fumigants and contact insecticides and suggested a direct relationship between toxicity and boiling point (up to 250° where the compound is frequently so non-volatile as to be inactive). Investigators occasionally discovered a new compound of promise, but such research was generally empirical in nature. For example, the moth repellant paradichlorobenzene was developed in this manner by Arnold Erlenback in Germany just before World War I. Its greater volatility and less unpleasant odor made it an immediate competitor of naphthalene, which had been the traditional component of moth balls for decades.

DDT

The discovery of the insecticidal properties of DDT by Paul Müller of the Swiss firm, J. R. Geigy, A. G., in 1939 opened up a new era in the warfare against insects. This compound, dichlorodiphenyltrichloroethane (or more properly, 2,2-bis-(p-chlorophenyl)-1,1,1-trichloroethane) had been originally synthesized by Othmar Zeidler in the late 19th century while he was a student in Adolf von Baeyer's laboratory at Strasbourg. Yet it remained only a chemical curiosity until Müller included it among a group of compounds being tested for mothproofing ability.

Compounds containing two p-chlorophenyl groups joined to a central atom or group were particularly toxic to moths. When the sulfone (SO_2) group of bis-(p-chlorophenyl)-sulfone was replaced by the fat-soluble $CCl_3CH=$ group, the easily prepared, distinctly toxic DDT resulted. Broad insecticidal value was soon established against beetles, flies, bugs, and roaches. Application was made for a Swiss patent on March 7, 1940. British patents were issued to the Geigy company in 1942; a United States patent to Müller (assigned to Geigy) was granted in 1943.

A DDT-containing product, Gesarol, was first used commercially during a potato beetle epidemic in Switzerland. Foreign branches of the Geigy company introduced it into Britain and the United States where military and agricultural agencies immediately became interested because imports of rotenone and pyrethrum had been seriously curtailed by World War II. The first tests in the United States were made by W. M. Davidson of the War Food Administration. He found Gesarol sprays and dusts effective against cabbage aphids, thrips, mealybugs, whitefly larvae, houseflies, carpet beetles, and German roaches.

Test results were so promising in Switzerland, Britain, and the United States that commercial production was spurred in all three countries. Testing for safety to human beings and warm-blooded animals had been carried out by R. Domenjoz in Switzerland, and the results appeared to indicate a comparatively low hazard.

Domenjoz had demonstrated the effectiveness of DDT on lice and fleas in 1941, and this was dramatically shown by its successful use in breaking a typhus epidemic in Naples in January 1944. The epidemic broke out shortly after the city was occupied by American troops late in 1943. When DDT became available in January, more than a million Neapolitans were dusted with it, and within three weeks the louse-borne disease was successfully brought under control. During the remainder of the war, DDT was used extensively for control of lice and mosquitoes. Wartime problems with typhus and malaria were significantly diminished as a result.

DDT proved particularly effective as a contact insecticide, although it also killed insects when ingested. Flies, after contact with the insecticide, first show excitement then suffer a progressive paralysis of the legs as the poison is absorbed through the tips of the feet. The insect gradually loses power of locomotion, turns on its back, and slowly dies. DDT proved particularly notable for its persistence. Walls sprayed with DDT solution remained toxic to flies for months.

Virtually all production was monopolized by the military services until 1945. By the time the war ended commercial production had reached a level where extensive diversion into agricultural use was possible. In the next decade it took the place of arsenicals and other traditional insecticides for many purposes. It was hailed as a wonder chemical which would revolutionize agriculture and forestry, eliminate insect-borne diseases like malaria, make cities and recreational areas bug-free. Mosquito-fogging became commonplace in American cities, and extensive foundation money was made available for use in spray programs aimed at elimination of the anopheles mosquito from malarial areas of the world.

The success of DDT stimulated research on structurally related compounds. In part this was aimed at discovery of chemically related molecules which might be even more effective. Synthetic studies were also aimed at understanding the relation of structure and toxic action. Among the many variants tested, none proved more toxic to common insects than DDT, and only one, methoxychlor, came into commercial production. Variant hypotheses credited the CCl_3 and the p-chlorophenyl groups with insecticidal value, but the matter remains in a state of uncertainty even today.

Only slightly later than the discovery of DDT was the discovery of the insecticidal value of hexachlorocyclohexane (commonly called benzene hexahydrochloride, benzene hexachloride, BHC, 666), a compound originally prepared in 1825 by Michael Faraday. Its insecticidal value was recognized in France by A. Dupire and M. Raucourt, and a patent for its preparation was taken out in 1941 by Louis Gindraux. It was used in France during World War II, but this was not generally known until 1945. In England it was developed concurrently by scientists in the laboratories of Imperial Chemical Industries, Ltd., and English development was largely responsible for its entry on the world market. Since the insecticide is particularly useful in control of grasshoppers, wireworms and other soil pests, cotton insects, mosquitoes, flies, and livestock pests, production was quickly pushed to a high level. However, BHC imparts a musty flavor to vegetables and is therefore unsuitable for use on edible produce.

Still other chlorinated hydrocarbons entered the commercial arena in the post-World War II period. These included Chlordane, Heptachlor, Endrin, Dieldrin, and Toxaphene. All of these chlorinated hydrocarbon insecticides are highly effective and are noted for their persistence against washing and weathering.

Wartime research was also responsible for the organic phosphate insecticides such as schradan, parathion, malathion, and TEPP. Gerhard Schrader, a German industrial chemist, undertook research on nerve gases about 1934. Fortunately, the products of this research were never used in military operations, but certain compounds were suggested as insecticides in a paper published in 1947. A number of these came into commercial production, the earliest one of importance being parathion.

The organic phosphates are contact poisons which diffuse through the cuticle and interfere with nerve impulse transmission. Acetylcholine, normally formed in the functioning of nerve cells, is soon destroyed by the enzyme cholinesterase. The organic phosphates inhibit the activity of the enzyme and hence favor the buildup of acetylcholine to levels where nerve functioning is impaired. Since the nerves of warm-blooded animals also generate acetylcholine, parathion and similar insecticides are hazardous to man, domestic animals, and wildlife. Application needs to be made by trained operators; deaths have resulted from failure to follow necessary precautions. The much less toxic malathion is gaining uses which parathion once had. Because organic phosphates decompose soon after application, they may be used on food crops shortly before harvest without danger of toxic residues.

Of the many other organic compounds which have been studied for insecticidal activity, the carbamates show particular promise. These compounds also appear to function through blockage of acetylcholinesterase activity. Though carbamates have long been known to be poisonous to mammals, recent research has led to forms which are insecticidal, non-persistent, and comparatively non-toxic to warm-blooded animals.

CONTROL OF WEEDS BY CHEMICALS

From the earliest days of agriculture, weed control was achieved primarily by mechanical means—pulling, cutting, hoeing, and cultivating. In recent decades, however, chemical agents have come into use. At first these were primarily soil sterilants—salt, borax, arsenites, carbon disulfide, and chloropicrin—which kill all vegetation and permit plant growth to resume only after the chemical is leached from the soil. Oil sprays were also used for non-selective killing of weeds, as on railroad rights-of-way.

A few selective chemicals such as ferric sulfate, sulfuric acid, and copper salts had limited use in the early part of the 20th century. In 1933 Sinox (sodium-dinitro-ortho cresylate), a yellow dye which kills broad-leafed annuals, was introduced in France and also had some use in America. Ammonium sulfamate was marketed in 1941 for killing chokecherry and poison ivy, but its high price limited it to small area use.

A new concept in weed control grew out of work on plant hormones at the Boyce Thompon Institute for Plant Research during World War II. Naturally occurring growth hormones had been isolated by Fritz Kögl and his co-workers at Utrecht in the 1930's. Indole acetic acid was among the first to be isolated. This led to studies which revealed growth-stimulating effects in certain synthetic compounds like 2,4-dichlorophenoxyacetic acid (2,4-D). Further research revealed that some of these compounds had a lethal effect on many broad-leafed plants when overexposed to the chemical. A patent was issued in 1945 for 2,4-D as a weed-killer, and its use in agriculture, and in maintenance of lawns, parks, and rights-of-way spread rapidly. It is a slow-acting poison to broad-leafed plants but comparatively non-toxic to grasses and to animal life, and is used in the form of salts or esters. Many related compounds were tested, and 2,4,5-trichlorophenoxyacetic acid was found superior for killing woody plants. Crag herbicide (sodium 2,4-dichlorophenoxyethylsulfate) has little toxic effect on plants but is toxic to germinating seedlings and is applied to the soil as a pre-emergence herbicide. Variants of 2,4-D are highly toxic toward certain plant species.

Certain carbamates have been developed as herbicides in control of grassy weeds. Isopropyl-N-phenylcarbamate (IPC) was found to be effective against quackgrass, Bermuda grass, and similar weeds, but comparatively non-toxic to broad-leafed plants. Related carbamates, complex urea derivatives, dinitrophenols, and miscellaneous other compounds, have had some success as selective herbicides. Aminotriazole was developed in the 'fifties as an herbicide especially suited to use against weeds in cranberry bogs. Of special interest is maleic hydrazide, which prevents sprouting of stored root crops such as onions, potatoes, and turnips, and is able to delay the growth and blossoming of other plants.

Various agricultural chemicals have also been developed which delay or speed up ripening, defoliate plants, induce seedlessness, stimulate growth of fruit, and prevent dropping of fruit while ripening. Defoliants applied to cotton shortly prior to picking have had an important role in making mechanical pickers practical.

CONTROVERSIAL ASPECTS OF CHEMICAL PESTICIDES

In June 1962 three articles in the *New Yorker* magazine marked the opening skirmish of a controversy which had been smoldering for more than thirty years.

The articles were a pre-publication condensation of a book, *Silent Spring*, which appeared the next autumn. The author, Rachel Carson, was a former biologist with the United States Fish and Wildlife Service and a free-lance writer whose books on the sea and its life had been enthusiastically received. *Silent Spring* dealt with the widespread use of chemical pesticides and the effect their use was having on man and wildlife. She gave example after example of instances where the use of pesticides in massive spray programs for control or eradication of insects such as the gypsy moth, elm beetle, spruce budworm, fire ant, and Japanese beetle had done extensive damage to wildlife, and to farm animals and human beings. While not contending that insecticides should never be used, she argued that they were being used in an irresponsible fashion, particularly in massive spray programs.

Reactions to the book were violent. Those persons who had been concerned about purity of foods and about conservation found Miss Carson an eloquent spokesman for the positions they had been supporting less effectively. Representatives of agriculture and the chemical industry considered her an irresponsible troublemaker determined to bring food production to a halt. President John F. Kennedy requested his science advisor, Jerome Wiesner, to create a panel to investigate the problem.

The report of the President's panel, presented in May 1963, pointed out that the use of pesticides was essential to high agricultural productivity and disease control, though admitting that they presented a genuine hazard to human health and to the welfare of wildlife. In addition the report pointed out various areas where knowledge was inadequate, where controls gave only questionable protection, and where extensive research was necessary; it also made recommendations for correcting such shortcomings.

In the area of human safety there had been concern about pesticide residues on foods since the time when arsenicals came into general use. The danger of traces of arsenic entering the diet was tragically demonstrated by a series of beer-poisoning cases in England in 1903, even though the source of arsenic was from contaminated sulfuric acid rather than pesticide. Britain established a legal tolerance for arsenic in foods at the time. Even though Congress had passed a Pure Food and Drug Act in 1906, similar action was not taken in the United States until 1927, when lead arsenate residues on fruit became a matter of serious concern. Even so, enforcement involved serious problems under existing laws, a matter that was only corrected in 1938 with passage of a new Food and Drug Act which simplified enforcement of the toxic-substances provision.

However, the new (1938) law proved inadequate to cope with the multitude of synthetic pesticides introduced after World War II. Technology continued to advance faster than adequate safeguards could be developed. The facilities of the federal Food and Drug Administration were severely taxed in attempting to keep up with the necessary toxicological studies, the hearings attendant to setting of satisfactory tolerance levels, and the analytical studies associated with enforcement. The difficulties were compounded, moreover, by the fact that food additives were also coming into extensive use at the same time. Hearings on food additives and pesticides were held in 1950 by a House committee chaired by Congressman John Delaney of New York. These revealed a chaotic state of affairs, with inadequate laws and facilities at a time of extensive change in the food industry. Remedial legislation in the form of an amendment sponsored by Congressman Arthur L. Miller of Nebraska was finally passed in 1954. The Miller Amendment required a new pesticide to be registered with the Department of Agriculture before it could be marketed. The registration was based on presentation of evidence of usefulness for a particular purpose, thus being a guarantee against sale of worthless products to farmers—a matter which had always been of concern and had resulted in the first federal Insecticide Act in 1910.

The registrant of a new pesticide was also required to submit results of toxicity studies and a method of analysis to the Food and Drug Administration. Such data on toxicity would then be used to create a tolerance for residues of the compound left on foods. The Administration established the practice of requiring acute and chronic toxicity studies on at least two species of animals, one of them non-rodent. Rats and dogs are most commonly used. Acute toxicity is generally expressed as the amount of chemical which is a lethal dose to 50 per cent of the test animals, expressed in milligrams of chemical per kilogram of animal (LD_{50} in mg/kg). Chronic toxicity is the level in parts per million (ppm) in food at which symptoms of illness appear or pathological abnormalities are observed in nervous tissues or glandular organs. Symptoms of chronic toxicity should also be sought, where appropriate, by respiratory exposure, skin exposure, and injection. Studies must cover several generations in order to detect reproductive abnormalities which may be caused by the chemical. On the basis of such data and on information concerning need and intended use, the Food and Drug Administration sets appropriate tolerance levels. A policy was established of setting these below one per cent of the chronic toxicity level, thus assuring a hundredfold margin of safety in extrapolating animal data to human beings. Residue levels may be set at zero when test data deem this appropriate. In accordance with the Delaney Amendment passed in 1958, any substance known to be carcinogenic (cancer-producing) to man or animals must be assigned a zero tolerance.

The Delaney Amendment was quickly involved in controversy when cranberries were seized in 1959 because they contained aminotriazole. This compound was registered in 1958, but because feeding experiments on rats showed development of thyroid tumors, the requested tolerance of one part per million was denied, and it was declared that the fruit must be entirely free of the chemical. If used after harvest there was no objection, but when used during the growing season the cranberry plant picks up aminotriazole, which becomes distributed throughout the plant, including the berry. The seizures made in 1959 resulted from improper use of the chemical leading to detectable residue in the berry. When Secretary of Health, Education and Welfare Arthur S. Flemming gave nationwide publicity to the seizures, there were loud charges that the amounts of pesticide present in the cranberries could not possibly cause cancer in human beings. Even if this were true, the facts were that the aminotriazole industry and the growers had been contemptuous of the rules. Even worse, the chemical had been used in 1957 even before the compound was registered. Three million pounds of contaminated cranberries were quietly seized and destroyed in that year.

A controversy developed in another area when the Food and Drug Administration decided that since dairy products were used by infants, convalescents, and aged persons, they should be free of chemical additives. DDT and BHC had been recommended at one time for use in controlling flies on dairy cattle and in their stables. These recommendations were withdrawn after it became evident that these insecticides became concentrated in the body fat of the cows and were secreted in the milk fat. However, the residue problem reappeared in new guise when Heptachlor and Dieldrin began to be used for control of the alfalfa weevil. When hay containing such persistent residues was fed to cows, the milk fat contained the residue in higher amounts, so control action became necessary. Some of the problems stemmed from faulty advice given to farmers by Department of Agriculture spokesmen and reflected a failure of co-ordination between government agencies.

Such lack of co-ordination was also evident in the massive spray programs attacked in *Silent Spring*. For example, a federal-state program was initiated in 1957 aimed at eradication of the imported fire ant from the southern states. The insect was accidentally brought from Argentina about 1925 by a cargo ship berthed at Mobile, Alabama. The insect, which has a painful sting and builds troublesome mounds, slowly spread so that by 1953 it was becoming a nuisance in ten states. In 1957 a massive spray program was initiated, and by 1964 more than seven million acres had been sprayed, at a cost to the taxpayer of more than $29 million. Yet during that time the acreage of infested land actually increased. In 1957 Heptachlor was used at a rate of 2 pounds per acre, and later, Dieldrin was applied at the same rate. The Pest Control Division of the Department of Agriculture had proceeded without consultation of the Department of the Interior or other agencies that might have been concerned with damage to wildlife. As a consequence, there was no opportunity for a controlled study of ecological effects; but large numbers of reptiles, birds, and small mammals were found dead in sprayed areas. A belated control study revealed that 85 per cent of the quail in a treated area had been killed.

Various studies in the field and in the laboratory have confirmed the dangers to wildlife of insecticide chemicals. Fish and birds are particularly susceptible. The problem is complicated by extensive species variation, some organisms showing surprising resistance, others unusual susceptibility. Some species actually concentrate the pesticide to a remarkable degree without being poisoned, for example, earthworms, bass, and bullheads. More susceptible animals higher in the food chain, such as robins and grebes, suffer badly. Experimental evidence is also accumulating that sub-lethal amounts of pesticides impair gonad function and thereby reduce the reproductive power of fish and birds.

NON-CHEMICAL PEST CONTROL

The criticism of pesticide use has redirected attention toward development of non-chemical control methods. Such procedures had been used from the time of early agriculture but had been largely abandoned during the period of enthusiasm for chemical pesticides.

Exposure to adverse conditions frequently results in development of resistance in a species through the survival of the most resistant members of the population. Use of insecticides has resulted in the development of flies and mosquitoes highly resistant to DDT, BHC, parathion, and other insecticides. In the same manner, exposure to insects can lead to development of resistant strains of host plants. In locations where an ecological equilibrium exists, a particular insect is seldom a serious pest, partially because host plants have developed such a natural resistance.

Perhaps the earliest deliberate use of this principle was associated with the attack on phylloxera in French vineyards. Resistant rootstocks from America, where phylloxera is native, were grafted onto French vines, thus introducing a resistance to the insect. This principle has been used in many ways since then. Through applied genetics it has been possible to develop many plant varieties with an inbred resistance to insect pests and diseases.

Another important method of attack involves the introduction and propagation of natural enemies. Pests frequently proliferate in a new environment because they are isolated from their own enemies. This suggests that control may be restored by introduction of predatory insects and diseases. The earliest known instance of such a practice occured in Yemen where by 1775 date palms were protected from destructive ants by introducing a predatory ant, batches of the latter being brought down from the mountains each year and placed in the palms. In 1873 a mite which attacked phylloxera was introduced into France from America by C. V. Riley.

Riley, as chief entomologist of the Department of Agriculture, was also responsible for introducing the vedalia beetle from Australia into California in 1888 to combat the cottony-cushion scale, which attacked citrus trees. This had been accidentally introduced in 1869 and became a major pest; the vedalia beetle quickly brought it under control.

Numerous other transplants have been made to achieve complete or partial control of plant pests, and the principle has also been applied to weed control. For example, Klamath weed control was achieved in California by two species of beetle from southern France. Insect diseases offer a further measure of control. The bacillus causing milky disease in the Japanese beetle was introduced in the late 1930's. *Bacillus thuringiensis* is pathogenic (disease-producing) to a number of insects, such as the cabbageworm, and is produced commercially for insecticidal use in several countries. Because the introduction of predatory insects and diseases carries with it the risk that the predator may itself become a pest, the biology of predator and host must be well understood before introduction to a new environment takes place.

Still another non-chemical approach involves sterilization, a technique developed to practical importance by E. F. Knipling of the Department of Agriculture. The screwworm fly, a livestock pest in southern United States, deposits its eggs on wounds of cattle, goats, deer, and related animals. Newly hatched larvae feed on the tissues of the animal until fully grown, when they fall off and pupate (develop from larva to adult form) in the soil. The female flies mate once and lay many eggs to begin a new cycle. Knipling showed that when male flies were sterilized by x-rays and released, matings resulted in sterile eggs. A full-scale test made on the Dutch island of Curaçao in the Caribbean led to eradication of the insect in 1954. Between 1957 and 1959, over 3 billion screwworm flies were raised, sterilized, and released in Florida, Georgia, and Alabama, successfully eradicating the insect in the southeastern states. This sterilization technique offers promise for control of other insects where the life history is suitable. Certain chemicals also act as sterilants, but their use in the field is accompanied by certain hazards which suggest great care before adoption of the process.

Still another promising development lies in the field of sex attractants. In many species, the female insect attracts the male by emission of a chemical scent. The female gypsy moth, a bulky, flightless creature, is dependent upon this scheme for mating, and males can detect a small concentration of the chemical at distances up to a half-mile. Department of Agriculture chemists have successfully isolated the scent and determined its chemical structure. Synthesis has led to related compounds of similar effectiveness. One named gyplure is highly effective in the field and, when mixed with poison in traps, shows promise of bringing about control of this pest which has been heavily sprayed but continues to flourish.

Other research on attractants led to the empirical discovery of a compound capable of attracting the Mediterranean fruit fly, an insect devastating to fruit trees which is periodically introduced into Florida and eradicated at great expense by spraying. The original attractant was improved through chemical manipulation and field tests to obtain siglure and trimedlure, both powerful attractants when used in suitable form.

Biological control methods have an advantage over chemical pesticides because they are specific for a particular organism whereas chemicals are toxic to all life. Thus, chemicals frequently eliminate not only the target species but honeybees, predatory insects, fish, amphibia, reptiles, birds, and mammals. In some cases, chemicals have intensified a problem by destroying more predatory insects than target insects. Non-chemical controls are generally more expensive than pesticides when only first costs are considered, but they may well be cheaper in the long run, when consideration is given to the total ecology.

Unfortunately, chemicals have frequently been used as a bludgeon rather than as a rapier. Yet when used imaginatively they are sometimes capable of doing a highly selective job. For example, spraying large acreages with Heptachlor or Dieldrin for fire ant control not only failed to eradicate the ant but proved to be a catastrophe for wildlife. Since 1961 control procedures have shifted to use of an oily bait mixed with a recently introduced chemical, Mirex (Kepone). Bait distribution in this manner is more costly than airplane spraying with Heptachlor, but it controls the ant without excessive hazard to wildlife. Even more recently entomologists have learned that the fire ant is controlled in Argentina by a predaceous ant which lives in the anthills built by the fire ant.

CONTROL OF PLANT DISEASES

Plants are subject to a variety of diseases, particularly those caused by fungus growths such as ergot, mildews, rusts, smuts, and blights. Until a century ago such diseases were controlled primarily by appropriate methods of cultivation, as had largely been true with insect controls: crop rotation was of some value, and seed might be planted early in order to be able to harvest the crop before conditions became serious, or in other cases, planted late in order to delay ripening until the period of greatest destructiveness had passed. Resistant plant varieties were recognized and cultivated. In serious cases a particular crop was simply not grown in an unfavorable locality.

With the rise of genetics as a science there was some success in breeding rust-resistant grains and mildew-resistant fruits. Further control was gained by treating seeds with fumigants such as formaldehyde, mercuric chloride, and other chemicals. Chemical sprays also came into use for disease control, particularly for mildews and blights. Copper sulfate solutions were used as fungicides in seed treatment as early as 1761 but use on plants was unsuccessful because of injury to foliage. By 1873 the effect of lime in reducing such toxicity was known, and it was developed as a fungicide under the name Bordeaux mixture. Millardet, a professor of botany at Bordeaux, was responsible for its use on downy mildew of grape, an American disease which appeared in France in 1878 and spread rapidly. Bordeaux mixture became widely used for plant mildews and potato blight, and remained the principal fungicide until 1910 when lime-sulfur became popular. It also had a toxic effect on certain insects.

Studies on soil fertility and plant nutrition demonstrated that some plant diseases are caused by lack of certain mineral elements in the soil. Until 1920 it was commonly believed that only ten major elements were essential to plant growth. Since then it has been established that a number of others are essential in trace amounts; these include copper, zinc, boron, molybdenum, and manganese. Absence of a particular element may result in poor growth, and frequently other pathological signs are evident—deformed structure, chlorosis, spotted leaves. Lack of boron was found responsible for heart rot in beets; and lack of zinc causes chlorosis in many plants, causing the leaves to lose their green color and frequently turn to yellow. Lack of proper mineral nutrition has been found to leave the plant more susceptible to fungus and insect attack, also.

RESTORING THE BALANCE

The progressive control over agricultural pests, both insects and diseases, which has been accomplished in the 20th century is one of the major reasons for the incredible increase in farm productivity and efficiency that marks our age. If the world's population is to be fed in the future, agriculture cannot turn its back upon this progress achieved through the advance of science and technology.

At the same time, it profits little if man saves food for himself only at the cost of making it inedible, or if his shortsighted concentration upon immediate profits through higher productivity destroys the natural ecological balance and devastates the landscape and the possibility of long-range productivity. Growing evidence reveals that present methods of control have, in some cases, wrought unlooked for and intolerable damage upon man's environment and even upon man himself.

The great growth in chemical knowledge and technique which has characterized the last century has given an easy method of pest control. Long used as a panacea, it is clear that chemical control must now be used as a specific, and that mechanical, biological, and other control methods must be developed as well. It has been a case where, in succeeding too well, technological advance in one area has tended to lessen advance in another, and the resulting disturbance of the ecological balance might have long-term results which could prove worse than the original problem. Yet further ingenuity in chemical technology may serve to reduce or eliminate the dangers which have accompanied the application of technology in an unthinking manner.

25 / Food Processing and Packaging
GEORG BORGSTROM

By 1900 the United States was a world power with an industrial might fully equal to that of the older nations of Europe. Cities had become the focal point for a steady stream of immigrants who arrived to staff the rapidly growing manufacturing companies of the nation. Before immigration to this country was severely curtailed in 1924, the United States received the largest share of the millions of people who had left Europe in one of the greatest migrations of all time.

Urban growth in America, as in other nations, brought profound changes in the structure of American society. Although homesteading on virgin land was still prevalent for at least two more decades, much of the land then settled was only marginally productive. At any rate, a larger proportion of food than ever before flowed through trade channels to urban consumers.

The food industry inevitably grew more complex. Processors handled a greater share of the food, and terminal markets and grocery wholesalers expanded their facilities to handle both the swelling stream of raw products from the farm and a growing volume of manufactured foods. These changes in processing were accompanied by and intimately connected with changes in packaging and distribution which, taken together, profoundly affected what people ate and the way in which they prepared it.

From 1900 to 1920, the food industry grew rapidly and increased in importance as research provided more economical ways to preserve and prepare more kinds of food. The volume of food consumed where grown declined sharply, and, to an increasing degree, farmers were buying their food from outside sources. The Great Depression of the 1930's affected all parts of the food industry, with agriculture itself making the slowest recovery of any sector of the economy. Nevertheless, with canning leading the way, food processing achieved unprecedented growth; by 1940 more than 65 per cent of all food in trade channels passed through some stage of processing, and by 1960 this figure had surpassed 80 per cent.

FOOD PROCESSING

Food processing has become one of the largest of American industries, involving approximately 11 per cent of the total manufacturing labor force—more than any other major industry with the exception of transportation equipment. Over five million men and women in this country process vegetables, pack meat, bake bread, and perform all other processing and distributing chores. Altogether, processing, transporting, and distributing nowadays take 60 cents of each food dollar.

In most countries of the world, food-processing facilities tend to be small in size. Even in such nations as the United States, the Soviet Union, and some of the European states, food units are comparatively smaller than the units for the manufacture of transportation equipment (autos) or iron and steel. In the United States, for example, there are more than 42,000 establishments involved in food processing, whereas there are only slightly more than 5300 making transportation equipment—despite the fact that the total labor forces of each of these two industries are about equal. Despite the relative smallness of the units in food processing, some of the most modern industrial enterprises are encountered in this field, where highly complex automation is required, for example, in flour mills, bakeries, and edible-oil industries. These continue side by side with small plants, less advanced, yet efficient and with good quality manufacturing.

Undoubtedly, the advanced position of the food industry will be maintained and still further accentuated as the population becomes more greatly concentrated. Within two decades from now, the population of the country will be located in 15 major megalopolises (gigantic metropolitan centers), more removed than ever from farming and fishing areas, and also from the industrial manufacturing of food.

Many salient features of the food-processing industry are in part attributable to the growing urbanization and industrialization already noted. Statistical studies of trends in food-consumption patterns in the United States reveal two major features. First, an almost revolutionary shift in the functions of the food industry. Whole branches of the industry have arisen to perform the work that consumers at the start of the century used to take care of almost entirely in their own homes. Most notable in this transformation are the expanding cooking and food-preparation activities of the food-preservation industries. The second feature is the emergence of a major food-service industry, that is, facilities in hotels, restaurants, factory canteens, hospitals, military establishments, and so forth. This second major trend toward institutional feeding is a consequence of the rapid collectivization of modern society, with the enormous ensuing proliferation of goods and services that are demanded. During World War II this trend was given a strong impetus in such countries as England, Russia, and Germany. In the United States, almost a third of food consumption takes place outside the home.

Even in the food prepared in the home, the work of preparation has been much lightened by the development of "convenience foods." The term "convenience food" has come to describe a product with ingredients that are

Fig. 25-1. A "basket" of filled cans being placed in a retort cooker. Once in the retort (which is actually a giant pressure cooker) the contents will be cooked and sterilized by steam under pressure. The recording device on the panels adjacent to each cooker automatically records time and temperature of each "cook" to insure complete sterilization of the foods. (Courtesy of *Libby, Mc-Neill & Libby*)

blended, mixed, or combined to replace comparable products prepared in the home. The canners were, so to speak, the first producers of convenience foods, and the earliest customers for these foods were explorers, military units, and travellers who needed dependable sources of prepared foods that required little cooking time. Soon canners turned to providing convenience foods for the home also. Other food-processing innovations followed suit, and there has been a gradual takeover of home cooking by the food-processing industry. As a result, "home cooking" no longer means "as mother made it." Instead, home cooking is increasingly coming to mean simply that the meals are prepared in home kitchens, although the meals themselves consist of instant, frozen-prepared, ready-mixed, pre-cooked, canned, or heat-and-serve convenience foods. Preparation has become a matter of minutes rather than the hours formerly required. This is truly a convenience for the housewife or, increasingly, the working mother.

CANNING

The canning industry grew rapidly during the 19th century, and by 1900 canned foods had found wide acceptance. During the first three decades of the 20th century, the major improvements in heat processing were the result of larger, more efficient retort pressure cookers and improved cooling systems. These developments, because of high installation costs and necessarily continuous operations, have favored large-scale processors with year-round production.

The enhancement in the quality of canned food may be attributed to technical advances which allow a more rapid heating of the cans by adopting higher processing temperatures and thereby shorter processing times, and by presterilization prior to filling the cans (so-called aseptic canning). An alternate way for rapid heating is rotating the cans in the retorts, allowing the heat to penetrate more rapidly through all the can's contents. Overcooked flavors, which earlier hampered the full use of canned foods, have been resolved by resorting to these techniques; the period for heating has thus become so short as to save the "fresh flavor" even of milk, banana puree, and other heat-sensitive foods.

Canning, initiated some 150 years ago, is overwhelmingly the leading method of food preservation in the developed world. It is the most reliable method of long-term preservation for many protein foods, as well as for fruits and vegetables. After processing, the products remain good for years under reasonable storage conditions. Moreover, the process can be satisfactorily operated with a high degree of flexibility, ranging from a minimum of complexity to a high degree of automation. Recent developments are aseptic filling, "end-over-end" canning, ultra-high temperature sterilization, further reduction of spoilage by better sanitation, and possibly the replacement of metal containers, such as tin and aluminum, with plastic materials.

Short-term preservation through pasteurization is used not only for milk but also for pickles, juices, beer, and wine. Pasteurization not only destroys bacteria capable of transmitting diseases but it also facilitates distribution by longer shelf-life. Although this method is well entrenched in the dairy field, it is facing the demand for higher temperatures to meet the onslaught of new armies of heat-adapted microbes—so-called thermoduric or thermophilic microbes. Alternate methods of killing microorganisms are ultrasonic or infrared irradiation, but these techniques are still in their infancy and less universal in their application.

CHILLING

Natural ice retained its position as a chilling medium far into the 20th century in both the United States and Europe. Only in the 1920's did the making of artificial ice become really large scale. Ice is used for transporting fresh fruits and vegetables, particularly in the United States and Canada, and icing stations have been organized at strategic points to service the transcontinental delivery of fruits and vegetables from California to consumption centers in the East. Leading articles being iced are tomatoes, lettuce, fresh potatoes, cantaloupes, and peaches. In most cases these products are chilled prior to loading through hydro-cooling, air-wind tunnels, or vacuum treatment. Large-scale pre-cooling plants have been constructed in the postwar period in France and Italy, often without serious attention to alternative, cheaper methods of preservation.

Ice or ice-chilled water is abundantly used in the handling and holding prior to processing of most perishable raw materials in the food industry: berries, cherries, peaches, poultry, fish, and the like.

Controlled-atmosphere (CA) storage is achieved by increasing the carbon dioxide content of the surrounding air and lowering the amount of available oxygen. This procedure, to lengthen the shelf-life of fruits (mainly apples and pears), assures that the fruit is put to "sleep" until a time in late winter and early spring when markets are less crowded. Such refrigerated storehouses for fruit were initially built in the United Kingdom (1932), and later in the United States, Canada, Holland, Switzerland, and Scandinavia. They are quite common among the apple-growers of Michigan and New York.

FREEZING

Freezing as a method of retailing food attracted serious commercial attention in the United States only in the 1920's, following the pioneering work of Clarence Birdseye. More than a thousand varieties of packaged frozen foods are currently available, including literally everything from soups to spreads, from complete turkey dinners with all the "fixings" to fine pastries for dessert.

Freezing is now the primary method for the bulk storage of raw materials used in the production of sausages, meat dishes, fish sticks, breaded shrimp, soups, and so on. During World War II, shipping space was saved when America provided food to the allies and to troops abroad by deboning and freezing meat in big cuts. Although several efforts have been made to popularize retailing of frozen meat, it has never, except in the case of hamburger meat, succeeded in gaining acceptance due to quality and cost factors.

In large, continental areas such as the United States, the Soviet Union, and Europe, freezing is the chief means of distributing and keeping perishable food in bulk and thereby of eliminating slack seasons in the food-manufacturing industry. Berries for preserves and syrups, and meat and fish for sausages and ready-made dishes are handled in this way. It is conceivable that in the future this application of freezing will be far more significant than retailing of frozen foods. As more and more food is pre-cooked for sale to the consumer, it seems likely that the process will be increasingly carried on in such a way as to preserve the food as well, and therefore make freezing less necessary.

DEHYDRATION

Dehydration, one of the classical methods of food preservation, has been vastly improved by various new technical devices and processes, such as puff-drying, accelerated freeze-drying (AFD method), and vacuum-contact drying. The latter method, which has improved quality, was developed in the 1930's by Scandinavian scientists, and is now employed with and without initial freezing. In 1954 the first large-scale plants for freeze-dried products, primarily fish and meat products, were opened in the Soviet Union, following the method earlier devised chiefly for the preservation of human blood, human milk, and other biological materials. The extended-plate method, developed by British and Canadian scientists, largely contributed to cheaper and better freeze-dried tissue foods, also giving them improved reconstitution properties.

RADIATION PRESERVATION

In the wake of the atom bomb, great hopes were attached to the use of various kinds of charged electrons and ions for the destruction of food-spoiling microorganisms. These expectations have not been fulfilled, for the consequent vitamin losses, together with other qualitative and undesirable effects, have made this method dubious.

Sterilization by radiation seems to be ruled out due to molecular disruptions, causing off-flavors under the doses required for food safety. The economic justification of using this procedure as an adjunct of refrigeration, freezing, or canning seems questionable, as either one of those methods offers sufficient protection and eliminates microbial spoilage without any such additional aid. At present, studies in this area are devoted to the possible use of such electronic radiation for partial reduction of the spoilage flora—in principle, a kind of pasteurization—with the limited aim of somewhat extending the shelf-life of certain items such as bacon, fish, and shellfish.

MEAT-PACKING

In the early years of America, livestock was concentrated on the Atlantic seaboard close to the major production and market centers, and commercial slaughter operations were performed by local butchers in small establishments. As the Midwest was settled, livestock production moved westward. The United States meat-packing industry was centered in the North Central states for more than a century. By 1920, about one third of the nation's meat-packing was done in Chicago, St. Louis, and Kansas City. Each offered better transportation advantages, in terms of railroads and inland waterways, than most other locations in the major producing areas.

The decline of meat-packing at these major centers can be attributed to various improved transportation facilities. Transportation costs generally favored shipment of dressed meat in preference to live animals. New methods to avert undue shrinkage made delivery to nearby markets attractive to both packers and farmers, and concentrations for slaughter became possible at almost any location.

In dressing, the handling of cattle requires heavy machinery due to the size of the animals. Much technical ingenuity and developmental work have gone into providing the slaughterhouses with effective mechanical devices for dispatching, handling, scalding, washing, depilating, eviscerating, hide-removing, and so on. Extensive conveyor systems form part of the standard equipment.

The complete dressing of hogs may be accomplished in 30 minutes, and several plants have a capacity of 600 hogs an hour. After chilling (24 hours) the pork sides are broken up into commercial cuts and routed to appropriate departments for further processing. About 40 per cent of the pork is sold as fresh meat, 50 per cent as cured or smoked, and 10 per cent as sausages.

As the old slaughter yards of Chicago and other centers have been shut down in favor of more local operations, the new facilities have become increas-

Fig. 25-2. Hogs on a conveyor system prior to disassembly of the carcass. (Courtesy of *Oscar Mayer and Company*)

Fig. 25-3. The continuous-process system for making
wieners. (*Oscar Mayer and Company*)

ingly automated. Indeed, the trade of slaughtering, once a skilled and lucrative
employment, if never one of much status, has shrunk to a small percentage of
its former dimension, and the ex-slaughterhouse employee is now one of the most
sobering examples of the technologically unemployed.

DAIRY PRODUCTS

The processing of dairy products has also undergone changes in the 20th century. The triumph over bovine tuberculosis and Bang's disease, supplemented
by pasteurization, now commonly applied, has everywhere made milk safer for
adults and children.

Homogenization is the most important single technical event in the processing of milk for the American market. Machines which disintegrate the fat

globules into particles so small that no cream line appears have standardized the composition of milk, improved its shelf-life, and on the whole, given it a higher taste appeal. Dairies have also come to add vitamins and minerals to milk to increase its natural food value.

In recent, more calorie-conscious years, low-butterfat, skimmed milk has gained in popularity. Specialty milk products such as cultured buttermilk, chocolate milk, "half-and-half," whipping cream, ready-mix whipping cream in pressure cans, coffee creams, and seasonal egg-nog drinks have further boosted the consumption of dairy products. Milk concentrates have found a market in those remote sections of Canada and the United States which have distribution difficulties in marketing fresh milk.

Modern cheese-makers still stick to traditional methods, but new machinery has been introduced and standardized starter cultures employed. Processed cheese has become a major mechanized product accounting for almost half of the United States cheese intake.

Margarine-making was improved substantially in the early 1930's, in time to make important inroads into butter sales volume during the Depression. Margarine outsells butter in the United States and is normally a cheaper food fat in most countries. However, in some countries, including Russia and Holland, butter holds a larger part of the market.

CEREALS

Cereals are processed in a variety of forms, the most popular in the West being bread, biscuits, and breakfast foods. Although processing is already highly automated, new continuous processes are constantly being devised. As the standard of living rises, consumption of carbohydrates declines, generally in favor of more sophisticated and usually more nutritious products. Visible fat and sugar intake have, however, risen considerably, largely resulting in an intake of empty calories, that is, those without accompanying enzymes and other metabolizing agents.

The production of baked goods since 1900 has moved out of the home and into the local commercial bakeries, allowing large-scale production of breads, cookies, and other goods, and finally back to the home again with prepared mixes. The freezing of dough has been a major technical aid contributing to this trend. The growth of the baking industry primarily reflects an increased demand for commercial bakery products, as well as the more general mechanization of production, and the expansion of mass distribution. By 1930, bakers could claim for the first time that they had produced more (60 per cent) than the homemakers (40 per cent).

One advance which helped to return baking to the kitchen was the development of "brown-and-serve," frozen, and ready-mixed bakery products. Flour mills early experimented with and developed packaged dry mixes for baked goods, one of the first being Aunt Jemima Pancake Mix, which appeared in the late 19th century. Biscuit mixes were successfully introduced in the early 1900's, and since the 1950's packaged cake mixes have become a popular item. Pantries need no longer be stocked with flour, baking powder, flavorings, toppings, and all the other ingredients required for cake-making.

No single food-product group can match in impact the emergence of this new industry, which has taken place largely since 1948. Besides innumerable cake mixes, one encounters mixes for doughnuts, biscuits, pie crusts, crackers, and pancakes, as well as dry soup mixes. More than one hundred types of mixes are on the market, each with four or five variants, and experimentation is now proceeding with bread mixes.

Among key discoveries that have rendered indispensable support to the manufacture of mixes are micro-encapsulation of fats, antioxidants, powdered shortenings, stabilized and instantized milk, and egg powders. Mechanical aids for effective mixing, blending, and grading are other prerequisites.

PACKAGING

Modern food packages have a number of functions. They protect their contents during storage, both before sale and in the home, from contamination by dirt and other foreign material; from infestation by insects, rodents, and microorganisms; and from loss or gain of moisture. They frequently are designed to protect the food from deterioration resulting from contact with air, light, heat, or contaminating gases. They may even serve as containers in which the food is heated for serving. Their odd sizes and weights are carefully designed either to confuse the consumer (as critics charge) or provide handy and exact quantities for standardized recipes (as industry spokesmen insist). Finally, they are often cleverly and colorfully designed to attract the eye and engage the loyalty of the customer.

Packaging is a key factor in the retailing of foods. The introduction of retail packaging has revolutionized food selling by: (1) facilitating handling; (2) relieving the food trade of cumbersome weighing; (3) permitting self-service; (4) providing facilities for on-the-spot advertising; and (5) providing protection against food contamination.

These attributes of food packages have contributed to the development and marketing of a whole new array of food products. Highly processed foods, the "convenience foods," such as ready-to-serve products, prepared dinners, mixes, and the like, may have peculiar and specific requirements that only special package formulations can meet. Only through the advent of new types of packaging materials has it been feasible to meet these many new and far-reaching demands of a complex, technically dominated society.

The packaging of a food product consequently is much more than the enclosing in a container. Though product protection is the main aim of packaging, durability, appearance, suitability to retail display, and consumer appeal must also be considered. Each individual food product, with its susceptability to chemical change, loss of volatile flavor components, and changes in moisture and texture, presents a special challenge to packaging experts. For any one food, the ideal material would maintain the fresh taste and appearance of the food for a long or indefinite period of time. This goal is never reached completely, but constant improvements toward this aim are made. Technology has brought about considerable changes in this field, both by offering an impressive array of new materials and by providing innumerable new machines designed for automatic packaging.

The number of establishments in the United States primarily engaged in the manufacture of containers and packaging materials totals over 5000. To this figure can be added 300,000 establishments using packaging to ship manufactured products to consumers. Some 900,000 people are engaged in manufacturing containers and packaging materials and providing service to the packaging field. Similar figures could be quoted from Canada, most Western European countries, and Australia.

The packaging field is one of the six major consumers of basic raw materials in the United States, using one tenth of all steel (an amount exceeded only by the automotive and construction industries), over half the paper and paperboard produced, two thirds of all polyethylene film, and nine tenths of all glass, aluminum foil, and cellophane. Glass and metal cans retain their leading position as food packaging materials, despite the inroads of new materials such as metal foils, plastics (moulded and in sheets), laminates, and others. This is in part due to the fact that the weight of glass containers, both jars and bottles, has constantly been reduced (by one third since 1930) as new ways of strengthening the glass have evolved. New methods have resulted in disposable (one-way, or no-return) bottles for milk, soft drinks, and beer, which have become one of the authentic artifacts of our civilization.

GLASS

Glass is maintaining its dominance in home-delivered milk (39 per cent of all milk consumed), of which approximately nine tenths is sold in bottles. Cartons, comprising 46 per cent of all consumer packaged milk, are mostly encountered in supermarkets, which sell half of all milk consumed. Glass is staging a slight comeback in supermarkets, however, particularly in two-gallon sizes or bigger. These new bottles are serviceable for 75 to 80 trips. The emergence of milk concentrates may increase the preference for bottled milk, since glass makes it easier to see what remains and how much is used on each occasion. Glass containers have some drawbacks, such as cylindrical shape, which wastes space in shipping and storage, and the proportionally greater weight, which adds to shipping costs.

METAL CANS

The can long ago took its place on grocery shelves alongside the glass container. One shortcoming is its cylindrical shape, and cans easily dent and lack transparency. Their strength and increasingly light weight are their major assets. Novelties are cans with built-in opening devices—pull tabs.

The manufacture of tin-plated cans, begun in the 19th century, has reached a high degree of mechanization and automation. The production rate of some machines now exceeds 800 units per minute. Tin shortages have led to tenacious efforts to reduce the required amount of this critical metal, as in the electrolytic method, and new cans entirely devoid of a tin cover—the food is directly protected by a lacquer against the steel plate—are now appearing on the scene. In addition, modern techniques for direct printing on the cans have outdated previous labelling techniques and have highly improved their "eye-appeal."

The tin can is in constant competition with the glass bottle. It is at present invading the soft-drink market, but glass bottles still accounted for well over 90 per cent of the sales of packaged soft drinks in the early 1960's. Steel containers increased their share of the United States beer market from about one fifth in 1938 to two fifths in 1960; yet the introduction of no-return glass bottles began swinging the tide back again, accounting for one tenth of beer business in 1963.

For a long time aluminum cans offered little competition to tin cans, but new methods of manufacture have brought down the price. The aluminum can is lighter and easier to open, and is made from a raw material more readily available. The techniques for both lacquer coatings and direct printing onto the outer surface have also been worked out for aluminum. Aluminum-coated steel cans are a new type with great promise. The foil-laminated fiber can is a forceful newcomer on the food-packaging scene, lower in price even than the aluminum cans, and it has rapidly conquered the frozen-juice market.

The pressurized can—aerosol dispenser with a spray nozzle—is an innovation which dispenses and induces a "whipping" effect through the gas injection. So far this invention has been used for food only on a very limited scale, largely for whipped cream and toppings. Difficulties persist with the preservation of the contents from microbes and in the development of the proper gases for each food product.

Collapsible metal tubes are still best known in this country as toothpaste tubes. Originally an American invention, they have for a long time been employed in Europe for the packing of a number of semi-liquid food products. In recent years they have rapidly gained ground in the United States, and a number of food packages of this type are now on the market for such items as juices, pastes, mustard, and so on. This package is made from tin or aluminum foil protected on the inside by lacquers.

FOOD WRAPPING MATERIALS

Papers, films, and foils compete strongly in the field of wrapping. This is in step with modern needs to increase packaging-line efficiency and to reduce shipping weights and handling costs. Food-wrapping materials must show considerable versatility and meet demanding specifications raised by individual food products. Essential property features of wrappers are their permeability by vapor, odor (both in and out), oxygen, carbon dioxide, and flavor volatiles. In order to strengthen one or more of these characteristics, foils and paper wrappings are laminated. Particular importance is attached to thermostable laminated products made from single films which can withstand the temperatures involved in the kind of heat treatment required in canning.

Aluminum foil has gained a strong standing in the food-packaging field, although laminated steel foils may become a competitor. Plastics are among the leading food wrappers; however, cellophane, introduced in the 1930's, retains its top ranking, closely followed by polyethylene plastic. Most of the plastic packaging materials have been made heat sealable, highly transparent, and with a smaller degree of chemical contamination than in metal foils.

A significant new feature in the use of plastic wrappers is the introduction of shrinkability. Stretch-wrap polyethylene, or plunge packs, and shrink-wrap polyethylene are being used where loose wrapping of commodities cannot be effected on automatic or semi-automatic packaging machines. After wrapping in this way, the material is shrunk back on the product or pack by means of heat.

The boil-in-bag method was introduced several years ago, but only recently has serious attention been devoted to this type of package. Processors are offering a complete line of such products that need only to be heated in boiling water for 10-12 minutes before being ready for the table.

CARTONS

The use of paper milk cartons soared from 1 billion in 1940 to 19 billion in 1965. Recently introduced to American markets, the polyethylene-coated milk carton had by 1967 almost completely replaced the earlier wax-coated one. This new coating removes the risk of peeling and the appearance of minute wax particles in the milk; it is also more leak-resistant.

The polyethylene-coated carton has also gained a strong hold in the frozen-food market, where the traditional package had been cartons with printed wax-paper overwraps. Single-wall or wrapperless cartons are gradually replacing these older ones, and in areas such as baked goods and frozen dinners, the wrapperless carton already dominates. The majority of the cartons used for frozen foods must be coated with wax or wax blends.

Eggs, with their brittle shells and susceptible freshness, present a unique packaging challenge. Through the years, corn husks, cardboard partitions in cartons, and finally 12-egg cartons with overwraps of transparent film have been used substantially to reduce cracking and to promote size- and quality-grading.

MULTI-PACK

Finally, the packaging industry has been vastly influenced by the introduction of the multi-pack, or a grouping of two or more unit packages in specially designed carrying cartons. Multi-packs promote the easy carrying of several units; mean less frequent shopping and provide against the inconvenience of running short of needed products; reduce waste, since the products purchased in smaller units can be kept unopened until used; and simplify shopping by combining different products that go together naturally, such as canned fruit and pie mix. Multi-packs provide an expanded surface for display and labelling advertising, and have even been designed to help distributors and retailers reduce costs of storing, handling, and taking inventory.

Multi-packaging sometimes employs several container types to good advantage: bags, bottles, overwraps, set-up boxes, thermoformed plastic-sheet containers, and various kinds of handles and gripping devices. It is sometimes simplified to a plastic sling or sleeve tying together two, three, or more packages.

EUROPE

Although many Europeans still buy their basic foods from open bins in small, specialty food markets, such outlets—inefficient, unsanitary, and (to Americans at least) quaint—are rapidly giving way to the American-style supermarket featuring pre-packaged goods. Already the European food scene exhibits an equally bewildering assortment of new packages. In many fields new ideas, new types of packages, and improved materials have been initiated in European countries, among them the new tetrahedron carton for milk and juices (Tetra-pak); a gas-tight, directly sealable coffee carton; collapsible tubes; and many more. Several packaging machines have been devised there as well. In Europe as in America, the impact of packaging on the food industry will probably be looked upon as the most significant technical contribution to food technology within this century.

ADDITIVES

As food technology has advanced it has enlisted the aid of numerous chemical additives and "improvers" to control or speed up processing. Such additives function as preservatives (against microbial growth), emulsifiers and stabilizers, oxidizing agents, antioxidants, pH regulators, sequestrants, which inactivate certain metallic ions, and humectants, which help to keep the food at desired moisture levels. Furthermore, there is a widespread use of artificial coloring materials, with the object of improving the appearance of goods, and thus their acceptability to the consumer.

There is opposition in some countries to the incorporation of additives into food. This is made up, in part, by proponents of the merits of natural foods, who regard it as prejudicial in principle to tamper with nature by using "artificial" fertilizers and food additives. Such processes as cooking, fermenting, and smoking are categorized as "natural," while canning, freezing, and most other food processing is condemned. Irrespective of such creeds, great caution must be exercised in the area of food additives.

The general intention of the food additives is to improve the properties of foods, to increase their shelf-life, or to shorten processing time and thus increase processing capacity. Their use is now closely regulated in most countries, and on the whole the authorities see to it that the public is neither deceived nor harmed by the quantities and kinds of additives consumed along with the foods they eat. In the United States, for example, large sums are spent on pre-testing food additives each year.

Although there are occasional occurrences which prove the need for constant vigilance, the overall situation should be kept in proper perspective. The price we pay for progress in a number of other areas of modern life is frequently much higher. Criticism against the addition of extraneous chemical compounds to food is not entirely without justification, but many people overlook the fact that very few chemicals play any role in preserving the major bulk foods which constitute the backbone of our daily diet. In this particular area of food preservation, modern food technology has come to rely on chemicals to a far lesser extent than at any earlier time in human history. The non-chemicalized sector has vastly grown, thanks to constant improvements in heat processing (canning) as well as in freezing and drying. At the beginning of the century, large amounts of salted, smoked, and otherwise preserved food were ingested, particularly in off-seasons. Modern food technology has transformed this situation, with beneficial results to the health of the individual.

DISTRIBUTION

At the beginning of the 20th century, grocery stores, meat markets, produce stores, and other individual types of stores served the cities, but the general country store remained the principal supplier in rural areas. A major change in food retailing occurred when food chain stores began to appear on the scene and challenge the very existence of the independent wholesaler and retailer. During the ensuing battle, the supermarket made its appearance, setting the pattern for the future development of retailing. The flow of food from the farm to the consumer came to be channelled primarily through processors, to grocery wholesalers and chain warehouses, and then to retail stores.

The lack of home storage of perishables was long the reason for almost daily trips to the food store. Mechanical refrigerators finally arrived to provide dependable home storage for perishables, and this, along with the automobile, helped reduce the frequency of shopping trips and made it practical to visit a supermarket only once or twice a week. The more than 43 million refrigerators and 12 million home freezers sold during the 1950's crowned this revolution.

In the stores, early ice coolers and mechanically refrigerated display cabinets gave way in the 1950's to open-type, self-service cases. This constituted a major advance in the mass merchandising of perishables and frozen foods. The measure of consumer acceptance of these new devices can be seen from the fact that in 1960, sales in departments requiring refrigeration (meat, dairy, produce, and frozen foods) accounted for about half the total sales of an average supermarket.

EVOLUTION AND REVOLUTION IN FOOD PROCESSING AND PACKAGING

During the first half of the 20th century, technological innovations in the processing, packaging, distributing, and marketing of foods wrought profound changes in the way people satisfied their fundamental need for nourishment. In many ways this development was only a logical and extended working out of trends already developing in the previous century: the concentration of flour milling in such cities as Minneapolis, the rise of large biscuit factories in the seaport towns, the concentration of slaughtering in midwestern cities such as Cincinnati and Chicago, the rise of refrigeration and commercial ice-making, and the development of large market areas in the rapidly growing cities.

In this century, the food industry has responded technologically to the new demands put upon it in a way similar to that of other 20th-century technologies. Mass production, standardization, and efficiency have become the technological goals which have influenced many decisions earlier made on quite different grounds. The results have, of course, been mixed. Greater variety and better nutrition are clear advantages, as is increased convenience. At the same time, these do not automatically result from change, and have been won only at the expense of some public watchfulness. It is hard not to agree, however, that the revolution in processing and packaging has been a beneficial, and perhaps necessary, development.

26 / Food from the Sea
GEORG BORGSTROM

In relative terms, no area of modern food production has a better record of productivity than fisheries. Their production has more than kept pace with population growth, and most countries have in recent years reported that their fisheries were more prosperous than at any previous time in history. The average annual gain in figures of total aquatic catches since 1948 is 9 per cent, which surpasses anything that has happened to any other food commodity. Furthermore, this development is proceeding at an accelerated rate, the years 1956-65 showing an average annual increase of 13 per cent.

THE POST-WORLD WAR II REVOLUTION

Many different factors account for the revolutionary transformation of fishing following World War II. In *technical* terms, fishing has moved on a large scale from the shelves of the continents to the high seas. At the same time, regional coastal fisheries in underdeveloped regions have experienced a high degree of mechanization and improved efficiency, even to building a number of specialized vessels designed to serve particular needs. Most revolutionary of all has been the great number of new technical aids that have been offered the fish industry for navigation and for the searching and locating of fish. The advances of technology in other fields have also aided fishing in other ways. For example, the wealth of new synthetic materials reduces the weight and at the same time increases the lifetime of netting and lines. Hulls of fishing boats are made of fiberglass, while several other non-corrosive materials have eliminated costly maintenance. Similarly, knotless plastic nets have greatly reduced weight and raised catching efficiency.

In terms of *catches*, the most noteworthy expansion has taken place in tuna fishing, which has grown immensely both in the Atlantic and the Pacific. Several new species (for example, saury in the Pacific, anchoveta in Peru, sea bream in the Pacific and the Indian Ocean, redfish in the North Atlantic and North Pacific, and hake in the South Atlantic) have been exploited on a major scale. Shrimping and the catching of other crustaceans also show large global increases. Another important development is the considerable growth in yield of herring and sardines by several fishing nations.

In terms of *utilization*, several major features have overriding significance. First is an unprecedented marshalling of refrigeration for saving these highly perishable catches, chiefly by more ample use of ice and by the development of freezing techniques and equipment. Chilling and freezing establishments have been set up in innumerable ports around the globe, and the technique has become standard equipment in a growing number of fishing vessels. Second, and of almost equal importance, has been the transfer to sea of the processing of aquatic catches by the construction of a large number of factory ships and the providing of trawlers with such facilities. Finally, there has been a massive investment in the creation of a highly modern and automated fish-meal industry.

In *international* terms, the postwar period has been notable in several respects. The great land giant of the Soviet Union has emerged as a major marine empire, and there has also been a resurgence of Japanese fisheries. These have been made possible by the development of distant fishing, rather than the older system of fishing "close to home." Another important event is the almost explosive creation of a fish-meal bastion on the South American coast of Peru and Chile, accounting for more than one third of the entire Pacific catch.

NEW COMPETITORS

The Soviet Union has made a large-scale investment in floating processing factories for the servicing of modern, highly mechanized fishing fleets, and Soviet fishing activities now extend to almost all oceans. Fishing activities are intense in the entire Pacific arch, stretching from the Sea of Okhotsk via the Aleutians into the Bering Sea as far as the Bristol Bay area, and then further east of the Alaskan peninsula and the entire Gulf of Alaska close to the North American mainland at Yakutat. Fishing is also pursued further south along the continent: Soviet fishing activities have been observed off Vancouver Island, California, and Baja California (Mexico). Trawl and herring fleets of the Soviet Union, in numbers in excess of 100 ships, have also moved into the northwest Atlantic, as far west as Greenland, the Newfoundland Banks, and George's Banks. With a series of large-sized vessels, more than 5000 tons, the Soviet Union has entered into world competition in tuna fishing, so far mostly in the Pacific. These tuna boats are in effect mother ships carrying 6 to 14 catching vessels.

With something like awe, the world is awaiting the commissioning by the Soviet Union of the new 47,000-ton mother ships of the Vostok type. At least thirteen of the vessels are planned which will be able to stay at sea for 125 days. A new series of ships half this size is also being built, and there are plans for constructing no less than 1200 modern fishing vessels and more than 200 big ships in thirteen different categories to attain an annual catch of ten million tons by 1970.

Following the lead of the Soviet Union, the nations of Eastern Europe—Poland, East Germany, Bulgaria, and Roumania—are investing widely in catching vessels, freezing trawlers, factory ships, and transport units. The Soviet Union has placed large orders for ships in the West (in the United Kingdom, West Germany, France, Denmark, and Sweden) and in Japan, and several Soviet shipyards in the Baltic and Black seas are devoted exclusively to providing for the fishing fleets. Most of the new big fishing trawlers are of the stern type, introduced on a large scale by the Soviet Union in the early postwar days. A number of Western countries have in recent years followed this same line, but on a smaller scale. Stern trawlers are now part of the fishing fleets of the United Kingdom, West Germany, Norway, Greece, Italy, Yugoslavia, Spain, and France.

Japan has not only restored her catch to pre-World War II figures but is constantly expanding its activities, extending them to important fishing grounds in all oceans. Many trans-shipment ports and fishing bases, literally encircling the globe, are operated by Japanese fishing companies. Since 1963 Japan's total catches have stayed level at around 6.3 million tons owing to several circumstances: for one, economic adjustments at home, and overfishing, both in coastal waters and parts of the Atlantic, caused by lack of previous biological studies of sustainable yields.

The creation of major industrial centers for fish-meal manufacturing in Peru, Chile, and lately in Ecuador is unprecedented both in magnitude and scope in the history of world fisheries. This phenomenon is based on exploiting the riches of the Humboldt stream in the Pacific Ocean, chiefly by extracting a fish known as "anchoveta." Peru alone landed more than 9 million tons in 1964, which constituted almost a fifth of the world's marine catch. These big harvests are brought to hundreds of reduction installations on shore and processed into oil and meal, both of which are largely absorbed by the European and American food markets for the raising of hogs and chickens. In recent years, Japanese enterprises have also operated Peruvian fish-meal plants. A similar but smaller reduction industry is located in southwest Africa, based on the sardine catch of the Benguela current.

With the high seas being scanned by huge fleets, our generation is witnessing a massive exploitation of the world's fishing grounds of unprecedented dimensions. The equatorial waters of Africa are at present scanned by fishing vessels from a number of nations—Russia, Japan, Spain, Portugal, France, Poland, East Germany, United States, and Brazil—in search of tuna, "sardinella," sea bream, and other fish. Soviet scientists have studied these waters intensely since 1956;

they have charted the Bay of Biscay, waters off the Canaries and Azores, and certain areas close to the African coast from Casablanca and Agadir in the north down to the Ivory Coast and Ghana. Detailed hydrographic data have been collected and observations made as to temperature preference for various commercial fish as well as their migration routes through the seasonal year. Also, farther south, exploratory expeditions have studied the fishing possibilities closer to the Antarctic. On the whole, Soviet investigations have established that these eastern sections of the Middle and South Atlantic are profitable fishing areas for mackerel, sardine, and several other species.

In irritation over foreign fleets dipping into the rich resources off the North American coast, Americans frequently overlook the fact that we ourselves are involved in the same kind of venture in other corners of the globe. Our Pacific tuna fleet some time ago found the resources off the California coast inadequate, and each year wandered farther south along the coasts of Pacific South America down to Chile in search of fish. More than nine tenths of the tuna processed at California plants originates south of our border. This has been true for a number of years.

Still not satisfied with the tuna catch, and in order to keep up with American population growth (around 3 million a year since 1955), a switch was made to the Atlantic in the 1950's. A new base, with four sizable canneries, was erected in Puerto Rico. American tuna vessels are now to be seen all around the Caribbean and off many foreign coasts far from United States waters.

VESSELS AND EQUIPMENT

The typical hook-and-line clippers of an earlier period required a 120-day trip to land less than 250 tons of fish; these catches furthermore required cumbersome quantities of bait. Since about 1955, most clippers have been converted into purse seiners (boats using purse-shaped fishing nets), which can easily land up to 1000 tons of fish. Thus, there has been a considerable increase in catches per unit of fishing effort, with fewer vessels catching more fish in less time. The size and capability of Peruvian fishing vessels have risen in step with the rocketing catches of anchoveta for fish meal. Whereas a few years ago anchovy seiners were rarely over 40 feet in length, a fleet of powerful steel seiners twice that length has recently entered the Peruvian fishing scene.

Steel vessel construction is now quite prevalent, and shipyards have been converted accordingly. Glass fiber and aluminum are used advantageously for hulls. A 65-foot aluminum boat weighs about 54,000 pounds less than the 78,000 pounds of a corresponding one made of steel. This reduced weight provides more speed with the same power and permits the carrying of more cargo; and by leaving the aluminum hull unpainted, no maintenance is required. There are close to 100 aluminum gill netters fishing for salmon in Alaska. Off the East Coast and on the Gulf of Mexico, some 230 aluminum purse-seine boats fishing for menhaden service the mother ships. These boats weigh 10,000 pounds less than the steel boats they replaced, reducing the weight by some 60 per cent.

All decked vessels and many open boats now have an electric generator directly connected with the main engine, while most vessels above 30 gross-tons have an auxiliary engine and a generator as well. Most craft of 50 gross-tons or more, as well as many smaller ones, are now equipped with auto-pilot, radar, and fish-finding apparatus (horizontal and vertical), in addition to the usual navigational and communication systems. Powerblocks, hydraulic and other winches are now standard equipment, the first-mentioned being absolutely essential in all vessels operating with purse seines.

Small vessels, or purse seiners, as well as long-liners and other types of vessels, now avail themselves of the benefits of hydraulically powered equipment. Winches have been designed for hydraulic operation, and many can be maneuvered from the bridge; clear, unobstructed decks have become possible through the use of such devices. This gear makes fishing easier, safer, and more productive. Hydraulic power is an essential element in this opening era of "push-button" fishing.

Historically, mechanization has been the prerequisite for the evolvement of large-scale fishing in Japan, Scandinavia, Western Europe, and North America. Few coastal vessels carried motors in 1945, but motorization partly coupled with automation has taken place on an almost unbelievable scale in postwar fishing—at all levels. While making work easier for the fishermen, the main object of mechanization is to extract more fish from the sea. Mechanization has been most conspicuous in the coastal fisheries of China, Ceylon, and other Asian, as well as some African countries. However, in these latter cases there has been some trouble with maintenance, the provision of spare parts and fuel, and the organization of depots.

COUNTRY	NUMBER OF BOATS MECHANIZED
Ceylon	500 (1960)
Hong Kong	2,366 (1960)
India	2,500 (1960)
Japan	165,000 (1958)
Malaya	7,884 (1959)
New Guinea	50 (1960)
Pakistan	220 (1960)
Philippines	1,198 (1959)
South Vietnam	1,700 (1960)

With the construction of new types of boats and improved gear, young fishermen have to be trained in their operation and maintenance. Local fishermen are not used to marine diesel engines, nor to deck equipment for handling gear. Mechanization can only succeed if an adequate training unfolds simultaneously.

Thus a dozen training centers have now been established in the different states of India, training more than 450 fishermen a year.

GEAR

With the exception of deep-sea trawlers, most fishing vessels now fish with more than one type of gear. This inevitably involves greater outlay both in gear and initial construction, but it allows an extension of the annual operational period. Most of the bigger motor vessels operate during more than one fishing season, using long-line and gill nets in one season and purse-seine or, rarely, drifts nets in another. Smaller decked vessels also fish in more than one season and go for different catches. This marks quite a break with an earlier tradition.

The gear weight has constantly been creeping upward to allow for more extensive fishing area in depth and distance. Newly built 725-foot trawlers have heavy winches that carry 700 fathoms of steel cables.

Fishing techniques and gear differ from area to area, even for catching the same species of fish. This is partly due to the different types of vessels used by different nations and their varying traditions. The same differentiation applies to the mechanization and modernization of boats and gear.

The use of synthetic instead of natural fiber for nets has, as mentioned above, increased steadily. Presently the cod gill net and the purse seine are made exclusively from synthetic fibers, though natural ones are still used in long lines and various types of twines and ropes. This development has almost eliminated cumbersome net repair work as well as costly preservation treatments. In 1962, for example, 78,000 tons of synthetic nets and ropes were in use in Japan as compared to about 9000 tons of natural fiber material, figures which demonstrate the rapid modernization. It is noteworthy that while the conversion to synthetics was 90 per cent for netting, about 80 per cent of the ropes used were still of natural fibers; this is explained by the low cost of manilla hemp as compared to synthetic fibers.

Another innovation is knotless netting, which has many advantages, such as higher strength, lower weight, and less resistance to water currents; higher mesh constancy and more accurate mesh size are other assets. Knotless nets have lower production costs, better resistance to abrasion, and are easier to handle. Furthermore, they are less prone to damage the captured fish; there is less adherence of dirt to the net; and finally, they dry quicker. These advantages are claimed for knotless netting of every type.

NEW CATCHING METHODS

Man is constantly devising better methods to harvest the great diversity of marine life dispersed throughout the seas. This is done by designing efficient detection and straining systems and by developing artificial means to induce fish to aggregate so they can be easily caught.

Of all the aids to fishing adopted during the past few years, echo-sounding has been perhaps the greatest boon. A few years back, fishermen used to check their way about the sea with a simple lead line. This not only measured the depth, but the hollow end was devised to bring up samples of the sea bed. In this way the relief of the sea bottom was outlined on charts. Today, however, every deep-sea fishing craft carries one or several echo-sounders, instruments that work by sending sound waves down to the sea bed and picking up the return wave or echo. The depth of the water is computed on the basis of the recorded time that it takes the echo to return. Up to World War II most fishing was, by and large, a groping in the dark. The echo-sounder developed during the war was a godsend, almost like looking into the depths and fishing by sight. Our generation is too close to this revolutionary change to see it in true perspective.

The practice of fishing guided by echo prospecting has become general since about 1950, when a recording-type sounder came on the market. Its usefulness has so far been limited to fish that travel in schools, but these dominate the catches—as for example, herring, menhaden, pilchard—of Norway, Alaska, the Pacific coast, Scotland, South Africa, the Soviet Union, and Japan. By relying on echo-sounders, the schools of fish can be located before the catching devices are set. Production has increased many times through these electronic finders, and new catching procedures have been built around them. The Norwegian herring schools, for example, are followed by echo-sounders as they approach the coast before the winter fishing starts. Through this device the important discovery was made that the herring stay at 75 fathoms in the daytime.

Efforts are being made to adapt the echo-sounder for locating fish on the sea bed. A visual type of machine is necessary for this purpose; such instruments present the soundings as a line of light from which the echoes flash out sideways in proportion to their signal strength. The sea bottom then shows as a base at right angles to the line, and echoes slightly above it can be spotted more easily.

Another key invention is Asdic, used in World War II for hunting submarines. This instrument, employed to find herring in the wide northern seas, has a swinging beam which is more advantageous than the fixed downward beam of ordinary echo-sounders, especially when the herring shoals are small.

Determination of water-mass boundaries and surface temperature by infrared procedures is also being studied. Single-wavelength light beams facilitate visual fish detection down to depths of 100-200 meters or even deeper. Sonar equipment is being improved for detecting the direction and speed of fishes, and high-resolution equipment for short-range identification of targets by studying three-dimensional patterns of fish schools is being tested.

Recording spectrophotometers for tracking organic odors in the sea are also being studied. This method might help to identify fish schools, and it might lead to the use of artificial odors to force or guide fish along a given path. Introducing water-soluble chemicals into air-bubble curtains might enhance their effectiveness as fish barriers. Reproducing sounds of prey or predator might be employed to attract or herd fish; or electrical fields might be used in conjunction with light, sound, or chemical stimuli to aggregate and lead fish. Retrievable floats with built-in detection systems could automatically signal to catcher vessels the presence of fish. A network of unmanned buoys might in the future detect fish and transmit data through satellitic telemetering to a shore-based "hydro-central" for computer analysis and later transmission of the computerized-data summaries to fishing centers; this might even lead to remote-controlled, self-propelled trawls.

There may also be other ways of capturing fish more efficiently, as for example, large traps attached to the shore or floating in the sea, which might attract and catch fish over a wide range of space and time. It has been suggested that new types of pumps, operated economically, might well crawl along the bottom of the sea and collect fish much as a vacuum cleaner functions on the floor of a house. Some of these ideas are presently undergoing tests. Manned underwater stations for research and harvesting constitute a conceivable alternative.

A new method for concentrating fish is by air-bubble curtains. Herring react as if this were an impenetrable wall; they become entrapped and can be directed into nets. A suction hose can then be lowered into the nets and pump the fish on board. Soviet studies prove that fish can also be directed by *ultrasonic* waves into nets. Anchovy in tropical African waters are captured like this. Fish can also be stunned by electricity; they become immobilized, cannot escape, and can easily be taken. The method can also be applied to fish already caught. In this way fighting is reduced, thereby improving quality and appearance and, in particular, eliminating excessive slime formation.

Fishing by means of electric current was first investigated as far back as 1912 and was used commercially after World War I, but it was then applied only to fresh water. Stunning fish and then taking them on board by means of suction pumps is practised by Soviet vessels in saury fishing off Kamchatka and sardine fishing in the Bay of Guinea. This procedure may be compared to light-attraction fishing—a kind of bulk fishing. Lights installed on the ship and fixed to the mouthpiece of a hose attract the fish. The suction pumps are powered by electric motors connected to rubber hoses, 5 meters (16.4 feet) long, with the trumpet-shaped mouthpiece at one end. Soviet fishing boats successfully employ these methods in the Caspian. Such light attraction is also widely used by the Japanese and the Russians in their saury fishing, north of the Japanese islands.

PROCESSING AT SEA

Processing at sea was first practised by the 15th-century Basques and Portuguese fishing the Grand Banks off Newfoundland, who resorted to salting their catches on board. Herring from the North Sea had originally been brought to shore for salt treatment until it was found that the fishing trips could be extended by a preliminary salting on board. After these early endeavors it took almost 500 years before further significant advances were made.

The extended trips to the fishing grounds demanded a means of preserving the catch other than by salting. Even well-iced fish cannot be kept more than 15 days. American Pacific tuna clippers early in this century acquired freezing wells to preserve their catches and to allow hunting in distant waters. Freezing might be termed a kind of pre-processing or semi-preservation, later to be followed by final processing. In effect, quick freezing made the factory trawler feasible.

In the postwar period, the Soviet Union created a large fleet of several hundred such freezing trawlers. The United Kingdom, in comparison, has three. Almost all fishing grounds are within operational reach of these boats and can be exploited. The ships, costing $3 to $5 million, require a large catch to pay off and are, in effect, small versions of floating whale factories. Filleting, handling, and processing normally account for part of the operation. Wastes are reduced into meal and oil. The crew, besides officers and engineers, comprises catchers, filleters, splitters, and washing and freezing technicians, 50 to 100 men in all.

Another operational pattern is represented by the mother ships, which keep the catching and processing functions separate. In such a unit the output required for economic operation has to be matched to the number of catchers employed. The areas of ocean over which the fleet may be scattered at various seasons and places also has to be determined. The method of transfering the catches to the mother ship is important, too. Early versions of the mother ships were the floating canneries or barges servicing the Alaskan salmon industry. Supplemented by freezer ships, they still are part of pioneering ventures now pushing into the riches of the Arctic, on the Yukon, for example.

Canning on mother ships was introduced in the 1930's by the Japanese to service their North Pacific salmon fleet. Both the U.S.S.R. and Japan process their catches of king crab and shrimp in these same waters, with mother ships of 14,000 to 19,000 gross-tons. The old herring mother ships of the Atlantic are being refitted by the Soviet Union with high-speed, vacuum-canning lines as well as fish-meal plants.

Soviet fishing fleets around the globe operate from all-purpose mother ships now reaching 22,000 tons in size. Sailing with twelve trawlers, they can process 150 tons of tuna and sardine in 24 hours, and are able to cruise for 125 days.

Fuel for the entire fleet is carried in the mother ship, which is also a floating cannery, with quarters for 600 sailors and workers. Crew members are in comfortable cabins with bathrooms, and the vessel has a mechanized kitchen and bakery, a health center with a fully qualified staff, and a printing plant of its own. One Soviet ship, a 10,000-ton diesel-type freezer, the *Sevastopol*, freezes 100 metric tons of whale blubber or fish per day. Based at Odessa in the Black Sea, it serves in season the Antarctic whaling fleet, and during the remainder of the year, various fishing fleets in the North Pacific.

The Soviet Union has led in the use of processing trawlers and mother ships, and Soviet satellites in Eastern Europe are following suit in building up their processing potential. In the 1960's a number of Western countries began entering into the race, in several cases, chiefly the United States and Britain, on a sizable scale. The United Kingdom is also experimenting using outmoded aircraft carriers as processing mother ships at sea.

On the whole, the development of offshore processing facilities has almost eliminated the need for placing shore facilities for final processing close to any fishing grounds. This was particularly significant for the Soviet Union, whose ships were fishing so far distant, since any readily attainable port could be selected. Another interesting consequence of processing at sea is circumvention of the auction system of selling fish, which in most countries is detrimental to quality, besides hampering speedy delivery.

FUTURE PROSPECTS

As world population increases, more fish will be needed to meet the vastly growing demand for food. New technology will be introduced to make fishing operations more efficient. The following trends can be expected: the number of species of fish landed will increase; there will be a greater utilization of the small fish, and fewer will be discarded at sea; thus the stocks of fish will be subjected to more intense exploitation, not only offshore but also onshore. Expanded fishing by international fleets will reduce the abundance and sizes of exploited species. The more common use of otter trawls will tax available stocks more heavily, resulting in smaller-sized fish as well as bigger catches with a greater variety of species. On the average, the prevalence of larger fish can be expected to drop.

There will be expanded use of improved fishing gear, equipment, and vessels. More efficiently towed nets, mechanized gear, and fish holding at sea (refrigerated sea water and bulk freezing), improved fish-detection equipment, larger stern trawlers and offshore long-liner seiners, and new types of purse seiners can be expected.

There will also be greater application of the accumulated knowledge of bottom topography, hydrographic barriers, fish migrations (diurnal or seasonal, vertical or horizontal), and of schooling. New products, improved quality, wider markets, and more efficient handling and processing methods will be developed. Research programs are being pursued in most leading fishing countries on all these aspects of the problem.

Fishing pressure on all grounds will mount with increasing world demand, and catch rates are bound to decline. Hence co-operative conservation measures are needed in most fishing grounds. The grounds off South Africa and Pacific South America will probably show a sharp fall in catch if they attract substantial increases in present fishing effort. There are no longer any major unexploited trawling grounds. While world stocks must be expected to decline and finally to level off at a markedly lower catch, other fishing grounds could be improved by a real effort to cut the number of catchers. The operation of controls is a priority task for world fishing—a kind of global conservation is called for.

The almost feverish urge to exploit the food resources of the ocean leads to the all-embracing question: how far can these riches be tapped without endangering the sustainable stock at an economic level? Fishing is an occupation subject to greater vicissitudes than most others. The demand for fish and fish products fluctuates, although this situation has improved somewhat because of better processing and storing methods. But more important is the fact that catches and fish supplies vary considerably. Changes in the migratory habits and other behavior of the fish, depletion of fish stocks, and vagaries of weather and currents make fishing unpredictable. Modern mobile fleets reduce these risks.

The rapid growth of world fisheries has raised concern about the risks of overfishing and has engendered demands for conservation measures. Competition for resources and world markets is jeopardizing long-range planning. Overfishing is a serious matter in many heavily fished waters of the world, such as the coastal waters of Japan and the continental shelves around Europe. The North Sea in particular, being so close to densely populated countries with a long tradition of fishing, is liable to overexploitation as new methods make fishing much more efficient.

Overfishing is international in nature and demands agreements which are difficult to attain. Limited success has been reached in restricting the size of mesh, and to a degree this may protect young specimens and thus enlarge the stock. Among examples of agreements that managed to avert overfishing is the North American joint control of the Pacific halibut.

MARICULTURE (SEA FARMING)

Certain kinds of shellfish (oysters and clams) have been cultivated for centuries in a manner analogous to that of farms. Carp, milkfish, tilapias, and others are also raised this way. The harvesting of the fish resources of the sea is essentially still a hunting procedure, but we will eventually be forced into cultivating the oceans. We therefore need to learn much more, particularly if fishing is not going to run into the many snags and failures mankind has experienced in exploiting the soils, chiefly due to a lack of understanding of fundamental biological relationships.

Doubtless we will see the development of an oceanic fish husbandry, presumably starting with the closing off of bays and inland sea areas, or marshalling lagoons along the coasts, or through the farming of continental shelf areas fenced into appropriate producing lots under control. Lagoon fisheries are already important in Italy, the Philippines, China, and many other parts of the world.

Fifty years from now, man may perhaps be farming the bed of the sea with giant tractors cultivating the sea bed. Fish may further be grown in compounds protected by electric fences. Periodically these compounds would be swept clear of fish by tractors. We must do something to improve on nature if we expect to get substantially increased yields, introducing some kind of farm method in the sea if we are going to continue reaping this harvest. The level of production can be raised by means such as temperature control, fertilizing, pest removal, disease control, and so forth.

The most significant single development along these lines is the inculcation of conditioned reflexes into fish, accomplished by Japanese scientists for trout and by Soviet biologists for cod (in the Barents Sea). These fish have been conditioned from the fingerling stage to gather, on sonic impulses, for feeding at a chosen spot, even if spread in open waters.

We should not overlook the fact, however, that the chief limiting factor of the ocean as a source of food remains the availability of oxygen. Man is drastically reminded of this almost each year when the excessive runoff from strong monsoons upsets the basic ecology of the oceans, inducing water bloom (red tides) and similar phenomena followed by mass losses of water life.

The rapid spread of agricultural pesticides over the ocean expanses—evidenced by the accumulating data on such pesticidal residues in aquatic catches—and radioactive fallout, concentrating in various organisms, are danger signs. These latter do not yet appear to have reached hazardous concentrations, but they are gradually building up around rivers carrying effluents from nuclear reactors—even though atomic energy has not even passed its infancy.

Water pollution, which has jeopardized or even destroyed fresh-water fishing in many industrialized countries, is starting to show its deleterious effect in coastal areas, drastically changing the oxygen balance and affecting fish life. This is not only true in the Great Lakes area, the Caspian, and the Black Sea, but also in the Baltic and its outlet to the Atlantic. Coastal pollution is also endangering Japanese homeland fishing, as well as that of Britain, Holland, Belgium, and many other countries. Man's failure to cope with these realities does not augur well for successful mariculture in the future.

27 / Food for the Future
WAYNE D. RASMUSSEN

For ten thousand years, since man harvested his first crop and tamed his first animal, increases in food supply have little more than kept even with increases in population. Periods of war, pestilence, and famine have offset periods of peace and plenty. Ever since the gloomy forebodings of Thomas Malthus's *Essay on Population* (1798), neo-Malthusian economists have suggested that man's very nature will lead to a constant population pressure upon the food supply. Man now faces one of his greatest challenges—to increase the supply of food at a rate sufficient to erase present deficits and to match the drastic increase in world population.

POPULATION PRESSURE

Throughout most of man's existence the number of births in any one year has not significantly exceeded the number of deaths. But over the last few centuries, and particularly over the last few decades, man has drastically altered this balance between births and deaths; the old equilibrium has been destroyed and a new one has not yet been established. The availability of food will be one factor in the establishment of the new equilibrium.

At the beginning of the Christian era, world population was about 250 million. This number slowly expanded, and had doubled by 1600. During these 16 centuries, population increased by about 3.5 per cent each *century*. By 1900, the annual rate of increase was nearly 1 per cent per year, and the world population stood at 1.5 billion. By 1960, the rate of increase was 3 per cent a *year*, and the population was 3 billion. In the mid-1960's, a world population of 3.6 billion was projected for 1970, and of over 6 billion for the year 2000.

The problem of matching food production to population growth does not occur in the developed or industrial nations of Europe, North America, and Oceania; the food deficits are in the less developed nations of Asia, Africa, and Latin America. A study published by the United States Department of Agriculture in 1963 showed that people in some 50 less developed countries did not have a balanced diet. There the population had outraced food production, and the number of people suffering from malnutrition had actually gone up since the early 1900's.

Most of the people who will be added to the world population in the last decades of the 20th century will swell the populations of the underdeveloped nations more than of the industrialized nations. In terms of rates of growth, Latin America has had a consistently higher rate during the 20th century than any other geographic area. By the year 2000, its population may be over 600 million, compared with 200 million in 1960. Asia is expected to reach 3.9 billion, compared with 1.6 billion in 1960. This poses a critical problem, for Asia is already densely populated, with a serious imbalance between population and conventional food-producing capability. Africa's population is also expected to increase, from 235 million in 1960 to 517 million in 2000.

Despite the persistent pressure of the rapidly growing population upon the world food supply, only a few nations have witnessed a limitation of population. While mortality rates have been reduced greatly, little has been done in most nations to encourage a reduction in birth rates, which have remained relatively constant. An exception is Japan, where a program of education and assistance in family planning was initiated in the late 1940's, with both government and private groups co-operating. By the end of a decade, the population increase had dropped below 1 per cent per year.

It is now medically and technically possible to undertake extensive programs to reduce the rate of population increase. Nevertheless, in many areas and particularly in areas where food deficiencies are greatest, no immediate reduction in the rate of population increase is foreseen. Hence, the pressure of population upon food resources seems likely to continue and intensify.

Technological advances in increasing the production of food through traditional means and from traditional sources have been discussed in earlier chapters. An important question facing the world today is whether these technological advances, intensified and adopted more widely, can meet the food needs of the human race in the year 2000. Some technological alternatives to or basic modifications of traditional means of food production and traditional sources of food have been proposed and are in an experimental stage. This chapter is concerned with such alternatives.

IRRIGATION

All life depends upon water. Man soon learned at the very beginning of history that not only his own existence, but that of his crops, required water, whether it was from rainfall or another source. Early in the history of civilization—5000 years ago in Egypt and 2500 years in China—man built dams to divert and conserve water for irrigation. Today, expanding irrigation is an absolute necessity to extend crop acreage; it may be the most productive of possible improvements on present crop land. Sufficient water at the proper time makes possible the full use of technology in farming—including the proper application of fertilizers, suitable crop rotations, and the use of more productive varieties of crops.

About 400 million acres were being irrigated throughout the world in the mid-1960's, amounting to 14 per cent of the arable land. There are two major ways in which this acreage might be increased. First, there is the possibility of making wider use of irrigation in districts that already have a high rate of output. Second, there is the possibility of irrigating non-productive land, especially in the arid zone. The greatest economic returns might well come from irrigating productive districts, but irrigation of the arid zone has a wider appeal to the imagination. Most of the arid zone, occupying more than one third of the land mass of the globe, is in the tropics. Generally, it is rich in solar energy and its soils are rich in nutrients, but water is lacking.

The United States offers an example of the increasing use of supplemental irrigation in humid regions and limited expansion of irrigation in arid regions. Supplemental irrigation, used primarily to make up for poor distribution of rainfall during the growing season, has increased very substantially since 1939. It safeguards against droughts, increases yields, permits production of products of higher quality, provides earlier maturity of crops, and maintains the grazing capacities of pasture.

Supplemental irrigation is carried on in the humid areas of the United States almost exclusively with sprinkler systems. The water is conveyed in pipes, usually laid on the surface of the field, and the soil acts as a storage reservoir. The water itself is pumped from a stream, lake, well, or reservoir. American farmers first used sprinkler irrigation about 1900, but the development of lightweight aluminum pipe with quick couplers brought a notable increase in the use of sprinklers after 1945. This technological change cut labor costs and demonstrated that sprinkler irrigation could be adapted to most sites and crops in the United States.

Minor improvements have been made in surface-irrigation methods, but none offers any notable advances over methods used thousands of years ago. Some attention has also been given to subirrigation, that is, the application of water beneath the ground surface rather than on it, usually by creating and maintaining an artificial water table at some predetermined depth; however, this method is not widely used. Surface irrigation is the type most often used to bring arid lands into cultivation in the United States, although sprinklers, mostly confined to humid regions, are used in several areas where wells are the source of water. In 1959, the total area of irrigated land in 17 western states was about 26.4 million acres. New facilities were being undertaken only slowly, and irrigation in some areas was being discontinued because of a lack of water or because the activity was uneconomic. The irrigation of arid lands is now expanding more rapidly in other parts of the world than in the United States.

Fig. 27-1. Water from the Snoqualmie River in Washington flows via this irrigation ditch to orchards in the Naches Valley. (From U. S. Department of Agriculture *Yearbook*, 1962)

In less than five years, from 1961 to 1965, about 55,000 acres of arid, low-altitude land was brought under irrigation in Rhodesia. The land had been covered with brush and scattered baobab trees, and its potential was great since much of it was fertile, daytime temperatures were high, and there was almost a complete absence of frost. Yet because rainfall was seasonal and unreliable, the land was used primarily for grazing African cattle.

Some irrigation was undertaken in the area during the 1930's, mainly for sugarcane, corn, beans, peas, and bananas, but more complete development waited until a railway had reached the area. The Rhodesian government assumed responsibility for building dams, and private investors undertook agricultural development, including the building of sugar mills. By 1965, Rhodesia was exporting rather than importing sugar, and substantial quantities of cotton, vegetables, seeds, tobacco, bananas, sorghum, and other crops were being produced. By 1990, the Rhodesian government proposes to irrigate a million more acres. This would be a notable achievement for a nation of about the size of New York State.

SOILLESS FARMING

Besides water, increasing production through irrigation requires land, a resource which is ultimately limited. Since the mineral requirements for plant growth have become known, the possibility of growing plants in tanks, with needed nutrients dissolved in the water in the tanks, has been proposed and studied. This idea of farming without soil has popular appeal as a possible answer to the future world food problem.

The term "hydroponics," invented by W. F. Gericke, who was connected with the University of California, is properly applied only to the growing of plants in water. Drawing upon past scientific work on nutrient solutions, Gericke presented his theory of water culture in 1929 and popularized the idea in 1940 with publication of *The Complete Guide to Soilless Gardening*. He pointed out that his theories were then being carried out by growers in California, New York, Illinois, Florida, and on Wake Island in the Pacific.

Gericke's plan included a tank filled with water, to which the required minerals had been added. The tank was covered with wire netting, on which was a porous mat of vegetable litter. This mat served as a seedbed, gave support to the growing plants, and protected roots from sunlight and changes of temperature. Plant roots require oxygen which was supplied by leaving an air space between the matting and the water level or by forced aeration of the nutrient solution.

The feasibility of growing plants in sand, to which nutrient solutions were added, was demonstrated about the same time that Gericke proposed his plan by H. M. Biekart and C. H. Connors of the New Jersey Experiment Station. The method was used in many greenhouses for growing carnations and roses. However, it had disadvantages: a large amount of the valuable chemical salts were lost when excess solution and accumulated chemicals were removed from the sand. Another problem was that the sand had to be virtually free of limestone, a requirement difficult to meet in some areas; otherwise, it was necessary to add an excessive amount of acid to the solution to bring it into the proper range of acidity for growing many crops.

The idea of filling the tanks with gravel or cinders and using a method of subirrigation of the plants was tested by R. B. Farnham of the New Jersey Experiment Station and independently by Robert Withrow of Purdue University. Such a system provided better support for the plants and avoided loss of both mineral nutrients and water. The solution readily drained off from the gravel or cinders and could be retained for future use. Aeration (insuring sufficient oxygen) was no problem since the plants were not constantly standing in the solution.

A hydroponic installation on Wake Island attracted attention before World

Fig. 27-2. U. S. Army hydroponic garden, Ascension Island. (Courtesy of *United States Department of Agriculture*)

War II. After the war, installations of various kinds were established in the Dutch West Indies, on Aruba and Curaçao; in British Guiana; on Ascension Island; and on Iwo Jima. These were mostly of the gravel type, but some work was done in South Africa using vermiculite instead of gravel. However, an expert wrote of soilless culture in 1964: "Under carefully controlled research conditions, yields have been high, but nearly all commercial ventures have failed." Thus, in spite of its popular and theoretical appeal, the future usefulness of hydroponics and other soilless methods of plant production in meeting the food needs of the world remains in doubt.

FRESH WATER

While soil may be replaced by a mat, sand, or gravel, all systems of farming (like most industries) depend upon an adequate supply of fresh water. The primary limitation upon irrigation in the recent past and present is a lack of such fresh water. Indeed, in many parts of the world, water shortage is the principal factor limiting agricultural development.

Various methods of relieving water deficiencies have been tested in areas where the potential supply of fresh water from conventional sources has been inadequate for the demand. Over the years, storage reservoirs, aqueducts, and canals have provided a more constant supply of water and have permitted its utilization at long distances from its source.

The use of ground water by pumping from wells or in other ways, at a rate at which replacement or recharging can take place, conserves water to some extent by encouraging less wasteful runoff. In this case, the surface water seeping down tends to restore the underground water level. On the other hand, in several places in the world, excessive pumping of usable ground water has resulted in salty or otherwise unusable water flowing into the ground-water reservoir.

The reclamation of waste water and, even more important, the prevention of water pollution, could make more water available for agriculture and other purposes. Efforts are being made in the United States to encourage industrial firms to treat their waste water, in order to reduce pollution and even to permit its reclamation and reuse.

The treatment of sewage in such a manner that its liquid content becomes nonoffensive and can flow in a stream without polluting it is becoming essential in densely populated areas away from the oceans. In some places, treated sewage water is used for agricultural irrigation. In newly developing countries, the possibility of utilizing sewage water after appropriate treatment as a source of water supply for farm or industrial purposes seems to be more limited than in industrial countries. The large quantities of such water available in the industrial countries are not found in developing countries, particularly in the water-short areas just undergoing economic development.

The most probable way in which fresh-water supplies will be increased in the future is by water desalination—that is, by removing dissolved inorganic salts from sea and brackish water. Covering about three fourths of the earth's surface, the oceans contain most of the world's water. Their water is part of nature's cycle of evaporation, rainfall, and return to the ocean through the streams. This unlimited supply of water, salty though it is, serves many of man's needs. It is a highway linking the continents, a storehouse of food, and the source of useful salts and minerals. Although some of its waters are used by man in their salty state, man's primary need is fresh water. The long-held dream of converting salt water to fresh in any needed amount is now a technological possibility. The problem now is basically economic, not technological.

Sand, sediment, and other foreign particles can be removed from water simply by filtration, but salt cannot be removed so easily. Saline water, although not chemically complex, is comparatively stable. Because of this stability the separation of saline solutions requires relatively large quantities of energy. Theoretical calculations of the cost of energy necessary to separate pure water from an infinitely large body of salt water indicate that such separation would be economically feasible only in very special and limited situations. Nevertheless, research and experimentation are continuing, with the United Nations giving particular attention both to improving the processes for separation and to obtaining large quantities of controlled energy at lower costs.

The problem of controlling large quantities of low-cost energy for desalination is not basically agricultural, of course. Nevertheless, it is obvious that man will, sooner or later, control one or more of such vast potential sources of energy as sunlight, the thermal difference between surface water and subsurface water in the oceans, wind power, and geothermal energy.

Almost since the first atomic bomb was exploded over Hiroshima, the application of nuclear power to water desalination has been proposed and studied. By 1955 the direct use of nuclear fission for the separation of salt from water did not seem probable, although it was possible to use heat from reactor plants in various desalting processes. During the next ten years, several ideas along those lines were tested. By 1965, particular attention was being given to the use of electricity produced in nuclear power plants as energy for desalination and, alternatively, of producing steam in a nuclear reactor and using such steam for desalination. However, the cost of power generation in nuclear plants is still higher than in conventional plants of equal size. The greatest opportunity seems to lie in very large, dual-purpose plants in areas where there is a high demand for both power and fresh water.

The United Nations in 1962 surveyed 74 developing countries and territories where fresh-water shortages existed. Information on 61 desalination plants showed that the great majority began production after 1950; however, a plant at Safaga in the United Arab Republic had been in operation since 1920, and others in Ancon, Ecuador, and Curaçao since 1930. The majority of the desalination plants surveyed by the United Nations, as well as most of those in developed nations, employed one of three distillation processes. All were based on the principle that when salt water is heated to the evaporation point, the resulting vapor is relatively salt-free. This water vapor can then be condensed and drawn off for use as "fresh" water.

Multiple-effect evaporation, also called the submerged-tube process, is the method most commonly used on board ship for refining sea water and is also the major method used for large, permanent, shore installations. Steam is generated in a fuel-fired boiler or evaporator. The vapor produced in this first-effect evaporator is condensed in the heating carts of an adjacent or second-effect evaporator, operating at a slightly lower pressure, thus furnishing heat for evaporating more sea water. By employing several such evaporators in series, the amount of heat that is ultimately wasted as cooling water in the last condenser is decreased as the number of effects is increased. A twelve-evaporation unit distillation plant began operation at Freeport, Texas, in June 1961.

A second process employs flash evaporation. Water at a particular pressure

Fig. 27-3. A long-tube vertical distillation plant at Freeport, Texas, which produces one million gallons of fresh water from sea water daily. Steam is admitted into the first evaporator, or effect, filling the space around the tube bundle and causing part of the sea water to boil as it goes through the tubes. A mixture of vapor and hot brine emerges at the bottom. The hot brine is pumped to the top of the second evaporator where, under slightly reduced pressure, it again falls through the tubes. Vapor produced in the first effect flows to the outside of the tube bundle in the second effect where it is condensed to fresh water by giving up its latent heat to the sea water falling through the tubes. This again causes part of the water in the tubes to boil. The same process is repeated through all 12 effects in the plant.

and temperature is released into a chamber of slightly lower pressure. The liquid flashes into vapor, and is then condensed. This process in modern, efficient plants uses less space than the multiple-effect evaporator, requires less fuel, and permits better regulation of output to meet demand. Large flash-distillation plants were opened in Kuwait in 1960. The possibility of large-scale desalination by this process in an emergency received public attention in the United States in 1964 when a multi-stage flash demonstration plant built and operated in San Diego by the Office of Saline Water of the United States Department of the Interior was moved to Guantanamo, Cuba, to meet the needs of the Navy.

Vapor-compression distillation is the third method of evaporation, and is the oldest still in use, having been originally patented by Pierre Pillitan of France in 1840. Saline water is evaporated by an outside steam source in a closed vessel. The vapor is then compressed, which raises its temperature. The high-temperature vapor is used to evaporate additional water vapor from the saline water source. The major portion of energy required is consumed in driving the compressor, with relatively little additional energy needed to generate steam in the evaporator after the process is begun. Portable units of this type have been used by military forces, and a large plant is operating in Roswell, New Mexico.

Although most desalination plants in operation in 1965 employed one of the distillation processes, several other methods were under study and development. The electrodialysis process, for example, was being developed on a commercial basis at several sites. The first commercial unit was built and installed in Libya in 1957, and a large unit was built in South Africa a few years later. Here the principle of operation is an electric current separating the salt into positive and negative ions; an electric force then passes these ions through special membranes, leaving fresh water behind. This method has proved most practical for demineralizing brackish water. The major limiting factor has been the life, cost, and efficiency of the membranes.

Fig. 27-4. This flash-distillation plant, at Guantanamo Bay, Cuba, produces 2.2 million gallons a day of fresh water for the U. S. Naval base. (Courtesy of *Westinghouse Electric Corporation*)

Membranes are also used in the reverse-osmosis process, first demonstrated at the University of Florida in 1953. Cellulose acetate membranes, for some unknown reason, reject salt but transmit water; sea water can be converted to potable water in a single pass through the membrane. Two thirds of the cost of water produced by reverse osmosis lies in the cost of membranes and their replacement.

Freezing techniques and solvent fresh-water extraction, like the reverse-osmosis process, were in various stages of experimentation in 1965. Purification of salt water by freezing is a well-known natural process. When freezing occurs, the salt separates from the water as it forms into crystals. The salt brine concentrate remains adjacent to the fresh water ice crystals and must be flushed away. However, the brine solution is so closely held between the ice crystals that the washing process is both difficult and expensive. Several methods of freezing and washing have been tested to simplify this process and make it less expensive.

The possibility exists that an economic program for using a solvent to separate fresh water from salt may also be developed. In theory, the process is simple. A solvent with the quality of absorbing a large amount of fresh water is mixed with saline water. The solvent and the fresh water contained in it are then separated from the residual brine. The solvent and water are finally separated by a temperature change which reduces the absorbent capacity of the solvent. The major problem is to find an efficient, low-cost, non-toxic solvent.

Another method, the ion-exchange process, has been found useful, if expensive, for small-scale desalination. This process usually incorporates resins, which substitute one kind of ion for another in the water. The resins can then be regenerated for reuse. This type of process is now most widely used in the United States for water softening.

Some of the methods discussed have been used for converting brackish to fresh water. Another approach to this problem has been to develop crops which can utilize brackish water directly. Although some crops grow reasonably well under these conditions, there are other difficulties in using brackish water for irrigation. A major one is that brackish water will often leave salt or other minerals in and on the soil. Eventually, it becomes impossible to use the soil for any crops.

There seems to be little doubt that large-scale, economic desalting of sea water will be a reality by 1980 and perhaps even by 1970. The United States, operating through the Department of the Interior with aid from the Atomic Energy Commission, launched a major research program to this end in the mid-1960's. The United Nations has also made desalination of salt water a major goal.

FOOD FROM THE SEA

There have been suggestions, however, that desalting sea water is not necessary for food production. The oceans themselves, filled with marine life, might supply all foreseeable food needs without intermediate processes such as water desalting and irrigation. It is evident that, as discussed in the preceding chapter, fisheries will continue to supply the world's increasing population with important quantities of food. Can man, however, draw even more directly upon the ponds, lakes, rivers, and oceans and utilize plankton as a primary source of food?

Plankton is the name given to marine life which drifts with the water currents. In contrast, nekton can swim against the currents and benthos are found attached to and crawling on the ocean floor. Planktonic life is important because all animal life in the sea is ultimately dependent upon it for existence. Most plankton is made up of microscopic plants and animals. Technically, the definition of plankton includes the largest jellyfish and the floating Sargassum weed, although the larger plants and animals are usually not considered in general discussions of plankton.

The classification and study of smaller plankton began in 1845, when Johannes Mueller, a German scientist, towed a small net of fine-meshed cloth behind a boat and collected samples. The *Challenger* expedition of 1872-76, under the leadership of an Englishman, Sir John Murray, added much to our knowledge. In 1889, Victor Henson, who first used the term "plankton," made a more detailed survey of the Atlantic; yet despite a great deal of research since then, there is still much to be learned about plankton.

The phytoplankton, which is plant life, carries on photosynthesis, using water, dissolved carbon-dioxide gas, and mineral salts to manufacture the food necessary for maintenance, growth, and reproduction. The zooplankton, animal life, feeds on the phytoplankton; and the zooplankton is important in the diet of small fish which serve as food for larger fish. Waste products of digestion and dead organisms of all kinds are converted by bacteria into simple chemical compounds that are again available for use by the phytoplankton. In addition to this traditional view of the oceanic organic life cycle, scientists in the 1960's called attention to the vast amount of organic chemicals dissolved in sea water. It was suggested that air bubbles in sea water brought some of these molecules together in a form which could be used by the zooplankton as food.

The oceans produce 150,000 million tons of phytoplankton each year, while man harvests only 30 million tons of fish. Plankton, both plant and animal, is available in seemingly unlimited quantities. It has been proposed that man catch plankton commercially, either for human food or animal feed. Plankton has a high protein and fat value and contains some of the vitamins, especially

Vitamin C. It can serve in a limited way to eke out a living for shipwrecked sailors. However, there are problems. First, plankton is not safe to eat in quantity because some of it has a nauseating flavor, while excessive quantities of its fats and vitamins could be fatal. Second, and most important, catching plankton on a large scale for food or feed is not yet commercially feasible.

Although plankton is plentiful, its total volume is small compared with the water in which it lives; the problem of separating it, in the case of marine plankton, from the sea water and salt is formidable. Plankton can be caught in nets. The larger the mesh of the net, the greater the loss of the smaller organisms through the net. The smaller the mesh, the more slowly will the water filter through and the more easily will the meshes become choked. A centrifuge can also be used: a short or slow spin recovers only the larger plankton, while a longer or faster spin is necessary to recover the smaller. Whether a net or a centrifuge is used, large quantities of water must be handled, and therefore large quantities of power must be available.

An expert on marine plankton, James Fraser, has suggested a ship with an "open mouth" below the water's surface as an efficient means of catching plankton. The ship's open mouth would lead to revolving, fine-meshed drums of metal netting, which constantly pass the plankton to the ends from which it can be extracted in concentrated form by pumps. It would be further concentrated to remove all the surplus sea water and then dried.

Such a ship is feasible from a technological viewpoint, but compared with costs of catching fish, it is uneconomical. Its original cost, its comparatively delicate parts, and its fuel requirements all compare unfavorably with the cost per protein unit of the catch of a conventional fishing trawler.

Finally, plankton is more difficult to preserve than fish. In the tropics, it becomes rancid or putrid within an hour or so. Even in colder regions, it cannot be stored with ice for any length of time. It must be deep frozen or, better, dried on the spot. In either case, the apparatus, power, and personnel to operate such facilities would add greatly to the cost. Clearly, while it is technologically possible to catch and preserve plankton for use as human food and animal feed, the economic costs make any such use by the 1970's or even later most unlikely.

PETROLEUM SOURCES

An entirely new source of proteins for food was proposed in 1964 by Alfred Champagnat, research director of the Société Française des Pétroles. It had been known for some years that a variety of microorganisms could live and actively reproduce on petroleum hydrocarbons. In 1957 a microbiological research unit was established by the company to evaluate the feasibility of using microorganisms to manufacture proteins from crude petroleum.

Champagnat's research group believes the petroleum-based microorganisms to be rich in proteins that contain all of the amino acids necessary to sustain animal life, and to contain them in about the same proportions found in proteins obtained from animal sources. The microorganisms are living beings which have adapted themselves to extract their carbon from hydrocarbons rather than from sugars or carbohydrates; as such they are capable of consuming certain paraffinic hydrocarbons found in petroleum. It might be possible to use the microorganisms to deparaffin petroleum as a step in the refining process, and to obtain an economic by-product in the protein. For the proteins resulting from petroleum fermentation, according to Champagnat, would be as normal as any vegetable and animal proteins.

When dried, the cells of the microorganisms burst open, thus becoming digestible. The dried and purified microorganisms appear as a powder or whitish flakes, without noticeable taste or smell. They can be stored for extended periods, generally in the same way as flour. Their greatest usefulness would likely be through mixing with cereals, since the particular amino acid deficiencies of the microorganisms would be made up by those found in most cereals. Champagnat suggests that, with full-scale effort, 20 million tons of petroleum-based protein could be produced each year, or about one half of the world's protein requirement in 1980.

The possible production of petroleum-based protein is limited by the availability of petroleum, particularly over a period of centuries. However, there is reason to believe that science and technology can point the way to the production and utilization of other unused sources of protein and vital nutrients, even though eventually we may be forced to turn away from some of our traditional habits and prejudices with respect to food.

THE PROBLEM

The population explosion so evident in the 1960's is cause for alarm, not for despair. Even within traditional bounds, advances in agricultural technology, including conservation and more effective use of water supplies, desalting sea and brackish water, widespread irrigation with desalted water, and more efficient fisheries, will probably supply the food needs of the world in 1980 and 2000 without widespread famine. In fact, famine in the latter part of the 20th century has become much rarer than it was a century earlier in spite of greater population pressure.

There is some reason to believe that a new population equilibrium will have been established before the year 2000. If it has not, then mankind may be forced to turn to plankton, algae, petroleum-based proteins, and other presently unconventional sources for its food, several of which are now technologically, though not yet economically, accessible.

Part **VIII**
Land Use and Resources

28 / The Resource Revolution
J. L. PENICK, JR.

In May 1908, President Theodore Roosevelt held an unprecedented Conference of Governors at the White House, to consider the problem of America's natural resources and their conservation. Reporting to his fellow engineers on the importance and results of the meeting, Charles S. Howe, president of the Case School of Applied Science (now Case Western Reserve University) and a conference delegate representing the Society for the Promotion of Engineering Education, cut to the heart of the matter. "This work of conservation," he wrote, "is the work of the engineer." Furthermore, he expressed his conviction that "the engineers of the country are capable of solving these problems, and that if they are given the necessary governmental and private aid the problem of conservation of our natural resources will be solved."

The belief that scientists and engineers—experts, to use the broader term—could alone solve the problems of resource management now appears less firmly based than it once did. Nevertheless, the involvement of such people in the Conservation Movement gave it its urgency and staying power, and the broader hopes of technical men like Howe have not yet been abandoned. In 1963 the Federal Council for Science and Technology (in a report on *Research and Development on Natural Resources*) wrote: "In the past the pendulum of public concern was swung from one of regarding America's resources as virtually inexhaustible to one of alarm that America was rapidly becoming a 'have-not' nation. But, in the last decade or so, a new course became apparent to many scientists and detached observers: knowledge and ingenuity were, in a sense, producing resources where none had existed before." It was not a concept that would have been totally foreign to Howe and those scientists and engineers who, working quietly in government bureaus at the beginning of the present century, founded the Conservation Movement.

431

ROLE OF THE FEDERAL GOVERNMENT

In the 19th century the federal government was rudimentary and primitive by modern standards, supporting itself on customs duties or through the sale of the public lands, in any case, without unduly taxing the citizen, and in general, remaining properly limited, as the prevailing laissez-faire doctrine of the day required. On one function every American could agree, however; the government was supposed to provide for the orderly settlement of the western territories. Most dramatically this involved cavalry to pacify the Indian and federal marshals to impose law and order, but more prosaically it meant periodic interest in scientific and technical concerns with which government, viewed in this narrow light, would otherwise scarcely have bothered.

It was natural that a nation possessing a vast hinterland should be concerned with internal expansion and development, and equally natural that the responsibility for exploring, surveying, and disposing of the public lands should have given the federal government a broad stake in the use of the nation's material resources. In the first decade of the 20th century this stake was translated into a great scientific and technical program, the Conservation Movement, the first such program of a government which has, as the century wears on, acquired broader responsibilities and harnessed much of American science and technology to national ends.

THE "ARID WEST"

In the decades after the Civil War the nation was riveted—East and West Coast —by transcontinental railroads, and a vast stretch of plains and mountains, once considered a desert unsuited for agricultural enterprise, was opened for settlement. The entire region, extending westward from a line roughly along the hundredth meridian to the fertile river valleys of the Pacific Coast, was different in character than earlier frontiers. The eastern half of the continent had a unity impossible to maintain in the western half. The "Arid West" was characteristically heterogeneous from an economic point of view, with one area valuable exclusively for mining, another for timber, another for arable farmland, and another, good for no purpose at all. The only unifying characteristic seemed to be aridity; but it sharply limited settlement, despite the prevailing agrarian ideology which called for the continued extension of agriculture regardless of nature's prohibitions. By the end of the 19th century, largely because of the western water problem, the federal government was committed to shaping policy for resource development.

At the forefront of this effort the United States Geological Survey operated on the assumption that old methods of settlement were inadequate to cope with the arid West, and attempted to translate that assumption into policy. It interpreted its mandate broadly. John Wesley Powell (1834-1902), its director, gathered together a wide range of talents from many technical disciplines: hydrology, geology, agrostology, and even ethnology. The Survey trained a generation of scientists to think of resource development as a whole with many related parts. Many of these men would occupy positions of leadership in the Conservation Movement headed by President Theodore Roosevelt (1858-1919). Equally important, the work of the agency cut across the interests of many groups, dramatically illustrating the character of the pluralism in which federal policy was rooted, and the extent to which one agency could embrace the elements of that diversity.

Powell's great contribution to resource policy was his insight into the dynamics of western economic and technical development. In his famous *Report on the Lands of the Arid Region,* submitted in 1878 to the Secretary of the Interior, he drew a picture of the West which few Americans were prepared to accept at the time, as a region in which only a small portion of land could ever be cultivated—and that only by irrigation at great expense—and in which the chief value of millions of acres was for grazing. He recommended that the lands of the West be classified according to the best use they could serve, and disposed of according to that classification. Powell warned that the arid West could not be developed without the tools of the Industrial Revolution and corporate finance: "To a great extent the redemption of all these lands will require extensive and comprehensive plans, for the execution of which aggregated capital or cooperative labor will be necessary. Here, individual farmers, being poor men, cannot undertake the task. For its accomplishment a wise prevision, embodied in carefully considered legislation, is necessary."

For a brief period beginning in 1888 Powell attempted to translate his recommendations into policy. He acquired congressional authorization for an investigation into the water resources of the West, which also empowered the Secretary of the Interior to reserve irrigable land from entry while the investigation was in progress. Seizing this as an opportunity to institute classification, Powell set aside virtually all of the arid region; however, the howl of surprised anger at having so much land suddenly removed from speculation and economic use forced Congress to reverse itself in 1889. All the reserved lands, except reservoir sites already identified, were restored to entry; meanwhile, Powell retired from public view.

A significant attempt at broad-gauged scientific planning had been thwarted, but the hydrographic investigations of 1888 proved to be the seedtime of the Conservation Movement. Scientists in the Geological Survey measured water supplies, studied ground-water movement and sedimentation, located reservoirs, and mapped areas that could be irrigated. Out of this effort grew the notion that water was a single resource with many potential uses, a notion that would later flower into the significant concept of multiple use (as in irrigation and power). Congress had rejected the theory that the West should be developed by federal planning, but as a result of the Powell episode, information had been collected which federal officials could use to plan a reclamation program.

FEDERAL RECLAMATION

In a region so vast, in which the scarcity of water dominates all considerations, the possibilities of irrigation had long been of great interest. By the close of the 19th century this included the possibility of direct federal construction.

The first settlers to practice large-scale irrigation successfully were the Mormons, who had developed the available water supplies of the valley of the Great Salt Lake through an ingenious system of canals and ditches. Their success dangled enticingly before the settlers and promoters of the arid West, and yet that success defined the limits of future development. The communal and co-operative organization of Mormon society anticipated Powell's insistence upon the necessity for "aggregated capital" and "co-operative labor."

In subsequent decades, as the arid region was opened to settlement, the efforts of individuals and private corporations accounted for most of the land brought under irrigation. By 1900, a total of only 7,527,690 acres of reclaimed land was under cultivation, most of it reclaimed by the simple process of diverting streams into nearby fields. The problem was not the unwillingness of private promoters, but rather their inability to develop any but the simplest of projects. They avoided the difficult sites requiring storage dams and expensive engineering works, and once the obvious sites were developed the possibilities for further irrigation declined rapidly.

In 1900 there were still over 500 million acres open to settlement under the general land laws, and promoters, speculators, and the ordinary settler would not accept the strictures of men like Powell that only a tiny portion could ever be arable. Using the National Irrigation Congress as their spokesman, and financed by the largest landowners in the arid region, the railroads, they pressed for direct federal construction of irrigation works. Reclamation, particularly irrigation, was urged as the panacea to lay forever to rest the idea that much of the region was unsuited for agricultural settlement; and optimistic estimates that as much as 100 million acres could be brought under cultivation by irrigation were by no means rare.

The movement for federal irrigation works, which culminated in the Newlands Reclamation Act of 1902, was a combination of adjustments between modern technical requirements and the agrarian assumptions of American development. The irrigation movement had support in government and out, from Powell-trained hydrographers like Frederick H. Newell (1862-1932) of the Geological Survey, to promoters and publicists like George Maxwell, a California water-law expert who hoped to cure social problems by bringing city-dwellers back to the farm. One and all they paid homage to the images of agrarian America: "The nomadic herdsman, the restless miner and the wandering laborer add little to the strength or safety of the community," Newell said, explaining the importance of reclamation, "but let one of these men become attached to the soil; let him own a small farm which is sufficiently productive to furnish his family with needed subsistence and comforts, and he becomes a citizen who can be depended upon."

The movement came to fruition during the 1890's, a time of great crisis in rural America. The People's Party and the Populist Movement were only symptoms of a more deep-seated disturbance; the nation was changing rapidly from a small-town, rural, decentralized, and non-technical civilization to a predominantly urban, national society, rooted in rapid technical change. Support for federal reclamation was an outlet for concern over this change.

Attitudes combining veneration for old ideals with deep faith in the unlimited horizons of science and technology were most dramatically expressed by Theodore Roosevelt, President throughout most of the first decade of the century. Deeply concerned with social and economic divisions in American life, no advocate of turning back the clock, and an exponent of greater organization and efficiency in economic affairs, Roosevelt was also an enthusiastic supporter of federal reclamation, which he hoped would buttress a declining rural life. "I warn my countrymen," he said, "that the great recent progress made in city life is not a full measure of our civilization; for our civilization rests at bottom on the wholesomeness, the attractiveness, and the completeness, as well as the prosperity, of life in the country." Applied science and advanced technology were to be enlisted in the service of cherished, but threatened, beliefs; with their help it would be possible to overcome not only the physical obstacles imposed by environment, but also to preserve frontier ideals by artificial means, to revitalize rural life, to protect the idealized yeoman farmer, whose virtues —vigor, manliness, independence, individualism, and democracy—were romanticized as the blood and bone of national life.

Legislation enabling federal reclamation was guided through the Congress by Representative (later Senator) Francis G. Newlands, who saw irrigation as the answer to the declining population of his arid state, Nevada. He introduced the proposal to finance federal irrigation from the proceeds of western land sales in the states, with complete discretion delegated to the Secretary of the Interior in the selection of the projects and apportioning of the funds. He hoped to forestall the possibility that disagreements among western politicians over the location of projects would retard the program, and to prevent the log-rolling so prevalent in rivers and harbors work. The Newlands Act of 1902 reflected the Progressive commitment to pre-industrial ideals, combined with a determination to use the most advanced techniques to solve social and political problems.

Administration of the act was entrusted to the Reclamation Service, under

Frederick H. Newell, and after 1907, when it separated entirely from the Geological Survey, to an independent bureau directly under the Secretary of the Interior. Through the Roosevelt years the Reclamation Service was regarded as a model conservation agency, both because of its supposed freedom from control by Congress, and because it was thought to have an independent source of income. The Progressive Conservation Movement was under the spell of a beguiling myth: a belief in the essential objectivity of the scientific administrator. The building of dams, tunnels, and power plants was a technical enterprise which, it was thought, should be managed on engineering principles and on the facts of the environment as determined by science, and decisions should be made by experts rather than politicians.

Perhaps inevitably, the Service made mistakes. It was inexperienced in high dam construction; it began by allowing settlers on the projects too soon; and it was open on occasion to the charge that political as well as purely technical considerations determined construction sites, while it frequently overemphasized engineering considerations to the detriment of the social and economic well-being of project settlers. It was equally beset by problems over which it had little or no control: by tangled and conflicting water laws, and the absence of a federal water law; by speculation which could not be prevented as long as project land could be taken up under the homestead laws; and by its own initial inexperience which led it to begin more projects than could be completed within the limits of the Reclamation Fund. The overextension of the fund before the end of the first decade of operation brought the engineers of the Service into serious conflict with the settlers.

In the 1920's agricultural depression joined with financial embarrassment to change drastically the character of federal reclamation. With survival the issue, the Service adopted a series of policy changes designed to take advantage of the West's growing demand for hydroelectric power. The Reclamation Service had previously produced power for auxiliary purposes, for construction needs or irrigation pumping; now it began to exploit power as a means of recovering costs, and so made possible a level of financial stability previously unknown to it. After 1930 it was committed to the full development of power on each project. It thus adopted a multiple-purpose approach to water which anticipated the co-ordinated river-basin development of the early New Deal.

Measured in terms of the grand dream of 1900, federal reclamation was a failure. It did not become the agent for scientific planning and the co-ordinated development of the arid West, as Powell might have wished and as many of his successors undoubtedly hoped. It did not halt the declining role of agriculture in the national life, nor stem the tide of migration to the cities. It fell somewhat short of turning the desert into a garden, at least on the scale dreamed of by its early enthusiasts; it was not, in short, the agent by which science and technology could reopen a frontier closed by nature to agriculture. On the other hand, viewed in historical perspective and against more hard-headed standards, the experiment was far from being a failure. The Reclamation Service plunged into a new field by undertaking large-scale water-storage works, and while it undoubtedly made mistakes as it gingerly moved ahead, it pioneered in the techniques of high dam construction and won for itself a worldwide reputation among engineers. By 1921 it had built reservoirs with a total capacity of 9,610,423 feet of water, constructed 11,258 miles of canals, and had brought 32,385 irrigated farms into being. The accomplishment seemed small enough when measured against the dream; but after all, John Wesley Powell had warned in 1879 that "vast areas many times greater than all the irrigable lands will remain to be utilized for other purposes."

A FEDERAL FORESTRY PROGRAM

The magnificent hardwood stands of the once heavily wooded East Coast had already been cut over when an active concern for forest resources first arose in America. Silviculture had an ancient history in Europe, but in the United States the technology of forest regulation was a response to conditions created by industrialism.

Not until the 1870's did the lumber industry spring from an infant to lusty, full growth. The activities of lumbermen in the Great Lakes region first attracted widespread attention, as improved techniques and more efficient corporate organization made possible forest exploitation on a scale and at a rate heretofore unknown. By the 1890's the pineries of these states had been cut over, and the transcontinental railroads had opened the pure stands of Douglas fir in the Far Northwest. In 1889 lumber production in Washington was equal to that of Minnesota; by 1909 it led the nation. Doubtless the social and economic implications of forest destruction first dramatized the need for protection of remaining stands. Hence the early forestry movement was concerned with saving trees or with planting them, rather than with the promotion of scientific and technical forestry.

Yet there was a close connection between forestry and irrigation, and the problem of western water development was the unifying theme of all conservation thought. Western irrigators had pioneered the theory that watershed vegetation affected water supplies, and the National Irrigation Congress supported the demand for a federal forestry program. That forest cover affected water retention and movement was accepted by the Geological Survey and all bureaus concerned with the public domain (except the Army's Corps of Engineers) a decade before the turn of the century. In 1891 urban and irrigation groups concerned with the protection of watersheds succeeded in having a section attached to an act dealing with the general land laws, which empowered the President to set aside forest reservations. President Benjamin Harrison (1833-1901) reserved

17.5 million acres from sales, although no provision was made for their administration or protection from fire and theft. President Grover Cleveland (1837-1908), acting on the recommendations of a study commission of the National Academy of Sciences, set aside an additional 21 million acres as national forest preserves.

The report of the NAS Forest Commission recommended the integration of the reserved forests into the general economy, and although there was wide disagreement on this point—the coalition that succeeded in getting the reservation act passed in 1891 had wanted the forests withdrawn from commercial use—the enactment of the Forest Management Act of 1897, as a direct consequence of the commission report, signalled a shift in the emphasis of the organized forestry movement.

The character of this shift was embodied in the views of Gifford Pinchot, a member of the Academy's Forest Commission who became head of the Division of Forestry in the Department of Agriculture following the retirement of the German-born Bernhard Fernow in 1898. Pinchot was a native American who called himself a "forester," and who already had behind him the practical experience of managing a forest on the Biltmore estate in North Carolina and several years' experience as a "forest consultant," as well as his participation on the Forest Commission. A Yale graduate with only a smattering of training abroad in his chosen field, never a scientist by either training or temperament, he was nevertheless fiercely dedicated to the belief that "practical" forestry could be successfully introduced in America without the years of scientific "preparation" and fact-finding insisted upon by Fernow. He assumed command of the old division determined to take forestry out of the laboratory and into the woods.

The core idea of Pinchot's "practical" forestry was sustained-yield management, a concept designed to maintain a constant supply of timber by insuring that annual cutting did not exceed annual growth. On the surface, a program built around such a core seemed out of line with the fluid, rapidly shifting economy of 1900, and yet there were solid reasons for predicting its success. Pinchot assumed command of his bureau with a free hand from the Secretary of Agriculture to develop his program. He began by offering assistance to the lumber industry in drawing up scientific management plans. Immediate requests for such aid flooded the division; some of the largest firms in the country, including the Weyerhaeuser Lumber Company, the Northern Pacific Railroad, and the Kirby Lumber Company of Texas, applied for aid. By 1905 such requests had been received from the owners of three million acres, and 177,000 acres were actually under sustained-yield management.

Behind this startling response was a shift within the organized forestry movement from emphasis upon saving or protecting trees to a more commercially oriented concern for future timber supplies. Already industries dependent upon wood were experiencing difficulty in acquiring satisfactory materials. Hardwood users wanted the Appalachians set aside as a sustained-yield area, and their trade associations lined up behind Pinchot and joined his bloc in the American Forestry Association. That bloc also included the major lumber concerns. Their industry was mobile and highly speculative, but with the shift to the Pacific Northwest, the last frontier of virgin stands had been reached. Pinchot began preaching management and planning at a time when lumbermen were becoming aware of the need for greater stability in their industry.

Pinchot and his foresters had their differences with lumbermen on the issue of federal regulation, but they had in common a desire to promote a stable industry by encouraging greater technical proficiency. Eventually a close alliance developed between the two camps. When in 1900 an initial endowment from the Pinchot family brought the Yale School of Forestry into being, the lumbermen raised $125,000 to endow a chair in the new school and opened their facilities and timberlands to forestry students for practical field training. Pinchot organized a forest-products section in the bureau in 1901 to study new uses for waste materials and new processes for manufacturing forest products. In 1909 when the work of this section was transferred to the campus of the University of Wisconsin, the Forest Service and lumber industry together supplied the necessary equipment. In 1901 there were enough trained foresters in the country to organize the Society of American Foresters which, together with representatives of lumber and wood-using industries, began to dominate the work of the American Forestry Association. This organization, formerly dominated by botanists, owners of large estates, and nature lovers, became an effective lobby for promoting the federal forestry program, both within and without the government.

Pinchot was equally as skillful in his dealings with Congress. The annual appropriation for his bureau jumped from $28,520 in 1899 to $439,873 in 1905. In one respect, however, he failed, at least at first. From the time he became chief forester Pinchot had one prime goal always in view; he wanted to have the forest reservations, administered by the General Land Office in the Department of the Interior, transferred to his control. From 1898 to 1905 he sought support for the transfer from every conceivable source. He courted the supporters of irrigation, such as the railroads and the National Board of Trade. With the aid of his allies in the wood industries, the American Forestry Association backed his efforts. Pinchot missed no opportunity to demonstrate that more western interests would benefit from his control of the forests than from control by the Department of the Interior, which frowned on their commercial use. He continually urged that the forests be opened to commercial use, and he consistently opposed groups such as the Boone and Crockett Club (of which he was a member), which wanted the forests to serve only as public parks and game preserves.

Pinchot took a strong stand for grazing in the forests. In 1901 he brought a western stockman, Albert Potter, to Washington to head a new division of grazing in the Bureau of Forestry. As he travelled through the West, Pinchot made contact with the leading grazing interests and particularly expressed views that contrasted with the past policy of the Interior Department, which had always sought to keep commercial use of the forests to a minimum. At its convention in 1901, and in succeeding years, the American National Livestock Association passed resolutions favoring Pinchot's ideas and recommending the transfer of the forest reserves to the Bureau of Forestry.

These efforts bore fruit in 1905. When the time came for the final push, Pinchot was able to crystallize sentiment in an American Forest Congress which, in his own words, "was planned, organized, and conducted for the specific purpose of the transfer by the Bureau of Forestry." The Congress was sponsored by a committee of arrangements which included the presidents of the Pennsylvania and Northern Pacific Railroads, the presidents of the National Lumber Manufacturers Association, the National Livestock Association, and the National Irrigation Association, the division heads of the United States Geological Survey, a number of friendly senators and congressmen, and the editors of numerous trade and industry journals. It was an impressive coalition, demonstrating Pinchot's great talents for marshalling support in and outside the government toward given ends.

With the transfer, the spectacular rise of the Bureau of Forestry was nearly complete. The bureau, renamed the Forest Service, saw its appropriations jump to $1,195,218 in 1906 and $3,572,922 in 1908. Ideas and theories of land management which had lain dormant in the bureaus now had a vast laboratory for experiment—150,832,665 acres in 159 national forests—and Pinchot fulfilled his promise to make commercial use of the forests.

Pinchot's policies promoted the broadening of the Conservation Movement. The legal basis for a new program of regulated and controlled use was the Forest Management Act of 1897, which empowered the Secretary of the Interior to "make such rules and regulations and establish such services as will insure the objects of [the] reservations, namely, to regulate their occupancy and use and to preserve the forests therein from destruction." The act did not specifically grant full commercial use of the forests, but neither did it exclude it, and building on this single clause, the legal officers of the Forest Service built a program requiring fees for grazing and permits for hydroelectric power development within the forests. Grazing became the principal commercial use of the forests, far exceeding lumbering. The significance of the expanded use of the existing legislation was that most of this program probably could not have won approval from Congress, although all of it was later upheld in the courts. As a Forest Service official said of this contribution to federal regulatory powers: "The Act of June 4, 1897, had placed us almost in the legal position of the agent of a private landowner with very broad powers to manage the property for the owner's welfare. The principles of real property law were available to use for the protection of the public interest."

THE CONSERVATION MOVEMENT

The gunshot that killed President William McKinley (b. 1843) in September 1901 brought into the White House a man who reacted strongly to the problems of his generation. Whether Theodore Roosevelt was a liberal or a conservative hardly seems as important as his awareness of the profound transformations at work in American life and his feeling of the need for institutional changes to meet the challenge. His heightened consciousness of rapid urbanization; his concern for the decline of rural life with its implications for traditional values; his fear of labor violence, general class conflict, and socialism; his pronouncements on monopoly and the "trust problem," all identified him as a spokesman of his generation. Except in the area of railroad regulation, Roosevelt's efforts to formulate a program by acquiring effective legislation were something less than completely successful, but no president has exercised existing executive powers more forcefully.

Pinchot and Newell had no trouble convincing Roosevelt that he should make a strong conservation statement in his first message to Congress. For many reasons Roosevelt came to look upon conservation as his most important domestic policy. Natural resources offered a theater of operations on a scale which could be duplicated nowhere else, and here policy touched on many other areas of interest to the President. His solution to the trust problem—to license corporations engaged in interstate commerce—had little chance of adoption, but corporations and individuals utilizing public resources could be licensed and regulated, and priorities on the use of various resources could be determined by the government, often without additional legislation.

The technical character of resource policy gave full sway to Roosevelt's belief that sensitive social problems were better solved by experts using the methods of science and good business rather than in the divisive fury of the political arena. Politics, to this very professional politician, often seemed to mean special interests, which in turn meant conflicting groups and class conflict. Hence the paradoxical efforts made to divorce the government from politics, which meant, as Roosevelt said, making it "as well planned, economical, and efficient as the best machinery of the great business organizations." Before Roosevelt, according to Pinchot, the government had been "debased by generations of political control." The diverse and scattered plurality of resource agencies—three separate government organizations, for instance, dealt with minerals, four with streams, and several with the forests, not to mention those for wild life, soils, soil erosion, and other questions dealing with land—offered abundant opportunity for co-ordination and consolidation of widespread government activity within an area of general technical unity.

Roosevelt's championing of the bureau doctrines of resource management, which had grown up since the time of Powell, received its first expression in the support he gave to federal reclamation, already discussed; but it is also symbolized by his close working relationship with Gifford Pinchot. The latter became a member of the famous "tennis cabinet"—a carrier of presidential influence to the bureau level, but also a carrier of bureau doctrine to the presidential level, a conductor cutting across the lines separating the cabinet departments and connecting the working agencies with the highest level of political power. With lines out also to numerous supporting groups in the private community, Pinchot was in a position to dominate federal resource policy in every area of the government.

LAND MANAGEMENT

The result was the promotion of a new program of land management, the principles of which had been forged by bureau technicians and scientists since the days of Powell, and tested on the National Forests by Pinchot after 1905. In 1903 President Roosevelt appointed a Public Lands Commission, with Pinchot and Newell as members. Their recommendations, forwarded to Congress in 1905, contained little that was new or startling. The report of the Public Lands Commission of 1879, including Powell's *Report on the Lands of the Arid Region*, had been much more comprehensive. Neither was there much significance in the referral of the report to Congress, which was no more prepared to accept a broad new resource program than it had been in the days of Powell. The report nonetheless was of great importance because it spelled out the theories of land management to be implemented by the Roosevelt administration between 1907 and 1909.

The core of the new program was reform of the existing land laws, which traditionally revolved around the principle of distributing land and resources to individuals. Roosevelt's resource leaders proposed that this system be replaced by public ownership. Resources were to be classified according to their actual value, and not sold but leased—a method of disposal which would permit federal officials to determine priorities and regulate the conditions of use.

The administration program for range lands illustrated all the elements of the new land management; in the end, it proved to be the most sensitive of all conservation issues because of the many interests it cut across. After the disastrous winter of 1887, whose freezing blizzards had killed many cattle on the open range, the livestock industry had transformed itself from a migratory to a permanently based industry. Many stockmen depended on federal grass, for which they competed with other possible users. The occasional intensity of this competition, among sheepmen, cattlemen, farming settlers, and watershed protection groups, made it a deeply partisan arena in which to formulate policy. For instance, federal officials became involved in conflict about the range after the national forests were opened to grazing in 1898. However, as priorities were established and remained in effect from year to year, conflict subsided. Security of use in the forests contrasted with the insecurity of the free range of the public domain. Stockmen became an important bloc in Pinchot's coalition, supporting transfer of the reserves to the Bureau of Forestry, because of the reluctance of the Department of the Interior actively to manage their own program in the forests, and because Pinchot advocated expanded commercial use of the forests. Seeking the same kind of stability for their industry on the free range as on the forests, stockmen began to advocate leasing of the grasslands. Lease bills were introduced regularly in Congress after 1901.

Although grazing had been at the center of Powell's thought, no federal agency comparable to the Division of Forestry existed for range until 1895, when the Division of Agrostology was organized under the Department of Agriculture. A botanist in this department, Frederick V. Coville, carried out the first scientific investigation of the range, and it was mainly on his recommendations that the Department of the Interior began to permit grazing on the national forests in 1898. Pinchot leaned heavily on him for technical advice. Coville was the moving spirit behind the investigation of grazing conditions in the West by the Public Lands Commission, and behind its final report recommending the classification and the leasing of the grazing lands of the public domain and their management in districts.

An administration bill embodying the recommendations of the Public Lands Commission was introduced into Congress as a rider to the 1907 appropriations bill. The controversy which sprang up immediately revealed not only anti-conservation sentiment, but also the inner tensions of the movement. The Reclamation Act of 1902 stemmed, in part, from a desire to prop up artificially a flagging individual ethic by preserving the family homestead, and irrigators and homesteaders had been part of Pinchot's grand coalition, along with giant corporate interests. Emotional commitment to the small-scale operator and admiration for the efficiency of the large economic unit existed side by side, but the proposed lease bill of 1906-7 brought out the basic anomaly of the situation.

To many of the resource policy-makers of the Roosevelt administration, the defeat of this leasing measure spelled out the limitations of trying to advance a program through traditional political channels. Pinchot later said it was impossible to have confidence in Congress because the "special interests" were in politics. Technical programs had to be advanced by technically trained administrators, according to technical rather than political considerations.

MINERAL LANDS

In one area the conservation program could move ahead without additional legislation. The Geological Survey had been made responsible for the "classification of the public lands" in its organic act of 1879, but the function had lapsed since the hydrographic survey of 1888. In 1906 Roosevelt withdrew 50 million acres of land containing coal-bearing rocks. Since coal land had formerly been sold at a flat rate which had no relation to the actual market price of coal, speculators had acquired coal land and made incredible capital gains by re-selling it at higher price. Although most of the valuable coal land was believed to have been acquired by 1906, the additional land was withdrawn so that it could be classified according to its value, after which it could be disposed of for something approaching the market price. These withdrawals continued, and by 1916 totaled 140,533,745 acres.

Shortly after the first coal withdrawals, the Geological Survey began to segregate oil-, phosphate-, potash-, and other mineral-bearing lands, which were classified and restored to entry for sale under the mineral laws—again, to check the practice of acquiring valuable mineral rights under agricultural laws designed to be lenient to the individual farmer. In 1914 Congress opened the surface of mineral lands to agricultural entry. The Roosevelt men had wanted to change basic methods of disposal, using lease rather than sale, and in the case of oil, by the barrel. Not until 1920, with the Mineral Leasing Act, was a consistent policy for these lands devised.

Other than classification, a well-developed conservation program for the public domain, similar to that initiated for the forests by Pinchot, had to depend primarily on unilateral executive action for its advancement, and conditions proper for this did not come about until 1907. In that year James R. Garfield replaced the more conservative and legalistic E. A. Hitchcock as head of the Department of the Interior. Garfield, the son of the assassinated American president, came from the Bureau of Corporations, over which he had presided during the years when the basic elements of the Roosevelt trust policy were formed; he tended to look upon the problems of conservation as germane to the trust problem generally—the need to control and regulate, rather than to destroy large-scale enterprise.

WATER AND POWER

With the grazing-lease bill dead, Garfield, Newell, and Pinchot, turned to the other area of control pioneered by the Forest Service, the extensive regulation of the water-power industry within the national forests, though it is probable that they would have attempted to apply this system to the public domain in any case. The large-scale production of electricity was just hitting its stride, and resource planners were determined that power sites should be taken up in different fashion than had been the case with valuable coal lands; however, the immediate occasion for devising water-power policy was in response to a significant broadening of conservation thought, rather than merely controlling the power industry.

The key role which water had played in conservation thought produced the sophisticated concept of multiple-purpose river development. The idea of water as a single resource with many potential uses had been bureau doctrine since the days of Powell. In 1907, largely through the efforts of Powell's closest associate, W J McGee (1853-1912), formerly of the Bureau of American Ethnology, Roosevelt appointed an Inland Waterways Commission, made up in part of Pinchot, Newell, and the chief of the Army engineers, with McGee serving as secretary. Their report recommended that waterways be controlled nationally, and that regional river systems be treated as units under a master plan for the use of the water for many purposes—flood control, navigation, electric power, irrigation, and industry. It recommended the creation of a permanent agency to co-ordinate waterway control nationally. The chief hydrographer of the Geological Survey, Marshall O. Leighton, another former associate of Powell, provided a specimen plan for the Ohio River system which included 100 reservoirs to impound the water of the entire region. Leighton argued that the government could produce and sell power to finance the project. Finally, the recommendations of the Inland Waterways Commission were embodied in a bill sponsored by Senator Francis Newlands.

The Commission's report, with the role it gave to hydroelectric power, worked to give a special twist to water-power policy on the public domain. From a legal standpoint there were two problems raised by the report. One was the question of federal jurisdiction over hydroelectric power development on navigable streams, particularly the Mississippi; and there was the question of their non-navigable headwaters on the public lands. The Inland Waterways Commission provided a philosophy for broadly integrated policy. Roosevelt attempted to use the General Dam Act of 1906 to regulate hydroelectric power on the navigable streams, much as Pinchot did with the forests. However, the Corps of Army Engineers considered navigation and flood control their inviolable preserve. The Corps dissented vigorously from the IWC report, and resisted the efforts of conservationists to use the General Dam Act as a means of regulating power on navigable streams. The Corps, as always, won.

As the Roosevelt years neared their end in the latter part of 1908, administration leaders, especially Garfield, Pinchot, and Newell, turned their attention to the one area of control still within their grasp, the formulation of a policy for the federal regulation of hydroelectric power on the non-navigable streams of the public domain. In December Garfield began withdrawing power sites from all forms of entry except for purposes of power development. Over four million acres were withdrawn before March, when Garfield retired as Secretary of the Interior. A permit system was devised similar to that used for the national forests, which charged a fee and regulated the terms of power development. There is no doubt, however, that the recommendations of the IWC were foremost in Garfield's mind, rather than just a desire to regulate power companies. Charges for power were to defray the costs of multiple-purpose river development if and when it emerged as a reality, and to safeguard sites for their future purpose, Garfield withdrew the great majority of water-power sites under the authority of the Reclamation Act of 1902, which clearly retained ownership for the government.

THE POPULAR CRUSADE

In 1907 and 1908 the failure of the administration lease bill for range lands was followed by the unwillingness of Congress to pass the Newlands bill and establish the waterways commission. Added to this was the open hostility of the Corps of Army Engineers. The entire conservation program seemed stalled. At this juncture Pinchot and Roosevelt decided to appeal directly to the people. To capture public attention, Pinchot and W J McGee organized the dramatic 1908 Governors' Conference at the White House, to which were invited not only the governors of all the states, but also representatives from all of the important engineering and technical societies of the nation; and a National Conservation Commission began an ambitious inventory of natural resources, under the direction of McGee.

These actions in the last months of the Roosevelt administration gave birth to the "Conservation Movement," a phrase which came into popular currency at that time—a product of the publicity talents of Gifford Pinchot and the willingness of Roosevelt to use the tremendous influence of the presidency to focus attention on the nation's "diminishing resources." What had been the concern of a handful of technical administrators and a restricted number of economic groups acquired a national audience. Enthusiasm was whipped up at some cost to accuracy. The rhetoric of conservation was plugged into the anti-trust sentiment of the Progressive era. To the public the Conservation Movement came to mean the movement to keep monopolistic trusts from exhausting the nation's material wealth within a few generations. As we have seen, the actual policies were not rooted in anti-trust sentiment, but rather in a desire to adjust the land-disposal policies of an agrarian past to the realities of modern industrial enterprise. This new popular interest disturbed many technical men who saw efficient utilization as the real goal and hoped that the problem would "be treated, not as a new cult, but as a practical development for which able men have labored conscientiously, persistently, and not unsuccessfully, for many years."

The great crusade of 1908 was scarcely an unmixed success. It was partly the logic of artificially induced enthusiasm that led to Pinchot's conflict with Roosevelt's successor, William Howard Taft, and his Secretary of the Interior, Richard Ballinger. Ballinger began by thoroughly undoing the water-power policy of Garfield. Although Taft was Roosevelt's hand-picked successor, he had taken the side of the Army engineers when he was Secretary of War, and he now took the side of Ballinger against Pinchot. In the last analysis, however, it was not a question of Taft's opposition to conservation, but rather his unwillingness to allow Pinchot to continue as a virtual "member of the cabinet for conservation." Barred from direct access to the President, Pinchot turned to appeals to both the general public and the interest groups, the other carefully cultivated source of his support. When Taft dismissed him in 1910 as chief of the Forest Service, Pinchot could no longer operate from within the federal government, and became completely dependent upon his broad-based support. The role which the dismissal of Pinchot played in contributing to the split in the Republican party in 1912—permitting the election of Woodrow Wilson on the Democratic ticket—showed to what extent conservation had become a political issue since the crusade of 1908.

After 1909, then, bureau chiefs concerned with conservation ceased to be endowed with extraordinary powers. Those powers had depended on the peculiar relationship of Pinchot and Roosevelt, and the condition could not be repeated. The great bureaus continued their separate programs, but without the vital co-ordination and inspiration of earlier years. Outside the government Pinchot led a coalition which commanded enough support in Congress to block measures that displeased it, but which was too weak to push through its own program. That program consisted of a mineral-leasing plan for the public domain and the waterways commission. In particular, Pinchot had come to stake all his hopes on multiple-purpose water development, but in 1917 the waterways commission died ignobly, and Pinchot realized he would have to settle for federal regulation of hydroelectric power as a substitute. In 1920 the Mineral Leasing Act opened up the mineral resources of the public lands, and a Water Power Act provided for hydroelectric power projects under federal regulation. Pinchot claimed the victory, but the Roosevelt program had been compromised; the leasing act provided for only a token rental fee, while regulation of hydroelectric power was no substitute for the broad planning of the envisioned waterways commission. The way was opened for significant conservation activity, but Powell's dream of national planning, so nearly implemented under Roosevelt, remained a chimera.

AFTER THE CRUSADE

Although the 1920's usually evoke thoughts of Teapot Dome, Elk Hills, and other big steals from the government by private interests, conservation programs made solid gains during the decade. A nationwide soil-conservation program was begun which laid the foundation for the work of the New Deal Soil Conservation Service. Its technical competence was as marked as its impotence to replace the short-grass resource that had been sacrificed to the agrarian myth, or to save the ruined farmers who had been as much the victims as the carrier of that myth. The Reclamation Service kept the idea alive of multiple-purpose river-basin planning, which finally received full expression in the Tennessee Valley Authority (TVA) of 1933. In the same year, the Taylor Act created a Grazing Service and set up grazing districts along lines recommended by Powell fifty years earlier. However, a jurisdictional dispute over control of the public grazing lands which ensued between the Departments of Agriculture and the Interior permitted the local grazing boards, controlled by the stockmen, to gain the upper hand; when, in 1947, the Grazing Service was finally eliminated as a separate agency of the Interior, it had long since been emasculated.

The New Deal gave birth to a proliferation of alphabet agencies concerned with natural resources: the Civilian Conservation Corps (CCC), the Works Progress Administration (WPA), the Public Works Administration (PWA), and so on. But the great range and variety of activity in the 1920's and 1930's could not obscure the fact that the creative era of conservationist thought had passed, at least in the technical programs. TVA, impressive as it was, was the dream of an earlier age. Furthermore, efforts of New Deal resource planners to extend regional development on a nationwide scale failed because a basic problem which had plagued conservationists since the first Roosevelt administration continued to defy solution. The technical know-how existed to blanket the country with innumerable "TVA's," but unanswered was the basic constitutional question of what type of agency could administer such a unified system of national planning. Departmental autonomy and bureau jealousies had been overcome for a short time by the special relation of Theodore Roosevelt and Gifford Pinchot. But this proved to be something less than a permanent solution, and the second Roosevelt administration was never able to come up with a substitute.

The range of conservation activity continued to broaden after World War II, but the central problem of administration remained as far from solution as ever. The jurisdictional struggle between the Department of the Interior and of Agriculture in the 1930's was significant precisely because Harold Ickes and Henry Wallace each dreamed of consolidating all conservation activity under their respective departments. Earlier in the century the first Conservation Movement had raised the question of whether purely technical programs could be adequately promoted through traditional political channels; subsequent years undermined the relevance of the question: there proved to be no purely technical programs. There were only technical programs with political implications.

29 / Regional Planning and Development
FOREST G. HILL

THE REGIONAL APPROACH

Regional economic development demonstrates the impact of technological advance and of related changes in resource patterns on man's natural environment and economic well-being. Changes in technology and resources, and also in public policy, can be analyzed in terms of their influence through time on individual regions. Today, as in the past, these changes affect various regions in quite different ways. If wise decisions concerning regional planning and development are to be made, the basic trends, problems, and policies concerning regional economic growth must be examined in their historical setting.

Regional as well as occupational specialization has long been a prominent feature of economic life. Impetus for the improvement of transportation went hand in hand with this spreading regional specialization. These interrelated developments benefitted from, and stimulated, technological change; in like manner urbanization, trade patterns, and interregional migration were promoted. Regions were carved out anew in recently settled and expanding countries. In older, well-settled nations, individual regions were gradually transformed through the interplay of industrialization, urbanization, and technological advances. These older areas went through a sequence of stages in regional development, while newer areas experienced similar transitions in the wake of moving frontiers of settlement. With rapid settlement and major changes in agricultural, transportation, and manufacturing technologies, these regional transformations occasionally proceeded with a spurt under boom-time conditions.

However, regional patterns were often sticky or inflexible. Regional specialization became hardened into a mould in terms of the applied technology, the evolved trade pattern, the structure of population and occupations, the prevailing policies serving the region's chief needs, and even the institutional shell of a region's basic values and traditions. The pattern thus developed with considerable structural rigidity, even though individual regions were subject to the continuing influence of technological advance, changing resource patterns, and shifting policies. Structural problems involved both the tension and conflict produced by these influences for change and the rigidity or inflexible character of the prevailing regional structure. At such times the regional growth rate often lagged, reflecting the obsolescence or stagnation affecting such regions.

Elimination or solution of these structural problems usually turned on technological breakthroughs, resource revolutions, and shifts in public policy. These
are the agents of regional economic change whose effects must be understood
and controlled today, and for these purposes it is necessary to know how these
forces have achieved their effects over substantial periods of time.

EARLY REGIONAL SPECIALIZATION

In the United States, regional specialization in economic activity began to take
hold during the colonial period. Ship-building and fishing became localized
and concentrated along the New England seacoast. The production of wheat,
beef, and pork was prominent in Pennsylvania and elsewhere in the middle
colonies. The southern colonies had their tobacco-growing areas, and frontier
areas began to specialize in herding and trapping activities. Especially toward
the interior, the individual regions in good part had to be self-sufficient, in view
of the urgency of many of their own immediate subsistence needs. However,
each region endeavored to produce one or more "cash crops" or marketable
staples. Specialized production was thus market-oriented; the surplus output
which was not needed locally was exported and sold outside the region to help
finance the import of commodities which it needed from the outside.

As the frontier of settlement moved westward, successive tiers of new regions
were carved out of the public domain. The historian Frederick Jackson Turner
romantically described how this frontier process worked: how successive waves
of trappers, miners, herdsmen, and then farmers occupied the open land, tamed
it, and brought a rebirth of civilization. However, during the 19th century these
empire builders soon included rising capitalists and industrialists, railroad
builders, and town developers. These occupiers of the West eagerly promoted
the production of cash staples which would yield the quickest and greatest
profit afforded by available market outlets. They eagerly sought exportable
products which were favored by the region's resource endowment and feasible
in terms of applicable production technologies and existing transportation facilities. Other necessary ingredients for a boom in the production of market staples, such as cotton, grain, or livestock, included labor skills and capital goods.
The availability, including the cost and quality, of these necessary ingredients
at critical points in time determined the character and rapidity of each region's
development.

New regions of specialized production were devoted not only to cattle, cotton, and wheat, but also to corn and hogs, hides and furs, minerals and lumber.
Each region developed the towns, transportation improvements, and organized
markets it needed for its own scheme of specialized production. Its land-use
patterns and social-overhead facilities, including transportation projects, warehouses, grain elevators, and other public facilities, were thus adapted to its

production specialties. Furthermore, its scheme of institutions and social values evolved in conformity with the exigencies for producing and marketing its export staples. The result was a pattern of separate regions, each with its own structure of resources, physical facilities, occupations, and markets, all encased within the region's institutional shell.

The "Cotton Kingdom" of the Old South provides an apt illustration of the manner in which physical facilities and social structure developed to conform with a system of staple production. Since slave labor could be used cheaply and supervised easily in a scheme of gang labor, slavery and the plantation system became part of the established order of things. This particular economic and social pattern, however, discouraged the extensive growth of towns, schools, migration to the South, and the development of entrepreneurial talent. The planters dominated social and political life, while local attitudes, customs, and laws buttressed the existing institutions. Although the Civil War marked the end of the institution of slavery and the breakup of large plantations, the Cotton Kingdom was merely recast. The cotton-producing economy was reorganized along the lines of sharecropping, small tenant farms, the crop-lien system of farm credit, and racial segregation. Since this changed institutional complex gained support through law and custom, it has persisted, with some modification, down to the present in the cotton-producing states of the South.

The rise and collapse of the open-range cattle industry on the great plains after the Civil War showed that regional specialization could develop quickly and stagnate or become obsolete just as rapidly in the context of westward expansion. This boom, with all its color and romance, ran its full course between 1865 and 1890. During the Civil War the longhorn cattle roaming the plains around west Texas multiplied rapidly. At the same time a great increase in the demand for beef resulted from urban population growth, advances in meat-packing and refrigeration, and construction of railroads into the plains regions of the West. Soon there were many long cattle drives from Texas to the rail-heads connecting with the new meat-packing centers of the Midwest. Long-horns were driven to northern pastures to be fed out for market and to stock new cattle ranges which extended into the Rockies and Canada.

As writers like Walter Prescott Webb have shown, such technological advances as six-shooters, windmills, and barbed wire, as well as railroads, promoted the range cattle industry around the 1870's. The bonanza ranchers used these new devices to good advantage on their cattle ranges. However, the further extension of railroads into the plains attracted many sod-busters or homesteaders—the small, land-hungry settlers who hazarded dry-farming methods on the plains. They, too, began to use barbed wire, settling first around watering places and then gradually breaking up the open range. Although enmities sometimes flared between cattlemen and farmers at water holes and fence lines, the more important battles were between representatives of the two groups in the state legislatures. Initially the state laws on such matters as taxes and fences favored the range cattle kings; for instance, fence laws forced the farmers to have a prescribed, and somewhat expensive, "legal fence" in order to claim damages when cattle trespassed on their growing crops. However, as soon as the farmers increased in numbers and political power, the legislatures passed fence laws lodging responsibility for damages, and even for fencing in their cattle, on the ranchers. The result was to reduce farmers' costs and to speed agricultural settlement. Railroads and fences marched across the plains. At the same time the range cattlemen were being hurt by drought, livestock diseases, and falling cattle prices resulting from expansion of cattle-raising in this country and in Canada, Argentina, and elsewhere. The range cattle business soon became unprofitable and yielded rapidly to dry-farming and diversified livestock farming.

By the end of the 19th century, a fairly definite, stable pattern of regional specialization was evident throughout the nation. The modern cotton, wheat, and corn belts had emerged by then; there were several major mining and coal-producing regions, and a few large oil fields had been discovered. The earliest manufacturing had been dependent on water power and had concentrated along the rivers of New England's coastline. Later, as coal and then petroleum became important as sources of power, manufacturing industries developed around New York and Pennsylvania and then further to the west along the Great Lakes. By 1900 the nation's industrial heartland extended from Boston down the Atlantic Coast to New York City and Philadelphia and westward between the Ohio River and the Great Lakes to Chicago. Expanding markets, transportation arteries, and sources of raw materials as well as fuel, pulled manufacturing westward along this large industrial belt. The iron and steel industry, taking advantage of the area's coal, iron ore, and limestone, as well as its interior markets, developed primarily in the region from Pittsburgh to Chicago. This area also attracted metal-fabricating industries and became the chief source of agricultural equipment such as plows, reapers, windmills, and wire fencing. The area had similar attractions for such resource-oriented processing industries as lumbering, flour-milling, furniture-making, and meat-packing.

As the 20th century began, the United States economy consisted essentially of the urbanized industrial zone in the Northeast running from Boston westward to Chicago surrounded by a series of raw-material-producing regions running from the Southeast and the Midwest to the Pacific Coast. This large hinterland was dotted with trading centers and contained a sprinkling of industry. The processing industries kept moving south and west toward new sources of supply. In addition, the Southeast had textile mills located in its Piedmont region and steel production at Birmingham, Alabama. The new oil fields of the Gulf Southwest and California provided sites for petroleum refineries. The growing cities across the nation were also attracting some consumer-oriented light manufacturing industries. And by 1900, the industrial Northeast had about lost its monopoly on manufacturing as the newer regions became more urbanized and diversified.

EARLY POLICIES INFLUENCING REGIONAL GROWTH

In a strict, modern sense of the term, regional planning of economic development took form late and on a limited scale in the United States compared to other large nations. However, this view may be oversimplified. Even in the absence of *general* planning of economic development in this country, there have always been policies consciously designed to influence regional development. Furthermore, in the absence of regional planning under *national* authority in the decades preceding the 1930's, there was some planned action at the state or local levels of government. In addition, public action along the lines of modern regional planning was not as negligible or insignificant during the colonial and early national periods as it was in the late 19th century, when the laissez-faire attitude was at its height. Since these views concerning the extent of early regional planning merit some attention and since policies affecting and promoting regional development have been utilized all along, these policies should be put in historical perspective.

Historians speak of the *planting* of the first colonies along the Atlantic Coast, but planting also required *planning*. The colonizing companies carried on this initial colonial planning, or corporate planning along quasi-governmental lines. In other early colonies the proprietors or other colonial officials engaged in similar planning functions. In New England, township-planning involved the laying out and the support of new areas for settlement.

Each of the thirteen colonies became largely self-governing, and engaged in considerable promotional and regulatory activity. Indeed, there was a home-grown, mercantilist tradition in the American colonies that sanctioned extensive governmental intervention and guidance in economic affairs. These governmental activities were quite varied and included land policy, defense, regulation of prices and wages, licensing of regulated businesses, and the granting of monopoly rights to promote transportation projects. During, and for some time after, the American Revolution, such state intervention and planning persisted. Circumstances resulting from the Napoleonic Wars and the War of 1812 gave renewed life to such state action, which turned downward significantly during the Age of Jackson and gradually diminished thereafter. However, the decline typically occurred later and more slowly in the newer or frontier states than in the older ones.

Federal policy bearing on regional development was far from insignificant during the early national period. Among the most important policies were those affecting land, tariffs, internal improvements, and money. Other such areas of public policy included agriculture, immigration, western exploration, and the advancement of science. Each of these federal policies at times had an important —and intended—regional impact, and many became sectional political issues.

When the states claiming western lands relinquished these claims, the way was clear for enactment of the Land Ordinances of 1785 and 1787. The first act instituted a systematic plan for surveying the public domain, and the second provided for the government of newly settled areas. Together they made it possible to survey and settle new areas, institute provisional government over them, and achieve eventual statehood for them. Individuals hungering for land were able to go west and help develop new self-governing states. "Manifest destiny" became more a private cause than a public one; it took on the character of a grass-roots imperialism.

The incentive and machinery for promoting western settlement were buttressed by an increasingly liberal land policy after 1800. Initially, the Hamiltonian view of selling public land to raise public revenue, and thereby moderating the speed of frontier expansion, held sway. However, the Jeffersonian policy of selling land cheaply and in smaller tracts soon prevailed. Such liberalization proceeded apace between 1800 and 1832, while the Pre-emption Act of 1841 permitted squatters to settle on surveyed public land and buy it later at a minimal price. However, public land policy was caught up in acute sectional controversy prior to the Civil War, and so were federal tariff and internal improvement policies. Thus the Homestead Act (1862), representing free land conditional upon occupancy for five years, was enacted only after the war had begun.

Sectional controversy over the protective tariff and internal improvements demonstrated that like land policy, they, too, had definite regional implications. In his efforts at national planning as Secretary of the Treasury, Alexander Hamilton bracketed proposals for the protective tariff as a device which would also yield revenue and for the application of federal funds to transportation improvements as means of expanding domestic markets. After the War of 1812 Henry Clay combined these two proposals in his "American System," and so did the new Republican party when it was formed in the 1850's. Although these policies found favor in the industrial Northeast, the leaders of the agricultural South concluded that they were contrary to its basic interests. Southern leaders opposed federal financing of internal improvements and also tried to limit the scope of river and harbor projects. In the agrarian West similar views were often held; however, as manufacturing began to develop along the Great Lakes, the Northwest began to favor protectionism when it was combined with government aid to transportation. The major federal land grants to railroads were enacted during the Civil War years and immediately thereafter while the South was politically weak.

During the 1850's the Army engineers applied a good deal of physical planning to their task of making surveys and plans for several possible railroad routes to the Pacific Coast. Army engineers had made numerous surveys for roads, canals, and railroads commencing with the General Survey Act of 1824. Their surveys for coastal defenses and transportation improvements following the War of 1812 involved some meaningful planning, with a view to the joint needs of defense and development. Their Pacific railroad surveys of the 1850's were of a similar character and had substantial engineering and scientific value.

Federal policy regarding money and banking always aroused sectional and regional feelings. The agricultural areas of the South and West, being debtor regions, usually preferred "soft-money" policies and either no federal control or at least more lenient federal control of banks—policies they hoped would raise farm prices and make debt burdens lighter to bear. States with strong financial interests, being creditor areas, tended to favor "hard-money" policies and firmer regulation of banks in order to protect the value of their financial assets and claims. Monetary controversy throughout the 19th century revealed that there was acute concern because government monetary policy produced different effects on various regions.

Federal and state governments during the 19th century actively promoted agriculture, immigration, exploration of the West, and the accumulation of scientific knowledge—policies which especially aided the settlement of new regions. The origins of many of today's major federal scientific programs, such as scientific aids to agriculture, conservation, geological surveying, and weather reporting, go back to the early national period, and the regional implications of many current programs continue to be stressed.

TWENTIETH-CENTURY REGIONAL DEVELOPMENT

During the 19th century America had a physical frontier and experienced lateral, or extensive, economic growth. Specialized regions were being created and settled, and migrants and capital goods were being attracted to these new regions. All the while, the older regions, as well as the newer ones, were stimulated and transformed internally by the process of frontier expansion and boom. In the 20th century, however, the physical frontier exists no more. Instead of extensive growth, the process has been one of the "filling in" or maturing of existing regions, or of intensive growth only.

This intensive, or vertical, development has included continuing urbanization and industrialization. Regions sharing prominently in these trends have continued to gain in population and in real income per person. Other regions have grown more slowly or not at all; several that have been losing population in absolute terms suffered a relative decline in real income per person. Leading and lagging regions have appeared side by side. Regional boom and stagnation have occurred simultaneously.

In several respects the period around World War I seems to represent a watershed in American economic development. Up to that time, railroad mileage, immigration, farm acreage, and agricultural exports were increasing; but not afterward. Since then the number of farms and the volume of agricultural employment have been decreasing. At the same time, sick or declining industries, depressed areas, and urban blight made their appearance. As of 1914 most Negroes lived in the South, mainly in rural areas. Within fifty years, however, the Negro population has become primarily urban and is more numerous outside the South. Such long-run shifts as these are connected to fundamental regional changes in recent decades.

For example, there have been enormous improvements in American agriculture, involving especially a large reduction in the number of persons employed in farming. Mechanization, the average size of farms, and output per worker and per acre have made great strides. Agricultural employment was reduced by approximately one half in the two decades following World War II, while total farm production was actually increasing. In other words, the rise in farm productivity, or output per worker, more than offset the fall in farm employment. During those decades productivity increased at a more rapid rate in agriculture than in manufacturing.

However, in the mid-1960's many small farms were inefficient, poorly equipped, and unprofitable. There have been estimates that some one million marginal farmers, together with their families, could be transferred out without harming agricultural production. These small, poor farmers are most predominant in the old cotton regions of the Southeast and in the Southern Appalachian area. Despite the fact that these rural areas have experienced heavy outmigration since World War I, the high birth rates in such areas have minimized or negated the decline in their population. Many of the poverty-stricken farmers who remain are Negroes, and many are tenants or sharecroppers. Their physical output is so small that government price-support programs yield negligible benefits to them, and they are increasingly exposed to the superior competition from better equipped farmers elsewhere. Long-run trends in cotton production, although downward in the Southeast, have been increasing in newer producing areas from Texas to California. The westward shift of cotton production has been impeded by government acreage limitations, which are based on past records of cotton production for each farm. However, the shift has been favored by highly mechanized methods of cultivating and picking cotton and sometimes by irrigation in the newer producing regions. To say the least, the old Cotton Kingdom faces prospects of continued decline in cotton production and further rural outmigration. Greater reliance on larger, more diversified farms will probably be necessary in the Southeast.

Small-scale and relatively unproductive farming has been common in the hilly "cutover" or deforested areas of the Appalachians, the Ozarks, and parts of New England and the western Great Lakes region. These areas, along with the

South's cotton belt and the Southwest's Latin American migratory farm workers, account for most of the country's rural poverty. Farming has become relatively large-scale and efficient in other agricultural regions, as in the Mississippi Valley area, the prairie and plains regions, and the Pacific Coast. The Midwest, for instance, with its regional specialization in wheat production, corn, and hogs, and diversified farming and livestock-raising, is relatively prosperous. This area has benefitted greatly from large-scale methods and rising productivity in agriculture, which have facilitated extensive rural outmigration.

Most rural counties throughout the nation have gradually lost population in recent decades. Indeed, several agricultural states in the interior, both east and west of the Mississippi River, have had declines in population during one or both of the last two census decades. Even in states with a growing population, which essentially means states with large, thriving cities, there has usually been net outmigration from the rural counties. The "pull" of cities, however, has varied greatly with business conditions. Urban migration swelled during the two world wars, the booming 1920's, and the prosperous years following 1945. Early during the Depression of the 1930's, however, a net return of people to rural areas held temporary sway. Requisite conditions for the needed rapid, stable migration out of low-income agricultural regions seem to include prosperity and full employment.

The first substantial Negro migration from the rural South to northern industrial areas occurred during World War I. World War II greatly accelerated this migration, permitting the first large movement of Negroes to the Pacific Coast. Since the 1920's Negroes in urban areas of the North have been able to obtain the unskilled jobs which previously had been taken by newly arrived immigrants. Within the South, however, rural whites have moved to the cities in greater proportion than rural Negroes. Since employment prospects for Negroes have seemed better elsewhere, most urban Negroes have taken residence outside the South. For such reasons as these, southern states typically have had a net outmigration of Negroes in recent decades, along with a net inward migration of whites.

Manifestly, a great redistribution of population has been taking place in recent decades from rural to urban areas, from town to city, from South to North, from East to West, and, in general, from the interior to the periphery of the country. Farming regions and thinly settled areas are being gradually depopulated. Except for a few major urban centers, the population is shrinking in large interior sections across the South and the West. Population is growing more concentrated in the North Atlantic coastal area, the highly urbanized region which the geographer Jean Gottmann calls "Megalopolis." Greater concentration is also developing in the manufacturing belt below the Great Lakes as well as on the Pacific Coast and the Gulf Coast.

The expanding urban population concentrations may be described as coastal if the Great Lakes are regarded as a seacoast. The location of these concentrations on coasts, large lakes, and rivers indicates the importance of water transportation and the great needs of urban and industrial areas for more water. Water has also become more important for recreation: fishing, boating, swimming, and other leisure activities. Indeed, water for recreational purposes is a major "amenities" resource which has been exercising an increasing locational "pull" on population, as shown by the experience of Florida and California. Mountains and deserts also have recreational or amenities value, along with beaches and lakes and streams. When recreational areas gain enough population, they attract various service activities and "footloose" industries.

As in the case of California, Washington, and Texas, defense production in recent decades has stimulated expansion of areas which have, in addition, recreational amenities as locational advantages. California has become the leading state in defense activities, especially for the production of aircraft and electronic and missile components and military research and development work. This state has also shared with Texas and other Gulf Coast states in the expansion of military installations and space programs, activities which have been attracting population and industry to the zone of warm climate and nearly year-round sunshine extending from California across the desert and Gulf states to Florida and Georgia. As a result, the dispersal of manufacturing activities has continued, favoring especially the Pacific Coast and the South. Growing urban markets in these regions have attracted consumer-oriented or "residentiary" industries. In recent decades, manufacturing employment has increased substantially on the Pacific Coast, to a lesser degree in the Gulf Southwest, and to some extent in the Southeast. Although employment in manufacturing has decreased in New England, it has expanded materially in the Great Lakes-Ohio River industrial belt. The Northeast has continued to be the nation's industrial heartland, containing nearly three fourths of its manufacturing jobs.

Total employment in manufacturing, however, reached a peak in 1957 which was not again approached until the brisk expansion of the mid-1960's occurred. Manufacturing has exhibited strong trends toward greater mechanization and automation, with resulting higher productivity and the decline of "blue-collar" employment. Unskilled and semi-skilled jobs have been shrinking in many manufacturing industries, in mining and other extractive industries, and also in construction, public utilities, and transportation, while service activities take on added importance with decreases in employment in goods-producing and goods-handling industries.

BASIC PROBLEMS

A survey of major regional trends in the American economy reveals several basic problems and needs. Continuing technical improvements and productivity increases in agriculture generally produce farm surpluses and regularly generate outmigration from rural areas. Manufacturing and other goods-producing, goods-handling activities in urban areas are subject to similar technical and productivity advances. If full employment is not maintained, however, the rural exodus will be hindered. In view of the extensive rural poverty and the many marginal farms, people may be leaving the farm too slowly. Yet, in the light of urban blight, congestion, racial tension, and unemployment, the rural population may be migrating to the cities too rapidly, and arriving lacking the knowledge and skills needed to adjust adequately to urban life and to obtain satisfactory employment.

These problems are tied to basic long-run trends; in a sense they are firmly structured in the American economy, and reflect the hard fact that changes affecting regions are not nicely dovetailed or synchronized. Structural changes proceed sluggishly, entail dislocation and pockets of unemployment, and pose serious challenges concerning how they are to be analyzed, guided, and coordinated. The rural exodus and the decline in blue-collar urban employment adversely affect one another. Depressed areas and rural poverty have a bearing on the inadequacy of education and skills among newcomers to the city. Racial tension grows under such circumstances, and aggregate demand and employment levels are, in turn, affected. Inflation, or recession, further complicates the problems of structural change and society's ability to deal with them.

REGIONAL PLANNING IN RECENT DECADES

During the first two or three decades of the 20th century national policies influencing regional growth in the United States remained very similar to those of the previous century. Only limited attention was given to the regional impact of national programs, such as those to promote agriculture or scientific knowledge. The programs increased in scope, while the conservation of national resources received much heavier emphasis. Steps were taken to enlarge the national forests and improve flood control. The Reclamation Act of 1902 instituted a program to reclaim and irrigate arid lands for agricultural purposes in the West, while the Federal Power Act of 1920 was designed in good part to protect hydroelectric power sites.

During the 1930's the Depression and the New Deal prompted a major increase in national and regional planning, as well as in programs for promoting agriculture, science, conservation, public power installations, and public works of all sorts. New government agencies were created in several of these fields, including public works and public housing. The Civilian Conservation Corps was active for a time as a developmental agency in the field of resource conservation. Another developmental agency, the Rural Electrification Administration, encouraged the use of electricity in rural areas by fostering a network of co-operatives and assisting them through government loans. However, the most significant planning and promotional agencies created during the New Deal period were the Tennessee Valley Authority and the National Resources Planning Board.

The Tennessee Valley Authority, created as an autonomous governmental corporation to plan and direct the multi-purpose development of an entire watershed covering all or part of seven states, was thus a major experiment in regional planning and development. Its chief activities included public power, flood control, navigation, soil conservation, and reforestation. In addition, it gave extensive technical aid to farmers in the region concerning soil-conservation practices and the use of fertilizers. The TVA became the model of a unified, comprehensive approach to the planning and development programs of an entire region. Its example has been widely studied and copied by other countries, especially underdeveloped ones. However, other regions and agencies in the United States copied not its organizational form but its integration of operational activities throughout one region. Since the established federal departments and agencies did not wish to yield ground to other TVA's in this country, they proceeded to employ inter-agency planning committees to co-ordinate or integrate their respective programs in operational terms for each major river valley. Through its own work and because of the stimulus it gave to inter-agency planning, the TVA has greatly advanced regional planning in the United States and abroad.

The National Resources Planning Board, an advisory agency of the New Deal period, promoted the formation of state and regional planning agencies and helped guide and co-ordinate their work. The NRPB made basic studies and reports on various problems of industrial, regional, and national planning, and on the relation of science, technology, and resources to such planning. Although the board itself was abolished during World War II, many of the state and regional planning boards it brought into being survived and became area-development agencies following the war. Private national organizations, such as the Committee for Economic Development, the National Planning Association, and Resources for the Future, have fostered and worked with these area-development boards.

Most of the developmental agencies and programs that issued from the New Deal—along with those which antedated it—were continued after World War II, although few significant innovations were made before the 1960's. An exception was the introduction of urban renewal. By 1965, several new developmental and planning programs had been enacted by Congress: the Area Redevelopment Act of 1961 created an agency to institute such work, although with very limited funds. A year later Congress passed the Trade Expansion Act and the Manpower Development and Training Act, both of which hold potential significance for regional development. The major legislation of 1964 included the Economic Opportunity Act instituting the so-called "War on Poverty" through several agencies designed to promote local action, and the Civil Rights Act of 1964.

The most notable legislative year, in the context of action to promote regional planning and development, was 1965, during which Congress passed the Public Works and Economic Development Act, the Appalachian Regional Development Act, the State Technical Services Act, the Water Quality Act, and the Highway Beautification Act. The first two of these may well become important; the first one reorganized the agency and program initiated by the 1961 act, while the second instituted a scheme of grants, loans, public works, and technical aid to help local areas and interests in several of the Appalachian states. The third act permits technical aid for planning activities at the state level. In concept and in practice, a great deal of the emphasis in these programs is placed on providing aid and attracting capital to depressed and lagging areas which otherwise would suffer greater outmigration in the absence of such special assistance. Little emphasis has been given to retraining and relocation programs designed to encourage and assist people to move elsewhere.

These recent acts provide an extensive basis for federal planning of regional development, and for promotion and support of such planning when carried on by state or local groups. Federal activity may increase materially on the basis of the legislation noted above.

Several other acts in recent years have strong implications for regional programs. Some of these concern education, vocational training, and civil rights. In addition, various recent acts facilitate joint federal-state planning of numerous programs. Furthermore, legislation concerning military procurement and other aspects of national defense allows some discretion concerning the regional impact of such activities. In terms of the legislation already enacted, the foundation has been provided for extensive federal action in the area of regional planning and development. Social and political factors and technological change affect regional economies and have played a major role in regional development in the past. It is clear then that future programs will have to take into account technological change in its social and political context.

30 / Urban Planning and Development
ROY LUBOVE

Urbanization, defined as a process of population concentration involving either a multiplication of points of concentration or an increase in their size, has always been influenced by technology. The location, form, and function of cities are determined, in part, by technological changes affecting transportation, communication, sources of power or energy, and industrial production. Thus, the 19th-century city, rooted in the technology of coal, iron, steel, and the railroad, has been succeeded by the metropolitan community of the 20th century, based upon electric power, the automobile, and an increasing flexibility in the spatial location of economic activities. In examining these two urban patterns, we will focus on (1) the types of community they produced, (2) the city-building process itself, and (3) the relationship between physical environment and social organization.

FIRST PHASE

Extending from the colonial period to the 1920's, the first urban phase was marked both by an increase in the number of cities and a concentration of greater proportions of the total urban population in the larger cities. This phase was completed about 1920, when the urban population of the United States first exceeded the rural. The number of urban places (population of 2500 or more) increased from 24 in 1790 to 2722 in 1920, when more than half the total urban population resided in cities of 100,000 or more. Between 1890 and 1920 the urban population more than doubled (from 22 million to 54 million), while the rural population increased by only 25 per cent.

This urbanization process has constituted a central theme of American life. It has been associated with the country's economic growth and the development of social and governmental institutions in many ways, including the following. Cities functioned as centers of commerce and industry, stimulated cultural-technological innovation and diffusion, and served as reception centers for successive immigrant groups. Class-, income-, and ethnic-stratification patterns which developed in cities profoundly influenced the broader pattern of social and economic mobility in the United States. Furthermore, city-building itself constituted a vast economic enterprise, a kind of people's capitalism, organized around the speculative acquisition, subdivision, and sale of land. And the concentration of large, heterogeneous populations in cities created distinctive problems of sanitary and social control which resulted, at an early date, in pressures to expand the service and welfare functions of government.

COMMUNITARIAN SETTLEMENTS

The colonial period foreshadowed a number of subsequent city or community types. The New England farm village of the 17th-century Puritans emerged as the fountainhead of the American communitarian tradition—a deviant from urban norms. Communitarianism included a number of non-sectarian groups, like the Owenites and Fourierists (Utopian Socialists of the early 19th century), but its main strength derived from the religious convictions of the Puritans and later pietist or millennarian sects of the 19th century, such as the Shakers, Rappites, Mormons, and Oneida Perfectionists. The distinctive feature of the

Fig. 30-1. Shaker community, Canterbury, New Hampshire. (Photos by author)

communitarian farm village, exemplified in the Puritan settlements of the early 17th century, was the subordination of individual goals and aspirations to those of the community. The homogeneity of the population and a commitment to the single, overarching goal of salvation provided a source of cohesion and discipline unusual in American community life.

Physical form and social aspiration were closely related in the communitarian farm village. Its small scale and compactness in comparison to the southern plantation system or the dispersed farmstead, which prevailed in the North and West, facilitated community supervision and control. In the case of the Puritans, new towns were established by groups rather than individuals. They devised a system of regional colonization in which new settlements reproduced the civic and religious institutions characteristic of the Puritan polity. The establishment of towns was conceived as a group or community function rather than a speculation for purposes of individual economic gain. In all these aspects —non-speculative attitude toward the land, co-ordination of physical plan and socio-religious aspiration, and controlled group settlement on a regional scale in towns limited in size—the early Puritans and the communitarians generally were atypical.

CAPITAL CITY

A second community type to emerge in the colonial era was the capital city; examples are Annapolis and Williamsburg, followed by Washington, D. C., in the 1790's. These towns introduced in dramatic fashion some of the leading design motifs of Renaissance-Baroque landscape architecture and site-planning: circles, radials, axes, rond-points. They launched the tradition of civic design and embellishment in America, and provided a source of inspiration to the architects, planners, and civic reformers active in the City Beautiful movement of the late 19th and early 20th centuries.

PORT CITIES

The commercial port cities of the colonial period—New York, Philadelphia, Newport, Charleston, and Boston—were more representative of future urban development in the United States than either the farm village or capital city. Heterogeneous in population, uncommitted to the transcendent communal goals of the sectarians, their existence was based upon economic functions and disciplines. Individual rather than public decision-making played an increasingly decisive role in determining their physical and social environment. Social organization became an incidental by-product of pecuniary aspirations: market disciplines, the price mechanism, and the imperatives of speculative and commercial capitalism shaped the life of the community.

Philadelphia and Charleston had originally been planned towns. Although designed with commercial purposes in mind, their founders had made some provision for public open space and civic institutions. In time, physical planning and development in American communities were disassociated from social planning and organization. Thus, it was not the social needs of the population which were uppermost in the minds of the commissioners for Manhattan Island, whose 1811 report led to the imposition of a rigid gridiron street system up to 155th Street; their explicit purpose was to serve the needs of trade and commerce, which they believed would benefit from a plan that facilitated the movement of goods and vehicles from river to river. This same street plan ultimately encouraged the subdivision of blocks into narrow, deep, rectangular lots and the evolution of a notorious tenement-housing style.

The problem was not that Americans preferred economic individualism and opportunity to the social controls and disciplines characteristic of the communitarians. The problem lay in the assumption that optimum social or civic advantages were necessarily inherent in a commodity concept of urban land and housing. This concept of economic liberalism minimized the need to anticipate the consequences of environmental change. As the commercial city of the colonial period evolved into the crowded industrial city of the 19th century, it became increasingly obvious that the city's success as an economic enterprise did not result in living conditions compatible with the biological and social needs of large segments of the population.

MILL TOWNS

A curious community type, a transitional phase in the development of the 19th-century industrial city, was the New England mill town. The founders of these textile communities—Lowell, Lawrence, Chicopee, Holyoke, Manchester, and Nashua—were determined to prove that industrialization in America need not reproduce the social conflicts and demoralization it had brought to Europe. Beginning at Waltham, Massachusetts, in 1814 and at Lowell in the early 1820's, the "Boston Associates" devised techniques of co-ordinated industrial, town, and social development which had few precedents. The mill town represented an experiment in large-scale, "quanta" planning, encompassing not only industrial engineering but city-building as well.

The structure and location of the mill towns were determined by technological necessity. Dependent upon water power, the mill complex spread alongside a river. Factory buildings and related facilities were often grouped to form a compact quadrangle. Parallel to the river, and approximately a quarter of a mile distant, a main road separated the mill area from the town. Company engineers dammed the river and dug a canal between it and the main road. Factory workers, most of whom were unmarried females from the farms and villages of New England, lived in the two- and three-story brick row houses situated between the canal and road. The mill complex was located on the other side of the canal, by the river.

An austere, functional design prevailed in the early mill town. Places of work and residence were close to one another, but separate. This was an efficient arrangement that avoided the indiscriminate mixture of land uses which contributed to the blight of residential environments in later industrial communities. Although the efforts of the mill-owners to supervise the morals and behavior of their female workers has been criticized as paternalistic, they did assume that those responsible for the economic development of a community were also responsible for housing and residential environment. By the standards of 19th-century industrial cities, the living and working milieu of the early New

Fig. 30-2. The canal in Lowell, Massachusetts. (Photo by author)

England mill towns was spacious and almost park-like. Even in the most purely speculative phase in the organization of a mill town—the subdivision and sale of land—the companies did not entirely ignore civic needs.

The substitution of an immigrant work force for the original Yankee farm girls, the growth of an absentee ownership lacking the paternalistic impulse of the founders, and competitive pressures in the textile industry combined, toward the 1850's, to sever the connection between physical and social planning. Working conditions deteriorated as did the environment of the mill towns. Their Shantytowns, which housed the unskilled labor engaged in construction and menial tasks, had always existed; but by the time of the Civil War, Shantytown had spread and become, indeed, universal.

THE EXAMPLE OF PITTSBURGH

Locational advantages, which included the availability of water power and a supply of unskilled labor, made possible the growth of the New England textile industry after 1815. In light of the strategic importance of locational advantages in the broader urbanization process in the 19th century, Pittsburgh emerges as perhaps the most representative city of the era; it also illustrates, however, the consequences of an urban-industrial development in which social and welfare planning ranked low among community priorities. Compared to industrial organization which was centralized, co-ordinated, and efficient, social planning was minimal and fragmented.

Pittsburgh evolved from a commercial entrepôt serving western and southern markets in the early part of the century to become the iron and steel capital of the world after the Civil War. The Pittsburgh district's competitive advantage lay in its proximity to the rich mineral deposits and other natural resources of western Pennsylvania. The use of coke after 1880 as the major iron-smelting fuel was particularly important in creating Pittsburgh's industrial pre-eminence, for in nearby Fayette County the beehive ovens of the Connellsville region produced the finest metallurgical coke in the United States. No other region could compete as long as coke costs represented the leading differential in pig-iron assembly (and, therefore, steel) costs. The abundance of coal and other raw materials also stimulated the growth of other major industries in the area, including the manufacture of stone, glass, and clay products and heavy electrical machinery. Pittsburgh retained its lead in iron and steel until technological changes enabled metals producers to use competing sources of coal. Proximity to expanding markets then became more decisive than proximity to a single source of coking coal.

Another resource which Pittsburgh and other industrial communities depended upon in the latter 19th century was a supply of unskilled and semi-skilled labor. This was provided by the "new immigration" from southern and eastern Europe beginning in the 1880's. In the Pittsburgh region the workers settled not only in the metropolis, but in isolated mining villages and in the mill towns which lined the Allegheny, Monongahela, and Ohio rivers. The memorable Pittsburgh Survey of 1907-8, which examined the living and working conditions of these immigrants and other wage-earners, found a wide discrepancy between the industrial efficiency of the area and the inefficiency of the social institutions which touched the daily lives of the population. The indictment included "an altogether incredible amount of overwork by everybody, reaching its extreme in the twelve-hour shift for seven days in the week in the steel mills and the railway switchyards . . . low wages for the great majority of the laborers employed by the mills . . . an absentee capitalism, with bad effects strikingly analogous to those of absentee landlordism . . . the destruction of family life, not in an imaginary or mystical sense, but by the demands of the day's work, and by the very demonstrable and material method of typhoid fever and industrial accidents . . . archaic social institutions such as the aldermanic court, the ward school district, the family garbage disposal, and the unregenerate charitable institution." Nothing disturbed the investigators more than the twelve-hour day, seven-day week for many steel-workers, resulting in a "system of speeding, unceasing and relentless, seldom equalled in any industry, at any time."

The fruits of the Pittsburgh Survey included Margaret Byington's *Homestead: The Households of a Mill Town,* a classic account of a community type spawned in the 19th century. Her study focused on the impact of economic and environmental change upon family life and social institutions. She criticized the failure of those responsible for the community's economic development to regard living conditions as a factor of production. "The mill which demands strong, cheap labor," she complained, "concerns itself but little whether that labor is provided with living conditions that will maintain its efficiency or secure the efficiency of the next generation."

Originally established as a residential suburb of Pittsburgh in the 1870's, Homestead's industrial phase opened with a glass factory in 1878 and a steel mill in 1881 (later absorbed into Andrew Carnegie's empire). The protracted, violent strike at the Homestead steel plant in 1892 precipitated the destruction of unionism in the Pittsburgh area steel industry, and insured that the worker would have little share in determining "his hours, his wages, and the conditions under which he works,—and which in turn vitally affect the well-being of his family."

According to the Census of 1900 the native white inhabitants of native white parents were already a minority 36 per cent of Homestead's population. A survey of the men employed in the steel mill in 1907 indicated that a majority were of Slavic origin. English-speaking and foreign-speaking groups led parallel lives with minimum social intercourse. Class stratification contributed to the breakdown of community cohesiveness. As in other mill towns, there were a large number of unmarried transients, mostly immigrant males; because of the nature of the employment, the population generally included a disproportionate number of males. The stabilizing influence provided by normal family relationships in other communities was less evident in Homestead.

It was not only the preponderance of males and the ethnic and class fragmentations which undermined Homestead as a civic entity; political and topographical obstructions also limited the community's capacity to identify and cope with its problems. The original steel works were situated in Homestead borough, a small triangle whose base parallelled the Monongahela River. The expansion of the mill along the river-front stimulated additional settlement to the east and west. These settlements were not absorbed by Homestead; instead, two new boroughs were created, Munhall to the east and West Homestead. Each of these autonomous jurisdictions had its own set of officials, ordinances, and tax levies. Thus, in contrast to the industrial sector, the civic sector was hopelessly atomized. Homestead, the central borough, had the largest population and concentration of low-paid workers, but tax revenues there were diffused and inequitable; most of the mill property was located in Munhall, yet its borough and school tax were little more than half the rate of Homestead's. Since assessors were inclined to value smaller properties at the highest rates, the large industries contributed a disproportionately small share of taxes.

Health and housing conditions reflected the planless, small-scale, unco-ordi-

Fig. 30-3. Pittsburgh housing, old style. (Photo by author)

nated process of development in the civic sector. Homestead's water supply was drawn from the Monongahela River, polluted by the sewage of numerous towns and villages, as well as by industrial wastes and acid discharges from mines. Individuals could draw water from wells, but these were frequently contaminated by discharges from privy vaults. In nearby Pittsburgh, but on a larger scale, lack of municipal regulation contributed to "inadequate, unsanitary, toilet accommodations, insufficient water supply, cellar rooms unfit for habitation, unsightly accummulations of rubbish, ashes and garbage in yards and cellars, [and] dilapidated old shacks that look as if a puff of wind would demolish them." Before Pittsburgh built its water-filtration plant in 1908, the typhoid death rate of 130 per 100,000 was the highest in the United States. Polluted water and substandard housing were partially responsible for the excessive mortality rate of 24 per 1000 in Homestead at the time of the Survey. No business corporation, certainly, would have allowed its production facilities to be developed in the disordered, sporadic manner of the housing environment. Beyond Munhall, for example, was "the Hollow," a "deep ravine with a meandering stream at the bottom and with irregular rows of houses, often hardly more than shanties, on either side." There were no streets leading to the "250 frame, box-like houses, many of them no larger than two rooms," in which unskilled mill workers resided.

Fig. 30-4. Cherry Street tenements, New York City, 1908. (Courtesy of *Museum of the City of New York*)

BACKWARDNESS OF THE BUILDING INDUSTRY

In view of overwhelming population pressures, there was perhaps no way to avoid many of the sanitary and housing problems which plagued Pittsburgh and most other American cities. The difficulties were intensified, however, by a faulty building industry, which remained, in contrast to other sectors of the economy, comparatively underdeveloped in terms of technology and management. Localized, small-scale, speculative, and technologically primitive, it confronted a challenge of mass production for which it was structurally unequipped. It did not benefit from economies of scale or mechanization. Major advances in building technology, such as the steel frame and elevator, had greater significance for commercial and office-building design than the wholesale construction of low-cost housing. Large aggregates of capital found more profitable investment outlets than housing, which remained the domain of the petty entrepreneur.

Subdivision practices in American cities, adapted to the limitations of the building industry, provided little inducement for design innovations. In New York City, for example, the standard 25- by 100-foot lot in tenement districts proved ideal for speculative use by developers working with a limited capital margin, but not for multi-family habitation. The builder erected one or a few tenements at a time. He had neither the desire nor opportunity to experiment with large building groups or site plans that might maximize light, air, ventilation, and open space. In the absence of mechanization or mass-production techniques, the only way to reduce housing costs and simultaneously improve the residential environment was through progress in site-planning and design; yet land-division practices and small-scale building operations precluded significant advances in this direction.

URBAN REFORM

By the late 19th century, dissatisfaction with the housing and living conditions of the wage-earning population produced a vigorous reform movement. In few cases, however, did the health and housing reformers, settlement and charity leaders, or sponsors of city planning and zoning address themselves to fundamental changes in the form and structure of cities. Their object, rather, was to define and legislate minimum standards in housing, public health, parks and open space, and other matters affecting the safety or welfare of the urban population. The major contribution of this urban-reform tradition was to challenge the assumption that social progress was an inevitable by-product of economic enterprise, and to establish norms of public intervention and control.

THE GARDEN CITY

A more radical reform approach, with important implications for city-building and social planning, originated in England. The Garden City, first proposed by Ebenezer Howard in *Tomorrow: A Peaceful Path to Reform* (1898), represented, in essence, a wholly new community type. Howard described it as a "magnet" combining the advantages of town (population concentration) and country (open space). The Garden City posed an alternative to the great urban aggregates which created problems of congestion in housing, health, and transportation, and in the preservation of space for recreational and civic purposes, and led to the speculative appreciation of land values which induced further congestion.

The Garden City raised some fundamental questions about the urbanization process. Were there optimum limits of size for a city (depending upon the social or economic objectives desired), and, related to this, could the advantages of urban concentration be attained through a regional grouping of smaller communities? Howard's answer was "yes." Another question concerned the scale of urban planning and development and whether quanta, or large-scale, planning was preferable to development by smaller parcels such as lots and blocks. The Garden City type was to be a large-scale enterprise, well planned, and community-owned.

Howard, in order to insure the first goal of limited size, proposed the creation of a permanent greenbelt surrounding the city. Use of the greenbelt for agricultural and recreational purposes would also contribute to the general objective of balanced communities, combining the advantages of town and country and containing diversified economies for the employment of the inhabitants. Howard favored a system of co-operative landholding. This, he believed, would insure that increments in land values benefitted the whole community, not just a few individuals, and would also minimize temptations to overcrowd or misuse the land. Finally, because the entire community would be planned, civic needs could be anticipated and facilities provided in adequate number. Following the organization of a Garden City Association in England in 1899, the First Garden City Ltd. was formed in 1903. It established the town of Letchworth, followed by Welwyn.

THE REGIONAL PLANNING ASSOCIATION OF AMERICA

The Garden City idea aroused some interest in the United States, but had no appreciable impact until the organization of the Regional Planning Association of America (RPAA) in 1923. A small, informal group which lasted for ten years, its accomplishments were largely attributable to a few architects and social critics, including Lewis Mumford, Henry Wright, Clarence S. Stein, and Benton MacKaye.

The RPAA accepted Howard's premises concerning limitations on the size of cities and the advantages of large-scale development, but went beyond him in devising a broader community-planning synthesis. Quanta development suggested to members of the RPAA the principle of organic or cellular growth—whether by superblocks and neighborhoods or on the scale of an entire community—in contrast to the mechanical pseudo-planning of cities. Thus, Mumford described contemporary city-building practice as "the addition of blocks and avenues to the original center, proceeding automatically and without limit." In the 1920's and 1930's Stein and Wright concretely demonstrated the advantages of large-scale site-planning and design at Sunnyside Gardens (Long Island), Radburn (New Jersey), and Chatham Village (Pittsburgh). In these communities they experimented with superblock subdivision, the grouping of open space into interior parks, and the separation of vehicular from pedestrian traffic.

Howard's concept of a federation of cities, limited in size, was expanded by the RPAA to include a broad program of regional reconstruction. This encompassed not only Garden Cities, or the later New Towns, to divert population from already overcrowded central cities, but renewal of the central areas, whose loss of population and deflation of land values would provide an economic basis for redevelopment (preferably by neighborhood or cellular units). In general, the RPAA visualized the emergence of a "regional city" pattern, in which a grouping of smaller communities or older central cities with satellite New Towns would ensure the advantages of urban concentration, but avoid both excessive concentration and low-density suburban diffusion.

The RPAA's community-planning synthesis differed in one other respect from Howard's older Garden City proposal: it was concerned, to a greater degree, with the implications of technology for the location and form of cities. The RPAA maintained that electricity, which could distribute power over greater distances more efficiently than steam, and the automobile provided a technological basis for dispersing and regrouping population according to its concept of the regional city. The location and growth of cities were less dependent than in the 19th century upon rail transportation or proximity to mineral fuel supplies; regional mobility afforded by the automobile diminished further the need to concentrate activities and institutions in central cities (particularly in their cores).

THE METROPOLITAN REGION: THE SECOND URBAN REVOLUTION

The RPAA recognized, in fact, that a process of deconcentration was already well advanced by the 1920's, when the rate of central city growth began to decline relative to the buildup along its fringes. A new community type had appeared, forcing a re-evaluation of traditional concepts of urban form and structure. From the viewpoint of the RPAA, the crucial question was whether this regrouping of population and institutions would produce a coherent pattern of community forms and relationships on the regional scale, or whether it would cause disintegration of the older, compact, urban fabric.

R. D. McKenzie's, *The Metropolitan Community* (1933), marked one of the first and most incisive interpretations of the new urban phase. "By reducing the scale of local distance," he explained, "the motor vehicle extended the horizon of the community and introduced a territorial division of labor among local institutions and neighboring centers which is unique in the history of settlement." Metropolitanization implied the emergence of a "supercommunity," which obtained its unity "through territorial differentiation of specialized functions rather than through mass participation in centrally located institutions."

In the context of the metropolitan division of labor, the central city itself assumes a specialized role. Rather than serving as a concentrated reservoir of diverse ethnic and racial groups and of cultural and economic activities, the central city loses many of its older economic functions, retains others, and experiences the increasing migration of middle-class citizens to the suburbs. More than a quarter of a century ago McKenzie perceived the locational shifts leading to the concentration in the central city of "certain functions, notably communications, finance, management, and the more specialized commercial and professional services," and, conversely, the regional dispersion of "manufacturing, the less specialized forms of merchandising, and institutions catering to

leisure-time activities." Later studies of the New York City and Pittsburgh regions have emphasized this changing role of the central city in the territorial
division of labor. There has been a departure of many retail, wholesale, and
manufacturing activities, balanced by an increasing concentration of small-
plant, style-conscious, or administrative-management activities dependent upon
external economies and rapid, face-to-face communication.

This second urban revolution, like the first, which directed a majority of the
population into cities by 1920, has severely strained older social and governmental institutions. Fragmented municipal jurisdictions and planning agencies
were not designed to deal with the functional relationships and problems on the
metropolitan-regional scale of such matters as transportation, air and water
pollution, waste disposal, platting and subdivision control, and the preservation
of open space. Much of the improvement in living standards and residential
environment associated with the metropolitanization process has in fact been an
outcome of increased national productivity and higher incomes rather than of
conscious direction or planning of the demographic and institutional changes
occurring within metropolitan areas. As in the past, market disciplines—to a far
greater extent than public or community policy—have been decisive in determining urban form, location, and growth.

Beginning in 1910, the Bureau of the Census included the "metropolitan district" among its enumerations. This was changed to the Standard Metropolitan
Area (SMA) in 1950 and the Standard Metropolitan Statistical Area (SMSA)
in 1960. The SMSA is defined as a central city of 50,000 or more inhabitants,
the county in which it is situated, and contiguous counties which meet certain
criteria (telephone calls, newspaper circulation, retail store activity, traffic
counts) indicating social and economic integration with the central city. The 168
SMA's of 1950, with a population of 89 million, had increased to 212 SMSA's
in 1960, with a population of 112 million.

An increasing percentage of the national population has concentrated in the
metropolitan areas since the 1920's. Equally important, the most rapid population growth has occurred outside the central cities. The Committee for Economic Development pointed out in 1960 that a majority of the metropolitan
population still resided in the central city, but no less than 80 per cent of the
population increase since 1950 had been in the suburbs. Of 13 million dwelling
units constructed in non-farm areas between 1946 and 1958, 85 per cent were
in the suburbs. A sample of 48 metropolitan areas indicated that the number of
production workers in central cities had declined from 66.5 per cent in 1929 to
53.6 per cent in 1954. By 1975, it is predicted, 60 per cent of the 140 million
persons residing in metropolitan areas will live outside the central cities. In
short, the American population is centralizing in metropolitan areas, whose
suburbs are witnessing the most rapid growth rates of all. The total population
of the United States increased by 18 per cent between 1950-60; but that of
metropolitan areas increased by 26 per cent (compared to 7 per cent else-

where). Within the metropolitan areas, the population of central cities grew by less than 2 per cent, compared to nearly 62 per cent in the suburbs.

THE PROBLEM OF GOVERNMENT

One might describe the metropolitan region as a giant network of functional relationships in search of a form and government. The territorial community, despite its common problems, does not coincide with governmental jurisdictions. The economic unity of metropolitan areas (expressed in terms of banking services, transportation, labor mobility, consumer purchasing, and manufacturing) exists in a context of governmental fragmentation which adversely affects the region's capacity to overcome its economic or social handicaps. As a consequence of the governmental vacuum, private and voluntary organizations often assume responsibility for studying and acting upon areawide problems.

The same vacuum has paved the way for widespread adoption of the special district authority. This quasi-autonomous substitute for government and planning on the metropolitan scale can be understood as an expedient designed to cope with functional problems transcending single jurisdictions while perpetuating free enterprise in land use and government policy. Special district authorities are characterized by limited functional responsibility and fiscal-administrative independence; rarely multi-purpose, they commonly deal with transportation, schools, recreation, health and sanitation, police and fire protection, water supply, or waste disposal. Their strategic role in metropolitan areas was delineated in a comprehensive study by John C. Bollens (1957), who found that special districts constituted approximately two thirds of the 116,000 governmental units in the United States. Thirteen out of every 20 governmental units were special districts—11 in the school and 2 in the non-school category. Moreover, 40 per cent of local government employees were paid by a special district, and giants like the Chicago Transit Authority and Port of New York Authority exceeded entire states in such categories as outstanding debt, number of employees, and annual revenue.

The special district rather than annexation, city-county consolidation, city-county separation, or metropolitan federation, emerged in answer to the fundamental metropolitan dilemma—a territorial diffusion of power and decision-making and the existence of problems which transcend single jurisdictions and require a more centralized administration. In contrast to the other approaches, the special district poses the least threat to the autonomy or corporate identity of local governments. Despite a post-World War II flurry, annexation had reached its zenith about the turn of the century. Apart from Toronto, Canada, the few approximations to metropolitan federation in recent years include the cautious experiments in Miami-Dade County, Florida, and Nashville-Davidson County, Tennessee.

One of the serious limitations of the special district is its minimal role in the co-ordination of policies and services, and in the development of comprehensive planning for metropolitan areas. Special districts have functioned as one of a multitude of corporate jurisdictions which compete in the broader context of "municipal mercantilism." Individual communities attempt to control their environment through a combination of fiscal and land-use policies, supplemented by aid from states or the federal government. Decisions affecting assessments, taxes, expenditures, zoning, and subdivision are particularistic and competitive. Suburbs vie with each other and the central city for outside financial assistance and for businesses which maximize tax revenue but require minimum community services. District authorities similarly compete for revenues and dominance, and it is not surprising that the most powerful are those which, according to Robert C. Wood, "exhibit an operating philosophy most closely akin to a market economy. The public agencies that define needs according to the criteria of the individual consumer, that have revenues dependent on direct-user charges, and that aim toward the satisfaction of the purchaser are the agencies that make the most influential decisions."

Since decisions and priorities in the public sector tend to reflect the competitive market values of the private sector, services which are non-revenue-producing or low in consumer preference often lack political support and adequate financing. A good example is the limited air-pollution control program in metropolitan areas compared to the expenditures affecting automobile use. Although physicians and public-health experts suspect that a relationship exists between air pollution and a variety of ailments (including chronic bronchitis, pulmonary emphysema, bronchial asthma, lung cancer, and non-specific upper respiratory diseases), the federal government did not launch a research and technical assistance program until 1955. A Division of Air Pollution was first established in the Public Health Service in 1960, and in 1963 a three-year, $90 million grant-in-aid program was launched which authorized three-quarter grants to regional authorities and two-third grants to single jurisdictions engaged in air-pollution control. In contrast to these federal efforts is the 90 per cent subsidy, $41 billion Interstate Highway program authorized by Congress in 1956 (amended in 1962 to make federal grants after July 1965 contingent upon broader metropolitan-planning procedures).

State and local action has been limited in scope, effectiveness, and financing. California in 1947 authorized the establishment of county air-pollution control districts, and Oregon in 1951 provided for an air-pollution study and control program. By the early 1960's, some 33 states and territories had a program of some kind, but only 17 were spending as much as $5000 a year. Fifty-seven per cent of the entire state expenditures of $2 million applied to California alone. Of the 85 local programs only 34 had budgets of $25,000 a year or more, and 7 of these were in California. California accounted for 55 per cent of the total local expenditures of $8 million, while the Los Angeles Air Pollution Control District was responsible for the expenditure of more than 41 per cent of all local money.

There is a relationship between the air-pollution problem in metropolitan areas and the rise of the automobile as the favored method of transportation. The automobile produces many fuel combustion contaminants. In Los Angeles, for example, the infamous smog is created by a combination of the nitric oxide from various forms of combustion and the hydrocarbons from autos. Nitric oxide reacts with oxygen to form nitrogen dioxide which, in turn, reacts under the sun with hydrocarbons to produce ozone and other contaminants. The experience of Donora, Pennsylvania, in 1948 and London in 1952 demonstrated that prolonged air inversion and heavy smog can be a lethal combination.

As public transit systems raise fares and reduce services in unequal competition with automobiles, auto use soars further (with its accompaniment of air pollution). In a number of communities, efforts are being made to develop a more balanced transportation network. These include the Bay Area Rapid Transit Project in San Francisco, the combined Congress Street Expressway and rapid transit in Chicago, the subway system in Toronto, and the Mass Transportation Demonstration Project in Massachusetts (involving fare reduction and service experiments in the Boston region and other parts of the state). The Massachusetts study concluded that the declining trend in public transportation use was reversible, that "selected, incremental" improvements could be self-sustaining, and that increase in volume of use was more dependent upon service frequency than lower fares.

It seems unlikely, however, that public transportation, any more than the central business district, can function as it did in the pre-automobile age. The American consumer's preference for the automobile and for low-density suburban settlement precludes the passenger volume which makes public transit economically feasible. In all probability, public transportation will make gains, but only as a supplement to the auto in the performance of limited, specialized services pertaining to downtown areas, commuter, and peak-load or rush-hour traffic. The federal Urban Mass Transportation Act of 1964, authorizing $375 million in grants and loans, assists those communities seeking improvement or expansion of their public transit facilities.

Even major changes in population distribution or community structure are less likely to diminish automobile use than to effect changes in circulation patterns. A New Towns program comparable to England's might alleviate commuting pressures somewhat and encourage a more balanced traffic-circulation system, but it is highly improbable that automobile use would suffer perceptibly. Changes in governmental and planning policy could, however, serve to contain the automobile; its use could be reconciled more successfully with residential safety and convenience, and the salvaging of valuable space currently devoted to roads and parking facilities, for example. Utilizing such techniques as the superblock, differentiated road system, and separation of pedestrian and vehicular traffic, Stein and Wright provided an object lesson at Radburn, New Jersey, in the 1920's.

HOUSING AND RENEWAL

Various federal grant and loan programs affecting transportation and other functions in metropolitan areas have done little to contain the automobile or prevent land misuse. Indeed, as population pressures increase, and urban fringe land is developed at the rate of 1 million acres a year, federal and state governments support programs which not only lack co-ordination, but which are frequently contradictory or archaic. Federal and state assistance to the New York Metropolitan Area, for example, is second only to the property tax as a source of revenue. This assistance helps the suburbs to preserve their autonomy and resist, if so inclined, co-operative efforts dealing with areawide problems. While the suburbs jealously guard their prerogatives, the central city, despite a declining population and tax base, is expected to serve a daytime population up to 50 per cent greater than its residential population and to provide disproportionately higher welfare services as the area of first settlement for low-income migrants.

Federal mortgage-insurance and road programs encourage the suburban migration, and federal and state assistance helps the suburbs survive economically. Simultaneously, the federal and state governments finance public housing projects as well as urban-renewal programs unrelated to areawide planning and with the contrary objective of reclaiming population or traditional economic-cultural functions for "downtown."

The clearance of slums and obsolete facilities through urban renewal serves a useful purpose, even though population continued to decline as much as 10 per cent in central cities during the 1950's and retail sales in central business districts dropped even more precipitously. One can, moreover, appreciate the desire of hard-pressed central city governments to increase revenues by using renewal to stimulate high-rental apartment or commercial construction. On the other hand, urban renewal has done little to increase the low- and middle-income housing supply and, indeed, has reduced the net housing stock through its operations. The renewal projects currently planned or in progress would affect only a fraction of the millions of substandard dwelling units in metropolitan areas.

Renewal, conceivably, could be more effective if related to tax reform in metropolitan areas. Slum property, as a rule, is taxed nowhere near its true market value, a situation which encourages slum formation while it delays the conversion of existing slums to higher use. Adoption of a differential or higher tax on land than on improvements might encourage improvement and better maintenance of property by owners, as well as more efficient land use throughout the metropolitan area. Low taxes on unimproved land lead to its speculative withdrawal from the market and a leapfrogging development process which is both wasteful of land and inconvenient as the commuting distance is lengthened. Another undesirable consequence of the speculative appreciation of land values, attributable, in part, to the existing tax structure, is the increased difficulty of acquiring land cheaply for recreation and other public uses.

FOREIGN PLANNING PROGRAMS

The United States has nothing comparable to the community planning or New Towns program instituted in Britain in 1946. Fifteen New Towns, containing a population of more than 500,000, had been established by public-development corporations by the end of 1962, and three more were designated. The New Towns in Britain testify, as did Letchworth and Welwyn earlier in the century, to the viability of Ebenezer Howard's original Garden City principles. They were planned as cities limited in size, but combining residence, employment, and other normal urban functions. In New Town design, use has been made of the superblock, pedestrian shopping plaza, cluster housing, and neighborhood sub-units.

Britain's Town Development Act of 1952 provided as a supplement to New Towns a means of reducing overcrowding in older centers, redistributing population, and controlling land use: it enabled local jurisdictions such as the borough council (exporting authority) to contract with other local jurisdictions such as the district council (receiving authority) to accept a population over-spill. As an inducement to the receiving authorities, the central government provides development subsidies. By the beginning of 1960, nearly 40 overspill schemes had been approved, the majority in the London and Birmingham areas. Even though fifteen New Towns had been completed as of 1967, the overspill problem still remained.

The impressive community-planning efforts in the Stockholm region of Sweden are based upon municipal land ownership and extensive public-development powers, a coherent mass-transportation policy, and regional planning. The regional plan, adopted by 47 communities and approved by the national government in 1960, attempts to concentrate population in large neighborhood units or satellite communities, like Vällingby and Farsta, located along radial transportation lines. The world-famous satellite town of Vällingby, nine miles from central Stockholm by subway, is four square miles in size and contains a population of approximately 25,000. The heart of the community consists of the colorful six-acre shopping center astride the subway tracks. Vällingby is the urban hub for four nearby residential communities, which form a crescent around a lake and forest preserve. The farmland site had been purchased by the City of Stockholm in 1930. Completed in the 1950's, Vällingby was designed by the Stockholm City Planning Commission.

COMMUNITY PLANNING AND HOUSING

Large-scale community planning in England and Sweden has important implications for housing policy. The wholesale development of entire neighborhoods and towns makes possible economies of scale otherwise unobtainable. The building of large, new communities on open sites minimizes the difficult relocation problems arising out of slum clearance and renewal in the United States, and creates opportunities for innovation in design and subdivision. Finally, low-cost housing, even more than land, has achieved the status of a public utility in Europe, where public housing programs began much earlier and have been far more extensive than in the United States.

The United States depended exclusively upon private enterprise to provide shelter for low-income groups in the explosive period of urban growth that extended from the late 19th century to World War I. Government intervention in the housing market was limited to negative, minimum-standards legislation, which could prevent the worst housing from being built but could not produce an adequate supply of good, low-cost housing. European nations during the same period, confronted with overcrowding and a deterioration of health and housing standards in their urban communities, experimented with a variety of constructive measures: public housing and low-interest loans to co-operative and other non-profit building organizations (particularly in England and Germany), loans to individual workers, and tax exemptions. Publicly assisted housing programs were expanded and improved during the 1920's, a period of extraordinary creativity in the architecture and design of low-cost housing. Public housing in England, Germany, Holland, and other nations of Western Europe, benefitted from extensive use of the superblock, the skillful grouping of row units, and neighborhood unit planning. J. J. P. Oud in Holland and Walter Gropius and Ernst May in Germany were among the architects of large housing developments which, according to Catherine Bauer, were epochal "quite as much in plans, social criteria, and construction methods as in aesthetic expression." For a brief period the architects and designers of the Bauhaus "International" persuasion shared with the political left and organized labor-consumer groups an impulse to improve the physical environment through rational, scientific planning and full utilization of modern building technology.

By the early 1930's, approximately 15 per cent of the population of Western Europe resided in homes built with government assistance. No less than 75 per cent of new residential construction in Western Europe since World War II has received some kind of government subsidy. In 1959, twenty-five per cent of all housing in Britain was publicly owned. Public housing represented 90 per cent of all housing built in 1950. Over 2 million public dwelling units were erected in Britain between 1945 and 1960 (when public housing accounted for approximately 50 per cent of new housing during the year). Public housing is also extensive in Sweden; public and non-profit co-operative housing account for half the new housing stock since 1945. The Swedish programs are supplemented by family-income subsidies or allowances. In the United States, on the other hand, fewer than 600,000 units of public housing have been built since a program was instituted in the 1930's.

European countries have not adopted the systematic renewal procedures initiated in the United States in 1949. Urban renewal is, nonetheless, widespread. It has occurred through rebuilding of war-devastated areas, inherited procedures for slum clearance and estate development, private investment, and in response to problems of downtown congestion, traffic, and obsolescence. It would seem, on balance, that European cities have less to gain from the emulation of American renewal practices than American cities might gain from scrutiny of European land, community-planning, and public housing policies. European experience in community-building is particularly significant in demonstrating the constructive role allotted public agencies, in contrast to the American tendency to offer inducements (as in mortgage loan insurance or urban renewal) to private enterprise.

MEGALOPOLIS

The governmental, housing, and planning challenges of the American metropolitan community may, in time, be superseded by those of the megalopolis, or "urban region." In a study of the urbanized Northeast extending from the New England to the Virginia seaboard, Jean Gottmann has argued that the "density of activities and of movement of all kinds is certainly the most extraordinary feature of Megalopolis, more characteristic even than the density of population and of skyscrapers." Here, even more than in the case of the metropolis, "we must abandon the idea of the city as a tightly settled and organized unit in which people, activities, and riches are crowded into a very small area clearly separated from its nonurban surroundings."

The disintegration of traditional forms and functions of cities, associated with the rise of the metropolis and megalopolis, has tempted some observers to sever the link between urbanization and territorial boundary. According to Melvin Webber, a planner, the term "urban" now suggests a cultural rather than a geographical phenomenon. In the past, he maintains, transportation and communication technology, as well as patterns of class stratification and mobility, encouraged compact, high-density settlement around a central core. By the mid-20th century, however, declining costs of communication and transportation, in addition to intensive specialization and increased mobility, created a radically different urban pattern. Proximity to fuel resources and rail transportation became less important in shaping the location, growth, and structure of cities than "non-transportable on-site amenities." And, as urbanites interact more frequently over greater distances, "the spatial patterns of their interactions with others will undoubtedly be increasingly disparate, less and less tied to the place in which they reside or work, less and less marked by the unifocal patterns that marked cities in an earlier day." An "urban realm" is evolving which is "neither urban settlement nor territory, but heterogeneous groups of people communicating with each other through space." Planning, therefore, must be adapted to flows of communication and interaction rather than to forms and structures based upon territorial proximity.

Some critics, including Lewis Mumford, perceive urban anarchy. "What began as a flight from the city by families," Mumford argues in *The City in History,* "has become a more general retreat, which has produced, not so much individual suburbs as a spreading suburban belt." Although the suburbs potentially "provided the elements of a new kind of multicentered city, operated on the regional scale, their effect has so far been to corrode and undermine the old centers, without forming a pattern coherent enough to carry on their essential cultural functions on anything like the old level."

The theory of the "urban realm" exaggerates the breakdown in relationship between territory and activity. For all our capacity to compress the frictions of time and space, it is highly unlikely that territorial proximity will become a secondary consideration in the daily lives of most people. Even ultra-mobile individuals—business executives, academicians, and other professionals—do not spend all their time in planes, communicating and interacting through the far-flung "urban realm." The domestic and child-rearing functions, and most forms of employment, remain rooted in territorial space. It is realistic to assume that questions of neighborhood and community-planning, urban form, and group relationships within a limited territorial space will remain important.

TECHNOLOGY AND COMMUNITY DEVELOPMENT

Suburbanization can be seen, in part, as a response to the dissatisfaction and frustration generated by the residential environment of American cities. Critics like Mumford argue, however, that while we are taking advantage of the economic and technological circumstances which permit diffusion and decentralization, we are not exploiting them imaginatively, thus allowing economic expediency to determine the form and structure of the metropolitan community. Rising national productivity and per-capita income levels, governmental programs of financial assistance, electric power, the automobile, and the continuous-flow assembly line, which have produced the existing metropolitan pattern, also permit a new approach to planning and community development hinted at in the British New Towns. This necessitates not tract development, but the creation of entire communities. Less congested than the older urban centers, more diversified than the suburbs, they would contribute to a more compact development of fringe land.

What will be the form and structure of the future metropolis? The answer to this depends upon whether or not an effective unit of government is devised somewhere between the municipal-county and federal-state level. Also, the balance between market disciplines and coherent public policy will affect population distribution and land use. The evolution of cities will follow from developments in these two related areas.

Part **IX**
Technology and the State

31 / Technology and Public Policy
MORGAN B. SHERWOOD

Technology and public policy are closely related phenomena. The relationship extends far back in time to the beginning of written history, and even into pre-history. Archaeologists identify the progress of old human cultures by designations like "Stone Age" and "Bronze Age," terms which refer to the relative sophistication of technological progress in ancient social orders; often, the more effective the tool or implement unearthed, the more advanced the culture it represents.

The new devices or tools modified social relationships and created new conditions and problems for the primitive societal organization. A shift to agricultural pursuits from hunting might call for a new type of tribal organization, and the development of superior weapons—no matter how crude by modern standards —might result in larger states with attendant organizational adjustments. Undoubtedly, ancient tribes not only reacted to the problems created by technological improvements, but also at times encouraged the use and further development of the new tools and techniques; it is equally reasonable to suppose that some of the improvements were deliberately suppressed for religious, political, or social reasons.

Professor R. J. Forbes has pointed out how the need for large-scale irrigation in Mesopotamia required more co-operation and led to bigger political units organized as "hydraulic provinces." The great pyramids were clearly the result of governmental "policy" decisions to satisfy the pharaohs' religious desires and glorify permanently the rulers of Egypt. The pyramids not only created engineering problems of design and construction, stimulating technological progress, but they also raised policy questions of labor supply and finance. The Classical civilizations emphasized public works, military technology, and efficient transportation and communication. The Greek governments built aqueducts to furnish good water for drinking and bathing. Cranes were utilized to raise the heavy elements of public edifices. Alexander the Great encouraged the development of mechanized warfare. The Hellenistic rulers, and later the Romans, acquired and improved the Persian road system in order to consolidate their great nations and empires.

The emphasis on public works and military technology was also apparent in Renaissance Italy. Leonardo da Vinci, for example, worked as a military and civil engineer for the rulers of Milan, Romagna, and France. In Leonardo's famous letter of application, dated about 1482, to Ludovico Sforza, duke of Milan, two paragraphs are devoted to his ability as a civil engineer and only one to his artistic talent; ten are concerned with his skill as a military engineer.

POINTS OF CONTACT

Governments promoted technology as a matter of policy, and such activities in turn helped the governments carry out other public-policy measures. Very often, technological progress created social problems that demanded the attention of governments. Thus, a glance at the relationship between public policy and technology reveals two major points of contact: first, governments make policy decisions about whether or not to promote technological innovation; second, they are confronted with the question of how to deal with social problems arising from the advance of technology. The decisions and solutions are never automatic and seldom easy: together they result from the policy process current at a given time in a given place.

Historically, governments have adopted a number of policies to promote technological progress. They have (1) guaranteed certain privileges to the innovator through patent systems; (2) passed restrictive legislation to discourage both the dissemination of technical information and competition from other more technically advanced states or communities; (3) supported technical education and training; and (4) made outright grants to bring about specific innovations, to establish laboratories and scientific institutions, and to support new technical industries.

PATENTS

What might have been a patent proposal, depending upon how one translates Aristotle, was advanced in ancient Greece by Hippodamos, but the earliest patent law on record was enacted in 1474 by the Republic of Venice. In the British colonies of America, the Massachusetts "Body of Liberties" (1641) stated that there "should be no monopolies but of such new inventions as were profitable to the country, and that for a short time only." Under that authority, in 1655, one Joseph Jenks was granted a patent on a new type of grass scythe. The General Court of Massachusetts apparently decided the privilege was for a "new invention," and was not a "monopoly."

By 1790, each American state had its own patent regulations, and the new national constitution empowered the Congress "To promote the Progress of Science and useful Arts, by securing for limited Times to Authors and Inventors the exclusive Right to their respective Writings and Discoveries." Accordingly, the first federal patent law was passed. The third patent issued under the law went to Oliver Evans, a key figure in the early history of American technology. Patent applications flooded in, making it difficult to hear and adjudicate each claim; in 1793, another law required only that the inventor swear to the originality of his device and pay a fee. The courts were soon inundated with patent litigation, and finally, a Patent Office was established in 1836 to investigate claims before issuance.

The first United States patent law was administered by an inventive American—then Secretary of State Thomas Jefferson. Although Jefferson thought that ingenuity should receive a reward and that an inventor should be "allowed a right to his invention for some certain time," he also apprehended the social danger of granting exclusive privileges. Patents, he said, "ought not to be perpetual; for to embarrass society with monopolies for every utensil existing, and in all the details of life, would be more injurious to them than had the supposed inventors never existed; because the natural understanding of its members would have suggested the same things or others as good."

The problems which Jefferson recognized have continued "to embarrass society" and to call for public solutions in every country with a patent system. The United States Patent Office was transferred from the Department of Interior to the Department of Commerce in 1925, in recognition of the closer connection of patent policy to the nation's business community. The transfer did not resolve patent problems once and for all. A dozen years later, the National Resources Committee, in a policy report on technology and planning, claimed that the Bell Telephone System had "suppressed 3,400 unused patents in order to forestall competition." The report stated: "The telephone came into existence over the bitter opposition of the telegraph companies. The radio telegraph was fought by the telephone companies. The radio telephone was fought by the telephone, telegraph, and radio telegraph interests. Although corporate organizations do develop and utilize many inventions, sometimes corporations will fight successfully against the passage of laws requiring them to adopt modern improvements." Whether it is profitable for a corporation to suppress inventions for any length of time is moot; nevertheless, a segment of the public remained suspicious that such a practice existed, and the question of suppression under the patent system was therefore an element in the continuing debate over patent policy.

The basic policy issue—how to encourage invention without supporting monopoly and its abuses—reached a new dimension in the United States following World War II, when the government began its massive support of research. The absence of a uniform patent policy for discoveries made, in whole or in part, under federal research contracts to private firms prompted Senator Russell Long to take note in 1961 of "the fantastic values involved here and the tremendous cost to the consumer to buy back something that he had paid for already . . . to buy it back at a monopoly price, are so enormous that it would seem to me that we are failing to protect the public interest if for a small cash saving we make it possible for persons to have these enormous patent monopolies that we are creating with $9 billion a year Government-financed research." Earlier, a debate over patent policy had delayed the passage of a National Science Foundation bill; the debate focused on the same concern about who was to get patent rights to inventions coming out of federally supported research.

In April 1965 President Lyndon B. Johnson appointed a Commission on the Patent System to determine the current state of the patent system and make recommendations for possible revisions, in response to complaints regarding the complexity and expense of patent litigation and delay in the granting of patents. The Commission's report, issued late in 1966, recommended various measures to speed up the processing of patents and to reduce expenses, to hasten the disclosure of innovations, and to bring American patent policy more in line with that of other nations; however, it said nothing about the question of ownership of patents resulting from government-sponsored research.

RESTRICTIONS AND LAISSEZ-FAIRE

Another way government policy promotes technology is through restrictive legislation—to protect a technological advantage by prohibiting the export of technical information and devices, and to protect technical industries through tariff barriers.

The first approach, a policy of secrecy, was employed in Byzantium during the time of Emperor Justinian, when silk manufacture was a state monopoly. In the last half of the 18th century, the English Parliament passed laws to prohibit the export of machinery and tools used in cotton manufacturing, and the woolen and silk industries; also designs, plans, and other information about industrial machines. In general, such policies proved to be ineffective, and were abandoned in favor of the patent system.

The second form of protective legislation to promote technology—the tariff —has been adopted for several economic reasons. Although there is considerable disagreement over their effects on technological progress, tariffs are, nevertheless, advocated in part as aids to technical industries. The English colonies in North America suffered under a kind of reverse tariff: the mother country passed a Woolens Act in 1699 which forbade the production of woolen cloth for export from the colonies; the Hat Act in 1732 prohibited the manufacture of hats; and the Iron Act of 1750 restricted the manufacture of particular iron implements. After the Americans won their independence, they used the tariff chiefly as a revenue measure; then the War of 1812 with Great Britain cut off imports and stimulated American manufacturing. Faced with British industrial competition after the war, the new United States industries called for a protective tariff on woolen, cotton, and iron manufactures; it was passed in 1816. American tariff policy wavered thereafter. Before the McKinley tariff of 1890, the country imported most of its tinplate from Wales. By 1900, a new American tinplate industry, benefitting from a tariff on imports, had replaced the Welsh product on the American market.

The British were, in the meantime, converting to a policy of laissez-faire (or free trade) in international commerce. In 1789, William Pitt proposed over 2500 resolutions to modernize the complicated tariff structure of Britain. The work was continued after the Napoleonic Wars. An act of 1825 repealed more than 1000 laws and gave the United Kingdom her first streamlined tariff structure. By then, British leaders were converts to 19th-century laissez-faire economics. Pitt himself acknowledged the influence of Adam Smith's *Wealth of Nations* (1776). The English free trade movement gained additional momentum in the 1830's and 1840's under the leadership of Richard Cobden, a cotton manufacturer. The Cobden Treaty of 1860 with France moved the latter nation temporarily toward anti-protectionism, and further treaties with other European countries reduced tariff barriers selectively.

On the other side of the question, the German economist Friedrich List, in his *National System of Political Economy* (1841), urged a policy of economic nationalism, which included a protective tariff for German states organized in the *Zollverein*, and extension of the German railroad network. List thought free trade was all right for Great Britain, a technologically advanced country that would prosper from an open world market, but that a laissez-faire policy was undesirable for newly developing industrial states. As a result of these and other objections, free trade never won a complete and final victory.

Recently in the 20th century the trend has been toward bi- and multi-lateral, reciprocal trade agreements, and the often dim relationship between tariff policy and technological progress has become even more obscure. Both protectionist and anti-protectionist elements have argued their cause in the name of a healthy industrial economy.

TECHNICAL EDUCATION

A third way by which governments promote—and influence the direction of—technology is by support of technical training and education. France pioneered in the education of engineers with institutions like the École National des Ponts et Chaussées, established in 1747, and the École Polytechnique, one of the first important engineering schools.

Other countries did not fail to appreciate the French policy toward technical education. In 1776, George Washington asked his minister plenipotentiary in Europe, Benjamin Franklin, to secure four skilled French engineers to assist in the Revolutionary War. The Frenchmen remained Washington's technical advisers throughout the conflict. The need for trained military engineers led Washington and others to urge the establishment of West Point, which was, during the first half of the 19th century, the new nation's main source of engineers for western exploration and civil and military construction projects. German states also followed the French lead. The Prussian Peter Beuth, as head of the Department of Trade, planned the foundation of the Berlin Industrial Institute (1821). In the United States, federal support of higher education took a giant step forward in 1862, when President Lincoln signed the Land-Grant Agricultural College Act, setting aside public lands for the establishment of state universities. The act promoted "such branches of learning as are related to agriculture and the mechanic arts." Despite a slow start in the 19th century, by 1959 sixty-eight land-grant colleges in America enrolled some 600,-000 students. Today almost every national government sponsors scientific and technical education through the direct support of colleges, universities, and technical schools of various types; through research and training grants; and through scholarships, fellowships, and loans.

Another general category of governmental activity to promote technology is outright grants for specific technical achievements or for laboratories and other scientific institutions and industries both in and out of government.

Prize money was an early type of outright grant for a specific technical breakthrough. Toward the end of the 16th century, King Philip II of Spain offered a prize of 100,000 crowns for a method of determining longitude at sea. The Dutch promised a similar award. Galileo himself competed for the prize. Samuel F. B. Morse, in 1843, received $30,000 from the American Congress for an experimental telegraph line from Washington, D. C., to Baltimore.

Samuel Langley's studies in aerodynamics at the Smithsonian Institution were supported in part by public funds. Experience in the Spanish American War moved the government to find a substitute for the balloon. Langley's carefully researched, power-driven aircraft was tested in 1903, and when it failed to perform properly, the press proclaimed the airplane a waste of public funds. Congressman Joseph G. Cannon said a few years later that he was thoroughly ridiculed for approving the $10,000 appropriation for Langley's flying machine: "I was cartooned as Mother Shipton riding through the air on a broom, and was given no end of notoriety because of that modest appropriation." Langley was Secretary of the Smithsonian Institution when he did his aeronautical research. The Smithsonian had been founded in the mid-1840's, with the government as trustee; along with West Point, the Coast Survey, and the Naval

Observatory, it was one of the nation's earliest scientific institutions. After Langley's failure, Alexander Graham Bell kept alive the Smithsonian's interest in aeronautical research, and the Institution organized an air-research committee.

In part because of the war in Europe, Congress in 1915 authorized support for a National Advisory Committee for Aeronautics (NACA). The NACA operated the Langley Aeronautical Laboratory and conducted research on the scientific problems of flight. These problems took on a new order of magnitude with the launching of the Space Age in 1957, and in 1958, on the advice of the Bureau of the Budget, the Nelson Rockefeller Committee on government organization, and the new presidential science adviser, the Eisenhower Administration sponsored a bill for a redesigned NACA to investigate and direct the United States space program. The National Aeronautics and Space Administration (NASA) was established in that year. Perhaps the two most important policy facets of the decision to create NASA were, first, that the committee approach was abandoned *de facto* for a stronger central administrator, and second, the new space program was to be put under civilian control.

Another 20th-century bureau served the more immediate demands of technology. In the last quarter of the 19th century, the United States Treasury Department began, on a very slight budget, to operate an office of weights and measures. Even so, American bureaus and technical industries often sent their instruments abroad for calibration. The private National Academy of Sciences noted in a resolution dated 1900 that "the facilities at the disposal of the Government and of the scientific men of the country for the standardization of apparatus used in scientific research and in the arts are now either absent or entirely inadequate. . . ." As a result of these and other pressures, the National Bureau of Standards was founded in March 1900. The NBS has, since that time, maintained linear, thermometric, barometric, electric, metallic, weight, tool, and other standards; tested baseballs; and developed an instrument (blind) landing system for airplanes, the proximity fuse, an atomic clock, and a base for false teeth, to name a few of its activities and achievements.

The technological demands of World War II and the postwar interest of the American government in research led to a new kind of relationship with technical, non-profit institutions. The National Science Foundation in 1957 reported twenty-two "illustrative" types of research facilities outside government but supported by federal agencies. The types of financial arrangements included:

(a) construction grants on matching basis, with recipient organization responsible for all operating costs; (b) construction at Federal expense and lease to institution; (c) construction at institution expense, with Government then paying a "user charge" under annual research and development contracts with the institution; (d) construction at Federal expense and operation through a "management contract" with institution or other organization; (e) direct Federal support of operation and maintenance through grants or contracts specifically designed to cover operating costs; (f) indirect Federal support of operation and maintenance through grants or contracts covering research projects at the facility and against which facility overhead and maintenance costs are pro-rated; and (g) various combinations or variations of the foregoing.

Research centers thus financed which remained after World War II include the Los Alamos Scientific Laboratory, administered by the University of California (atomic energy research), and the Jet Propulsion Laboratory at the California Institute of Technology. Other federally supported, non-profit, civilian research institutions, like the RAND Corporation, will be discussed elsewhere.

GRANTS TO PRIVATE ENTERPRISE

In addition to financial support for "in-house" laboratories and for research centers outside the governmental hierarchy, public policy has also aided some private technical industries.

In colonial New England, the Massachusetts General Court granted John Winthrop, Jr., 3000 acres of land to develop a salt works. In France, also in the mid-17th century, Pierre-Paul Riquet de Bonrepos convinced Louis XIV's great minister, Colbert, of the wisdom of constructing a canal across the isthmus connecting France and Spain. Riquet eventually received provincial as well as national support for his private canal-construction company, and the Grand Canal of Languedoc was completed in 1681. In America, state governments took the lead in canal-building. In 1817, New York State began the construction of the Erie Canal, between the Hudson River and the Great Lakes. Completed in 1825, it was an immediate success. Other states soon planned and built their own canals, but not always with equal financial results. For canal-building during the first half of the 19th century—and wagon roads too—the federal government often granted right-of-way lands and sometimes made additional land grants to aid in defraying the expense of construction.

Similar grants were also made by states and by the central government for railroad construction, and in 1862 the Transcontinental Railroads Act was passed, authorizing grants of land as a basis for credit to finance the coast-to-coast railways. The total public land received by all railroads was about 131.5 million acres, of which approximately 91 million acres was for the Pacific lines. The states granted another 48.9 million acres. The national government also loaned the railroad companies more than $64.5 million at six per cent interest. In retrospect, it was a shrewd policy; by 1898, the railroads had paid over $63 million on the principal and $104.7 million in interest. What was more important, the new transportation routes helped to open the West for settlement and industry; stimulated other manufactures, such as steel; promoted related technological innovations; and provided the training ground for a new cadre of engineers.

In numerous other ways public policy has promoted technology through financial assistance. For example, governments have dispatched agents to investigate the technological accomplishments of other countries, and have encouraged the dissemination of technical information by publication or by sponsoring special meetings. For the American contributions to England's great Crystal Palace Exhibition of 1851, the United States government provided only maritime transportation, but for later world's fairs, the Congress made more substantial appropriations. The country sponsored its own fairs in 1876 and 1893. The increased respect for the value of participation was related to the success of the American exhibits. At the Crystal Palace, United States farm machinery out-performed competitors; indeed, American exhibitors won more medals in proportion to the number of items displayed than many European countries.

In 1884, to promote the new electrical industry, Congress appropriated $7500 for a conference of electricians. A National Inventors Council was organized in the United States in 1940; during the five years of war that followed, the Council received over 200,000 ideas for innovations, talked to over 14,000 inventors, and saw more than 100 inventions put into production or use. Today, on a more routine level, both the Department of Commerce and the National Science Foundation have offices to expedite the interchange of technical information.

PROBLEMS OF SOCIAL DISLOCATION AND ECONOMIC PRESSURES

After promotional activities, the second major area of contact between public policy and technology is the necessity of dealing with the social problems created by technological progress and by governmental activities designed to encourage such progress. We have hinted how a patent may result in monopoly, how a tariff to protect one industry may affect others adversely, and how new technical industries and transportation facilities may alter economic and social conditions. Since other chapters consider facets of this subject and because it is the core of many volumes of political and economic history already written and to come, the point will be investigated only briefly here.

Alexander Hamilton's financial program for the new American nation called for the payment of the national debt at par and the creation of a national bank; the two measures were, along with tariffs and bounties, designed to encourage domestic manufactures by creating capital and stabilizing credit. The issues raised by Hamilton's economic nationalism served to divide the nation's leaders into political factions that formed the basis of the American political party system.

In England, and later in most of Europe and in the United States, mechanization and the factory system created labor problems that necessitated govern-mental interference. The authors of the satirical volume *1066 and All That* have described the British reaction:

The new situation created by the Industrial Revelation was boldly met by the statesmen of the day with a wave of Acts, such as Tory Acts, Factory Acts, Satisfactory Acts and Unsatisfactory Acts. The most soothing of these enacted that children under 5 years of age who worked all day in factories should have meals (at night). This was a Good Thing, as it enabled them to work much faster.

The tariff and free trade issue divided political and economic interests in England. The focal point of the British argument was the Corn Laws, which protected local farmers with a tariff on grain imports, to the dissatisfaction of many manufacturers. In the United States, the economic roles were reversed: agricultural factions, particularly in the South, objected to duties on imported manufactured goods. The question of support for canals and other internal improvements also contributed to political factionalism, and the increasing sectional conflict delayed a decision over a route for the transcontinental railroad. The Pacific Railroad Act was signed by Lincoln in 1862, after the outbreak of hostilities between North and South.

The American courts have also been forced to react to problems raised by technological innovation. Robert Fulton and Robert Livingston received the exclusive right to operate steamboats in New York State, and from this monopoly Aaron Ogden was given the privilege of operating steamboats across the Hudson River to New Jersey. Thomas Gibbons began to compete with Ogden, and the New York courts upheld the latter's monopoly; however, the United States Supreme Court in 1824 supported Gibbons, under the federal right to regulate interstate commerce. The decision was one of many affecting technical industries.

The problems created by technological progress in the 20th century defy summary. Technology has even been blamed for the Depression of the 1930's and a thousand other spectacular social ills. Applied governmental contract research in universities has been criticized for diverting higher education from its main goals. Nuclear energy has created potent foreign as well as domestic problems. The promotion of air and automobile transportation has produced a wide variety of social problems that have drawn the attention of public officials at every level of government. Individual technical bureaus have become entangled in numerous political disputes. For example, the earliest serious domestic controversy of President Eisenhower's administration involved the seemingly insignificant question of whether a particular additive prolonged the life of auto batteries. The manufacturer said it did; the National Bureau of Standards said it did not. When the NBS director, Allen V. Astin, was asked to resign, the scientific community protested, claiming that the objectivity of science was being subverted by partisan politics. Astin kept his job.

THE POLICY PROCESS

A third major connection between technology and public policy is in the policy-making process itself. With rare exceptions, the government, throughout American history, has approached technological issues pragmatically, one at a time, the same way it has dealt with most national concerns. When the need for military engineers became obvious, West Point was founded; when the British dumped goods on the American market after the War of 1812, a tariff to protect the country's infant industries was passed; when internal communication and transportation were needed, canal- and railroad-building were promoted; when steam navigation became popular, a Navy Bureau of Steam Engineering was created to study the associated problems; when manned flight was young, the NACA was established; and so forth. Policy-planning for technology is mainly a 20th-century phenomenon, but the government still tends to seek solutions to problems as they arise. Creation of the Atomic Energy Commission and an office to study desalination of sea water are two examples of recent approaches.

During the early years of this country, the Congress, the Executive, and the courts made policy decisions, often without advisory assistance. Sometimes a special agency was founded, or an investigating committee organized; the latter was the case in the 1880's, when the Allison Commission of Congress looked into the organization of federal scientific pursuits. The National Academy of Sciences, a private institution, was chartered by Congress in 1863 to report to and advise the government when called upon; it was asked for advice now and then, but not until the 20th century was the advisory approach employed extensively. During World War I, the National Research Council, its members drawn from many scientific institutions, was joined to the Academy. The Academy also had its own Committee on Government Relations for a few years after 1925, and in 1933 the Science Advisory Board—also attached to the NAS-NRC—was created by Executive Order. As a high-level science advisory group, the Board competed in the 1930's with a science subcommittee of the National Resources Committee (later the National Resources Planning Board).

The National Resources Committee took its policy and planning functions seriously, and issued long and controversial reports on the social implications of science with such titles as *Technological Trends and National Policy, Relation of the Federal Government to Research,* and *Industrial Research;* the last was prepared for the Planning Board by the NAS-NRC. Though the Planning Board was elevated to the Executive Office of the President, it disappeared during World War II, when its advice ran afoul of the powerful organization of Army engineers, a group that has managed to resist close Executive control. With the severe demands upon technological resources occasioned by World War II, the Office of Scientific Research and Development was organized. The practice of contracting out research gained a secure foothold in the OSRD.

Co-ordinating committees proliferated after World War II. In 1947, a President's Scientific Research Board published a hastily compiled report with policy recommendations. The Interdepartmental Committee on Scientific Research and Development, a co-ordinating group composed of government agency representatives, became involved in, among other things, the problem of patent policy. A Science Advisory Committee of the Office of Defense Mobilization was designed to help answer high policy questions; it was the direct ancestor of the President's Science Advisory Committee, established after Sputnik I. Other advisory groups were organized at the departmental level. One—the Research and Development Board in the Department of Defense—spawned dozens of technical subcommittees, panels, and subpanels, reducing the committee approach to an absurdity. The trend now appears to be toward stronger central administrators and advisers.

All the committees mentioned were technical in nature, and intended to provide the government with specialized advice in matters of scientific policy. Problems were bound to arise. Who was to make policy: the technicians or the duly elected and appointed representatives of the people? Although not originally formed to deal with this problem, a promising staff agency was born in 1921, with passage of the Budget and Accounting Act. Located in the Treasury Department until 1939, when it was elevated to the Executive Office, the Bureau of the Budget soon became the President's general staff agency. The Bureau's main function in relation to science and technology was to make a reconciliation between technical advice and the nation's general policy posture. Since recommended technological and scientific projects had one thing in common—the dollar—the budget became a major policy instrument of the federal government, just as it became a chief instrument of municipal reform during the Progressive era. Dollar-project balancing has developed into a fairly precise, rational, policy procedure, especially in the Department of Defense.

Today, public policy for technology is essentially a matter of reconciling private economic and occupational interests with the public interest, and the key concerns are the same as those in other areas of society: Can private interests do the job, and if not, is the problem of sufficient importance to warrant governmental activity? If it is, how much of a claim, in terms of available resources, does the activity have in relation to all the other demands made upon public resources? How well these questions are answered will determine how well public policy deals with what Lewis Mumford considers our "over-commitment to technology."

32 / The Problem of Social Control
LESLIE H. FISHEL, JR.

Appearing before the Temporary National Economic Committee in 1939, Charles F. Kettering, the head of General Motors Research Division, testified: "We are way behind technologically . . . , I am trying to invent a way to get new industries started." Kettering, an inventive genius, was correct. Although American industry spent more for research than any country in the world, except for Russia, the United States seemed backward in many respects in 1939. Germany had great automobile freeways (autobahns) and was experimenting with rockets. Twenty years earlier, England had established a government department of scientific and industrial research with an initial budget of £1 million, and in the 1930's the Soviet Union began the large-scale co-ordination of research. In the United States research was still fragmented. The explanation lay in differing attitudes toward social control.

THE IDEA OF SOCIAL CONTROL

The concept of social control—shaping the use of national resources for national benefit—gained favor in Europe after World War I but remained dormant in the United States. While European nations, smaller in size and resources, recognized the profound implications which science and technology could have on a national basis, the United States identified these implications in bits and pieces, and then ever so reluctantly. The men who sparked innovation thought in terms of greater technological efficiency without regard to its total impact on society. Kettering was relatively far-sighted, but he spoke from the point of view of an industrialist whose chief concern was satisfying a market demand through the exploitation of scientific and technical knowledge. Consideration of technological and societal issues was neither broadly conceived nor very constructive. For example, problems concerning patents, technological unemployment, industrial profits, crop fertilization, and dam construction were handled separately.

England, Sweden, and in an infamously extreme way, Nazi Germany, were all trying to do more with technology than satisfy pressures for high profits and consumer products. Over and above these twin demands, each sought to utilize technology for national purposes so that the fruits of technological progress would add fiber and strength to their nation as a whole. In the United States, the question might have been phrased in this way: how can technology be adapted to make the American experiment a truly democratic one in which every individual can maintain his basic rights, exercise equivalent privileges, and confront a wide range of opportunities? Between the wars, Americans were slow to raise and grapple with this issue.

The Great Depression following the 1929 stock market crash was a case in point. Characteristically, Americans cited technology as a major cause of that economic holocaust, but they seldom viewed technology as a force which could be constructively used to alleviate the depressed conditions. Henry Wallace, as Secretary of Agriculture, was a minority voice when he asked how far should government "concern itself with the conservation of those human and material resources which technology and corporations have tended to misuse and waste?" It was not only corporations—although they were a favorite target of Wallace's —it was American society, its government and its people, who failed to see in technology the potential for greater total use of the nation's physical and human resources.

THE CONSUMER IN A BUSINESS SOCIETY

Although the United States had been "first" with some inventions and types of industrial production before World War I, it was not until after 1918 that the full impact of a technological society began to make its mark. In a real sense, Americans woke up suddenly to the fact that their industrial power was technologically based, that it was changing rapidly, and that whatever other ramifications this had—and most Americans did not care about those—it meant more efficient and more luxurious consumer products.

In one way, Americans were prepared for the change. World War I had familiarized American soldiers and war workers with gasoline and diesel engines, the airplane, rapid mass production in factories, high-power small arms and ordnance, and heavy machinery. Since it was the first war of machinery, Americans were not unaware of the vague promise of technological advance that might be realized after the Armistice.

In the textile industry, for example, the mechanization begun in the 18th century was still advancing. The Northrup automatic loom came into use before the turn of the century, and a significant improvement, a warp-tying machine, was introduced after the First World War. This machine tied 250 threads a minute and did the work of 15 operators. The Northrup machine was adopted by new mills in the South, but established New England mills could not afford it, since installation meant new plant layouts as well as extensive capital investment. Southern mills prospered during the 1920's. New England mills had their peak year in 1923, but by 1927 there were more spindles in the South. The impact of this on the consumer market was obvious—more cloth at lower prices

—but the impact on society generally was more complex. Skilled craftsmen lost out to semi- and unskilled labor, and one region's economy suffered at the expense of another's prosperity; on the level of a community or a family, it sometimes meant economic disaster or salvation.

Every widespread consumer innovation had deep-seated and far-reaching repercussions on the economy, and on the physical and mental well-being of the nation. For example, as electricity became more commonplace in urban areas in the 1920's, six million Americans trooped off their farms and headed for electric lights, refrigerators, stoves, and similar city conveniences. As offices adopted easy-to-use machinery for adding, subtracting, calculating, billing, addressing, duplicating, dictating, folding, and sealing during the 1920's, women took over the office work of the nation. By 1930, there were for the first time more women than men in office work, almost two million of them. Families dressed in machine-laundered clothes, lived in vacuum-cleaned homes, filled their refrigerators with foods packaged in newly invented cellophane or canned by new high-speed machines. The radio brought news and nonsense with breathtaking speed; the automobile extended the family's horizons. In the summary phrase of sociologist Robert S. Lynd in 1932, the consumer emphasis had changed from making a living to "buying a living."

The consumer's problem, Lynd added, was "one of selection to a degree never before known." Herbert Hoover, as Secretary of Commerce in the mid-1920's, had called 900 conferences to reduce the number of varieties of manufactured products. Although Hoover's efforts were rewarded with some reductions—for example, 78 kinds of blankets were reduced by industrywide agreement to 12, and 49 kinds of milk bottles were reduced to 9—the consumer was still faced with a bewildering mélange of products and bombarded by an accelerating volume of advertising. Between 1909 and 1929, periodical and newspaper advertising expenditures jumped from $200 million to over $1 billion annually. In 1929, radio added expenditures of $75 million and an additional $600 million was spent for advertising in other forms. Advertising "makes new thoughts, new desires, new actions . . . ," President Calvin Coolidge commented, adding that "it is the most potent influence in adopting and changing the habits and modes of life." Manufacturing technology created both the products to sell and the vehicles by which to sell them, and the consumer was trapped by this exploitation of his own latent desires.

However, the problem of social control was not yet recognized as a problem. The business community was governed only by its own abilities to adapt innovation for profitable production and by its own good judgment. Organized labor was still in its infancy and without the leverage to exercise any countervailing power. The government was content to cater to the needs of business with high tariffs, low taxes, minimal credit restrictions, and the encouragement of business associations.

The trade associations which flourished during the 1920's established industrywide licensing systems, supported the price structure at high levels, underwrote and often controlled industrial research, and publicized industry's products and shaped its public image. By the end of the decade there were between 1000 and 1800 trade associations, most dedicated to improving industry's efficiency and profit margin and to reducing competition. Limited mainly by the internal struggles of the manufacturing companies within an association, these trade groups shaped technological processes for industrial gain. Hoover remarked as President (1929-33) on the "almost unnoticed . . . great revolution . . . in the whole superorganization of our economic life. We are passing from a period of extremely individualistic action into a period of associational activities." Technology was a Pandora's box, to be opened and admired at will, without regard to the consequences.

THE RISE AND FALL OF TECHNOCRACY

The time bomb of unbridled technological exploitation exploded almost without warning in the fall of 1929. The Depression which followed the stock market crash plunged the United States into the most intensive reappraisal of its economic and social trends that it had ever undertaken. Beneath the pollyanna assurances that everything would turn out well, the voices of industry and government rose in shrill, Babel-like confusion, decrying the crisis and pointing fingers of responsibility in all directions.

It remained for a group of scholars, organized by Hoover as the President's Research Committee on Social Trends, to call attention to the basic imbalance in American society. In an introductory statement to their report (1932), the Committee asserted that "closer communications favor centralization in social life, in domestic politics and in international relations." They called for more intensive studies of the social structure, to give direction and purpose to public policy and to avoid the continued "pursuance of a policy of drift." They labelled as the key problem the need to realize "the interdependence of the factors of our forward movement so that agriculture, labor, industry, government, education, religion and science may develop a higher degree of coordination in the next phase of national growth." In short, the Committee was calling for planning. Unhappily, that word was literally a "red flag" because the Soviet Union had already adopted it and boasted about its planned economy. Americans were already hypersensitive about aping any segment of the Soviet system.

Actually the concept of social and economic planning had American roots. In the 20th century the pioneering writings of the economist Thorstein Veblen (1857-1929) called upon engineers to adapt their inventiveness to social institutions. After World War I, a small group of technically oriented men, including Veblen and the mathematician Charles Steinmetz of General Electric, met informally over a period of years to discuss the problem. By 1928, the American Economic Association was calling for a national economic plan in the United States, and the United States Chamber of Commerce and the American Federation of Labor made similar suggestions. In 1932, Howard Scott, who had years before met with Veblen and Steinmetz, launched a movement to stabilize the economy and social structure of the country by measuring all goods and services in energy units rather than dollars. He called this movement Technocracy.

Scott was a man of mystery. He had earlier flirted with a radical union, the Industrial Workers of the World (IWW), and had once owned a small floor-wax factory. He claimed to have been studying the output of energy and its relation to technological progress for twelve years in a precursor organization known as the Technical Alliance. Flamboyant and evasive, Scott was responsible for the flurry of publicity about Technocracy in late 1932 and early 1933.

He first came to public notice following a speech before a branch of the American Statistical Association in June 1932. He called for "the development of a social system based on scientific control of national resources and manpower." In August of the same year he announced that his survey of energy was nearing completion and that it was being carried on under the auspices of Columbia University. Under that respectable umbrella, Scott's pronouncements gained a wider audience. *The New York Times* scoffed at Scott's claims, asserting that his data merely confirmed the obvious fact that machine production had accelerated along with unemployment, and that his predictions and speculations were those of "a plain human being like the rest of us." But the general public, baffled by unemployment and buffeted by financial hardship, was titillated by technocratic pronouncements.

For the next few months the pot boiled over, as Scott and his associates repeated their claims. Cartoonists harpooned Technocracy, the pulpit damned it, and industrialists scorned it. One industry representative claimed that the public had gone "technocrazy," and Will Rogers professed not to know whether it was a disease or a theory. Columbia disassociated itself from Technocracy in January 1933, and the few scholars who had stood with Scott, like Walter Rautenstrauch of Columbia and Leon Henderson of the Russell Sage Foundation, resigned their membership in his organization. Scott was repudiated on all sides, and although his organization still exists, the movement itself collapsed, disappearing from the news and from influential channels of policy-making. Scott vanished from public view almost as suddenly as he had appeared.

The Technocrats' comic-opera antics—what one critic called their constant "air of parade"—clouded Technocracy's contribution to the problems of technological advance and their solution. While their energy theory was enmeshed in gobbledygook and their prediction of 20 million unemployed was a calculated scare tactic, the Technocrats achieved more than they realized.

In 1932, when many were talking about technological unemployment, the Technocrats forced prominent men to examine it closely and express their conclusions publicly. Karl T. Compton, president of the Massachusetts Institute of Technology, ridiculed technocratic ideas but went on to theorize about the causes and possible solutions of technological unemployment. Gerard Swope, president of General Electric, in a panel discussion of Technocracy sponsored by the American Association for the Advancement of Science, called for a guaranteed period of employment and some form of unemployment insurance for workers.

Besides evoking a defensive response from national figures, Technocracy called the public's attention to the need for social planning more dramatically than could established organizations or a presidential committee. Swope agreed to industrial planning on a national level, by trade association agreement if possible, but by congressional action if necessary. It is more than fortuitous that Technocracy first reached public notice during the closing months of the 1932 presidential campaign and that the counter attack on it was mounted immediately after the election. During the campaign Franklin D. Roosevelt had called for planning to create a more equitable distribution of wealth, and approximately twelve months after he took office, Leon Henderson, an early sponsor of Technocracy who had left the movement, joined one of the New Deal's most aggressive planning agencies.

Planning was in the air. Although not of the technocratic variety, it stemmed from the same unrest that had catapulted Technocracy into the limelight, fed on the popular fervor which the Technocrats helped to create, and grappled with the technological problems which the movement had underlined.

THE NEW DEAL

President Roosevelt's inaugural message in March 1933 was more than inspirational. He castigated profit-chasers and called for a war-emergency approach to the economic crisis with "direct recruiting by the Government" to enlarge employment and "stimulate and reorganize the use of our natural resources." He suggested a population redistribution to relieve urban congestion and make more effective use of cultivated land. He warned of the need for an army-like discipline to achieve the objectives of recovery.

The economic crisis which faced the new administration in the spring of 1933 was so acute that there was little time for analysis of causes, only the pressure to get the country moving again. Hundreds of men and women, academicians and professionals the likes of which had never before been seen in the Capital, flocked to Washington. They came with enthusiasm and energy, and with some preconceptions about the nation's economy and future course. From the universities came men like Raymond Moley and Rexford Tugwell of Columbia and Thurman Arnold and Abe Fortas of Yale, while Felix Frankfurter sent dozens of Harvard men to various New Deal agencies. Few of them were originally students of technology, but all became students of a technological society. They were for the most part city-bred and urban-oriented, intellectuals displaced from the ivory tower, wily but not wild-eyed, and ready to experiment. They provided the innovative spark of the New Deal.

One of their number stood apart. Karl T. Compton was already a man of international reputation, a physicist and president of the prestigious Massachusetts Institute of Technology. He was called to Washington to head the newly established Science Advisory Board (1933-35), a federal agency which he hoped would provide the springboard for a resurgent scientific attack on the problems of the nation. For two and a half years, Compton struggled to impress government agencies and the White House with the need for massive support of science. He argued that technology and applied science could be a significant restorative for an ailing nation and that these practical disciplines depended upon a thriving, well-co-ordinated science establishment in industry, the universities, and government.

In 1933, after initially suggesting government expenditures for scientific research totalling $16 million over a six-year period, Compton enlarged his vision the next year, and with the support of the nation's scientific leaders, suggested annual federal expenditures of $5 million for the support of science and technology outside of government. When this was not approved, he scaled down his request to less than $2 million over a two-year period. Even though his spending proposals were matched with a clearly delineated federal structure to channel and direct the research, and were backed by documented needs for research, Compton's proposals were coolly received and finally denied. Frustrated and disillusioned, he left Washington in 1935, not quite understanding why he and his colleagues had been unable to demonstrate the key role which government-supported science and technology should play in the nation's recovery.

It was not unusual during the New Deal to see able men leave Washington with a sense of failure, since the genius of the New Deal, "that man in the White House," was to extract from every contributor the maximum in ideas and stimulation and to let these and their instigators rub and polish against each other until a practicable policy and procedure appeared. This was trial and error, and the errors were enormous, but it was also a typically American way of doing things. More than that, it allowed the New Deal to accelerate a revolution—the introduction of government into almost every phase of American life —without becoming a revolutionary government. It was, in short, a democratic experiment which eschewed dictatorship, a bungling, almost non-directional movement which was without totalitarian efficiency. In large measure, this very approach, the antithesis of a systematic scientific method, minimized the influence of scientists and engineers and subordinated the government's interest in and emphasis upon technology.

THE TENNESSEE VALLEY AUTHORITY (TVA)

Perhaps the best example of the New Deal's exploitation of able men and its lack of policy with regard to technological innovation and application is the Tennessee Valley Authority. Long before 1933 the Tennessee River Valley had been stripped of its natural wealth by lumber, oil, and gas interests, whose legacy to the region was poverty. World War I had stimulated the construction of a dam near Muscle Shoals, Alabama, to make possible the manufacture of nitrate, which was no longer needed after the cessation of hostilities. During the 1920's, efforts to expand the now-unused federal plant into a series of power dams were killed. But President Roosevelt, influenced by Arthur E. Morgan, president of Antioch College and an accomplished engineer, wove together several suggested uses for the Tennessee Valley; and during the first Hundred Days of the New Deal, Congress passed the TVA Act.

From the beginning, the TVA was multi-purpose. Empowered to produce power, manufacture fertilizer, and provide flood control, it was also instructed to prevent erosion, support soil conservation, stimulate small industry, resettle improverished city-dwellers, reforest scrub areas, reduce unemployment, and retire marginal farmlands. "It touches and gives life," said the President, "to all forms of human concern." To the three-man controlling commission the President appointed Arthur Morgan as chairman, H. A. Morgan, a Tennessean influential in agricultural extension work, and David Lilienthal, a young lawyer from Wisconsin by way of Harvard and a Chicago law firm whose specialty was public utilities. It was only natural in such a vast undertaking that the directors would disagree, but it was characteristic of the New Deal that the directors disagreed on matters of basic policy.

The policy differences ran deep. Chairman Morgan was a man of wide social vision who looked on TVA as an opportunity to re-create a region. He wanted to build co-operatives, reform the educational system, and improve the health of the region, as any social visionary would, but he believed that this had to be done by centralized planning and a firm controlling hand. Let anyone refuse to co-operate and Chairman Morgan was willing to let the weight of law and publicity descend upon him. His zeal was for social planning from above and conformity from below. His colleagues on the Authority had a different approach. H. A. Morgan coined the phrase "grass-roots democracy," and Lilienthal used it forcefully. No planning, Lilienthal argued, could proceed without the participation and acquiescence of those who inhabited the land. Lilienthal was

Fig. 32-1. TVA's Wheeler Dam, 16 miles above Wilson Dam at Muscle Shoals, Alabama, aids in flood control, navigation, and power production on the Tennessee River. Construction on the dam began in 1933, and the first power was generated in November 1936. (Courtesy of the *Tennessee Valley Authority*)

for decentralizing policy-making in order to let the people concerned make the basic decisions, and for centralizing the administration of that policy. He looked upon the region, its people, and its organizations, as partners with government in the restorative work of TVA.

For four years, the three directors divided up responsibilities; Lilienthal was in charge of power installation, H. A. Morgan, of agricultural responsibilities, and Chairman Morgan, of dam construction and the social areas of TVA concern. Attacked from the outside by private power interests but making substantial progress in flood control, dam construction, and power production, TVA created what the historian Broadus Mitchell has admiringly called "a social resurrection." Yet the basic issues of policy and planning were left undecided. Was TVA to become a machine for centralized social planning and progress or was it to become merely a vehicle for ecological improvement? The answers could not be provided by a simple policy statement. Too much depended upon the temper of the times and the politicians' sensitivities to them, and on the abilities of individual administrators. By 1937, as the New Deal moved into its reform period, the friction of ideas and personalities had overheated, and Chairman Morgan resigned. The issue of planning versus ecological development became obsolete as TVA braced for attacks from private power interests.

The impact of TVA is too vast for summary. In terms of electrification alone, kilowatt-hour costs tumbled and consumption spurted upwards as lights and electrical appliances were turned on in thousands of homes in the valley. Here was a striking example of technological progress brought about through government intervention. But the larger questions of control and experimentation in a technologically advancing society were left unresolved. Having no separate facilities for research and development, the TVA utilized the work of outside laboratories. While this manifested a constructive degree of co-ordination, it precluded innovative research in a place and at a time when the results might have been fruitful.

The widely publicized economic virtues and vices of the TVA tended to obscure its potential for planning and downgraded the long-range social and economic benefits which had no immediate dollar value. The economic formula which ultimately resolved the conflict between public and private power advocates was politically, not technologically, inspired. And the opportunity which the TVA in its early days offered as a pilot project for planning in a developing technological region was lost in the maze of economic and political charges and counter charges.

SOME NEW DEAL TECHNOLOGICAL MEASURES

The transcendent importance of economic problems so shaped the early New Deal that little else mattered. Industrial productivity had in March of 1933 skittered to a low of 63 (based on a *New York Times* average norm of 100); between twelve and fifteen million people were out of work; average hourly wages in manufacturing were down to 87 (where 1923 = 100). Prices fell, but not as low as technological efficiency would have permitted. Using 1923 = 100, the output per man-hour in manufactures was up almost 50 per cent to 144 and the unit labor cost down 40 per cent to 59. Yet in the spring of 1933 the hue and cry about the technologically caused Depression faded before the overwhelming need to get factories humming and people working and consuming.

In only a few of the New Deal programs was the technological emphasis clear, and even in these it was subordinated to more pressing economic problems. The Civilian Conservation Corps (CCC), established in 1933, put 300,-000 men into parks and forests of the nation in its first year. During its nine-year life, it utilized the technical knowledge and supervision of many federal agencies, including the Soil Conservation Service, the Biological Survey, the Bureau of Agricultural Engineering, and the War and Interior Departments, in its efforts to restore and reclaim the country's natural resources. But the major impetus for the program was the reclamation and restoration of the young men who served in the Corps.

The Public Works Administration (PWA), carefully administered by Interior Secretary Harold Ickes, built schools, sewage plants, hospitals, docks, and a host of essential public structures. PWA funds and engineering know-how helped New York construct its Triborough Bridge. Ickes himself urged the Pennsylvania Railroad to electrify its New York to Washington track, and the PWA provided the funds. His purpose, according to the New Deal historian, Arthur M. Schlesinger, Jr., was to "beautify the national estate," and he used private contractors and technical knowledge to accomplish it. PWA funds were also used to strengthen the military—with ships, planes, ordnance, and military installations—until Congress prohibited this use.

The Works Projects Administration (WPA) was created in 1935 and was, along with other relief measures, administered by the controversial Harry Hopkins. In June 1938, Hopkins reported that all of the agencies under his direction had utilized 3 per cent of their appropriations since 1933 for science and research, although included in this amount were traffic studies and research in museum modelling as well as research of a more truly scientific nature. The WPA also provided professional, technical, and clerical assistance to tax-supported university research projects. WPA funds assisted federal agencies with their research and development needs: soil conservation, plant entomology, Indian affairs, and the military, to name a few. Even in the arts, WPA funds contributed to technical experimentation with the silk screen process, the development of an inexpensive carborundum print process, and the improvement of manufactured paint colors. Because Depression unemployment had affected men and women with technical skills, government work relief penetrated the sciences and technology during the New Deal.

THE NATIONAL RECOVERY ADMINISTRATION (NRA)

In the early New Deal, the project which scored the highest in expectation was the National Recovery Administration, symbolized by a blue eagle. Created by the National Industrial Recovery Act (1933), the NRA was established as an independent federal agency under General Hugh Johnson. Primarily an economic measure, it aimed to revive industry, the heart of the nation's technological power. Taking its cue from the trade association practices of the 1920's, the NRA promulgated codes of fair practice which exempted industries from competition and allowed price-fixing, generally to the advantage of the larger companies within each industry. Apprehensive about any challenge to the NRA's constitutionality, Johnson used publicity and the blue eagle symbol to whip up public support for the codes and their enforcement. In spite of the flurry of publicity, Johnson's fears were realized when the Supreme Court in 1935 declared the NRA unconstitutional.

The NRA's problems were part economic, part philosophic, and part personal, but at base was a failure to understand the nature of the technological push which had both generated prosperity and contributed to depression. In allowing industry to maintain prices without competition, the NRA failed to create purchasing power which could support the price structure. Small businessmen rose up in arms against big-business favoritism disguised as fair practices, while farmers and consumer groups railed against rising prices. Philosophically, the NRA's trade association approach, with the government as partner, alienated New Deal intellectuals within and without the NRA. Some, like Rexford Tugwell, stood for rational planning on a national scale, with the government playing a larger role in the partnership; others, like Leon Henderson, argued for a controlled competitive market, policed by intensive antitrust action, with consumer advisory groups sharing influence with industry, government, and labor. General Johnson's impetuousness contributed to codifying almost every conceivable industry, big and little, wholesale and retail, instead of concentrating on the major ones. The result was a grossly overburdened bureaucratic machinery irretrievably bound by inconsistencies and red tape.

At no point in the industrial activities of the NRA was close attention paid to the potential of technology as a way of increasing production and profit and of fostering new industrial opportunities. The tenor of NRA and the New Deal was rather one of apprehension about further technological unemployment, and Karl Compton's assertions, after the demise of the NRA, merely underlined the vacuum:

Labor-saving and quantity production devices [he wrote in 1937] are largely mechanical and the science of mechanics is already well-established. Economic pressure will continue to force the development of labor-saving devices on the basis of our present mechanical knowledge, and independently of any further scientific advances. Future scientific discoveries, however, are most likely to be in other fields than mechanics, as in chemistry, electricity, biology, or medicine . . . Even if we were to grant the economically disturbing effects of scientific progress, we should still face the immediately practical fact of unemployment and concentrate on an attempt to make science do what it has done many times in the past; i.e., give birth to some great new industries.

Throughout the 1930's, the New Deal addressed itself to the problems of a depressed society. Within this range of activity, however, the role of technological progress was hardly recognized, although in almost every instance, research and development had brought about both the inequities and the corrective measures. Industrial and agricultural production accelerated because of technological advances; the mobility which broke down family responsibilities came about because of technological advances; the exploitation of natural resources, the concentration of people in cities, these and other conditions which the New Deal tried to rectify grew out of technological change. And the measures which government took to correct inequities were founded on technology—rapid communication, improved construction machinery, the expanding science of agriculture, and so on.

THE NATIONAL RESOURCES COMMITTEE

And yet for all that, as Compton pointed out, the New Deal did not directly confront technology as a force to be controlled and channelled, except in two instances. One exception was the National Resources Committee. Growing out of a planning group under the NRA, it was independent by 1935. Its function was to study problems involving national resources and assist state and local planning groups.

During the four years of its existence the National Resources Committee expanded previous studies of water, land, minerals, public-works, and industrial policies and initiated new studies of education, science, technology, population, health, housing, urbanism, transportation, and energy. It was, in essence, a pre-planning body, surveying existing areas of knowledge and bringing together facts and figures, so that state and local groups could organize and plan concrete programs.

Its most significant project was authorized by the President in 1937 and the results published between 1938 and 1941 in a series under the general title *Research—A National Resource*. This study examined the role of science in the nation and reported its extensive growth in and out of government. The major implication of the report, that science and technology deserved central organizational recognition within the government, was, however, not implemented. The NRC's successor in 1939, the National Resources Planning Board, became involved in the war effort and was dissolved in 1943 in a wartime reorganization of federal scientific and technological agencies.

THE TEMPORARY NATIONAL ECONOMIC COMMITTEE (TNEC)

In a sense, the second New Deal confrontation with science and technology also grew out of the NRA. The Supreme Court's 1935 decision outlawing the NRA marked the death-knell of industrial self-regulation concepts which had dominated the agency. As the economy moved slowly upward to 1937 and then suffered a sharp reversal, three different approaches came to the fore. One which went back to President Woodrow Wilson's "New Freedom" stressed the need for competition in a free market with strict governmental controls on monopoly and the interested participation of consumers, labor, government, and

industry. The second approach was taken from the ideas of the British economist John Maynard Keynes, whose major work was published in 1936, and who
emphasized the role of government spending as a balance wheel in the economy. The third approach, that of economy in government and a balanced
budget, was voiced by Secretary of the Treasury Henry Morgenthau.

By 1938, with recession gripping the nation, several presidential advisers who
were followers of the economic precepts of Louis D. Brandeis (who had out-
spokenly attacked the monopolistic practices of big business before his elevation
to the Supreme Court) and of Keynes pressed Roosevelt to create a committee
to study the monopoly structure of industry. In spite of the pleas of Morgenthau, who worried about deficit spending, Roosevelt asked Congress for such a
study. "Private enterprise," he wrote, "is ceasing to be free enterprise and is
becoming a cluster of private collectivisms." When Congress established the
Temporary National Economic Committee (TNEC), the New Deal again confronted the challenge of technology and its implications. The leaders in organizing the TNEC were Thomas G. Corcoran and Benjamin Cohen, two lawyers
who had studied with Felix Frankfurter, and Leon Henderson, a former Tech-
nocrat and chief economist of the NRA.

The TNEC investigation began in December 1938 and lasted eighteen
months. The committee sat for 775 hours of testimony and listened to 552 wit-
nesses. Its published hearings, exhibits, and reports would fill two good-sized
shelves. It suffered from several overriding disabilities. Since it was a political
inquiry conducted in full view of the public, whatever was said had to be stated
with caution and an eye to newspaper and radio headlines. What was more
important, in the elapsed time between the request for the inquiry and the first
hearing, President Roosevelt had suffered a rebuke in the 1938 elections and
had become more sensitive to the deepening foreign crisis. Both developments
made a reconciliation between government and industry more pressing, and
Roosevelt privately reassured reluctant businessmen that the sharp words of his
congressional message would be muted and that the investigation would not be
an attack on industry but an opportunity for industry to state its case and polish
its public image. Under these new conditions, the government's confrontation
with research and development was bound to be more exploratory than exact-
ing, more an exchange of ideas than an invitation to social and economic
reform.

The problem of technological unemployment came under close scrutiny at
the hearings. It was clear that workers were displaced by technological improvements; one reliable estimate asserted that 57 workers in 1939 could do
what 100 workers had done in 1923. In industry after industry, the evidence
accumulated—and the list was extensive. The testimony also revealed a significant by-product of technological unemployment—a definite decline in the use of
skilled workers. This phenomenon made the ground fertile for industrial unionism

and foreshadowed future debates over the effects of automation on labor. But it was equally clear that technology was only one factor at work in creating unemployment and that there was no way to isolate the data in order to evaluate them.

Management had counter claims to offer. The new technology had created new industries and new services which not only took up the slack, but which created a higher standard of living. The automobile, a frequently cited example, required new roads and highways, service stations, petroleum products, home garages, and a miscellany of parts, while the increased mobility it offered encouraged more hotels and improved recreational facilities, and accelerated the expansion of suburbs.

Another facet of the inquiry dealt with the research potential of industry, and it became obvious that industrial research was a healthy baby, indeed. Between 1921 and 1938 the number of personnel engaged in industrial research had tripled; in petroleum it increased five times, in radio and phonograph industry sixteen times, in food and textiles two and a half times, and so on. The research process itself was changing, with group projects replacing the individual scientist or engineer. "I think that one of the hardest problems we have had is to get scientific men to sit down and work on a common problem," Kettering reported to the committee. If a problem can be divided up among metallurgists, chemists, physicists, and others, ". . . then our particular job is to correlate so that when their work comes together, it is the thing we are trying to get made." As Vannevar Bush, a vice president of M.I.T. affirmed, this was "a very new and I think beneficial phase, a group phase." Just months away was the Manhattan Project.

Early in the investigations the committee heard testimony about the patent system which, in its long history, has periodically been under fire. One problem with the patent system was the advantage it gave to corporations with money to come up with patentable innovations. Less than one per cent of the corporations with research staffs employed 33 per cent of all research workers in 1938, so that these firms had an advantage in securing patents which would give them further advantages. Industrywide licensing procedures gave large companies greater control over their competition and in some instances held back innovation. But in the long run, even critics of the patent system had to admit that whatever its defects, it was a sound and democratic process.

Midway in the proceedings, as the proponents of free versus managed technological economy politely argued themselves to a stand-off, the committee heard the feeble voice of the consumer in the persons of the consumer counsel for the Agricultural Adjustment Administration and some private citizens. Their plea was that technology had so strengthened corporations that the consumer no longer had a free choice in the marketplace. Price differentials were slim or non-existent, they argued, and products not labelled. Advertising pressures, they complained, appealed to the emotions and prejudices rather than to reason. Technology had

enabled industry so to vary its products and containers and so to pressure pro-
spective consumers that the confused purchaser no longer decided in terms of
his needs, but rather in terms of his response to marketplace symbols.

The TNEC hearings finally came to an end in 1940, a victim of politics and a
deteriorating international situation. A year earlier, Vannevar Bush had dropped
the prophetic hint to the committee that "if we get into another great difficulty,
we will need research personnel in all fields who will be useful for war research." As the international situation worsened, demanding fuller American
attention, there was no room for debate over the government's economic and
technological policies. By the spring of 1940, the first of several war research
agencies, the National Defense Research Committee, was established. It was
time to stop talking and start planning.

THE FAILURE TO PLAN

The decades between the two world wars were dominated by the presence of
technological advance and, until World War II, by a concomitant inability to
direct technology toward widespread national purposes. During the 1920's the
controls lay outside the government, in an industry which was organized and
expanding at the expense of, and with the passive acceptance of, the government and the general public. Technological progress was subordinated to economic demands to such an extent that national and social needs were largely
ignored.

The Depression created an awareness of the great thrust and potential of
technological progress and evoked some pointed calls for planning. The New
Deal utilized the latent powers of the federal government, but concerned itself
almost exclusively with economic recovery. Yet by the time spokesmen for
science and technology were able to catch the ear of the President, his administration was beleaguered by political opposition at home and the threat of war
abroad. Not until the war was almost upon the nation did the government recognize the need for co-ordination in research and development and the importance of scientific advisers at the highest policy levels.

There are several historically significant reasons for this lack of recognition
during the two critical decades 1920-40. The more general explanations are
commonly understood: the nation's tradition of individual enterprise; its suspicion of a professional elite; its supreme optimism in its ability to ride rough-
shod over crises (an optimism which was almost destroyed by the Depression); and a political system whose stability resisted innovation. But there are
other, more specific, interpretations which may clarify the general problem of
technology and social control in this period.

One of these relates to scientists and engineers themselves, men like Compton, Kettering, Bush, and their colleagues. Brilliant and inventive, these men

were neophytes in a political atmosphere. They needed time, perhaps even a generation, before they could work with confidence in areas of public policy. It is worth noting that after World War II, Compton took the lead in greatly expanding the offerings in social sciences and humanities at the Massachusetts Institute of Technology in an effort to broaden the background of future technological leaders.

A by-product of this insularity was the initial inability of social scientists and humanists, the politicians and the industrialists, really to understand what science and technology were about; the jargon, the methodology, and the relation of what was then called pure science to applied science were alien concepts to most of the nation's leaders. Henry Wallace, a devotee of scientific agriculture, was an exception to the rule.

In still another sense, the backwardness of the social sciences before World War II handicapped the whole process of planning. Information needed to solve problems like technological unemployment, predictions of consumer demand, the impact of new technological developments, and comparable enigmas, was not available in reliable or usable form. Until the computer gave social scientists the ability to digest and interpret huge masses of raw data, would-be planners were working with little more than intuition and outdated information.

If planning concepts during these decades were largely intuitive, the general public could only guess about the problem of technology and social control. Their view of technology was based on consumer products and prices. Although an average middle-aged man in 1940 could trace developments in his lifetime from horse-drawn buggies to airplanes and from the scrub board to the washing machine, few could detect the subtleties of a process which disoriented the family, impinged on the economic system, and altered the role of government in American life. Until the public could appreciate that drift was no longer a sound working policy and that technological progress called for the substitution of greater control, there would be, under the American system, no improvement.

Here, indeed, was and is the nub of the problem. Could technological progress be controlled within the established American system without infringing upon the individual rights which are a cornerstone of that system? The answer which emerged at the end of the 1930's, under the cloud of war, was affirmative, but the war itself was no adequate test tube because of needed wartime controls. It remained for postwar generations to see the dimensions of the problem more clearly than the between-the-wars generation which first identified it, and to take on the challenges of technological progress.

33 / The Challenge of Underdevelopment
JACK BARANSON

One of the major international developments in the years following World War II was the disintegration of the great colonial empires which had been amassed by the European powers over the course of four centuries, ever since the age of exploration and colonization. Throughout Africa and Asia new states have come into being. These emerging nations, imbued with nationalistic zeal for prestige and power, and desiring economically viable states in order to satisfy the material needs of their people, now seek to develop their economies through technological advance. Our own stake in a stable and peaceful world dictates that the benefits of modern technology, now shared by only a handful of the world's population, should serve also those who live in as yet undeveloped countries.

The importance of introducing improved technology in underdeveloped areas has thus been generally recognized. A basic difficulty has been that technologies designed for industrially advanced societies are most often of a scale and sophistication unsuited to the production environments and market demands of developing economies. Typically, technologies that have proven efficient in industrially advanced countries almost invariably result in higher costs or inferior products when transmitted to economies in the early stages of development. Underdeveloped countries either lack the necessary labor and managerial skills or are short on capital, materials, and foreign exchange. Where materials are available, they are often of inferior quality or local suppliers are unreliable; in addition, the products themselves are bound to be different from those produced for affluent economies where incomes are higher and consumer tastes different. Thus, a basic problem of transmittal involves choosing or adapting technologies that will enable recipient societies to utilize more effectively existing resources at emerging stages of development. Adapting technologies to social capabilities and economic conditions can ease the burden of restructuring societies to fit modern techniques and should lessen considerably the human and economic costs.

TECHNOLOGY AND ENVIRONMENT

The choice of which technologies to transplant depends upon cost and feasibility, which, in turn, are influenced by economic and social environments. Technological choices also depend upon whether private profit considerations prevail or broader strategies of social development are taken into account. The ability of an underdeveloped country to innovate and adapt to change is usually low, which means that strategies for technological transformation have to be adjusted accordingly.

There is a two-way interaction between technology and environment. Technology here refers to characteristics of production systems including their scale and organization; factor combinations of labor, materials, and equipment; managerial aspects; and design characteristics of the products themselves. On the one hand, the cost and feasibility of production techniques are conditioned by the economic, sociocultural, and physical aspects of environment. The availability, price, and quality or productivity of factors, are basic determinants of rational technical choice. Political and psychological considerations often compel non-economic choices of more advanced techniques for reasons of prestige and status seeking. Factor price and performance, as we will see, are related to economic conditions and cultural environments.

On the other hand, technology acts as an instrument of environmental transformation. Economically proficient techniques of production can help to educate large numbers of people in industrial skills; provide more effective transportation, power, and communication systems at emerging levels of development; and render endowed physical resources economically exploitable.

ECONOMIC ENVIRONMENTS

Product design and production engineering are influenced by conditions of demand and supply. The size and extent of markets influence the scale and location of production. Market demands also influence the design and price range of the products themselves. Wage levels, capital costs, and the prices on raw materials and other intermediate goods have a direct effect upon the particular mix of labor, capital, and material that comprises a production technique. Implicit in the cost computation are relative productivities of labor and machines and the quality of available materials.

In most underdeveloped countries there are controls on the use of foreign exchange and other trade restrictions. This means choices in production techniques are also conditioned by import restrictions on capital equipment, materials, and manufacturing components that are not available in the domestic economy. The cost and availability of power, transport, and other services have an indirect influence upon factor costs and, therefore, upon factor combinations. The location and organization of production are also conditioned by the economic geography of transport and power facilities.

CULTURAL FACTORS

Individual characteristics and patterns of social organization have a direct bearing both upon products demanded and productive capabilities. Product design

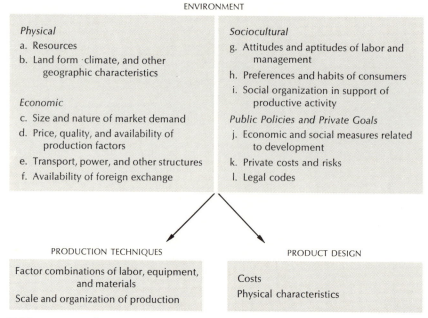

ENVIRONMENT

Physical
a. Resources
b. Land form ·climate, and other
   geographic characteristics

Economic
c. Size and nature of market demand
d. Price, quality, and availability of
   production factors
e. Transport, power, and other structures
f. Availability of foreign exchange

Sociocultural
g. Attitudes and aptitudes of labor and
   management
h. Preferences and habits of consumers
i. Social organization in support of
   productive activity

Public Policies and Private Goals
j. Economic and social measures related
   to development
k. Private costs and risks
l. Legal codes

PRODUCTION TECHNIQUES

Factor combinations of labor, equipment,
and materials
Scale and organization of production

PRODUCT DESIGN

Costs
Physical characteristics

Table 33-1. Influence of environment upon product design and production techniques.

is influenced by the preferences and habits of consumers. Processed foods, for example, must respond to local affinities and tastes. Vehicles and engine design need to be adapted to local driving habits. Housing and appliances must be accommodated to indigenous modes of living. Durability features often have to be built into equipment in response to local habits of maintenance.

Productive capability and related choices among technological alternatives depend upon labor force skills, managerial proficiencies, and patterns of social organization. The cottage industries that played an important role in the industrial development of Japan, and continue to act as sub-contractors in modern industrial complexes, were based upon special artisan skills and unique patterns of social organization. Labor skills and managerial proficiency are critical elements in quality control standards built into many modern industrial systems. Cultural values and patterns of social organizations have a bearing upon industrial discipline, the quality of output, the efficiency of particular man-machine combinations, and the scheduling of operations both within the plant and with outside suppliers.

PHYSICAL ENDOWMENT

The physical geography of a region and its resource endowments are important elements in technological choice. For example, engine design is influenced by climate, altitude, and the slope of the terrain in highway systems. Geographic locations of resources and markets and the existing transportation systems have a bearing upon the scale and location of productive facilities.

Resource endowment itself is relative to the technology that can be brought to bear. For example, a new technique to process low-grade taconite iron ores has, in effect, given the United States "new" iron ore reserves for its steel industries. Japan was able to overcome agricultural land deficiencies by developing silkworm cultivation and an intensive rice culture that had a high product yield per unit of land. Also, the Dutch have reclaimed land from the Zuider Zee for agricultural purposes.

PUBLIC POLICIES AND PRIVATE INTERESTS

Most economies in the early phase of industrialization have acute shortages of capital resources and foreign exchange—particularly where the government pursues policies designed to accelerate industrial development. In those countries there is a special premium on technologies that economize on capital, foreign exchange, critical skills, and certain key materials, such as steel. Wider utilization of used machinery, which is cheaper to buy than new machinery, is one way of conserving capital and foreign exchange—this was done in the early industrialization of Japan and the Soviet Union. Running machines on multiple shifts or at higher speeds with more intensive use of labor for maintenance and repair is another way of conserving capital.

Private firms must base their technological choices on market costs and factor availability, which, in turn, are influenced by foreign-exchange controls and governmental licensing of materials and equipment. Since factor prices do not always reflect relative factor yields, there are often considerable disparities between private and social costs. For example, in many underdeveloped countries, the social goal of reducing unemployment results in policies designed to increase the labor content in production; this might result in social gains for the country at large, but it might also make for uneconomic production costs for the private producer. Moreover, governmental measures designed to benefit domestic suppliers through protective tariffs or enforced local procurement inevitably pyramid production costs and often cause production standards to deteriorate. Therefore, reconciling efficient production with social goals remains a fundamental issue of economic development.

FACTOR COMBINATIONS IN PRODUCTION

The labor, capital, and materials that comprise a production technique distinguish one technology from another. Thus, a labor-intensive technology is one that uses relatively high inputs of labor and relatively small amounts of capital equipment. In the road-construction field, a technique using bulldozers and road levellers would be capital-intensive, as opposed to the labor-intensive technique of using brigades of laborers with shovels and picks. Economic determinants of factor combinations are the relative prices and productivity of factors. If thirty men can do the work of one bulldozer over a given time period, but their combined wage is less than the rental value equivalent of the bulldozer, then a labor-intensive technique is more economical. In industrially advanced economies, bulldozers are used because of the relatively high wage rates which make machines more economic than hand labor. In transmitting technologies to low-income economies, production techniques need to be adjusted to differences in factor prices and productivity.

One difficulty in choosing among alternative techniques stems from the cultural orientation of industrial engineers. When a Western engineer designs a plant for overseas operations, he is aware of alternate techniques and knows the performance and operating costs of various equipment using Western labor and operating in Western environments. But this is rarely the case in considering alternative techniques for underdeveloped economies, where the quantity and quality of product yield is much less certain. The proper relationship between cost of inputs and value of output in alternative man-machine combinations in newly industrializing environments must be determined largely through trial and error.

Choices in factor combinations depend upon whether market conditions or developmental criteria are used. For example, firms choose optimal production techniques based upon factor prices (which are usually determined by market conditions), but these do not always reflect the relative scarcity of foreign exchange and capital equipment (which must be taken into account by those concerned with the overall economic development of the country). This, in fact, is why most underdeveloped economies have rigid import and resource-allocation controls—because domestic prices are often at levels where demands far exceed supplies. Thus, a capital-intensive technique may be optimal from the producer's own viewpoint—if he can get the necessary licenses to import capital equipment (machinery and the like) and the resource allocations for required materials (steel, for example). But a more labor-intensive technique using a material other than steel may be preferred from a *social* viewpoint, so that a critical resource such as steel is conserved and used in combination with more abundant factors, such as unskilled labor, thereby increasing overall output. However, certain productive factors can only be brought into use with an expenditure of resources that involve social costs. For example, skilled labor might involve additional expenditures on education, or certain mineral development might require long-term investments in new transport facilities.

SCALE AND ORGANIZATION OF PRODUCTION

The scale of production is largely a function of the size and distribution of the market, subject to economies of scale, that is, unit production costs decreasing with increased scale of plant. Among Western economies, as incomes and markets have grown and markets improved, more efficient and larger scale production techniques have been developed for many industries, including the chemical and metallurgical processing industries, metalworking, and other transformation industries, where larger scale equipment can produce at lower costs. These industries are also characterized by a high degree of integrated activity to schedule the flow of materials and intermediate goods among interlacing suppliers and plants. Interplant linkages, timing, and the control of quality and standards are other vital elements in modern industrial systems.

Implicit in some large-scale production are specialization and interchange of intermediate goods to produce final products. At advanced stages of industrial development, individual plants rely upon a wide range of specialized producers to supply them with semi-finished goods that they would otherwise have to produce themselves in smaller volume and at higher costs. For example, a standard diesel engine for trucks contains over 700 parts, produced in the United States by as many as 200 plants. Among economies in the early stages of development, deficiencies in both consumer demand and factor supply inhibit such large-scale, specialized production. On the demand side, incomes are low and domestic markets small. On the supply side, the capability range of specialized producers is narrow. Shortages in foreign exchange curtail critical imports necessary to supplement domestic procurement. Part of the adversity of limited domestic markets and inadequate indigenous suppliers could be overcome through international trade and production for mass, world markets.

PRODUCT DESIGN

Products are designed to fit market demands and production environments. Design characteristics must also be adapted to physical environments, patterns of customer usage, and prevailing legal codes. For example, the work capacity and price of a diesel truck engine should be adjusted to the transport economics, highway conditions, and traffic regulations of the underdeveloped country. If the engine is to be manufactured in an underdeveloped economy, further adjustments in components and parts may be necessary to accommodate locally available materials and other intermediary goods.

Aside from differences in cultural and physical environments, underdeveloped countries have special requirements for product design. Because of relatively low incomes, inexpensive models of consumer goods are needed. Furthermore, the dearth of maintenance and repair facilities places a premium upon durability and reliability of products.

FITTING TECHNOLOGY TO A SOCIETY

The nature and pace of technological adjustment will vary with the social condition encountered and the strategy of development that is pursued. In a sense, it is a question of technological pegs and environmental holes. Among the alternatives in fitting one to the other are: refashioning the technologies, restructuring environments to accommodate transmitted technologies, or combinations of the two. How successfully technological transition is accomplished depends upon the social capability to innovate and adapt to change. Economically proficient technologies enhance developmental capabilities by economizing on scarce resources or utilizing abundant factors that would otherwise stand idle or underemployed. Thus, technology is both a creature of environment and an instrument of social change.

In transmitting technology there are two basic choices, either to (a) duplicate the product prototype and production system with *minor* adjustments to accommodate differences in scale of production and relative factor availability in the underdeveloped country, or (b) make *major* adjustments in product designs and production systems to accommodate differences in the stage of development as it relates to product need and productive capability. While the first method economizes on adaptation costs, there may be a high penalty in terms of real costs and quality of output, for an underdeveloped country may be turning out an inferior product at three times the cost. The second method may involve high research and development costs to design a product for indigenous needs and to determine what the economy is capable of producing at reasonable cost. This, however, is the system under which many products are originally designed and production engineered. These research and engineering costs are not to be feared—they may indeed recover the economic losses from "over-design" and production inefficiency. The preference for adjustment or re-design of technological systems depends in part upon an intelligent estimate of the probable time lag in achieving proficiency in transmitted technologies, which may vary widely from country to country.

In the past, industrial techniques have largely been transmitted through private business building plants abroad and providing related technical assistance. Efforts to transmit techniques to underdeveloped countries have not been as effective as the transfer of technology from one industrially advanced country to another. Similarly, efforts to increase agricultural output through technical assistance and agricultural extension services have encountered substantial obstacles. Perhaps in both industry and agriculture too much emphasis has been placed upon duplicating Western environments and not enough upon adapting techniques. The state of the art of technological transmittal is itself underdeveloped. There is particular need to reinforce engineering design capabilities at the plant level and to re-examine the public role in advancing technology.

TECHNOLOGICAL ELASTICITY OF A SOCIETY

Underdeveloped countries are somewhat in the same position as the French peasants who were advised to eat cake if they had no bread. In a similar fashion, the less-developed countries have been told that, if they are short of capital, they should adopt labor-saving techniques. But part of the difficulty lies in a basic inability either to use foreign technology or to adapt techniques to their stage of development.

Labor-intensive techniques adopted in Japan have often been cited as a developmental model for industrializing societies; however, there are reasons why a country like Japan can adopt capital-saving techniques and the underdeveloped countries cannot. To begin with, Japan has, in addition to abundant labor, the engineering and technical skills to adapt foreign techniques to domestic conditions. For example, during a period of economic boom in Japan, production orders were coming in much more rapidly than demands for new machine tools could be filled, and Japanese industrial firms sub-contracted to the large number of small shops and factories found in Japan today.

In order to convert machine-intensive into labor-intensive techniques, hundreds of technical drawings must be made, requiring the services of large numbers of engineers and technicians. Then a highly skilled and large industrial labor force takes over. When modern machine techniques are converted to labor-intensive techniques, heavier demands are made upon machine operators to read blueprints, set up tools, and substitute human skill for machine accuracy. Furthermore, a primary element of Japan's technological flexibility that is generally lacking in underdeveloped countries is the system of sub-contractors that work as part of the industrial complex. To function effectively, these small machine shops and town factories must be able to co-ordinate their activities within the larger industrial complex. This includes meeting engineering standards and production schedules and presumes a high degree of industrial organization.

Thus, underdeveloped countries are faced with a very real dilemma. Capital-intensive techniques, on the one hand, place excessive demands upon their reserves of foreign exchange to import the necessary equipment. On the other hand, labor-intensive techniques demand human resources and proficiency in social organization which developing economies sorely lack. As indicated in the Japanese case, engineers and technicians are needed to convert techniques, higher levels of machine skills are demanded to maintain standards, and heavier demands are placed upon industrial organization to schedule and co-ordinate production.

ROLE OF TECHNOLOGY IN SOCIAL TRANSFORMATION

Obstacles to development may be described in terms of scarcities in domestic resources or foreign exchange. Scarcity is a somewhat elusive term. Where market mechanisms prevail, supplies adjust to demands through price fluctuations. In most underdeveloped countries price mechanisms are generally not allowed to operate freely. It is argued that since the demands for certain goods and commodities are in excess of forthcoming supplies, either inflation would result if the market were left unchecked or critical resources would be diverted from more "vital" developmental needs. Hence, this argument provides the rationale for foreign-exchange controls, import restrictions, price regulations, and domestic licensing of materials and equipment. At prices set where demand exceeds supply, certain goods are bound to be "scarce," and the same applies to overvalued exchange rates.

In this qualified sense, technologies that economize on "scarce" resources or minimize foreign-exchange expenditures aid development. Technologies that reduce capital requirements in the early stages of development are similarly beneficial, as are those that find commercial uses for "sub-marginal" resources, waste materials, or domestic commodities. For example, certain technical innovations have, in the past, provided the basis for agricultural commodities entering world trade—cases in point are a decortication process to reduce the bulk of sisal hemp, a milling process to prevent deterioration of sugar cane, the sulfate process for wood pulp, and the mechanical cream separator that commercialized Danish butter. Similar innovations might enable certain currently "unusable" agricultural products of underdeveloped areas to become items capable of export and hence earners of much-needed foreign exchange.

DESIGN CAPABILITIES AT THE INDUSTRIAL PLANT LEVEL

Centralized research activities have been rationalized in terms of the scarcity of technical skills in underdeveloped areas. While there is undoubtedly a place for industrywide research in centralized laboratories, it cannot take the place of technological adaptation at the plant level. Indeed, most of the problems of adaptation can only be formulated at the plant level—such things as the need to expand engineering capability to design and adapt new products and production techniques. Continuing adaptations can follow as markets and production environments change or evolve.

It is especially important to design products that accommodate both market demand and productive capability. This calls for a unified concept of design combining product and process characteristics; design and production engineers are needed to adjust for the performance differences of equipment, labor, and managerial systems. Too often, industrial engineers have inadequate knowledge of equipment performance under local conditions in the underdeveloped region. As often as not, it is merely assumed that labor and managers will eventually adjust to equipment and techniques that have proven efficient elsewhere.

INTERCHANGE OF PEOPLE AND INSTITUTIONAL RELATIONS

The most successful efforts at transmitting industrial techniques include an interchange of people; this means not only that technical experts visit developing countries, but that engineers and technicians have an opportunity to work with their counterparts abroad. It is important that production and design engineers be exposed to ideas and experience that are as nearly as possible related to the home country conditions. For example, a parts manufacturer in India may learn much from the side-street garages of Birmingham that make parts for the British engine industry. And engineering students from developing countries, through the International Association for the Exchange of Students for Technical Experience, are being given opportunities to work with firms located in industrially advanced countries. But it is essential that the interchange between operational environments also take place beyond the training level so that what is learned can be effectively transmitted and not merely stored for future reference.

Design engineers from developing countries should be afforded opportunities to work in the advanced design division of Western corporations, both to convey to the Western engineers a sense of reality in matters affecting product and process design for underdeveloped environments and to take back with them ideas and techniques that can be currently adapted at their home plants. This approach places a different emphasis upon innovation and adaptation of technique rather than straight apprenticeship to learn how to do things the Western way.

TECHNOLOGICAL RESEARCH INSTITUTES IN DEVELOPING COUNTRIES

Technological research institutes in developing countries have helped in the development of manufacturing processes which utilize indigenous materials. Many of these institutes, such as the Ceylon Institute of Scientific and Industrial Research (CISIR) and the Institute Centroamericano de Investigación y Technología Industrial (ICAITI) have been established under international technical assistance programs. ICAITI has developed new techniques for the preservation of tropical foodstuffs and the processing of turpentine and essential oils from local resources, and a high-protein corn meal to replace the less nutritious flour commonly used in Central America. The CISIR in Ceylon has worked on new or improved techniques for the desiccation of coconut, for the processing of citronella and cinnamon oils, and for the manufacture of cheap shoes and rugs from banana-stalk fiber.

At the East African Industrial Research Organization in Nairobi, Kenya, research laboratories are engaged in such projects as the agricultural processing of coffee, jasmine, and tannin; ceramics research on vitreous bowls, drainpipes, brick, and tile; metallurgical studies on the removal of arsenic from copper; and developing building and construction materials from local resources. Other laboratories in African countries are working to develop the economic potential of a variety of local resources: natural rubber and palm oil in Liberia; phosphate ore, fish meal, and soil-cement brick in Uganda; and coconut-husk fibres and protein grasses in Nigeria. In Rhodesia, advanced research is being done on the extraction and refining of various metals and on new techniques in geological prospecting.

Technological research institutes are especially useful to small-scale industries which lack their own laboratory facilities and need advice on the design and selection of manufacturing equipment. The Indian government has sponsored prototype production centers to help select and adapt technologies for such industries. These centers arrange for foreign collaboration, help engineer equipment design, and train technical personnel. They also set up pilot-plant production using local labor to test equipment for suitability in the field.

Efforts to adapt technologies can probably be improved through arrangements abroad with counterpart institutions—especially in countries that are technologically closer to underdeveloped countries. For example, the Japanese have been especially adept at developing labor-intensive techniques, and their product designs are often much closer to the incomes and needs of developing countries. Food-research institutes in India working on cheap sources of proteins have much to learn from institutes in Japan working on algae and proteins from ocean sources. The Israelis have also demonstrated technological ingenuity in making the most of their limited resources.

GOVERNMENT-INDUSTRY CO-OPERATION

Effective co-operation between government and industry is essential if technological transformation is to take place, since governments inevitably influence the production environment through domestic and trade policies. Consultative bodies to advise government and industry on the formulation and implementation of controls affecting production would help reconcile efforts to achieve efficiency at the plant level with the total industrial effort of the country. The government can also participate in research efforts to advance indigenous technology.

Co-operative efforts between government and private industry in the highly industrialized nations can perhaps serve as models—or at least as stimulus for similar endeavors in underdeveloped nations. In the United States, federal and state governments have exercised an important role in pioneering new technologies in the fields of transportation, agriculture (nitrate fertilizers), and defense-related industries, including satellite communications and nuclear power. Similarly, the Japanese government has supported technological advance through its Science and Technics Agency. In the United Kingdom, government-sponsored industrial laboratories engage in research to advance technology.

In some underdeveloped nations government investment authorities have played an important role in attracting viable industry. Both Puerto Rico and Israel have built pilot plants which were eventually sold to private investors. The

Israelis have built a world network designed to seek out foreign investors with technical know-how or access to foreign markets.

Markets and viable techniques are two critical elements for a successful industrial enterprise. Special laws to encourage foreign investment of this kind provide for exemption from custom duties on the import of equipment and raw materials, a sharing in labor-training costs, special export incentives, and certain tax exemptions. Industrial technologies that can realize export earnings in effect alleviate foreign-exchange scarcities.

UNITED NATIONS RESEARCH PROGRAM

The United Nations Secretariat has sponsored, through its Industrial Development Centre, substantial research on the problems of technological adaptation. The Centre has concentrated on prototype studies to build a body of knowledge to deal with industrial development problems. The program is designed to provide a synthesis between economics and engineering in advancing industrialization, and considerable attention has been devoted to the adaptation of processes and equipment to local conditions. Individual industries have, therefore, been studied with a view toward identifying processes and equipment suited to the resource endowment of a developing country. For example, a study of Japanese cottage industries indicated how certain aspects might usefully be applied to reduce rural unemployment in developing countries. Equipment-output ratios and capital-intensity requirements have been examined in order to find feasible substitutions of labor for capital.

INTERNATIONAL MANUFACTURING SYSTEMS

Industries that establish facilities for manufacturing abroad provide, in many ways, a unique opportunity to transmit technology. Being familiar with the special techniques of a manufacturing system, foreign firms can provide the technical assistance and engineering design capabilities so badly needed by developing countries. By and large, adaptation has been limited to minor adjustments in the choice of equipment to accommodate differences in the scale of production or in substitution of unavailable local materials. Major changes are needed in the technologies that have been transmitted. International manufacturing systems may also offer help in reformulating technological needs in terms of emerging productive capabilities.

AGRICULTURE

Technological adaptation in the field of agriculture must be treated as a special case, for social and economic conditions associated with advanced techniques of production in the field of agriculture are especially restrictive. Modern techniques involve, for example, intensive use of capital equipment, large amounts of chemical fertilizer, and the use of new strains of seed and new techniques of soil management. Social innovations in support of modern agricultural systems include agricultural experimental stations, extension services, and well-integrated commodity and credit markets.

In underdeveloped countries, the social and economic prerequisites necessary to utilize an agricultural extension system effectively are lacking. Typically, 80 to 90 per cent of the population of an underdeveloped country are engaged in subsistence agriculture. People live largely in rural communities bound by tradition which are very slow to accept social change or changes in production techniques. Agricultural extension services which have had such phenomenal success in industrialized societies are extremely difficult to implant in rural, traditional societies. Part of the social inertia is traceable to landholding systems that give little incentive to an impoverished peasantry to increase output for landowners and tax collectors in areas such as India and Latin America.

From an economic standpoint, subsistence agriculture has great difficulty in generating an economic surplus to finance investments in fertilizer, seed-development, and irrigation projects that are necessary to sustain more productive techniques. It is difficult for peasants living at the subsistence level to invest in the future or to risk the little they have on new patterns of living. Nor does mechanized equipment make much economic sense in areas with huge amounts of surplus labor that overcrowd the arable land. Given the limited resources available to developing economies, the most advantageous investments are probably in fertilizer and simple tools.

Penetrating rural communities with better soil-management techniques and improved seed varieties is itself a formidable task. Considerable funds have been spent by the Rockefeller Brothers on enterprises to build agricultural experimental stations in Latin America. But there is perhaps a twenty-year lag between the new crop varieties developed and social acceptance of and economic readiness for them. In many countries, the pressing need is for an improved storage and distribution system; and in this area improved techniques can alleviate food shortages greatly.

DEPRESSED AREAS IN DEVELOPED COUNTRIES

Even developed countries have depressed areas which are characterized by poverty and underemployment analogous to that of underdeveloped countries. Origins and causes vary, but the general situation reflects the inability of certain regions to keep pace with dynamic change in the rest of the economy. Shifts in consumer demands may have caused certain industries to decline or technological advance made obsolete certain products or production techniques. Foreign competition or the migration of industrial plants to more favorable environments are other factors contributing to regional decline. Economic changes causing shifts in the demands for and location of certain occupations and skills have also led to unemployment in certain regions. Depressed areas result when a region is unable to adapt its labor skills and develop alternate economic activities.

Technological change has caused certain industries to decline and has drastically reduced or altered labor requirements. As of 1960, productivity gains and mechanization in American agriculture reduced the number of gainfully employed farmers by one half in a twenty-year period, while farm output increased by more than 50 per cent. Labor requirements in the textile industry in this country declined by 30 per cent in a decade—the combined effect of increased foreign competition, the decline of export markets, and a 60 per cent gain in productivity. Labor requirements in coal mining dropped 60 per cent in twenty years—the result of shifting demand to other fuel sources and of improved technology amounting to an 80 per cent productivity gain. Isolated communities in southeastern Kentucky, West Virginia, and western Pennsylvania, with limited alternative employment opportunities, were especially hard hit—more so than the New England textile mills where employment in machine industries was sometimes possible. With the decline of manpower requirements in the railroad industry, repair and maintenance shops in such areas as Altoona, Pennsylvania, suffered.

Broadly speaking, technological change has displaced the need for brawn and certain artisan skills and has upgraded intelligence requirements to operate expensive farm machinery or industrial equipment. Regions with low levels of education and skills fared the worst.

Eastern Kentucky is an extreme, but by no means unique, example of a distressed area. In addition to low incomes, high unemployment, and low standards of living, the region is characterized by high birth rates and low levels of education. In recent decades, the major industries have been coal mining, wood processing, and clay products. Lumbering and coal mining have faced long-term decline as resources were depleted or other more productive regions entered into competition. Mechanization has reduced labor requirements, so that employment has fallen off even where demand has been sustained. In the face of declining economic opportunities, the younger, better educated, and more energetic have migrated elsewhere, leaving behind an even lower quality of productive human resources. The unskilled and untrained previously employed in logging and coal mining who remain have particular difficulty in finding jobs elsewhere. Outmigration has created ghost towns, lowered the morale of those remaining, and depressed the investment outlook, thus further limiting opportunities for alternate employment. These adversities are compounded by the remoteness and isolation of the region, which limits access to markets and suppliers. Local topography makes road construction relatively high, and excessive costs of water-supply and flood-control systems add further to the cost of industrial installation. The technological revolution in transportation and production techniques in other parts of the economy has further undermined the competitive advantage in resource-based industries. All these factors combine to limit the advantages of the region in competing for resources with other parts of the country.

Poverty pockets, such as those in eastern Kentucky, pose somewhat analogous problems to those of underdeveloped countries. Both are faced with the problems of raising the incomes and quality of life for those who cannot or will not migrate to more prosperous parts of the world. The essential problem is one of human resource development to raise education levels and improve the social capability to adapt to change. Resource-based industries of the type described in eastern Kentucky, are especially vulnerable, as the best forest stands become depleted or economically accessible coal strata become exhausted. Technological innovations can help alleviate the condition in poverty pockets only to a limited degree. New "auger" mining techniques for the type of coal deposits found in eastern Kentucky have, for example, prevented the industry from declining even further in the face of the more efficient strip mining developed for surface coal deposits in other parts of the United States.

Government funds have been allocated for research and technical assistance to depressed areas to help meet competition in declining industries and develop indigenous resources. Public funds have been authorized to develop processing techniques for low-grade iron ores in distressed areas of Minnesota and to investigate the technical feasibility of storing liquid petroleum gas in shale formations found in depressed areas of eastern Pennsylvania. Other subsidized research has covered new forest products development, and one project is investigating the production of animal feed from aquatic plants indigenous to a depressed area of Texas.

Among industrially advanced countries, economic measures and related policies for dealing with underdeveloped regions place strong emphasis upon retraining and relocating manpower to expanding areas of the economy. Such relocation and outmigration are rarely possible in underdeveloped nations. In countries like Sweden, the United States, and Great Britain, remedial legislation has emphasized efforts to increase labor mobility. A relatively minor emphasis has been placed upon technical assistance to distressed areas to provide for the hard core of underemployed who are either unwilling or unable to relocate. Paradoxically, in an industrially advanced economy, depressed regions are in an economic sense "overdeveloped"—that is, human and physical resources could be used more effectively elsewhere. However, where the socioeconomic decision has been made to develop employment opportunities in a region, technology can be advantageously applied to develop products or techniques based upon local resources and environments.

THE CHALLENGE OF UNDERDEVELOPMENT

The challenge of underdevelopment has been viewed here largely in terms of economic efficiency. Although little has been said of the social and psychological implications of technological change—except as they influence economic efficiency—criteria for technological adaptation should be viewed in the larger context of social adjustment, taking into account the broad effects upon mental health or ethical values of the good life. Gandhi's preference for village industry in this sense takes a larger view of socioeconomic adjustment. The same applies to urban planners like Constantine Doxiadis who build economic, social, and aesthetic considerations into their technical design.

The condition of poverty and underemployment, whether it occurs only in a depressed area or is a national phenomenon, reflects an inability to adapt and transform. Technology provides a means for transition and adjustment. Countries like Israel and Japan, although relatively underdeveloped, have managed to make economic progress largely as a result of their ability to adapt to their resource endowment and adjust to changing demands in the world economy. Among the industrially advanced countries, a small country like Sweden has been more successful than the United States in keeping unemployment down through measures to reallocate resources and adapt economic and technological change. Technological capability is therefore merely part of overall ability to adapt to a changing world.

Part **X**
Technology in War·

34 / Organization of Military Research
DONALD C. SWAIN

In 1900, as a new century began, the American people found themselves in a strangely reminiscent mood. Journalists from coast to coast analyzed and appraised the main trends of the last hundred years, and dozens of authors rushed into print with popular accounts of the American past. Widely recognized even then as one of the outstanding features of the 19th century was its remarkable record of technological success. At the turn of the century, America's enormous industrial capacity stood as a monument not only to the ruthless ambition and boundless energy of the Gilded Age, but also to the progress of 19th-century technology. Men like Eli Whitney and Thomas A. Edison, whose careers spanned the century, had helped to create a strong tradition of technological innovation and change. By 1900 the people of the United States were deeply imbued with the idea that technological change meant progress.

Under these circumstances, one might suppose that a systematic program of technological improvement within the military establishment would also have become an American tradition. In fact, quite the opposite was true. The technical and scientific branches of the Army and Navy had lapsed into stagnation. In spite of the rise of the new technology, the United States government had not materially modified the pattern of organized military research since the Civil War. Nearly half a century was to pass and two devastating world wars were to be fought before science and technology would be firmly and effectively wedded to national defense.

AMERICAN BACKWARDNESS IN TECHNICAL MILITARY RESEARCH

During the 1890's, the American military establishment, handicapped by inadequate appropriations and shortsighted leadership, devoted only a small part of its energies to the development of new weapons. The Navy simply adopted most of the technological changes pioneered by the British fleet. The Army, which in terms of both size and armaments ranked among the weakest in the world, contented itself with a few unimaginative investigations of old problems. Although the "Splendid Little War" of 1898 culminated in a prestigious victory over Spain, the Cuban campaign revealed the true dimensions of American military weakness. Far-reaching reforms were necessary before America's military might would match her new stature as a world power.

Secretary of War Elihu Root began these reforms shortly after the Spanish-American War by installing a modern staff system in place of the outmoded Army command structure, which was a relic of the Civil War. Out of Root's organizational changes came a certain invigoration of the Army's small research program. The Signal Corps, for example, began experimenting even before World War I with radio communications and aviation, both of which held immense military potential. But at the same time, the Quartermaster Corps demonstrated its continuing lack of imagination by tinkering with mule wagons instead of turning its attention to the possibilities already apparent in automotive engineering. The Navy did not reorganize itself until 1915.

As World War I engulfed Europe and threatened to involve the United States, military and scientific leaders recognized that the major obstacle to the establishment of a vigorous program of military research was the fact that the military had no practical organizational device for drawing upon the expertise of civilian scientists and technical experts. During the Civil War the federal government had attempted with some success to utilize civilian experts as advisers for military research. In 1862 the Navy Department appointed a Permanent Commission of prominent scientists to handle the flood of inventions and technical suggestions that poured into Washington. Composed of Joseph Henry, Charles Henry Davis, and Alexander Dallas Bache, the Commission performed creditably, although it never became an active research agency.

Congress chartered the National Academy of Sciences (NAS) early in 1863 to provide scientific advice to the President and also to serve as the American counterpart of the Royal Society and the Académie des Sciences. Under the forceful leadership of Bache, the Academy organized special committees to study such problems as protecting the bottoms of iron ships from salt-water damage and correcting the magnetic deviation of compasses on iron ships. But the modest research achievements of the NAS had little impact on the outcome of the war. Its efforts, as in the case of the Navy's Permanent Commission, were more important in terms of setting a precedent for this kind of scientific activity than in terms of tangible results. In the years after the Civil War, the Permanent Commission disappeared and the National Academy of Sciences suffered an eclipse. The rapidly declining Academy became a strictly honorific society, struggling to find the financial resources necessary for survival. By 1900 it had fallen into virtual decay.

In 1915, shortly after the sinking of the *Lusitania* by German submarines, the Navy Department took the initial steps that were to bring civilian technicians into the war effort. Falling back on precedent established during the Civil War, Secretary of the Navy Josephus Daniels appointed the Naval Consulting Board, with Thomas A. Edison as chairman, to evaluate "all ideas and suggestions" sent in by inventors. It was imperative, the Secretary believed, to establish the "machinery and facilities for utilizing the natural inventive genius of Americans." The Naval Consulting Board was composed mostly of engineers and inventors drawn from the ranks of industry. By the end of World War I, these men had screened more than 100,000 suggestions and inventions, only a few of which proved to be valuable. The Board soon realized that the pressing technical problems of submarine warfare were not going to be solved by random suggestions from patriotic American citizens.

In 1917, the Board recommended the establishment of a Naval Research Laboratory with a staff of full-time civilian scientists who would apply their knowledge and ingenuity to the task of solving specific naval problems. Congress appropriated $1 million for the purpose of building the laboratory; however, the war ended before construction could begin, and the Naval Research Laboratory had to wait until 1923. By finding so few worthwhile ideas among the thousands of voluntarily submitted inventions, the Naval Consulting Board demonstrated beyond any doubt the inadvisability of depending upon "the natural inventive genius of Americans." The American military establishment would be forced to adopt the problem-solving approach already pioneered by the Department of Agriculture, putting teams of scientifically trained specialists to work on technical problems of utmost urgency.

The National Academy of Sciences, though sadly lacking in vitality, provided the second avenue by which the federal government eventually obtained scientific advice and assistance during World War I. Within the Academy were a handful of reformers who saw in the war an opportunity to revitalize their organization. George Ellery Hale, the director of Mount Wilson Observatory, and Robert A. Millikan, a physicist from the University of Chicago, were the leaders of this reform campaign. At Hale's insistence, the Academy boldly tendered its services to President Woodrow Wilson. The President promptly accepted, but the problem then became one of working out an effective mechanism for co-ordinating a nationwide scientific program.

It was universally agreed that the slumbering National Academy of Sciences could not be expected to manage this program. It was also agreed that participants in the emergency scientific work should not be drawn exclusively from the Academy, for most of its members were old and out of touch with the latest scientific developments. A method had to be found to bring talented younger scientists into the program. The National Research Council (NRC), established in 1916 as a subsidiary of the National Academy of Sciences, proved to be the answer. With its numerous committees, subcommittees, and specialized panels, the NRC became the vehicle through which hundreds of individual scientists could participate in the wartime science program. The National Research Council solicited the co-operation of both university scientists and industrial specialists to carry out its mission. Moreover, it won the co-operation of the great foundations who showered their largesse on the NRC when federal funds proved inadequate.

As chief executive officer of the National Research Council, Robert Millikan became the focal point of a large scientific enterprise. By February 1917, the NRC was functioning as the research branch of the Council of National Defense, with a wide range of responsibilities in military research. At about the same time, the Council of National Defense asked the Naval Consulting Board to serve as its inventions committee.

The National Research Council proved its worth in 1917 and 1918 by functioning as a central clearing house for the wartime scientific program. It established a valuable research Information Service, and its panels and committees performed useful services for both the Army and Navy. Among other things, the NRC co-ordinated a wide-ranging study of the most vexatious of all the technical problems of World War I—how to detect the presence of submarines. Before the end of the war, Millikan and many other NRC scientists accepted commissions in the armed forces because this seemed to be the most practical means of acquiring research support.

Several other scientific organizations contributed to the war effort in 1917-18. The National Advisory Committee for Aeronautics (NACA), which had been created by act of Congress in 1915, undertook "the scientific study of the problems of flight." Composed of representatives from the Army and Navy, the Smithsonian Institution, and other federal scientific agencies, and including "seven citizens who know the needs of aeronautics," the committee cautiously organized itself and had just begun its pioneering research when the war ended. Its most valuable scientific and technological achievements would come later. The Army's newly organized Chemical Warfare Service conducted extensive experiments with poison gases, which had already been recognized as weapons of immense and horrible potentiality. Nevertheless, of all the World War I scientific organizations, the National Research Council most nearly resembled a central scientific agency.

"BACK TO NORMALCY"

Unfortunately, as soon as the fighting stopped in November 1918, the American military research program began to deteriorate. Civilian scientists, including

Millikan himself, promptly took steps to resign from government service in order to return to their university positions. As the American people embarked on a frantic search for "normalcy," Presidents Harding and Coolidge placed strong emphasis on fiscal economy. Moreover, the State Department turned to disarmament treaties and to the renunciation of war as an instrument of national policy. Nearly all phases of the military research program suffered severe cutbacks shortly after the 1920's began.

The National Research Council continued in existence (it had become a permanent fixture in 1918 by virtue of an Executive Order signed by Woodrow Wilson) but it soon diminished in both size and influence. In the pattern of its parent organization, the National Academy of Sciences, the Council went into a period of rapid postwar decline. It made the transition to peacetime by turning its attention to the international exchange of scientific information and by strictly limiting its activities to a small budget provided almost entirely by private philanthropy. It essentially lost touch with the research activities of the federal government and surrendered its position as the central co-ordinating agency for American science. The time had not yet arrived for a permanent wedding of science and technology to national defense.

During the 1920's, the nation's military research agencies remained in the doldrums. The Army's Chemical Warfare Service managed to survive, but only at the cost of drastically reducing its research program. The Signal Corps and the Quartermaster Corps had no choice but to accept minimal research budgets. When faced with a similar fiscal squeeze, the Navy adopted a generally apathetic attitude toward the need for research, except in the case of the newly constructed Naval Research Laboratory, where a handful of civilian scientists began the experiments that led to the development of radar.

The vigorous research program of the National Advisory Committee for Aeronautics was the only real exception to the generally downward trend in military research in peacetime years following World War I. Although its budget was never very large, the NACA consistently expanded. Because of its unique organization, which linked it not only to the Army and Navy but also to the Smithsonian Institution and to private centers of aeronautical study, the NACA followed an independent and successful course. Its research center at Langley Field, Virginia, grew and compiled a distinguished record for organizing and carrying out complex studies of the problems of flight. Research sponsored by NACA during the 1920's and 1930's paid off handsomely during World War II.

The Great Depression of the 1930's had a disastrous impact on government-supported science activity. The downward spiral of appropriations for research forced virtually every scientific agency of the federal government to retrench. The National Bureau of Standards, the Bureau of Mines, the Forest Service, the United States Geological Survey, the Agricultural Experiment Stations, and the Bureau of Fisheries, all of which had active scientific staffs, saw their research programs severely curtailed. The New Deal spent millions of dollars in an attempt to combat the deleterious effects of the Depression, but in trying to compensate for huge emergency expenditures, Congress found scientific programs eminently expendable; they were the first to feel the economy axe. Franklin D. Roosevelt, acting at the behest of Secretary of Agriculture Henry A. Wallace, appointed the Science Advisory Board in 1933 to advise him on national scientific policy. But when this Board proposed a "New Deal" for science, the President rejected the idea on grounds that it would cost too much money. Federally sponsored scientific research, including military research, continued to decline until late in Roosevelt's first term.

Annual appropriations for military research had hovered around $4 million since the 1920's. In 1935, the Army received an extra $5 million for research, most of which went to the Air Corps. In 1936, a series of threatening international episodes triggered a reappraisal of the American defense posture, and new appropriations were earmarked for the military establishment. At this point the Army General Staff made a curious decision. Instead of drastically expanding its military research program, it decided to emphasize the procurement of weapons already developed and to bypass the time-consuming research process.

By 1940, with a bloody war raging in Europe, the Army's decision of 1936 loomed as a great mistake. Thoughtful observers already were agreed that the outcome of World War II would probably hinge on weapons not yet developed. For the sake of national defense, therefore, the United States would have to mobilize her total research capacity in an attempt to make up for lost time. The application of science and technology to weaponry now became a matter of utmost national importance, and the search for an effective administrative mechanism to co-ordinate a gigantic wartime science program began.

No attempt was made to make the National Academy of Sciences or the National Research Council the central co-ordinating organization for American science. Just as Millikan and Hale had recognized the inadequacies of the Academy in 1916, a new generation of American scientists realized the inadequacies of the Council in 1940. An entirely new organizational device was needed.

THE NATIONAL DEFENSE RESEARCH COMMITTEE

At this crucial juncture, four extraordinary research administrators stepped into the breech. Having emerged as leaders of the scientific community in the 1920's and '30's, these men were privy to the nation's highest scientific councils. Together they represented the various "estates" of American science: Vannevar Bush, president of the Carnegie Institution of Washington, represented the great foundations; Frank B. Jewett, director of Bell Laboratories, represented industrial science; James B. Conant, Harvard's president, represented the universities; and Karl T. Compton, former chairman of Roosevelt's Science Advisory Board, could speak from experience in the field of government-supported research. In 1940, upon the advice of these four, President Roosevelt appointed the National Defense Research Committee (NDRC), patterned after the successful NACA.

The NDRC's mission was to take charge of the emergency scientific program. Made up of eight members, including representatives from the Army and Navy, the Committee was dominated by civilian scientists who insisted on their right of independent judgment. Although the Department of Commerce established a National Inventor's Council to handle a new flood of suggestions from inventors, neither the Army nor the Navy held out any hope that random inventiveness would provide solutions to highly complex technical problems. Military leaders had abandoned that naive hope as a result of their experience in World War I. As the months passed, Vannevar Bush emerged as the dominant figure in the inner councils of the NDRC.

At the outset, the National Defense Research Committee decided not to engage in research of its own. Instead, it developed a system of contracts which allowed the best scientists and engineers in the nation, regardless of geographical location or institutional affiliation, to do the research. Outstanding universities and large industrial firms could thus be tapped for their scientific and technical expertise. Originally put to effective use by the NACA, the device of the research contract gave the NDRC an enormous flexibility and proved to be a great breakthrough in the administration of the wartime research program. Research contracts would also revolutionize the conduct of scientific research in the postwar epoch.

OFFICE OF SCIENTIFIC RESEARCH AND DEVELOPMENT

By the late spring of 1941, it became quite clear that a more comprehensive administrative agency would be required to supervise the nation's sprawling wartime research operation. Although the NDRC had performed with distinction, its authority extended only to weapons research, which was after all a rather limited field. Bush proposed that an Office of Scientific Research and Development (OSRD) be established to take responsibility for virtually the entire program of wartime research and development. The NDRC would become a part of OSRD and would continue to co-ordinate weapons research. Filling an urgent need for co-ordination in the medical sciences, a Committee on Medical Research (CMR) would take its place in OSRD as the co-equal of NDRC. At the top of the pyramid, functioning as "Czar" of the wartime scientific effort, would be the director of the OSRD. Roosevelt created the Office of Scientific Research and Development by Executive Order in June 1941, and named Bush as its director.

The OSRD compiled an extraordinary record during World War II. Using research contracts with great ingenuity, it marshalled the scientific resources of the United States as never before and became the most effective central scientific agency in the history of American science. It maintained close relations with the research agencies of the Army and Navy and provided essential interservice liaison. Research looking toward the development of atomic weapons began under OSRD. Contract researchers, co-ordinated by Bush's office, developed the proximity fuse, the Duck (an amphibious military vehicle), and short-range rockets; other OSRD specialists suggested technical improvements in a wide range of both weapons and military equipment. The CMR was responsible for the application of mass-production techniques to the manufacture of penicillin.

By the end of World War II, the OSRD commanded universal respect and admiration in Washington, and the nation's highest officials had become convinced of the great military value of scientific research. The awesome mushroom cloud towering over Hiroshima dramatically symbolized the union that finally had taken place between science and national defense.

Altogether, more than $3 billion passed through the OSRD's hands, with the wartime scientific budget reaching a peak of about $1 billion for fiscal year 1945. This monumental flow of money from the federal coffers into the nation's research laboratories became the key to the emerging close relationship between the federal government and American science and technology. Having grown accustomed to massive federal support, an entire generation of American scientists and engineers found it difficult to give up that support once peace returned. World War II, we now realize, radically altered the hitherto casual relation of science to American government.

In addition to the OSRD, which performed the vital co-ordinating function, many agencies of military research distinguished themselves during World War II. The National Advisory Committee for Aeronautics employed hundreds of technicians in its research laboratories. Wind-tunnel experiments and design changes in the internal-combustion engine, pioneered by NACA, raised the performance of propeller-driven aircraft to the highest level possible, although NACA fell somewhat short in the development of jet-propelled aircraft. The Naval Research Laboratory showed the way to vastly improved radar performance, the culmination of its electronic experiments initiated in the 1920's. The Army Signal Corps developed lightweight and very efficient field communications systems, exploring the potentialities of miniaturization in radio transmission and reception. The Chemical Corps made new and potentially devastating additions to the stockpile of poison gases that the Army carefully maintained but never used. The Ordnance Corps did valuable work in the development of rockets, and the Army engineers took over the Manhattan Project (initiated by the OSRD), which produced the world's first atomic bomb. By the summer of 1945, the wartime scientific operation had assumed colossal proportions. "The mighty edifice of government science," A. Hunter Dupree has written, "dominated the scene . . . as a Gothic cathedral dominated a thirteenth century landscape."

CREATION OF THE NATIONAL SCIENCE FOUNDATION

Long before the end of World War II, members of Congress, government officials, and professional military men began to wonder what might be done to perpetuate the close relationship that the federal government had with science and technology. It seemed perfectly obvious to most military observers that postwar defense planning would, of necessity, revolve around an extensive military research program. With the advent of the Atomic Age, millions of individual Americans arrived at the same conclusion.

The question was how to continue in peacetime this desirable relationship between science and government. Many high government officials, including President Harry S. Truman, wanted the OSRD to remain as the central scientific agency for American science after the war. But Vannevar Bush was unalterably opposed to the idea, believing that the OSRD's success derived essentially from unique wartime circumstances. Bush had earlier made a study of the needs of postwar science in response to an invitation from President Roosevelt. As a result he had recommended the establishment of a National Science Foundation (NSF) to co-ordinate and support not only military research and medical research but also basic research. Senator Harley M. Kilgore of West Virginia, who had spent three years investigating the shortcomings of America's wartime scientific mobilization, made the same general proposal. After five years of debate and compromise, Congress finally passed an act authorizing the establishment of the NSF in 1950; however, by that time separate agencies had been created to co-ordinate and support both medical and military research. The support of basic research thus became the primary mission of the National Science Foundation.

MILITARY RESEARCH AND DEVELOPMENT

During the debate over the NSF, the defense establishment took steps to stimulate and co-ordinate military research. Co-operating with high-ranking professional military men, the National Academy of Sciences made an abortive attempt to set up a Research Board for National Security, but the Bureau of the Budget vetoed the idea for compelling administrative reasons. Thus died another attempt to revitalize the National Academy of Sciences through an alliance with the military. In 1946, after lengthy consultations, the Army and Navy agreed to establish the Joint Research and Development Board (JRDB), a committee of civilian and military scientists, to provide high-level scientific advice and co-

ordinate all military research projects. The Truman administration clearly intended the JRDB to prevent expensive duplication within the separate weap-
ons-research programs maintained by each branch of the armed forces.

When the Department of Defense came into existence in 1947, the JRDB
became the Research and Development Board (RDB), with essentially the
same functions. Vannevar Bush agreed to become the chairman of the RDB
and by so doing aroused considerable optimism about the Board's future. As a
devotee of the committee approach to research administration, Bush drew
upon precedents established by the NRC, NACA, NDRC, and OSRD; he organized dozens of specialized panels and committees, composed mostly of university scientists, to advise the Defense Department. But after a few months
of utter frustration, he resigned his position as chairman. The RDB eventually
failed because implementing policies for the co-ordination of military research
in peacetime proved to be more difficult than anticipated, and because the
RDB had "elevated the committee-panel approach to the absurd." The Research and Development Board continued in existence until 1953, when Congress authorized two new Assistant Secretaries of Defense, one for research and
another for development, to replace the RDB. In 1956, the Army, Navy, and Air
Force each designated an Assistant Secretary for Research and Development.
An administrative stepchild before World War II, military research now had
representation in the highest councils of the Defense Department and the three
uniformed branches.

Of the many administrative techniques pioneered by the OSRD during
World War II, the research contract was by far the most important. The United
States Navy, Air Force, and Army all developed large postwar programs of
"intramural" research, that is, research conducted in laboratories operated directly by each service. But enormous "extramural" research programs soon
dwarfed the scientific and technical work conducted within the defense establishment itself. The key to the success of these extramural scientific programs
was the flexible research contract. Civilian scientists by the hundreds received
contracts to engage in scientific studies of direct or indirect importance to the
national defense. Later, the Defense Department and the separate services
began awarding research grants as well as contracts.

Expenditures for "R & D" went steadily upward, rising from less than $1
billion in 1947 to almost $6 billion in 1960. By using a flexible system of con-
tracts and grants, the Pentagon was able to draw upon the special scientific
talent of the universities and private industry. Inevitably, the mounting federal
investment in scientific research had a stimulating effect on the pursuit of
"pure" science, for the highly sophisticated kind of military research in vogue
after World War II depended to a surprising extent on basic research in the
hard sciences.

The Navy may claim credit for having produced perhaps the most extraordinary postwar military research organization, the Office of Naval Research (ONR), created by act of Congress in 1946. The Navy had sponsored a vigorous research program during World War II, and the Naval Research Laboratory, directed by Rear Admiral H. G. Bowen, compiled a distinguished scientific record, as did other less well-known naval agencies like the Bureau of Ships. Under Rear Admiral J. A. Furer, the Office of Research and Inventions demonstrated the value of a special agency for the co-ordination of the Navy's various independent research programs. But most important, the Navy had a collection of career and reserve officers vitally interested in expanding the peacetime naval research program. Admirals Bowen and Furer, Captain R. D. Conrad, and about a dozen junior reserve officers, who called themselves the "Bird Dogs," led the drive toward a greater scientific commitment within the Navy, persuading and "educating" dozens of high-ranking officers and politicians who were in a position to influence the policy-making process. Success crowned their efforts in 1946 when Congress authorized the Office of Naval Research. Having sprung from a maverick campaign to put scientific research on an organizational par with the other naval bureaus, the ONR quickly became a maverick organization.

An ingenious use of research grants and contracts and a thorough-going commitment to the ideal of basic scientific research were the keys to the ONR's early success. Within two years, a large number of university scientists were receiving financial assistance with virtually no strings attached. The new office had recognized that the Navy would benefit by stimulating research in a wide range of scientific fields, with special support for physics, chemistry, and radio astronomy. Its financial commitment to basic research became so extensive and its grants program achieved such wide success that the National Science Foundation simply adopted many of the ONR's procedures and goals when it came into existence in 1951. The ONR's extramural research program, combined with the competent intramural research conducted at the Naval Research Laboratory, gave the Navy a deserved prominence in the field of military research after World War II.

ATOMIC ENERGY COMMISSION

Unquestionably, however, the paramount scientific agency of the federal government from 1947 to 1958 was the Atomic Energy Commission (AEC), whose responsibilities included the development of atomic and thermonuclear weapons. The phrase "born under a cloud" had special meaning for the AEC because congressional action on atomic energy came largely in response to the mushroom cloud that rose like an enormous question mark over the Japanese landscape in the summer of 1945.

Congress began studying the problem of what to do about the development of atomic energy less than a month after the war ended. The animated debate on this question overshadowed all other questions of science policy then before Congress. Several controversial issues arose, but probably the most debated was the question of whether civilian officials or professional military men should head atomic research. Senator Brien MacMahon and the Federation of Atomic Scientists managed to block the Army's proposal for military control. In the end, Congress decided that a five-man civilian commission should administer and control atomic development.

A memorable series of atomic tests at Eniwetok in the Pacific initiated the familiar AEC pattern of theoretical weapons research followed by extensive field tests, a pattern that Soviet Russia also adopted. With the development of the hydrogen bomb, a new round of testing took place which ended only with the Nuclear Test Ban Treaty of 1963. By the decade of the 1960's, the AEC had developed a highly sophisticated arsenal of atomic and thermonuclear weapons, which formed the backbone of our national defense. There is no better example of the application of science and technology to military problems than in the field of atomic energy.

NATIONAL AERONAUTICS AND SPACE ADMINISTRATION

In the constantly changing government science program the predominance of the Atomic Energy Commission proved to be short-lived. In 1957, the United States found itself suddenly jolted into an awareness that a new age had dawned. By orbiting the first earth satellite, the Soviet Union not only inaugurated the Space Age but shocked the American government into a re-examination of its vast scientific program. Sputnik I was still in orbit when the members of Congress began erecting a gigantic organizational monument to the new age, the National Aeronautics and Space Administration (NASA). With the NACA as its nucleus, NASA soon became the predominant federal scientific agency.

Although NASA's purpose was to lead in the peaceful scientific exploration of outer space, its operations had a definite impact on military research. Contracts and grants from NASA generated unprecedented new support for scientific research in geophysics, chemistry, rocketry, and many other technical fields which undoubtedly benefitted the missile-development programs of the Defense Department. In addition, the Air Force, Navy, and Army each maintained its own missile-research projects.

A Navy team coupled the Polaris missile with the nuclear submarine to fashion a highly flexible and mobile weapons system of outstanding importance. The Air Force and Army have shared about equally in the development of the giant intercontinental ballistic missiles which are slowly rendering manned-bombers obsolete. The Army's missile-research center at Huntsville, Alabama, and the Rocket Propulsion Laboratory at Edwards Air Force Base in California are among the best known military research centers in the United States today. The research and development expenditures of the Department of Defense stood at almost $8 billion in 1964, more than ten times those in 1947.

THE "KNOWLEDGE INDUSTRY" AND THE MILITARY

One of the most fascinating developments in the organization of military research since World War II has been the rise of the "idea industry." The RAND Corporation is probably the best example. Founded in 1946 as a part of Douglas Aircraft Company, RAND (the initials stand for "Research and Development") has thrived simply by providing the Air Force with advice on specialized problems that range all the way from "nuts and bolts" technology to matters of highest strategic policy. At its spacious headquarters in Santa Monica, California, the RAND Corporation employs more than eight hundred people and annually spends more than $13 million. Its employees pride themselves on not being members of the federal establishment, though most of their time is spent on government projects. Aerospace Corporation in El Segundo, California, is another well-known example of this new and unique industry. Sensing the organizational potential of these research institutes, leading universities have lately begun to establish consulting centers on their campuses. The Stanford Research Institute of Palo Alto, California, the Applied Physics Laboratory at the Johns Hopkins University, and the MITRE Corporation of Cambridge, Massachusetts, fall into this category. The Operations Evaluation Group (OEG), the Weapons Systems Evaluation Group (WSEG), and the Institute for Defense Analysis (IDA), though operating exclusively within the Pentagon, are other examples of privately operated consulting organizations that provide the government with specialized advice and overall policy evaluation. "We live in the age of the specialist," Edward L. Katzenbach, Jr., has noted, "and just as tooting one's own horn is now contracted out to a public-relations firm and one's anxieties to a psychoanalyst, so all kinds of technical problems and even questions of high policy are more and more being handed over to outside advice." Selling ideas to the federal government has become a big business.

The vast expansion of this part of America's defense industry represents the logical extension of the research contract system that worked so well for the OSRD. The federal government has achieved remarkable flexibility in all areas of military research by being able to utilize the services of non-civil service specialists. Many highly competent experts, who would refuse to consider a government position because of the relatively low salary and red tape, will gladly work for RAND or one of the other consulting firms which pay top salaries and offer such attractive fringe benefits as a kind of academic atmosphere and occasionally even sabbatical entitlements.

The Defense Department thus purchases ideas and advice on a contract basis in addition to hiring its own experts. This system naturally appeals to Congress, for it offers a spur to the national economy while at the same time limiting the growth of the Defense Department bureaucracy. Moreover, the system produces successful results. This new defense industry is another mark of the increasing sophistication of the American military research organization in the decade of the 1960's.

35 / The Mechanization of War, 1880-1919
EDWARD L. KATZENBACH, Jr.

In August 1914, after nearly a century of freedom from world war, the great powers of Europe plunged the world into a holocaust of unprecedented scale and character. Before an armistice was declared on the morning of November 11, 1918, thirty sovereign states had become involved in the madness, four empires had been overthrown, and seven new nations born. For this humanity had offered up 20,000,000 lives—half of them noncombatant. It was a war for which many nations share responsibility, but which none really wanted, and for which none was truly prepared. Although the war had been anticipated for years and planned to the smallest detail, in the actual event the plans had worked only to make the war inevitable and they proved worthless once the fighting began.

To a large degree, the gallows humor of the First World War stemmed from the fact that although a whole new technology of warfare was introduced, it was not absorbed in the strategy and tactics of the war. Indeed, it has been said that no inventions helped win the war, but one—the submarine—came close to losing it. An unprecedented number of new devices and machines in addition to the submarine were first used on a large scale during these years—the airplane, tank, machine gun, poison gas, and barbed wire. The net effect, however, was to create a stalemate which ruined all plans for a short war and frustrated every attempt to achieve the much-sought breakthrough. Until the manpower and industrial resources of the United States were thrown into the balance late in 1917, both the gallantry of the men and the stupidity of the officers were mocked by the new technology of warfare.

The military generation which fought World War I never understood what technology had done to their profession. That is why half a century after the war the only heroes are those like the eccentric Lawrence of Arabia, who operated farthest from the Western front. Despite occasional biographers, history has branded the generals of both the Allied and Central Powers—those mustached, monocled, booted, dapper gentlemen—as dunderheads and butchers.

The contrast between the military leaders of World War I and those of World War II is significant. Almost intuitively the generals of World War II understood that the technological revolution had changed warfare by offering choices as to time, space, and the means of marshalling men and materials. From these choices decisions were made, and reputations with them. The generals of World War II are, in the perspective of a quarter of a century, most capable men with moments of brilliance.

The intellectual problem of the military is to translate the characteristics of a piece of hardware—a gun, a machine, a vehicle—into a doctrine for its use, that is, to relate technological possibility to space and time, to mass, and to human psychology. The military in World War I failed to do this. It is a tragic paradox that what they did best in the way of planning helped bring on the war, and what they least comprehended made of that war a bloody morass.

THE EVE OF WORLD WAR I: THE TYRANNY OF THE MOBILIZATION TIMETABLE

The military grasped the relationship between transportation technology and the mobilization of masses of troops and materiel for an *initial strike*—the first clash of arms which they believed would be the last. Time was all important, and this they knew. No one in the higher reaches of command, however, ever seems to have thought of the relation of weapons technology and mass combat once the first battle had failed its objective. Therefore, they never had any idea at all how to conduct a long war.

When it came to mobilizing, the military were well prepared. The Prussian General Staff had known and understood the importance of the railroads since the 1850's, and in 1914 they were able to rush 250 troop trains a day to the frontiers. The French appreciated it only after the War of 1870, when the fact that all railroads led to Paris proved disastrous. The French, in turn, taught the British about these matters in the years of tipsy international relations between 1905 and 1914. Even the Russians understood the importance of the timetable, which is why they used different railroad gauges from those of the Germans.

Indeed, the technical consideration of mobilization became the single most important fact in international relations. This being so, mobilization was thought of as an allied as well as a national concern and led to a situation in which the policy of one nation was inextricably tied to that of its allies. Thus, the least temperate and/or most frightened nation could, and as it turned out, did, take the stronger and more stable to war.

It is not too much to say that in the years after 1905 the railroad timetable of the military was the final arbiter of foreign policy. For example, Moltke, the Chief of the Imperial German General Staff, virtually gave a blank check to an expansionist and irresponsible Austrian foreign policy by writing his Austrian counterpart that should Austria find it necessary to invade Serbia, thus causing Russia to mobilize, this would "constitute *causus foederis* for Germany." He went on to say that this would lead to French mobilization, and this was, in fact, the way it happened in 1914. Military necessity, or what passed for it, had tied German policy to Austria's apron strings.

Much the same thing happened to the British. Just on the eve of World War I, British statesmen discovered, to their great consternation, that the military had tied British policy to French. British and French planners had allocated precious boxcars to a British expeditionary force assigned to the mission of holding the French left flank.

In the years before the war, the diplomats were out of contact, and hence out of phase, with the military. The German military, as in the case of Moltke, committed their nation's policy to that of Austria; and military attachés abroad, bypassing their diplomatic superiors, reported directly to the Kaiser—frequently giving information and advice contrary to that of their ambassadors. The British military, as already noted, linked British foreign policy to French by agreement on a military timetable. Moreover, the diplomats, knowing in a general way that Austria and Russia were flighty and undependable because of their conflicting interests in the Balkans, were not aware that these two powers, having the longest mobilization timetables, had to begin to mobilize first.

The public seemed in many ways more concerned with the military situation than were the diplomats. There was great interest in war in the pre-World War I days; the topic was constantly in the press, and military problems were discussed in parliamentary bodies. In the 19th century, war was the concern of the citizen. Along with universal suffrage, universal military service became part of the democratic obligation. The public was enthusiastic and frightened. Peace movements, although relatively small, exercised growing influence on public opinion. So did various arms-control measures, or at least their rationale. Socialism became as attractive for its pacifist as for its economic slogans. In the last years of the 19th century and in the first years of the 20th century a new factor, namely, the general public, was added to the military.

As the potential of increasing the size of the mobilization base through mechanized transportation grew, more and more men were fitted into uniform. Military policy had, in fact, made a tinderbox of Europe. A spark anywhere could ignite the powder keg. This the timetable had done. And knowledge of the importance of the timetable had created a dangerous psychological imbalance: fear increased apace. The coming of war was actually almost a relief to many, and to many a matter of joy, a day of release.

There were, however, two aspects of technology which neither the military nor the public appreciated. The military had planned for a short war, one to be fought by uniformed personnel, each service on its own. They had never looked squarely at the implications of a long war which had to be co-ordinated.

Although Lord Kitchener, Chief of Staff of the British Army and Minister of Defense in the early stages of the war, and the younger Moltke, German Chief of Staff before the war, both apparently mentioned that the war might last longer than was generally thought, not much attention was paid to them. Kitchener was thinking back to the bloody Boer War (1898-1901), and Moltke was worried in general.

Most military men, looking back to the War of 1870, expected an eight weeks' war. The development in weapons technology from 1870 to 1914 did not impress them, nor did they ever foresee that weapons could change the very meaning of the numbers of troops, the duration of war, and hence its very nature. Even in retrospect this is difficult to understand, for the prewar military generation lived through one of the greatest military revolutions of all time.

NEW WEAPONS AND PROBLEMS

The most difficult weapons to clear for final mass production are the simplest— sword, lance, bayonet, and rifle—and the French Lebel had been adopted only in 1886, after ten years of squabbling. The improved Mauser of 1898, the 1903 Springfield, the Lee-Enfield, the Ariska, and the Mannlicher-Carcano rifles finally gave the modern infantryman a decisive advantage over the bowman of Crécy, an advantage which had often seemed indecisive during the first two hundred and fifty years of gunpowder.

By 1900 or shortly thereafter, the slip-fed, breach-loading, repeating rifle was in the hands of the troops of all the major powers. Self-firing weapons were on the assembly lines of the arms manufacturers. The machine guns of Maxim and Hotchkiss were in the arsenals of the great powers by the time of the Russo-Japanese War (1904-5), and narrowed the numbers of the great powers. As the Chinese ambassador remarked when he first saw a machine gun fire, the cost of bullets alone would make his nation a second-class power forever. At roughly the same time a glycerine recoil mechanism enabled artillery weapons, firing at 20 rounds per minute, to become themselves rapid-fire weapons. The French "Seventy-Five" (75-mm. cannon) was in production shortly after the turn of the century. Barbed wire, which had been manufactured automatically since 1874, was in military use at the end of the century.

In March of 1887, the American inventor Hiram S. Maxim fired 666 rounds in a minute at a field trial at Enfield, England. In the Matabele War of 1893 fifty infantrymen with four Maxim machine guns defended themselves against 5000 African warriors who charged five times in an hour and a half with great bravery—and 3000 dead. If the Winchester and the Colt won the American West, the Maxim won the world. It was the machine gun which, in a sense, carried the "white man's burden."

Even with data on reliability and rate of fire and with the evidence of the

Fig. 35-1. Machine Gun Corps antiaircraft post, 1917. (Courtesy of *Imperial War Museum*, London)

Matabele War and others, any studied appreciation of the meaning of the machine gun and weaponry related to it was simply not in evidence. Essentially, the reason was that the tactical use of these weapons posed an enormous challenge to the military mind, for now a man with a rifle equalled a platoon, men with a machine gun, a battalion. Was the machine gun an offensive or defensive weapon? Should it be used on the flanks or in the rear as was artillery? Should it be used with infantry units or in weapons companies of its own? Above all, how many were enough? These questions were not easy to answer.

Even more difficult was the question of strategy. Technology had destroyed man's ability to fight war in the terms in which he had earlier known it. There were no flanks to be turned, no breakthroughs to be made, and no deep raids to be ordered. Barbed wire prevented surprise. The bravery of the white man with the rifle proved little more effective against the machine gun than had the spear of the black man. By 1915, it should have been clear in high quarters that technology had stalemated war. The Queen of Battle, the Infantry, was mired in mud. Just as the castle had once been, and the town later became, the objective around which a war of attrition was fought, so in World War I the nation became a fortress. The only difference between nation and castle was that walls (trenches) were dug, not raised, and moats (barbed wire) were raised, not dug.

Attempts to fight fire with fire—or technology with more technology—largely failed, in part at least because no one really believed that innovation was possible. The Germans first used poison gas in April and May of 1915. The effect on the Allied lines was so devastating, however, that the Germans were not prepared to exploit their advantage, and by the time they were ready to do so in December of that same year, the Allies were prepared with gas masks and poisons of their own.

The tank, developed in Great Britain by the Admiralty under the name of "land battleships" when the army refused to work on it, was handled much the same way. In September 1916 the British committed their 20 tanks to battle, to the consternation and demoralization of the Germans. Not, however, until November 1917, in the Battle of Cambrai, were the British prepared to launch a meaningful tank attack, using 380 of the vehicles. Once again the Germans were unprepared, but the British were also; with no real idea of what tanks could or should do, the latter nearly snatched defeat from victory by changing plans midway through the battle.

THE ROMANCE OF WAR

The ideas of the military on the nature of war in 1914 were not consonant with the realities technology had established. In warfare, as in other affairs in life,

Fig. 35-2. A view of warfare at the Somme Crossings. The men of the 20th British Division and the 22nd French Division are seen in hastily dug rifle pits covering a road, 1918. (Courtesy of *Imperial War Museum*, London)

a clear vision of reality was blurred by value systems. Only when the tank came into being to poke holes through the ramparts, the airplane added a third dimension to war, and the amphibious assault was developed to attack from the sea, did mobility return to the battlefield. As it was, any analysis of technology should have indicated to military advisers that massive attacks would be futile and costly, and they in turn should have advised their governments accordingly. They did not. The reason was that the generals and their staffs had little feel for technology: they were, in fact, hopeless romantics.

This explains why the German cavalry, all ninety-three regiments with pennants flying from their lances, trotted off in 1914 to a war they would never fight. Of course, they should have known better. Each fall, at the German army's annual maneuvers, a team of referees would rule that one or another of several regiments of cavalry were shot out of action by artillery. But the Kaiser, whose favorite troops they were, would as regularly overrule the decision. Thinking such as this was not simply an aberration of German romanticism. The same general attitude prevailed elsewhere in Europe and explains why the cavalry survived the development of repeating, automatic, and semi-automatic weapons, the introduction of gasoline and diesel-fueled engines, and the invention of airborne weapons. The horse cavalry made those minor adjustments that time dictated absolutely; it continued to live out an expensive and decorous existence with splendor and some spirit into an age when it should have been only a memory. Even in the United States, the most mechanized nation on earth, the cavalry remained in a position comparable to that which it enjoyed in Poland up to the start of World War II. The *arme blanche* (the "white arm," as the cavalry was called), which linked man, sabre or lance, and horse, in a sort of spiritual weapons system, became a monument to public and military backwardness.

The bayonet and *pantalons rouges* (red pants) of the French army were similarly symbolic. The French were, on the eve of World War I, chivalric, or more accurately, quixotic. But unlike Don Quixote, who only charged windmills, the French charged machine guns—which they considered unsporting weapons, unfair and unethical.

In essence, the French believed that a proper state of mind (*élan*) would of itself achieve battlefield mobility. This emphasis on the human spirit was a fetish everywhere in Europe in 1914. In France it amounted to a sort of spiritual dedication not unlike that inculcated into the Japanese soldier in World War II. The difference between *banzai* and the charge *à outrance* (to the utmost) was largely linguistic. In short, the monocle, the shako, the lance, the swagger stick—those diverse symbols of courage and *insouciance*—tended to obscure the war as it really was. The romantic could not face the technical or even admit that it was there.

Like the horse cavalry, naval power was oversold in the years before World

War I, but navies flourished largely because of technology not in spite of it. They too had a romantic appeal to the public. This was important, and more revolutionary than anyone at the time seems to have realized, for with the advent of universal suffrage, the public of each nation had become the final arbiters of warfare. Theirs was the choice of weapons, of strategy, and even of tactics. They set the arena of war, dictated weapons and enemies, and made gladiators of the professional military. The military, in turn, had to become publicists in their own causes. So, as the ways of war became matters of public policy, military professionalism came to encompass propaganda.

Navies became particularly skilled in propaganda, although this was less true in France than in Great Britain, Germany, and the United States. From the 1880's to World War I navies were enormously successful in obtaining the public dollar. This was not due altogether to their own skills. They were aided by the public's interest in the whole new world across the seas. One could hardly be interested in African exploration, trade with China, or missionaries in the South seas, without thinking of navies. Steam power, the telegraph, the new printing presses, and the machine gun combined to bring colonies close to home, to make them seem romantic and important to the man on the street, and from a military point of view, to render them cheap to subdue and acquire.

MECHANIZATION AND THE OCEANS

Colonialism and navalism went hand in glove, of course. Colonies could be neither acquired nor defended without navies—at least so those who believed in them maintained. Navies were the insignia of world power, and filled a symbolic need for even the smallest and poorest of nations, those who could support only a few old ships. Navies were said to give a nation "a place in the sun." They certainly gave the "white man's burden" a lift and kept the sun from setting on the British Flag. Indeed, in its enthusiasm for its own "Great White Fleet," the United States quite forgot that the army had provided the great bulk of new territorial acquisitions and money bought most of the rest.

The public acceptance of large navies might never have been gained without bands of citizens who were organized into Navy Leagues. These, in turn, became great propaganda lobbies with funds from industry: coal and steel, shipyards, and armaments manufacturers banded together. From the very first years of the 19th century, for example, the United States Navy bought planks, masts, pitch, and cordage with an eye cocked on congressional interests. Lobbies can serve a worthwhile purpose in democracies, but one cannot help but feel that the ways in which the Navy Leagues were encouraged to fan the flames of nationalism and colonialism gave a new and sinister aspect to the ties between industry and navies on the eve of World War I. They created fear and dulled reason. The fever of the time can still be recaptured in novels such

Fig. 35-3. The *Dreadnought*, introduced into the British fleet in 1906. (Courtesy of the *Mariners Museum*, Newport News, Va.)

as Saki's *When William Came* and Erskine Childers's *The Riddle of the Sands*, both of them concerned with the possibilities of an invasion of Britain, and lending support to the proponents of a powerful fleet.

One of the most noteworthy aspects of naval development is that change in this field was so often spectacular. This was particularly true in the case of the introduction of the Dreadnought (battleship) into the British fleet in 1906. Like the atomic bomber, there was simply nothing like it in terms of sea power. Like the bomb, it established a new era in warfare. Yet because it seemed to make other seaborne weapons systems obsolete, it created a crisis for the island power that had built it. So powerful did the dreadnought class of ships appear to contemporaries that it seemed to renew the whole arms race. The dreadnought was, in this respect, similar to such other new developments in military technology as radar, the snorkel, the homing torpedo, the proximity fuse, and the ICBM (intercontinental ballistic missile). The dreadnought also introduced another quandary of major weapons systems—the calculus of security. How many dreadnoughts would constitute a margin of safety? What was a margin of safety?

The answer one gave depended on one's theory of warfare, and theory had become so rigid by the eve of World War I that it excluded contingency planning. It confined itself exclusively to the problem of enemy sea power. British naval authorities, like those of the United States, virtually banished armies from their thinking as an element of national military power. Joint planning between services was virtually non-existent. The theorists of German navy-building programs considered naval power to be a particular aspect of national power addressing itself to specific and separate issues.

Sea power to the British Admiralty revolved around the concept of "command of the sea." The articles on "Sea-power" and "Command of the Sea" in the 1911 edition of the *Encyclopaedia Britannica*, generally considered to be the most authoritative source possible, represented truth to the thoughtful citizen. Here is a portion of what Admiral Sir Cyprian Arthur George Bridge, G. C. B., had to say in his section on "Command of the Sea":

In war the British navy has three prominent duties to discharge. It has to protect the maritime trade, to keep open the communications between the different parts of the empire and to prevent invasion. If Great Britain commands the sea these duties will be discharged effectually. As long as she does that, the career of cruisers sent to prey on her commerce will be precarious, because command of the sea carries with it the necessity of possessing an ample cruiser force. As long as the condition mentioned is satisfied her ocean communications will be kept open, because an inferior enemy, who cannot obtain the command required, will be too much occupied in seeing to his own safety to be able to interfere seriously with that of any part of the British empire.

The theory was a stark one: it meant absolute superiority. The difficulty with the doctrine is that no one ever had defined—or could define—"absolute superiority." It was on the impossibility of deciding this that the theory of German sea power was based.

Admiral Von Tirpitz, the Chief of the Imperial Navy, was the author of a doctrine of sea power, the underlying assumption of which was psychological. The theory, directed, of course, against Great Britain, was built along these lines: peace would be maintained so long as an enemy feared to attack but felt that an attack against him would be impractical and foolhardy. It therefore followed that what Germany should do was to build a fleet sufficiently great, though not equal to, that of the British to prevent the latter from risking war—a naval stalemate. Of course, what the percentage should be was never spelled out; but it was also obvious that it was one on which two already belligerent parties could never agree. In Britain the theory created irrational panic, not rational fear.

These doctrines came primarily from surface-minded sailors who looked back to the Battle of Lepanto (1571), the defeat of the Armada (1588), Trafalgar (1805), or more recently, Shushima Straits (1905), where in the Russo-Japanese War, the Japanese had sunk the Russian fleet in one of the world's most ludicrous battles. The cruiser was thought to be a threat to commerce, but it turned out not to be the threat under steam that it was under sail; for with a relatively short range and without refueling at sea, it could not be a dangerous weapon. This was not true of the submarine, which could sneak back into port for fuel and provisions.

Fig. 35-4. A German submarine (U-boat) of World War I. (Robert T. Little Collection, the *Mariners Museum*, Newport News, Va.)

But as war broke, no one appreciated the real possibilities of the war at sea. The British admirals watched the German fleet. The German fleet stayed in port. After all, its mission—to prevent war—had already failed. As the war progressed and attrition became recognized as the prime objective, submarines were added to the German fleet. This presented Allied navies with their most difficult decision—whether or not to convoy.

The question was essentially one of dispersion versus concentration of force, and in the absence of modern analytic techniques there was a great deal of visceral thinking on the subject. Turn-around-time for convoys and holding the fast ships down to the pace of the slow ones were matters which had to be weighed against ship sinkings. The brilliant Admiral William S. Sims of the United States Navy eventually persuaded the British to convoy. This played a major role in cutting down Allied shipping losses to the German U-boats.

THE HOME FRONT

The glory of war, such as it was, went to those who won the Iron Cross, the Croix de Guerre, the Medal of Honor, or the Victoria Cross. But what kept the war going was the talent behind the lines, the ability of a free society to re-structure itself for war. Mechanization of the factory and of agriculture made it possible to support so gigantic an effort.

Each of the belligerent nations had to go through a whole series of shocks wide ranging in scope and content—none of which had been foreseen. France, for example, had severe unemployment in the initial months of the war; while certainly not as crucial as the Battle of the Marne, it nevertheless created a serious situation behind the lines. The German military had a mental block, even after the possibility of a long war was recognized, that prevented them from acknowledging that industries were an aspect of the new military professionalism. In Great Britain a free trade government had to learn to accept rationing and any number of state restrictions. In short, the idea that in the case of a long war an industrial society had to transform itself into a nation-in-arms came as a new idea and was met with improvisation. That democracies were able to adjust so quickly to an unaccustomed war-emergency "dictatorship" was remarkable. As it turned out, democracies were flexible, and the public, adjustable and willing to make sacrifices for the national cause.

Much has been written on the organization of the home front. The acceptance of rationing, of Great Britain's extremely severe Defense of the Realm Act (or "Dora," as it was called), of industrial restriction, and of enforced co-ordination was remarkable. Intense nationalism made this transformation possible. But what is so frequently not given the attention it deserves is the technology which made the buildup possible on the Western front.

What is very striking is the contrast between the American Civil War and World War I from the point of view of technological support. It is as difficult, for instance, to imagine World War I without the typewriter as without the machine gun. The fast printing press made the rapid dissemination of regulations and ration stamps possible. The telephone and the telegraph made unified

Fig. 35-5. A Curtiss JN-4 "Jenny," an American-built plane of World War I. (Courtesy of *The Smithsonian Institution*)

action expeditious. Filing systems, loose-leaf memoranda, and record duplication made possible fast recall.

World War I was one of the first wars in which disease, particularly typhus and cholera, had not played a role as important as that of generals' decisions. It was also one of the first in which dysentery and beriberi were not—except on the Eastern front—rampant and serious. The home front was responsible. Drug manufacturers were as important to the outcome of the war as arms manufacturers. And so were the canners of food. A World War I ditty, dreadful as it is, makes an important point,

> We can sing without bands
> Parade without banners;
> But no modern army
> Can eat without canners.

The production line in the canneries of the United States alone produced 500 million cans of food for the army. Agricultural machinery was sufficiently advanced so that over a million men could leave the farm while agricultural production increased.

Factory production was at least as remarkable. Few Americans realize that the French arms manufacturers were so efficient that they supplied not only their own armies but those of the American Expeditionary Force (some 1,390,-000 by Armistice Day) as well. Of forty-three United States aviation squadrons in France on Armistice Day, only 10 used American planes. Most of the rest, 4874 in all, were of French manufacture. Of a total of 4194 artillery pieces, 3532 were of French manufacture, as were 227 of the 289 tanks used. An official picture of the United States Army in action in World War I shows a doughboy with a French rifle. When one thinks of the mechanization of war, one must remember that the mechanization of the home front is as important to the outcome as what goes on at the fighting front.

THE RETREAT FROM TECHNOLOGICAL VICTORY

The importance of the home front was forgotten after the war. The United States did set up the Industrial College of the Armed Forces, to be sure, and made some tentative plans for industrial and labor mobilization in case of war —plans which were ignored when the next war actually came.

Indeed, most of the lessons of World War I were ignored. The French, convinced that the trench was the wave of the future, built the Maginot Line. The United States continued to pour money into its own Maginot Line—the coast artillery. Tanks were largely forgotten, and the lance returned as the chief weapon of the British cavalry. In the United States, the cavalry continued to charge across the plains of Kansas firing .45 automatics—weapons inaccurate even when not fired from the very unstable platform of a horse.

It remained for the defeated powers to understand the new technology. The Germans turned to the tank and the bomber. While the United States was spending only 1.19 per cent of its budget on research and development between the world wars, the German army spent large sums on new designs and prototypes—in secret, of course.

It is understandable perhaps that armies and navies should, in forced withdrawal from society at large, ignore the advances in technology which society was making. What is difficult to understand, however, is that there were so few military men who reflected on the technological lessons of World War I—and of those who did few were influential. Nearly all were associated with the newer, and hence "unproven," weapons such as tanks and airplanes, and their thinking was machine-oriented. There was virtually no thought given, particularly by the services of the victorious powers, to inter-service co-ordination. The generation of World War I passed over questions about the role of society as a whole in warfare, and the relation of time, space, mass, technology, and human psychology to the science and art of war.

36 / Three-Dimensional Warfare: World War II
RALPH SANDERS

On the first day of September 1939, units of the German Army smashed across the Polish border. World War II had begun. Twenty-six days later Warsaw fell, and, except for the sharp Russo-Finnish War, Europe settled down to the uneasy "phony war" during the winter months of 1939-40. Then, on April 9, 1940, Germany moved against Norway; on May 10 the Nazi troops invaded Denmark, Luxembourg, Belgium, and the Netherlands. The Battle of France opened on June 5, and German troops were in Paris within nine days—and France surrendered. Great Britain survived the Battle of Britain (August 8-October 31), and the world settled down to almost five more years of unprecedented destruction. On June 22, 1941, Adolf Hitler, the short-term ally of Soviet Premier Josef Stalin, attacked Russia, and less than six months later, on December 7, 1941, Japan precipitated United States entry into the war by its attack on the American naval base at Pearl Harbor in the Hawaiian Islands. During these years the most talented technical people and the combined industrial capacity of the world's major nations were concentrated on the technology of war.

Nevertheless, World War II was fought largely with weapons developed before hostilities began. The belligerents did not have time to push through new lines of fundamental research and then apply that research before the outcome of the war was decided. Major technological innovations in Germany, such as ballistic missiles, jet aircraft, and snorkel submarines, arrived too late to stave off her defeat; the American atomic bomb merely sped an inevitable Japanese collapse. The warring nations fought chiefly with guns, tanks, submarines, surface ships, and aircraft—all developed prior to the war; however, improvements in basic military technologies often proved decisive in the course of combat.

NEW ELEMENTS OF WARFARE

The war's distinguishing features were fourfold: the widespread application of science to the military effort, the coming of age of air warfare, the near worship of mobility, and a shift to weapons systems.

The United States long before had called upon scientists to improve its military hardware. The establishment of the National Academy of Sciences (NAS) during the Civil War wrought an early link between government and scientists. The demands of the First World War prompted President Woodrow Wilson to request the Academy to expand its practical services by creating the National Research Council (NRC). This Council helped fashion the future pattern of scientist-government co-operation by enlisting the services of eminent scientists on a host of working technical committees.

It was in World War II that scientists first entered the inner councils of government to organize a massive effort that deeply influenced the conduct of the war. Alarmed by the Nazi invasion of France and preparing for possible American involvement in the conflict, President Roosevelt in June of 1940 established the National Defense Research Committee (NDRC) to correlate and support wartime research. While the NDRC did excellent work, three major gaps were exposed: (1) inadequate exploitation of research findings by engineering development; (2) lack of machinery for co-ordinating NDRC research with that of the military services and other agencies; and (3) insufficient research into military medicine. In answer to these, President Franklin D. Roosevelt created the Office of Scientific Research and Development (OSRD) in June 1941 and placed it under the direction of Dr. Vannevar Bush, a distinguished scientist who was already chairman of the NDRC, which was now absorbed into the new agency.

The OSRD was to be the top science authority and operating agency throughout the war. It had funds, could initiate promising scientific and medical research, carry developments to the stage of operating models, and let contracts with industry and universities. The military departments, however, remained the final judges of the military value of the developments sponsored by the OSRD. Because the OSRD was part of the Executive Office of the President, Dr. Bush had direct access to the Chief Executive.

Through OSRD and its myriad operating committees, scientists and military men formed an effective partnership. A host of outstanding research centers, such as the Woods Hole Oceanographic Institute, carried on important war work. Before it disbanded in 1946, the OSRD had awarded more than 2500 contracts amounting to $536 million. It provided the United States with the very strengths that Germany and Japan often failed to muster in organizing science and technology for war: effective planning and co-ordination, a decision-making echelon free from parochial interests, and intelligent communication between research people and the military.

American scientists also co-operated closely with their British counterparts, largely through the efforts of Sir Henry Tizard (1885-1959), scientific adviser to the British government who headed an important mission to this country in August 1940. The Tizard mission brought American scientists abreast of substantial British achievements in weaponry. And, in developing the proximity fuse, jet propulsion, various radar devices, fire-control systems, heavy flame-throwers, RDX explosives—and the atomic bomb, the United States profited from intimate British help and frequently from previous British development.

In addition to improving the design of military hardware, scientists applied a new, systematic, mathematical technique—operations analysis—to tactical problems. This technique became invaluable to the military man trying to solve difficult problems of choice generated by a technology that increased the complexity of warfare. When first employed to devise effective ways of hunting submarines, operations analysis disclosed the laws of probability governing visual and radar sighting and other naval search patterns.

World War II was also characterized by the intense use of air power, an application which received its baptism of fire in World War I. Land and sea were no longer the sole battlefields; man made the atmosphere of his planet another highway to enemy territory. Some thirty years of improving the military airplane made possible this new dimension. Most of the dramatic technological innovations in military weapons—radar, the atomic bomb, the proximity fuse, electronic fire-control equipment, and incendiary bombs—either originated with or were chiefly used to improve or impair the airplane as a weapon system. German V-2 ballistic missiles were later to extend the new aerial dimension to outer space.

Disillusioned with the static warfare of World War I, the belligerents sought mobility by emphasizing the mechanization of military striking forces. To supply and maintain this new military machine, a greatly expanded logistic chain came into being. Logistic units, involving service and supply organizations, had to be heavily mechanized and provided with mobility equal to that of the fighting units. The ratio of service to combat troops grew, requiring radical changes in military organization. Mechanization did not eliminate the need for mass armies; as machines replaced men in many functions, the men were shifted to other tasks, some created by the mechanical trend in warfare.

World War II witnessed, moreover, a definite shift from reliance on individual weapons to weapons systems—that is, to a family of closely related items, all of which had to function to produce results. In 1918, the airplane represented an independent instrument of warfare; in World War II Britain was saved by a well-knit combination of aircraft, radar, and rapid communications. The carrier strike force, composed of many ships, planes, guns, and electronic gear, represents a highly integrated, super weapons system—a technological feat which makes co-ordination of component parts a prime task.

TYPES OF TECHNOLOGY

In modern wars, nations develop five broad categories of technologies: (1) delivery, (2) intelligence, (3) payload, (4) protective, and (5) production. Simply stated, delivery technologies are designed to move a payload from one spot to another. The delivery unit can be vehicles, such as tanks, ships, submarines, and aircraft; projectile components, such as bullet and shell casings and rockets; instruments which hurl projectiles, such as guns, artillery, and rocket-launchers; or combinations of these. The payload itself destroys or impairs an enemy's ability and will to wage war. World War II was largely fought using improved varieties of traditional high-explosive and metallic warheads, although chemical warheads, other than poison gas, also played an important role. The war ended with the most destructive warhead the world had ever seen—the atomic bomb.

The purposes of intelligence technologies are threefold: to identify and locate targets; to direct a delivery technology to a target; or to transmit information. For example, radar was developed to identify and locate airplanes; fire control, to guide a delivery technology to a target; and microwave, to improve the transmission of military information. Electronics provided the most significant innovations in intelligence technologies during World War II.

Delivery and intelligence technologies aim primarily to achieve or deny access. Military commanders aim to hit an enemy and prevent him from striking back. Radar was first intended to help deny access to hostile aircraft; when designed as airborne microwave it helped aircraft to strike at submarines. Obviously, communications equipment served both roles.

The belligerents fashioned some efficient protective technologies, that is, technologies which resist or counteract payloads once applied. For example, military medicine reduced mortality rates from disease and battlefield injury; advances in armored equipment saved lives, as did fortifications.

Finally, those charged with mobilizing industry excelled in perfecting large-scale production technologies, sometimes under very difficult circumstances. Too often we fail to realize that new weapons demand new production techniques and that quantity proved as crucial as quality in determining the outcome of the war.

DELIVERY TECHNOLOGIES

In analyzing the 1940 blitzkrieg (lightning warfare) victory over France and the Low Countries by German forces, the British Prime Minister, Winston Churchill, highlighted two delivery technologies—the airplane and tank. The opening battles of the war were lost not only because the Allies committed strategic errors, but because of the "unforeseen power of the armored column" and the great strength and fierceness of the German "main power, [the] air force." The Germans welded the airplane and the tank into a most powerful military force, one that prevented the enemy from regrouping; the Luftwaffe (German Air Force) became the first tactical air force, and the blitzkrieg, the grand tactic of quick ground victory, once air superiority was assured.

By 1918, observation planes, fighters, and multi-engined heavy bombers had appeared; subsequently, designers chiefly concentrated on improving these types to meet tactical needs. Aircraft engines profited from two developments in the 1930's. The supercharger permitted military aircraft to operate at greater speeds and high altitudes, and the controllable-pitch constant-speed propeller allowed maximum utilization of power at various altitudes. During World War II, aircraft were highly specialized with from one to four reciprocating engines and an aluminum airframe housing armament and electronic equipment.

At the outbreak of hostilities, all fighter aircraft were short range. Nevertheless, the British Hurricane and Spitfire proved themselves during the Battle of Britain in the summer of 1940, and the Germans fought with the speedy (and numerically superior) Messerschmitt.

The United States entered the war with a whole series of fighters but lacked one of long-range capability. On October 14, 1943, bombers flying over Schweinfurt, Germany, and beyond the range of existing fighter escort planes, sustained severe losses from German fighters. For protection of their bombers on such raids which penetrated deeply into enemy territory, the Americans developed the long-range Mustang fighter escort, equipped with British Rolls-Royce engines and disposable fuel tanks. The British acknowledged the Mustang to be the best American fighter of the war.

In 1939, although Germany boasted the strongest air arm in Europe, its bombers were largely limited to close support of ground troops. It made extensive use of slow-moving, but fairly effective dive bombers, had a few medium bombers, but never developed an independent strategic air force. British airmen, conversely, seeing great promise in large bombers striking the heart of the enemy's territory, destroying industrial might, and sapping its morale, introduced a series of greatly improved, heavy, four-engined bombers.

American airmen, sharing the British view, fought the war with a family of heavy, medium, and light bombers, all designed prior to Pearl Harbor. The first

Fig. 36-1. The P-51 Mustang fighter escort of World War II. (Courtesy of *The Smithsonian Institution*)

operational B-17 was delivered to the U. S. Army Air Corps in 1937; the B-29, introduced late in the war, was similarly designed in the late 1930's. During the war, the United States concentrated chiefly on improving the armament, radio communications, fire-control systems, and the power of engines of its planes. The more powerful engines permitted additional bomb loads for longer distances. The Americans also developed leakproof fuel tanks to prevent fire when wings were hit.

Bombing raids against Axis military forces and other targets caused heavy damage to the enemy economies. In Europe alone, almost 2.7 million tons of bombs were dropped. Massive attacks against German and Japanese cities proved particularly destructive. During the summer of 1943, Hamburg was subjected to a series of Royal Air Force (RAF) incendiary raids which produced such severe "fire storms" that many thousands of civilians, trapped in shelters, suffocated for lack of oxygen. While strategic bombing did not cripple German war production, it so devastated certain crucial sectors of the economy that the German war machine faltered.

Jet aircraft and missiles came too late to alter the outcome of the war. In contrast to reciprocating (piston) engines, the turbojet engine obtains propulsion by forcing the products of combustion to the rear, producing an equal and opposite forward thrust. It differs from a rocket engine in that it uses air for combustion, while the energy for the rocket engine's combustion is self-contained in its oxidizer. Studies on jet propulsion began as far back as 1923, but it was not until 1930 that Frank Whittle, RAF officer and engineer, obtained British patents for a turbojet engine. The Germans became jet enthusiasts and conducted the first flight of a jet-propelled aircraft in 1939. It was the British, however, who formed the first jet squadron in 1944; the Germans followed in January 1945; and the Americans, in December, too late to use the jet aircraft in combat. The Germans further equipped their ME-262 jet with the highly effective 55-mm air-to-air rocket.

The Germans pioneered the revolutionary flying bomb (V-1) and the long-range ballistic liquid-fuel rocket (V-2). The V-1, an "air-breathing," pilotless jet plane with a range of 150 miles, carried a high-explosive warhead. With a top speed of nearly 400 mph, it could be controlled in flight by an automatic pilot, magnetic compass, and altimeter. The V-2 was a single-stage, surface-to-surface, supersonic rocket, which followed a parabolic trajectory. It weighed five and a half tons and had a range of 200 miles and a warhead of some 210 pounds of explosive. Its top speed of 3500 mph was well beyond that of any Allied manned vehicle. The rocket comprises a chamber closed at one end. When fired, gas pressure escaping from an open nozzle exerts full force upon the closed end, producing a thrust in the direction opposite to the nozzle.

Fig. 36-2. Diagram of the German V-1. (Courtesy of *Colonel G. B. Jarrett, Aberdeen, Md.*)

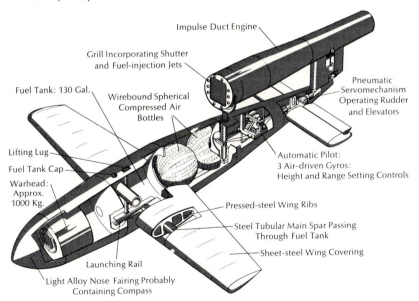

Impulse Duct Engine

Grill Incorporating Shutter and Fuel-injection Jets

Fuel Tank: 130 Gal.

Wirebound Spherical Compressed Air Bottles

Pneumatic Servomechanism Operating Rudder and Elevators

Lifting Lug

Fuel Tank Cap

Warhead: Approx. 1000 Kg.

Automatic Pilot: 3 Air-driven Gyros: Height and Range Setting Controls

Pressed-steel Wing Ribs

Steel Tubular Main Spar Passing Through Fuel Tank

Sheet-steel Wing Covering

Launching Rail

Light Alloy Nose Fairing Probably Containing Compass

Fig. 36-3. *Above,* German V-1 diving. *Below,* the explosion. (Courtesy of *Colonel G. B. Jarrett*)

Although the Chinese invented the black powder rocket and an American physicist, Robert H. Goddard (1882-1945), pioneered liquid-fuel engines, the Germans perfected it as a long-range weapon. Work began under Major General Walter Dornberger about 1932. The German military seriously considered its possibilities by 1935 and two years later opened up their main rocket-research station at Peenemunde on the Baltic Sea. This center cost $120 million and employed a peak of 2200 scientists and technicians. The Germans studied long-range missile bombing of Britain in 1941, one year before they launched their first successful test of the V-2. Churchill saw reconnaissance photographs of long-range missiles in April 1943, two months before Hitler gave the V-2 program the highest priority. The first V-1 struck London in June 1944 and the

Fig. 36-4. Cross-section of the German V-2 rocket.
(Courtesy of *Colonel G. B. Jarrett*)

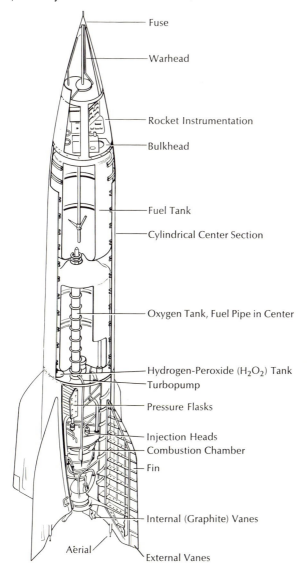

Fuse

Warhead

Rocket Instrumentation

Bulkhead

Fuel Tank

Cylindrical Center Section

Oxygen Tank, Fuel Pipe in Center

Hydrogen-Peroxide (H_2O_2) Tank

Turbopump

Pressure Flasks

Injection Heads

Combustion Chamber

Fin

Internal (Graphite) Vanes

Aèrial

External Vanes

first V-2 three months later. In 1945, Germany's V-2 rocket was the world's finest. This important spoil of war passed into the hands of both the United States and the Soviet Union.

Using jet aircraft, the proximity fuse, radar, and improved fire control, the Allies were able to blunt the V-1 attacks, but there was no defense against the V-2. Air raids against Peenemunde and launching sites succeeded only in a temporary slowdown in the growth of the German missile capability. Only the capture of the launching sites near the very end of the war in Europe ended the V-2 attacks. Despite its poor accuracy, the weapon was responsible for the death of 2700 persons in Great Britain and 5000 in Antwerp. Had the V-2 become available six months earlier, General Dwight D. Eisenhower believed, it could have seriously hampered preparations for the Normandy invasion by attacking the staging areas. The Germans also experimented with the A-10, a transatlantic rocket capable of hitting the United States.

On the ground, the tank became the major vehicle used to break through enemy positions. The first tank attack had been launched during the First World War by the British, hoping to break out of the military stalemate of im-mobilized, trench warfare. This powered, heavily armored vehicle with cater-pillar tracks could traverse trenches, barbed wire, and other defenses; however,

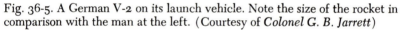

Fig. 36-5. A German V-2 on its launch vehicle. Note the size of the rocket in comparison with the man at the left. (Courtesy of *Colonel G. B. Jarrett*)

Fig. 36-6. A Sherman tank of the United States Army moving up to the front in World War II. (Courtesy of *Colonel G. B. Jarrett*)

the British were unprepared to exploit the breakthrough achieved by their initial tank attack. By the beginning of World War II improvements in hull construction, controlled differential steering, rubber jointed tracks, thicker armor, and power plants of high horsepower-to-weight ratio made the tank a formidable weapon. Mobile tactics replaced static warfare and made use of a large variety of tanks ranging in weight from 10 to 75 tons, carrying armor plate six inches thick or more, and mounting guns from 37 to 120 mm. Speed varied from a slow crawl to 60 miles per hour.

In general, German tanks were bigger, faster, and more heavily armored than those of the Allies. Mindful of their experiences with heavy Soviet tanks and showing great ingenuity, the Germans tended to build even heavier tanks, especially the 47-ton Panther and the 75-ton Tiger II, the latter equipped with an extremely effective 8.8-cm. caliber gun. In 1940, the United States Army, though well equipped with light tanks, lacked heavies and mediums. Later the Sherman medium tanks, which replaced the oft-criticized Grant, provided the main punch of U. S. armored strength. Advanced models had cast upper hulls and high-velocity 75-mm. guns; a few had 105-mm. howitzers. In 1944 the

Germans could oppose the Shermans with their heavies which, though far from perfect, had much tougher protective armor and more powerful guns. The American response was numerical superiority and special tactics. Recognizing the need for a heavy tank, United States Ordnance developed the Pershing, probably the best heavy tank to see action; however, it arrived in Europe after the worst fighting was over.

At sea, the submarine took a heavy toll of shipping. The Allies and neutrals lost some 23.5 million tons of shipping, while American submarines all but eliminated the Japanese merchant fleet. American submarines were not only twice as large as the German, but also faster, more heavily armed and capable of longer cruises. Germany adapted a Dutch invention, the "Schnorkel," a hinged stack which could be extended above the surface to provide an air intake for the diesel engines and an exhaust for hot gases. No longer required to surface for recharging batteries, German submarines could operate underwater for days at a time, thereby reducing chances of detection; yet this caused the crew great discomfort and was subject to mechanical problems in rough seas. Moreover, introduced in 1944, it came too late to help the Axis.

Torpedoes, depth charges, and mines saw frequent service in naval warfare. Torpedoes, self-propelled underwater missiles, were adapted to submarines, airplanes, and patrol boats. The Germans introduced homing, acoustic torpedoes, called "Gnats" or "Wrens," which were guided by the sound of a ship's propeller. The British, by towing a noisemaker, called Foxer, from the stern of a ship, diverted the acoustic torpedo from its target.

The depth charge, a cylindrical can containing about 600 pounds of TNT, was the chief weapon used against submerged submarines. The Allies perfected the more highly destructive Torpex depth charge and the Hedgehog, a mount which threw 24 small missiles ahead of the ship. Since the missiles exploded only upon contact, no unsuccessful explosion disturbed the sonar search for the enemy sub.

Serious shipping losses were caused by the more than 450,000 mines laid by the Allies and Axis. When the Germans introduced a magnetic mine, the British countered with a "degaussing" process which, by electric current, neutralized the magnetic effect of the hull.

During the war all Anglo-American ground operations began with successful amphibious assaults. The Allies produced a whole family of landing craft which hit the shore without swamping, thanks to the fact that only a small area forward touched the beach. In addition to facilitating initial attacks, these vessels also provided over-the-beach logistic support. The Allies also produced vehicles which could operate on both land and water. The DUKW, (the "Duck"), an amphibious jeep, proved effective in the surf and on the beaches, while the Weasel, a track-laying vehicle suitable for swamps and mud, was converted into a self-propelled amphibian that could operate in deep water.

INTELLIGENCE TECHNOLOGIES

The most far-reaching intelligence technology used during World War II was radar—"radio detection and ranging." The outbreak of hostilities in 1939 accelerated the pace of electronic development (especially on radar and its variations) to tackle the crucial problems of observation, fire control, and navigation.

Simply stated, radar is an electronic sighting device which discloses distant objects by means of a reflected radio signal, an echo. The heart of this device is an electronic tube, which generates the electromagnetic waves that are reflected by objects in their path. Radar enormously extends the effectiveness and accuracy of human vision. It can "see" in darkness and fog; can determine distance rapidly, accurately, and continuously; can detect objects up to 200 miles away; and display these data within seconds for many objects over a vast area.

Radar grew out of radio-wave research begun in 1887 by Heinrich Hertz, the famed German physicist. In 1921 Dr. Albert Hall of General Electric invented the "magnetron," a vacuum tube which made it feasible to generate adequate power at wavelengths of less than 50 centimeters. The magnetron was a crucial advance because by narrowing the wavelength it increased the accuracy of determining angles of elevation, or azimuth. The British, more than others, intensified research to improve the magnetron. Largely through the efforts of Tizard, five radar stations became operational in England by 1935, and fifteen more joined the system within a few years.

The Germans lagged in radar development. They started early enough, in 1936, and by the outbreak of the war achieved a respectable early warning system. But Germany lacked effective co-ordination among military and technical officers, industrial laboratories, and university scientists. The military also tended to dictate to the scientists, and it pursued rocket and missile research far more actively than it did electronics development. Only the Peenemunde rocket group had a qualified electronic engineering section.

The Allies developed radar types to cope with changing military needs. In the Battle of Britain, for instance, radar helped pinpoint approaching German aircraft, and enabled the RAF to husband its fighters. When daylight attacks failed, the Germans switched to night bombing. Anticipating this shift, the British, with the help of the Radiation Laboratory at the Massachusetts Institute of Technology, developed airborne microwave search radar for night fighters. When submarine warfare became a menace, the Allies developed similar airborne radar for submarine search. As the submarine threat waned, they shifted to the problem of bombing at night or through cloud overcast. Finally, with the Allied invasions of North Africa, Italy, and Normandy, they put radar to work improving air-ground tactics. The concept of using radar for ground control and strategic air operations apparently never occurred to the Germans, although some of their equipment could have been adapted to these purposes.

Radar's great success prompted the belligerents to work hard designing counter measures. Thus, while the Nazi battleships *Schornhorst* and *Gneisenau* moved from Brest to a safer port under cover of fog and snow, the Germans successfully jammed British radar. Because the Allies took the air offensive over Europe, they had greater need to perfect counter measures against the enemy radar. They dropped metallic strips called "window" or "chaff" which, by returning so many echoes, hopelessly cluttered German radar screens. They later added an electric jammer, Carpet. This combination proved very effective inasmuch as the measures taken by the Germans to overcome the effects of "window" and "chaff" against their antiaircraft radar made it all the more vulnerable to Carpet.

The Allies adapted radar to produce one of the most remarkable intelligence technologies of the war—the proximity fuse. Also called the variable-time (VT) fuse, it contained a tiny radar transmitter and receiver which, after picking up waves reflected from the target, detonates a projectile at a distance measured to cause maximum damage. This fuse eliminated the errors associated with mathematically calculated and manually set time-fuses. Its accuracy improved the effectiveness of air bursts from five to twenty times.

Although the British first experimented with proximity fuses, the Applied Physics Laboratory of the Johns Hopkins University developed the first operational fuse. The Americans originally designed it for the shell of the Navy 5-inch, 18-caliber antiaircraft gun. The Germans made many attempts to perfect this device, but failed to produce a standardized service item. Afraid that the Germans might copy a captured fuse, the United States at first limited its use to the Pacific naval war, where it proved effective against Japanese kamikaze suicide attacks. The Allies rescinded the prohibition against its use in Europe in 1944, when Britain faced impending German V-1 attacks. Hundreds of "buzz-bombs" were thus destroyed in mid-air.

When used in land warfare the proximity fuse greatly increased the fragmentation effect of artillery shells by detonating some 20 to 30 feet above the ground target. In this role, it helped significantly to stem the German advance during the Battle of the Bulge in December 1944–January 1945.

Improved fire-control mechanisms became imperative as existing mechanical devices proved inadequate against fast-moving aircraft. Mathematicians were set to work developing reliable and accurate tracking mechanisms capable of calculating three-dimensional measurements: distance, direction, and speed. To aid heavy antiaircraft, the Allies developed the M-9, an electrical device utilizing both optical and radar equipment which eliminated all operations except tracking. The M-9 performed magnificently against the German V-1 attacks. The more difficult problem of fire control for lighter 20- to 40-mm. guns was brilliantly solved by the Mark 14 sight, a gyroscopic lead-commuting device.

The Allies developed other antiaircraft devices as well as more effective air-borne systems, including an improved central fire-control system for the B-29. On the other hand, the German military, once more unwilling to communicate with science, failed to appreciate good design proposals offered to them.

PAYLOAD TECHNOLOGIES

Without a doubt, the atomic bomb proved the war's most dramatic technological achievement. On July 16, 1945, scientists at Alamogordo, New Mexico, under the direction of Dr. J. Robert Oppenheimer, exploded the first plutonium bomb. The results were immediately forwarded to President Harry S. Truman, then in conference at Potsdam. Ten days later the President issued his surrender ultimatum to Japan. After the Japanese failed to accept by the July 31 deadline, on August 6 an American B-29 bomber dropped the first atomic bomb, containing U-235, on Hiroshima; a second, containing plutonium, fell on Nagasaki three days later. These bombs had more explosive power than 20,000 tons of TNT, by far the single most destructive force in history. Four square miles of Hiroshima were devastated and 80,000 people killed; some 40 per cent of Nagasaki's buildings were razed and 39,000 killed.

Because of shorter development lead times, important new chemical warheads were developed after the war began—flame-throwers and incendiaries with thickened fuel, and large area smokescreen generators capable of sustained performance. The Germans used magnesium bombs on the British with telling effect, and the British retaliated in kind. The United States, at first short of magnesium, designed a less effective thermite bomb (powdered aluminum and iron oxide) with which General James Doolittle raided Tokyo in April 1942. Later the United States developed efficient magnesium bombs.

To improve penetration of bombs through the slate roofs of German buildings, American engineers attached an iron nose. When used in the Pacific theater of operations, however, these bombs crashed through the flimsy Japanese house roofs and buried themselves in the ground, causing little damage. The answer was a lighter bomb that would produce a less intense but wider flame. It was found that metallic soap could thicken gasoline, thus producing "napalm," or jellied gasoline, a remarkably effective incendiary material. The 100-pound napalm bomb (M-47) and the 6-pound bomb (M-69) soon began to roll off assembly lines. In January 1945, a massive M-69 incendiary raid destroyed fifteen square miles in the center of Tokyo. The same incendiaries were equally effective against German targets.

Military men quickly saw that jellied gasoline opened a new field for flame-throwers. Previous portable units, using gasoline or fuel oil, had a range of only about 25 yards. By thickening, the range was increased to 60 yards for back-borne sets and 150 yards for those mounted on tanks. On Iwo Jima and other

Pacific islands, flame-throwers effectively killed and dislodged Japanese from caves and dugouts.

The Allies also made great strides in improving chemical smokescreens to hide targets from the enemy. Based on the work of Irving Langmuir, a Nobel Prize winner, the United States fashioned the M-1 Mechanical Smoke Generator which helped save the tenuously held Anzio beachhead in Italy in 1943.

RDX, or cyclonite, proved the most important conventional explosive developed during the war. Its originators, the British, persuaded the United States Navy to conduct research on this explosive. The Navy became convinced of RDX's superiority over existing explosives, especially for mines, depth charges, and torpedoes. The result was Torpex, a combination of RDX, TNT, and aluminum, which increased destructiveness by at least 50 per cent. The Allies also used RDX mixture in bombs dropped on submarine pens and in sinking the German battleship *Tirpitz*.

PROTECTIVE TECHNOLOGIES

The medical profession made great strides in protecting military personnel against disease and in saving the lives of the wounded during World War II. These advances stemmed from intensive applied rather than basic research, which all but stopped during the war. A few statistics will illustrate medicine's impressive record. During World War I as many United States soldiers died from disease as in battle, while only 23 per cent died from non-battle causes during World War II. Less than 3 per cent of the wounded died compared to 11 per cent during the First World War. This record was accomplished by no one single technological development. It was due to the widespread use of effective drugs and medicines, including anti-malarials, blood and blood substitutes, antibiotics, vaccines, and insecticides; improved surgical techniques; well-equipped medical facilities at the front and aboard ship; and highly skilled and motivated personnel.

Millions of man-hours were lost during the war due to malaria; in the southwest Pacific, half of all hospital cases suffered from this disease. While improved mosquito control helped somewhat, one drug, Atabrine, was finally responsible for the sharp drop in malaria patients. After massive use of this drug during 1944, the incidence of malaria fell from 20.6 per cent to 7.8 per cent.

Blood and blood substitutes saved countless lives and returned many wounded men to combat. Doctors had long known the benefits of transfusions of blood and blood fractions. Wartime innovations consisted in obtaining large quantities of blood, quick processing, and rapid delivery to the battlefield in usable forms. The use of blood plasma, rather than whole blood, for example, did away with problems of refrigerated transportation and made it possible to give transfusions on the battlefield and thus save many lives.

The greatest medical miracle of World War II was penicillin. This wartime miracle of antibiotics was a triumph of applied research. Although Sir Alexander Fleming announced penicillin's discovery in 1929, the drug did not come into common use until after hostilities began, and only after problems of mass production and quality had been solved. Co-operation between commercial firms and government scientists solved laboratory problems; American firms tested the drug and then mass produced it for use in all combat theaters. Industry developed packaging methods to preserve the quality of the drug over long-distance transportation, and these permitted storage in small places and facilitated administration under difficult circumstances.

Despite the effectiveness of the new weapons, conventional fortifications often proved an efficient protective technology against them. Nothing was demonstrated more convincingly than the unique power of defending forces, under cover of conventional earthworks, to survive "saturation" fire by air bombs and naval artillery. It is estimated that the massive preparatory bombardment by Americans of the Japanese-held Pacific islands of Kwajalein, Tarawa, and Makin killed only about 4 per cent of the defenders, who had dug in deeply. Nonetheless, these bombardments did insure the amphibious landings of the American forces and severely damaged the enemy's communications.

TECHNOLOGIES OF PRODUCTION

One of America's greatest wartime feats was the development of production technologies capable of providing Allied troops with a decisive quantitative superiority in weapons. Mass-production techniques were applied even to the new and complex instruments of wartime with astonishing success. Industries learned to work within very close tolerances, sped up metalworking by widespread use of very hard tungsten carbide cutting tools, developed process control and inspection operations for the new electronics industry, made advances in production volume and fabrication know-how in light metals, perfected substitute raw materials, and improved packaging and shipping techniques. American factories poured out vast amounts of war materiel—over 86,000 tanks and 296,000 aircraft. British and Commonwealth production added to this huge inventory.

Basing their initial strategy on quick victory through use of the blitzkrieg, the Germans had not originally planned for a sizable expansion of wartime industry. After the Nazis encountered difficulties in Russia, they realized their mistake, and from 1942 German production experienced a spectacular improvement under Albert Speer, a remarkable organizer. By the time peak production was reached in August 1944, output had tripled. Speer accomplished this feat despite repeated Allied bombings, but this amazing performance could not deter Germany's defeat.

THE HUMAN FACTOR

Technology helped mightily to determine the course of World War II, and such major combatants as the United States and the Soviet Union emerged from the war convinced that national capabilities in research and development on new weapons and the organization of new weapons systems were critical to the maintenance of world power in the future. Yet, in the final analysis, technology lessened somewhat, but did not dominate, the human element in warfare—courage, loyalty, skill, and organizational ability. These qualities were crucial in determining the outcome, in the laboratory and the factory, as well as on the battlefield.

37 / The Contemporary Spectrum of War
EUGENE M. EMME

As rapid technical change came into the art and science of warfare in the 20th century, historical experience declined proportionately as a reliable teacher of military strategy, doctrine, and tactics. This historical trend was etched in bold relief on August 6, 1945 by one bomber, one bomb, and one city called Hiroshima. The future of warfare had been drastically altered. Thereafter, superior technology and diplomacy were to become as important as the organization and numbers of military forces in the prevention of war, as well as in the conduct of effective military operations.

The velocity of changes in weaponry had accelerated rapidly during World War II. Radar, jet aircraft, large liquid-fuel rockets, and the atomic bomb were major innovations. Among the historical trends reflected in the increased influence of technology upon warfare after 1945 were the following: (1) the dehumanization of combat and attrition and the rise of noncombatant casualties because of the enlarged radius of mobility and firepower available, largely through the medium of air power; (2) the destruction of undeployed military forces, of logistic lines of supply, and of productive forces far behind the surface battle lines brought about by aircraft, submarines, and liquid-fuel missiles; (3) the emergence of man-machine complexities of total mobilization—including resources, manpower, finance, organization, research and development, production, and pipelines of fuel, munitions, and weaponry—of decisive influence upon the outcome of a war itself as well as its prevention; and, finally (4) the expansion of the range of military operations to global radii which not only altered the meaning of offense and defense but which also placed the highest premium upon weapons-system development.

A fantastic evolution of weapons-systems changes in the two decades following the end of World War II reinforced these trends. The contemporary spectrum of warfare thus derives largely from technology.

The acceleration of military technology was both a determinant and a consequence of a bipolar world, the geopolitical result of World War II, whereby political and military strength were concentrated in two powers, the United States and the Soviet Union. Germany and Japan, Russia's traditional sources of containment in the heart of Eurasia, had been crushed by defeat. China and all of Europe had been weakened by the years of extended warfare. A combination of subversion and insurgency soon saw China sucked into the Communist orbit. The states of Eastern Europe contiguous to Russia fell under Soviet control enforced by the never-demobilized Red Army. An "iron curtain," as Winston Churchill said, clanged down from Eastern Germany on the Baltic to Bulgaria on the Black Sea. Kremlin pressure was exercised directly in the Middle East, while Communist parties mushroomed in countries of Western Europe. The Truman Doctrine for Greece and Turkey (1947) and the Marshall Plan (1948) for Western Europe successfully consolidated politico-military boundaries between East and West. Four-power occupation of defeated Germany proved most uneasy as the Soviets imposed a blockade on the surface access routes to the political island of occupied Berlin in 1948. Only by a massive airlift of food and coal were the United States and Britain able to preserve the status quo on the general arrangements made at the Potsdam Conference (1945) for peace in Europe.

The United States demobilized the bulk of its wartime forces in 1946, and placed high hopes for the maintenance of peace on its monopoly of atomic bombs and on the infant United Nations. American proposals presented by Bernard Baruch for the international control of atomic energy, submitted to the United Nations on June 14, 1946, were rejected. In the face of Soviet aggrandizement into the power vacuum of Central Europe and the Far East, the United States reluctantly stockpiled nuclear weapons and accelerated its reconstruction of strategic air power with jet-powered aircraft. Improved B-29 "Superfortresses" (B-50's) with tankers and 10,000-mile range B-36 heavy bombers provided global range nuclear capability until the twin-jet B-47 "Stratojet" bombers and later the B-52 "Stratofortress" became operational.

Hopes that American monopoly of nuclear firepower would support world peace were shattered with the first Soviet nuclear test in 1949. President Harry

S. Truman immediately ordered the development of thermonuclear (fusion) weapons to proceed, thus leading to another thousandfold increase in explosive power available in a single bomb device. Nuclear weapons and their delivery systems were the taproot of military technology and security strategy henceforth. In the words of Walter Millis: "It was not the theorists who were changing, it was war itself, more and more terribly weaponed by the possibilities of modern science and technology."

SOVIET POLICY

While Washington and Moscow became centers for a polarized global conflict, the technological essense of the "cold war" was not fully apparent at its inception because of traditional viewpoints and the nature of Communist subversion. Immediately after the war the Kremlin had found itself in a strategic crisis. The powerful Red Army, conventionally weaponed with artillery, tanks, battlefield rockets, and infantry, was pre-eminent in backing Soviet expansion and control in areas contiguous with Russian territory. But lacking the atomic bomb and long-range air forces, the Soviet Union was obviously vulnerable to atomic air attack in the event of war with the United States, the only power base opposing its consolidation of Eurasia. Highest priorities were thus immediately assigned to break the American nuclear monopoly and to develop first-class aviation and intercontinental rocket forces as well.

On March 15, 1947, after reviewing the capabilities of captured German V-2 rocketry, Premier Josef Stalin said: "Such a rocket could change the fate of war. Do you realize the tremendous strategic importance of machines (intercontinental rockets) of this sort? They could be an effective straightjacket for that noisy shopkeeper Harry Truman. We must go ahead of it, comrades. The problem of the transatlantic rockets is of extreme importance to us." At the same time, leading American scientists and engineers were testifying before Congress and advising the President that intercontinental rockets were "impossible."

Exploitation of the ten-year lead in rocket technology manifested by the German V-2 was an option selected by the Soviets, one which resulted in intercontinental ballistic missiles with nuclear warheads and the Sputniks. Because the Russians began with the development of rockets of intercontinental range with high-explosive warheads, and also because of their backward nuclear technology, they constructed a large rocket of great thrust which gave them superior rocketry in the opening years of the Space Age. In the meantime, the Soviet Union tested its fission bombs in 1949 and acquired a thermonuclear bomb in 1954. It also developed its air force. The MIG-15 swept-wing jet fighter with Soviet pilots proved a worthy match for the best American fighter aircraft, the F-86, during the Korean War. By 1955 the Soviets had developed an intercontinental heavy jet bomber, called the Bison, at the same time ex-

Fig. 37-1. German V-2 rocket shortly after takeoff.
(Courtesy of *Colonel G. B. Jarrett*, Aberdeen, Md.)

hibiting a wide range of aeronautical advances in fighters, turbo-prop transports, and helicopters. Western strategists argued over "deterrence" and "counter force" strategies in the late 1950's and early 1960's as a result of the revolution in military technology and the Soviet Union's exploitation of this technology which made it a first-rate military power.

KOREAN WAR

The geographically contained Korean War, which began on June 25, 1950, caused the United States not only to remobilize its conventional army, air, and naval forces, but also to undertake urgent technological developments for the maintenance of a power base for worldwide stability.

With the creation of a unified Department of Defense in 1947 to include an independent Air Force alongside the Army and Navy, the problem of severely limited funds exploded into inter-service arguments over various weapons systems. The B-36 versus the aircraft carrier debate, while argued in terms of institutional concepts, actually grew out of the question of the ability of different weapons systems to meet the needs of national security in a large war as well as in lesser conflicts. The "bigger-bang-for-a-buck" budget which had earlier been projected for fiscal year 1951 provided $14.2 billion for defense, the historic pre-Korean War budget of Defense Secretary Louis Johnson. As events turned out, the limited monies for research and development proved excessively restricted, forcing the cancellation of basic rocket studies. The needs, as seen in early 1950, did not seem to include an intercontinental ballistic missile, much less an earth satellite.

All this, of course, changed overnight with the American decision to defend South Korea under United Nations auspices. The defense budget jumped in 1951 to $47 billion. For the United States the race for superior weaponry had begun in earnest with the first Soviet nuclear test in 1949, the demands of Korea, and the buildup of NATO forces after 1950.

In 1956, when General Nathan F. Twining returned from his visit to Russia, he summarized:

> Of late there has been a wealth of visible evidence that the mightiest of all potential aggressors is determined to surpass the technology in general of the United States, and our airpower in particular. I need no trip to Moscow to convince me of this. The evidence can be seen in the form of the big jet bombers and swift jet fighters. . . . The evidence can be heard in reports of atomic explosions originating deep within the Soviet land mass . . .
>
> More than anything else during my trip to Moscow, I was impressed by the determination to erect a tremendous technological base, backed up by a huge educational system, and fed by vast numbers of youths who have little choice in the matter. . . . The Soviet problem is not to encourage more young men and women into technical careers. It is more to weed out the less adept and select the best for further education and more productive careers.

In August of the following year, the Soviets announced that they had tested an intercontinental ballistic missile (ICBM). Six weeks later this was confirmed in spectacular fashion by their rocket launching of the first man-made earth satellite, Sputnik I. Whatever the shortcomings of the Soviet leadership to solve fundamental economic and social problems within its monolithic governmental structure, military technology and development were neither neglected nor found wanting.

THE TECHNOLOGICAL CHAIN REACTION

The second decade after the end of World War II ended the pivotal American monopoly on global nuclear military capability. It witnessed also a further acceleration of weapons-systems advances. It is possible only to highlight representative milestones chronologically here. Table 37-1, "Milestones of Military Technology Since World War II," provides a rudimentary appreciation of the evolution of major weapons systems.

Table 37-1.   Milestones of Military Technology Since World War II

AIR SYSTEMS	UNITED STATES	SOVIET RUSSIA
Medium Piston Bomber	1943 (B-29)	1947 ("TU-29")
Atomic Bomb[1]	1945	1949
Heavy Piston Bomber	1947 (B-36)	1954 (TU-31)
Medium Jet Bomber	1949 (B-47)	1954 (TU-16)
Swept-wing Sonic Fighter	1949 (F-86)	1950 (MIG-15)
Thermonuclear Explosion[2]	1952	1953
Heavy Turbo-prop Bomber	——	1955 (TU-20)
Heavy Jet Bomber	1955 (B-52)	1955 ("Bison")
Supersonic Fighter	1954 (F-100)	1959 (MIG-21)
Jet Transport/Tanker	1955 (KC-135/707)	1956 (TU-104)
Supersonic Bomber	1959 (B-58)	1964 ("Blinder")
Hypersonic Bomber	1964 (RB-70)	?
Air-to-air Seeker Missile	1953 (Sidewinder)	1964 ("Atoll")
Air-to-air Missile (Nuclear)	1956 (Genie)	?
Air-to-ground Missile (Standoff)	1959 (Houndog)	1963 (?)
ARMY SYSTEMS		
Atomic Artillery	1953	?
Nuclear-tipped Missile (200-300m.)	1958 (Redstone)	1961 (T-1)
Ground-to-air Missile	1958 (Nike Hercules)	1957 (M-2)
Anti-satellite Missile	1964 (Nike Zeus)	
NAVAL SYSTEMS		
Snorkel Submarine	1945	1946
Missile Cruiser	1955 (*Boston*)	?
Nuclear-powered Submarine	1955 (*Nautilus*)	1962
Nuclear-powered Aircraft Carrier	1961 (*Enterprise*)	?
Ballistic Missile Submarine	1962 (*Ethan Allen*)	?
STRATEGIC BALLISTIC MISSILES		
ICBM (range: 5,500 n.m.)	1959 (Atlas D)	1958 (T-3)
IRBM (range: 1,200 n.m. plus)	1958 (Thor)	1962 (T-2)
Anti-missile Missile	1964 (Nike Zeus)	1963
SPACE SYSTEMS		
Weather Satellite	1960 (Tiros I)	?
Missile Launch Warning Satellite	1960 (USAF)	?
Observation Satellite	1961 (USAF)	?
Navigation Satellite	1963 (Transit)	?
Nuclear Detection Satellite	1963 (Vela)	?

Source: Based on public sources, including various editions of Jane's *All the World's Aircraft,* and the British Institute of Strategic Studies, *The Military Balance, 1963-64.*

[1] Nuclear tests first conducted by Britain in 1952, France in 1960, and Red China in 1964.

[2] Thermonuclear test conducted by Britain in 1957 and by Red China in 1967.

Fig. 37-2. The USS *Robert E. Lee,* one of America's nuclear-powered submarines. (*Mariners Museum,* Newport News, Va., B. J. Nixon)

From the first supersonic flight of the X-1 rocket airplane in 1947 to the supersonic F-100 fighter required five years; from the first multi-jet bombers of 1947 to the heavy United States B-52 and Soviet "Bison" took nearly eight years. It took almost a decade to develop the nuclear-powered submarine, actually the first true submarine of unlimited range that did not need to surface. When the nuclear submarine technology proved by the *Nautilus* was combined with a solid-fuel-propelled rocket carrying an intermediate range ballistic missile (IRBM) which could be launched underwater, the Polaris, an entirely new global weapons system, was added to jet bombers and ICBM's. These latter became of even greater importance when fusion warheads (*c.* 1954) could be scaled down in size and weight for lofting on the most advanced liquid-fuel rocketry.

The crash program under the Air Force Ballistic Missile Division to catch Russian rocket technology and match the development of the first generation ICBM took only five years. Four years later (1958), man himself had orbited in space along with scientific and utilitarian satellites, some of which had immediate military usefulness for early warning of missile attack, surveillance, and communications. Second generations of ICBM's and IRBM's came in much less time, as did also the later generations of solid-propellant Minuteman and Polaris. The intricacies of missile guidance, warhead re-entry, systems reliability, and deception, as well as countering anti-missiles, continued to demand intensive basic scientific research and engineering marvels.

WEAPONS FOR LIMITED WARS

In his final report as Commanding General of the United States Army Air Forces in 1946, Henry H. Arnold said: "Today's weapons are tomorrow's museum pieces." This statement certainly proved valid for the fulcrum of the world balance of military power—the strategic weapons system.

Neither the B-36 bomber nor the nuclear sting of the first jet aircraft, land- or carrier-based, was used in anger before being retired for reasons of technical obsolescence. Some were useful for training or for export to allies. After almost a decade of readiness for instant nuclear war, B-52's of the United States Strategic Air Command were fitted out for high-explosive rather than thermonuclear bombs and employed in saturation attacks in the rain forests of Vietnam in 1965. Obsolete weaponry from World War II, along with more recently developed conventional weapons, remained useful for the local security of smaller nations. Air force attack bombers (B-26) "mothballed" in 1945 were very effective during the Korean War, while the last propellor-driven attack bomber of the American fleet (AD-8) proved ideal for tactical operations in South Vietnam. In the overall spectrum of warfare, conventional and obsolete weapons, from small arms to reciprocating-engine aircraft, were to remain important in conflicts limited in geographical extent or restricted in weapons. However, the United States was forced to engage its best jet fighter, the F-86, to tangle with Soviet MIG-15 jet fighters committed over the Yalu River during the Korean War.

The connection between military conflict and diplomacy, technology, and politics is self-evident. While the apex of military technology has been nuclear-armed weapons and their delivery or countering systems, the history of international affairs has witnessed many crises associated with a sequence of lesser conflicts. In the 20th century, the rise in Asia, Africa, and Latin America of underdeveloped nations expressing their self-determination has confounded the conflicting interests of the great powers. These developments have sometimes erupted into open military conflicts, which have drawn the strategic interest of the major powers and created a spectrum of definitions of war. Thus, whereas restraining nuclear warfare on a global scale has been the highest consideration in the decisions and policies of both the White House and the Kremlin, such decisions have never been far removed from the problem of escalation of local and limited conflicts. Furthermore, the avoidance of general nuclear war has not stabilized the frequency or the intensity of localized conflicts in which conventional military technology prevails.

THE BALANCE OF TERROR

At the dawn of the Atomic Age, it was widely held that general warfare as an institution of the modern nation-state had become obsolete, and that warfare as an instrument of policy no longer served the national interest. Fatalities of 100,000 caused by one bomb were unthinkable by any standard. Following World War II general warfare has been averted, despite a most strained period of international difficulties. During the American monopoly on nuclear weapons, the Finletter Report, "Survival in the Air Age," stated to the Truman administration in January 1948 that unrestrained general war was not likely so long as the United States coupled its nuclear monopoly with an effective global delivery system. The Finletter Commission recommended a 70-group air force and also projected a period of alteration in the nuclear fulcrum of world politics in the 1950's, when it was predicted the Soviet Union inevitably would develop an atomic bomb and an aerospace delivery technology. This forecast was widely challenged in 1948. The jump from kiloton to megaton nuclear bombs and warheads, from thousand-ton equivalents of TNT to million-ton yardsticks, occurred much more swiftly than anyone who was concerned about the technological ingredients of war and peace in a bipolar world had estimated or desired.

The dilemma of nuclear weaponry has directly influenced the military strategy and weapons development of both the United States and the Soviet Union. In this, surprise atomic attack and the strategic problem of homeland defense, including civil defense, have been the central concerns of statesmen and strategists alike. With the emergence of a set of nuclear powers in the late 1950's, Winston Churchill coined the apt term, "the balance of terror." The creation of deterrents to general war involving nuclear weapons assumed new urgency.

During the period of American monopoly, all suggestions to employ nuclear weapons for the sake of world stability, that is, in preventive war, had been rejected; Western strategy chose political means to achieve its ends. Collective security, manifest first in the formation of the North Atlantic Treaty Organization and later in other treaties, brought the American pledge to use its full military power to defend its global allies in the event of attack. Technology made collective security feasible on a global basis, as evidenced by the worldwide system of American air and naval bases in addition to the commitment of token ground forces backed by swift airlift and sealift.

The spectre of a general nuclear war aimed at the cities—the nerve centers of modern society—became a living nightmare when the American nuclear deterrent was challenged in the late 1950's by the appearance of Soviet thermo-nuclear capability and global delivery systems. To the wholesale blast, thermal, and radiation effects of atomic weapons on a large target area such as a city were added the enormous megatonnage of thermonuclear weapons with their local as well as their downwind fallout of deadly radiation. Poisoning of the surface of large land areas in a thermonuclear war, and the slow contamination of long-life isotopes (Strontium 90 and others) resulting from atmospheric nu-clear tests, aroused new concern.

Adequate air and civil defense became even more difficult when ICBM sys-tems replaced manned bombers as a threat in the event of general war. Such ballistic missiles provided only fifteen minutes of warning before a massive attack at intercontinental ranges. Thus the premium against surprise attack was higher when the Soviet ICBM, confirmed by the Sputniks, appeared in 1957.

The problem of blunting a massive nuclear missile attack by effective civil defense measures has yet to be squarely faced. Some theorists insist that effec-tive passive defenses to ensure the survival of some of the human race would only help bring about the catastrophe. Sound arguments against these fearful theorists have not yet been fully persuasive. The interrelation of offense to de-fense remains ever-changing because of continued technological change. Elab-orate detection and warning systems, including space satellites, hardened and dis-persed missile sites, airborne bomber alerts and Polaris submarine patrols, quicker-responding solid-fuel ICBM's, anti-ICBM systems—these and other at-tempts to receive warning and launch a nation-killing retaliatory strike (that is, the second strike) in the event of a surprise nuclear attack today dominate military strategy. These or similarly imperfect strategic systems may continue to dissuade a potential aggressor. At present no workable alternative system for international stability other than superior technology has yet appeared.

ARMS CONTROL

Control of armaments, the contemporary form of disarmament hopes, appears to some to offer a means to counteract the imperfections of thermonuclear de-terrents and the limitations of the United Nations in maintaining world peace. Constrained steps toward some means of East-West disarmament were under-taken throughout the 1960's. Nevertheless, a global themonuclear war "too awful to contemplate" has not yet been rendered improbable by any such steps achieved to date.

Effective control of nuclear weapons involves incredible technical complex-ities as well as the political hazards associated with international controls over inspection of stockpiles, development tests, and the vagaries of human nature. The Limited Nuclear Test Ban Treaty of 1963 covering atmospheric tests, as well as the United Nations resolution not to place nuclear weapons in space,

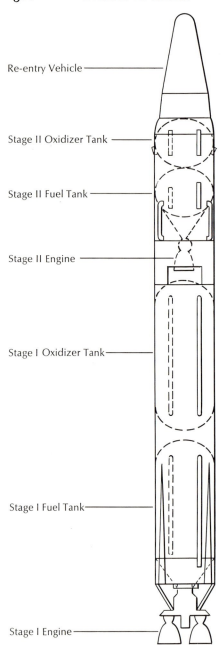

Re-entry Vehicle

Stage II Oxidizer Tank

Stage II Fuel Tank

Stage II Engine

Stage I Oxidizer Tank

Stage I Fuel Tank

Stage I Engine

Fig. 37-3. Diagram of a Titan II ICBM. The missile is 103 feet in length. (Adapted from *U. S. Air Force* figure)

have to date been the only achievements. However, discussions of a nuclear non-proliferation pact, which would limit such weapons to countries already possessing nuclear capabilities, were carried on during 1966-67 with some prospects of success.

Unilateral breaking by the Soviet Union in 1961 of the brief and self-imposed nuclear test moratorium, coupled with ICBM-rattling by successive Kremlin leaders, have offered little comfort to Western leaders. However, the Cuban Missile Crisis of 1962, a direct confrontation of power between Moscow and Washington, seemed to provide evidence that Soviet leaders had also come to regard a thermonuclear war as not feasible, and co-existence with the West as practical in a period of nuclear parity.

SPREAD OF NUCLEAR WEAPONS

The influence of nuclear weaponry in defining world powers has been further conditioned by the proliferation of technology. Nuclear tests by Britain in 1952 and by France in 1960, as well as Britain's thermonuclear shot in 1957, did not alter appreciably the East-West aspects of the aerospace nuclear balance. A nuclear explosion by Red China in 1964, however, shook the future of Far Eastern and world affairs and caused concern about additional expansion of the so-called "nuclear club" of nation-states. Should Israel, the United Arab Republic, India, Pakistan or other nations acquire nuclear capabilities, the diplomatic consequences might prove difficult to solve in any way but by force. Nuclear weapons also offer the opportunity for smaller nations to acquire "equalizers" of military technology, a situation compared to the American frontier days when a "runt with a six-gun" could do individual combat with a giant so armed. The problem of Chinese atomic capability has been compounded by China's announcement (1966) of the development of a rocket missile-delivery system and in 1967 of a thermonuclear bomb.

Beyond the problem of the proliferation of nuclear weapons are aspects of weapon development related to the precise technology of nuclear weapons themselves. These are related to the relative size of weapon effects regarding radiation fallout. The United States early sought to scale down nuclear warheads below the 20-kiloton Hiroshima size for effective tactical application, perhaps in a limited war (using atomic cannon, tactical A-bombs, and the like). Kremlin leaders, for their part, were openly boastful of their 80-megaton weapons, even threatening to place them into "orbital rockets."

MILITARY TECHNOLOGY IN THE SPACE AGE

The beginning of the Space Age opened up an entirely new medium of potentially great significance to the problems of war and peace. Constantly orbiting satellites can be used for military reconnaissance and also as weapons carriers, ready to deliver nuclear weapons to enemy territory. Although both the United States and the Soviet Union have eschewed the idea of nuclear weapons in space, there is no guarantee that all other nations will follow suit when they develop space and nuclear capabilities, or that the situation between America and Russia might not alter radically in the future. Unlike the military leaders of World War I, who looked largely to the past for their strategies and weapons, those of the mid-20th century seem alert to the potentialities of the new technologies of war.

The older technologies of ground, sea, and air warfare have by no means been made obsolete; localized conflicts, such as in Korea and in Vietnam, have demonstrated their continued usefulness. And here, too, military technology has made strides in the development of superior firepower and greater mobility.

Paradoxically, advancing military technology has made more delicate—and dangerous—the task of maintaining peace, due to the threat of vast annihilation and the possibility of small-scale conflicts with their risk of escalation.

38 / Technology and Strategy

I. B. HOLLEY, JR., and THEODORE ROPP

The greatest book on war was written by the Prussian officer Karl von Clausewitz (1780-1831). *Vom Krieg* (On War) is based on the author's analysis of his era's "Great War" against Napoleon—a war less important for technology than for its revelation of the power of nationalism. Though some of the details in *Vom Krieg* are hard to follow, its main themes are very clear. War is a violent political act "to compel our adversary to do our will." Legally, modern war is a *violent conflict between states.* Many states have been more successful in curbing internal violence than they have been in combining with other states to prevent direct or indirect aggression while retaining the right to use other types of violence, rioting, and subversion.

From Clausewitz, the political factors in a given war can be summarized as the aims of the opposing states and the resources at their disposal. Since his day, modern nation-states have struggled to increase their ability to mobilize men and resources. A military dictionary of 1802 does not use the term "mobilization." The *Encyclopaedia Britannica* edition of 1911 used the word for placing peacetime armed forces on a war footing, but the first edition of the same work to appear after World War I applied the term to every element of society.

Clausewitz saw force, that is to say, "physical force," as the *means* of strategy. The *object* of strategy was to impose one's will upon the enemy. To attain this object, the enemy had to be disarmed: "Disarming is by definition the proper aim of military action." The issues raised by two world wars and by contemporary developments in weaponry are whether or not this can be done without destroying the opposing society, without committing state suicide, and without irreparably damaging man's entire natural environment.

THE HOLLOW TRIUMPH OF THE OFFENSIVE

Given the Clausewitzian definition of force as the means by which a nation imposes its will on an enemy, a rapidly advancing technology produced frequent changes in the balance between offense and defense. World War I (1914-18) was the first general European war in which the belligerents attempted to use the full resources of modern technology. Machine guns, rapid-firing field guns, barbed wire, underwater mines, and many other devices, first aided the defensive. After three years of bloody stalemate the advanced industrial powers eventually surmounted the barriers raised by the new arsenal of defensive weapons, ingeniously developing such offensive devices as the airplane, tank, and submarine. The resulting war of attrition, and its massive economic strains, shortages, and dislocations, did not lead to the predicted social collapse of the industrialized great powers. They rebuilt their economies in less than ten years and continued to develop the concepts and weapons which had broken the deadlock.

War showed that modern warfare demanded more machines, more state controls, greater national self-sufficiency, and more peacetime research and development than nations were accustomed to. Not surprisingly, these lessons were applied in different ways in the two decades before another world war broke out in 1939. The defeated Russians and Germans both overemphasized totalitarian controls; the Germans accentuated the possibility of quick land victory; the French overemphasized the defensive. British rearmament began too late and Italian rearmament too soon, which is to say the Italians stocked huge quantities of weapons that proved to be obsolete when war finally came. The distant United States used the minimal appropriations granted by isolationist Congresses to develop prototype weapons as models for subsequent mass production and relied upon elaborate paper plans for industrial mobilization which seriously underestimated the time required to shift a complex economy to wartime production and to provide for combat training. Both Germany and Japan underestimated British and American interest in the balance of power and their willingness to fight for it. These experiences demonstrated that military policy in peacetime is as dependent upon political as technological considerations.

During World War II modern offensive weapons were used against every major center of heavy industry throughout the world except those in North America and western Siberia. The real prophets of this war were the American naval officer Alfred Thayer Mahan (1840-1914), who had stressed *The Influence of Sea Power upon History* in 1890, and the Italian infantry officer Guilio Douhet (1869-1930), whose *Command of the Air* was published in 1921. Douhet claimed "The aeroplane is the offensive weapon *par excellence* . . . because of its independence of surface limitations and its superior speed," and that consequently, "The disintegration of nations [which] in the last war was brought about by [attrition] will be accomplished directly by . . . aerial forces."

Though total war turned out to be more complex than either Mahan's or Douhet's extreme followers had predicted, the Second World War was fought across thousands of miles of open ocean and the whole of the European arena from the Caucasus and the Egyptian desert to Morocco and Northern Ireland. Mechanized weapons were combat-tested from the Arctic to New Guinea, in almost every geographical environment. By mid-1945 the largest research and development project in history had combat-tested an "absolute weapon," the atomic bomb, whose possession seemed to give its developers the power to impose their political will on any state.

The illusion of absolute political power arising from the possession of a technologically absolute weapon vanished in less than ten years. The Korean War (1951-53) was not "won" by the most powerful state because that state was afraid to risk a general conflagration which would undo the postwar recovery of its allies in Western Europe. And once again the great industrial powers had been able (1) to repair war damages and raise their standards of living more rapidly than underdeveloped countries which had not been directly affected by the war, (2) to step up the development and production of new weapons, and (3) to modernize their conventional or non-nuclear forces. The stockpiles of weapons amassed by the great industrial powers were unprecedented both in lethality and flexibility. Each of the superpowers, the United States and the Soviet Union, confidently asserted its ability to destroy most of the other's industries and population centers with offensive nuclear weapons. Yet neither had found a proven defense. The dilemma posed by this triumph of the offensive was soon painfully apparent.

THE NUCLEAR DILEMMA

A dilemma is a pair, or a definite number, of choices, both or all of which seem unsatisfactory. Whether the superpowers could destroy each other was unknown, but their leaders acted as if they believed that their only defensible positions were "hardened," that is, armored, underground launching sites or mobile missile-launchers and command posts, both on land and sea, from which their surviving forces would win the war. Whether the "victor" could rebuild his society, let alone that of the "loser," or even call on neutral aid was questionable because of possible drastic changes in the natural environment through nuclear, biological, or chemical contamination. Winston Churchill, the great wartime prime minister of Britain, had predicted in 1955 "All deterrents will improve and gain in authority during the next ten years. It may well be, that . . . by a process of supreme irony . . . safety will be the sturdy child of terror, and survival the twin brother of annihilation."

The nuclear dilemma, sometimes called the "balance of terror," enormously complicated all efforts to form alliances to defeat or to promote Communist expansion in a period of social and national revolutions. Competing alliance systems were not new, but those erected after 1945 were worldwide, had more numerous points of possible conflict, and were composed of people of cultures as different as those of Vietnam and the United States who were trying to collaborate effectively. Several other powers, Britain, France, and China, joined the "nuclear club," partly for prestige and partly because it gave them the dubious ability to force a nuclear war on their reluctant allies. Smaller states were well aware of the blackmailing power which ideological alliances gave them over the decisions of much larger states.

In the field of nuclear warfare it was clearly apparent that technology had presented even the superpowers with a set of unacceptable choices. Moreover, the fear of escalating a conventional war into a nuclear one imposed somewhat comparable though less easily recognizable restraints on the use of traditional weapons. At the same time, other technological advances such as the speed, certainty, and volume of information from a worldwide communications network, had both shortened the time available for decision-making and increased the number of factors which had to be considered.

THE NEW WARFARE

Had strategy no options but destruction or surrender? Had these cumulative technological and political developments made the only rational choice that of "the New Warfare," defined by one pioneer proponent as "the means by which a nation (or group of nations) seeks to impose its will . . . by all means short of total war, and without disturbing its own economy to an extent which is unbearable, or unacceptable, to its people"? International conflict was now regarded as a spectrum ranging from total, tactical nuclear, and conventional war, through wars by proxy, subversion, and insurgency, to cold and economic war, on down to more or less peaceful co-existence.

In analyzing possible choices, American strategists led in joining Operations Research to gaming theory. Game theory is simply the choice of optimal strategies based on a mathematical appraisal of various courses of action, maximizing advantages or gains and minimizing costs or losses. The use of this tool by decision-makers in "computer wars" or "computer solutions" rules out certain choices and permits closer analysis of others. But computers cannot consider (Latin for "contemplate" or "weigh") unquantifiable factors, unless these are given arbitrary (Latin for "judgment") values. The resulting solutions may be quite unscientific. This is particularly so when applied to operations involving guerrilla warfare, counter-insurgency, civic action, and political propaganda in non-Western or underdeveloped areas, especially those areas for which the Chinese Marxist Mao Tse-tung developed both the theory and tactics of revolutionary warfare in the 1930's.

Since game theory deals with rational or predictable reactions, statistical methods which have proved most effective in developed Western societies may be positively misleading in other societies and situations. Public-opinion polling techniques that succeed in free countries may break down in the climate of fear often prevailing in less favored societies. What is "unbearable" in terms of Western values may seem normal to the peoples of emerging nations. Indeed, as Clausewitz had noted a century before Mao, revolutionary and nationalist passions can stimulate extraordinary degrees of social sacrifice.

Fortunately for the West, the formulas of both Russian and Chinese Marxism proved partly unworkable for similar reasons. Though more practised in subversion, propaganda, and war by proxy, the Communists were not overly successful in subverting the new states which postwar nationalist revolutions left on their borders from Korea to the Near East and Africa; "irrational" attractions of nationalism remained too strong for easy subversion by traditional Marxism. Where these states were not subjugated by Communist armed forces (as in Hungary), they often preferred ideological neutrality behind a curtain of Western armed force, though they were not unwilling to take military and other aid from both power blocs when they could get it (as in Egypt or Indonesia).

In spite of its mathematical aura, the strategic concepts of the New Warfare are even more blurred than those of the old. To what Clausewitz called war's "strange trinity"—(1) hate and enmity, (2) the play of probability or chance, and (3) political action—has been added a fourth phenomenon—major technological complications. Military, economic, and political power now rest on a combination of industrial, military, scientific, and administrative competence.

All military, economic, and political planning has international overtones, though men still think in nationalistic terms and are still easily aroused by nationalistic slogans. Modern transportation alone has exposed the illusion of individual national security and economic self-sufficiency. For example, all of the tin ore required by the United States for the production of engine bearings, bronze, and numerous other military components must be imported from such distant producers as Bolivia, the Congo, and Indonesia. Weapons technology has made total nuclear war obsolete or at least highly impractical as a political tool and has sharply limited the use of either nuclear or conventional weapons in such developed areas as Central Europe. Even revolutionary warfare may become less useful in underdeveloped areas, which can employ modern technology effectively only in a relatively stable political environment. The German experience in Central Europe in the 1930's showed that underdeveloped states that take military or economic aid from larger industrial powers give those powers hostages for their political behavior. For example, in letting the Germans build refineries for their oil, the Rumanians made themselves dependent upon German markets, facilities for repairs, and spare parts.

Twenty years after the end of the Second World War, five of the seven great powers of 1939 were not rearmed to the level which their economies could support because they were sure of Allied assistance. The super powers and all but two of the great powers had agreed not to test nuclear weapons in the atmosphere, and the super powers were cutting back the production of fissionable materials. Whether this would lead to disarmament was partly a political issue, since such agreements involve choices between various military, technological, and even ideological goals. Clausewitz—who emphasized war's complexities—would surely have felt that these choices were more complex than ever. There were more irrevocable decisions and less time in which to make them. These decisions would affect more people over wider geographical areas, and inescapably involved a wider variety of ever more powerful weapons. The choices were still further complicated by the development of non-lethal chemical weapons designed to immobilize whole populations without damaging their productive facilities. As a consequence of all these developments, the great problem of strategy in the 20th century was the urgent necessity for devising better means for decision-making. Inevitably, political-military policy-making led to an increased interest in policy (or the social) sciences.

UTILITY OF THE SOCIAL SCIENCES IN THE NEW WARFARE

Technology is the science of the industrial arts. Its relation to war was seen by Clausewitz in his observation that "Force, to meet force, arms itself with the inventions of art and science," and in his descriptions of a soldier as a man who is "levied, clothed, armed, trained, sleeps, eats, drinks, and marches *merely to fight at the right place and the right time.*" Most of the official history of the United States Office of Scientific Research and Development in the Second World War properly deals with "New Weapons and Devices," that is, military tools or hardware. The more important of these tools have been described in preceding chapters. But the demands of the New Warfare go far beyond the development of rockets, missiles, and nuclear warheads. Now more than ever those in command have been forced to seek methods in the selection, procurement, and utilization of weapons no less scientifically sophisticated than those used in their development.

Analysis of the comparative economic impact of two rival weapons systems can be decisive in the choice between them. This necessity for rigorous analysis of social, economic and political factors has vastly complicated the problems of strategic decision-making. No social scientist would claim that computers can produce instant strategy or instant social psychology, but the importance of the social sciences in decision-making can be suggested by a tongue-in-cheek sixteen-track computer war-game simulator of what Clausewitz called that "veritable chameleon, combat." When playing such a war game, the factors which must be quantified are related to the special skills involved. These include: (1) international relations (diplomats); (2) public administration (bureaucrats); (3) public opinion (journalists) and (4) policy formation (political scientists); (5) economic development (economists) and (6) economic potential (geographers and demographers); (7) social structure (anthropologists); (8) social change (sociologists); (9) ideology (philosophers); (10) individual motivation (psychologists); (11) group motivation (artists and historians); (12) the administration of science (physical and biological scientists) and (13) the organization of production (engineers and business managers); (14) military doctrine (soldiers); (15) leadership (statesmen and politicians); and (16) Clausewitz's "wild card" or X-factor—chance.

While this illustration has been deliberately employed to point up the absurdity of quantifying the unquantifiable, social scientists have played an increasingly important part in military affairs. A single example, drawn from World War II, will serve to illustrate the character of this rapidly developing activity. The United States Army Air Corps, confronted by the need to train tens of thousands of pilots and crew members with the least cost in time and with scarce facilities, turned to professional psychologists for help. A battery of tests was quickly designed to select from more than a million candidates those whose mechanical aptitude, mathematical reasoning, and speed of perception suited them for flying. A relatively modest investment in time and effort produced enormous savings; better initial selection not only lowered the accident rate during training and thereafter, but also substantially reduced the scale of organization required to turn out trained pilots and crews to meet the level of production—nearly 100,000 aircraft in 1944 alone—achieved by industry in the United States.

STRATEGY AND SKILLED MANPOWER

While manpower problems such as the selection of pilots have been vastly complicated by technological advances, at the same time rising educational standards have provided an even larger pool of talent to draw from. Nonetheless, the provision of skilled manpower poses enormous difficulties. Complicated weapons magnify the burden of training and maintenance; new models require retraining. In the Second World War new aircraft were sometimes kept out of combat until new crews could be trained from scratch because the retraining of veteran crews would have broken the rhythm of operations. Since navies were the first mechanized services, some of the earliest mechanical training aids were invented by naval officers. One famous example was Sir Percy Scott's electro-magnetic pencil "dotter" to enable gun-pointers to practise without using ammunition.

But training is more than a question of mechanical gadgets; it requires command decisions. As Captain Herbert Richmond, one of the key theorists of the Royal Navy, noted in 1909 before he took command of *Dreadnought,* the ship designed around Scott's gunnery devices, " 'Time! Time!' is the cry. More is wanted on all hands. The gunnery-men want more time to teach their men to shoot. The formalists want more time to drill, others want time for cleaning ship, others time for giving the human element a chance. But I hear few who ask for time to solve strategical questions."

A half-century later neither training aids nor strategic thought have yet caught up with technology. Even far less complicated infantry weapons, such as radarscopes and radios, cannot be efficiently maintained by short-tour draftees or weekend soldiers; much of the combat value of reservists depends on repeated maneuvers simulating combat conditions, maneuvers for which funds are seldom appropriated. Similar problems beset the whole economy supporting the soldier in the field. There, too, the skills of the technicians must be constantly updated. And the most intricate "black box" equipment of the military services must frequently be maintained by civilian factory specialists.

A nation's educational level literally permeates its entire military organization. The European professional soldier's traditional preference for farm boys vanished as the health of the city recruits improved, their revolutionary or proletarian fervor declined, and their mechanical skills and education became more important. European conscript armies taught patriotism, hygiene, and mechanics simultaneously. But a German could be trained in a shorter time than a Russian because the latter often had to learn to read and write in the army. Good food and pure water, to take another example, were also essential to mobility and morale. The "ration dense" C and K rations of the United States Army in World War II were "foods which, through processing, have been reduced . . . to a small compact package without appreciable loss of food value, quality, or acceptance." Acceptance of such innovations is in large measure socially determined, but educated soldiers are more easily taught to eat new messes. During the war, it was repeatedly observed that well-educated men from upper-income families found the prescribed army diet palatable and well balanced, while others complained of having to eat too many vegetables.

The relation between military and civilian technology, educational level, morale, and mobility, can be shown by an example drawn from military medicine.

Helicopters evacuating wounded men during the Korean War were a far cry from stretcher-bearers struggling in the mud of the Somme during World War I. There, medical facilities which were adequate in quiet sectors broke down completely during major offensives. At Pozières in 1916, three Australian divisions with about 36,000 infantry lost 23,000 officers and men in less than seven weeks when it took "five or six relays of stretcher bearers, each team six to eight strong," many hours to reach the ambulance, a few miles back, with a single casualty. A mortally wounded Brigadier was ten hours on the journey. Yet the soldier's knowledge that the bearers would try to save him outweighed the man-hours "wasted" in this often fruitless attempt. And the social, technological, scientific, and logistical factors of modern war were concisely linked in the contention of General J. F. C. Fuller, the noted British military writer, that the Burma campaign of 1944-45 was won by "leadership, . . . soldiership, . . . air power, medical care, and engineering." Clearly, contemporary combat demanded total mobilization.

STRATEGY AND TOTAL MOBILIZATION

The First World War forced governments to control manpower, transport, food, raw materials, and production by a selective draft, by priorities, by rationing, and by price-fixing. But this social planning was not achieved without opposition. In the United States and England, organized labor often opposed both military and labor conscription, and businessmen resented the intrusion of the government into their most intimate affairs. Costs, profits, production methods, and trade secrets all had to be disclosed when working on certain types of military contracts. The wartime experience, however, subtly acclimated both businessmen and governmental officials to working with one another; businessmen came to a far wider acceptance of governmental intervention in their affairs than would have been possible before the war. And for their part, the military men saw the necessity of utilizing the most advanced business techniques in mobilization planning. In the United States military officers were, for example, assigned to take degrees at schools of business administration. And in 1924 the Secretary of War established the Army Industrial College to train officers in the techniques of economic mobilization.

Although the mobilization plans contrived by the newly trained officers proved faulty in many respects when the coming of World War II put them to the test, the increasingly intimate association of the civilian and military communities greatly facilitated this second large-scale national mobilization. Fairer controls, particularly on profits, and improved techniques of contracting, better understood by those on both sides of the bargaining table, generated wider support for the war effort. So, too, did the skillful use of local civilian volunteers in a wide variety of organizations behind the war effort, both public and private. By mid-century, the demands of more than a decade of cold war had forced the nation even further in the direction of an effective symbiosis of civilian and military activities. Nowhere was the choice of tools and techniques more difficult than in the evolution of guerrilla and special warfare as instruments of national policy.

Special warfare, as conceived in the years immediately following World War II, was to be waged by highly trained special forces capable of paradrop delivery behind enemy lines. Once in the target area these units were to organize disaffected elements of the local population into guerilla bands to harass the enemy. This conception presupposed the existence of a "hot" or declared war and a clearly discernible enemy. But experience, especially that in Southeast Asia, repeatedly demonstrated that the enemy was not so readily defined. Military forces of the United States stationed in friendly nations as advisers and technical instructors often found that the immediate menace came more from disaffected elements of the host nation's own population than from infiltrating foreign invaders. To meet this threat, training in psychological warfare was introduced in the schools for the soldiers assigned to special forces. Since deeds speak louder than words, training in psychological warfare was soon supplemented by courses in counter-insurgency or the art of forestalling disaffection and revolt by removing their root causes through constructive civic action to improve the education, health, and welfare of potentially dissident elements.

The interpenetration of military and civilian activities could scarcely have been more complete. The result was not a modern Sparta, not a garrison state on Prussian lines, but quite the reverse. The soldiers had become increasingly civilianized, or at least the skills they required were those conventionally identified with the civil sectors of society. Psychological warfare required technical competence in broadcasting, printing, and other means of communication. More significantly, it required a highly sophisticated knowledge of the people to be persuaded. To be effective, a psychological warrior must know and be sensitive to not only the politics of his target population, but the full range of its culture, its unique characteristics, its vulnerable points and ultimate values. Similarly, without a detailed knowledge of the values and beliefs held by the disaffected residents of an aboriginal village on a crucial national border, the most elaborate program of civic improvement can backfire and destroy an entire counter-insurgency effort. In short, the exigencies of contemporary warfare have forced military men to encompass not only technology but the full range of human endeavor. The tabu of a Malay tribe, the dietary practices of a Middle Eastern community, and the dialect of a remote African village have become subjects of pressing concern to military men.

The most effective propagandists of World War I were those advertisers and politicians of the Western democracies conscious of the masses. Not surprisingly, the totalitarian states which dominated Central and Eastern Europe by the 1930's took lessons in propaganda from them and added some twists of their own. Propaganda analysts knew when cartoons were more effective than print or photographs, when movies were more effective than stills, and how color increased the impact of them all. Words and music carried special national connotations, but pictures and the radio could also span national frontiers. Totalitarian states made listening to foreign broadcasts a crime and often tried to stem the tide by giving production priorities to radio sets that could be controlled by central switches or were too weak to reach foreign stations. Such sets were among the few consumer goods allowed to people in the race for industrial mobilization.

By the 1960's instantaneous picture transmission had become a major factor in conveying or undermining national images. And both visual and vocal images could be stored on magnetic tape to be reproduced in quantity whenever the occasion demanded it. Electronic devices were increasingly important in international trade and as significant to modern nations as printing had been in the welding of those 16th-century nations who dominated the international political scene by the beginning of the 20th century. Clearly, the implications of these technical developments on strategy in the New Warfare still further complicated the selection of tools and objectives. Once again the range of choices confronting Western strategists offered a bewildering variety of alternatives. In deciding upon appropriate programs of economic aid, civic action, counterinsurgency, and overt military action, Western policy-makers had to consider a wide span of technical, ideological, social, political, and geographic circumstances.

THE DILEMMA OF DISARMAMENT

Another of the dilemmas of modern strategy is reflected in the dilemma of disarmament. The most immediately pressing problem is the control of specific weapons of mass destruction. The same technologies which have produced these weapons offer instruments for their control. Most of these weapons require large industrial complexes for their production, testing, and operation. Earth satellites which, from miles high in the sky, can photograph objects as small as a truck, so as to reveal any kind of industrial or military buildup, are obviously powerful instruments for arms control. So are seismographic and radiological monitoring devices which can detect and measure nuclear explosions thousands of miles away. The intelligence officers who advise statesmen get far more information continuously and more quickly than was the case ever before. Of necessity, modern states must develop better methods for sifting, evaluating, and communicating this information.

A second problem of disarmament is its potential effect on general scientific and technological development. Certain improvements might be inhibited, but the release of trained scientists and engineers from projects of marginal military value could result in dramatic advances in other fields. A related problem is the shift from military to civilian production without creating massive unemployment. The experience of the Western powers in accomplishing such massive shifts after two world wars provides experience but not formulas for dealing with this issue.

But the great problems of disarmament are political. Limited—as well as general and complete—disarmament depends on genuine, if only tacit, political agreements to relieve tensions among the great industrial powers before they can be lifted from underdeveloped nations. A half-century of warfare has given psychologists and psychiatrists great insight into the conditions under which men will fight well. But men of good will must still seek that "moral equivalent" for war which the American psychologist William James (1842-1910) suggested might be found in peaceful projects requiring the same self-sacrifice and leadership demanded by battle. The solution to this political and psychological dilemma thus remains the primary responsibility of those states whose technological development has given them the power to destroy each other.

39 / The Transfer of Military Technology to Civilian Use
RICHARD S. ROSENBLOOM

Along with the need for food and shelter, the defense of self and society is a fundamental human requirement long served by man's technological accomplishments. Historians concerned with the role of technology in warfare have pointed out the fruitful interaction between technical capabilities and the requirements of waging war. This is a reciprocal relationship. Technological advances have proved a decisive advantage to the victor in many battles. But the intensive application of valuable resources to military innovation has, in turn, accelerated the rate and altered the direction of technological change. There is no better example of this than the effects on warfare of 20th-century developments in aviation, electronics, and the control of nuclear energy, and the reciprocal impact which the stimulus of defense needs has had on the advancement of those technologies.

We shall not dwell on these important points, well covered in preceding chapters. Here we will consider how the fruits of military technology can find important uses in peacetime endeavors, specifically, the process sometimes called "spinoff," by which inventions having their origin in military needs can form the basis for useful innovation in a civilian economy.

Our concern here is with the spread of technology rather than its origin or initiation. We will postulate a framework for analysis, consider the significance of the process of technology transfer within the broader area of technological innovation, and review accomplishments and prospects for the facilitation of this process in the mid-20th century. The significance of this topic results from the convergence of an opportunity and a need. The opportunity is created by the fact that the possibilities inherent in an invention commonly transcend the bounds of the field to which it is initially applied. The need is there because man, forced by social and political imperatives to commit an excessive share of his limited resources to military pursuits, has long sought to convert the fruits of military inventiveness to peaceful uses.

A FRAMEWORK FOR ANALYSIS

Science, invention, innovation, and social acceptance are the significant links in the chain of technological change. An invention is a novel and useful combination of knowledge about the material universe. An innovation, in contrast, implies the use of an invention (which need not be new) in a manner which is novel at the time. Long time lags between these successive steps—suggestion of a scientific idea, the accomplishment of an invention, its incorporation in an innovation, and the successful accomplishment of the innovation—are common in history. The distinguished historian Lynn White reminds us, for example, that societies have long had difficulty in bridging the gap between invention and innovation:

. . . a new device merely opens a door; it does not compel one to enter. The acceptance or rejection of an invention, or the extent to which its implications are realized if it is accepted, depends quite as much upon the condition of a society, and upon the imagination of its leaders, as upon the nature of the technological item itself.

It is important to recognize that invention and innovation are distinct activities and may be widely separated in time and space. The significant feature of an invention is that it discloses an operational method of creating something new. An innovation, however, is a more complex event, combining diverse activities: it may require the successful application of new technology, capital, facilities, and personnel. Substantial resources may be committed in the face of risks of failure. As it takes hold, an innovation may be altered markedly in response to unforeseen circumstances. In the end, if an innovation is to be successful, it must gain social acceptance. These points are well illustrated by the histories of two fundamental inventions: the steam engine and wireless telegraphy.

Watt's basic invention was made in 1765. His invention was only the first step; it was Watt's association with an imaginative and resourceful businessman and the organization of the firm of Boulton and Watt which converted the steam engine into a true innovation. The first engine was not installed until 1776, and it took several more years and £40,000 of Boulton's capital to reach the point of profit. To achieve success, the firm had to create an entirely new system of manufacture, devise new methods of pricing and credit, establish parts inventories, and break new ground in the management of innovation as well as in the technology of invention.

The story of Marconi is similar. With notable single-mindedness of purpose, he invented a practical machine for wireless telegraphy based on the scientific principles stated ten years earlier by Heinrich Hertz. Marconi then created a worldwide business organization to exploit his invention. Although the firm lost money for more than a dozen years, growth was rapid once the innovation caught hold—in two years profits wiped out the losses incurred in starting the enterprise.

TECHNOLOGY TRANSFER

By transfer of technology we mean the acquisition, development, and utilization of technology in a context different from that in which it originated. The simplest aspect of this is the process of diffusion, the means by which a given invention is incorporated in innovations meeting essentially identical needs in similar settings. Examples of this are the adoption of hybrid corn by farmers throughout the country and the spread of diesel locomotives on different railroad systems. Although it may seem to be simple copying, the process of diffusion is a complex one, consisting of several stages, which may take place over an extended period of time. Just as there may be a long time lag between the appearance of an idea or invention and its use in an innovation, a substantial interval usually separates the first adoption of an innovation and its spread. Studies of the diffusion of important 20th-century industrial innovations show that ten to twenty years commonly elapse from the date of first use to the time that an innovation is employed by most of its potential users.

Diffusion is not the only means for transfer. Sometimes the new technology is used in secondary innovations meeting needs different from those of the original innovation. In that event another step is added to the process: the technology must be adapted before it can be adopted, that is, somone must see an analogy between the characteristics of the original invention or innovation and the requirements of the new situation.

The transfer of technology, therefore, may take place by means of *imitation* or by *analogy*. When an invention has been successfully utilized in a certain context, and can serve similar needs in some other context, the original innovation can be imitated. This is the way in which an innovation gains social acceptance and the means by which the broadest social benefit ultimately is derived. Transfer by analogy poses distinctly different problems and is less well understood.

Analogy underlies all inductive reasoning. It implies the identification of structural or functional similarities in otherwise dissimilar situations or things. Transfer by analogy is illustrated by such diverse examples as the adaptation of the steam engine, originally used to pump water from mines, to serve as a prime mover for factories; the adaptation of cotton-spinning machinery to serve the needs of the woolen industry; and the application of solar energy cells, developed for satellite use, to power portable radios for personal use.

The transfer of military technology to civilian use can be realized through a range of mechanisms extending from direct imitation to a highly imaginative adaptation of a concept or technique to wholly new circumstances. The means required to transfer the technology will vary according to the degree of analogy required to match the original and secondary settings. Since transfer implies innovation, it will involve the complex ingredients of successful innovation and will probably be accompanied by the long time lags which normally mark the various stages between innovation and diffusion.

HISTORICAL EXAMPLES

History provides numerous examples of important civilian innovations stemming from military technology. Before directing our attention to contemporary aspects of the transfer of military technology, we should consider briefly its role in the past.

Although the destructiveness of warfare is happily unique to that activity, many of the functions required to support a military force—the provision of food, mobility, and communication—are pervasive requirements of advanced societies. Technological innovations satisfying these needs have been stimulated by and found application in both military and ordinary affairs. Innovations in small arms, from the crossbow to the Colt revolver, have been motivated by or utilized in the hunting of game and the maintenance of domestic order, as well as in the practice of war. Military medicine, starting as early as the 16th century, has made notable contributions to the prevention and cure of disease. Historically, at least with respect to these fundamental social needs, the transfer of technology from military to civilian uses has been relatively simple to achieve, has occurred often, and has been of a reciprocal nature.

A number of inventions of great importance to modern Western societies have originated as military innovations. The preservation of food by canning, the jet aircraft engine, and the electronic computer, for example, were first fully developed in response to a military need and are now ubiquitous in military and everyday civilian life. The successful canning of food was first achieved by the Frenchman Appert at the beginning of the 19th century in response to a prize offered by Napoleon, who wanted a means of preserving food for his army. The jet engine was developed independently by British and German air forces during the Second World War and first incorporated in a commercial passenger transport by the British in the early 1950's. The first realization of a "computer" was the electro-mechanical Mark I built by International Business Machines (IBM) at Harvard University in the early 1940's. The first electronic computer, ENIAC, was a result of a military project at the University of Pennsylvania at the end of World War II, and its successor, EDVAC, was the first stored-program computer. Electronic data processing found rapid postwar application in scientific uses and was first employed for business data processing in 1954.

In each of the examples just cited, the military invention was applicable in its original form directly to civilian requirements. There are other military devices, however, which have no civilian counterpart and thus do not offer an opportunity for "direct" transfers of this sort. Yet, at the heart of every invention lies an *idea* which is applicable to other settings, even if its specific embodiment is not. In these cases a different sort of transfer occurs, for it is not the military device, but the principle underlying it which is adopted in a civilian innovation.

In recent history, for example, the development of servomechanisms was greatly accelerated by World War II advances in fire-control and gun aiming devices. While devices for aiming artillery have few peacetime applications, the concept of the servomechanism and the advances it stimulated in the underlying sciences and technological arts have found important applications. Another example where an idea, rather than a specific technique, was transferred, can be found in the widespread current use of games for management training; stemming directly from the war games conducted for centuries by the military, it was first transferred to business in 1957. In short, technology transfer is a single term which is used to refer to a variety of ways in which technology applied to one purpose can find useful application in others.

CONTEMPORARY PROBLEMS IN TECHNOLOGY TRANSFER

Whatever man's aspiration toward effective peaceful utilization of military technology—from the biblical recognition of the relevance of swords to plowshares, to the recent Project Plowshare, by which the United States Atomic Energy Commission explores the peaceful uses of nuclear explosives—efforts in this regard have met with imperfect success. The diffusion of new technology in society is itself a slow process, and the need to develop analogous uses for a new device or idea introduces additional delays and possibilities of failure.

Yet, albeit slow and haphazard, the transfer of technology has been important in a number of historical settings and is a significant part of the relationship between technology and society, not unique to the Space Age.

As we consider the United States in the 1960's, however, some differences emerge. As with many other aspects of modern society, technology transfer occurs in a radically changed political, economic, and technological context. A change in the character of the military technology itself, a qualitative shift, may have reduced the potential for achieving imitative transfers of the new technology. In the past, most civilian applications of military technology were based on close analogies (or near identities) between civilian needs and military requirements, as those we have examined in food preservation, transportation, and communication. These military needs continue as warfare enters the Space Age (although this continuity is sometimes masked by a new terminology). In the present era, however, when the technologies for life support, communications, power, and control must serve under extreme conditions in special environments, their relevance for corresponding civilian uses is more doubtful. For most contemporary military innovations to realize potential civilian applications will require a greater degree of perception of analogies, and we must be prepared to make more substantial transformations in the original technology.

These changes have several important implications. To the extent that secondary innovation must come by analogy, rather than by imitation, we must contend with a new element—creative adaptation. The practical significance of this is great; not only is there an additional step in the process, but one which requires creativity and imagination. This means a further increase in the lead time from the original invention to the spread of the derivative innovation. Even though the idea of a fruitful adaptation may occur shortly after the introduction of the source invention, the derivative invention will probably have to go through some process of development and refinement before it is suitable for implementation.

Another implication of the greater contemporary importance of analogy is that potential users usually cannot be identified until after adaptation of the source invention has taken place, unlike imitation, where definition of the innovation usually defines the potential users, as doctors for new drugs, and farmers for agricultural developments.

One effect of the greatly accelerated rate of military research and development in America has been a large qualitative change in military technology such that the opportunities for civilian utilization have been reduced rather than enhanced. Nevertheless, important shifts in public attitudes toward science and engineering mean that although it is now more difficult to transfer military technology to civilian use, there is significantly more interest in doing so.

One reason is that in place of "tinkerers and geniuses," who accounted for a large share of inventions and innovations in an earlier era, in 20-century America inventive activities have been institutionalized. Scientists and engineers, working in organized research and development projects, have become the main source of new technology in modern society. Before World War II, most organized research and development was privately supported and directed toward profit-making innovation. In the Space Age, by contrast, only a small part of national efforts to develop new technology for military use and space exploration are governed by economic criteria. In the United States in the 1960's, a majority of research and development work is supported and directed by agencies of the federal government, which motivates a new interest in the transfer of military technology to other uses.

The concentration of research and development in a few industries and for a few purposes is easy to document. In 1964, approximately one half of the scientists and one third of the engineers in the United States were employed in research, development, or their administration and management (and many of the others taught or worked in production operations). Although 75 per cent of these scientists and engineers were employed by private industry, the work done by half of those in industry and three-fifths of the total group was financed by the federal government. Both the work performed and the federal funds in support of research and development were concentrated in a very few industries. At the end of 1964, for example, aircraft, electrical-electronics, and chemical industries employed 64 per cent of the scientists and engineers at work in industry on research and development and spent 68 per cent of the funds for these in industry. During 1964, federal funds supported 90 per cent of research and development in the aircraft and missile industries and 62 per cent in the electrical equipment and communications industries.

This high concentration of federal support in a few industries is mirrored in the distribution of privately supported research and development in industry. A few industries, notably electrical-electronics and chemical, now account for a majority of private spending on research and development. The few "science-based" industries account generally for a disproportionate share of technological innovation and are the principal "growth companies." This concentration does not mean that the benefits of innovation are necessarily concentrated among a narrow group of either producers or consumers. Quite the contrary. Science-based industries—which are the industries with significant research and development—tend to manufacture "producers goods," that is, products which are sold to other manufacturers rather than to ultimate consumers. As a consequence, the benefits of innovation in these industries are diffused throughout the economy. If we consider the case of the chemical industry, particularly the branch devoted to plastics, we find that in two decades following World War II, innovations in synthetic materials, stimulated by the aggressive marketing policies of the manufacturers, transformed large sections of such fundamental and "unscientific" industries as textiles, containers, and the building trades.

The desirability of economic growth—a goal that seems increasingly impor- tant in the modern political milieu—and the apparent dispersion of limited in- ventive resources to many national goals, have given rise to some important questions. First, to what extent does this change in the aims of organized research and development represent a weakening of the technological forces contributing to economic growth? Further, to what extent and by what means can the technological results of programs directed toward other goals be utilized to further economic growth and change? The latter question concerns the feasibility of finding means which will more effectively and speedily produce civilian benefits from the sizable technical efforts directed toward military (and other federally supported) purposes. The former question is concerned with the desirability or, as some have put it, the urgency of finding such mechanisms.

The political and economic forces of our time have provided a strong moti- vation for those who would accelerate this process of transfer. In the United States, the transfer of military technology has ceased to be something that takes place more or less autonomously and has become something which must be "made to happen." The effectiveness of various means for "making it happen" is debated not only among scholars but in the public press and in Congress. Ad- mittedly, the character of the relevant military technology has changed so radically in such a short time that it is becoming more and more difficult to find civilian analogues. Yet it seems clearly desirable to try to facilitate and to pro- mote the more effective transfer of technology, whether stemming from federal or privately supported research and development efforts.

PATHWAYS TO TRANSFER IN THE SPACE AGE: DIRECT APPLICATIONS

There are two principal pathways by which the fruits of modern, large-scale military research and development might find useful application in the civilian economy. The first means is through the direct application of inventions to ap- propriate civilian use. Indirect applications and intangible benefits constitute the second. We shall consider these in turn.

As noted earlier, the jet engine, radar, and a multitude of less prominent military inventions were applied directly to civilian needs in the decade follow- ing World War II. Contemporary parallels, stemming from technical advances in the 1950's not yet translated into routine civilian usage, are communications satellites, nuclear power generation, and supersonic air transport. All these in- ventions are based on military advances in important technologies: rocketry, miniature electronics, nuclear weapons and propulsion systems, and aeronautics. Yet despite their apparent direct applicability to civilian needs, a long interval separates successful military realization of the invention from its civilian utiliza- tion. Communication by satellite was first demonstrated in 1958 (Project SCORE) and had earlier been described in a prophetic paper by J. R. Pierce; however, almost a decade had elapsed before commercial use passed the experimental stage. The generation of electric power by controlled nuclear fission offers a potential which is staggering to the imagination, yet over twenty years after the public first learned of nuclear fission, the economics of nuclear power are still on the borderline, and conventional steam generating stations are still being constructed in the United States. Supersonic bombers were flown operationally by the air force before 1960, but commercial transports will not be available until after 1970, and there is still a sharp debate over the wisdom of investing in their development.

Direct applicability to civilian needs, it would seem, does not assure that utilization will be rapid, inexpensive, or automatic. Although major breakthroughs in technology, such as nuclear arms and rocketry, create important opportunities for "direct" application to the civilian domain, the realization of those opportunities depends upon society's ability to bridge the gap between invention and innovation. In all these cases, the major problems of the innovator have yet to be faced, even though the technology has been demonstrated in some other context.

Consider the role of the development process. An invention demonstrates a useful principle; multiple paths lead from it to alternate possible realizations. In the process of development, engineers and scientists seek a mix of operational characteristics best suited to the intended operating context. This involves "trade-offs" between competing criteria in order to achieve a balanced result.

The civilian application of a military invention must meet economic criteria which can only have been of secondary importance in the shaping of the new technology for its original military purposes. Furthermore, the trade-offs between characteristics desired for civilian use are necessarily different than they were for the military. The design of a military jet engine is likely to emphasize thrust at the expense of operating economy; a satellite solar cell will be designed for maximum reliability, at a necessarily high initial cost. These trade-offs would be reversed in the civilian development of these devices.

Development of new technology is risky, takes time, and requires the commitment of substantial resources. When the scale of an innovation is large, for example, or its social implications are powerful, significant institutional or political changes will also be required to carry the innovation through the stages of development and implementation. It is thus no mere coincidence that the three major innovations we have cited—nuclear power, satellite communication, and supersonic transport—have brought about a shift in the relation between government and business and a change in the structure of the government itself. Because the implications of nuclear fission and rocketry transcended the military requirements which had caused the initial great leaps forward in these fields, we have such powerful new agencies as the Atomic Energy Commission and the National Aeronautics and Space Administration. The Communications Satellite Corporation is a unique business venture, the "chosen instrument" of our government in dealing with other nations in an area where international co-operation is made imperative by the nature of the job to be done. But it is also a firm with private stockholders, and its activities will compete with privately held businesses in this country. To develop a supersonic transport, the United States must combine the resources and skills of various corporations in the aerospace industry with those of the federal government in both its military and non-military aviation activities. Working out the new political and economic relationships for each of these innovations has necessarily been a matter of public debate, the intensity of which has been strengthened by the magnitude of the vested interests on various sides of the issues.

It is, of course, quite reasonable that the development of a fundamental and large-scale innovation proceeds best within an institutional framework suited to the requirements of the innovation; the study of innovation in industry has shown this to be so—fundamental changes are not usually introduced by the established firms in an industry. In the same way, the National Aeronautics and Space Administration, devoted wholly to peaceful exploitation of space, has advanced those activities far more rapidly than would have been possible if the nation had continued the practice, followed in the early satellite programs, of giving full responsibility to military agencies for which peacetime use was necessarily a secondary concern. Similarly, the development of communication satellites, it was argued, would be advanced more effectively through a corporation chosen for that purpose, and solely devoted to it.

When dealing with a fundamental innovation, whether it be the steam engine or communication satellite, the two major tasks facing an innovator are the development process and the industrial framework for development. These tasks probably account for a large portion of the time lag. In the case of direct application of military technology, we must be careful not to make the error of assuming that having the invention is an assurance of successful innovation. The rewards still go to the societies and the institutions which are effective in bridging the gap between invention and innovation, a process that calls for the expenditure of resources, the underwriting of risks, and the development of new organizational and managerial techniques, along with new technical configurations.

INDIRECT APPLICATIONS AND INTANGIBLE BENEFITS

Spectacular achievements such as communication satellites tend to dominate public awareness of the benefits of military technology. Of equal importance, however, are the indirect and intangible benefits. These are of three sorts; the first is represented, in the case of communications satellites, by advances in manufacturing techniques, electronic components, the processing of materials, small portable energy sources, and so on, which can be incorporated as incremental improvements in many manufacturing processes and in the design of industrial and consumer products. These may be termed improvements in "general technology." Military research and development have also contributed substantially in the postwar years to the advancement of science. Finally, there are a number of "intangible by-products" of military research and development, including the development of important underlying ideas and the advancement of the general level of technical competence.

Individually, incremental improvements in general technology make possible gains in the efficiency of industrial operations or advances in the quality of performance of new or established products. Although the gain from application of a new welding technique may be small, the aggregate benefits of many such advances, applied in many industries and firms, can be quite large. Furthermore, the convergence of a number of such improvements, along with technical advances arising in other fields, may make possible new fundamental inventions of substantial individual significance. Most important inventions in the past have, in fact, been contingent upon developments in materials, energy sources, and other aspects of the technological competence of the society as a whole.

As is true for direct applications, realization of the potential inherent in general technology is neither simple nor immediate; incremental benefits usually need to be adapted to the requirements of the new field for which they are relevant. In many instances the identification of relevance and the process of development and adaptation will have to be carried out through a new institutional context. A different sort of organizational innovation will be required to take advantage of the host of potential by-product applications of this sort. Examples of this are "civilian technology programs" in the government and information centers and independent services which have been organized to help businesses identify opportunities in military (and space) technology. Of growing importance will probably be the State Technical Services Act of 1965, passed by Congress in the belief that "the benefits of federally financed research, as well as other research, must be placed more effectively in the hands of American business, commerce, and industrial establishments."

A second indirect path by which military research and development contribute to progress in the civilian economy is through the advancement of science itself. Our recent history holds some striking examples of this contribution in the development of nuclear and solid-state physics, in the emergence of operations research as a professional discipline during and after World War II, and in the contributions to the life sciences stimulated by the manned space program. The problem here, of course, is not of identifying military developments which are relevant to civilian applications, but of understanding how to couple science effectively with practical affairs. This will take time. Two decades after the emergence of operations research, the widespread and effective application of its methods has not been fully realized.

The third indirect route to the utilization of military technology takes advantage of important underlying ideas and general technical competence. These may be termed the intangible technological by-products of military research and development. As a consequence of large-scale postwar military research and development, the American economy in the 1960's includes a number of organizations with the managerial and technical competence to undertake large-scale, scientifically based engineering programs. We have developed a greater public awareness of the power of new technology and to some extent a greater business interest in exploiting the potential of that technology. Finally, there is an increased level of governmental sophistication both in technical matters—as a result of its considerable experience as customer and manager—and in the formulation of policy for science and technology. Because these benefits are in their nature intangible, it is difficult to point to significant results in the short run. Their long-term significance, nevertheless, is potentially very great. An attempt to take advantage of these benefits has been made in California, where the governor has undertaken contracts (1965) with major firms in the aerospace industry to investigate solutions to four major problems of modern urban life: transportation, air and water pollution, information collection, and crime and the control of criminals.

CONCLUSION

Societies have long exploited military technology for civilian purposes; it is an inseparable part of the process by which technology, in general, is utilized in a society. The fundamental questions we face are: How can science be coupled effectively to technology? How are inventions translated into innovations? What is the nature of the social response to fundamental innovations? Accomplishments in this area have hinged on the answers to these long-standing—although still poorly understood—questions about technology and society in general.

There are, of course, some distinctive features to these questions as they arise in contemporary American society. Because of the large scale and public character of the major innovations, some of them have had a disproportionately large effect on public awareness. In response to qualitative changes and the greatly increased scale of military research and development, new institutions are being developed to help translate the results of military research and development into useful terms for the civilian sectors of the economy. A heightened awareness of the importance of technological change in economic growth has lent further impetus to these changes. Yet the problems of facilitating institutional adaptation to promote innovation are not essentially different in kind because the roots of the technology lie in the military domain. A society which is technologically responsive should perform equally well the similar tasks of adapting military technology for civilian use and of originating and exploiting new technology wholly within the civilian sector.

Part **XI**
Scientific Research, Technology, and Automation

40 / Industrial Research and Development
W. DAVID LEWIS

The application of science to industry on a large scale and in a systematic manner is a development of momentous importance that has taken place only within the past century. Previously, contact between the scientist and the mechanic or inventor was likely to be at best haphazard, with the result that substantial lapses of time might occur between the discovery of a new principle and its practical application. Despite significant technological progress which took place from time to time with the development of ingenious machinery, precision techniques, and repetitive processes, many manufacturing methods continued to be based upon wasteful and inefficient practices that had evolved over the course of generations on an empirical, trial-and-error basis. In other cases, industrial growth was hindered by the natural limitations of certain key raw materials and a lack of knowledge about how to overcome them.

By the late 19th century, however, businessmen and government officials who were becoming increasingly aware of the potential utility of applied science began to invest large amounts of time, money, and effort in exploiting it for profit and power. The possibilities of industrial research were strikingly revealed in England during the mid-1850's, when a chemist named William Henry Perkin synthesized a mauve-colored dye from a coal-tar derivative and proved through intensive experimental development that this substance could be profitably produced on a commercial basis. Despite this pioneering venture, England's lead in applied science was soon lost to Germany, where government support for scientific education had helped both to advance knowledge about natural phenomena and to produce a university system capable of turning out large numbers of technically trained graduates. In Germany there also emerged a group of highly competitive dye manufacturing companies whose directors willingly provided the laboratory facilities and working conditions necessary for systematic research in coal-tar colors and derivatives. The pursuit of scientific knowledge for purposes of industrial advancement led quickly to German domi-

nance in the manufacture of dyes, pharmaceuticals, and other chemically related products.

As the benefits of applied science became more and more obvious, the use of
organized industrial research became increasingly widespread throughout economically advanced areas, becoming a force of great consequence in its influence on human affairs.

THE INTERNATIONALISM OF SCIENCE

In the broadest sense, science knows no national boundaries, being devoted to
the search for truth wherever it is to be found. This is especially evident with
regard to fundamental experimentation aimed at the discovery of previously
unknown principles and relationships, but it is also true to a considerable extent in the industrial application of scientific research. For example, major steps
leading to the eventual appearance of commercial television were made in at
least four countries, Germany, Russia, Great Britain, and the United States;
similarly, work on the development of catalytic petroleum cracking, diesel
railway traction, jet engines, magnetic recording, radio, and a variety of other
products and processes took place in a number of different nations, with key
breakthroughs sometimes occurring almost simultaneously in separate places.

From an early date, the international character of scientific and technological
innovation has been emphasized by the way in which business corporations
have overlapped political boundary lines and by the spread of a complex web
of patent, cartel, and licensing agreements which are respected and enforced
throughout a large number of participating countries. Furthermore, in recent
years considerable research of industrial significance has been conducted under
the auspices of supranational bodies such as the European Atomic Energy Community, founded in 1958 and dedicated to peacetime applications of nuclear
science. It seems clear that such trends will continue.

Despite these considerations, it is meaningful to study the development of
industrial research within a national context, for the practical consequences of
scientific investigation have led governments to take an ever-increasing interest
in channelling and exploiting efforts in this area. In addition, the particular
needs, resources, and traditions of various countries have had important effects
upon the characteristics of the research activities they undertake. It is logical,
for example, that certain Scandinavian nations and Canada have developed
programs to investigate the utilization of wood pulp, iron ore, hydroelectric
power, and products of the fishing industry, and that Switzerland, with limited
resources, has encouraged research aimed at maintaining superior quality in
manufactured goods and achieving excellence in specialized fields, as in the
production of fine chemicals and pharmaceuticals. It is also obvious that certain
countries have been better able to develop extensive programs of applied sci-

ence because they possess superior assets in terms of skilled personnel, strategic raw materials, financial resources, or overall industrial capacity. In this regard, as elsewhere, the great powers have occupied positions superior to those of their neighbors.

GERMANY

Having seized a position of leadership in applied science by the end of the 19th century, Germany intensified its efforts during the early years of the 20th century. Government support, already heavily enlisted in scientific education, was utilized after 1911 in the establishment, in co-operation with various private firms, of the so-called Kaiser Wilhelm Institutes for carrying out research in such fields as chemistry, physics, and biology.

After making a great contribution to the German military effort in World War I, industrial science was relied on to help lift the country out of the economic consequences of its defeat, and played a key role in the nationalization movement that took place in German industry during the 1920's. The research efforts of large firms like I. G. Farbenindustrie in chemistry, Siemens-Halske and the Allgemeine Electrizitäts Gesellschaft in electricity, Krupp and Vereinigte Stahlwerke in metallurgy, Telefunken in radio, and Zeiss in optics, assisted in the recovery of prewar markets and later contributed to the Nazi drive for national self-sufficiency and military power. Following the collapse of the Third Reich, the scientific and technical staffs of renascent firms, Krupp and Agfa, for example, again played a part in the dramatic recovery program which by 1964 had brought the West German Federal Republic to second rank among the countries of the world in foreign trade and third in gross national product.

GREAT BRITAIN

In Germany, the growth of large industrial combinations with extensive financial resources facilitated the rise of correspondingly sizable company laboratories; in Great Britain, the generally prevailing pattern of small firms resulted in a characteristically different approach to industrial research.

After shortages in key materials following the outbreak of the First World War had alerted political leaders and businessmen alike to the need for a more positive cultivation of applied science, a Department of Scientific and Industrial Research was established in 1915 under government sponsorship. With the collaboration of various British trade groups, a number of research associations were set up within different fields of production to investigate problems of interest to member firms on a co-operative basis. This provided a means of sharing the heavy financial burdens of scientific experimentation, but the direction of research efforts, being the product of joint decisions by a number of separate and often competing units, inevitably lacked the sharpness of focus which could be attained in programs carried on by single, heavily capitalized business units. Interestingly, some of the most significant products of British industrial research, like polyester fibers, were developed by a few large firms such as Imperial Chemical Industries, Ltd., on the basis of earlier experimentation by smaller organizations which could not afford to carry them through to the stage of full commercial exploitation.

In Britain also, an emphasis on fundamental research and persistent low public estimation of engineering (as opposed to science) contributed to a characteristic lag between the discovery of promising ideas and their practical implementation. So serious had this problem become by 1964 that Parliament created a Ministry of Technology, hoping that in this way a means might be found of increasing the country's slow economic growth rate and augmenting its volume of exports.

FRANCE

In France, a nation with a notable scientific heritage, organized industrial research developed in a slow and spasmodic manner throughout the first four decades of the 20th century. Traditions of intense trade secrecy, lack of effective communication between educational institutions and manufacturing firms, and a characteristic pattern of small, family-owned business units, along with a generally passive attitude toward innovation so long as customers were satisfied with existing products, were among the circumstances that discouraged progress in applied science, despite the work of individual inventors who made valuable contributions in the early development of synthetic fibers, tungsten carbide, and petroleum cracking processes, or of a few firms like the Comptoir des Textiles Artificiels, which helped develop cellophane.

By the late 1930's, however, an energetic research program had been inaugurated under government auspices, and following World War II France became increasingly involved in technological innovation. Most of this effort came from nationalized industries engaged in the production of automobiles, aircraft, machine tools, coal, iron, and electricity, but considerable progress was also made by private companies manufacturing commodities such as aluminum and chemicals. In part, the change seemed traceable to governmental initiative, but it was also evident that a remarkable alteration had taken place in public attitudes toward means of economic progress.

JAPAN

A characteristic willingness to borrow ideas from the West, combined with the fostering care of a paternalistic government and the existence of large business organizations with ample financial resources, has formed the background for steady progress in applied science in Japan throughout most of the 20th century. Following the example of the Kaiser Wilhelm Institutes in Germany, the Japanese created in 1917 a National Institute for Physical and Chemical Research, which established laboratories throughout the country to carry out investigations financed jointly by government and industry. The setting up of a National Research Council in the United States in 1916 was followed by a similar move in Japan four years later.

During the period between the two world wars, Japanese industry underwent a rationalization movement much like that in Germany, climaxed by a pronounced drive toward self-sufficiency and military preparedness in the 1930's. The role of applied science in these developments was as pronounced as it was in the era of reorganization, recovery, and business expansion that took place after 1945. In the latter period the Japanese again demonstrated a remarkable capacity for capitalizing on Western developments, making great progress, for example, in electric railway transportation, the production of transistors and other electronic devices, and the manufacture of specialty steels.

THE SOVIET UNION

Neither basic nor applied science was promoted in Russia in an extensive or vigorous manner by the Czarist government during the late 19th and early 20th centuries. Nevertheless, as the country industrialized rapidly throughout this period, there was also a considerable growth in the number of trained scientists and engineers. Some of these emigrated after the Bolshevik Revolution (1917) and made outstanding contributions to industrial research in the United States and elsewhere; others remained and played key roles in the new Soviet economy.

From the beginning, the new rulers made elaborate provisions for the encouragement of science and its application to industry. Technical institutes were established in various sections of the Soviet Union, and the Russian Academy of Sciences, originally founded by Peter the Great, was ultimately reorganized to co-ordinate research activities in accordance with government directives. Massive changes were also made in the higher educational system after shortages of specialists in key areas became apparent following the inauguration of the first Five Year Plan in 1927. By the 1930's, Russia was devoting a larger proportion of its national income to science than any other country, and this effort continued in the postwar era. Thanks, in part, to the high prestige and special financial rewards accorded to scientific workers in Soviet society, their number had reached an estimated 4 million by 1961, accounting in great measure for the immense strides which the country had been able to take in the development of its industry and technology.

THE UNITED STATES

Large-scale industrial research was slower getting under way in the United States than in Germany, but by the beginning of the 20th century a basis had been established for significant future achievements in this field. A survey of the way in which industrial research developed in America shows clearly not only the conditions which stimulated the growth of applied science, but also the manner in which organizational change accompanied its ever-widening use.

The American experience in this field is also instructive in two additional respects. From one point of view, it reveals the influence of the competitive forces characteristic of a capitalist economy and the way in which science could be used as a weapon in commercial warfare. On the other hand, it also demonstrates that the industrial utilization of science fostered a degree of co-operation, first between business units themselves and then among various types of business, governmental, and private organizations, that expanded and deepened over the course of time. As the relationship of science and technology to the public welfare became more and more apparent, it was increasingly necessary to consider the wise allocation of human and non-human resources so as to prevent serious imbalances, the wasteful duplication of effort, and unnecessary losses of time and capital.

EARLY EXAMPLES

A concern for applying theoretical knowledge to practical pursuits has long been a characteristic American trait, observed by native residents and foreign visitors alike. From the late 18th century onward, scattered examples of co-operation between science and technology gave promise of greater future developments. For example, a remarkable group of Philadelphia chemists, led by Robert Hare and James Woodhouse, carried on experiments of industrial value in illumination, gas analysis, and metallurgy during the early years of national independence. Another chemist, Samuel L. Dana, made significant contributions to the bleaching of textiles throughout a period of employment with the Merrimack Manufacturing Company of Lowell, Massachusetts, lasting from 1834 to 1868. During these years a number of trained investigators including Joseph Henry, Benjamin Silliman, Jr., James Booth, Augustus A. Hayes, Lammot du Pont, and James Beck, also applied scientific principles with varying degrees of success in the fields of telegraphy, analysis of petroleum deposits, smelting and refining of metals, manufacture of explosives, and the production of the commodities sugar, salt, and potash.

Such portents as these reached greater fulfillment in the late 19th century, when three major developments contributed to more systematic use of scientific research for practical purposes. First, by this time, basic knowledge in various areas of natural science—thermodynamics, electricity, chemistry, and bacteriology—had advanced to a point at which profitable exploitation was possible on a relatively large scale. This coincided with a process of rapid industrialization which was ultimately to make the United States the world's leading manufacturing nation. Finally, this period of American history also witnessed a marked expansion of educational opportunities in science and engineering as state colleges and universities were established under the Morrill Land-Grant Act of 1862. A number of new private institutions, Lehigh, Cornell, Johns Hopkins, and the University of Chicago, opened their doors, and technological institutes were founded in various parts of the country. The stage had thus been set for widespread and fruitful contact between science and industry wherever specific circumstances provided the impetus.

ANALYSIS AND TESTING

One of the first ways in which the potential value of applied science became apparent to American businessmen was in connection with the analysis and testing of raw materials and finished or semi-finished products. Various circumstances typified the development of transportation and industry during the late 19th century: severe competition, declining prices, and heavy capital requirements. These led increasing numbers of entrepreneurs to stress a high volume of operations at a low unit cost through the utilization of standardized ingredients, uniform processes, and interchangeable parts. This, in turn, made it necessary to develop methods of precise testing and measurement, and led to the hiring of trained personnel who alone had the expert knowledge to perform such work. Andrew Carnegie, for example, began to employ chemists in the 1870's to make ore analyses, and other firms soon followed his lead.

One of the skilled pioneers in industrial testing was Charles Benjamin Dudley, who went to work for the Pennsylvania Railroad in 1875 after receiving a Ph.D. in chemistry from Yale. During the course of a long career at the company's shops in Altoona, Pa., he conducted important studies on the composition and properties of rails, and developed standard specifications for mechanical components, paints, fuels, lubricants, and lighting devices used by his employers. In 1898 Dudley played a leading part in founding the American Society for Testing Materials, an organization which continues today to promote and develop analytical methods, and served as its president from 1902 until his death in 1909.

BASIC STANDARDS

Although introduced into the operations of business firms largely as a means of cutting costs and enabling individual producers to gain an advantage over their competitors, scientific testing and analysis soon came to play a major role in the co-operative efforts of manufacturers and private professional organizations to adopt industrywide standards in the interest of greater overall efficiency and economy. By the early 20th century the federal government had become involved in this effort to the extent of establishing a National Bureau of Standards, authorized by Congress in 1901 and modelled in part upon European institutions like the Physikalische-Technische Reichanstalt in Germany and the National Physical Laboratory in Great Britain.

Maintaining close ties with business from the beginning, the Bureau of Standards performed notable work in the precise determination of weights and measures and the formulation of uniform standards in the fields of electricity, optics, thermometry, chemistry, metallurgy, structural engineering, and so on. In addition, it supplied information to manufacturers on a variety of problems and actually carried out applied research in fields where firms were too small and widely scattered to afford their own programs of experimentation. Another important aspect of the Bureau's activities was its co-operation with such business organizations as the National Electric Light Association and the General Cotton Manufacturers' Association, which became especially pronounced during the 1920's under the guiding influence of Secretary of Commerce Herbert Hoover.

Testing and analysis have continued to be of major importance in the industrial application of science down to the present time; indeed, the necessity for such efforts became increasingly pronounced as the American economy eventually moved out of an age of mere standardization and into one of automation. The significance of such work in providing employment for scientists, however, gradually declined in a relative sense. Although the development of testing procedures and the determination of physical constants often required considerable ingenuity and imagination, routine testing itself tended to be monotonous and unattractive to highly trained personnel; in time it was increasingly assigned to non-professional employees and even handled by mechanical or electronic devices. Meanwhile, the efforts of industrial researchers came to be applied to an ever greater degree to eliminating production bottlenecks, exploring the merits of different processes, finding substitute raw materials from which goods could be turned out at lower cost, reducing waste, finding profitable uses for by-products, and improving the quality of various manufactured commodities.

EARLY INDUSTRIAL RESEARCH

Such activities were consistent with the needs of an increasingly rationalized economy based upon large-scale production. A firm which utilized research for projects like these at an early stage was the Standard Oil Company. It derived great profit during the 1880's from the work of chemist Herman Frasch in making possible the use of sulfurous petroleum deposits, and again in the early 20th century from the success of William M. Burton in developing a cracking process capable of obtaining greater yields of light gasoline fractions from crude oil, thus meeting a key need in the emerging automobile age. Similar examples occurred during the same period in the sugar industry, where refining techniques were much improved; in the field of photography, where the Eastman Kodak Company was particularly successful in developing new products and processes; and in the manufacture of explosives, which became increasingly rationalized through the efforts of trained chemists like Francis Gurney du Pont.

Despite the early success of these ventures, many companies initially hesitated to commit themselves to organized research on a large scale. In some cases, businessmen were reluctant to risk money in experimental equipment or feared the effect of introducing unforeseen changes into plants whose personnel had become accustomed to long-established methods of production. Other entrepreneurs were willing to hire scientists and engineers for routine work but preferred to rely chiefly upon part-time consultants drawn from university faculties or other sources for more basic ideas. A similar approach was to wait for discoveries to be made by outside investigators and then purchase the resulting patents. Thus the rights to Charles M. Hall's electrolytic method of producing aluminum and Michael Pupin's loading coil for amplifying impulses in long-range telephony were secured by industrialists only after their potential usefulness had already become apparent. In other cases, important products, such as Bakelite and carborundum, were initially manufactured on a commercial scale by their own discoverers.

RESEARCH INSTITUTIONS

The slowness of many companies to develop research programs of their own had various results. One was to facilitate the rise of independent commercial laboratories which did scientific work for industrial clients on a fee basis. Arthur D. Little, Inc., is still prominent in this field; founded in 1886, it was most active in handling problems relating to the manufacture of paper before it branched out into other areas.

Equally important was the way in which colleges and universities became involved in a variety of commercial relationships through the consultative activities of staff members and the establishment of experimental stations on a number of campuses for the investigation of industrial problems. A venture of this type, motivated at least in part by a distrust of the businessman's capacity for managing scientific work, was a program of industrial fellowships inaugurated by a chemistry professor, Robert K. Duncan, at the University of Kansas from 1906 to 1910 and subsequently transferred to the University of Pittsburgh, where it became the basis of the Mellon Research Institute. This plan, under which manufacturers brought problems to the university and endowed a fellowship to have them investigated there by students or other staff personnel, eventually spread to other countries, including Canada, Great Britain, Australia, and Japan.

At the same time that many businessmen were holding back from making use of science or seizing only upon applications which gave promise of quick profits, others were beginning to realize that systematic and well-organized programs of research, continuously supported with ample financial resources, offered outstanding prospects of long-range growth in certain key fields of enterprise. The firms that pioneered in this new phase of development shared two main characteristics. First, they tended to be based wholly or in large part upon the technological exploitation of fundamental scientific discoveries; also, they were almost always among the largest companies in their respective fields and held positions of market leadership under oligopoly or virtual monopoly conditions. Realizing that it was necessary to keep constantly abreast of possible technical innovations in order to maintain such dominance, and aware of the large profits that could accrue from one significant breakthrough, they could well afford to invest in long-range research gambles even if a number had only margin. l prospects of success. Eventually, some of these companies came to see the wisdom not only of supporting intensive programs to exploit the practical potential of known scientific concepts and ideas, but also of allowing a few gifted staff members to engage in fundamental studies of natural phenomena conducted without thought of immediate applications.

THE ELECTRICAL INDUSTRY

These characteristics were shared by various American corporations which instituted ambitious research programs in the early 20th century. The electrical and communications industries, however, were particularly important in the development of large, multi-faceted company laboratories of a truly modern variety, primarily because they were based directly upon recent fundamental scientific discoveries whose commercial exploitation required organized invention on a scale not previously known in this country.

The complexity which came to typify research and development programs in these areas was well illustrated at an early date by the work of Thomas A. Edison in devising a practical system of incandescent lighting. This involved intensive work on interrelated elements—parallel circuits, vacuum bulbs, high-resistance filaments, improved dynamos, complex distribution systems, voltage regulators, safety apparatus, and metering devices. In order to carry out such a project, Edison needed a large staff of assistants with varying skills, elaborate experimental equipment, extensive shop facilities, and ample financial backing. And although more of an empirical inventor than a scientist, many of Edison's

Fig. 40-1. Thomas Edison's Menlo Park laboratory as reconstructed at Green-field Village. (Courtesy of the *Henry Ford Museum*, Dearborn, Michigan)

activities were similar to those of later industrial research directors, and his Menlo Park establishment in New Jersey was in certain respects a prototype of future company laboratories.

Continued technical advancement in electricity eventually created problems demanding greater scientific and mathematical competence than such men as Edison possessed. This was particularly true after expanding markets and fundamental difficulties in power transmission forced the utilization of alternating current, which could readily be stepped down from high to low voltages, rather than the simpler, more technologically limited direct current previously in use. By acquiring basic European patents and overcoming practical difficulties through intensive development, the Westinghouse Company seized an initial lead in adapting alternating current to American commercial exploitation; but the business firm which in time capitalized most effectively upon the new situation was the Thomson-Houston Electrical Company of Lynn, Massachusetts, with which the Edison interests were to merge in 1892 after a stubborn and unsuccessful effort by the latter to resist the changes taking place in the industry. Thanks in considerable measure to the scientific and mathematical capabilities of Elihu Thomson and Charles P. Steinmetz, the newly formed General Electric Company which resulted from this merger rapidly achieved dominance in its field and in 1900 established the first truly modern industrial research laboratory in America at its new headquarters in Schenectady, New York. Here, under the leadership of Willis R. Whitney, formerly a chemistry professor at M.I.T., a large staff of scientists and technical personnel was formed and kept constantly at work on a variety of problems involving electrical phenomena. By engaging in continuous innovation, the company hoped to keep abreast of any new developments in its area of commercial interests, thus maintaining its dominance and guarding against future competition.

General Electric's lead was soon followed by other large firms which had seen from their own experience the benefits of applied science. The Du Pont Company, long concerned with problems of quality control and throughout its history an important innovating force in the explosives industry, had built a laboratory at Carney's Point, New Jersey, in 1891 for experimental work on smokeless gunpowder, and established business relationships with outside inventors like Hudson Maxim. Following a major reorganization of the firm in 1902, the new directors inaugurated a broad program of research in explosives by setting up the Eastern Laboratory at Gibbstown, New Jersey, under the direction of a professional chemist, Charles L. Reese.

The Parke-Davis pharmaceutical company, which had shortly before derived great profit from the enzyme and hormone discoveries of a Japanese chemist, built a large new laboratory in 1902, and the Corning Glass Works, which had formerly received consultative help from Cornell University, commenced a research program in 1908. Another large and technologically progressive firm, the Eastman Kodak Company, opened an excellently equipped laboratory at Rochester, New York, in 1913 for continued experimentation in photography under the leadership of the British-trained chemist C. E. K. Mees, who became an outstanding authority in the organization and administration of industrial research.

The extent to which some business leaders were willing to provide facilities for applied science was best revealed after 1907 by the American Telephone and Telegraph Company, which had previously maintained scattered engineering and development units but relied chiefly for a number of years upon acquiring the rights to important patents from outside inventors. This policy changed when a new president, Theodore N. Vail, took over leadership of the firm and centralized its research activities in New York City under the direction of John J. Carty, a company engineer. By 1921 the Bell Telephone Laboratories, operated by the parent firm's Western Electric Company subsidiary, were by far the largest in America, occupying a thirteen-story building with approximately 400,000 square feet of floor space and employing more than 1500 men to work on a great variety of technical and scientific problems. Because of the experimental achievements of such persons as Harold D. Arnold, whose improvements on the De Forest triode tube contributed greatly to the development of long-range communication, and John R. Carson, who pioneered in the field of high-frequency transmission, A.T.&T. continued to dominate technological progress in its industry and also established itself in an excellent position to take advantage of the commercial opportunities that opened up in the field of radio in the years that followed.

Although the large research laboratories just described shared many common characteristics, different patterns of management were evident for a number of years. Some directors, like John J. Carty, were severely practical in their approach, preferring to allow fundamental investigations to remain exclusively the province of universities and other non-profit-making institutions. That there were limits beyond which it was unwise to go in the opposite direction was indicated by the experience of the engineer C. E. Skinner, who was ultimately dismissed as director of the Westinghouse research program for failure to exert enough pressure on staff members for quickly profitable results. A policy of moderation in this regard was followed at General Electric by Willis R. Whitney, who gave priority to requests for help from company divisions but nevertheless allowed some of his staff to carry out long-range investigations which were not always aimed at specific practical goals. Under his leadership, scientists were allowed to publish their findings in scholarly journals, permitted to attend professional meetings on company time, and provided with facilities similar in many respects to those found in higher educational institutions. The favorable result of these practices was that General Electric developed profitable innovations, for example, the tungsten filament, and at the same time retained the services of outstandingly creative scientists like Irving Langmuir, who later won a Nobel Prize for fundamental research on surface films. Eventually Whitney's approach became typical in the administration of most large American industrial laboratories.

EFFECTS OF WORLD WAR I

With the advent of the large corporate laboratory, industrial research was firmly established in the United States on a scale transcending mere testing, trouble-shooting, and process development. Science had become a source of innovation and a component of economic growth. And it is important to note that this degree of relative maturity had been reached before the onset of World War I, which has sometimes been credited with playing a decisive role in America with regard to relations between science and technology. Although this is a defensible point of view, its applicability in specific instances should be closely examined so as not to neglect the importance of long-range trends.

From the standpoint of industrial research, it must be granted that the obvious connection between Germany's scientific establishment and its military prowess, combined with great shortages of commodities such as dyes and pharmaceuticals following the outbreak of the war in 1914, went far to convince many influential Americans of the necessity to give organized science strong support. The establishment of the National Research Council in 1916 signified the beginning of an era in which government would play an ever more active role in the allocation of the country's scientific resources. Among the new agency's subdivisions was a committee on industrial research, which spearheaded a drive to promote applied science under the leadership of John J. Carty, aided by an advisory board containing a number of outstanding business executives.

In addition to the impetus which was thus given to a general expansion of applied science during the war years, specific research opportunities of great importance were opened up in many fields, including the chemical industry, which became an object of great solicitude on the part of government officials and private interests alike. Through the confiscation of German patents and the inauguration of intensive research and development programs by American chemical firms themselves, a determined effort was begun to achieve national self-sufficiency in the manufacture of dyes, fine chemicals, and scientific instruments, which had previously been obtained largely from abroad. Under the spur of wartime demands for the increased production of various commodities, scientists were called upon in larger numbers than ever before to rationalize manufacturing techniques, and companies which had not previously engaged in such activity now found it expedient to do so.

Nevertheless, the contribution which the war made to the development of American industrial research should not be overestimated. The drain of scientific talent into projects of a military or semi-military nature, for example, caused the temporary cessation of research in various areas of peacetime application and interfered with the progress of fundamental exploration in basic science. Furthermore, as the noted industrial scientist and administrator Frank B. Jewett pointed out in 1918, the mere multiplication of industrial research projects and facilities during the war did not necessarily signify a corresponding increase in the quality of work being done, nor even indicate of and by itself that the nation's long-range capacity for effective research and development had been materially strengthened. Finally, it should always be kept in mind that applied science was well entrenched in the United States before the fighting began and that many of the tendencies observable in its evolution reappeared as soon as the conflict stopped.

POST-WORLD WAR I DEVELOPMENTS

One trend, already apparent before World War I and continuing afterward, was the establishment of large, centralized laboratories by major firms which occupied strategic positions in technically based industries and sought to out-distance their competitors by keeping in the vanguard of possible innovations in their field. The impact of the automobile revolution, already well under way by 1914, was reflected in the inauguration of an extensive research and development program by General Motors in 1919 under the direction of Charles F. Kettering, who had previously organized an automotive engineering company in Dayton, Ohio. The experimentation which took place under the new program in improving valve mechanisms, transmission systems, plated parts, finishes, brakes, shock absorbers, and other automobile components, formed a natural concomitant to the annual model change that General Motors pioneered in response to consumer discontent with uniformly standardized vehicles like the Model-T Ford. The needs of the motoring public were also evident in the appearance of large-scale research in the fields of rubber manufacturing, where firms like Goodyear and B. F. Goodrich sought to improve the quality and performance of tires and other accessories.

The rise of the radio industry, the scientific and technological basis of which was present in the prewar period, was similarly accompanied in the 1920's by intensive experimentation and development as the mass-market potentialities became increasingly obvious. Much of this research was carried on in the already well-established laboratories of General Electric, A.T. & T., and Westinghouse, whose scientific staffs continued to expand rapidly throughout the decade. These years also saw the rise of electronics experimentation by other firms such as the Philadelphia Storage Battery Company (later renamed the Philco Corporation) and Raytheon.

Although quantitative growth and the appearance of ever larger laboratories in certain fields of enterprise could have been expected on the basis of previous trends, a number of developments in the period following World War I indicated that a new stage in the practical application of science had been reached. One of these, an increasing product diversification in research-oriented industries, may be ascribed partly to special circumstances growing out of the war, from which the United States emerged as the world's most abundant source of investment capital. That the existence of large amounts of money seeking an outlet in productive enterprise could push manufacturing concerns into new lines of activity was shown in the case of the Du Pont Company which, through a process of merger and internal growth, became a vast and multi-faceted chemical empire dependent upon frequent innovation and expansion to keep its operation capital profitably employed. The research scientist played a key role in this regard, and the history of Du Pont in the postwar era was punctuated by the appearance of new products—Duco lacquers, synthetic ammonia, improved motion-picture film, moistureproof cellophane, and neoprene synthetic rubber. In part, however, the trend toward diversification reflected not only the search for investment opportunities but also a basic tendency of scientific investigations to open up varied research areas for future development once a laboratory program was well established.

A second tendency which marked this era, namely an accelerating trend toward co-operative research, manifested itself in two ways. As the potentialities of applied science became more apparent, numerous smaller firms which had previously neglected research or used it only sparingly began to desire programs of their own; often, however, they lacked funds with which to establish these efforts on anything but a small scale. This brought an increasing volume of business to independent commercial laboratories, the spread of which was marked by the establishment of the Battelle Memorial Institute of Columbus, Ohio, in 1929. On the other hand, it induced a number of businesses to turn to their trade associations for help, with the result that a variety of co-operative research establishments appeared. Although this approach was less prevalent in America than in England, it did spread in the United States in the petroleum, paper, textile, lumber, leather, cement, and paint industries. In some cases, efforts of this type were carried on in co-operation with educational institutions, as with Lawrence College in paper research or Ohio State University in petroleum studies. Thus the linking together of public and private, profit and non-profit, educational and non-educational organizations in the common pursuit of applied science continued throughout this period as before.

The use of co-operative research techniques was not, however, limited to small enterprises during the postwar era. For various reasons, even large corporations found joint efforts occasionally desirable, especially when interlocking directorates and other financial ties between different firms made for a natural community of interest and facilitated the exchange of information. Such a relationship existed between Du Pont and General Motors, which worked jointly on a project for the synthesis and commercial production of Freon refrigerants. Even more complex was the development of anti-knock gasoline, in which General Motors, Du Pont, Dow Chemical Corporation, and Standard Oil all had a part, along with a chemistry professor at Clark University. The sheer complexity of many products which became items of mass consumption during this period often necessitated sharing the fruits of research even when experimentation was carried on independently by separate firms. The patent rights to various radio components, for example, were so scattered in 1919 as to force the creation of a new business entity, the Radio Corporation of America, in which A. T. & T., General Electric, and Westinghouse each had a share. The spread of cross-licensing agreements in the radio and automobile industries stimulated many companies to carry on research projects so as to derive fees and royalties from the utilization of their inventions by competing firms.

A growing degree of maturity with regard to applied science was marked during the 1920's by an intensified concern for maintaining a proper balance between various aspects of the nation's overall scientific and technological effort. In particular, it was increasingly realized that a steady flow of industrially useful ideas was ultimately dependent upon the vigor with which basic research, motivated primarily by the desire for new knowledge rather than for financial gain, was carried on.

While business leaders were not inclined to invest indiscriminately in fundamental research, a realization of its long-range profit potential induced some firms to make formal provision for it in areas of investigation which were of obvious relevance to their commercial interests. For example, in 1927 C. M. A. Stine, research director at Du Pont, persuaded company officials to allocate $250,000 per year for fundamental explorations in polymer chemistry. This project, conducted under the outstanding chemist Wallace H. Carothers, led ultimately to the development of nylon, first placed on the market eleven years later after a total outlay of about $27 million. The profits from this venture amply repaid the firm for its investment, but the costs it entailed show why only large corporations with ample resources could engage in efforts of this nature.

THE DEPRESSION

The extent to which industrial research had entered into the American economy is indicated during the 1930's by a rise in the number of company laboratories and of personnel employed in them, despite the fact that this was the most severe business depression in the nation's history. Although research budgets were cut temporarily by important firms such as General Electric, and the total national effort in this field suffered a demonstrable drop during the years 1931-33, there was a decided upward trend for the decade 1930-40 as a whole.

The Depression stimulated a number of companies to intensify research efforts aimed at cutting costs, explaining, in part, the development of such innovations as the continuous casting of aluminum and the adaptation of diesel electric traction for use on American railroads. In addition, it gave added impetus to quality improvement as a means of gaining a competitive edge in dwindling markets. It is also important to note that ambitious projects leading ultimately to the emergence of new items of mass consumption were pushed ahead during these years which saw notable progress in the development of automatic transmission, petrochemicals, synthetic fibers, Kodachrome film, silicones, fluorescent lighting, and television equipment.

A conviction that industrial research offered a means of combatting adverse economic conditions led to the publication of an increasing number of books and articles devoted to popularizing this activity during the Depression, and to intensified governmental efforts to encourage the growth of applied science. The continuing operations of the National Research Council in this regard were supplemented by the exertions of special federal agencies such as the Works Progress Administration (WPA) and the National Resources Planning Board, which issued notable reports in 1938 and 1941 on the development, practice, and potentialities of industrial research. These efforts attempted to encourage small- and middle-sized businesses to institute research programs, for the continuing dominance of large corporations was of concern to New Deal administrators, who feared increasing concentration in American industry, and also to citizens generally interested in a more balanced use of the country's scientific capacity. A WPA survey near the end of the Depression period estimated that fully half of the nation's industrial research personnel were employed by only 45 firms, with the other half distributed thinly among approximately 1700 business units.

The increasing size, complexity, and cost of many development projects also created uncertainty about the future prospects of individual inventors, who lacked the financial resources for research conducted on so grand a scale. Nevertheless, it should be noted that highly significant work was carried on during these years by individuals: Edwin H. Land, in synthetic light polarization; Chester Carlson, in xerography; and Philo Farnsworth, in television.

In brief, the Depression period was one of considerable achievement in industrial research, an era in which the evolutionary currents of the preceding decades were generally continued and many of the innovations that became crucially important in future consumer markets first began to appear. For this reason, it would once again be unwise to overstress the importance of wartime events, in this case those occurring between 1941 and 1945, in affecting the long-range development of applied science outside the military sphere.

WORLD WAR II

It is undeniable that World War II accelerated the practical development of pre-existing ideas and discoveries in areas of peacetime applicability—pharmaceuticals (for example, penicillin), aircraft (jet propulsion), electronics (radar), and atomic power. Yet it interrupted a variety of projects in other fields, including some significant efforts in basic research. One of the latter, a program in solid-state physics which the Bell Telephone Laboratories had commenced late in the prewar years, was resumed after the conflict and ultimately led to the development of the transistor, first announced to the public in 1948.

World War II nevertheless had an obvious impact upon the future course of applied science, especially in that it accustomed government leaders, businessmen, and taxpayers alike to the massive expenditure of federal funds for programs in this field. This phenomenon continued in the postwar period of confrontation with the Communist powers. Thanks in considerable measure to such governmental outlays, which reached nearly 60 per cent of the nation's total research and development budget in the late 1950's, science and technology were harnessed on a scale which dwarfed previous efforts in the field. The number of scientists and engineers employed by industry in such work rose from an estimated

37,000 in 1940, to 70,577 in 1950, 157,300 in 1954, 222,800 in 1957, and 277,000 in 1959. During roughly the same period, the funds spent for industrial research and development increased from approximately $660,000,000 in 1941, to $1,980,000,000 in 1950, $3,020,000,000 in 1954, $6,280,000,000 in 1957, and $9,600,000,000 in 1959. By 1962 it had reached almost $12 billion. The combined impetus of expanding consumer markets on the one hand and the search for military security and national prestige on the other brought profit-oriented and non-business institutions into a closer relationship as government scientists, industrial laboratory personnel, college and university professors, and graduate students, worked on a variety of related projects.

POSTWAR AND COLD WAR

The military and space-related aspects of postwar research and development are beyond the scope of this essay and are covered elsewhere in the present volume. It is pertinent, however, to note some of the social and economic consequences of the growing interdependence of public and private organizations in the pursuit of research objectives. A particularly interesting manifestation of this trend has been an increased concentration of government facilities, industrial laboratories, and technically oriented firms close to outstanding centers of learning such as Cambridge, Massachusetts, and Berkeley, California, where the recruitment of trained personnel, the assigning of research contracts, the formation of consultative relationships, and the dissemination of new and potentially useful knowledge can proceed with maximum speed and efficiency.

Another characteristic is the increasing similarity of large governmental, industrial, and university laboratories as the tasks to which they are devoted become more closely associated. There is, furthermore, a blurring of lines between commercial and non-commercial research as companies come to recognize the possible civilian applications of military or space projects. The launching by the National Aeronautics and Space Administration of the Bell Telephone System's Telstar I in July 1962 and the subsequent creation by Congress of the Communication Satellite Corporation dramatized this, and the periodic carry-over of knowledge from military-sponsored research into areas of peacetime application, as in aircraft and electronics, precipitated a lively discussion in business and trade publications about the opportunities involved in "spinoff," the term coined to describe this phenomenon.

The connection between industrial research and economic growth became apparent in the postwar period, when products which had been in an embryonic stage for years became everyday consumer items and themselves began to be replaced by even more recent discoveries. Burgeoning profits were realized in the electronics, pharmaceutical, and petrochemical industries on sales of semiconductors, antibiotics, tranquilizing drugs, hormone compounds, synthetic fibers, detergents, plastics, and other laboratory-created commodities. Similar gains were realized elsewhere from the development of Polaroid cameras, instant copying devices, ball-point pens, long-playing records, wide-screen motion pictures, and kindred innovations. One leading American corporation calculated in the late 1950's that 80 per cent of its sales revenue came from products unknown a decade before, while another predicted that 60 per cent or more of its receipts in 1975 would come from items as yet undeveloped or uninvented.

The impact of applied science is evident not only in the progress of single business units or fields of enterprise but also in the prosperity of certain geographic areas that can attract technically oriented firms, and the correspondingly depressed state of those that have not adapted so readily to changed conditions. The expenditure of billions of dollars for research and development purposes has intensified competition among states and regions to attract "growth industries," and stirred political conflicts over the awarding of "prime contracts." Meanwhile, the massive costs of various military and industrial projects have stimulated great policy concerns about increasing the effectiveness of managerial techniques in research so as to guard against the gross waste of public and private funds; and the occurrence of anticipated shortages of trained personnel, in the face of unprecedented demands for their services, has caused government officials, businessmen, and economists alike to ponder ever more seriously how best to allocate the country's scientific resources in the future.

THE "RESEARCH REVOLUTION"

The importance of science as a force for conscious and continuous technological innovation in the modern world has prompted some observers to speak of a "research revolution" as having taken place. They point out the possible consequences in terms of impaired economic growth, mass unemployment, diminishing investment opportunities, and declining national security that may occur should there be a slackening or some other malfunction in this crucial area. To the extent that the use of the term "revolution" may imply a sudden break with the past, such a view may be partially misleading, for the applied science of today has deep historical roots. Nevertheless, such language forcefully indicates the degree to which industrial research, once relatively unknown and undeveloped on the American scene, has become a social force of imposing consequence.

41 / The Development of Automation
JAMES R. BRIGHT

The history of automation involves two elements: automation as a phrase of social force, and as a set of technical facts. These two proceeded independently until about 1952-54, when technological progress and the new term merged into common recognition, literally influencing national and worldwide industrial activity.

THE ORIGIN AND GROWTH OF THE CONCEPT

In late 1946, D. S. Harder, then a manufacturing engineering executive for the Ford Motor Company, was in an engineering conference studying layout and equipment plans for Ford's proposed engine plant at Cleveland and stamping plant at Buffalo. During the review, he asked for "more materials handling equipment between these transfer machines. Give us some more of that automatic business . . . that 'automation.'" He was referring to the specialized machinery designed to feed castings, forgings, and metal sheets into conventional machine tools such as transfer machines and stamping presses. The word so aptly described automatic handling and work-feeding devices that it was immediately adopted by Ford's manufacturing engineers. In April 1947, Ford formed the first automation department in any firm and gave the title "automation engineers" to those manufacturing systems specialists designing the materials-handling, work-feeding, work-removing mechanisms that linked production equipment.

The word "automation" first appeared in print in 1948 in an article by Rupert Le Grand, "Ford Handles by Automation," in *American Machinist,* describing the activities of Ford's automation group. It gave the first definition of automation:

the art of applying mechanical devices to manipulate work pieces into and out of equipment, turn parts between operators, remove scrap, and to perform these tasks in timed sequence with the production equipment so that the line can be put wholly or partially under pushbutton control at strategic stations.

While automation thus began with the *automatic handling of parts in process in the metalworking industry,* it soon merged into a far broader technological context with deep social overtones. The key event was a paragraph by Norbert

Wiener, a professor at the Massachusetts Institute of Technology, in his book, *The Human Use of Human Beings* (1950). That book grew out of his earlier work (1948) entitled *Cybernetics*. By cybernetics Dr. Wiener meant "control and communication in the animal and the machine," and he compared control devices such as mathematical calculators and automatic pilots to the human nerve system and brain. With increasing frequency the word cybernetics was found in literature dealing with control systems. *The Human Use of Human Beings* was a philosophical projection of the impact of cybernetic concepts on society. Wiener anticipated that computing machinery would be adapted to a host of judgment situations that occur in manufacturing and distribution; mechanization would rapidly invade other areas of human endeavor where, as before, the machine would be more efficient than man:

> I should give a rough estimate that it will take the new tools 10 to 20 years to come into their own. A war would change this all overnight. . . .
> Under these circumstances, the period of about two years which it took for radar to get onto the battlefields with a high degree of effectiveness is scarcely likely to be exceeded by the period of evolution of the automatic factory . . . thus a new war will almost inevitably see the automatic age in full swing within less than five years.

Weiner then made his now-famous prediction, which launched the furor over automation and still continues to cause social concern:

> Let us remember that the automatic machine, whatever we think of any feelings it may have or may not have, is the precise economic equivalent of slave labor. Any labor which competes with slave labor must accept the economic conditions of slave labor. It is perfectly clear that this will produce an unemployment situation, in comparison with which the present recession and even the depression of the thirties will seem like a pleasant joke.

The book had a tremendous (and unwarranted) influence on the public. Regardless of what Wiener intended to convey, he established in the minds of many people that (a) electronic controls were merely in their infancy; (b) these controls were about to make possible computation machinery that could be adapted to decision-making problems in war, business, and social areas; (c) therefore, the automatic factory was not only possible, it was an imminent reality and a certainty within a decade; (d) it followed that millions would be displaced within 20 years at the latest, which would result in a violent depression; (e) thus, *cybernetics*, the *automatic factory*, and *automation* become interchangeable and parallel concepts. This had evil and terrifying implications as far as human labor was concerned: the machine, which had replaced man's muscles, was now about to replace his brain. Automation became a social concern.

Automation gathered new impetus when John Diebold's book, *Automation—*

the Advent of the Automatic Factory (D. Van Nostrand Company, Inc.), appeared in 1952. This book defined automation as

. . . a new word denoting both automatic operations and the process of making things automatic. In the latter sense it includes several areas of industrial activity, such as product and process redesign, the theory of communication and control, and the design of machinery. The connotation intended is delineation of these otherwise loosely related studies as being a distinct area of industrial endeavor, the systematic analysis and study of which will yield fruitful results.

Diebold, attempting to balance Wiener's emphasis on automatic controls, wrote:

Paradoxically, the current obsession with the novelty and spectacular performance of automatic controls diverts attention from the problems of their application to industry. Although automatic control mechanisms are *necessary* for the achievement of fully automatic factories, they are not *sufficient* in themselves. The full promise of the new technology cannot be realized so long as we think solely in terms of control. . . . The amount of attention given to the control problem has kept nearly all discussion of automatic industrial processes revolving around the control devices and the control systems. . . . These uses of control devices incite journalistic fantasy, for it is all too easy to draw superficial parellels between the operation of certain military equipment and the operation of industrial machinery. Most of what has been published about the peacetime industrial use of the new technology, even when not outright science fiction, has presented the problem as primarily one of control. The result has been diffuse and loose thinking.

A little more than a year later, Diebold appears to have reversed his thinking. Automatic control was no longer "overemphasized"; it was now "the key concept."

In particular, what are the key concepts which top executives should understand in order to make intelligent decisions involving automation in their plants? . . . (1) the *common denominator* of the widely different forms of the new technology is the concept of *feedback* control, or self-correction. It is the use of electronic controls employing feedback that gives rise to an entirely new technology: automation. . . . This represents quite a different meaning. The fact that it is not distinguished from the more general and less significantly new idea of automatic operation . . . is unfortunate, though understandable at this early stage.

Despite these pronouncements, many engineers in the automotive and other parts of the metalworking industry continued to define automation, in hundreds of papers, as the automatic handling of work-in-process. However, in July 1954 the Reinhold Publishing Corporation brought out the first issue of a magazine called *Automatic Control,* with Diebold as editor. In the leading article he added another phrase that caught the eye of many journalists:

. . . there is a new concept fundamental in our technology today which gives us cause to speak of a *second industrial revolution*. This concept is *automatic control*, involving the application of the principles of self-regulation to any process, machine or product. Thus where the first industrial revolution replaced manual labor by machines, today's industrial revolution means the replacement of manual control by machine control.

In August 1954 editors of a new magazine, *Automation,* published by the Penton Publishing Company, defined automation as "the art and science of manufacturing as automatically and economically as feasible." Thus, in the six years after 1948, automation had grown to include broader and broader technical and social concepts. To most industrialists it implied continuous automatic production made possible by automatic control.

THE FUROR OVER AUTOMATION

A new development simultaneously widened and intensified automation excitement. In 1952 the first computer was sold to the Bureau of the Census, and by 1955 several hundred more were on order or installed. Many non-manufacturing industrialists began to equate automation with data processing; this new meaning of automation was applied to computers and accounting, and to finance and business activities concerned with the mechanization of paper work. Insurance companies, for instance, found automation an apt term to describe computer progress. Automation became a commercial and financial term of the nation.

Technical and popular interest in the term mushroomed during these years. There is probably not a technical, business, or trade paper that did not carry half a dozen (or a hundred) articles on automation between 1952 and 1955. Almost every professional engineering society—mechanical, electrical, and others —held seminars on the subject. The popular press was filled with articles on automation. United States government agencies and European nations held conferences on automation, and Russia eventually created a Ministry of Automation.

The automation furor was next compounded by the activities of the unions, initially the UAW-CIO, beginning in 1954. In preparation for the 1955 bargaining sessions, the United Auto Workers published extracts of various speeches and claims from the literature that delineated their attitude toward automation. Perhaps most typical and significant was Walter Reuther's report, *Automation,* to the UAW-CIO Economic and Collective Bargaining Conference on November 12-13, 1954. His report contained 19 direct quotations taken from such sources as Wiener's book, speeches of Ford executives, and the business press. These comments were used to develop arguments for new approaches to wage bargaining. If the quotations correctly described industrial progress through automation, one could hardly blame the unions for their alarm.

Management, engineers, and top executives of leading firms promptly denounced these claims as exaggerated, declaring that automation did not represent anything technologically or economically different from what had occurred in the past. As a typical example, Benjamin J. Fairless, Chairman of the Board of United States Steel Corporation, counterattacked:

Among the engineers who coined it, the word automation is merely a term which conveniently describes certain mechanical controls and processes. There is nothing frightening about it, nor is there anything basically new about mechanical principles to which it applies.

But to thousands of our people who do not understand its meaning, it suggests a brand new class of machines—different from any which we have ever had before—and so superior to man himself that, ultimately, they may rise, like Frankenstein's monster, to destroy us all. Thus the word alone is enough to conjure up visions of a wholly-automatic factory where machines with super-brains will grind out products, 168 hours a week, without any human payroll whatever.

And these fears, of course, are just plain silly. There are no such factories and no such machines; nor will there ever be, either in my time or yours! But propaganda is a powerful thing; and it is growing louder.

Hundreds of other top management officials tried to restore a balanced perspective through similar speeches, but with little success; nor did industrialists or "experts" succeed in educating the public on the "true" meaning of automation (whatever that may be) or its effects. They could not agree with one another, nor were they consistent in their own views. Wiener allowed, in the 1954 edition of his *Human Use of Human Beings*, that he had been too pessimistic about the impact of automation; Harder, in later speeches, emphasized automation as a much broader "philosophy of manufacturing"; and Diebold, as we have seen, completely reversed his stand on the importance of control.

The popular press, inspired, in many cases by Wiener's alarming statement of a depression which would "make the 1930's look like a pleasant joke," continued to publish extreme claims without any critical analysis, and so convinced the public that automation was a real threat. A typical example is one of the first "scholarly" symposiums published on the broad aspects of automation. The prestigious *Saturday Review* devoted its January 22, 1955 issue to "The American Factory and Automation"; under the subtitle "A Description of the New Manless Manufacture," it quoted a senior manufacturing executive, John I. Snyder, Jr., as follows:

Our own company, U. S. Industries, Inc., operates perhaps the only fully automatic factory now producing. It is a government-owned, 155 mm. shell plant in Rockford, Illinois. The plant was designed for very high production, using 20% less manpower, both direct and indirect, and conventional plans . . .

The editors blithely ignored the fact that if it used only 20 per cent less manpower, it certainly was not "fully automatic," and was hardly "manless manufacture." Engineering and business literature contains hundreds of similar inconsistencies and exaggerations. *Business Week* (March 29, 1952) described Ford's new Cleveland engine plant (the first to be labelled as "automated") using this title: "Automation: A Factory Runs Itself." A careful study of the Ford plant in 1954 showed that over 4500 people worked there, more than 2700 of these being production-line workers. Surely a plant employing 4500 people does not "run itself," but that was a frequent claim, often heard even in presumably carefully edited business periodicals.

Perhaps the culmination of this national attention was reached when the Congress, in October 1955, conducted hearings in response to union pressures and public and government concern over the apparent technological threat to employment. Union officials, government specialists, labor-relations experts, and managers and engineers associated with the steel, electrical, automobile, machine-tool, computer, and communication industries, as well as a sprinkling of college professors and consultants, all gave their views on automation.

In many cases they simply rehashed previously quoted items, and much of the testimony was highly inconsistent. Walter Reuther, for example, stating that automation was upgrading the skill required in the work force, included in his testimony exhibits from *American Machinist,* one of which carried the headline "Tape-controlled Lathe Run by Unskilled Worker."

Management was equally inconsistent. Describing his automatic plant at Rockford, Illinois, John Snyder, Jr., testified that the skill requirements had increased significantly. He appended a description of his factory, published in the magazine *Machinery,* which explained, however, that the "push-button" plant had been built so that it could be staffed by unskilled housewives during the wartime shortages of skilled labor.

There was further confusion in that "automation" became synonymous with any and every kind of technological change. Non-technical people—union leaders, labor-relations specialists, politicians, sociologists, and others, imputed every kind of productivity gain to automatic machinery and/or to the computer. There was scarcely a single reference to the productivity gains brought about by advances in new materials, product design, plant layout, or similar factors. Any kind of machinery affecting labor was labelled as automation, whether or not it was automatic. Thus, railroad unions cited diesel locomotives and their effect on the employment of locomotive firemen as an example of automation; and maritime unions called container ships automation.

Apparently, no definition can overcome the impetus of public usage. In general, automation covers *anything significantly more automatic than previously existed.* The word seems to fill a semantic void in our technical and social life; it is frequently used to describe any aggressive effort to achieve new levels of automatic operation. Despite several other congressional hearings and thousands of additional articles, the only distinct clarification that has been made since 1950 is formal recognition by the government that automation and technological change are not the same; in 1964 President Johnson appointed a committee significantly styled "The National Commission on Technology, Automation, and Economic Progress."

The Commission's report, *Technology and the American Economy,* and its six volumes of appendices were published in 1966. The report is obviously a compromise, containing concessions to the traditional positions of some of its labor members. However, it does verify that the dire predictions of 1955 have not materialized; and it recognizes that more than automatic machinery is involved. The appendices contain dozens of papers giving current statistics and different points of view.

SOME EFFECTS OF THE FUROR

We have now followed the social history of a simple, coined word which came to stand for a technological trend and became the focus of much social and economic concern. Its major technical-economic effect was to call management's attention to automatic manufacturing, and so to support and inspire literally thousands of firms to move toward more highly mechanized production systems during the 1950's. It simultaneously drew society's attention to the social problems of technological progress, leading to new studies, wage agreements, retraining programs, and the creation of government agencies, such as the Department of Labor's Office of Manpower, Automation, and Training.

THE DEVELOPMENT OF AUTOMATION TECHNIQUES

Automatic machines existed long before machinery was applied to economic purposes. Automata, meaning "devices that move by themselves," have a history extending at least back to ancient Egypt. It has been argued that man has a strong, innate tendency to employ mechanistic explanations of nature and to imitate nature by mechanical means; this instinct, it is said, first led to the construction of automata. The mechanical refinement needed to make elaborate automata eventually laid the technical foundations for fine mechanisms, control devices (particularly those based on cams), and the precise instrumentation needed in scientific work. Through the centuries, five classes of automata have been built: religious and historic monument devices, astronomical models, devices for amusement, table decorations, and androids (mechanical men). These devices became intricate and complex, combining the arts and skills of the fine mechanician, the watchmaker, and often the jeweler.

The extreme ingenuity shown in these elaborate automatic machines prompted the great scientist Helmholtz to write (1847): "Nowadays we no longer attempt to construct beings able to perform a thousand human actions, but rather machines able to execute a single action which will replace that of thousands of humans." Automation's possible impact on labor was thus recognized long before complete automation itself became possible.

TOWARD AUTOMATIC PRODUCTION

Intriguing and technically marvelous as these pre-industrial automatic mechanisms were, they were not directed at creating goods. To understand the evolution of automatic manufacturing we must follow these three developments: (1) machines to perform the production operation; (2) machines to move materials from one work station to the next, including feeding the production machines; and finally (3) control systems that regulate the performance of production and handling systems.

A major advance in *any one* of these three areas often so impresses observers that the label of "automatic" factory is applied. Yet, unless all *three* factors are provided, *for all events in the activity,* we do not have a fully automatic factory. Let us examine each of these in turn, realizing that they gradually blend together as machinery was refined from the Industrial Revolution to the present day.

AUTOMATIC PRODUCTION MACHINES

Automatic machines for production actions can be traced back at least to the early 1800's in many fields, and were commonplace in almost every field of manufacturing by the 1870's. In textiles, for instance, the industry's history, beginning in the early 1700's, reflected increasing mechanization, the application of power to integration of successive operations, and automatic control. As an example of "automation," the textile process would qualify before 1800.

Perhaps the earliest system of automatic machines (though not linked by an automatic handling system) for parts manufacture, as distinct from bulk materials, was the pulley-block machinery built by Marc Brunel for the British Admiralty. From 1802 through 1808 he installed a set of 44 machines, driven by a 32-hp. steam engine. Three types of blocks were simultaneously produced by the machinery, which cross-cut lumber to length, ripped planks, bored, mortised sheave holes at 110 to 150 strokes per minute, shaped the pulley-block faces and grooves, and performed appropriate operations on the sheaves. With this equipment, 10 men replaced the 110 men needed to make 130,000 pulley blocks per year by conventional means. This machinery remained in use until 1854 and is now in the Science Museum in London. Charles Tomlinson noted the effect of automatic machinery on skill; his *Cyclopedia of Useful Arts and Manufactures,* published in London in 1854, points out that "the attendance of a few common labourers under the direction of a master of the wood-mills is quite sufficient" to carry on the process!

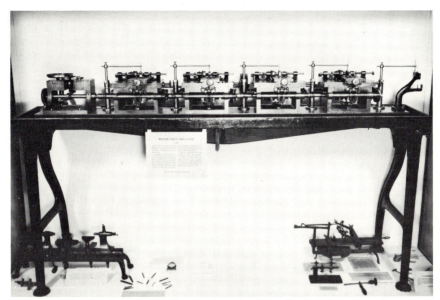

Fig. 41-1. The first known transfer machine, built by the Waltham Watch Company in 1888. Parts such as steel staff blanks, arbors, and pinion blanks were made in a series of four turnings. The part was moved by a feeding plate to the first lathe, and by transfer arms between lathes. It was automatic except for work feeding and removal at the ends of the line. (Courtesy of *The Smithsonian Institution*)

A landmark in progress toward full automatic production was the transfer machine. This may be described as a number of machining stations mounted upon a base (or bases so closely integrated that the effect is the same), and having a work-feeding device integral with the machine and common to all stations. Usually this built-in handling system moves all workpieces in the process simultaneously to the next station. It holds workpieces in proper orientation, and positions them to a precise location during machining operations. Transfer machines usually include devices for removing metal turnings, and embody necessary jigs, fixtures, coolant, power supply, compressed air, and so forth.

The transfer machine concept has been widely misrepresented by economists, automation enthusiasts, and journalists who claim it originated in Detroit in the 1950's, and with naive condescension they further dismiss it as mere "Detroit automation" of no major significance. They are wrong on three counts. First, the transfer machine principle was applied by the Waltham Watch Company as early as 1888.

Next, the transfer machine was first applied in the automobile industry by

Morris Motors, in England, about 1924. Their machine was 181 feet long, 11 feet high, and weighed 300 tons. There were 53 work stations, using 81 electric motors, totalling 267 horsepower. A rough cylinder-block casting was loaded in one end and 224 minutes later, the finished block, including bearing blocks, crankshaft bearing, and all studs, reappeared. Production rate was one block every four and one-half minutes. Third, transfer machines have been standard practice in high-volume engine manufacturing in Detroit since the mid-1930's. Graham-Paige Motors Corporation installed the first true transfer machine in 1929. The further advance of automatic jigs and fixtures (to grip the cylinder blocks tightly during machining) in a transfer-machine system probably was first applied by Graham-Paige in 1931.

These transfer machines, in which a number of work stations are combined on one machine base, with an integral handling system, became commonplace in the automotive field in the 1930's, and spread to appliance manufacturing, electrical parts production, and many high-volume, metalworking activities by late in the decade. They appear today in typewriter manufacturing as well. Although very impressive, they do not constitute "automatic factories," because they only do a part of the total required operations. However, they are extremely important in cutting labor cost, increasing quality through uniformity and reduced tolerances, and in reducing manufacturing cycle time.

AUTOMATIC CONTROL

The most common and earliest control device is the cam, which mechanically adjusts the position of a lever or a machine element as it rotates. Thus, it causes the machine automatically to carry out a fixed set of events—a "program" control. The cam can be found in many early machines. Its ultimate development was reached as early as 1822. Thomas Blanchard, at the Springfield, Massachusetts, Armory, invented a lathe to produce automatically the irregular shapes of military gunstocks. The desired master shape was placed in a tracing cradle; a profiling system of cams then adjusted cutting tools so as to shape a similar gunstock from a rough block of wood. Such cam-controlled devices have long been used in machine tools. For instance, the automatic screw machine, cam controlled, was developed during the Civil War. The turret lathe was made automatic by cam control in 1876.

The mechanical cam has severe limitations in speed, degree of movement, number of changes, sensitivity, and size. Hence, electrical, hydraulic, and pneumatic control techniques emerged in the late 1800's and were developed in very sophisticated forms by World War I. These were still fixed "programs" of actions. Eventually, instrument systems were applied to control machines by measuring a critical variable, sensing a change, and translating the degree of change into a response that modified operations and restored the process to appropriate condition.

This principle of "feedback" control has been widely hailed as the heart of automation. While this is true in controlling many chemical and electrical processes, there is relatively little feedback control in most of today's automatic machinery. Program control by mechanical cams, electrical relays, tapes, and punched cards is far more common, simply because many activities do not require the self-correcting precision of feedback control.

A fundamental control concept of today—the punched card and punched tape—can be traced at least to 1725, when Basile Bouchon in France invented perforated-paper-sheet automatic needle selection in forming textile patterns. The idea was subsequently improved by Falcon and Bouchon in 1737 and in 1762. In 1747 Vaucanson eliminated the attendant by mechanizing the forward motion of the perforated selecting cylinder. In 1804, Jacquard first applied this idea on a practical scale to the draw loom. The punched tape ultimately was applied to control the player piano, and to control the monotype for casting lead type (1897). The punch card was adopted by Hollerith in the 1890's for tabulating equipment used in United States census work. Today it is a familiar element of the computer and other types of business machines.

Tape control, either magnetic or punched-hole, undoubtedly was the greatest advance in machine-control history; it enabled a very long and complex program to be imposed on a machine, yet it could easily be altered or replaced. Arma Corporation built a punched-sheet (like a player-piano roll) controlled lathe in 1948.

The next advance in tape control began with a United States Air Force research project at M.I.T., about 1950, and spread to commercial equipment in 1954-55. This was numeric control, in which successive positions of tools, tables, speeds, and feed rates were indicated on the tape by a numeric system expressed magnetically or as punched holes, hence the name "numeric control." The use of numbers of 4 to 8 digits (or positions) affords fine discrimination; and the tape affords a long succession of instructions. A form of computer enables the machine to interpret the taped instructions for its actions. By 1965 numerical control machine tools numbered close to 10,000, and accounted for perhaps 20 per cent of the current output of the machine-tool industry.

Today, the ultimate in control is the computer, which acts as both a programmer and/or a feedback control system, and can direct a single machine or a total production system. The first computer-control applications were made about 1957-58 to electric power generating plants and oil refineries, and were used largely to monitor performance and log data. At one generating station, the computer monitored 14 variables, and logged critical data, even sounding an alarm as safety limits were exceeded. Texaco's Port Arthur refinery went into production in 1959, under full digital computer control. Imperial Chemical Industries operated the first computer-controlled chemical plant in 1959. In 1960, Monsanto's Louisiana ammonia plant and B. F. Goodrich's vinyl plastic plant at Calvert, Kentucky, became the first American chemical plants in which the

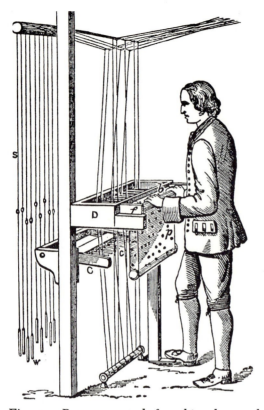

Fig. 41-2. Program control of machines by punched
tape has its roots in Bouchon's development of 1725,
shown here. It eventually led, via contributions by
Falcon, Vaucanson, and Jacquard, to the Jacquard
loom of 1804. The punched holes control the selection of needles, and thus the weaving pattern.
(Courtesy of Division of Research, *Harvard
Business School*)

computer activated the controls, thus "closing the loop." Human intervention
was no longer involved.

Since then, steel rolling mills, blast furnaces, many chemical processes, and
other continuous-process systems have been put under computer control. As of
1965 about 600 computer-controlled plants had been installed or were under
construction throughout the world.

CONTINUOUS MOVEMENT

Automatic machines plus automatic control do not alone result in an automatic
production system. Automatic movement of material through the entire produc-

tion sequence also is necessary. The role of movement has been literally ignored by the economist, sociologist, and the public, and has had only spotty attention from a handful of historians of technology. Although today's engineer is conscious of and continuously employs mechanized handling, his textbooks do not make clear its contribution. One looks in vain for a discussion of the principles of continuous movement and consideration of the sources of the productivity increases that result. Continuous movement is the most dramatic form of automation to the observer. Where did it come from, and what is its significance?

Screw conveyors and bucket elevators (the chain of pots) are found in Greek and Assyrian times respectively. The hoist and windlass and the crane were also tools of antiquity. Conveyors seem to be comparatively more recent; Leonardo da Vinci was familiar with the principle of the belt conveyor, and the roller conveyor, with rollers fixed to a wood frame, appears in medieval manuscripts on building construction. However, the early use of conveyors in industrial operations is evident only in mining and construction, where the bucket elevator was used to raise ore, earth, and water.

Automatic handling as part of a production process was first identified in the biscuit-baking ("hardtack") process at the Deptford Victualling Department of the British Navy, 1804-33. A Mr. Grant modified the existing hand process by mechanizing some actions, such as mixing, rolling the dough into sheets, and cutting. He introduced what may have been the first powered-roller conveyor line. As part of this system, square pieces of dough were placed on boards (3 ft. x 6 ft.), which were then passed under rollers, where the dough was reduced to proper thickness and then cut into shapes before baking. The empty boards were moved from the oven to the mixer table by a series of rollers. A novel feature was powering the rollers by a steam engine, so that empty boards from any stations were automatically returned to the mixer.

In 1802 Fourdrinier made paper in an endless roll, and by 1835 Hill had printed on paper in a continuous roll. From the 1830's on there were many attempts at continuous processing. Feeding hides, sewn together as a continuous sheet, through tanning baths, continuous brickmaking, and sugar-cane processing are other examples. Processing *while moving* gradually became a recognized industrial principle contributing to automatic operation.

A typical example is the "travelling" or "railway" oven for baking bread, exhibited in 1862 by Vicars of Liverpool. It consisted of a long oven chamber with suitable registers and dampers to regulate temperature. An endless chain, with provision for adjusting its speed, ran through the chamber. Loaves to be baked were placed in tile-bottomed wagons, equipped with steam-tight covers and attached to the power-driven cabin. Thus bread moved through the oven at a speed and temperature controlled by the foreman. Empty wagons were returned through an upper chamber. This seems like a forerunner of the dragline conveyor.

The arsenal of Venice, in the 1300-1500 period, used moving "assembly lines" to equip war galleys; as the galleys were towed down canals, supplies were handed out from successive buildings. As many as ten galleys per day were so completed.

Continuous movement as a means of increasing productivity seems to have lain unrecognized until the 1870's. About this time the meat-packing industry of Cincinnati and Chicago evolved a "dis-assembly" line in slaughterhouses. Carcasses were hung on monorail trolleys and pushed from worker to worker. Eventually the trolleys were connected with ropes or chains, and powered movement brought carcasses past workers at a steady pace. Productivity increased because of the timed work pace, job specialization, and the minimization of unnecessary movement by the worker and the materials. Still, the concept did not penetrate the metalworking industry until April 1913. In his biography Henry Ford says, "The idea [for a moving assembly line] in a general way came from the overhead trolley that the Chicago packers use in dressing beef." May 1, 1913 was the date when a line for the moving assembly of flywheel magnetos was installed. The magnetos were simply pushed, on rails, from one work station to the next. Assembly time dropped from about 20 man-minutes to 13 man-minutes; after movement was powered by a chain, the time dropped to 5 man-minutes.

This sensational gain suggested trial of the same technique with chassis assembly. Using the conventional stationary assembly stations for each chassis, assembly required 12½ man-hours per car. In August 1913, the first trial was made using a rope to pull the chassis 250 feet, past piles of components. Six assemblers moved with the chassis, and total assembly labor time dropped to less than 6 man-hours. The system was gradually refined—by applying powered movement through a chain drive, giving assemblers stationary locations, providing parts and work stations at optimum heights to minimize stooping and awkward positions, and shortening the line. By April 30, 1914, assembly time had been reduced to 93 man-minutes.

This fantastic gain, reported in several American engineering journals, was met with disbelief here and abroad. But shortly it launched companywide, and then nationwide, exploration of new ways to achieve productivity gains, and set the pace and spirit of American manufacturing enterprise. Until the advent of the computer, the moving assembly line epitomized the vitality and efficiency of American mass production, which clearly led the world. It also became the symbol to many workers, social critics, labor leaders, and others, of grinding monotony and relentless pressure.

The principle of continuous movement swept through the automobile industry and other mass-production, metalworking industries due, in part, to the demands of World War I. By 1920 the concept had been applied to the assembly of engines, to painting automobile bodies, and to the manufacture of almost all automobile parts, as well as to refrigerators and similar items.

Fig. 41-3. Beginnings of the moving assembly line, the most powerful productivity concept in history, at Ford Motor Company about May 1913. Magnetos were slid from one worker to the next for successive assembly operations. Labor time was more than halved. Eventually, automatic mechanical movement was supplied by conveyor, and productivity further increased. (*Courtesy Ford Motor Company*)

AUTOMATIC MANUFACTURING

Automatic production machines, integrated handling systems, and automatic control devices were ultimately blended together to achieve a highly automatic, continuous manufacturing system. The first known attempt to create an "automatic factory" was Oliver Evans's design for a grist mill, several of which were built in the Philadelphia area in 1784-85. Evans claimed to have improved or applied five machines (including belt conveyors, bucket elevators, batch weighing scales, and screw conveyors) so that all movement throughout the mill was automatic. No labor was required except to set the mill in motion ". . . which lessens the labor and expense of attendance of flour mills fully one half."

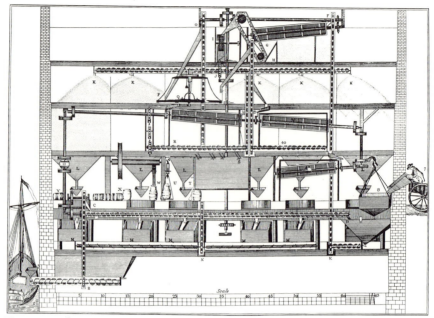

Fig. 41-4. Oliver Evans's grist mill of 1785, the first known attempt to create a "fully automatic" factory. Operations were linked by screw conveyors and bucket elevators. (From *The Young Mill-Wright and Millers Guide*, Philadelphia, 1795)

Here the goal of automation was defined and apparently achieved. However, the idea did not take hold in the industry; and the concept of full automation did not then become a factory-builder's or engineer's accepted target. Many production systems devoted to packaging, bottling, canning, and processing foods, as well as in making electric lamps, printing, textiles, components of machinery, automobiles, appliances, ammunition, and similar high-volume products, used highly automatic *sequences* before the 1920's. Yet they were not "automatic factories" since many operations and movement between machines were not automatic.

The next avowed attempt to create an "automatic factory" seems to have been the A. O. Smith Corporation's Milwaukee automobile frame plant, begun in 1919 and operating by 1920. In addition, this seems to have been the first attempt at *automatic assembly*. The machinery formed parts of automobile frames and then riveted them together. Each frame required 552 operations, which were performed in a 1½-hour cycle and produced a frame every 8 to 10 seconds. This plant was the personal goal of the company president, L. R. Smith, who announced in an article: "We Build A Plant to Run Without Men." Nevertheless, about 200 workers were required to operate the machines, compared to 1200 previously. The system, with modifications, remained highly efficient and competitive until the early 1950's.

The three lines of progress indicated previously (automatic production machines, automatic materials movement, and automatic control systems) continued to develop in almost every high-volume industry (some major exceptions, perhaps, were the shoe and garment industries). Process industries dealing with a limited number of bulk materials—petroleum refineries, chemical plants, packaging lines, soap and food plants, feed mills, flour mills, and so on—rapidly integrated into highly automatic systems during the 1930's and 1940's. By any technical and functional comparison of mechanization they would have to be called "automated" or very close to it. Nevertheless, it was in the production of assembled, metal products that "automatic factories" made the greatest impression. A British industrial observer wrote in 1925, "Continuous production is, of course, no new thing. It has been practised for many years in the food, soap, textile, newspaper, and other industries. It is, however, comparatively new to the engineering industry [metalworking] . . ."

The next major attempt (exclusive of the lamp industry) seems to have been the 155-mm shell plant designed by the W. F. and John Barnes Co. for the United States Army in the latter days of World War II. It was put into operation just as the war ended. Because the shells weighed 125 pounds, and because skilled male help was scarce, the plant was designed to operate with unskilled women workers. Thus, automatic mechanical handling, push-button activated, was provided from the receipt of billets and moving through all machining and heat-treating operations, including the removal of scrap, coolants, fumes, and so forth. Automatic gauging and inspection also were provided, as well as electric lamp "trouble-indicator" circuits. The key goal was mechanical handling linked to automatic production machines; but control was often by push-button from local work stations at major machines. (Today we would mechanize the control system.)

AUTOMATION: FACT AND CONCEPT MEET

When the Ford Motor Company announced the first "automated" engine plant —planned in 1948-49 and operating in 1950—the word and the fact at last met in one plant. What was the plant like? First, it was *not* automatic; it employed more than 4500 people. Even the most automatic element, the cylinder-block line, used 36 operators and 11 inspectors per shift. Next its most automatic elements did not use "feedback" (then a much-touted concept) to any great extent. Also, automatic assembly of the engine was not incorporated to the slightest degree.

The unique advances in this plant were four:

1. The most striking element was the "automated" cylinder-block line. "Au-

Fig. 41-5. One of the first automatic assembly machines, at Admiral Corporation, Chicago, about 1955. Punched radio and TV chassis boards are loaded at the left. Each chassis board then indexes from station to station, where components are successively added by machine or by a worker. These indexing machines were quite flexible because the work head at any station could be easily replaced for a different operation or part; or a worker could be used if desired. (Courtesy of *Admiral Corporation*)

tomation," as Ford then used the term, meant "selective sequence loading" devices to connect the transfer machines that turned the rough casting into a finished engine block, ready for assembly. Sets of transfer machines were needed to perform each successive operation, such as boring, milling, drilling, and tapping. The output of each machine had to yield the same number of blocks within a given time (a balanced line). Selective sequence devices solved the physical problem of taking the blocks from, say, two machines, turning them over or reorienting them, then dividing the number so as to feed them into, say, three machines for the next operation. They performed this handling, orienting, division (or consolidation), and work-feeding of blocks emerging from the previous transfer machine(s). To the casual observer, it appeared as though a line some 500 feet long was processing the blocks without any human help.

2. Automatic crankshaft production was another feature. Prior to 1947, 29

separate machines were used to machine the crankshaft surfaces and holes. Ford built three 8-station transfer machines with automatic loading arms that fed and removed crankshafts at both ends of the line.

3. Automatic small parts production. Many small parts—oil pans, valves, pistons—were automatically machined; and automatic work-feeding devices were used to serve the machines.

4. Continuous movement through the complete engine-assembly, testing, painting, and shipping cycle by means of powered devices and a free overhead conveyor. The machined block was attached to a carrier and moved along without detachment from the conveyor.

This plant was the subject of intense scrutiny by the industry and by labor. It inspired a succession of improved engine plants: Pontiac, 1954-55; Dodge-Plymouth, 1956; and others. Each advanced automatic production, assembly, and testing a bit further.

Concurrently, automatic assembly of radio and television chassis was tried out. Sargrove in England had devised "electronic circuit-making equipment," 1935 through 1948. His system failed as a commercial venture, presumably due to lack of flexibility; but it clearly foreshadowed the automatic insertion and soldering techniques applied in 1955-56 by Admiral and other electronic equipment producers.

The automation label, in the late 1950's, was commonly applied to any and every new automatic machine. However, chief ventures at that time were the automatic assembly of electronics components—radio and TV chassis—and automatic assembly of many small metal sub-assemblies, such as voltage regulators, horns, electric motors, and the like.

THE COMPUTER JOINS THE AUTOMATIC PRODUCTION LINE

Computer control of continuous-process activities, steel mill rolling lines as well as in power plants, refineries, and chemical plants, has grown rapidly. However, computer control over the manufacturing of discrete parts and assembly operations is rare. The first (and possibly only) computer-controlled production line, with automatic processing and movement, was built by the North Carolina Works of Western Electric, Hickory, N.C., about 1960.

This pioneer line manufactures deposited-carbon resistors at the rate of 20 per minute, in four sizes and of many resistance values. Not only are the production operations performed automatically, but the acts of inspection, assembly, testing, and movement between stations have feedback-control loops through which critical processes are modified as inspection results dictate.

Three noteworthy "automation" principles are emphasized in this installation:

1. The primary goal of automation in this, as in many current projects, is not labor reduction or increased productivity. Product quality and reliability are

the prime targets. The increasing complexity of military electronic systems demands more reliability. Therefore, the goal of not over one failure in 200 million component-hours of operation was set—about 4 per cent of the failure rate at the time. Only mechanization could possibly minimize variation in manufacturing to this degree, and then only with precise process control.

2. The achievement of a highly automated line must begin with analysis of the process and its relationship to the goal. In this case, it was first necessary to identify the causes of failures, and to trace these to material and manufacturing deficiencies that needed correction and/or control.

3. Automating the operations and the control would not alone achieve the goal. It was also necessary to change the physical design of the product, to change materials, to change or modify processes, to change and modify production equipment, and even the sequence of processing events.

Strangely enough, these lessons of automation were stated very clearly years ago, but technical society is rather weak on the use of history. Many plants of 1950-60 ran into trouble because of lack of flexibility to adjust to changes in volume, product design, or even product mix. Incoming raw materials were an unsuspected source of inflexibility. As early as March 1925, Frank G. Woollard, in an article in *The Automobile Engineer* (London), identified the problem when he pointed out that:

Regularity, then, is the keynote of continuous production: regularity in sales as to quantity and type; regularity in material as to quantity, quality and time; regularity in processing, workmanship and inspection, and . . . where continuous production also implies working the plant on a basis of 24 hours to the day, regularity has a very special meaning, because a shortage means absolute loss of output . . .

AUTOMATION BENEFITS

From a bird's-eye view, we have seen the growth of mechanization in three areas—production equipment, control, and handling systems—finally merge into an automatic production line. In the early 1960's interest in automatic manufacturing subsided somewhat although progress continued. Important technical developments now lie at the ends of the production line—in storage, transportation, and distribution. Automatic warehousing and advances in mechanizing the transportation system become the areas of greatest attention.

Originally, lower labor cost, increased productivity, and increased capacity were the goals of most automation efforts; in many recent operations, labor costs have become a rather small percentage of manufacturing cost. So automation programs are gradually motivated by new objectives. A 1958 study found twenty-four motives for automation in thirteen plants, including such things as increased capacity in a given space or time, reduction of scrap, improved quality. improved safety, reduced housekeeping, less skill required in the operating work force, more attractive working conditions, reduction in lead time, centralization of control, and reduction of material cost. The fundamental disadvantage of automation is lack of flexibility in one form or another.

As new demands are placed on industry—for higher wages or better quality —further automation is encouraged. It will be applied to achieve whatever economic, technical, and social objectives are important to industrial society at a given time.

42 / The Impact of Cybernation
DONALD N. MICHAEL

"Cybernation" refers to the electro-mechanical manipulation of material things by automation and the electro-mechanical manipulation of symbols by computers, and to the simultaneous use of computers and automation for the organization and control of material and social processes. Using the word "cybernation" saves continually repeating "automation and computers" and eliminates the sense of rigid mechanization that tends to be semantically associated with the word "automation."

"Cybernetics," a term invented by Norbert Wiener, refers to the systematic description of the processes of communication and control in man and machines in which performance or goal-seeking activity is determined by the system's ability to adjust its behavior in terms of errors between where "it is" and where "it wants to go." Wiener derived the term from the Greek word for "steersman." The theory and practice of cybernetics underlies all systematic design and application of automation and computers. Cybernation, then, refers not only to automation and computers, but also to the philosophy behind their systematic application to society.

THE TERMS OF INQUIRY

Speculation about the long-range implications of cybernation will be limited here to the next twenty years more or less, because those who will be the adults of that world are alive today. Thus, we can recognize something of the values the next generation will bring to that world as they influence and determine its directions and actions. All aspects of the world are changing so fast and so profoundly that to speculate much beyond two decades might require views of the world and its values quite different from those we have the experience to extrapolate from: we would quickly be in the realm of fantasy.

When we try to anticipate some of the major trends and circumstances in the next two decades we encounter three formidable obstacles: ignorance of crucial unpredictable events; misunderstanding of the long-term implications of trends which now appear significant for the period; and the unanticipated consequences of planned actions implemented to avoid the problems and embrace the opportunities which, from our vantage point, the future seems to hold. Nevertheless, we must try to imagine what the trends of the next twenty years might be so that we can begin now the actions needed to prepare for them. While we cannot predict, we can anticipate that which we ought to be prepared to deal with just as we plan our national defenses—not for what *will* happen, but for what *might* happen.

It is important to recognize that the impact of cybernation is just beginning: the practical application of sophisticated equipment dates from around 1950-60. If the growth curve of the application of this technology is typically exponential, it probably has yet to reach real "take-off" proportions. Since the high level of application and impact is still to come, no assessment of effects to date can be considered a sufficient basis for prognosis.

All great technological developments—and certainly this will be among the great ones—have consequences which defy comprehension by the usual formulas. For example, it is difficult to discern precisely what effects associated with it can be ascribed to cybernation as such, because cybernation is only one factor—if an extraordinarily important one—affecting and affected by a society exposed to high rates of technological and social change. What is more, it is only in the last few years that even a few people have come to appreciate that cybernation's impact on man and society may be so different in degree from the impact of technological developments in the past as to create a profound difference in kind. Therefore, our understanding is limited because understanding the effects will require detailed study over a long period of time—and that time is just beginning. Hence, the categories of impact presented here can be only a selection, and within these categories the events and conjectures presented are also selections.

THE SOCIAL CONTEXT

Many who are optimistic about the impact of cybernation justify their complacency by arguing that man's effort to reduce his burden of work is age-old, that we have been through the impact of technological change before, that there is nothing really new about cybernation. However, as we shall see, the differences from the past in tomorrow's demographic and social factors indicate that in social context and technological potential we are moving into a radically new situation. Let us look briefly, then, at the general social context in which cybernation will evolve, recognizing that the impact of a technology cannot be sensibly forecast without knowing something about the context in which it will operate. Although we will concern ourselves primarily with the implications of cybernation for the United States, to varying degrees, these will probably be paralleled in other nations which are cybernating. Clearly, however, they will differ as the values and material and economic circumstances of these nations differ from ours.

One new aspect of our situation will be substantially increased economic competition from other developed nations. They, too, are beginning to apply cybernation to production and to planning international strategy. In order to compete effectively, we will have to use cybernated techniques for minimizing labor costs, maximizing efficiency of production, and optimizing marketing strategies. Such actions will probably accelerate labor displacement.

Another factor will be the general situation in the emerging nations. By and large, barring extraordinary changes in the relations between the rich and the poor nations, the rich will get richer while the poor will make only slight gains. Hunger, privation, dictatorial governments, and social struggle will be their lot—this, at a time when, more than ever before, we have avowed their right to the good life and at a time when we probably will be the beneficiaries of increasing, cybernation-induced leisure. These circumstances pose major moral and ethical challenges for us.

The most radical change in our condition will be in population growth and its composition: about 230 million people in the United States by 1975; 250 million by 1980. Beginning in 1965, there will be at least one million more young people available for the work force each year. But many will not be able to enter it: they will compete unsuccessfully with older, more skilled workers, many of whom will be displaced by cybernation.

Even with no further developments in medicine, by 1975 the population over age 65 is expected to increase about 20 per cent. This increase will exacerbate the already difficult political and emotional problems associated with giving meaning and dignity to the lives of older people. The difficulty of the task will be compounded because not only will there be more older people, but more will be retired or will have been fired early from jobs made obsolete by cybernation. Moreover, developments in medical technology make it very likely that even more than the predicted portion of the elderly will live longer.

About 80 per cent of our people will be living in urban environments by 1980, with corresponding increases in the growing social and technological complications that large urban complexes involve.

Another major background factor which will evolve over this period is the greatly enhanced potential and application of the behavioral sciences to predict and manipulate human behavior. For the sophisticated computer can do two things for the behavioral scientist which he has always needed but never had. First, economic, demographic, and social data can be collected with great speed and in great quantities as it reflects the state of society *today*—not as it was five or ten years ago, as has been the case. Second, the computer allows the behavioral scientist to build complex models of institutional and human behavior. In the past he has always been restricted in the number of variables he could deal with simultaneously. But with the computer, the scientist can make his models as complex as his creativity allows, try out these models, make predictions, and check them against current data.

This deeper understanding of society will provide leaders with an enormously expanded potential for good and evil. They can simulate the likely outcome of alternative programs and policies by programing into the computer these models of behavior along with alternative economic or social policies, so that the policies and behavior will interact, each altering the other. Then the planner, studying the description of the interplay as produced by the computer, will have a more detailed understanding of how the plans he is considering might affect the groups concerned and, in turn, be affected by them.

Thus, while our social problems will be compounded many times over, partly being accelerated by cybernation, they might also be partly resolved by cybernation, for to understand, interpret, plan, and provide for this kind of complexity requires the capabilities of computers and the productiveness of automation. But cybernation alone, as we shall see, cannot solve all the critical problems it will produce, nor can it adequately counterbalance them through the new opportunities it will provide.

OPINIONS ABOUT CYBERNATION

One of the most direct effects of cybernation has been a growing preoccupation with its implications. Increasingly, organizations and spokesmen with interests ranging from religion to leisure to education have begun to recognize that cybernation is important to them. Most of their statements have been notably lacking in imagination and understanding of both the potential of cybernation and the pertinent social changes developing in society which are significant for estimating the impact of cybernation.

For the most part the emphasis has been on the implications of cybernation for work; only a few commentators have concerned themselves with its implications for leisure; and except for very recent attention to the privacy of computerized dossiers, almost none have explored the implications for decision-making, policy-making, and the democratic process. Increasing attention has not, however, led to a consensus on the nature of the problems or opportunities cybernation presents: as usual, vested interests have resulted in selective perceptions. Views range from seeing cybernation as simply an extension of traditional technologies and social aims, to seeing in it a sufficient pre-condition for sweeping changes in the social structure and social values. For example, Dean Wallis of the University of Chicago's Graduate School of Business said "the problem of general unemployment from automation is a nonexistent will-o'-the-wisp problem," and President John F. Kennedy called the problems of unemployment arising from the impact of cybernation "the major domestic challenge of the 'sixties."

There is a strong tendency to consider the effects of cybernation primarily in terms of economic criteria. Only in a few places, and slowly, is it beginning to be understood that the consequences of cybernation in terms of values, attitudes, and behavior may be such that other criteria, such as self-respect or democratic participation, may be at least as important in many situations as are the conventional criteria of efficiency and productiveness. Many see cybernation as inevitably enriching our economy; others see it as looming disaster. Most public statements seem to represent attempts to anticipate or influence opinion rather than to reflect it; except for those directly affected by cybernation, there is no reason to believe an informed public opinion now exists on these matters. At any rate, the opinion studies which are available are too limited in scope or sampling to give a clear picture of the present mood or knowledge of the general public.

EMPLOYMENT

What is the present effect of cybernation on the number and types of jobs? There is no clear answer available. Estimates range from 4000 to 40,000 displacements a week caused by cybernation. Doubtless, new jobs have been created by cybernation (such as programmers and special-skill maintenance men), but no estimates have been suggested as to how many such jobs have been produced. The problem is complicated because the introduction of cybernation sometimes means that people are not hired who otherwise would have been. Then, too, there are an unknown number of jobs which for humanitarian and public-relations reasons are still held by people who, upon retirement or withdrawal from the work force (for example, women marrying), will not be replaced.

Overall, while many new technologies will alter the future job market, it is quite clear that, barring unforeseen developments, cybernation will have by far the most important consequences. During the 1960's, Walter Buckingham has written, it will be necessary to create perhaps as many as four million or more jobs every year to provide for the average yearly growth in the labor force of some 1.35 million and the possible replacement, as a result of rising productivity, of as many as 2.5 million or more workers.

While there will continue to be unskilled jobs, if the size of the unemployed, unskilled labor force increases, as is very likely, those unskilled jobs for which good wages can be paid on the basis of labor scarcity will steadily decline. During the next decade at least, this growing army of competitors for the remaining menial tasks will be reinforced by high numbers of school dropouts, unskilled women returning to the work force, blue- and white-collar workers with insufficient training in how to learn and relearn, as well as the hard core of functionally disemployed: victims of illiteracy and physical, emotional, or mental inadequacies.

The economic and ethical problems involved in coping with this problem on the needed scale will be enormous. A highly detailed national system of job-planning data will have to be devised—one which necessarily would compel industry to reveal some of its long-range plans for the future. New arrangements will have to be invented to provide the economic and psychological support necessary to encourage the unskilled or semi-skilled to go where jobs are available. At the very least, this may mean an extended social welfare program transcending state residence requirements, and a mortgage-guarantee program which would make it possible for low-income people to move even if their house were unsold.

If the social and economic problems of the large unskilled group threaten to disrupt the nation, the government will have to acknowledge that a decent standard of living is a citizen's right rather than a wage-earner's privilege. It will also have to enlarge its public-works programs to encourage the employment of the untrained.

While there is considerable feeling that cybernation is definitely displacing the unskilled (and in some cases reducing what were skilled jobs to unskilled ones), only recently has there been a growing awareness that cybernation challenges the job security of many workers customarily classified as skilled. For example, numeric control, the technology of guiding the machine tool by a computer, is just beginning to make inroads into the skilled blue-collar community of metalworkers, welders, metal-cutters, machinists, and the like. It is destined to climb to greater proportions because of the economies involved in fabricating and manufacturing in this way. Numeric control includes, intrinsically, a good part of the maintenance of the machine tool and most of product quality control; consequently, it is beginning to displace the skilled people employed in these activities as well.

Clerical and office workers are also beginning to feel the impact of cybernation. The *Wall Street Journal* reported on May 5, 1964, that the rate of increase in office staff hiring dropped in 1963 to one third of the rate in the 'fifties. This seems chiefly due to one thing—the replacement of office workers by computers. As population grows and as office activities become more complex and deal with wider markets, it becomes more efficient to use computers. This is increasingly true even for small organizations because time can be rented on central computer tools set up for part-time users. All that is needed is a teletype to feed inventory, payroll, and other information into a computer, pre-programed to serve a given organization and a similar device to feed it back in appropriate, processed form.

In 1960, 30 per cent of the female work force was "clerical," a group which comprised 68 per cent of all clerical workers. Women now are about a third of the total work force, and are expected to retain that proportion into the 'seventies. In 1970, about 28 per cent of the fourteen-to-nineteen-year-old women and 45 per cent of those twenty to twenty-four are expected to be available for work; consequently, there will be serious economic and retraining problems if, as is likely, there is too little advanced training for women in more needed skills, and too little motivation in both girls and their parents for them to acquire such skills.

Middle-level managerial jobs are already being altered or displaced by machines. Much of the routine decision-making that middle managers do—determining inventory levels, optimum distribution procedures, and so forth—can be done by computers using such mathematical techniques as operations research and systems analysis, combined with sophisticated behavioral science and economic theory.

Moreover, because in the future there will be fewer people to be supervised, due to labor displacement by automation and computers, fewer managerial supervisory personnel will be needed. Often, preparing information to help top management make decisions will be better done by a computer than by a middle manager—much faster, more reliably, and in many more formulations. As a result, decision-making processes will move more to the top managers, allowing them to work together in a much more organized way and to effect more internal control and efficiency. All these trends will tend to reduce the proportion of customary middle-management job opportunities, also meaning that those remaining will require relatively more skill than is usually the case today.

The same holds for the mediocre engineer. The following is illustrative of the trend: in the past, many electrical engineers were employed to design motors and transformers to the specifications of the customer. The customer would specify cost per unit, operating temperature, overload capabilities, and so forth, and the engineer would design the item to meet the customer's requirements by combining the information found in standard references according to specified optimizing procedures. Today the customer's specifications are fed into the computer and the computer designs the optimum motor or transformer. It goes further than that in some cases—the computer may go on to control the automatic fabrication of the product. There are corresponding developments under way in civil, mechanical, aeronautical, and marine engineering.

The overall impact of technological change has been to shift the work force from blue-collar productive jobs to white-collar service jobs; doubtless this trend will continue. There is a widely held assumption that growth in service jobs will adequately cope with all cybernation-produced displacement. However, there are reasons to believe that the rate of increase in relatively unskilled service jobs in the United States over the next two decades or so may not be as great as it has been.

As the population increases and as the high productivity of automation keeps production prices low, attractive markets will develop for many types of specialty products that will perform a vast number of services in the house which require outside help now. Many maintenance jobs will disappear, in addition, because new technologies will produce items that are cheaper to throw away than to repair, or which have components that are replaced rather than maintained. Furthermore, when the demand is large enough, it becomes economically advantageous to cybernate many service tasks. In the United States, vending machines are already a $3 billion a year industry, and this is just the beginning—there are supermarkets on the drawing board now which eliminate almost all personnel, even the cashier.

On the other hand, cybernation will generate important new types of service jobs. One such job will be that of data abstractor to work along with the computerized translator and abstractor, performing the necessary abstraction of material that computer programs cannot handle. As the information explosion increases, so too will the need for such people. Another type of occupation will be that of the sub-professional: the teacher's aide, nurse's aide, minister's aide, social worker's aide, and so on. These will be responsible jobs which relieve the hard-pressed professional of his routine tasks so that he can work more directly as a professional. The need for such person-to-person attention will increase as the problems of the occupationally displaced multiply, and as the requirements for education and opportunities to learn new leisure-time activities grow larger—all consequences of cybernation.

With regard to leisure time, it has been suggested that an enlarged recreation industry will supply endless low-skill jobs. It might, but it is also likely that as the demand for facilities increases, the economic advantages of cybernating them or using other new technologies to eliminate manpower will increase, too. For example, artificial turf for game surfaces will soon be available. And the handyman who used to repaint rowboats at the beginning of the resort season no longer has that job because the boats are made of fiberglass or aluminum. As population grows and leisure grows, there will be more opportunities to "do it yourself"—to maintain one's house, to plan one's own itinerary, and so on. Indeed, there will not only be opportunities, but the incentives to do these: they are attractive ways to use leisure time.

Computers now in the laboratory can already make the kinds of rule-of-thumb decisions most people are faced with in the routine tasks that make up their productive lives. But computers cannot now think at the level of a first-rate mind facing a real task that requires creative thought. Whether computers will eventually become highly creative is something that cannot be decided *a priori*, simply because we do not know precisely the nature of creative thought. What is clear is that the computer will only expand the creative capabilities of those few who are both trained and have the innate talent to be more creative than the computer. Those who assert that the computer will be a blessed release from the boredom of trivial intellectual activity ignore the fact that such activity is the only kind most people will be occupationally skilled for in the next two decades.

The highly skilled, professionally-trained leaders throughout our economy and society will find in the computer an unprecedented aid, one that will not, however, reduce the need for or shortage of such people. As far into the future as we can see, we are going to be short of such top-flight professionals—business executives, artists, ministers, educators, engineers, and so on—who will be called upon to deal with an increasingly complex society. What is more, these professionals will need more knowledge to carry out their jobs well. Having powerful tools with which to manipulate society, the highly skilled will have to think much more in terms of long-range planning and in terms of the ethical and moral consequences of their acts. Since they will have to keep in touch with the latest thought in their areas, their formal education will be unending—as will be the demands on them.

Artists will be increasingly in demand, and a larger proportion of them will be fairly well paid, even for mediocre abilities, if the economy remains reasonably prosperous. The recent steady growth of audiences for the arts suggests that greater numbers of potential amateurs—due to population growth, better education, and more leisure and money—will enter the commercial market. Doubtless the role of the artist will grow increasingly attractive to those who have talent, and while cybernation will no doubt produce interesting and attractive aesthetic products, it will not alter the fact that an artistic production is what it is because it reflects man's estimate of the human condition.

DIRECT EFFECTS ON THE WORKER

To understand the effects of cybernation on work we should distinguish its effects on various work activities—chiefly physical or blue-collar, white-collar (e.g. clerical, statistical, and secretarial), work that is essentially creative (e.g. scientific research, artistic production, and management activities), and those tasks which require people to relate creatively to other people. The effects probably will be different in these various groups because the degree and types of change introduced by cybernation will differ in each case, and because people with different backgrounds, aspirations, and personalities are associated with these levels of work. At present we know little about the psychological effects on any of these groups because not enough systematically related and wide-ranging research has been completed, though studies presently under way, especially at the Department of Labor's Office of Manpower, Automation, and Training, should substantially improve our understanding in the next few years. What follows is based on Professor Floyd Mann's review of studies which have thus far been made on the psychological and social impact of cybernation. Evidence from subsequent studies completed or under way seems compatible with his observations, published in 1962 in a volume on *Automation and Technological Change*, edited by John T. Dunlap.

Evidence shows that both white-collar and blue-collar employees who now work in cybernated systems generally have more important jobs with greater responsibility; they have to produce at a higher rate, and live with the realization that a breakdown in the system is now more costly or disrupting than it was previously. As a result, there is greater pressure and feelings of tension. The studies suggest that when the cybernated equipment is first put into operation, those with jobs related to it find it more challenging and interesting, because of the novelty. However, while the blue-collar worker appears to be asked to perform a broader range of duties, the trend with white-collar workers seems to be toward a narrower range. The results seem to be that there is no profound overall difference in work satisfaction, and what little differences have been measured indicate that blue-collar workers are somewhat more satisfied, while white-collar workers are slightly less satisfied with their new job environments. Again, it should be emphasized that the studies have not been conducted over long time periods yet, and the long-range effects on job satisfaction are not known.

Both white-collar and blue-collar workers increasingly sense that technological changes will importantly affect their working lives. White-collar workers are coming to recognize what blue-collar workers have long known: technological change introduces uncertainty. Many skilled persons will be subject to replacement by the latest cybernated device or by a younger, better-informed work force. This means a continuing potential threat of downgrading or retraining for the skilled, and along with it the emotional difficulties of job insecurity which will be new to skilled workers.

Changes in organization within both plant and office, which are inevitable when computers and automatic production lines are introduced, change social relationships as well. Among other things, conversation on the job and other informal, social arrangements are often reduced during the working period because fewer people are needed to perform cybernated tasks and they may be physically separated. There are changes in the pathways to job promotion and the procedures by which efficiency is judged; these wipe out investments in time and experience which people have expected to be applied to their future careers. And with smaller work forces and fewer supervisory tasks, openings for job promotion are often sharply altered or reduced. These changes, therefore, destroy traditional expectancies about how things will be done and how people will be evaluated.

Since social relationships developed in and the attitudes associated with the work environment are a great source of support and guidance for the worker, changes are necessarily upsetting. These difficulties are not limited to the blue- and lower white-collar levels, since, according to one report, ". . . there is also little doubt that computer installations are severely resisted at the management level by groups who fear a shift in the balance of power at a management level. This in fact has taken place in many installations."

As of today a man who graduates from a business or engineering school thinks he is set for life. He does not expect to go back to school, to take tests, to have his future income or suburban status threatened; therefore, retraining experiences are often emotionally difficult.

LEISURE

The trend toward increased leisure time is already evident in some new union contract arrangements. While the number of hours worked per day or the days worked per week could be shortened, the continuous-flow characteristics of cybernated systems and the inefficiencies of multiple work shifts probably point to longer vacations or "sabbaticals" for some every few years. Increasingly, a substantial portion of the population will have more free time.

In the next decades, most first-rate professionals and managers will continue to work long hours for reasons indicated earlier. What is more, those seeking membership in this professional elite will have to begin studying earlier and harder; and because of the shortage, they will probably be encouraged to work longer than the usual retirement age.

Semi-professionals and those with middle-level skills will contribute enough in their social role to command good or adequate salaries but they will not be in demand for long hours of work. They will have both the time and money to utilize their free time well, if they choose to. Also in this leisured group will be adolescents whose career plans do not require long hours of study and who have the money to acquire the commodities produced for leisure use.

Then there will be a population—how large is moot—relatively poorly paid or unemployed. These will be the slum-dwellers, a disproportionately larger percentage of the Negro population than of the white, the poverty-stricken from the rural areas, the mentally and emotionally underendowed, the un-skilled, those made unskilled by cybernation, the high school dropouts, and students from schools which do not provide the opportunity for longer study hours or the stimulus to use them. These will have plenty of time on their hands but not the money or the motivation to use it as "free time." In most cases, they will not have the education to do so either. What they will have—along with the struggling populations of the emerging nations—is a deep and growing resentment of those with both free time and the wherewithal to enjoy it. Serious social and political repercussions might ensue unless wise measures are taken in time.

Increasing numbers of retired and aged will find they have more free time, and for many in the population retirement will come earlier as cybernation and the increasing size of the younger work force exert pressure on society to move the economically unproductive out of the labor market. Making life meaningful for this growing group will become an increasingly serious problem, for without some changes in our values and even perhaps political action directed to their special needs, these people will feel left out of the vigorous life of the younger population—and with this feeling will come resentment.

The vast majority of America's population is unaccustomed to, untrained for, and unexposed to a qualitatively wide range of free time leisure-oriented activities; also, it is in large part the product of a Protestant ethic which equates leisure with idleness and the devil—or at least with a state of mind which makes most people uncomfortable if they are not working. Indeed, many will become more anxious as the increasing rate of job obsolescence—from blue-collar to junior executive—deprives a good part of the working population of the sense of having found an occupational niche. As a result, taking a second job may become more frequent if laws are not passed to prohibit moonlighting in order that work may be spread around. Second jobs may become desirable not only to overcome the ennui of free time but to compensate families for income loss when the working wife loses out to cybernation.

Travel, more time with the family, and adult education ranging from pottery-making to occupational retraining are examples of means for dealing with additional free time. But for many, boredom, anxiety, and marital problems will increase as individuals find in themselves or others inadequate personal resources for this new way of life. The satisfying use of leisure time involves a state of mind that probably cannot be developed quickly. We know little about how to inculcate the psychology and style of leisure, and doing so on a national scale as rapidly as additional leisure becomes available will be a major challenge for our values and methods of education.

DECISION-MAKING: THE INDIVIDUAL AND GOVERNMENT

Over the next two decades, the methods of science and engineering will be applied more often to social situations. And in the forefront, facilitating this approach, will be the methods and technology of cybernation. The increasing complexity of today's demands, the chronic shortage of top-flight skills to meet these demands, combined with a deeper understanding of the behavior of men as individuals and in groups, the stress on science and logic, and the tools available for social analysis—all will result in a more systematic organization of an ever-larger range of activities in order to maintain control over and stability in society. In all these situations, the computer will be a major and necessary element providing the basis for processing and interpreting data about the society and for simulating the consequences of policies and programs applied to the society.

For example, as our population grows and as everything becomes more complex and interrelated, there will have to be much more integrated, nationwide, long-range planning. There will undoubtedly be an expansion of government as the dominant device for social control. In this way, cybernation will have profound implications for the democratic process.

Computers are especially useful for dealing with social situations that pertain to people in the mass, such as traffic control, financial transactions, mass-demand consumer markets, allocation of resources, and so on. They are so useful in these areas that they undoubtedly will seduce some planners into trying to invent a society with needs and goals that can be met in aggregate rather than in terms of the individual. Indeed, the whole trend toward cybernation can be seen as an effort to remove the variabilities in man's on-the-job behavior and off-the-job needs which, because of their non-statistical nature, complicate production and consumption. Somewhere along the line, the idea of the individual may be completely swallowed up in statistics if those who depend on the computers attend chiefly to those social components which can be computer-processed. The dominant values may thus become those which are compatible with this logical-statistical approach to analyzing and manipulating the world. The planner and those he plans for may become divorced from one another, and the alienation of the individual from his government or from other individuals may grow greater.

But it may also be that by dealing with some social problems statistically, opportunities will increase in other areas to deal with the individual on a more personal level than can be the case when all services are overworked. Whether the integrity of the individual is lost or enhanced through cybernation will depend on how well we understand the needs of the individual and adjust the appropriate political processes to a cybernating society.

Other related factors will tend to undermine the customary form of American democracy. Will the average citizen know enough to assess the long-range plans proposed for him by his government? Probably not; computer-based models are complex, and the ancillary techniques for manipulating them require a very high degree of training to understand fully the premises and implications of the plans and interpretations. The intricacies of arguments for and against the possible adverse effects of nuclear weapons testing fallout, or on the effects of pesticides on the ecology are lost on most citizens. This situation will probably get worse, not better, over the next two decades, for the problems will grow in complexity far faster than we can be taught to deal with them.

Better understanding of the nature of public opinion, better methods for collecting such data, and more refined conceptual models that can indicate how to use this feedback further to influence public opinion, will increase the capacity of leadership to gain public consent. One stimulus to development in this field will be the pressing need for public support for long-range programs. Given these persuasive methods, the ominous possibility arises that these might be perverted in the pursuit of private ambitions rather than of the broad public interest.

EDUCATION

Clearly, cybernation will have a major impact on the processes and purposes of education. The ability to work skillfully, to use leisure rewardingly, to partici-pate as citizens in a changing democracy, and to acquire the values appropriate to the kind of world we have been describing will depend finally on education.

In each of these areas, the demands cybernation makes on the educative system will be great and in some ways radically different from those imposed by past technological changes. This impact has already begun to be felt. For example, as a consequence of anticipated unemployment produced by tech-nological change, government-subsidized vocational education was broadly re-vised in 1963. It is still too early to tell whether or not—or how quickly—this moribund educational activity, which has far too long concentrated chiefly on preparing people for work in agriculture and home economics, can respond appropriately to the cybernated age. It remains to be seen whether traditional interests and teacher inadequacies, as well as fundamental questions about *who* shall be vocationally educated for *what,* can be overcome on the scale needed to revise this form of education so that it meets the vocational training needs of tomorrow's world.

For all but the unskilled, education will have to be a life-long process. The professional will need frequent updatings in knowledge and technique. The technician will probably change his basic occupation two or three times during his working life as technological change makes his last occupation obsolete. Each time he will have to unlearn the old and learn something quite different. Today, life-long learning and unlearning are by no means the norm even at the professional level of society, where doctors, lawyers, and teachers more often than not avoid this difficult task of readjusting their view of the world, their command of their discipline, and thereby their image of themselves. The psychology associated with a life-long motivation to learn and unlearn is confined to a tiny fraction of any society; making it the standard is one of the major value changes cybernation will demand.

Youngsters aspiring to a top professional role will study longer and harder than those with more limited ambition. What is more, those aiming for the leisured life will have to be educated in the use of leisure as well as in the knowledge needed for well-paying but not overly time-consuming jobs. This contrast in school experience as well as in life expectations will tend to separate the two groups into two different educative patterns.

College will no longer be primarily the preserve of youth. Older people learning new things and new jobs, in order to compete with cybernetic machines and to make lesiure meaningful, will make up a substantial part of the student body. Increasingly, cybernation will provide the means for teaching automatically and responsively in terms of the varying abilities of the student. Large classes can often be taught better this way; for rote learning of facts and methods such devices are at least as good as mediocre teachers. (Whether this will result in the substantial displacement of mediocre teachers remains to be seen.) But teaching wisdom, integrity, and the attributes which make a wise and good leader, decision-maker, planner, or a plain human being, still requires a human being with those qualities and the ability to inspire and cultivate them in others. The greater the need for such people, given the complexity of the issues they must deal with and the complexity of the techniques used for dealing with them, the greater the tendency will be to save such teachers for these hard-working social servants-to-be.

CONCLUSION

Work, leisure, education, public opinion, and the processes of decision-making are each dependent on the others for their modes and consequences of expression. The social system is itself a cybernetic system. Therefore, it is naive to expect the benefits of cybernation to manifest themselves in all areas just because they are evident in some of these areas; it is also naive to expect solutions to all the problems that cybernation presents to be obtained by changes in any one of these areas alone. Over the years ahead, the United States will face a formidable challenge to its wisdom, foresight, and social flexibility in planning on the scale needed to reap the benefits and avoid the problems that cybernation will generate.

Part **XII**
Space, Culture, and Technology

43 / The Challenge of Space
EUGENE M. EMME

The last four decades of the 20th century appear to be destined for an increasing velocity of technical change. One of the triggers of swift change is the unprecedented exploration of space, with its related acquisition and exploitation of new knowledge, as well as a host of new engineering techniques. The influence of space science and technology has already been dynamic, sometimes profound, and indicative of even greater changes in human affairs, since no horizons are yet in sight which might constrain the basic challenge of space.

Perhaps never before have interrelated alterations in fundamental knowledge, practical engineering, and universal perspective been so quickly thrust upon mankind. In less than a hundred months, gigantic teams of managers, scientists, engineers, and technicians—governmental, industrial, and academic—became involved in charting previously inaccessible reaches of nature beyond the earth's envelope of atmosphere and gravitational force. Billions of dollars and rubles are being invested in this task. The optical cataract, or radiation filter, of the atmosphere has been removed from the eyes of astronomers for the first time. Basic relationships between the planet Earth and its source of energy—the sun —are undergoing intensive study and analysis. In addition, the sciences and arts of war and peace have not been immune to the impact of space exploration. All of this has happened within the span of less than a decade since the first man-made moon, Sputnik I, orbited the earth on October 4, 1957.

FACETS OF SPACE EXPLORATION

The chain reaction of events that followed the shock of recognizing that the "technologically backward" Russians had made the first step into space is generally referred to as the "Space Age." Two major world wars in the first half of the 20th century had consequences for this new age wider and more complex than those of mere military innovation. The mobilization of science in human affairs accelerated through technology. Space mobility, too, based initially upon the need for advanced rocketry, has come to serve as a fundamental transportation technology. The prospect that man is not confined forever to his planetary homeland may revolutionize future history, perhaps not unlike those revolutions attributed in the past to the development of agriculture, the control of fire, or the working of metals leading to machines.

It was only 350 years between the time Galileo pointed his telescope at the moon and the time that man was able to hit the moon with his devices and plan to land on it and return to earth. It has been 180 years or so since man first flew in a balloon, and just over 60 years since the Wright brothers initiated practical and controlled aerodynamic flight in the lower atmosphere. Ultimately, aviation revolutionized warfare and commerce by shrinking the time-distance dimensions of the world for weapons and for statesmen, artists, politicians, and tourists alike. More Americans cross the oceans and continents by jet today than by any other means. Within a half dozen years after the missile-birth of the Space Age, over a dozen men and one woman had orbited the earth. It will not be many years until a hundred earthlings will have flown in space. Over 400 satellites and space probes have already been flown.

Space-flight technology in all of its aspects hurries on. The first scientific reconnaissance of the planet Venus was achieved by Mariner II in December 1962, and of the planet Mars by Mariner IV on July 14, 1965. The first close-up pictures of the pockmarked surface of the moon were acquired by Ranger VII in July 1964, thereby increasing a thousandfold man's vision of the lunar surface through earth-bound telescopes. This and Rangers VIII and IX were merely a beginning. In 1966 Luna 9 and Surveyor I soft-landed on the moon. Within a few years a man will set foot upon the surface of that natural satellite of the earth; the moon could prove to be a scientific Rosetta Stone offering clues to 100-million years of the geological history of our solar system.

Weather observation and communication relays in orbiting satellites are already in daily service to earthbound activities. The ten Tiros weather satellites are among the spectacular contributors; Telstar, Relay, and Syncom, though only test satellites, have already served home television programming, while the incalculable economic and social potentials of communications satellites have global implications. Few scientific and engineering disciplines have not been influenced by the needs and consequences of space science and technology. The social sciences and humanities, likewise, are awakening to the implications of Space Age analyses and insights. Educational institutions at all levels have found themselves victims of "cultural lag."

What is the challenge of space in the history of technology? It might be said that space technology is at once a revolutionary tool of the sciences; a national instrument for power and prestige; an international impetus for both co-opera-

Fig. 43-1. Photograph of the surface of the planet Mars taken from digital data, radioed by Mariner IV on July 14, 1965. Note the lunar-like craters. The photograph was taken from a distance of about 7800 miles from the planet. (*NASA* photo)

tion and competition among nations; and a projection of man's historic exploration of his accessible environment. No thoughtful person can ignore the aspects of the space venture. Man's time for space mobility is here.

THE TECHNOLOGICAL TAPROOT

The technical basis of space mobility is the liquid-fuel chemical rocket. Carrying its own oxidizer for the combustion of high-energy fuel, rocket propulsion functions in the atmosphere as well as in the vacuum of outer space.

Black powder, used both for rockets and gunpowder, has long been known in the Western world. Rockets were a practical device long before Newton's principles actually explained reactive thrust. Chinese "fire arrows" were known

Fig. 43-2. Robert H. Goddard with his rocket just
before the first flight of a liquid-propellant rocket,
at Auburn, Massachusetts, March 16, 1926.
(Courtesy of *Mrs. Robert H. Goddard*)

in the 10th century, and versions were used in the Tatar campaigns in northern
Europe as well as by the Moors in the Iberian peninsula during the 13th century. Successful Indian rocket barrages against British regulars at Seringapatam
in 1792 and 1799 inspired the development of the Congreve rockets, which became standard in most European armies. "The rockets' red glare" has been
known to Americans since 1814, along with the traditional festival fireworks
Americanized for the Fourth of July.

By the middle of the 19th century, the art of solid-propellant rocketry was
largely dropped by the military because of improvement in the accuracy and
effect of artillery through rifled barrels, breech-loading, and high explosives. On
the other hand, large black-powder rockets had never been controllable. It is
not generally recognized that the modern evolution of the liquid-fuel rocket was
first sparked by early advocates of space flight rather than by the military. Its
eventual military utility only accelerated liquid-fuel rocket development.

Konstantin E. Tsiolkovsky of Russia, Robert H. Goddard of the United

States, and Hermann Oberth of Rumania, among the first to be interested in the scientific exploration of space, were the progenitors of liquid-fuel rocket development. They directly inspired disciples who organized the enthusiastic interplanetary and rocket societies of the 1920's and 1930's in Germany, Russia, Britain, and the United States. The world's first successful liquid-fuel rocket flight was performed by Goddard at Auburn, Massachusetts, on March 16, 1926. This primitive flight of 184 feet, in effect, became for astronautics what the Wright brothers' flight at Kitty Hawk in 1903 became for the history of aviation.

Two major technological innovations appeared during World War II: the ballistic missile, especially the spectacular five-and-a-half-ton German V-2, and the atomic bomb. The ten-year German experience in liquid-fuel rocketry in the V-2 of 1945 immediately passed to the United States and the Soviet Union as a technological spoil of war. When it was realized that nuclear warheads could be accurately delivered at great distance by rockets, the cold war race for the first generation of intercontinental ballistic missiles (ICBM's) was on.

This race started relatively late (1954) for the United States, whose monopoly of atomic bombs and superior global jet air power provided a weapons system which had been considered adequate for maintaining world peace for some time to come. The Soviet Union, however, because of its nuclear and air-power deficiencies, initiated intensive projection of the V-2 technology within six months after the destruction of Nagasaki. Because of its relatively backward nuclear technology, and therefore larger and more cumbersome bombs, the Soviet Union had to design and develop an even larger ICBM rocket than the United States, an important consideration when large-thrust rockets became central to the so-called "space race."

THE SCIENTIFIC IMPETUS

The rise of the liquid-fuel rocket as a new tool of science likewise stemmed from the V-2 technology in 1945. Space—previously an inaccessible portion of nature—became with rocketry a new laboratory for all scientific disciplines interested in the workings of time, motion, matter, energy, and life processes. The United States Army fired the first of its hundred captured V-2's at White Sands Proving Ground, New Mexico, in June 1946. It invited scientists in governmental and university laboratories to conduct upper atmospheric experiments with these rockets which reached into near space. Thus was created the important Atmospheric Research Panel, which became so vital to later space-science activities, particularly the inception of the International Geophysical Year.

The Jet Propulsion Laboratory of the California Institute of Technology also launched from White Sands its war-developed Wac-Corporal rockets. On February 29, 1949, a V-2 with a Wac-Corporal second stage, called a "Bumper Wac," reached a record altitude of 244 miles over White Sands, yielding valuable information about ion densities. As the supply of V-2's ran out, the Applied Physics Laboratory of the Johns Hopkins University developed the Aerobee sounding rocket, while the Naval Research Laboratory developed the Viking. Probing of near space and of the upper atmosphere to altitudes of 150 miles were of increasing scientific interest. The evolution of the sounding rocket led to the scientific feasibility of earth satellites and space probes as missile development also made greater rocket thrusts available.

SATELLITES

By late August 1957, the Soviet Union announced that it had successfully fired a long-range ballistic missile which had reached its intended target area. Only six weeks later, on October 4, 1957, Sputnik I orbited the earth, and its "beep, beep" was heard around the world. Advanced rocket technology could not have been more spectacularly demonstrated than by the launching of the first earth satellite. This event, followed by Sputnik II (carrying the space dog Laika) one month later, had a lasting impact, particularly on American public opinion, and initiated the response known as the "Space Age." This chain reaction of events was also to characterize subsequent phases of the era of space flight, not the least of which has been the further stimulation of rocket and related technology to evolve a genuine space-transportation system.

The idea of an earth satellite had been much in vogue after 1945, but sponsorship of such a venture did not spring from the logic of military need. Not until the International Council of Scientific Unions recommended (October 1954) that earth satellites should be launched during the forthcoming International Geophysical Year (July 1957–December 1958), did the United States and the Soviet Union pick up this proposal and institute launching programs. The basic American decision had been to institute the IGY satellite program (Project Vanguard) under non-military auspices. Project Vanguard, under civilian direction in the Naval Research Laboratory, was ordered not to interfere with the high-priority military program for a ballistic missile; therefore the project had to design, develop, construct, and test its own three-stage rocket. This requirement delayed the program, and it was not until after Sputnik I that the first American satellite was launched. This was Explorer I, hastily launched on a military rocket by the Army Ballistic Missile Agency on January 31, 1958. The first American satellite carried James A. Van Allen's IGY experiment which discovered the radiation belts in the earth's outer atmosphere (the belts now named after Van Allen). His discovery was considered the most important contribution of the entire IGY. It was not until March 17, 1958, that Vanguard I was finally launched. As anticipated, it made great contributions to

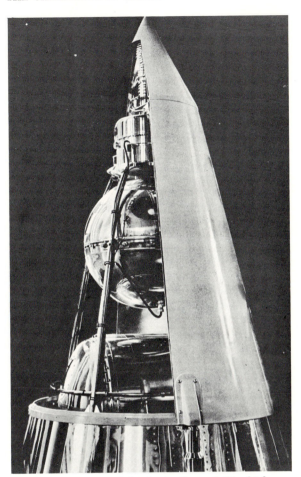

Fig. 43-3. Cutaway of the Soviet Sputnik II which
in 1957 carried the dog Laika into space. It contained scientific research instruments and an
hermetically sealed cabin for the animal. (Courtesy
of *Library of Congress*)

basic science and rocket technology. By then America's space efforts and Russia's space exploits had created what world opinion regarded as a "space race."

The scientific importance of space exploration has remained its basic impetus.
Immediately after the Sputniks, Lloyd V. Berkner, chairman of the Space Science Board of the National Academy of Sciences, wrote:

From the vantage point of 2100 A.D., the year of 1957 will most certainly
stand in history as the year of man's progression from a two-dimensional to a

three-dimensional geography. It may well stand, also, as the point of time at which the intellectual achievements forged ahead of weapons and national wealth as instruments of national policy. The earth satellite is a magnificent expression of man's intellectual growth—of his ability to manipulate to his own purposes the very laws that govern his universe.

In essence, this basic idea was incorporated in the National Aeronautics and Space Act of 1958, a product of the American process of national decision-making signed into law by President Dwight D. Eisenhower on July 29, 1958. It declared that "it is the policy of the United States that activities in space should be devoted to the peaceful purposes for the benefit of all mankind." The act created the National Aeronautics and Space Administration (NASA) to carry out the exploration of space for its own sake, leaving to the Department of Defense and military services those aspects of space technology of potential military application. Space activity was in the general view considered too important to be the exclusive administrative domain of either a scientific or a military agency. As a co-ordinating and administrative agency, NASA was to work out the delicate interrelationships among other governmental agencies, the aerospace industries, and academic institutions—a situation which led to over 90 per cent of the money being spent outside of NASA proper.

In 1958 the United States encouraged space exploration for "peaceful purposes." These purposes were emphasized before the United Nations on November 17, 1958, by the Senate Majority Leader, Lyndon B. Johnson, just as Bernard Baruch had presented the American proposal for the international control of atomic energy to that same body in 1946. This precept of peaceful use has underlain all of American space policy since the Space Age began. To date, progress in the development of international space law has been modest. Based upon the recommendations of its Committee on the Peaceful Uses of Outer Space, the United Nations has passed initial resolutions covering requirements for the safety and rescue of astronauts, and for keeping weapons of mass destruction out of space. On January 27, 1967, sixty nations, including the United States but excluding France, signed an international agreement for the peaceful uses of space.

The tradition of international scientific co-operation established during the International Geophysical Year has continued in space activities. Tracking of satellites and space probes requires worldwide ground facilities. Scientists of most nations have pressed for personal inclusion in the new area of space conquest. From 1960 on, the international programs of the United States under NASA, from specific experiments in sounding rockets to satellite launchings, have involved over sixty nations in varied but mutually beneficial associations. For example, during the International Year of the Quiet Sun, worldwide sounding rocket activities have been co-ordinated. The U.K.-U.S. Ariel I (1962) and Ariel II (1964), the Canadian-U.S. Alouette (1963), the Italian San Marco I

(1964), and the French FR-I (1966) were highly successful, joint earth-satellite ventures. The European Space Research Organization (ESRO) and individual nations other than the United States and the Soviet Union now have plans for launching satellites of their own.

Agreements for the barter of information have been negotiated between the United States and the Soviet Union, although only limited exchanges have been made thus far. Exploratory steps for American-Russian space co-operation have proved inseparable from the total context of international affairs. The late President Kennedy's proposal before the United Nations for a joint manned lunar program, for example, found inadequate technical and political bases.

The impetus to basic scientific research provided by the accessibility of the previously untouchable reaches of space should not be discounted, despite the criticism by some scientists of the level of investment in space activities, particularly in the United States. Such criticism appears somewhat surprising to historians and others who are traditionally inclined to view science as the pursuit of the unknown rather than the pursuit of narrow interests. After all, if it were known what might be learned in space, it would not be necessary to go there. Sir Bernard Lovell, director of the famous British Jodrell Bank Experimental Station, declared at the height of the American space dialogue during the summer of 1963:

> The challenge of space exploration and particularly of landing men on the moon represents the greatest challenge which has ever faced the human race. Even if there were no clear scientific or other arguments for proceeding with this task, the whole history of our civilization would still impel men toward the goal. In fact, the assembly of the scientific and military with these arguments creates such an overwhelming case that it can be ignored only by those who are blind to the teachings of history, or who wish to suspend the development of civilization at its moment of greatest opportunity and drama.

It may be that once the existence of extraterrestrial life forms, however primitive, is confirmed—enforcing the revolutionary idea that man is not alone and perhaps not unique in his universe—the contemporary critics of space research will be routed, as were the inquisitors of Galileo. Although one may often share the doubts of Albert Einstein that truly intelligent life exists beyond earth, one cannot argue with astronomers who point to the tens of thousands of bodies in the universe capable of supporting a physical environment similar to that of the earth.

MAN AND SPACE

The opening phases of the Space Age were highlighted by the initial scientific discoveries of the first Explorers and Sputniks, the first Tiros pictures of the world's cloud cover from above, and the spectacular missions of the Luniks as

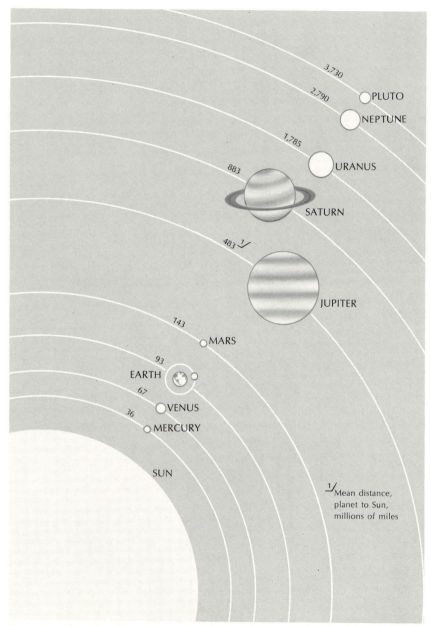

Fig. 43-4. The solar system, showing relative location of the planets and mean distance from the sun. (*NASA* drawing)

well as the Pioneer V probe to 18 million miles in 1960. The kindergarten era of space mobility came to an end when man himself orbited the earth in 1961. Within a month after the first orbital space flight by the Russian cosmonaut Yuri Gargarin in Vostok I on April 12, 1961, the American decision had largely been made to land a man on the moon within the decade of the 1960's. On May 25, 1961, President Kennedy presented this "opportunity" for national decision in a stirring presentation to the Congress and the American people. He viewed space achievement as a contest which the United States could win in open competition.

The American space program subsequently expanded fivefold over its previous three-year growth. An open information policy with regard to the highly successful Mercury flights during 1961-63 not only permitted most Americans to participate via live TV but also permitted the launchings to be witnessed by international observers. No neutral observer has witnessed Soviet manned space launchings. In a sense Alan Shepard, John Glenn, and the other Mercury astronauts became effective spokesmen for the merits of an open society. Thus the chain reaction initiated with Sputnik I appears to be continuing and to be reaching into many areas of social and political life as well as science and technology.

Contrast between the United States and the Soviet Union in orbital payload-weight capability was most apparent with regard to comparative space flight exploits from 1961 to 1964. Project Mercury used the best available American rocket booster, the Atlas; but the first woman in space, Valentina Tereshkova, who completed 48 orbits in Vostok VI during June 16-19, 1963, achieved more orbital time than all of the Mercury astronauts combined. This was precisely the technological basis which underwrote the decision for a lunar landing in this decade—to overcome the early Soviet lead in rocket thrust by a decision to begin development of the necessary booster rockets. The American decision to build a genuine space transportation technology has already been manifested in the successful flights of the giant Saturn I and is becoming apparent in the fabrication of the super-giant Saturn V rocket and its launching facilities for the manned lunar mission. In 1966 the United States completed the Gemini program. The astronauts achieved the first orbital rendezvous as well as other record achievements for manned flight, including extended flight up to two weeks' duration. Clearly the conquest of space is rapidly approaching its exploitation phases.

Space here does not permit a detailed recounting of the successes of Project Mercury or Project Gemini or the unmanned satellites and probes, nor of the future course of the Apollo space flight program. Without reviewing the philosophical challenge presented by man's physical exploration of his solar system, it appears that a dramatic new age of discovery is upon us. The discovery of the New World; the settling of the American frontier; the conquest of the highest mountains, the Arctic and Antarctic, the ocean depths, and the atmosphere—

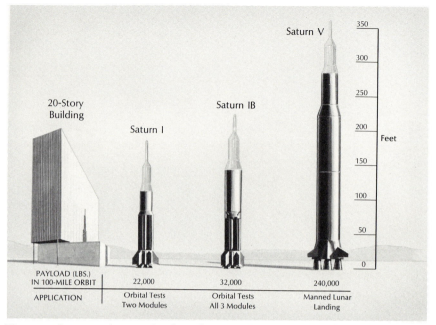

Fig. 43-5. Saturn rockets used in launching Apollo spacecraft. (*NASA* drawing)

these responses to the challenge of curiosity and adventure in history are in many ways analogous to the space venture. Beyond the scientific goals of space flight by man, important tasks such as manning orbital or lunar laboratories or perhaps police stations to keep space peaceful emerge as logical needs of the future.

Basic military needs for space technology cannot be ignored. Reconnaissance, early warnings of missile attacks, and detection of nuclear explosions in outer space are already operational features of military space systems. Increasing military functions in space for astronauts are evident. While the United States has consistently stressed its intention not to place weapons of mass destruction in space, the international order does not yet exist for keeping space peaceful. The first feeble steps of the Nuclear Test Ban Treaty of 1963 and the Space Treaty of 1967 were just that, no more and no less. The application of space technology to military purposes could present grave future dangers.

The strategic importance of space to national security is intimately related to the acquisition of new knowledge and techniques. It is likewise part and parcel of the fundamental problem of world peace on earth. The challenge of space includes the competitive aspects of international affairs, and suggests to some the features of a "moral equivalent of war" which William James once thought necessary in order to institute peace in accord with human psychology.

Beyond the political and economic impact of the space challenge on national power and purpose, there is also impact on local resources and manpower in areas such as Cape Kennedy, Houston, and Southern California. The total impact on society of this investment—perhaps the largest single non-military undertaking ever made by man—remains to be documented and analyzed by future historians. Simply to call it another "technological explosion" seems an inadequate and uncritical description.

PROSPECT AND RETROSPECT

We cannot foresee fully the scientific, strategic, economic, political, military, or intellectual influences of the undertaking in space. The power and prestige of the major nations, the workings of society as a whole, and the lives of individuals

Fig. 43-6. Astronaut Edward H. White II as he walks in space. He remained outside the Gemini IV spacecraft for 21 minutes on June 3, 1965, secured to the spacecraft by a 25-foot umbilical line. (*NASA* photo)

and their offspring would seem inevitably to be increasingly influenced. It is not known what we will learn or discover on the moon and the neighboring planets any more than Columbus could know about coking coal, petroleum, rich farm-land, and all of the other resources which were to make the United States great in world influence and material prosperity. Questions answered by space missions create more questions.

Historically, as man has steadily conquered and understood his environment, he has made intellectual and material progress in civilization. Thus, there are valid reasons for believing that the exploration and exploitation of space is one of man's greatest scientific and dramatic adventures. We can only guess at the sequence or timing of specific events.

In this age of science in which we live, the capabilities of space flight have already provided us with the ability to perform feats which primitive man only granted to the greatest gods in his limited universe. The universal complexities of nature, not just earth-bound data, become increasingly known, but the supreme design we cannot yet know or fully understand, as we are only now beginning to piece together the cosmic jigsaw puzzle. This challenge should define one of the greatest chapters in the history of mankind.

44 / The "Two Cultures"
KENNETH E. BOULDING

In 1959 C. P. Snow, English scientist, scientific administrator, and novelist, delivered a series of lectures later published under the title *The Two Cultures and the Scientific Revolution*. This book introduced a new phrase—the two cultures—into currency and stimulated widespread discussion of the role of science in modern life. It was Snow's argument that modern culture was becoming increasingly bifurcated between the traditional literary or humanistic culture and the increasingly important scientific culture, in which he included technology. He excoriated the upholders of the humanistic culture for their snobbish refusal to recognize that science itself had, in the modern period, become a valid culture demanding recognition in the present world. Custodians of the literary culture answered, somewhat snippishly, that there was only one culture, and that scientists by and large did not have any culture.

Snow's concept of the polarization of modern society is, of course, oversimplified. There are, in fact, not two but many subcultures with which we must deal, and deciding how to bring about communication among them is a general rather than a specific need. One may know how to make a rocket go up without knowing where it should come down, but to separate completely the two knowledge systems may be fatal to mankind. Somehow, integration must be achieved.

THE CONCEPT OF CULTURE

The word "culture" is itself used in different senses in ordinary speech and in the social sciences, and leads to some confusion. In ordinary speech, we often use it to mean those aspects of human life which involve a cultivated taste, especially in the arts. We think of culture in terms of opera, art galleries, classical music, good taste in architecture, furniture, or dress, and so on. To call a person "uncultured" is a form of abuse, implying that he has unrefined tastes or does not belong to the cultural elite.

In the social sciences, however, and especially in anthropology, the word culture is used simply to refer to a social system in all its aspects. The culture of the Hopi Indians, for instance, consists of their language, norms of behavior, forms of organization and community structure, family and kinship patterns, technology and methods of production, and so on. In this sense, then, culture means the general description of a society as a total system, and in this sense everyone is part of a culture of some kind, for no human being can exist in isolation from others. Even Robinson Crusoe carried with him the artifacts, memories, and knowledge of his own culture, though in isolation he began to modify the culture he possessed.

We often use the word "subculture" to mean a sub-system within a larger social system, and we use this term again as a total description. Thus, we find occupational subcultures. Truckers, for instance, have a pattern of life, even of speech, which is very different from that of doctors. There are organizational subcultures. A school, a hospital, a city, or a neighborhood will develop certain patterns of its own, even though it shares patterns of speech, behavior, and organization with other groups in the society in which it is embedded.

Although they all have some apparatus for preventing change and maintaining the old patterns, cultures and subcultures continually change. The very fact that human beings are born, age, and die, forces change; furthermore, some processes of learning, whether a result of inputs of information from outside the culture or the result of internal information generation, likewise lead to change. Where, however, the existing structures and patterns of a culture are highly valued by the persons who belong to it, change will be resisted, and will be interpreted as "bad." Thus the university continually tries to maintain the quality of its staff, its integrity, and academic freedom; a nation resists threats from outside or internal challenges to its legitimacy; a family, too, will resist attempts to undermine the mutual affection of the members; and so on. The overall dynamics of a culture is the result of the interaction of the forces making for change and the countervailing forces making for stability. Perfect stability and equilibrium is unknown in nature, though some systems, such as the solar system, approximate it. No biological or social system even comes close to perfect stability. We have to judge the "health" of a system by its ability to maintain desirable patterns of change. What we mean by "desirable," however, raises large issues which cannot be adequately discussed here.

THE "SOCIOSPHERE"

Social systems, then, consist of people, the roles they occupy (that is, the patterns of behavior they exhibit), and the inputs and outputs which go into these roles and the channels they follow. The inputs and outputs may be material, as when raw materials and people go into a factory and produce automobiles, or they may be inputs and outputs of information. A role in a social system, then, can be thought of as a transformer of inputs into outputs.

The role occupant does not have to be a person; it may be a machine, a combination of a person and a machine, or a group of persons in combination with a group of machines. Some inputs modify the transformation process itself, and create a different input-output relationship. Some material inputs may do this, in which case we think of them as investment. Information inputs also do this when they create new knowledge and new ways of transforming inputs into outputs.

On the whole, the *information* inputs and outputs, and the knowledge they create, dominate social systems, and even biological systems. Though the availability of sources for *material* inputs and outlets for material outputs considerably affects the operation of a system, the role of information and knowledge in social systems can hardly be overestimated. Even something we consider physical capital, such as a machine, is really a knowledge structure imposed on the material world which began as a knowledge structure in the human mind. Material inputs and outputs set limits and boundaries on the system, but information makes the system function.

We can picture the entire social system, then, as a "sociosphere," almost like the biosphere or the atmosphere, which consists at any one moment of all the people in the world, all the roles they are occupying, all the knowledge inside their heads, all the lines of communication among them, all the commodity flows among them, all the material capital (the houses, factories, machines, and so on) with which they work, and the organizations in which they participate. Change in the sociosphere comes partly from the accumulation of material capital, more fundamentally from the accumulation of knowledge, which will determine what people can do. Even when material capital is destroyed it can be recreated if the social system of which it is a part is unimpaired. We see this, for instance, in Japan, where the cities destroyed in World War II are now rebuilt and thriving; we see it in a city such as Leningrad or the central part of Warsaw, which has been rebuilt exactly as it was. These examples show very clearly how the information and knowledge aspects of a culture dominate its material substructure.

SCIENTIFIC KNOWLEDGE AND FOLK KNOWLEDGE

The last three hundred years have seen an enormous change in the sociosphere, mainly because of the development of a relatively small human subculture known as science. Science specializes in the cumulative increase of knowledge. This cumulative increase, can, of course, be traced back a long way. Only in the last three hundred years, however, has the increase of knowledge become, as it were, a specialized trade, making it possible now to distinguish between what is often called "folk knowledge" and "scientific knowledge."

Folk knowledge is acquired in the ordinary experience of life, and a great deal of it is useful. We all have images in our mind, for instance, of the geography of our house, school, or local community; we know about the members of our family and our friends, and the people with whom we have day-to-day, face-to-face contact; and we learn many things in ordinary conversation from our friends and relations; and so on. None of us, indeed, could operate for a single day without folk knowledge.

In pre-scientific societies, almost all knowledge is folk knowledge; and the knowledge capital of the society is transmitted from generation to generation largely through the family, by word of mouth, and face-to-face contacts. The introduction of writing about five thousand years ago profoundly modified this process and probably introduced an irreversible change; for once language can be written down, the past can speak to the future, and the knowledge capital of a society is no longer dependent on the fragile memories of old men.

The processes by which knowledge is acquired—whether folk knowledge or scientific knowledge—are essentially alike. In both cases, true images of the world in our minds can be derived only by the successive elimination of error. There is no way in which we can compare directly the image of the world that we have in our minds with the world as it presumably exists outside us. We have the opportunity to detect error after we make an inference regarding some message or input of information anticipated in the future, for when the future date arrives we can compare the expected input with the actual input. If these do not correspond, obviously something is wrong. (Even when they correspond, this does not necessarily mean that we are right. We may have made a correct prediction by accident.) Disappointment, however, forces us to reexamine the situation, and we can usually do one of three things: (1) we can reject the present message, which is inconsistent with our expectations, and say it was a false message; (2) we can, on the other hand, reject the inference which gave rise to the expectations—and with each of these choices our basic image of the world remains unchanged; (3) if, however, we can neither reject the inference nor the message, we must revise our image of the world, for we have then detected an error.

This process goes on all the time, even in ordinary life in the accumulation of folk knowledge. Suppose, for instance, I have an image in my mind of where the post office is located, and go to mail a letter and discover it is no longer there. My disappointment forces me to reorganize my image of where the post office is. I don't try to mail a letter in a nonexistent mailbox on the grounds that it has always been there and therefore must still be there. I don't reject the evidence of my senses and say I must be going blind because I can't see the post office. In a simple case like this, the error-detection process operates extremely well and produces genuine knowledge.

As we move away from the kind of systems involved in ordinary daily life to larger and more complex systems, whether in the physical or the social world, folk knowledge becomes less and less reliable. Folk knowledge, for instance, tells us that the earth is flat. Ordinarily this assumption will not get us into much trouble if we don't travel for long distances. Even in driving about the United States, for instance, a flat road map is quite adequate, and we do not usually have to take into account the curvature of the earth. The scientific image of the earth as a spheroid can be developed only by much more accurate inferences and observations than ordinary life provides—and such scientific images are essential if we are going to be an astronaut, for to believe then that the earth is flat, will get us into very serious, indeed fatal, trouble!

THE N-CULTURES

The "two-cultures" problem arises because within the educated community there seem to be two subcultures, two constellations of communication networks, that do not interact very much with each other—the scientific, engineering, and technological subculture on the one hand and the literary, artistic, and perhaps political subculture on the other. The problem of communication between the two is perhaps more acute in European countries than in the United States because of the nature of the European educational system, which forces specialization at an early age. Even in the United States, however, the problem is real, although it would be more precise to call it the "n-cultures" problem. It is not merely that we have only two non-communicating cultures; we have a great many of them.

It is one of the fundamental principles of economics that specialization without trade is useless, for the farmer would freeze and the tailor would starve. The same principle applies to the world of information and knowledge. Specialization permits greater productivity in a particular field and a particular line of knowledge, but if it is not accompanied by exchange and even by a class of people who specialize in intellectual exchange, the bits of specialized knowledge do not add up to a total knowledge structure for mankind. And within the scientific community, the inability of specialists to communicate with specialists in a different field hampers the progress of the various specialties and also the total growth of knowledge. In part, this problem has been handled in the sciences by the development of what might be called interstitial fields such as physical chemistry or biophysics. It is countered, also, by the development of good scientific journalism, such as we find, for instance, in *Science*, the magazine of the American Association for the Advancement of Science, or in the *Scientific American*. The value of publications of this kind can hardly be overestimated. Nevertheless, the n-culture problem remains, and the fact that politicians, businessmen, artists, writers, poets, musicians, engineers, and scientists, often move in non-intersecting circles means that each may have knowledge and skills that are important to others but which are unavailable because of the lack of communication.

The social sciences can play a crucial role in bridging the gap which exists among the various cultures, and especially the two-culture gap between the humanistic and literary kind of knowledge and scientific knowledge. The social scientist himself is in a key position as a part of the systems he studies. He can not only approach the study of social systems from the point of view of an outside scientific observer—taking careful observations, making careful measurements, making predictions by mathematical or logical inference, and then seeing whether these are confirmed or falsified; but he also has an "inside track." The physicist has never been an atom or an electron; but the social scientist has participated himself in a great many social systems. Genuine knowledge can be derived from the inside track, and indeed provides many of the hypotheses and insights which the social scientists may then proceed to test by more rigorous methods.

Literary and humanistic studies represent a process of reflection and sifting of the accumulated records of folk knowledge. As such they represent a scholarly type of knowledge which is intermediate between the unsophisticated folk knowledge of ordinary life and the more testable images of science. Humanistic knowledge is in no sense to be despised; indeed, if one wants to understand the human being, a reading of Sophocles or Shakespeare may instruct us more than the latest psychological experiments. I have elsewhere defined science as the art of substituting unimportant questions which can be answered for important questions which cannot. This wisecrack clearly belongs to the humanistic subculture and is pretty hard to test. Nevertheless, it contains elements of truth; and as we move from the humanities through the "soft" into the "hard" sciences, we often find that our knowledge becomes less significant as it becomes more exact.

The technologist who is so absorbed in his own technique that he has no time for that expansion of his personal experience and, if we like, folk knowledge, which comes from acquaintance with the great literature of the world, or who has a mind so completely oriented toward verbal and mathematical symbols that he cannot appreciate the messages of art, music, or religion, will fail in his own technique, no matter how good it is. Somewhat in the mood of the former wisecrack, I once defined an engineer as a man who spends his life finding the best way of doing something which shouldn't be done at all. This indeed is always the danger of the technician. It is what is known in the technical language of programming as sub-optimization. The problem is summarized by the story of the engineer who said all he wanted to do was to reduce costs, until it was pointed out that costs could be reduced to zero by the simple process of shutting down the plant and liquidating the enterprise.

THE ROLE OF THE SOCIAL SCIENCES

Perhaps one of the most important questions which faces mankind at the present time is whether the increase and spread of knowledge in the social sciences, of a testable and cumulative kind, can meaningfully affect the decision-making processes of governments, businesses and large organizations, and of individuals and households. There is a good deal of evidence, indeed, that it can, and that as we acquire more knowledge of the relationships, the significant variables, and the magnitude of the parameters of social systems, we will be able to avoid the disastrous consequences which failure to understand these systems has often caused in the past. The record of famine, depression, war, and social collapse, which has characterized past history, is at least in part a product of human decision-making and inadequate technologies.

We still do not have the social technology capable of creating a world social system in which men can live out their lives with the expectation of peace, plenty, and the fulfillment of their potentialities. The technology here must be thought of not only in terms of machines and material inventions, but also in terms of social inventions, such things as government itself, the United Nations, decision-making through consent, and such homely things as a deductible-at-source income tax, which was probably one of the major social inventions of the 20th century.

Economics is the oldest of the social sciences, and indeed one of the oldest of all the sciences, having developed its basic theoretical structure under Adam Smith in 1776, before the development of scientific chemistry. It is not surprising, therefore, to find that the impact of the social sciences on social systems is most apparent in the application of economics. The great economic development of the last two hundred years in Western countries itself is not unconnected with the profound insights of Adam Smith regarding the social and developmental function of the price system.

If we contrast the twenty years between the two world wars, say from 1919-39, with the twenty years after the Second World War, 1945-65, we see a remarkable difference. The first period saw the Great Depression in the West and the disastrous First Collectivization in the Soviet Union, and it ended with Hitler and the Second World War. In the second period, there has been no major depression, though some small ones; rates of development in many countries have been unprecedented, indeed, two or three times what they were before the Second World War; a large number of colonies have become new nations, and some of these have started on the road to development. It would be both immodest and untrue to attribute the whole difference between these two periods to the growth of economic knowledge. Nevertheless, the rise of better information systems as reflected in national income statistics and a certain frame of theoretical reference provided by Keynesian economics has made a noticeable contribution to the difference between the two periods.

The international system has barely begun to feel the impact of the accumulating knowledge of the social sciences, but this, perhaps, is the next field of advance. It is still largely true that international systems operate by folk knowledge; and the gap between the two cultures, in this case between the developing science of international systems and the folk knowledge of the major decision-makers, is wide and hard to bridge. The information collection and processing system, on which the decisions of states are made, is primitive in the extreme as judged by scientific standards. Indeed, one could hardly do better, if one were setting up a system for producing misinformation and false images, than the system which relies extensively on diplomats and spies. There is a problem of sampling here, and also a problem of what is called the "value filter," which screens out information which is unacceptable to the recipient. In the scientific community there are defenses against these corruptions of the information system. In the international system, unfortunately, these defenses are still very primitive. It is not surprising, therefore, that the international system is so appallingly costly, and that it operates so badly.

A world system that spends $140 billion on the war industry and still gives no real security to the world must be reckoned a failure, and the problem of how to devise a better system for doing what unilateral national defense can no longer provide is one of the major tasks of mankind. The intellectual effort going into the solution of these problems, however, is at present much smaller than it should be; and we are certainly not going to solve them with the kind of resources which are now being applied. Still, some progress is being made, and the abolition of war does not seem so utopian an objective as it did a generation ago.

SPACESHIP EARTH AND THE HUMAN BEING

There are long-run problems facing the human race which may be very difficult to solve. We do not yet, for instance, have a stable, high-level technology. Our existing technology is based on fossil fuels and ores, and is thus limited; we will be all right for a hundred years, or perhaps two hundred, but within strictly historic time we may face a totally exhausted earth. Fortunately, a technology based on the concept of Earth as a self-contained spaceship is by no means impossible, and indeed seems to be on the way. This would involve placing man in a self-perpetuating cycle, drawing on the atmosphere and the oceans as the only basic resource, and importing energy either from the sun or from nuclear fusion on the earth.

For the spaceship society, we must also achieve population control, which we are a long way from accomplishing. We do not even know how large a population the earth could support in a stable, high-level economy. One hopes for the sake of the unborn that it will be large, for world population is all too likely to go to six billion by the end of this century, and we are not likely to catch it before then.

A final problem related to the problem of the two cultures is that of human development, that is, the full development of human potential in terms of the enjoyment of life, variety of experience, sensitivity of concern, appreciation of beauty, love, affection, community, and so on. The very concept of development implies some ideal or at least some direction of change which we regard as ideal, by which we can measure achievements.

The social sciences can, perhaps, help here by expanding our knowledge of what men have in fact regarded as ideal, and by attempting to explain the circumstances under which one set of ideals becomes prevalent. Our ideals themselves are derived largely from people we have known, imagined, or encountered in literature, poetry, religion, and art. We can, perhaps, find out something about the relation of prevalent ideals to the survival of societies and subcultures; or we can study the way in which its ideals affect the character of a society. Where, for example, there is an exaggerated ideal of masculinity, where the status of women is low, or where achievement goes into rivalry rather than into production, economic development may be hampered. The social sciences study the relation of these ideals to the nature and development of a society. The ideals themselves, however, come out of the folk culture or out of humanistic culture. This is true even for science itself, which has ideals of objectivity, dispassion, honesty, and so on. These ideals come not from science itself, though they are the prerequisites for the development of science.

A PROBLEM OF CHOICE

There are questions here that the framework of science and technology cannot answer. No matter how far we go in technology, all that technology gives us is power; and power without an objective is meaningless and ultimately self-destructive. This is an area scarcely penetrated as yet by the social sciences. We have, therefore, to rely a great deal on the humanistic vision expressed in poetry, art, and religion. We can grow in knowledge and begin to apply the human mind to the critique of the *ends* of man and his social systems, just as we can to the improvement of *means.*

Thus the increase of power technology produces raises all the more insistently those questions about the "chief end of man" which religion and philosophy, poetry and the arts, have always raised. When we are impotent, the question of whether we want the wrong things hardly arises; we cannot get them any-way. As our power increases, the question of *what* we want to do with it ac-quires overriding importance. At this point even the social scientist must take a back seat, for such knowledge is perhaps unobtainable, and wisdom is all that we have left.

45 / Technology's Challenge
MELVIN KRANZBERG AND CARROLL W. PURSELL, JR.

Early in 1966 the National Commission on Technology, Automation, and Eco-nomic Progress, in its report to the President, declared that "future historians will probably describe our time as an age of conscious social change." The effect of this change is widespread and includes, according to the Commission, "the rapid growth of population, the massive flow of peoples from rural areas to the cities, the steady growth of national wealth and income, the rise of op-pressed and submerged peoples, the spread of mass education, the extension of leisure, the venture into space, and the frightening increase in the destruc-tiveness of military weapons. Change is worldwide in scope." The Commission concluded that "if there is one predominant factor underlying current social change, it is surely the advancement of technology."

THE PROMISE OF PROGRESS

The coupling of technology with science has, within the present century, made technology a potent means for the conscious alteration of large segments of society. The idea that men might become masters of their own fate was a heady one for technologists at the beginning of this century. Leo H. Baekeland (1863-1944), inventor of Bakelite, an early plastic, enthusiastically claimed victory for science in 1910:

To put it tersely [he wrote], I dare say that the last hundred years under the influence of the modern engineer and the scientist have done more for the bet-terment of the race than all the art, all the civilizing efforts, all the so-called classical literature, of past ages, for which some respectable people want us to have such an exaggerated reverence.

All of the naiveté, daring, and egoism of young America was summed up in Baekeland's further declaration that:

The modern engineer, in intellectual partnership with the scientist, is asserting the possibilities of our race to a degree never dreamt of before: instead of cowering in wonder or fear like a savage before the forces of nature, instead of finding in them merely an inspiration for literary or artistic effort, he learns the language of nature, listens to her laws, and then strengthened by her revelations, he fulfills the mission of the elect and sets himself to the task of applying his knowledge for the benefit of the whole race.

This was the authentic voice of the pioneer, the trail-blazer into the unknown. The faith of such men was summed up at the end of World War II by Vannevar Bush in the title of his report to the President: *Science—The Endless Frontier.*

MAJOR TRENDS

Toward the end of the 19th century two major changes took place which had a profound impact upon the history of the 20th century. First, in the words of Alfred North Whitehead, "the greatest invention of the nineteenth century was the invention of the method of invention." By 1900 it was no longer necessary to sit back and wait for inspiration to strike an inventive genius at work in his garret. To an increasing degree, especially in the new science-oriented industries such as the chemical and electrical, it was becoming possible to invent almost any device or system needed by industry, and to produce new synthetic materials to meet any given specifications.

Second, the method of technological innovation travelled slowly from Great Britain, where it was born, and from Germany, where it had grown rapidly, to the United States, where it was to mature into a way of life. Science and technology in the United States were democratized in accordance with the fundamental commitment of the nation. The egalitarian ethos made it inevitable that the fruits of technological success should be widely spread throughout the population. Henry Ford took a toy of the upper classes and made it a necessity for an entire population. Frederick W. Taylor, insisting that workers had to be involved in the management of industry, developed Scientific Management to fit manpower into the machine system. While neither of these democratic experiments has turned out to be uniformly beneficial, they are representative of efforts undertaken in the 20th century.

INSTANCES OF CHANGE

Nowhere was the rationalization and democratization of technology in the United States better displayed than in the efforts to build man and the machine into a coherent and efficient system of production, distribution, and consumption. The classic statement of Scientific Management, which led the effort, was published in 1911 by Taylor, a mechanical engineer. The principles of Scientific Management evolved from a plan to investigate and control the work processes carried on in the machine shop. Coupled with the principle of mass production by Ford in his famous automobile assembly line of 1914, the concept spread to other industries and other nations. The stopwatch and the assembly line became the symbols both of America's industrial dominance and her culture.

Mass production implied and required mass consumption. The goods which rolled from the production lines had to be distributed to retail outlets and then marketed in such a way as to bring them to the attention and within the means of the average consumer. The spread of consumer credit, the rise of advertising, and the invention of such social institutions as the supermarket contributed to the efficiency of consumption, which rose along with production. The system has worked so well that Americans have found themselves facing the prospect of a truly affluent society—one in which, to the majority, consumption is more important than production, and where the pioneer ethic of work-and-save is thought not only obsolete but possibly even a threat to continued prosperity.

The automobile, which has revolutionized transportation in the 20th century, had its beginning in the 19th. Although a few people realized its importance before the turn of the century, no one could have anticipated the full impact of this one machine. Its influence on the economy has been enormous: the automotive industry is, today, the largest in the world; one firm, General Motors, is larger in its financial ramifications than any government in the world, except for the United States, Great Britain, and the Soviet Union. The statistics are staggering. Early in 1966 there were some 82,000,000 motor vehicles in the United States alone—well over the total number of *people* in the country in 1900. Furthermore, American auto-makers alone put more than 200,000 new vehicles a week onto the highways of the nation.

The story of the airplane is equally spectacular. Most of the components for successful manned flight were present in 1900, although no one had yet put them together successfully. Then, in 1903, the Wright brothers succeeded where others had failed. The airplane was then brought to final perfection during World War II. Using engines essentially like the 12-horsepower unit used at Kitty Hawk, planes with 400 horsepower were developed during World War I, and 3000 horsepower was not uncommon during the Second World War. A whole new evolution began in 1947 when the Bell X-1 was flown at supersonic speeds. Mach 2 (twice the speed of sound) was achieved in 1953 and Mach 3 in 1966. Even more spectacular were man's first ventures into space. The space programs in both the Soviet Union and the United States provided a remarkable demonstration of how scientific and technological teamwork could bring about the fulfillment of one of man's most fantastic dreams.

Most of the technical miracles of the new century, including those in trans-portation, were based on new or more efficient use of energy sources. Neither gasoline nor electricity was new, although the latter, despite its wide use before 1900, continued to excite some observers with its seemingly inexhaustible power. Nuclear energy was another matter entirely: its introduction, through the awesome power of the atomic bomb, deeply disturbed those who gave thought to its moral implications. Many people, however, preferred to speculate about its future benefits to mankind than dwell on its destructive power. In the few decades since the discovery of nuclear energy, there have been many pre-dictions, not yet all fulfilled, about its eventual ability to provide man with what he had never had before—virtually unlimited energy at his disposal.

Further scientific advances were made in the communications field, beginning with the telegraph in the first half of the 19th century. The telephone in 1876, then the radio early in this century, carried forward the harnessing of electricity to aid communication. More recently television and the communications satel-lite have expanded the range of the process.

Not only is it possible to spread information faster and increasingly more effective ways, there is now—at least on one level—more information to commu-nicate than ever before. The sheer accumulation of data, itself a by-product of the growing complexity of society, is being dealt with by a wide range of new devices called "computers." They have already proved themselves in automat-ing both factories and offices; furthermore, they are giving man the ability to solve complex and difficult questions of both a scientific and social nature.

In no area was innovation more successful than in agriculture. During the last half of the 19th century, the United States government undertook to com-municate the findings of agricultural science and technology to the American farmer. Proper techniques of irrigation, conservation, fertilization, cultivation, stock-breeding and feeding, the development of new hybrid crop strains, and serums against animal diseases, all made agriculture in the mid-20th century a prime example of how productivity could respond to the stream of innovation suggested by research.

The kind of innovation which Taylor brought to the shop, which the research laboratory brought to the factory, and which the Department of Agriculture brought to the farm, was also applied to the natural resources of the nation. In the first decade of this century the conservation crusade, inaugurated by scientists and engineers engaged in resource development, extended the concept of rational management to the raw materials of industry. The idea of regional planning, first thought of only in terms of the arid West, gradually came to be applied to more populous areas. The "systems" approach is now being applied in the field of urban planning and development.

The role of the state became critical. The concept of laissez-faire had been, in the previous century, a scholar's model, a powerful weapon in controversy,

and perhaps an ideal to be pursued; certainly it was never an accurate description of the actual day-to-day relationship between the government and economy
of any nation in the world. Everywhere, usually on a more or less piecemeal
basis, the government intruded into the marketplace with the hope of achieving
socially desirable ends. Embargoes, tariffs, premiums, patents, grants, monopolies, loans, taxes, and tax rebates, all were common devices and widely supported.

In different countries and at different times, this pattern of relationship between public and private began to deteriorate. Whereas previously one of the
sectors would for a time dominate the other, or both would be in precarious
balance, science and technology began to erase the traditional distinctions
between the two. This was particularly the case where the technology was so
complex and expensive (for example, in the development of a supersonic airplane) that private enterprise could not afford to undertake the task itself. In
certain highly important sectors of the economy, such as aerospace and electronics, the distinction between public and private became so blurred as to be
almost meaningless.

The best example of the massive integration of technology and the state can
be found in military preparedness. During World War II, nations began to
realize that technological innovation, already successfully applied to industry,
could be equally fruitful when applied to the arts of war. The traditional struggle of civilian leaders to exercise control over the military, countered by the
efforts of the military to maintain their freedom of action, has been greatly
complicated by a major factor: the inability of either one to order the conditions
and results of technical innovation.

CRITICS AND CRITICISMS OF TECHNOLOGY

Every technological change has had social repercussions, and these repercussions have not always been beneficial to mankind. In many cases, technology
has made possible the exploitation of human beings by others. The depressed
condition of factory workers during the early Industrial Revolution is enough
to show that technological change has its darker side; the imperialistic domination of colonial peoples by European states in the 19th century is another example of how technology can be utilized by some men to exploit others. Technology is also feared because it has magnified man's potential to spoliate nature
and, much worse, destroy himself.

What, ask some critics, has technology done for man's moral and intellectual
progress? The reply of some is that technology fosters a materialistic outlook
that is opposed to human values. Lewis Mumford, for example, claims that our
advanced technology threatens to de-humanize man, transferring "the attributes
of life to the machine and the mechanical collective." Similarly, the develop-

ment of the production line, it has been said, has made man act mechanically, and now automation threatens to make him the slave of the very machines he has created.

The critics of technology may be divided into several groups. There are those who fear change of all kinds and hark back to the "good old days"—to an idyllic, rural, "non-technological" past. But, as we have seen, there is no "non-technological" past in human history; and the "good old days" were old but not necessarily good. This longing for the golden age is by no means new; in the 19th century John Ruskin, the English literary and art critic, looked back to medieval England—"ye merrie olde Englande" of cakes and ale and Morris-dancing on the green. But "olde Englande" was not so "merrie" for the vast majority of its inhabitants, who lived in fear and poverty, in superstition and filth. Similarly, the American small town of the beginning of the century, to which many of our contemporaries look back yearningly, may not have been so idyllic: how are we to account for the fact that so many Americans fled from the small towns? Perhaps the provincial, parochial, gossipy, and uncultivated world of the small town did not appeal so much to human desires as the challenge and excitement of the big city.

Not all the contemporary critics of technology are motivated by a nostalgia for the past. Many do recognize that technology has benefitted man by meeting his material needs, but they still look askance at its sociocultural repercussions. They claim that technological values have superseded more important values—concepts of freedom, individualism, and creativity—and have made technology, instead of man, the end of human life. Are their fears grounded in fact? Can human freedom, individuality, and creativity be retained in an age which is becoming increasingly technologically oriented?

Perhaps we must define what kind of freedom we have in mind, for technology has actually extended human freedom along some lines. For most of human history, men lived in constant poverty, barely above the subsistence level; the advances of technology, by making possible a great outpouring of food and other necessities, for the first time gave Western man a new freedom—freedom from want.

But what about freedom of the individual? In the past, especially in the rural areas, people had more space; they were less "fenced-in" than in today's urban society. That kind of spatial freedom vanished with the onrush of urbanism; but people apparently want to live together in large agglomerations. In the metropolis, society has become so "fragmented" that man has acquired freedom in an existentialist sense; while he lives among large numbers of people, he feels more lonely, and must act without past tradition or authority to guide his conduct.

In many ways the average man has more freedom today. Before the industrial framework of our modern society was built up, the overwhelming majority of citizens had no say regarding their conditions of work. Through union organizations, the laborer can control the working conditions on his immediate job much more than could the individual employee under the thumb of the factory-owner or foreman. Similarly, the development of political democracy, which was concomitant with the growth of industrialization, has given the common man a say in political decisions.

TECHNOLOGY AND DEMOCRACY

Some sacrifice of unbridled individualism is necessary if men are to live together. By requiring an increasing division of labor, technology has made compulsory some form of co-operation and understanding among human beings in order to carry on the productive process. If each worker were to follow his own bent, he might not awaken until noon or he might decide to go fishing instead of going to work; in either case, the production line would cease to function.

It is possible, however, that the rigid discipline of the production process is now becoming a thing of the past. The automatic factory, requiring scarcely any workers, is on the verge of making the assembly line, and the industrial discipline associated with it, obsolete. In other words, the discipline imposed by the assembly line might be regarded only as a temporary stage of industrialization; we have now passed that stage, and in place of making people work instead of going fishing, we may possibly be faced with the even more difficult problem of getting society to accept the idea that everyone *should* be out fishing.

The real problem of man's freedom in relation to technology has thus completely changed face. It is no longer a question of whether the machine enslaves man—for it is now abundantly clear that the machine can liberate man from onerous tasks and degrading labor; the problem becomes one of whether or not man can handle the new freedom which has come to him through technology. Looked at from the long-range perspective of history, we might say that mankind has passed from the tyranny of nature through that of the machine into an era of true freedom, all of which has been made possible through technological advance. Nevertheless, traditional habits and attitudes make us look askance at the new freedom from toil which the machine has granted us, and we begin to look back with longing to the old conditions of work which we sought to escape.

There is yet another way in which technology has reinforced the power of the group against that of the individual. Almost from the beginning of human history, warfare has been intimately related to technology. To the extent that technology has made warfare more complex and more costly, it has helped to increase the power of the state. A strong state need not necessarily be undemocratic, however.

Throughout antiquity, in Egypt, Mesopotamia, Greece, and Rome, manual labor was largely done by slaves, who were considered as property and had few—if any—rights as individuals. In the Middle Ages windmills and water wheels eased the burden somewhat, but the serfs, who were numerically the largest group in the population, still possessed few rights, and those only by virtue of the custom associated with their plots of land, not as individuals. Although the decline of manorialism and feudalism loosened the bonds of serfdom, not until the political and social revolutions of the 17th and 18th centuries was the idea accepted that each individual possesses certain inalienable rights and that societies should be directed toward the guarantee and maintenance of those "natural" rights.

At the same time that the state was being organized in behalf of the individual, great technological changes, which we lump together under the term Industrial Revolution, were also taking place. In changing the productive mechanism, the Industrial Revolution also transformed the individual's way of life and therefore the conditions of all society. Technology made possible modern industrial society, which provided the conditions for contemporary democracy.

We can see the democratizing force of technology at work in many different ways. For example, the machine is color-blind; it does not care whether the hand which operates it is black, yellow, or white. Proof of this democratic impact of advancing technologies can be seen in the progress toward integration in the southern United States. The development of a new industrial South has created tensions between the old and the new order, yet it is slowly but inexorably bringing an end to inequality. This situation is not peculiar to the United States; the demands of a modern industrialized society in India have breached the caste system in many places.

Moreover, the advance of technology among our "people of plenty" is closing the great gap between the rich and the poor. All but the poorest in our economy of abundance can enjoy much the same amusements, foods, clothing, and transportation.

MAN, NATURE, AND THE MACHINE

Another type of freedom is broadened by advancing technology. Man is no longer dependent upon the weather and has been spared many of the rigors of natural catastrophes. A drought in the Midwest or a frost in Florida will not greatly affect our food supplies—we have ample reserves, methods for preserving food, and means to ship in food from elsewhere. In the winter our homes are heated, and in the summer they are air-conditioned; we no longer have to conform to the vagaries of the weather.

Technology has also freed man from back-breaking tasks. In work such as mining, a great many operations have been mechanized to remove much of the most arduous labor. And in certain factories, human manual labor has been taken over almost completely by machines. While the use of machines to relieve the worker from strenuous physical labor has been universally applauded—except by those who might be thrown out of work by such rationalization of production—there have been severe objections to the automation of "brain power"; that is, when technology begins to take the burdens off man's mind as well as off his back. Such criticism forgets that much so-called mental work is really repetitious, boring, and enervating.

Actually, automation requires an upgrading of the work force. There is no longer room for the unskilled laborer, for the machine has taken over his job. People of limited horizons, faint ambitions, and inferior capabilities cannot perform the sophisticated tasks which modern technological society demands of them. Besides, machines will no more destroy human imagination and creativity than did the invention of photography in the 19th century mean the end of painters, or the invention of the bicycle or the automobile, long-distance runners, or the phonograph, live musicians.

TECHNOLOGY, LITERATURE AND THE ARTS

Does advancing technology really have a deleterious effect on imagination and creativity in literature and the arts? Ever since the Industrial Revolution artists, composers, and writers have attacked technology for demeaning aesthetic appreciation and artistic creativity. Yet, when one looks at the arts in the 19th century—when society was coming under the sway of industrial technology—one finds riches in poetry, art, and music. The 20th century has also witnessed a flowering in all the arts.

Once we realize that technology is not inherently inimical to the arts, we find two constructive ways in which technology has contributed to the human need for aesthetic creation. The first is that technology has created more time and leisure for the cultivation of the arts by a larger segment of society; the second is that there are certain aesthetic elements within technology itself.

Until the Industrial Revolution, literature and the arts were virtually an aristocratic monopoly. Today more people are able to engage in aesthetic and intellectual activities, transforming these from the property of a select few to the heritage of all. Mass culture has become possible, in addition, by means of technical advances—long-playing records, art reproductions available at low cost, paperbound books, and television and movies, the latter two representing new art forms developed through technology. Although critics might claim that the taste of "mass culture" is debased, the fact is that technology has provided the means whereby public taste may be elevated.

Although many of the items mass produced are not beautiful, there are certain aesthetic qualities within technology itself. This is particularly so when aesthetic elements are judged in terms of functional design. The mathematical precision and symmetry which characterize our most advanced designs are indeed works of art. Although these may not correspond to the artistic standards set by earlier critics, the sleek, functional lines of modern products have already made themselves felt. The creation of new art forms derived from advances in technology is a challenge for the future; our own time has witnessed only the beginning experiments.

STRIKING A BALANCE

Technology has produced many paradoxes. It has quickened transportation and communication, which can bring men closer together; yet men can meet together more readily only to quarrel more frequently, and the faster, more efficient means of communications can be used to spread hatred rather than goals of peaceful co-operation.

On balance, modern technology has given man, to a great extent, control over his own activities, and therefore, presumably, over his own destiny. In some areas this has worked an unmixed blessing; in agriculture, for example, the use of machinery combined with scientific knowledge has produced abundance in some areas of the world, and shipping and storage developments have allowed that area to share its surplus with others far removed. Furthermore, this miracle of production has taken place in a relatively small proportion of the world's arable land, so that the possibility of future extension is bright.

In other areas, the results have not been so happy. At the beginning of the century, military innovators covered over their success with the confident claim that by making war increasingly horrible they were making it increasingly unthinkable, and therefore, impossible. The carnage of World War I made this optimism unfashionable for thirty years, until the formation of the current concept of the "balance of terror." The prospect of massive nuclear annihilation may have helped prevent international warfare among the major powers since the end of World War II, but it has certainly not prevented aggression or "minor" wars, and there is no guarantee that it will continue to prevent world catastrophe in the future.

The ambivalence of technological change is shown by two other major developments during this century. First, there has been a rationalization of our lives, a wider application of the scientific method based on systematically gathered and verified *facts*. Second, this dependence on facts has led to the growing importance of those who can understand and act upon these facts; in short, the technical expert. Since experts, almost by definition, are fewer in number than non-experts, and since it is efficient to reduce categories and decisions to a minimum, this concentration of experts has led also to a centralization of expertise and therefore of power.

These two developments should not be deplored. Very few people would say that we should not know the facts of a case or that the facts ought not to govern. Neither can it be maintained that the tendency to centralize policy-making is without benefits. Nevertheless, it should certainly be admitted that these are mixed blessings, and every effort should be made to maximize their good and minimize their bad tendencies.

The field of conservation affords one of the best examples of the dependence on scientific fact. In one country after another, first in the Old World, then in the New, scientists and engineers began to realize that the method of exploiting resources, based upon private profits and short-term interests, was wasteful and extremely destructive. Late in the 19th century, government scientists in the United States attempted to find a new method: one based upon the gathering and the analysis of facts and the formulation of development plans consistent with those facts. The result has been the steady accumulation of data which, in turn, form a basis for regulating resource use in behalf of the community, both for the present and future.

The economies that come from taking advantage of research and development are one more example of the old saying, "the rich grow richer." Since 1952 American industries, already strengthened by the economy of the home market, have massively invaded the European field. Between 1952 and 1963, American investment increased by a factor of 5: to $4.1 billion in the European automobile and aviation-equipment industries; $2.8 billion in petroleum; $2 billion in chemicals; $2 billion in non-electrical machinery; $1.5 billion in electrical machinery; and $1.3 billion in food products.

At the same time, European industries are becoming increasingly dependent upon licenses to use American patents, rather than investing in research and development themselves. When European investments and markets in the United States are considered, it is obvious that a transatlantic community of technological interest is rapidly expanding. Such a community, of course, has existed at least since the Industrial Revolution, for no nation has ever been successful in keeping its technological secrets from others. The important fact is, however, that this interdependence is becoming greater and, of equal importance, is increasing the distance between the already technologically advanced nations and those less developed.

THE CONTROL OF TECHNOLOGY

Technology per se can be regarded as either good or bad, depending on the use which man makes of it. Lynn White has said, "Technology opens doors, it does not compel men to enter." Basic to White's position is the view of technology as a means, which man is free to employ as he sees fit. Nuclear power provides a good example, for the power within the atom can be used for constructive or destructive purposes, as man chooses.

However, a different view of the moral neutrality of technology might emphasize the constraints it places upon human choice rather than the freedom of decision which White stresses. Employing another metaphor, we may say that technology builds a bridge. It is a rigid structure, going from point A to point B. The rigidity of the bridge restricts man before he sets foot on it; he can go only from point A to point B on that bridge. On the other hand, the bridge enables him to go from point A to point B, a journey which might otherwise have been impossible for him to take.

It is not always easy to distinguish between means and ends, and there is always the possibility that means become ends in themselves. Man is not compelled to enter Dr. White's open door, but an open door is an invitation. Who determines which door to open? And who can foretell exactly what lies behind the opened door?

Technology may be ambivalent, but it does not exist in the abstract; it exists in society, and it exists to meet human and social goals. Part of the trouble arises from the fact that in fulfilling certain goals, technology creates new problems which seem to run counter to other goals. For example, in providing for man's material wants, technology has produced an economy of abundance which apparently fosters a materialistic outlook. While liberating man from the constant struggle against nature for his existence, technology has also limited the freedom of the individual in behalf of the collective nature of production and distribution; in giving man leisure for artistic and literary pursuits, technology may have produced a quantitative set of values inimical to aesthetic appreciation. While providing an abundance of material goods which man might share with less fortunate neighbors, technology has also made possible the exploitation of man by his fellow man. And demanding on the one hand, societal living to fulfill technological requirements, technology has also given man the capability of destroying society.

Can technology assist in the solution of the problems which it has helped to create? There is no doubt that many problems can be solved by the application of more technology. For example, scientific technology has made it possible for more people to live longer on the face of the earth. The "population explosion" requires food and the satisfaction of other material wants—just the kind of problem that our contemporary technology is well equipped to solve. The same may be said about other problems, such as water resources, air pollution, and traffic congestion. Modern technology has a capacity for the constructive solution or alleviation of all these problems, which in some ways it has helped to produce. In such cases technology is part culprit, part victim—and part rescuer.

Many of the problems and ills of our society are not the fault of technology at all. They are the results of an improper and unwise use of technology, caused frequently by human greed, stupidity, or short-sightedness. These are human ills, and technology can only help abate them; social inventions are necessary if we are to resolve them.

Man has always used tools, and for an equally long time tools have influenced the evolution of man and his social structure. To say that technology is a major determinant of our age, therefore, is not to name a new influence on mankind. It must be stressed, however, that the coupling of science with technology—the rise of scientific agriculture, atomic energy, space travel, as well as in Scientific Management and systems analysis—has greatly widened the range of what man may accomplish.

However one judges the problem, technology lies at the center of the 20th century and its dilemmas. In three major areas it defines the boundaries of the possible and offers both the rewards for success and ghastly penalty for failure: the overriding concern for peace, the rising demand from exploited peoples all over the world (and here at home) for justice, and the need to close the gap between the material abundance supplied by technology and the want which still besets the lives of most of the world's people. Without social justice there can be no peace; without the development of technology which creates abundance there is not likely to be social justice; and without peace we are unlikely to concentrate on the technologies appropriate for peace.

This does not mean that there is no hope; it is to say that our major problems are related and intimately intertwined with the existence and state of various technologies. Nor does it mean that the ends and means are identical. Technique is not a substitute for a policy, but technology is necessary for the implementation of policies. Although one may question whether man has the *will* to survive, it cannot be questioned that he possesses the *way*. While the study of the past does not prove that man's progress is necessarily guaranteed, the study of the history of technology does reveal that the possibility of progress is always present in human affairs. It shows us how the human mind and hand can solve complex, disturbing problems and contribute to man's betterment. Technology thus gives us hope that other problems may be conquered by the use of reason, ingenuity, and imagination.

Readings and References

The fact that technology lies very close to the center of the modern human condition has not escaped the notice of many social critics and apologists. Since no listing of such books could possibly be comprehensive, the titles given below are designed merely to direct the interested student to a few of the best and most useful works in the hope that he will then be led deeper into the subject. In order to keep the bibliography within reasonable bounds, nearly all of the non-English works have been excluded. Attention is focused on the most accessible works, hopefully, those readily available in college and public libraries. In addition to the books listed here, several specialized periodicals contain articles of importance, among them *Technology and Culture, Transactions of the Newcomen Society,* and the *Journal of Industrial Archaeology,* the last two of which are English publications. Occasional articles on aspects of the history of technology appear in *Isis, Business History Review, Journal of Economic History, Economic History Review, Chymia, Minerva,* and many others.

Technology in the 20th Century

One of the most thoughtful of recent books on the general problem of 20th-century technological development (Chapters 1, 2, 3, 45), by a distinguished historian is Elting E. Morison, *Men, Machines, and Modern Times* (Cambridge, Mass., 1966). No serious student of the human impact of machine civilization can afford to ignore Lewis Mumford's classic work, *Technics and Civilization* (New York, 1934, paperbound edn. 1963), and his most recent study, *The Myth of the Machine: Technics and Human Development* (New York, 1967), with its animadversions against the "megamachine." In addition, two special volumes have attempted to bring together scattered papers on the subject: Charles R. Walker (ed.), *Modern Technology and Civilization: An Introduction to Human Problems in the Machine Age* (New York, 1962) covers a wide variety of subjects in its selections, while John Burke (ed.), *The New Technology and Human Values* (Belmont, Calif., 1966) is shorter and more integrated.

A number of conferences have been held on this general subject, and the following volumes record the results of several. One is the "Encyclopaedia Britannica Conference on the Technological Order," *Technology and Culture,* III (Fall, 1962), 381-658. This has been published in a hardbound edition, Carl F. Stover (ed.), *The Technological Order* (Detroit, 1963). The Columbia University Seminar on Technology and Social Change has produced three volumes: Eli Ginzberg (ed.), *Technology and Social Change* (New York, 1964); Aaron W. Warner, Dean Morse, and Alfred S. Eichner (eds.), *The Impact of Science and Technology* (New York, 1965); and Dean Morse and Aaron W. Warner (eds.), *Technological Innovation and Society* (New York, 1966). Unique because of its wide coverage and quasi-official source is the Report of the National Commission on Technology, Automation, and Economic Progress, *Technology and the American Economy* (Washington, D.C., 1966), which is supported by six staff studies in depth of such problems as "Adjusting to Change" (Vol. III) and "Applying Technology to Unmet Needs" (Vol. V).

The imaginative literature of the 20th century has by no means ignored the machine and its effect upon man. Among the many works which have greatly influenced our thinking is the play *R.U.R.* (Rossum's Universal Robots) written by the Czech author Karel Čapek, a work which gave us the word "robot." The play, available in an Oxford Press paperback edition, was first published in 1923. Probably better known, and indeed often taken as models of the anti-utopian novel in the 20th century, are Aldous Huxley, *Brave New World,* and George Orwell, *1984,* both available in paperback editions. The whole genre of science fiction—characteristic of though not limited to the 20th century—has been surveyed several times, but never more interestingly than in Kingsley Amis, *New Maps of Hell* (New York, 1960).

The existence of "two cultures" (Chapter 44) has often been noticed, but the classic statement is, of course, that of C. P. Snow in his widely read and discussed *The Two Cultures and the Scientific Revolution* (1959), published as a paperback with an addendum entitled *The Two Cultures: and a Second Look* (New York, 1964). The commentaries on Snow's views are legion, but the most vigorous—and indeed abusive—has been F. R. Leavis, *Two Cultures? The Significance of C. P. Snow* (London, 1962). The interactions of science and society in the modern age may be sampled in two volumes of collected articles: Bernard Barber and Walter Hirsch (eds.), *The Sociology of Science* (Glencoe, Ill., 1962) and Norman Kaplan (ed.), *Science and Society* (Chicago, 1965).

Organization and Rationalization

The concept of efficiency of production, workers, and management, will forever be associated with the name of Frederick W. Taylor. The standard biography is still Frank Barkley Copley, *Frederick Winslow Taylor* (2 vols., New York, 1923). Taylor's major ideas are best conveyed in his very readable *The Principles of Scientific Management* (New York, 1911); a wider range of his comments are collected in Frederick W. Taylor, *Scientific Management: Comprising Shop Management, The Principles of Scientific Management, Testimony before the Special House Committee* (New York, 1947). Usable biographies of major Taylor disciples are L. P. Alford, *Henry Laurence Gantt: Leader in Industry* (New York, 1934) and Edna Yost, *Frank and Lillian Gilbreth: Partners for Life* (New Brunswick, 1949). The best intellectual study of the subject is Samuel Haber, *Efficiency and Uplift: Scientific Management in the Progressive Era, 1890-1920* (Chicago, 1964).

The most comprehensive general studies of the growth of mass production (Chapter 4) are Roger Burlingame, *Backgrounds of Power* (New York, 1949) and Sigfried Giedion, *Mechanization Takes Command* (New York, 1948). For the introduction of assembly-line production in the automobile industry the most authoritative source is Allan Nevins, with the collaboration of Frank E. Hill, *Ford, The Times, the Man, the Company* (Vol. I, New York, 1954). Briefer accounts are Christy Borth, *Masters of Mass Production* (Indianapolis, 1950), Roger Burlingame, *Henry Ford: A Great Life in Brief* (New York, 1955), and John B. Rae, *American Automobile Manufacturers. The First Forty Years* (Philadelphia, 1959).

The best account of the rationalization of production in the extractive industries is Harold A. Barger and Sam H. Schurr, *The Mining Industries, 1899-1939* (New York, 1944). The effect of the power excavator on mining technology is well treated in Harold F. Williamson and Kenneth H. Myers, II, *Designed for Digging* (Evanston, Ill., 1955). Warren C. Scoville, *Revolution in Glassmaking* (Cambridge, Mass., 1948) is the authoritative account of the coming of mass production to the glass industry.

It is impossible, of course, to separate management (Chapter 5) completely from other factors discussed in many chapters, but in addition to books listed elsewhere, one may turn to Adam Abruzzi, *Work Measurement: New Principles and Procedures* (New York, 1952) and Ernest J. McCormick, *Human Factors Engineering* (New York, 1964). Interrelations with the worker are particularly considered in Fritz J. Roethlisberger and William J. Dickson, *Management and the Worker* (Cambridge, Mass., 1940), Victor H. Vroom, *Work and Motivation* (New York, 1964), Charles R. Walker and Robert H. Guest, *The Man on the Assembly Line* (Cambridge, Mass., 1952), and Thomas North Whitehead, *The Industrial Worker* (Cambridge, Mass., 1938).

More general considerations include Daniel Bell, *The End of Ideology* (Glencoe, Ill., 1960) and Robert Blauner, *Alienation and Freedom* (Chicago, 1964). An excellent collection of essays will be found in Charles R. Walker, *Modern Technology and Civilization* (New York, 1962). Raymond E. Callahan, *Edu-*

cation and the Cult of Efficiency (Chicago, 1962) covers the application of managerial techniques to the public schools in the United States. Loren Baritz, *The Servants of Power: A History of Social Sciences in American Industry* (Middletown, Conn., 1960) is a provocative account of one method adopted by management in industrial relations.

On labor (Chapter 6) the reader should turn first to Milton J. Nadworny, *Scientific Management and the Unions* (Cambridge, Mass., 1955). An early appraisal is given in Robert F. Hoxie, *Scientific Management and Labor* (New York, 1915), and a description of what happened in one shop is given in Hugh G. J. Aitken, *Taylorism at Watertown Arsenal* (Cambridge, Mass., 1960). William Gomberg, *A Trade Union Analysis of Time Study* (2nd edn., Englewood Cliffs, 1955) offers yet another perspective.

Also focusing on unions are Jack Barbash, *The Practice of Unionism* (New York, 1956), particularly chapters VII-IX, and Sumner H. Slichter, *Union Policies and Industrial Management* (Washington, D.C., 1941). Broader consideration is given in Conrad Arensberg *et al.* (eds.), *Research in Industrial Human Relations* (New York, 1957), Richard A. Beaumont and Roy B. Helfgott, *Management, Automation and People* (New York, 1964), E. M. Hugh-Jones (ed.), *Human Relations and Modern Management* (Amsterdam, 1958), Clark Kerr *et al.*, *Industrialism and Industrial Man* (Cambridge, Mass., 1960), Gerald Somers *et al.* (eds.), *Adjusting to Technological Change* (New York, 1963), and Thomas G. Spates, *Human Relations Where People Work* (New York, 1960). Two works treating collective bargaining specifically are Sumner H. Slichter *et al.*, *The Impact of Collective Bargaining on Management* (Washington, D.C., 1960) and Industrial Union Department, AFL-CIO, *Conference on Industrial Engineering Problems and Collective Bargaining Policy* (Washington, D.C., May 27-28, 1957).

The literature on distribution and marketing (Chapter 7) is vast. General historical studies include Harold Barger, *Distribution's Place in the American Economy since 1869* (Princeton, 1955), John William Ferry, *A History of the Department Store* (New York, 1960), Godfrey M. Lebhar, *Chain Stores in America, 1859-1950* (New York, 1952), and Malcolm P. McNair and Eleanor G. May, *The American Department Store, 1920-1960* (Boston, 1963). The country store of the southern United States is discussed in Thomas D. Clark, *Pills, Petticoats and Plows* (Indianapolis, 1944). Individual firms are treated in Boris Emmet and John E. Jeuck, *Catalogues and Counters: A History of Sears, Roebuck and Company* (Chicago, 1950) and Ralph M. Hower, *History of Macy's of New York, 1858-1919* (Cambridge, Mass., 1943). The literature on supermarkets includes the Loewy Report to the Super Market Institute, *Super Markets of the Sixties* (Chicago, 1960), Rom J. Markin, *The Supermarket: An Analysis of Growth, Development, and Change* (Pullman, Wash.,

1963), and M. M. Zimmerman, *The Super Market: A Revolution in Distribution* (New York, 1955).

Transportation is traced in Harold Barger, *The Transportation Industries 1889-1946: A Study of Output, Employment, and Productivity* (New York, 1951) and the history of one particular line is told in Wayne Broehl, *Trucks, Trouble and Triumph: The Norwalk Truck Line Company* (New York, 1954). Wilfred Owen, *Automotive Transportation: Trends and Problems* (Washington, D.C., 1949) is also useful.

One fairly recent technique for studying these problems is given in Robert D. Buzzell, *Mathematical Models and Marketing Management* (Boston, 1964), while political factors are treated in Daniel Bloomfield (ed.), *Chain Stores and Legislation* (New York, 1939) and Joseph C. Palamountain, Jr., *The Politics of Distribution* (Cambridge, Mass., 1955). Several other useful works of an economic or descriptive nature are Richard M. Clewett (ed.), *Marketing Channels for Manufactured Products* (Homewood, Ill., 1954), Reavis Cox, *The Economics of Installment Buying* (New York, 1948), Victor Gruen and Larry Smith, *Shopping Towns, U.S.A.* (New York, 1960), George Sternlieb, *The Future of the Downtown Department Store* (Cambridge, Mass., 1962), and E. B. Weiss, *Management and the Marketing Revolution* (New York, 1964). The problems of agricultural products are surveyed in the USDA, *Marketing: The Yearbook of Agriculture, 1954* (Washington, D.C., 1954).

The material consequences and attendant phenomena of mass production (Chapter 8) are touched upon in virtually every serious book on the human condition in the 20th century. General works include Adolf Berle, *The American Economic Republic* (New York, 1963), and three books by Robert Theobald, *The Challenge of Abundance* (paperback edn., New York, 1962), *Free Men and Free Markets* (New York, 1963), and *The Rich and the Poor: A Study of Rising Expectations* (paperback edn., New York, 1961). Milton Friedman, *Capitalism and Freedom* (Chicago, 1962) is a conservative appraisal, and Marshall McLuhan, *Understanding Media* (New York, 1964) is a provocative work of wide influence.

One of the most important books of the postwar period has been J. K. Galbraith, *The Affluent Society* (Boston, 1958), a work of great insight, literary grace, and wide audience. A less optimistic answer to Galbraith was given in Michael Harrington, *The Other America: Poverty in the United States* (paperback edn., Baltimore, 1963), a work of great humanity which is given much of the credit for the concern evidenced in the War on Poverty. On this same score one should read Gunner Myrdal, *Challenge to Affluence* (New York, 1963) and Robert Theobald (ed.), *The Guaranteed Income* (New York, 1966). A forceful if pessimistic statement about the fate of human values in the modern world is made in Jacques Ellul, *The Technological Society* (New York, 1964).

Some of the doubts expressed by Ellul were also discussed by a "father" of the computer, Norbert Wiener in *The Human Use of Human Beings* (Boston, 1958).

It is often impossible to disentangle the social (Chapter 9) from the material consequences of mass production, so that for this subject one should consult works already cited—those of Bell, Galbraith, Harrington, Walker, and Guest. Especially recommended is Robert Blauner, *Alienation and Freedom: The Factory Worker and His Industry* (Chicago, 1964), which compares the influence of mass-production technologies, especially on workers. On this same subject the reader will benefit from Charles R. Walker, *Toward the Automatic Factory: A Case Study of Men and Machines* (New Haven, 1957) and Georges Friedmann, *Industrial Society: The Emergence of the Human Problems of Automation* (Glencoe, Ill., 1955). Two general studies by Elton Mayo are *The Human Problems of Industrial Civilization* (New York, 1933) and *The Social Problems of Industrial Civilization* (Boston, 1946).

Books also recommended include Robert H. Guest, *Organizational Change: The Effect of Successful Leadership* (Homewood, Ill., 1962), J. G. March and H. A. Simon, *Organization* (New York, 1958), Douglas McGregor, *The Human Side of Enterprise* (New York, 1960), F. J. Roethlisberger, *Management and Morale* (Cambridge, Mass., 1947), Arthur N. Turner and Paul R. Lawrence, *Industrial Jobs and the Worker* (Cambridge, Mass., 1946), and A. Zaleznik *et al.*, *The Motivation, Productivity, and Satisfaction of Workers* (Boston, 1958).

Industrial Research

The history of industrial research (Chapter 40) has until recently been a much neglected field. A valuable book on the European aspects of this topic is John J. Beer, *The Emergence of the German Dye Industry* (Urbana, 1959). A pioneering account of American activities, to which subsequent students have been much indebted, is Howard R. Bartlett, "The Development of Industrial Research in the United States," in National Resources Planning Board, *Research—A National Resource* (Washington, D.C., 1941), Part II, pp. 19-77. On various 20th-century developments an especially useful work is John Jewkes, David Sawers, and Richard Stillerman, *The Sources of Invention* (New York, 1961), containing case histories of numerous research achievements. Material on recent accomplishments is also provided in John R. Pierce and Arthur R. Tressler, *The Research State: A History of Science in New Jersey* (Princeton, 1964). The relationship of the United States government to applied science is explored in A. Hunter Dupree, *Science in the Federal Government: A History of Policies and Activities to 1940* (Cambridge, Mass., 1957). Some general historical perspectives, as well as information on contemporary trends in industrial research, are provided in John J. Beer and W. David Lewis, "Aspects of the Professionalization of Science," *Daedalus* (Fall, 1963), 764-84, and in Donald A. Schon, *Technology and Change* (New York, 1967). Of central importance is Jacob Schmookler, *Invention and Economic Growth* (Cambridge, Mass., 1966), the long-awaited study by a distinguished and influential economist.

The application of science in specific fields of American enterprise needs more scholarly attention than has thus far been devoted to it. Technical developments in the electrical industry, however, have been treated in a number of works, of which the following are particularly valuable: Kendall Birr, *Pioneering in Industrial Research: The Story of the General Electric Research Laboratory* (Washington, D.C., 1957); Malcolm MacLaren, *The Rise of the Electrical Industry during the Nineteenth Century* (Princeton, 1943); and Harold C. Passer's outstanding volume, *The Electrical Manufacturers, 1875-1900* (Cambridge, Mass., 1953). A good study of the interaction of science, technology, and business in the field of communications is W. Rupert Maclaurin, *Invention and Innovation in the Radio Industry* (New York, 1949). Frederick A. White's *American Industrial Research Laboratories* (Washington, D.C., 1961) is a misnamed book, being a study in the development of scientific instrumentation during the 20th century. Within its field, however, it is an authoritative work. A concise essay on this whole problem is Kendall Birr, "Science in American Industry," *Science and Society in the United States*, edited by David D. Van Tassel and Michael G. Hall (Homewood, Ill., 1966), pp. 35-80.

For information on various individuals important in the history of American industrial research, students should especially consult the numerous brief biographical accounts of eminent chemists, physicists, engineers, and inventors in the *Dictionary of American Biography* (20 vols. and Index, New York, 1928-1937), with two supplementary volumes issued in 1944 and 1958. The following books, which vary in quality, also deal with specific noteworthy persons: Thomas A. Boyd, *Professional Amateur: The Biography of Charles Franklin Kettering* (New York, 1957), John T. Broderick, *Willis Rodney Whitney: Pioneer of Industrial Research* (Albany, 1945), John W. Hammond, *Charles Proteus Steinmetz: A Biography* (New York, 1924), Matthew Josephson, *Edison* (New York, 1959), Henry G. Prout, *A Life of George Westinghouse* (New York, 1922), Frederick L. Rhodes, *John J. Carty: An Appreciation* (New York, 1932), and David O. Woodbury, *Beloved Scientist: Elihu Thomson, A Guiding Spirit of the Electrical Age* (New York, 1944). Also valuable in this regard, especially for the presidential addresses it contains, is a *Memorial Volume Commemorative of the Life and Life-Work of Charles Benjamin Dudley, Ph.D.* (Philadelphia, 1911), issued by the American Society for Testing Materials. A biography of C.E.K. Mees is much needed, but his ideas can be studied in his own works, such as *The Organization of Industrial Scientific Research* (New York, 1920), *The Path of Science* (New York, 1946), and

From Dry Plates to Ektachrome Film: A Story of Photographic Research (New York, 1961).

Statistical information on the development of industrial research in the United States during the 1930's is available in compact form in George Perazich and Philip M. Field, *Industrial Research and Changing Technology*, Report No. M-4, Works Project Administration, National Research Project (Philadelphia, 1940). Although this information is not entirely reliable, it is important to note that it actually underestimates the size of the national industrial research effort during this period. For statistical data on trends since World War II, see particularly Fritz Machlup, *The Production and Distribution of Knowledge in the United States* (Princeton, 1962), pp. 157-58, and the annual reports on *Funds for Research and Development in Industry*, published by the National Science Foundation.

Transportation

For information on automobiles and trucks (Chapter 10), one may turn to the volumes by Nevins and Hill, Borth, Burlingame, and Rae listed above. There are two additional volumes by Nevins and Hill, *Ford, Expansion and Challenge, 1915-1933* (Vol. II, 1957), and *Ford, Decline and Rebirth, 1933-1962* (Vol. III, 1963). An excellent reference book is *Automobiles of America*, compiled by the American Automobile Association (Detroit, 1962). The Selden patent case is analyzed in detail in William Greenleaf, *Monopoly on Wheels: Henry Ford and the Selden Automobile Patent* (Detroit, 1961). An excellent analytical study of organizational problems in the automobile industry is Alfred D. Chandler, Jr., *Giant Enterprise* (New York, 1964). Two pioneers of the industry are discussed in Wilfred C. Leland and Minnie Dubbs Millbrook, *Master of Precision: Henry M. Leland* (Detroit, 1966) and Glenn A. Niemeyer, *The Automotive Career of Ransom E. Olds* (East Lansing, 1963).

European automotive history can be studied in L. T. C. Rolt, *Horseless Carriage: The Motor Car in England* (London, 1950), E. Diesel, G. Goldbeck, and F. Schildberger, *From Engines to Autos* (Chicago, 1962), and G. Maxey and A. Silbertson, *The Motor Industry* (London, 1959). A reliable and readily accessible source of information on highway development is Ross M. Robertson, *History of the American Economy* (2nd edn., New York, 1964), Chapter 19. Philip P. Mason, *A History of American Roads* (Chicago, 1967) is a brief survey of the subject from colonial times to the present.

On rail and water transport (Chapter 11), one may consult Harold Barger, *The Transportation Industries 1889-1946* (New York, 1951). General works include William W. Hay, *An Introduction to Transportation Engineering* (New York, 1961) and Lewis K. Sillcox, *Mastering Momentum* (New York, 1941). For the railroads, John F. Stover, *American Railroads* (Chicago, 1961) is the standard brief account. This may be supplemented by Cecil J. Allen, *Locomotive Practice and Performance in the Twentieth Century* (Cambridge, 1949), Robert Selph Henry, *Trains* (New York, 1957), Ralph P. Johnson, *The Steam Locomotive* (New York, 1942), and Walter A. Lucas, *Locomotives and Cars Since 1900* (New York, 1959). The story of one line is given in Merle Armitage, *Operations Santa Fe* (New York, 1948). Three volumes are particularly good for maritime transportation: C. F. H. Cufley, *Ocean Freights and Chartering* (London, 1962), Laurence Dunn, *The World's Tankers* (London, 1956), and the older Robert Riegel, *Merchant Vessels* (New York, 1941).

For the development of the airplane (Chapter 12) one should begin with Marvin W. McFarland (ed.), *The Papers of Wilbur and Orville Wright* (2 vols., New York, 1953). The efforts of Alexander Bell and Casey Baldwin are traced in J. H. Parker, *Bell and Baldwin: Their Development of Aerodromes and Hydrodromes at Baddeck, Nova Scotia* (Toronto, 1964). For another pioneer read James Howard Means, *James Means and the Problem of Manflight during the Period 1882-1920*, Smithsonian Publication 4526 (Washington, D.C., 1964). A handsomely illustrated volume is *The American Heritage History of Flight* (New York, 1962). Something of the excitement that marked the early years of aviation may be gotten from Charles A. Lindbergh, *The Spirit of St. Louis* (New York, 1953). American military craft may be studied in F. G. Swanborough, *United States Military Aircraft since 1909* (New York, 1963), and various problems are covered in a book by a leading scientist, Theodore Von Kármán, *Aerodynamics: Selected Topics in the Light of their Historical Development* (Ithaca, 1954). Other useful books include Henry L. Smith, *Airways: The History of Commercial Aviation in the United States* (New York, 1942) and Edgar B. Schieldrop, *The Air* (New York, 1958).

For developments outside the United States see Henry L. Smith, *Airways Abroad* (Madison, 1950) and Charles H. Gibbs-Smith, *The Aeroplane* (London, 1960). A popular history of the support given to research by the United States government is George W. Gray, *Frontiers of Flight: The Story of NACA Research* (New York, 1948) and a special aspect may be traced in Robert Schlaifer and S. D. Heron, *Development of Aircraft Engines and Aviation Fuels: Two Studies of Relations between Government and Business* (Cambridge, Mass., 1950). Something on lighter-than-air craft may be gained from John Toland, *Ships of the Sky: The Story of the Great Dirigibles* (New York, 1957) and Richard K. Smith, *The Airships Akron and Macon: Flying Aircraft Carriers of the United States Navy* (Annapolis, 1965). A particularly important work on the subject is Robin Higham, *The British Rigid Airship, 1908-1931: A Study in Weapons Policy* (London, 1961).

Materials and Construction

To study the problem of materials (Chapter 13) one must piece together the story from scattered and fugitive sources. No comprehensive history of industrial chemistry in the 20th century exists, but the story of the beginnings of the German industry is well told in John J. Beer, *The Emergence of the German Dye Industry* (Urbana, 1959) and William Haynes, *American Chemical Industry* (6 vols., New York, 1954) contains a vast amount of data on firms and personalities. A prolific popularizer of the heroic deeds of chemists, especially those associated with the "Chemurgic" movement, is Christy Borth, who has written, among other works, *Pioneers of Plenty: Modern Chemists and Their Works* (rev. edn., New York, 1942). The London *Journal of the Society of Chemical Industry* issued a special Jubilee Issue in 1931 and other periodicals in the trade have done likewise. Albrecht Schmidt, *Die industrielle Chemie . . . und Erinnerungen an ihren Aufbau* (Berlin, 1934) has long chapters on the history and development of special fields. For an early history of the German dye industry one may consult T. W. Delahanty, *The German Dyestuff Industry*, U. S. Department of Commerce, Misc. Series 126 (Washington, D.C., 1924).

On the construction and appointment of buildings (Chapters 14 and 15), one should begin with two books by Carl W. Condit, *American Building Art: The 20th Century* (New York, 1961) and *The Chicago School of Architecture* (Chicago, 1964). For information on any subject in this field one may consult Gerd Hatje (ed.), *Encyclopedia of Modern Architecture* (New York, 1964). A history aimed at broad coverage is Jürgen Joedicke, *A History of Modern Architecture* (New York, 1959). Two special aspects are covered by the same author in separate volumes: *Office Buildings* (New York, 1962) and *Shell Architecture* (New York, 1963). Also of particular importance are Robert E. Fischer, *New Structures* (New York, 1963), Leonard Michaels, *Contemporary Structures in Architecture* (New York, 1950), and Curt Siegel, *Structure and Form in Modern Architecture* (New York, 1962). Two useful works specifically on concrete building are the Portland Cement Association, *Cement and Concrete Reference Book* (Chicago, 1964) and Aly Ahmed Rafaat, *Reinforced Concrete in Architecture* (New York, 1958).

For both the construction of buildings and their fitting out (Chapter 15) one may turn to the standard work, James M. Fitch, *American Building: The Forces that Shape It* (Boston, 1948). A book cited elsewhere, which has had a great influence on this and other problems of technology, is Sigfried Giedion, *Mechanization Takes Command* (New York, 1948). On air conditioning see the biography of a leading advocate, Margaret Ingles, *Willis Haviland Carrier: Father of Air Conditioning* (Garden City, N.Y., 1952), and Willis H. Carrier,

"Progress in Air Conditioning in the Last Quarter Century," *Transactions of the American Society of Heating and Ventilating Engineers,* XLII (1936), 321-48.

Useful books on special topics include Vern O. Knudsen, *Architectural Acoustics* (New York, 1932), National Electrical Manufacturers Association, *A Chronological History of Electrical Development* (New York, 1946), Louis S. Nielsen, *Standard Plumbing Engineering Design* (New York, 1963), William T. O'Dea, *The Social History of Lighting* (London, 1958), and Lawrence Wright, *Clean and Decent* (London, 1960). A fine collection of relevant documents and incisive comment on the social and artistic context of housing in one critical period in American history is Roy Lubove, *The Urban Community: Housing and Planning in the Progressive Era* (Englewood Cliffs, 1967).

Energy

For the traditional sources of energy (Chapter 16) one should look first at S. H. Schurr, B. C. Netschert *et al., Energy in the American Economy, 1850-1975* (Baltimore, 1960). For petroleum the definitive classic is Harold F. Williamson *et al., The American Petroleum Industry: The Age of Energy, 1899-1959* (Evanston, 1963), which may be supplemented with the American Petroleum Institute's *History of Petroleum Engineering* (Dallas, 1961) and the "Diamond Jubilee of the Petroleum Industry" issue of the periodical *Oil & Gas Journal* (Aug. 27, 1934). A general study sponsored by the federal government was V. E. Spencer, *Production, Employment, and Productivity in the Mineral Extractive Industries, 1880-1938,* Works Project Administration, National Research Project Report No. S-2 (Philadelphia, 1940). J. M. Gould, *Output and Productivity in the Electric and Gas Utilities, 1899-1942* (New York, 1946) is standard for those firms. Electric power may be studied in Philip Sporn, "Growth and Development in the Electric Power Industry," *Electrical Engineering* (75th Anniversary Issue, May 1959), 542-55 and C. F. Wagner, "Electric Power Transmission," *Electrical Engineering,* the same issue, 581-8.

On atomic energy (Chapter 17), one should begin with the very excellent Richard G. Hewlett and Oscar E. Anderson, Jr., *The New World, 1939-1946,* Vol. I of *A History of the United States Atomic Energy Commission* (University Park, Pa., 1962). Alvin Glassner, *Introduction to Nuclear Science* (Princeton, 1961) provides an excellent summary of the basic technology of atomic energy and the scientist or engineer unfamiliar with atomic energy should consult John F. Hogerton, *Atomic Energy Deskbook* (New York, 1963). Henry D. Smyth, *Atomic Energy For Military Purposes* (Princeton, 1945) is the classic account of that subject published at the end of World War II. An analytical study of the economic factors involved in the development of nuclear power is Philip Mullenbach, *Civilian Nuclear Power: Economic Issues and Policy Formation* (New York, 1963). An interesting description of the Soviet atomic energy program pieced together from scattered reports and statements by Soviet scientists is Arnold Kramish, *Atomic Energy in the Soviet Union* (Stanford, 1959).

The beginning point for the future problems of energy (Chapter 18) is Schurr and Netschert, *Energy in the American Economy, 1850-1975*, listed above. *New Sources of Energy*, Proceedings of the United Nations Conference in New Sources of Energy of 1961 (New York, 1963), includes several volumes, with a large number of papers on wind, solar, and geothermal energy sources and processes for their use, particularly in the newly developing countries. A specific study is L. P. Gaucher, "Energy Sources for the Future for the United States," *Journal of Solar Energy*, IX (1965). Longer studies include M. K. Hubbert, *Energy Resources*, Publication 1000-D, National Academy of Sciences–National Research Council (Washington, D.C., 1962), P. C. Putnam, *Energy in the Future* (New York, 1953), and E. Ayres and C. A. Scarlott, *Energy Sources—The Wealth of the World* (New York, 1952). Farrington Daniels, *Direct Use of the Sun's Energy* (New Haven, 1964) is standard on that subject.

Communication and Information

The history of the radio and other electronic devices (Chapter 19) is not well covered in monographs. We are fortunate, indeed, in being able to start with an excellent general study, W. R. Maclaurin, *Invention and Innovation in the Radio Industry* (New York, 1949). Two works of general usefulness are Donald McNicol, *Radio's Conquest of Space* (New York, 1956) and C. F. J. Overhage (ed.), *The Age of Electronics* (New York, 1962). The helpful tradition of publishing historical material was carried on by the *Proceedings of the Institute of Radio Engineers*, L (May 1962), in their 50th anniversary issue. Useful information on the subject may be obtained from the Institute of Electrical Engineers, *Thermionic Valves, 1904-1954* (London, 1955), E. H. Armstrong, "Some Recent Developments in the Audion Receiver," *Proceedings of the IRE*, III (1915), 215-47, "Operating Features of the Audion," *Electrical World*, LXIV (1914), 1149-52, by the same author, and John A. Fleming, "How I Put Electronics to Work in the Radio Bottle," *Popular Radio* (March 1923), 176. One of the pioneers of radio tells his own story in Lee de Forest, *Father of Radio: The Autobiography of Lee de Forest* (Chicago, 1950). Another first person account aids our understanding of radar: Robert Morris Page, *The Origin of Radar* (Garden City, N.Y., 1962), a study by a Director of the Naval Research Laboratory in Washington, D.C. On the same subject see also I. A. Getting, "Radar," in C. F. J. Overhage's *Age of Electronics* cited above.

For ancient forerunners of calculating devices (Chapter 20) one may look at M. R. Cohen and I. E. Drabkin, *A Source Book in Greek Science* (Cambridge, Mass., 1958). An attempt to trace its development is Jeremy Bernstein, *The*

Analytical Engine: Computers, Past, Present, and Future (New York, 1964). For the most part, however, students of the computer seem more concerned with its future than its past. Still useful are W. J. Eckert and R. Jones, *Faster, Faster: A Simple Description of a Giant Electronic Calculator and the Problems It Solves* (New York, 1955), Martin Greenberger (ed.), *Computers and the World of the Future* (Cambridge, Mass., 1962), and Pierre de Latil, *Thinking by Machine: A Study of Cybernetics* (Boston, 1957). Other books worth consulting on the subject include Mortimer Taube, *Computers and Common Sense* (New York, 1961), Shirley Thomas, *Computers* (New York, 1965), M. V. Wilkes, *Automatic Digital Computers* (New York, 1957), and Dean E. Wooldridge, *The Machinery of the Brain* (New York, 1963).

On the subject of the social impact of mass media (Chapter 21), one might begin with the unconventional Marshall McLuhan, *Understanding Media: The Extensions of Man* (New York, 1964). More conventional approaches include Joseph T. Klapper, *The Effects of Mass Communications* (Glencoe, Ill., 1960) and Wilbur Schramm (ed.), *Mass Communications* (2nd edn., Urbana, 1960). A wide-ranging collection is Francis R. Allen *et al.* (eds.), *Technology and Social Change* (New York, 1957). Frank Luther Mott is standard for the subject of *American Journalism* (New York, 1947), and Robert C. Davis, *The Public Impact of Science in the Mass Media* (Ann Arbor, 1958) discusses the handling of one important subject.

On radio see Asa Briggs, *The History of Broadcasting in the United Kingdom*, especially Vol. II *The Golden Age of Wireless* (London, 1965), which covers the years 1927 to the outbreak of World War II. Television has been the subject of many books, among the most useful of which are Gary A. Steiner, *The People Look at Television* (New York, 1963), Gerald Beadle, *Television: A Critical Review* (London, 1963), and Raymond Williams, *Britain in the Sixties: Communications* (Baltimore, 1962). The spread of American television over the world is chronicled in Wilson P. Dizard, *Television: A World View* (New York, 1966). A stimulating critique is given in Daniel J. Boorstin, *The Image: A Guide to Pseudo-Events in America* (paperback edn., New York, 1964).

Agriculture and Food

The literature on agriculture, especially American agriculture, in the 20th century is very large but surprisingly only a small part of it is the work of historians, and they tend to emphasize political aspects of the subject. An excellent jumping off place is the *Yearbook of the United States Department of Agriculture: 1899* (Washington, D.C., 1900), which contains an overall contemporary view of the situation at the turn of the century. In more recent years these Yearbooks have concentrated on particular subjects: those for 1936 and 1937 are invaluable for discussions of genetics and its application to agriculture; that of 1947 covers the years of World War II and has material on plant- and animal-breeding and fertilizers; the 1957 Yearbook, *Soil*, has new material on fertilizers; and that for 1961, *Seed*, is excellent for plant hybridization. The Yearbook for 1962, *After a Hundred Years*, a centennial volume, contains material on a variety of subjects.

The official history of the United States Department of Agriculture in Gladys L. Baker *et al.*, *A Century of Service: The First 100 Years of the United States Department of Agriculture* (Washington, D.C., 1963). For federal-state relationships in research see H. C. Knoblauch *et al.*, *State Agricultural Experiment Stations: A History of Research Policy and Procedure*, USDA Misc. Pub. No. 904 (Washington, D.C., 1962). T. Swann Harding, *Two Blades of Grass: A History of Scientific Development in the U. S. Department of Agriculture* (Norman, Okla., 1947) is the standard history of the subject. A shorter and more recent guide is given in Reynold M. Wik, "Science and American Agriculture," *Science and Society in the United States*, edited by David D. Van Tassel and Michael G. Hall (Homewood, Ill., 1966), pp. 81-106. For bibliographic aid one must still rely on Everett E. Edwards, *A Bibliography of the History of Agriculture in the United States*, USDA Misc. Pub. No. 84 (Washington, D.C., 1930). The Agricultural History Center, University of California, Davis, Calif., is beginning a program to update Edwards: the first effort in that direction has been Carroll W. Pursell, Jr., and Earl M. Rogers (comps.), *A Preliminary List of References for the History of Agricultural Science and Technology in the United States* (Davis, 1966). The files of *Agricultural History, Journal of Farm Economics*, and *Rural Sociology* contain many fine articles of major interest.

On the application of science to agriculture (Chapter 22), besides the items listed above and others in this section, see Henry A. Wallace and William L. Brown, *Corn and Its Early Fathers* (East Lansing, 1956), a vivid account of the development of hybrid corn. The American Association for the Advancement of Science has published the results of a symposium on *Liebig and After Liebig: A Century of Progress in Agricultural Chemistry* (Washington, D.C., 1942). A standard work widely used in agricultural colleges is G. H. Collings, *Commercial Fertilizers: Their Sources and Uses* (5th edn., New York, 1955). Vincent Sauchelli (ed।)., *Chemistry and Technology of Fertilizers* (New York, 1960) reviews fertilizer technology and gives some historical background.

A. Hunter Dupree, *Science in the Federal Government: A History of Policies and Activities to 1940* (Cambridge, Mass., 1957) is excellent on the rise of the USDA's research empire. Wayne D. Rasmussen (ed.), *Readings in the History of American Agriculture* (Urbana, 1960) emphasizes the history of technological change in American agriculture; Donald D. Durost and Glen T. Barton, *Changing Sources of Farm Output*, USDA Production Research Report 36 (Washington, D.C., 1960) evaluates the importance of the technological factors affecting farm output in the United States; and *Agriculture and Economic Growth*, Economic Research Service, Agricultural Economic Report 28 (Washington, D.C., 1963) relates technological change in agriculture to general economic growth.

Specifically on farm mechanization (Chapter 23), one may consult for background Percy W. Bidwell and John I. Falconer, *History of Agriculture in the Northern United States, 1820-1860* (Washington, D.C., 1925) and Lewis C. Gray, *History of Agriculture in the Southern States to 1860* (Washington, D.C., 1933). What Reynold M. Wik does for the United States in *Steam Power on the American Farm* (Philadelphia, 1953), Clark C. Spence does for Great Britain in *God Speed the Plow* (Urbana, 1960). Darragh Aldrich treats the developer of the steel plow in *The Story of John Deere: A Saga of American Industry* (Minneapolis, 1942) and the development of the harvester is told in William T. Hutchinson, *Cyrus Hall McCormick* (2 vols., New York, 1930).

Early evaluations of the tractor may be found in Barton W. Currie, *The Tractor and its Influence upon the Agricultural Implement Business* (Philadelphia, 1916) and Lynn W. Ellis and Edward A. Rumley, *Power and the Plow* (New York, 1911). James H. Street, *The New Revolution in the Cotton Economy: Mechanization and its Consequences* (Chapel Hill, 1957) is the best book on that subject. The interrelations of social and technical factors in the harvesting of cotton, citrus, and lettuce in Arizona may be found in Harland Padfield and William E. Martin, *Farmers, Workers and Machines: Technological Change in Farm Industries of Arizona* (Tucson, 1965). An older but more general study was made in Leo Rogin, *Introduction of Farm Machinery in its Relation to the Productivity of Labor in the Agriculture of the United States during the 19th Century* (Berkeley, 1931).

Two older works are the handsomely illustrated Benjamin Butterworth, *Growth of the Industrial Arts* (Washington, D.C., 1892) and R. L. Ardry, *American Agricultural Implements* (Chicago, 1894). More recent discussions are Holland Thompson, *The Age of Inventions: A Chronicle of Mechanical Conquest* (New Haven, 1921), Merrill Denison, *Harvest Triumphant* (New York, 1949), and the USDA Yearbook *Power to Produce* (Washington, D.C., 1960). The last may be compared with the excellent study *Technology on the Farm: A Special Report by an Interbureau Committee and the Bureau of Agricultural Economics of the United States Department of Agriculture* (Washington, D.C., 1940).

On the problems of pest and disease control (Chapter 24), there are basically two types of studies: those which deal with the pesticides themselves and those which are primarily concerned with their effects. In the first category are A. W. Brown, *Insect Control by Chemicals* (New York, 1951), D. E. Frear, *Chemistry of the Pesticides* (3rd edn., New York, 1955), F. A. Gunther and L. R. Jepson, *Modern Insecticides and World Food Production* (New York, 1960), P. H.

Müller and S. W. Simmons (eds.), *The Insecticide Dichlorodiphenyltrichloro-ethane and Its Significance* (2 vols., Basel, 1955), H. H. Shepard, *The Chemistry and Action of Insecticides* (New York, 1951), and T. F. West and G. A. Camp-bell, *DDT and Newer Persistent Insecticides* (New York, 1952). A broader scope is adopted by L. P. Reitz (ed.), *Biological and Chemical Control of Plant and Animal Pests* (Washington, D.C., 1960) and a special problem is taken up in R. H. Painter, *Insect Resistance in Crop Plants* (New York, 1951).

R. L. Metcalf, *Organic Insecticides, Their Chemistry and Mode of Action* (New York, 1955) covers that interesting development. Another important book in this area is P. DeBach and E. I. Schlinger, *Biological Control of Insect Pests and Weeds* (New York, 1964). D. R. Hoagland, *Lectures on the In-organic Nutrition of Plants* (Waltham, 1944) is older but still useful. L. O. Howard, *A History of Applied Entomology*, Smithsonian Misc. Coll., LXXXIV (Washington, D.C., 1930) is one of the few historical efforts in this field.

On the effects of pesticides, the classic popular but solid account is Rachel Carson, *Silent Spring* (Boston, 1962). One of the many studies triggered, at least in part, by Miss Carson's book was the prestigious President's Science Advisory Committee, *Use of Pesticides* (Washington, D.G., 1963). Among the many official and private evaluations, not all of which postdate *Silent Spring*, are J. C. Ayres *et al.*, *Chemical and Biological Hazards in Food* (Ames, 1962), R. F. Bernard, *Studies on the Effects of DDT on Birds* (East Lansing, 1965), D. J. Kuenen (ed.), *Symposium: The Ecological Effects of Biological and Chemical Control of Undesirable Plants and Animals* (Leiden, 1961), R. L. Rudd, *Pesticides and the Living Landscape* (Madison, 1964), and the Wilson Ornithological Society Conservation Committee, "Some Effects of Insecticides on Terrestrial Birdlife in the Middle West," *The Wilson Bulletin*, LXXIII, No. 4 (1961).

The Committee on Pest Control and Wildlife Relationships of the National Academy of Sciences issued three publications in 1961-62 entitled *Pest Control and Wildlife Relationships*. During the 89th Congress, 1st Session, a Subcom-mittee on Appropriations of the House of Representatives issued a report on *Effects, Uses, Control, and Research of Agricultural Pesticides*, in *Department of Agriculture Appropriations for 1966* (Washington, D.C., 1965), pp. 165-208. Finally, one may consult the Surgeon General's Committee on Environ-mental Health Problems, *Report of the Committee on Environmental Health Problems to the Surgeon General* (Washington, D.C., 1962).

Of the several methods of preserving foods (Chapter 25), refrigeration has received the most attention from historians. One should begin with the use of natural and artificial ice as chronicled in Richard C. Cummings, *The American Ice Harvests: A Historical Study in Technology, 1800-1918* (Berkeley, 1949), and then move on to mechanical refrigeration in Oscar Edward Anderson, Jr., *Refrigeration in America: A History of a New Technology and Its Impact*

(Princeton, 1953). Recent descriptions of the process include A. D. Althouse and C. H. Turnquist, *Modern Refrigeration and Air Conditioning* (Chicago, 1956), S. Cotson and D. B. Smith, *Freeze-Drying of Foodstuffs* (London, 1963), and R. W. Vance (ed.), *Cryogenic Technology* (New York, 1963). A comprehensive work is D. K. Tressler and C. F. Evers (eds.), *Freezing Preservation of Foods* (2 vols., Westport, Conn., 1957), the first volume of which covers the freezing of fresh foods, and the second the freezing of precooked and prepared foods.

One of the few historical accounts in the field is J. C. Drummond, W. R. Lewis, *et al.*, *Historic Tinned Foods*, International Tin Research and Development Council, Publication No. 85 (2nd edn., London, 1939). The packaging field is described in L. C. Barail, *Packaging Engineering* (New York, 1954). Other special processes and aspects of the industry are outlined in R. A. Clemen, *Byproducts in the Packaging Industry* (Chicago, 1927), I. E. El'piner, *Ultrasound: Its Physical, Chemical and Biological Effects* (New York, 1964), W. B. van Arsdel and M. J. Copley, *Food Dehydration* (2 vols., Westport, Conn., 1963), U. S. Army Quartermaster Corps, *Radiation Preservation of Foods* (Washington, D.C., 1957), and U. S. Atomic Energy Commission, *Radiation Preservation of Foods* (Washington, D.C., 1965). One recent and well-illustrated book which describes a wide range of current practices in food processing, and attempts to look ahead toward future changes, is Magnus Pyke, *Food Science and Technology* (London, 1964).

Although the literature on fishing (Chapter 26) is very large, once again the historical literature is much smaller. One may turn to L. Cutting, *Fish Saving: A History of Fish Processing from Ancient to Modern Times* (London, 1955) and H. A. Innis, *The Cod Fisheries—The History of an International Economy* (2nd edn., New Haven, 1954). The recent efforts of various nations are outlined in E. A. Ackerman, *New England's Fishing Industry* (New Haven, 1949), G. Borgstrom, *Japan's World Success in Fishing* (London, 1964), the same author's *The Soviet Fishing Revolution* (London, 1966), and A. von Brandt, *Fish Catching Methods of the World* (London, 1964). Special areas are covered in G. Borgstrom and A. Heighway (eds.), *Atlantic Ocean Fisheries* (London, 1961) and C. F. Hickling, *Tropical Inland Fisheries* (London, 1961).

More general studies include A. Hardy, *The Ocean Sea* (2 parts, London, 1956 and 1959), C. F. Hickling (ed.), *Fish Culture* (London, 1962), G. Borgstrom (ed.), *Fish as Food* (4 vols., New York, 1960-65) and I. J. Bottemanne, *Principles of Fisheries Development* (Amsterdam, 1959). Whaling is treated in A. Ash, *Whaler's Eye* (New York, 1962), conservation in T. V. García-Amadro, *The Exploration and Conservation of the Resources of the Sea* (2nd edn., London, 1959). Finally, a specifically technological work is H. Kristjonssen, *Modern Fishing Gear of the World* (London, 1959).

The problem of future food supply (Chapter 27) has attracted a good deal of attention. Two good surveys are Lester R. Brown, *Increasing World Food Output*, USDA, Foreign Agricultural Economic Report No. 25 (Washington, D.C., 1965) and, by the same author, *Man, Land & Food*, USDA, Foreign Agricultural Report No. 11 (Washington, D.C., 1963). Both of these emphasize growing population and possible food supplies, with possibilities for solving the problem in conventional ways. A less conventional source, "Proteins from Petroleum Fermentation—A New Source of Food," was the subject of a research report by Alfred Champagnat summarized in *Scientific American*, CCXII (Jan. 1965), 49-50. The issues of *Food Technology*, XVII (Jan.-June 1963) contain articles relating present technology and future needs. James Fraser, *Nature Adrift: The Story of Marine Plankton* (Philadelphia, 1962) is a comprehensive, non-specialized account. A discussion of America's Food for Peace program is contained in George S. McGovern, *War Against Want* (New York, 1964). Two studies of water desalinization are *Water Desalination in Developing Countries*, United Nations Publication No. 64 (New York, 1964) and U. S. Department of the Interior, *Report to the President: Program for Advancing Desalting Technology* (Washington, D.C., 1964).

Natural Resources

In connection with the resource revolution (Chapter 28), several significant studies of the Progressive conservation movement have appeared in recent years. Samuel P. Hays, *Conservation and the Gospel of Efficiency: The Progressive Conservation Movement, 1890-1920* (Cambridge, Mass., 1959) interpreted the movement in terms of technical administrators seeking to establish technical programs, rather than as a fighting faith of liberals bent on reforming democracy and economic justice. The latter view is defended by J. Leonard Bates, "Fulfilling American Democracy: The Conservation Movement, 1907-1921," *Mississippi Valley Historical Review*, XLIV (June 1957), 29-57. Both of these should be read in company with Elmo R. Richardson, *The Politics of Conservation: Crusades and Controversies, 1897-1913* (Berkeley, 1962). A. H. Dupree, *Science and the Federal Government: A History of Policies and Activities to 1940* (Cambridge, Mass., 1957), Chapter 12 is the best brief account of the movement.

Those interested in the challenge of the arid West in the 1880's should consult John Wesley Powell, *Report on the Lands of the Arid Region of the United States* (Washington, D.C., 1879), and relevant chapters in Henry Nash Smith, *Virgin Land: The American West as Symbol and Myth* (New York, 1957). However, no one should approach this subject without first reading Walter Prescott Webb, *The Great Plains* (New York, 1931). Gifford Pinchot's personality and character are revealed in his autobiography, *Breaking New Ground*

(New York, 1947). For a full-dress evaluation of his career see M. Nelson McGreary, *Gifford Pinchot: Forester-Politician* (Princeton, 1960).

E. Louise Peffer, *Closing of the Public Domain: Disposal and Reservation Policies, 1900-1950* (Stanford, 1951) has the definitive treatment of grazing and range-land policies. Those seeking more specialized treatment of federal reclamation should consult Dorothy Lampen, *Economic and Social Aspects of Federal Reclamation* (Baltimore, 1930). For an account of the significant broadening of the conservation movement in the 1920's, see Donald C. Swain, *Federal Conservation Policy, 1921-1933* (Berkeley, 1963). The preservation of natural beauty as a federal policy is taken up in John Ise, *Our National Park Policy: A Critical History* (Baltimore, 1961), and Robert Shankland, *Steve Mather of the National Parks* (New York, 1951).

Richard M. Highsmith, Jr., J. Granville Jensen, and Robert D. Rudd, *Conservation in the United States* (Chicago, 1962) is a good textbook on the subject. On water conservation and engineering, one may consult Arthur Maass, *Muddy Waters: The Army Engineers and the Nation's Rivers* (Cambridge, Mass., 1951); Dean E. Mann, *The Politics of Water in Arizona* (Tucson, 1963), a political study in one area by a specialist in aridity; and a history of an Ohio flood-control project, Arthur E. Morgan, *The Miami Conservancy District* (New York, 1951). An engineering and conservation monument is covered in U.S. Department of the Interior, *The Story of Hoover Dam*, Conservation Bulletin No. 9 (Washington, D.C., 1961). Some of the latest ties between science, technology, and conservation are described in Federal Council for Science and Technology, *Research and Development on Natural Resources*, report prepared by the Committee on Natural Resources (Washington, D.C., 1963).

Regional planning and development (Chapter 29) have been treated in a number of books whose titles indicate the particular regions considered: Mary Jean Bowman and W. Warren Haynes, *Resources and People in East Kentucky: Problems and Potentials of a Lagging Economy* (Baltimore, 1963); Ronald R. Boyce (ed.), *Regional Development and the Wabash Basin* (Urbana, 1964); Harry M. Caudill, *Night Comes to the Cumberlands: A Biography of a Depressed Area* (Boston, 1963); Margaret S. Gordon, *Employment Expansion and Population Growth: The California Experience, 1900-1950* (Berkeley, 1954); Melvin L. Greenhut and W. Tate Whitman (eds.), *Essays in Southern Economic Development* (Chapel Hill, 1964); Seymour E. Harris, *The Economics of New England: Case Study of an Older Area* (Cambridge, Mass., 1952); James M. Henderson and Anne O. Krueger, *National Growth and Economic Change in the Upper Midwest* (Minneapolis, 1965); Calvin B. Hoover and B. U. Ratchford, *Economic Resources and Policies of the South* (New York, 1951); Carl Frederick Kraenzel, *The Great Plains in Transition*

(Norman, Okla., 1955); Ralph R. Krueger, Frederic O. Sargent, Anthony de Vos, and Norman Pearson (eds.), *Regional and Resource Planning in Canada* (Toronto, 1963); William H. Nicholls, *Southern Tradition and Regional Progress* (Chapel Hill, 1960); and Ladd Haystead and Gilbert C. Fite, *The Agricultural Regions of the United States* (Norman, Okla., 1955).

Broader and more general studies include: John Friedmann and William Alonso (eds.), *Regional Development and Planning: A Reader* (Cambridge, Mass., 1964); Donald R. Gilmore, *Developing the "Little" Economies: A Survey of Area Development Programs in the United States* (New York, 1960); Edgar M. Hoover, *The Location of Economic Activity* (New York, 1948); Walter Isard and John H. Cumberland (eds.), *Regional Economic Planning: Techniques of Analysis for Less Developed Areas* (Paris, 1961), which is worldwide in scope; Harvey S. Perloff, Edgar S. Dunn, Jr., Eric E. Lampard, and Richard F. Muth, *Regions, Resources, and Economic Growth* (Baltimore, 1960); the older but still useful study by the U.S. National Resources Committee, *Regional Factors in National Planning and Development* (Washington, D.C., 1935); and Gunnar Myrdal's classic *Rich Lands and Poor* (New York, 1957).

Oscar Handlin and John E. Burchard (eds.), *The Historian and the City* (Cambridge, Mass., 1963) contains a useful bibliography on urban history (Chapter 30). John W. Reps, *The Making of Urban America: A History of City Planning in the United States* (Princeton, 1964) is a heavily illustrated survey extending from the colonial period through the early 20th century. Two works by Lewis Mumford, *The Culture of Cities* (New York, 1938) and *The City in History: Its Origins, Its Transformations, and Its Prospects* (New York, 1961) are landmarks in urban literature. An early classic is Adna F. Weber, *The Growth of Cities in the Nineteenth Century* (Ithaca, 1899).

N. S. B. Gras, *An Introduction to Economic History* (New York, 1922) and R. D. McKenzie, *The Metropolitan Community* (New York, 1933), are among the first accounts of metropolitan form and structure. Valuable from an ecological and statistical viewpoint is Amos H. Hawley, *The Changing Shape of Metropolitan America: Deconcentration Since 1920* (Glencoe, Ill., 1956). Committee for Economic Development, Research and Policy Committee, *Guiding Metropolitan Growth* (New York, 1960) points out trends and problems. Among the cities given particular study, New York and Pittsburgh stand out. For the latter see the *Economic Study of the Pittsburgh Region,* conducted by The Pittsburgh Regional Planning Association, published in 1963, Edgar M. Hoover, study director: (1) *Region in Transition;* (2) *Portrait of a Region* (by Ira S. Lowry); (3) *Region with a Future.* Lowdon Wingo, Jr. (ed.), *Cities and Space: The Future Use of Urban Land* (Baltimore, 1963) and Melvin M. Webber (ed.), *Explorations into Urban Structure* (Philadelphia, 1964), contain a number of provocative essays dealing with urban form, design and land use. Scott Greer, *The Emerging City: Myth and Reality* (Glencoe, Ill., 1962) focuses upon the implications of metropolitan development for urban social organization.

A substantial number of publications are available which deal with the politics and government of metropolitan areas, among them Scott Greer, *Governing the Metropolis* (New York, 1962), Winston W. Crouch and Beatrice Dinerman, *Southern California Metropolis: A Study in Development of Government for a Metropolitan Area* (Berkeley, 1963), and John C. Bollens (ed.), *Exploring the Metropolitan Community* (Berkeley, 1961). An interesting historical interpretation appears in Seymour Mandlebaum, *Boss Tweed's New York* (New York, 1965).

William Dobriner (ed.), *The Suburban Community* (New York, 1958) provides a good introduction to the social organization and ecology of the suburbs. Transportation issues are discussed in Lyle C. Fitch and Associates, *Urban Transportation and Public Policy* (San Francisco, 1964), A. S. Lang and R. M. Soberman, *Urban Rail Transit: Its Economies and Technology* (Cambridge, Mass., 1964), George M. Smerk, *Urban Transportation: The Federal Role* (Bloomington, 1965), and George W. Hilton and John F. Due, *The Electric Interurban Railways in America* (Stanford, 1960), a detailed historical study.

Historical accounts of urban housing and planning development include Sam B. Warner, Jr., *Streetcar Suburbs: The Process of Growth in Boston, 1870-1900* (Cambridge, Mass., 1962), Lloyd Rodwin, *Housing and Economic Progress: A Study of the Housing Eperiences of Boston's Middle-Income Families* (Cambridge, Mass., 1961), Roy Lubove, *The Progressives and the Slums: Tenement House Reform in New York City, 1890-1917* (Pittsburgh, 1962), and by the same author, *Community Planning in the 1920's: The Contribution of the Regional Planning Association of America* (Pittsburgh, 1963). One aspect of the current situation is covered in Martin Anderson, *The Federal Bulldozer: A Critical Analysis of Urban Renewal, 1949-1962* (Cambridge, Mass., 1964).

A good introduction to the problem of air pollution in urban and metropolitan areas is "A Study of Pollution—Air," *A Staff Report to the Committee on Public Works*, U.S. Senate, 88th Congress, 1st Session (Washington, D.C., 1963). Surveys and interpretations of urban problems designed for the general reader include Wilfred Owen, *Cities in the Motor Age* (New York, 1959); Edward Higbee, *The Squeeze: Cities without Space* (New York, 1960); The Editors of Fortune, *The Exploding Metropolis* (Garden City, N.Y., 1958); and Jane Jacobs, *The Death and Life of Great American Cities* (New York, 1961). For a contrast between British and American urban policy see William Ashworth, *The Genesis of Modern British Town Planning: A Study in Economic and Social History of the Nineteenth and Twentieth Centuries* (London, 1954), Charles M. Haar, *Land Planning Law in a Free Society: A Study of the British Town and Country Planning Act* (Cambridge, Mass., 1951), by the same author (ed.), *Law and Land: Anglo-American Planning Practice* (Cambridge, Mass., 1964), and Stanley Anderson, *Britain in the Sixties: Housing* (Baltimore, 1962). Also useful for comparative purposes is Paul F. Wendt, *Housing Policy—The Search for Solutions: A Comparison of the United Kingdom, Sweden, West Germany, and the United States since World War II* (Berkeley, 1962).

Technology and the State

No single volume available deals exclusively with the history of technology and public policy (Chapter 31), though many books on the history of technology touch upon the subject. For the United States, one must turn to Dupree, *Science and the Federal Government*, cited above. Very little has been published directly on technology in international affairs; a pioneer work in this field is Eugene B. Skolnikoff, *Science, Technology and American Foreign Policy* (Cambridge, Mass., 1967). Richard R. Nelson, Merton J. Peck, and Edward D. Kalachek provide some contemporary case studies as the basis for their policy recommendations in *Technology, Economic Growth, and Public Policy* (Washington, D.C., 1967).

Two general works on the U.S. Patent Office are G. A. Weber, *The Patent Office: Its History, Activities, and Organization* (Baltimore, 1924) and F. L. Vaughan, *The United States Patent System: Legal and Economic Conflicts in American Patent History* (Norman, Okla., 1956). Recent congressional investigations of patent policy include U.S. Congress, Senate, Select Committee on Small Business, Hearings *Patent Policies of Departments and Agencies of the Federal Government—1959*, 86th Congress, 1st Session (1960) and Senate, Committee on the Judiciary, Subcommittee on Patents, Trademarks, and Copyrights . . ., Hearings, 87th Congress, 1st Session (1961). Two recent publications from the Executive branch are the Federal Council for Science and Technology, *Annual Report on Government Patent Policy, June 1965* (Washington, D.C., 1965) and subsequent reports, and the Report of the President's Commission on the Patent System, *"To Promote the Progress of . . . Useful Arts" In An Age of Exploding Technology* (Washington, D.C., 1966). Also concerned with the problem of patents is a report of an advisory committee of private citizens to the Secretary of Commerce: *Technological Innovation: Its Environment and Management* (Washington, D.C., 1967).

British secrecy policies are mentioned in Witt Bowden, *Industrial Society in England Towards the End of the Eighteenth Century* (New York, 1925). L. A. Harper discusses *The British Navigation Laws* (New York, 1939). F. W. Taussig's *Tariff History of the United States* (7th edn., New York, 1923) is a detailed study of that subject. A relevant example is detailed in C. W. Pursell, "Tariff and Technology: The Foundation and Development of the American Tin-Plate Industry, 1872-1900," *Technology and Culture*, III (Summer, 1963),

267-84. For an interpretive essay on technical education see Eric Ashby, *Technology and the Academics* (New York, 1958). The story of West Point is outlined in Sidney Forman, *West Point: A History of the United States Military Academy* (New York, 1950). The land-grant colleges are discussed in A. C. True, *A History of Agricultural Education in the United States* (Washington, 1929). The NACA is examined in G. W. Gray, *Frontiers of Flight: The Story of NACA Research* (New York, 1948) and the activities of the National Bureau of Standards are told in Rexmond C. Cochrane, *Measures for Progress: A History of the National Bureau of Standards* (Washington, D.C., 1966).

The Commerce Department in general is treated in National Academy of Sciences–National Research Council, *The Role of the Department of Commerce in Science and Technology* (Washington, D.C., 1960). The proliferation of federally supported technical facilities is detailed in National Science Foundation, *Federal Financial Support of Physical Facilities and Major Equipment for the Conduct of Scientific Research* (Washington, D.C., 1957). For recent statistical data, the handiest reference is the NSF's *Federal Funds for Science* series.

The Organisation for Economic Co-operation and Development has issued a series of booklets describing research in several countries entitled *Country Reports on the Organisation of Scientific Research*. Twenty-one nations are surveyed, including the United States, which is covered in a volume by Mary E. Corning, *Country Reports . . . : United States* (Paris, 1963).

Merle Curti considers the role of the industrial exhibition in "America at the World Fairs, 1851-1893," *American Historical Review*, LV (1950), as does Eugene S. Ferguson, in "Expositions of Technology, 1851-1900," Chapter 44 in the first volume of this text. An excellent and exhaustive study of events leading to the organization of the Atomic Energy Commission is Hewlett and Anderson, *The New World*, cited above. For a sketch of recent relations between science and government see National Academy of Sciences–National Research Council, *Federal Support of Basic Research in Institutions of Higher Learning* (Washington, D.C., 1964), pp. 16-56. For a policy statement on federal-university relations see American Council on Education, *Sponsored Research Policy of Colleges and Universities* (Washington, D.C., 1954). The National Resources Committee, *Technological Trends and National Policy* (Washington, D.C., 1937) should be required reading. Don K. Price, *Government and Science* (New York, 1962) is a thoughtful interpretation of that subject, and a brief survey of the historic relations is given in Carroll W. Pursell, Jr., "Science and Government Agencies," *Science and Society in the United States*, edited by David D. Van Tassel and Michael G. Hall (Homewood, Ill., 1966), pp. 223-49. A collection of documents and readings on the subject may be found in J. L. Penick, C. W. Pursell, M. G. Sherwood, and D. C. Swain (eds.), *The Politics of American Science: 1939 to the Present* (Chicago, 1965).

The problem of social control (Chapter 32) is discussed in many places.

Some old but still significant publications of the United States government include the President's Conference on Unemployment, Committee on Recent Economic Changes, *Recent Economic Changes in the United States* (Washington, D.C., 1929), President's Research Committee on Social Trends, *Recent Social Trends in the United States* (Washington, D.C., 1933), National Resources Committee, *Technological Trends and National Policy, Including the Social Implications of New Inventions. A Report of the Subcommittee on Technology, June, 1937* (Washington, D.C., 1937), National Resources Committee, *Research—A National Resource* (3 vols., Washington, D.C., 1938-41), and the Temporary National Economic Committee, *Technology in Our National Economy*, Monograph No. 22, 76th Congress, 3rd Session (Washington, D.C., 1941).

On the Depression itself see Broadus Mitchell, *Depression Decade: From New Era Through New Deal, 1929-1941* (New York, 1947), and for the problem of monopoly during these years see Ellis W. Hawley, *The New Deal and the Problem of Monopoly: A Study in Economic Ambivalence* (Princeton, 1966). A rather unsuccessful attempt to trace the rise of a technical elite is traced in W. H. G. Armytage, *The Rise of the Technocrats: A Social History* (London, 1965). A provocative survey of the social history of the American economy is Thomas C. Cochrane and William Miller, *The Age of Enterprise: A Social History of Industrial America* (New York, 1942). In addition to many of the books cited for Chapter 31 and others, the interested reader may turn to Francis R. Allen *et al.*, *Technology and Social Change* (New York, 1957); Ritchie Calder, *Science in Our Lives* (East Lansing, 1954); Henry Elsner, Jr., *The Technocrats: Prophets of Automation* (Syracuse, N.Y., 1967); and Frank Arkwright, *The A B C of Technocracy* (New York, 1933).

The literature on the developing countries (Chapter 33) is already large. Jack Baranson has compiled an annotated bibliography, *Technology for Underdeveloped Areas* (Oxford, 1967), which provides an excellent guide to the published materials and official reports on this topic. On the economics of technological change, A. K. Sen, *Choice of Techniques: An Aspect of the Theory of Planned Economic Development* (rev. edn., Oxford, 1962) treats social and profit techniques, as does Jan Tinbergen, *The Design of Development* (Baltimore, 1958). Daniel L. Spencer and Alexander Woroniak have edited *The Transfer of Technology to Developing Nations* (Washington, D.C., 1966), the report of a conference of economists dealing with the problem of technology transfer in underdeveloped countries. The classic study of sociocultural influences of technology is Margaret Mead, *Cultural Patterns and Technical Change* (paperback edn., New York, 1955). For entrepreneurship and innovation see pertinent chapters in Lucy Mair, *New Nations* (London, 1963), Adamantios Pepelasis *et al.*, *Economic Development* (New York, 1958). Growth models are suggested in Irma Adelman, *Theories of Economic Growth and Develop-*

ment (Stanford, 1961), Albert O. Hirschman, *The Strategy of Economic Development* (New Haven, 1959), and Stephen Enke, *Economics for Development* (Englewood Cliffs, 1963).

On technology and industrial development, see the United Nations Bulletins entitled *Industrialization and Productivity,* and for a case study George Rosen, *Industrial Change in India: Industrial Growth, Capital Requirements, and Technological Change, 1937-1955* (Glencoe, Ill., 1958). Various aspects of the general problem of products and systems are treated in Ruth Gruber (ed.), *Science and the New Nations* (New York, 1961) and Richard L. Meier, *Science and Economic Development* (New York, 1956). Population problems are discussed in Richard L. Meier, *Modern Science and the Human Fertility Problem* (New York, 1959), education in Jack Baranson, 'Implementing Technology Programs for Underdeveloped Countries," *Oregon Business Review,* XXI (June 1962), 3-4, housing in B. Y. Kinzey and Howard Sharp, *Environmental Technologies in Architecture* (New York, 1963), and village technologies in General Engineering Laboratory, *An Integrated Program of Technical Support for Village Development* (Schenectady, 1961). Some depressed areas which exist within our otherwise industrially advanced country are covered in Mary Jane Bowman and W. Warren Haynes, *Resources and People in East Kentucky* (Baltimore, 1963), Sar A. Levitan, *Federal Aid to Depressed Areas* (Baltimore, 1964), and Committee for Economic Development, *Distressed Areas in a Growing Economy* (Washington, D.C., 1961).

War and Space

Concerning the organization of military research (Chapter 34), the best general study of the relations between science and government is Dupree, *Science and the Federal Government,* cited above. For the period since 1940 see J. Stefan Dupré and Sanford A. Lakoff, *Science and the Nation: Policy and Politics* (Englewood Cliffs, 1962). I. B. Holley, Jr., *Ideas and Weapons: Exploitation of the Aerial Weapon by the United States during World War I* (New Haven, 1953) and L. N. Scott, *Naval Consulting Board of the United States* (Washington, D.C., 1920) are valuable specialized studies of World War I. George W. Gray, *Frontiers of Flight: The Story of NACA Research* (New York, 1948) is unusually informative. A. Hoyt Taylor, *The First Twenty-Five Years of the Naval Research Laboratory* (Washington, D.C., 1948) is also useful. There are two good books on the OSRD: James Phinney Baxter III, *Scientists Against Time* (Boston, 1946) and Irvin Stewart, *Organizing Scientific Research for War: The Administrative History of the Office of Scientific Research and Development* (Boston, 1948). Hewlett and Anderson, *The New World, 1939-1946,* cited above, contains detailed information about the development of the first atomic bomb as well as the establishment of the AEC.

"The Bird Dogs" trace the origins of ONR in "The Evolution of the Office of Naval Research," *Physics Today*, XIV (Aug. 1961), 30-35. An article by Edward L. Katzenbach, Jr., "Ideas: A New Defense Industry," *Reporter*, XXIV (March 2, 1961), 17-21, knowingly describes one of the most important recent developments in the organization of military research. In his book *American Scientists and Nuclear Weapons Policy* (Princeton, 1962), Robert Gilpin examines the political influence of scientists in the nuclear age. Clarence G. Lasby, "Science and the Military," *Science and Society in the United States*, ed. David D. Van Tassel and Michael G. Hall (Homewood, Ill., 1966), pp. 251-82 is a brief summary. The struggle over British policy during World War II is told in C. P. Snow's widely read Godkin Lectures of 1960, *Science and Government* (paperback edn., New York, 1962). Another version of these same events is told by The Earl of Birkenhead, *The Professor and the Prime Minister: The Official Life of Professor F. A. Lindemann, Viscount Cherwell* (Boston, 1962).

The vast field of the mechanization of warfare (Chapter 35), especially as carried out in World War I, may be approached through Holley, *Ideas and Weapons*, cited above (for aviation). The tank is covered in Giffard Le Q. Martel, *In the Wake of the Tank: The First Fifteen Years of Mechanization in the British Army* (London, 1931), the machine gun in G. S. Hutchinson, *Machine Guns: Their History and Tactical Employment* (London, 1938), and the navy in E. L. Woodward, *Great Britain and the German Navy* (Oxford, 1935). More general are Richard D. Challener, *The French Theory of the Nation in Arms, 1866-1939* (New York, 1955), Edward Meade Earle (ed.), *Modern Strategy* (Princeton, 1940), and Frank P. Chambers, *The War Behind the War* (New York, 1939). An enthusiastic account of American weapons is Frank Parker Stockbridge, *Yankee Ingenuity in the War* (New York, 1920).

The best guide to the weapons of World War II (Chapter 36) is the eight-volume history of the OSRD. The general volume by Baxter, *Scientists Against Time*, is cited above, as is the administrative history, Stewart, *Organizing Scientific Research for War*. The other volumes are E. C. Andrus, *Advances in Military Medicine* (Boston, 1948), Joseph C. Boyce (ed.), *New Weapons for Air Warfare* (Boston, 1947), John E. Burchard (ed.), *Guns and Targets* (Boston, 1948), William A. Noyes (ed.), *Chemistry* (Boston, 1948), C. G. Suits, George R. Harrison, and Louis Jordan (eds.), *Applied Physics: Electronics, Optics, Metallurgy* (Boston, 1948), and Lincoln R. Thiesmeyer and John E. Burchard, *Combat Scientists* (Boston, 1947).

The Office of Military History, Department of the Army, has published within its *United States Army in World War II* program a historical series narrating the activities of *The Technical Services*. Several of these volumes contribute valuable information to the study of technology during World War II. A subseries on the role of the Ordnance Department contains two pertinent volumes. One should consult Constance M. Green, Harry C. Thompson, and

Peter C. Roots, *The Ordnance Department: Planning Munitions for War* (Washington, D.C., 1959), Harry C. Thompson and Lida Mayo, *The Ordnance Department: Procurement and Supply* (Washington, D.C., 1960), Dulany Terrett, *The Signal Corps: The Emergency* (Washington, D.C., 1956), George R. Thompson, Dixie R. Harris, Pauline M. Oakes, and Dulany Terrett, *The Signal Corps: The Test* (Washington, D.C., 1957), and Wesley F. Craven and James L. Cate, *The Army Air Forces in World War II: Vol. 6, Men and Planes* (Chicago, 1955).

Other books of merit include G. M. Barnes, *Weapons of World War II* (New York, 1947), Vannevar Bush, *Endless Horizons* (Washington, D.C., 1946), *Modern Arms and Free Men* (New York, 1949) by the same author, and Eugene M. Emme (ed.), *The Impact of Air Power* (New York, 1959). An excellent summary of production technologies used during World War II, replete with meaningful statistics as well as their analysis, is the War Production Board, *Wartime Production Achievements and the Reconversion Outlook* (Washington, D.C., Oct. 9, 1945). For Great Britain's war effort see J. G. Crowther and R. Widdington, *Science at War* (New York, 1948); for Canada see Wilfred Eggleston, *Scientists at War* (Toronto, 1950); and for Germany see Leslie E. Simon, *German Research in World War II* (New York, 1947).

Missiles, and their place in modern warfare (Chapter 37), are discussed in a growing number of books. The best biography thus far of America's rocket pioneer is Milton Lehman, *This High Man: The Life of Robert H. Goddard* (New York, 1963). Various aspects of the early years of rockets are treated in Eugene M. Emme (ed.), *The History of Rocket Technology* (Detroit, 1964). One line of development may be followed in Ernest G. Schwiebert, *A History of the U.S. Air Force Ballistic Missiles* (New York, 1965). A useful guide to developments is Eugene M. Emme, *Aeronautics and Astronautics: An American Chronology of Science and Technology in the Exploration of Space, 1915-1960* (Washington, D.C., 1961). The German rocket effort is described by an important leader in Walter Dornberger, *V-2* (New York, 1954), and the transfer of this technology to the United States is described in Dieter K. Huzel, *Peenemunde to Canaveral* (Englewood Cliffs, 1962) and in James McGovern, *Crossbow and Overcast* (New York, 1964). The strategy context is discussed in Eugene M. Emme (ed.), *The Impact of Air Power: National Security and World Politics* (Princeton, 1959) and in many of the books listed below.

Technology and strategy (Chapter 38) are discussed in a number of the books already cited, such as Baxter, *Scientists Against Time*, Dornberger, *V-2*, and Holley, *Ideas and Weapons*. Two general and popular works of merit are Bernard and Fawn Brodie, *From Crossbow to H-Bomb* (paperback edn., New York, 1962) and James R. Newman, *The Tools of War* (New York, 1942). Robert V. Bruce, *Lincoln and the Tools of War* (Indianapolis, 1956) describes how the problem ought not to be handled, and Vannevar Bush, *Modern Arms and Free Men* (New York, 1949) drew upon his war successes to comment on the future. A pioneer in the development of jet aircraft speaks in Sir Frank Whittle, *Jet* (London, 1953); the development of the tank is chronicled in E. D. Swinton, *Eyewitness* (London, 1932); and A. M. Low traces the story of small arms from the *Musket to Machine Gun* (London, 1943). Derek Wood and Derek Dempster, *The Narrow Margin: The Battle of Britain and the Rise of Air Power, 1930-1940* (New York, 1961) treat a key period. Two general works are John Frederick Charles Fuller, *Armament and History* (New York, 1945) and Edwin Tunis, *Weapons: A Pictorial History* (Cleveland, 1954). Lewis L. Strauss, *Men and Decisions* (New York, 1962) is an eyewitness account of many strategic decisions. Theodore Ropp, *War in the Modern World* (Durham, 1959) is a good survey.

For the particular problems raised by the atomic bomb, one may consult the controversial Herman Kahn, *On Thermonuclear War* (Princeton, 1960), Henry A. Kissinger, *Nuclear Weapons and Foreign Policy* (New York, 1957), Raymond Aron, *The Great Debate: Theories of Nuclear Strategy* (New York, 1964), and Bernard Brodie, *Strategy in the Missile Age* (Princeton, 1955). A good selection of articles appears in M. Grodzinsl and E. Rabinowitch (eds.), *The Atomic Age* (New York, 1963).

One of the problems resulting from the massive government support of military and space technology has been the effect upon civilian industrial technology (Chapter 39). A brief but stimulating essay on the changing pace of research will be found in Derek J. de Solla Price, *Science Since Babylon* (New Haven, 1961). Two independent studies of what is sometimes referred to as the problem of "spinoff" are Everett M. Rogers, *Diffusion of Innovations* (New York, 1962) and Richard S. Rosenbloom, *Technology Transfer—Process and Policy* (Washington, D.C., 1965). Merton J. Peck and Frederic M. Scherer, *The Weapons Acquisition Process: An Economic Analysis* (Boston, 1962) describes the nature, structure, and execution of the process. Implications for the civilian sector are discussed in U.S. Congress, Joint Economic Committee, *Impact of Military Supply and Service Activities on the Economy*, 88th Congress, 1st Session (Washington, D.C., 1963). The National Security Industrial Association has published the *Proceedings of R & D Symposium on the Impact of Government Research and Development Expenditures on Industrial Growth* (Washington, D.C., 1963). Two other studies of the problem are National Bureau of Economic Research, *The Rate and Direction of Inventive Activity: Economic and Social Factors* (Princeton, 1962) and Committee on Utilization of Scientific and Engineering Manpower, *Toward Better Utilization of Scientific and Engineering Talent* (Washington, D.C., 1964).

The problems of civilian vs. federal technical progress are nowhere more clearly seen than in the area of space exploration (Chapter 43). Although carefully placed under civilian rather than military control, the space program is also clearly quite separate from (and some charge, inimical to) the problem of stimulating the private sector of the nation's economy. Since this argument turns largely on questions of goals and values rather than on hard technical data or considerations, it is not likely to be solved in terms of technology. Nevertheless, many books—only a few of which can be listed here—have begun the description of the space program itself. Many of the works cited above in connection with Chapter 37 are useful, especially Emme's chronology entitled *Aeronautics and Astronautics, 1915-1960,* and the annual series published by NASA since 1963 entitled *Astronautics and Aeronautics: A Chronology on Science, Technology, and Policy.* Two histories of NASA have already appeared: covering the legislative history is E. Allison Griffith, *The Genesis of the National Aeronautics and Space Act of 1958* (Washington, D.C., 1962), and tracing the administrative history is Robert L. Rosholt, *An Administrative History of NASA, 1958-1963* (Washington, D.C., 1966).

There are several histories of specific events and programs in this young Space Age. The first satellites were a part of the International Geophysical Year, which is chronicled in Walter Sullivan, *Assault on the Unknown: IGY* (New York, 1961). America's first manned flights are covered in Loyd Swenson, Charles Alexander, and James Grimwood, *This New Ocean: A History of Project Mercury* (Washington, D.C., 1966). Bessie Z. Jones, *Lighthouse in the Sky* (Washington, D.C., 1965) is a history of the Smithsonian Institution's astrophysical observatory.

Although not strictly histories, the following describe aspects of space in an informed and valuable manner: Harold Wheelock, *Mariner Mission to Venus* (New York, 1963) covers that important trip; Kenneth W. Gatland (ed.), *Telecommunications Satellites* (New York, 1964) treats a subject of economic importance, as do Donald N. Michael, *Proposed Studies on the Implications of Peaceful Space Activities for Human Affairs* (Washington, D.C., 1960) and Simon Ramo (ed.), *Peaceful Uses of Outer Space* (New York, 1961). More general works include Hugh Odishaw (ed.), *The Challenges of Space* (Chicago, 1962) and Vernon Van Dyke, *Pride and Power: The Rationale of the Space Program* (Urbana, 1964). The best collections of materials on the international problems are U.S. Department of State, *Documents on International Aspects of the Exploration and Use of Outer Space, 1959-60,* Senate Doc. No. 18, 88th Congress, (May 1963) and U.S. Congress, Senate, *United States International Space Programs: Texts of Executive Agreements, Memoranda of Understanding, and Other International Arrangements, 1959-65,* Staff Report . . . Committee on Aeronautical and Space Sciences, 89th Congress, 1st Session (July 30, 1965).

Automation

Several books of value for the history of automation (Chapter 41) are men-tioned above under the sections on *Organization and Rationalization* and *Com-munications:* for example, Wiener, *Human Use of Human Beings*, Giedion, *Mechanization Takes Command*, Arnold and Faurote, *Ford Methods and the Ford Shops*, and the Report of the National Commission of Technology, Auto-mation, and Economic Progress, *Technology and the American Economy*. Two additional works that should be consulted are James R. Bright, *Automation and Management* (Boston, 1958) and the U.S. Congress, Subcommittee on Economics Stabilization, Hearings, *Technology and the American Economy* (Oct. 1955).

A postwar Ford department (later disbanded) is described in Rupert Le Grand, "Ford Handles By Automation," *American Machinist*, XCII (Oct. 21, 1948), 107-22. In addition to the book listed above, Wiener's ideas may be also seen in his earlier work *Cybernetics* (New York, 1948). John Diebold (who is sometimes incorrectly given credit for creating the word "automation," which actually began to appear in the metalworking and technical societies press throughout 1949-50) has written *Automation—The Advent of the Auto-matic Factory* (New York, 1952) and "Automation—The New Technology," *Harvard Business Review* (Nov.-Dec. 1953). The ideas of Benjamin F. Fairless were stated in "Our One Indispensable Weapon," an address presented at the Annual Dinner of the Greater Johnstown Chamber of Commerce, Johnstown, Pa., Feb. 11, 1955; those of John I. Snyder, Jr., in "The American Factory and Automation," *Saturday Review*, XXXVIII (Jan. 22, 1955), 16ff. References to the Ford Cleveland plant are found in Bright, *Automation and Management* and in *Business Week* (March 29, 1952), 146-8. For early attempts to measure automation see Chapter 4 of Bright's study. Historical aspects of the subject before the 20th century may be traced in many histories of technology, but see particularly Derek J. DeSolla Price and Silvio Bedini, "Automata in His-tory," *Technology and Culture*, V (Winter, 1964), 9-42.

Brunel's block-making machinery is described in Charles Tomlinson, *Cyclo-pedia of Useful Arts and Manufactures* (London, 1854); for transfer machines see *Automotive Industries* (Feb. 13, 1924) and J. P. Lannen, "Automatic Jogs that Have Cut Automobile Costs," *Machinery*, XXXVII (Aug. 1931), 897. The method of making ships by continuous movement through a production process is covered in Frederick Chapin Lane, *Venetian Ships and Shipbuilders of the Renaissance* (Baltimore, 1934). Grant's biscuit-making process was out-lined in Peter Barlow, *Encyclopedia of Arts, Manufactures, and Machinery* (London, 1851), pp. 801-4. Henry Ford's autobiography is *My Life and Work* (New York, 1922); Oliver Evans's work is described in his guidebook,

The Young Mill-Wright and Miller's Guide (Philadelphia, 1795). L. R. Smith described his automobile plant in "We Built A Plant To Run Without Men," *Magazine of Business* (Feb. 1929), and a film of the plant made in 1922 is still (1966) in the possession of A. O. Smith. A British observation on the problem is given in Frank G. Wollard, "Some Notes on British Methods of Continuous Production," *Automobile Engineer, London* (March 1925).

The impact of automation (Chapter 42) is still a matter of debate and speculation. Most of the works cited above in connection with Chapter 8 and 9 are pertinent here as well: particularly Galbraith, *Affluent Society*, Ellul, *Technological Society*, Harrington, *The Other America*, McLuhan, *Understanding Media*, Myrdal, *Challenge of Affluence*, the report of the National Commission on Technology, Automation and Economic Progress, *Technology and the American Economy*, and the books of Robert Theobald and Norbert Wiener. In addition, one should consult the collection of articles edited by Morris Philipson, *Automation: Its Implications for the Future* (paperback edn., New York, 1962), two books by the economist Robert L. Heilbroner, *The Making of Economic Society* (Englewood Cliffs, 1962) and *The. Worldly Philosophers* (rev. edn., New York, 1961), and Arthur O. Lewis, Jr. (ed.), *Of Men and Machines* (New York, 1962).

Other works specifically on automation are William W. Brickman and Stanley Lehrer (eds.), *Automation, Education and Human Values* (New York, 1966), Gilbert Burck (ed.), *The Computer Age and Its Potential for Management* (New York, 1965), John Diebold, *Beyond Automation* (New York, 1964), John T. Dunlop (ed.), *Automation and Technological Change* (Englewood Cliffs, 1962), Martin Greenberger (ed.), *Management and the Computer of the Future* (Cambridge, 1962), and Herbert A. Simon, *The Shape of Automation* (New York, 1965). Less specifically on automation, but none the less important, are Myron H. Bloy, Jr., *The Crisis of Cultural Change* (New York, 1965), Kenneth E. Boulding, *The Meaning of the Twentieth Century* (New York, 1964), Henry B. Clark, *The Christian Case Against Poverty* (paperback edn., New York, 1965), Harvey Cox, *The Secular City* (New York, 1965), Donald Michael, *The Next Generation* (paperback edn., New York, 1965), and D. K. Price, *The Scientific Estate* (Cambridge, Mass., 1965).

Contributors

Jack Baranson, an economist with the International Bank for Reconstruction and Development in Washington, D.C., has participated in economic development missions to underdeveloped areas and has written on the problems of industrialization and technology transfer. He is the compiler of an annotated bibliography on *Technology for Developing Economies.*

Jack Barbash, Professor of Economics at the University of Wisconsin, specializes in labor and industrial relations research and consulting. He was formerly staff director for the U.S. Senate Subcommittee on Labor and Labor-Management Relations. Among his books are *The Practice of Unionism, Labor's Grass Roots,* and *The Government and Structure of American Labor Unions.*

Georg Borgstrom, Professor of Food Science and Geography at Michigan State University, is an authority on world food resources and food preservation. Among the best known of his books are *The Hungry Planet* and the four-volume *Fish as Food,* which he edited.

Kenneth E. Boulding, Professor of Economics at the University of Michigan, is president of the American Economic Association and director of the Center for Research on Conflict Resolution. His published works include a dozen books and many articles in a wide range of fields, including all phases of economic theory and practice, organizational theory and structure, conflict resolution, peace research, and international systems.

James R. Bright is Professor of Business Administration at the Harvard University Graduate School of Business Administration. Among his books are *Automation and Management* and *Research Development and Technological Innovation.* In preparing his chapter, Professor Bright was assisted by Miss Mary Henderson, who performed library research on early automation systems.

Robert C. Davis, of Case Western Reserve University, is a specialist in the sociology of science and the history of the behavioral sciences. As a member of the Survey Research Center at the University of Michigan, he directed the study on *The Public Impact of Science in the Mass Media.*

Peter F. Drucker, Professor of Management at the Graduate Business School of New York University, has served as a management consultant to several of the country's largest corporations, as well as to agencies of the United States government, and to the governments of Canada and Japan. Among his many books are *The Concept of the Corporation, The New Society, The Future of Industrial Man,* and *The Landmarks of Tomorrow.* The recipient of many awards and honors, Dr. Drucker has served as president of the Society for the History of Technology.

John A. Duffie is Professor of Engineering, director of the University-Industry Research Program, and director of the Solar Energy Laboratory at the University of Wisconsin. He is the author of many technical papers in the fields of mechanical engineering, chemical engineering, and solar energy.

Eugene M. Emme, Chief Historian of the National Aeronautics and Space Administration, Washington, D.C., is the author of numerous official studies and articles. Among the books which he has written or edited are *Aeronautics and Astronautics, 1915-60; A History of Space Flight; The Impact of Air Power;* and *The History of Rocket Technology.*

Eduard Farber, is a consultant on industrial chemistry and a professor of Chemistry at the American University. In addition to his technical writings, he is the author of articles and books in the history of chemistry, including *The Evolution of Chemistry* and *Great Chemists.*

Bernard S. Finn is Curator of the Division of Electricity of the Smithsonian Institution. His writings include articles on the development of electrical devices and a book of *Sources in Thermoelectricity.*

Leslie H. Fishel, Jr., is Director of the State Historical Society of Wisconsin in Madison. In addition to publishing articles in scholarly historical journals, Dr. Fishel is co-author of *The American Negro: A Documentary Story.*

Robert H. Guest is Professor of Organization and Administration at the Amos Tuck School of Business Administration of Dartmouth College. He has written many articles and is the author of *Organizational Change: The Effect of Successful Leadership* and co-author of *The Man on the Assembly Line* and *The Foreman on the Assembly Line.*

Richard G. Hewlett is Chief Historian of the United States Atomic Energy Commission in Washington, D.C. He is co-author of *The New World, 1939-1946,* the first volume of the official history of the Commission.

Forest G. Hill, Professor of Economics at the University of Texas, is an authority on American economic history and regional economic growth. In addition to writing many articles, he is the author of *Roads, Rails and Waterways: The Army Engineers and Early Transportation* and co-editor of *American Economic History: Essays in Interpretation.*

Irving Brinton Holley, Jr., Professor of History at Duke University, specializes in the history of aviation and in military history. He is the author of *Ideas and Weapons* and *Buying Aircraft: Air Materiel Procurement for the Army Air Forces.*

Aaron J. Ihde is Professor of Chemistry and chairman of the Integrated Liberal Studies Program at the University of Wisconsin. Appointed by the Governor to the Wisconsin Food Standards Advisory Committee, he has done much technical research in food chemistry. He has written and edited numerous articles and books on the history of chemistry, including *The Development of Modern Chemistry; The Physical Universe, Readings and Exercises;* and *Selected Readings in the History of Chemistry.*

Edward L. Katzenbach, Jr., now in charge of educational activities for the Raytheon Corporation, has previously served as Deputy Assistant Secretary of Defense (Education) of the Department of Defense, and as director of the Commission on Administrative Affairs of the American Council on Education. He is the author of many articles on military subjects in scholarly journals and encyclopedias.

Melvin Kranzberg, Professor of History and director of the graduate program in the history of science and technology at Case Western Reserve University, is editor-in-chief of *Technology and Culture,* the quarterly journal of the Society for the History of Technology. He has been a vice president of the American Association for the Advancement of Science, chairman of the Historical Advisory Committee of the National Aeronautics and Space Administration, and vice president of the Society for French Historical Studies. He is the author and editor of books and articles in general history and in the history of science and technology.

W. David Lewis, of the State University of New York at Buffalo, has specialized in various aspects of American social history and in the history of technology, including the development of the industrial research laboratory. He is the author of *From Newgate to Dannemora: The Rise of the Penitentiary in New York, 1796-1848* and co-editor of *Economic Change in the Civil War Era.*

Roy Lubove is Associate Professor of Social Welfare and History at the University of Pittsburgh. He is the author of *The Progressives and the Slums: Tenement House Reform in New York City, 1890-1917; Community Planning in the 1920's: The Contribution of the Regional Planning Association of America;* and *The Professional Altruist: The Emergence of Social Work as a Career, 1880-1930.*

Theodore F. Marburg is Professor of Economics at Marquette University. He is the author of articles and book chapters on business and marketing history and has written *Small Business in Brass Fabricating.*

Donald N. Michael, Professor of Psychology and a program director at the Center for Research on the Utilization of Scientific Knowledge at the University of Michigan, has published many papers and books on practical and theoretical problems concerning man's ability to adjust to the social and psychological changes produced by developing technology. His books include *Proposed Studies of the Implications of Peaceful Space Activities for Human Affairs, Cybernation: The Silent Conquest,* and *The Next Generation: Prospects Ahead for the Youth of Today and Tomorrow.*

Bruce Carlton Netschert, of National Economic Research Associates, Inc., has worked with United States government agencies and with Resources for the Future, Inc., studying future supply prospects for energy and mineral resources. Among the books of which he is author or co-author are *The Future Supply of Oil and Gas; Energy in the American Economy, 1850-1975;* and *The Future Supply of the Major Metals.*

James Lal Penick, Jr., of Loyola University in Chicago, is the author of articles dealing with the history of conservation in the United States. He is co-editor of *The Politics of American Science, 1939 to the Present.*

Carroll W. Pursell, Jr., is Assistant Professor of History at the University of California, Santa Barbara. He is one of the editors of *The Politics of American Science, 1939 to the Present,* and has published articles on the history of American science and technology in many journals.

John B. Rae is Professor of History at Harvey Mudd College. He was formerly chairman of the Liberal Studies Division of the American Society for Engineering Education and is an advisory editor of *Technology and Culture.* His books include the prize-winning *American Automobile Manufacturers* and *The American Automobile.*

Wayne D. Rasmussen is Chief of the Agricultural History Branch of the United States Department of Agriculture in Washington, D.C. He has served as president of the Agricultural History Society and has written many articles on agricultural technology, the interaction of technological and economic changes, and agricultural policy. He is the author of *A History of the Emergency Farm Labor Supply Program, 1943-47,* editor of *Readings in the History of American Agriculture,* and co-author of *A Century of Service: The First One Hundred Years of the United States Department of Agriculture.*

Theodore Ropp is Professor of History at Duke University, chairman of the Board of the Historical Evaluation and Research Organization, a trustee of the American Military Institute, and former member of the Secretary of the Army's Historical Advisory Committee. He is the author of *War in the Modern World* and has written many articles on military history.

Richard Rosenbloom is Associate Professor of Business Administration and research associate to the Program of Technology and Society at Harvard University. Specializing in problems in the administration of research, development, and technological innovation, he is the author of *Technology Transfer-Process and Policy* and of a number of articles and papers on related subjects.

Melvin M. Rotsch is Professor of Architectural History at Texas A&M University. In addition to having architectural experience in the United States and abroad, he has published articles on landscape, planning, and architectural history in professional journals.

Ralph Sanders is Associate Professor of Political Science at the Industrial College of the Armed Forces and professorial lecturer at American University. He is the author of *Project Plowshare: The Development of the Peaceful Uses of Nuclear Explosives* and co-editor of *New Dimensions in the Cold War* and *Science and Technology: A National Resource.*

Morgan Sherwood teaches the history of American science and technology at the University of California, Davis. He is the author of *Exploration of Alaska, 1865-1900* and co-editor of *The Politics of American Science, 1939 to the Present.*

Thomas Malcolm Smith, Associate Professor of the History of Science at the University of Oklahoma, was formerly scientific historian, Headquarters, Air Research and Development Command of the United States Air Force. He is the co-author of *Architects of Aviation* and co-editor of *The Challenge of our Times.*

Donald C. Swain is Associate Professor of History at the University of California, Davis, specializing in the 20th-century history of American scientific research. He is author of *Federal Conservation Policy, 1921-1933* and co-editor of *The Politics of American Science, 1939 to the Present.*

Robert Theobald, a British socioeconomist who is now an economic consultant in New York City, has written widely on the effects of abundance, made possible through technological developments, on the American society and economy. Among his publications are *The Rich and The Poor, The Challenge of Abundance,* and *Free Men and Free Markets.* He is also editor of *The Guaranteed Income: Next Step in Socioeconomic Evolution.*

Charles R. Walker was, until his retirement, Senior Research Fellow in Industrial Relations and director of the Technology Project of Yale University. He is the author of *Steeltown: An Industrial Case History of the Conflict Between Progress and Security* and *Toward the Automatic Factory,* co-author of *The Man on the Assembly Line,* and editor of *Modern Technology and Civilization.*

Reynold M. Wik is May Treat Morrison Professor of American History at Mills College. He is the author of the prize-winning *Steam Power on the American Farm* and of many articles on scientific and technological developments in American agriculture.

Ernest W. Williams, Jr., is Professor of Transportation at the Graduate School of Business at Columbia University. He specializes in transportation, economic geography, and business policy, and has occupied a number of government posts dealing with those matters. His books include *Freight Transportation in the Soviet Union, The Regulation of Rail-Motor Rate Competition,* and *Economics of Transportation.*

Subject Index

abacus, 310-12, 313
abundance
    Basic Economic Security (BES), 111-15, 116
    crisis of, 103-16
acceleration of technology, 3-4
acetyl-salicylic acid, 188
acoustical control, 232
additives, food, 400
Admiral Corporation, 652
adrenaline, 188
advertising, 83, 331, 501, 697
aerodynamic research, 163-65
aeronautical engineering. *See* airplane, aviation, rockets, satellites, *etc.*
aerosol dispensers, 397
Aerospace Corporation, 547
Africa, industrial systems in, 74
Agricultural Adjustment Administration, 513
agriculture, 8-9, 698
    dairy products, 393-94
    fertilizers, 348-53
    fruit-picking, 365
    genetics, science of, 338-39
    hybrid corn, 339-43
    interrelatedness of factors, 353
    livestock, 345-48
    scientific, 337-53
    soybeans, 344-45
    in underdeveloped countries, 527-28
    wheat, new varieties of, 343-44
    see also food, insecticides, mechanization of agriculture, pest control
Agriculture Department, U. S., 133, 134, 341, 344, 345, 346, 352, 354, 356, 367, 371, 374, 380, 381, 383, 414, 438, 443, 448, 537, 698
aircraft carrier, 168, 582
air conditioning, 228-32, 233
air-cooled engine, 122, 158, 172
Air Force, U. S., 544, 546, 582, 645
airlines, development of, 173-76
air mail, 173
airplane, 3, 8, 28, 697
    agricultural use of, 368

air defense systems, 179
airframe and airfoil design improvements, 163 ff
air safety system, 177 ff
bombers, 168 ff, 565 ff
development of commercial airframe, 174
development of component systems, 162-63
engine development, 157 ff
equipment problems, 161-62
first success, 155
military stimulus to development, 154, 167 ff
military use of, 168-71, 554, 559, 561, 565-67 577, 579, 580-81, 582 ff, 598, 609
propulsion design, 158 ff
Spirit of St. Louis, 172
systems and control improvements, 160 ff
as weapons system, 563
Wright biplane, 155
see also aviation, jet aircraft
air-pollution control programs, 476-77
Alamogordo, New Mexico, 260, 575
Alcoa Building, Pittsburgh, 215
Allis Chalmers, 361
alloys, 184
aluminum, 184
aluminum foil, 398
American Association for the Advancement of Science, 504
American Bantam Car Company, 132
"the American century," 5-6
American Concrete Institute, 204, 207
American Federation of Labor (AFL), 66, 503
American Forest Congress, 440
American Forestry Association, 439
American Foundation on Automation and Employment, 105, 111
American Management Association, 56
American Marconi Company, 301, 302
American Society for Testing Materials, 204, 621

American Society of Mechanical Engineers, 103
"American system," 9
American Telephone & Telegraph Company (AT&T), 300-302, 626, 627, 629, 630
aminotriazole, 378, 380-81
ammonia and ammonia compounds, 185, 351, 378
amplifying equipment, electronic, 232
amplitude modulation (AM), 301
analog computor, 313
Annapolis, Maryland, 464
antiaircraft devices, 575
antibiotics, 193-94, 576
Appalachian Regional Development Act (1965), 461
Applied Physics Laboratory, 547, 574, 678
arc lamp, 224, 225
architecture
  "Chicago school," 199 ff
  "De Stijl" movement, 201
  "International school," 205-6, 408
  see also construction and individual architects
Area Redevelopment Act (1961), 460
Argonne National Laboratory, 263, 264, 265, 268, 270
arms control, 587-89
Army, U. S., 307, 320, 544, 546, 560, 582, 677
  Air Corps, U. S., 566, 596
  Ballistic Missile Agency, 678
  Corps of Engineers, 445, 446, 454-55
  Industrial College, 598
  Signal Corps, 542
Around the World in Eighty Days (Verne), 30
arsenic, 373-74, 379
artificial breeding associations, 347-48
Asdic, 408
aspirin, 188
assembly line, 38, 45-47, 93, 648-49
Atabrine, 576
Atlantic Cable, 307
Atmosphere Research Panel, 677
Atomic age, 273-75, 586
atomic energy, 21, 255, 256-75, 287, 546, 632
  economics of nuclear power, 273-75
  European programs, 265-66, 270-71
  Fermi pile, 259-60
  first reactor, 259-60
  fission, 256-57
  Geneva Conferences on, 271, 274, 275
  international control of, 579
  military development of, 258 ff
  power reactor development, 266 ff
  uranium isotopes, 257 ff
  see also Atomic Energy Commission, atomic weapons, nuclear reactor
Atomic Energy Act (1946), 261, 266, 268, 274

Atomic Energy Commission, U. S., 261 ff, 266, 268 ff., 273 ff, 424, 497, 545-46, 605, 609
atomic weapons, 27, 542, 562, 563, 575 ff, 580 ff, 592, 595, 608, 677, 698
  fallout, radiation, 589
  hydrogen bomb, 546
  Manhattan Project, 260-61
  spread of, 589
  thermonuclear, 546, 580, 583, 585
  see also atomic energy
audion, 297, 298
Australia, food packaging in, 396
automation, 20, 26, 52, 99, 151, 513
  automatic control, 644-46
  automatic manufacturing, 649-51
  automatic production machines, 642-44
  benefits of, 654-55
  collective bargaining and, 69-71
  computer joins, 653-54
  continuous movement, 646-48
  definitions of, 635-40 passim
  furor over, 638-44
  manufacturing trend toward, 458-59
  techniques, development of, 641-42
  transfer machine, 643-44
  unemployment from, 659
  see also computer, cybernation
Automation—The Advent of the Automatic Factory (Diebold), 636-37
Automation Commission, 103-4, 105, 107, 111-12, 115
automobile, 3, 7, 8, 19, 30-31, 87, 90 ff, 101, 401, 477, 513, 697
  automotive revolution, 125-29
  brake system, 127
  compact car, 128
  diesel engine, 128
  early models, 122 ff
  electric, 122, 123
  electric starting system, 127
  on the farm, 365-66
  free wheeling, 127
  horseless-carriage era, 121-24
  later innovations, 127
  model changes, annual, 127
  modern prototype, 121
  overdrive, 127
  patent conflict over, 125 ff
  steam-driven, 119-20, 123-24
  transmission systems, 122, 127
  see also automobile assembly line, automobile industry, engine, Model T
automobile assembly line, 38, 45-46, 47, 55-61, 93-95, 648, 649
automobile industry, 133, 643
  and American economy, 135-36
  Ford and Olds, 125 ff
  foreign, 128 ff
  growth of, 121 ff
  mass production in, 128 ff
  production techniques, 42-48
autorack, 147

aviation
  aerodynamic research, 163-65
  air-mail service, 173
  airlines, 173-76
  balloons, 165, 168
  development of, 153-80
  development of civil aviation, 171 ff
  dirigibles, 165-67
  lighter-than-air ships, 165-67
  Lindbergh flight, 172
  research and development, 154
  support facilities, 177-79
  see also airplane

Badische Anilin-und Soda-Fabrik, 191
Bakelite, 186, 187
balloons, 165, 168
barges, 146, 152
Basic Economic Security (BES), 113-15, 116
bathing facilities, home, 220-21, 223
Battelle Memorial Institute, 630
Battle of Britain, 561, 573
Battle of the Bulge, 574
Battle of Cambrai (1917), 553
Battle of the Marne (1914), 129, 559
Bauhaus, Dessau, Germany, 205, 206, 480
Bay Area Rapid Transit Project, San Francisco, 477
Bay View Terrace Apartments, Milwaukee, 208
beehive oven, 240, 467
Bell Telephone Laboratories, 303, 306, 632, 636
benzene hexachloride (BHC), 376, 381, 382
Berlin blockade, 579
bicycle, 122, 135
binder, harvesting, 355
blimps, 167
blitzkrieg, 565, 577
block signal controls, 141
blood and blood substitutes, 576-77
Boeing Aircraft Corporation, 173-74, 176, 579
Boer War, 551
Bordeaux mixture, 384-85
"Boston Associates," 465
boxcar, 147
Brave New World (Huxley), 32
bridge construction, 213
British Daimler Company, 121
British Marconi Company, 302
broadcasting. *See* radio, television
building
  codes, 205, 207, 215
  industry, backwardness of, 470-71
  see also construction, housing, urban planning and development *and individual buildings and architects*
Bull Traction Machine Company, 360
Bureau of Fisheries, 539
Bureau of Forestry, 440

Bureau of Mines, 350, 539
Bureau of Public Roads, 134
Bureau of the Budget, 493, 498, 543
buses, 131-32

C.N.I.T. Hall, Paris, 212
Cadillac Motor Car Company, 126, 127
calcium carbide, 184
calculus, 314
California Institute of Technology, 11, 164
Camus system, precast housing units, 219
Canada
  atomic energy program, 265, 274
  food packaging, 396
  natural gas industry, 247
canning, 386 ff, 397-98, 605
carbamates, 378
cargo shipping, 149 ff
Carrier Corporation, 229
Carson, Pirie, Scott Building, Chicago, 198, 199
Cartercar, 122
cartons, food packaging, 398-99
Case Western Reserve University, 431
Cash Buyers Union, 83
cast-in-place piling, 205
catalog sales, 83
catalysis, electricity and, 184-85
cattle breeding, 345-48, 440
caustic soda, 184
cavity magnetron, 305
cellophane, 398, 618
cellulose, 186
Census Bureau, U. S., 8, 474, 638
central-heating systems, 227
cereals, processing, 394-95
Ceylon Institute of Scientific and Industrial Research, 525
chain reaction, nuclear, 256-57, 259, 266
chain stores, 79, 81, 85-86, 401
Chamber of Commerce, U. S., 503
charge accounts, 90
Charleston, South Carolina, 464
chemical engineering. *See* chemical industry, energy resources, insecticides, *etc.*
chemical industry, 9, 14, 183-95, 607
  antibiotics, 193-94
  chemical process units, 194
  development of, 183-84
  drugs, 188-89, 192-93
  dyestuffs, 187-88, 189, 192-93
  electricity and catalysis, 184-85
  petrochemicals, 189-90
  plastics, 185 ff, 190-92
  progress to 1930, 189
  vitamins, 189, 193-94
  see also disease control, insecticides, pest control, *and individual chemicals*
Chemical Warfare Service, U. S. Army, 539

"Chicago School" of architecture, 199
Chicago Transit Authority, 475
Chlordane, 377
chlorine, 184
City in History, The (Mumford), 482
city planning. *See* urban planning and
    development
Civil Aeronautics Board, 178
civil aviation. *See* aviation
civil engineering. *See* architecture, build-
    ing, housing, roads, water, *etc.*
Civilian Conservation Corps (CCC), 448,
    459, 508
Civil Rights Act (1964), 460
Civil War, American, 168, 451, 536, 537,
    559, 562
Clark University, 630
coal
    "coal-oil" lamp, 223
    coal-tar distillates, 187, 189
    coke industry, 240
    consumption, 253
    distribution of, 280-81
    improved preparation methods, 239-40
    mechanization of mining operations,
        237 ff
    methods of underground mining, 238-
        39
    reserves, 280-82
    surface mining, 239
    as source of energy, 237-40, 253-54
Cobden Treaty (1860), 491
Coignet system, precast housing units,
    209
coke industry, 240
cold war, 256, 262, 580, 633-34
collective bargaining, 64, 69 ff, 74
Columbia University, 503
column-and-beam construction, 209
Commerce Department, U. S., 178, 362,
    489, 495, 541
commercial vehicles, 129-33
Commission on Industrial Relations, U. S.,
    65
Commission on the Patent System, 490
Committee for Economic Development,
    460, 474
Committee on Medical Research (CMR),
    541
Committee on the Peaceful Uses of Outer
    Space, U. N., 680
Commonwealth Edison Company, 268,
    269, 272
communication
    early, 323
    electronic, 8, 293-309, 698
    motion picture, 326, 327
    new media, 326 ff
    newspapers, 324-25, 328
    printing, 324
    radar, 305-6
    satellites, 608, 609, 674, 698
    telegraphy, 325 ff
    see also mass media, radio, television

Communication Satellite Corporation,
    609-10, 633
communitarian settlements, 462-64
Compagnie Générale de Télégraphie sans
    Fils, 302
Comptoir des Textiles Artificiels, 618
computer, 148, 253, 515, 594, 605, 638,
    645, 653-54, 667
    abundance and, 104-5
    analog, 312
    auxiliary devices, 322
    binary system of calculation, 321
    "branching," 316
    Differential Analyzer, 320
    digital, 313, 320-22
    early designs for, 316 ff
    EDVAC, 605
    electronic, 320-22
    ENIAC 320, 321, 605
    machine-tool influence, 315 ff
    Mark I (1944), 319-20, 321, 605
    marketing use of, 91
    and mathematical calculator tradition,
        310 ff
    punched cards, 318-19, 645
    sources of, 310 ff
    time-sharing, 321
    uses, 309-10
    see also mathematical calculator,
        H. Aiken, C. Babbage
concrete
    reinforced, 204-10
    shell structures, 210-13
    transit-mixer, 207
    see also construction
Congress of Industrial Organizations
    (CIO), 67
conservation
    arid West, 432-34
    Conservation Movement, 431, 432, 433,
        441-42, 446-48
    forestry program, 437-41
    land management, 442-43
    mineral lands, 444
    reclamation, 434-37
    water, 444-46
Consolidated Edison Company of New
    York, 269
construction
    Camus system, 219
    challenge of mass production, 470-71
    Coignet system, 209
    column-and-beam, 209
    concrete shells, 210-12
    high-rise, 196 ff
    Jesperson system, 209
    Koslov system, 209
    lift-slab, concrete, 208
    new methods, 209 ff
    prefabricated, 209 ff
    reinforcement and stressing, 207 ff
    Sectra system, 209
    skeleton-frame, 196 ff, 207
    skyscraper, 9, 197 ff, 214-17, 227

slip-form system, 208
Tersons system, 209
tilt-up concrete, 208
consumer credit, 90, 697
consumer goods, 49
Consumers Power Company of Michigan, 273
Consumers Public Power District of Nebraska, 268
container ships, 151
continuous-mining machine, 238
controlled-atmosphere storage, 390
"convenience foods," 387-88
conversion of energy, 279
co-operative wholesaling, 86
Cornell University, 621, 626
Corning Glass Works, 626
Corn Laws, 496
corn picker, 364
Cotton Kingdom, 451, 456
cotton picker, 363-64
Council of National Defense, 538
craft unionism, 70
crag herbicide, 378
critics of technology, 6-7, 32-33, 699-701
cross-licensing agreements, 630
croton oil, 372
crude oil, 237, 253, 255, 284
Crystal Palace Exhibition (1851), 221, 495
Cuban missile crisis (1962), 589
cultural factors of underdevelopment, 517-18
cybernation
    direct effect on worker, 663-65
    education and, 668-69
    employment and, 659-63
    impact of, 655-69
    leisure time and, 665-66
    opinions about, 658-59
    social context, 656-58
    see also automation
Cybernetics (Wiener), 636
cyclonite (RDX), 576

Daily News Building, New York City, 201
dairy products, 393-94
Darwinism, 3
DDT, 368, 375-76, 381, 382
Defense Department, U. S., 498, 544, 547, 548, 581, 680
Defense of the Realm Act, British, 559
defoliants, 378
dehydration of food, 391
Delaney Amendment (1958), 380
delivery technologies, 565-72
department store, 79, 80, 81, 82, 89, 90
depressed areas, 459, 528-30
Depression (1930's), 32, 66, 72, 90, 96, 127, 172, 202, 203, 214, 246, 337, 386, 394, 457, 459, 496, 500, 502, 508, 514, 539, 631-32
depth charge, 572, 576

desalination of water, 419-24, 427
    electrodialysis process, 423
    flash distillation process, 421-22
    freezing, purification by, 424
    ion-exchange process, 424
    reverse-osmosis process, 424
    solvent method, 424
    submerged-tube process, 421, 422
    vapor-compression distillation method, 423
"De Stijl" movement, 201
detergents, 190
deuterium, 257
Deutschland, 148
developing countries. See underdeveloped countries
Diedrin, 377, 381, 384
diesel, 128, 130 ff, 152
    freight advantage of, 144 ff
    locomotive, 143-46
    on shipboard, 149
digital computer, 313, 320-22
dirigible, 165-67
disarmament, dilemma of, 600-601
distribution
    handling of goods, 89-90
    organization of, 77-91
    see also cargo shipping, freight, food, marketing, resources
DNA, 339
Douglas Aircraft Company, 173, 174, 175, 176, 547
Dow Chemical Corporation, 630
Dreadnought, 556, 597
drugs, 188-89, 192-93, 576-77
Du Pont Company, 626, 629, 630
Duquesne Light Company, 267
Duryea automobile, 121
Dutch elm disease, 370-71
dyestuffs, 187-88, 189, 192-93

East African Industrial Research Organization, 525
Eastman Kodak Company, 623, 626
Eau Grison, 374
Echo communications satellite, 307
echo-sounders, 408
École des Beaux-Arts, 199
École National des Ponts et Chaussées, 491
École Polytechnique, 11, 491
Economic Opportunity Act (1964), 260
economic problems and public policy, 495-97
"Edison effect," 296
Edison Electric Company, 224
education
    cybernation and, 668-69
    future of, 114-15
    mass media and, 332-34
    technical, 11-12, 491-94, 525-26
EDVAC computer, 605
Eiffel Tower, 201
Einstein Observatory, Potsdam, 206

Eisenbeton, Der (Mörsch), 204
Electric Vehicle Company, 126
electrical engineering. *See* communication, computer, electricity, radio, television, *etc.*
electrical industry, 14, 495, 624-27. *See also* T. Edison *and individual companies*
electricity
   catalysis and, 184-85
   direct production of, 247 ff, 255
   early uses of, 247
   electrical appliances, 221, 223
   electric automobile, 122, 123
   electric locomotive, 143
   electric motor, 247, 254, 367
   as energy source, 237, 247-53, 254
   for fishing, 409
   furnace, electric, 184
   generation of, 247 ff, 253
   hydropower, 247 ff
   lighting, 17, 224-26, 366-67
   "power pools," 252
   for railroad, 142-43
   transmission of, 249-50
electrodialysis process, water desalination, 423
electronic digital computer, 320-22
electronics, 577. *See also* communication, printed circuits, radio, television, transistor, *etc.*
electron-scanning tube, 303
elevator, passenger, 196, 197, 199, 203
Empire State Building, New York City, 196, 201-3
emulsifiers, 190
Endrin, 377
energy resources
   biological, 237, 286-87
   capital resources, 275, 278
   coal, 237-40, 253, 254, 280-81
   consumption, shifts in, 253 ff
   conversion, 279
   crude oil, 237
   economics and supplies of, 276-79
   electric power, 237, 247-53, 254
   factors influencing development, 276 ff, 288-89
   fossil fuel, 279-80, 281
   future sources, 254-56, 275-89
   geothermal, 287
   hydropower, 250-52
   income energy resources, 275, 278
   natural gas, 237, 246-47, 253, 283-84
   oil shales, 255, 284
   patterns of use, 288-89
   petroleum, 240-46, 281-83
   pooled resources, 252
   solar, 286
   stored energy, 275
   tidal power, 285
   "tar sands," 255, 284
   transport of energy, 276
   water power, 284-85
   wind power, 285-86
   wood, 237
   see also atomic energy *and under specific resources*
engine
   air-cooled, 122, 158, 172
   eight-cylinder, 126-27
   gas-turbine, 158, 159
   piston, 157, 159
   see also diesel, internal-combustion engine, locomotive, steam power
England. *See* Great Britain
ENIAC (Electronic Numerical Integrator and Computer), 320, 321, 605
Erie Canal, 494
Essay on Population (Malthus), 414
Europe. *See under specific technologies and individual countries*
European Atomic Energy Community (Euratom), 271, 616
European Space Research Organization, 681
Experimental Boiling Water Reactor (EBWR), 268, 270, 273
Experimental Breeder Reactor, 263, 264, 268, 270, 273
explosives, 576

Farbenwerke Bayer, 193
Federal Aviation Administration, 178
Federal Communications Commission, 304
Federal Power Act (1920), 459
Federation of Atomic Scientists, 546
feedback control, 645
fertilizers, 348-53
Finletter Commission, 586
fire control in warfare, 573, 574
fish industry, 402-13, 616
   catching methods, 407-9
   fish-meal, 403-4
   future prospects, 411-12
   gear, 407
   in Japan, 403, 404
   mariculture (sea farming), 412-13
   processing at sea, 410-11
   Soviet Union, 403-5
   vessels, 402, 403-4, 405-7, 410-11
fission, 256-57
flame-thrower, 575-76
flash boiler, 123, 124
flash distillation, water desalination, 421-22, 423
flow of materials concept, 38
fluorescent lamp, 226
fluorine compounds, 374
food
   additives, 400
   baked goods, 394-95
   canning, 386, 388, 389
   cereals, 394-95
   chilling, 389-90
   dairy products, 393-94
   dehydration, 391
   distribution, 86 ff, 386, 401
   fish, 402-13

food-service industry, 387
freezing, 390-91
for the future, 414-27
meat-packing, 391-93
packaging, 386, 395-400, 401-2
population explosion and, 414-15, 427
processing, 386-88, 401-2
radiation preservation, 391
wrapping materials, 398
see also agriculture, fish industry
Food and Drug Administration, 379, 380,
  381
forced-air circulation heating system, 227
Ford Motor Company, 44-48, 49, 51, 125,
  132, 365, 635, 649, 651-53
Forest Commission, U. S., 438
Forest Service, U. S., 439, 440, 444, 447,
  539
forestry program, federal, 437-41
fossil fuels, 279-80, 281
fractionation, 243, 244
France
  atomic energy program, 259, 266, 270,
    271, 274
  automobile industry, 120, 121, 128,
    129
  aviation development, 165
  chemical industry, 193
  construction in, 203-4, 205, 208, 211,
    212
  industrial research, 618
  national road system, 133
  nuclear tests, 589
  radio development, 301, 302
Franklin motor car, 122
freeways, 135, 136
freeze-drying, 391
freezer, home, 401
freezing, salt water purified by, 424
freight
  domestic traffic, 153
  freight car, 142, 147
  reduction of rates, 147
  rail services, 146 ff
Freon-12, 230, 630
frequency modulation (FM), 303, 304,
  305
Frigidaire, 49
frozen foods, 390-91
fuel cell, 255
fuels. See energy resources *and specific
  fuels*

Galalith, 187
game theory, 593-94
Garden City movement, 471-72, 473,
  479
gas
  gas-cooled atomic reactor, 273
  gasoline, 243, 245, 254, 630
  industry, 246-47
  gas lighting, 223, 224
  liquefied, 247
  gasoline motor, 358
  natural, 223, 237, 253

pipelines, 221, 246
gas range, 221
gas-turbine engine, 158, 159
gas-turbine locomotives, 145-46
Gemini program, 683
General Dam Act (1906), 445
General Electric Company, 14, 263, 265,
  269, 302, 303, 625-26, 627, 629, 630,
  631
General Electric Research Laboratory, 9,
  14, 18
General Motors Corporation, 48, 49, 125,
  130, 144, 629, 630, 697
General Survey Act (1824), 455
generation of electricity, 247-49, 253
genetics, science of, 8, 338-39
Geneva Conferences, 271, 274, 275
Geological Survey, U. S., 350, 432-33,
  434, 437, 444, 445, 539
geothermal energy, 287
Germany
  automobile industry, 120, 121, 128
  aviation development, 158, 165-67
  chemical industry, 184, 185, 193
  coal mining, 239
  community planning and housing, 480
  construction, 204, 205, 208, 210-11
  industrial research, 615-16, 617
  radio development, 301, 302, 303
  social control of technology, 499
Gesarol, 375
glass containers, food packaging, 396-97
glass-making, 48-49
Goodrich Tire and Rubber Company,
  629, 645
Goodyear Tire and Rubber Company,
  129, 629
government-industry co-operation, 526-27
Governors' Conference (1908), 446
Graf Zeppelin, 166
Graham-Paige Motors Corporation, 644
Grand Canal of Languedoc, 494
Grand Coulee Dam, 251
Great Atlantic and Pacific Tea Company,
  85, 86, 87
Great Britain, 39, 64
  atomic energy program, 258, 259, 265-
    66, 270-71, 272, 274
  automobile industry, 121, 129
  aviation development, 158
  chemical industry, 184, 191
  community planning and housing, 480
  concrete construction, 204
  industrial research, 615, 617-18
  New Towns program, 479, 483
  nuclear tests, 589
  plastics, 191
  radio development, 301, 302, 303, 305
  social control of technology, 499
  textile industry, 95-96
  workers' movements, 74
Great Depression. *See* Depression
Great Northern Railroad, 143
Grocer and Country Merchant, 81
guaranteed income, 111 ff

Guaranteed Income, The (Lovenstein), 107
Guggenheim Aeronautical Laboratory, 164

Hammersmith Ironworks, Saugus, Massachusetts, 38
handling of goods, 89-90
harvester, 362, 363-65
Hayden Planetarium, New York City, 211
heating, 218, 226-28
helicopter, 598
helium, 166
Heptachlor, 377, 381, 384
herbicides, 378
heterodyne receiver, 301
hexachlorocyclohexane, 376-77
highways, 129, 132, 133-35
Hiroshima, 256, 259, 575, 578
Holland, community planning and housing in, 480
home facilities
    acoustical control, 232
    air conditioning, 228-32
    bathing, 220-21
    heating, 218, 226-28
    kitchen appliances, 221-22
    lighting, 218, 222-26
    in mid-19th century, 217-19
    sewage disposal, 219-20
Home Insurance Building, Chicago, 197
Homestead, Pennsylvania, 467-69
homogeneous reactor, 264-65, 268, 270
homogenization, 393-94
Hoover Dam, 249
hopper cars, 147
horseless-carriage era, 121-24
household appliances, 221
housing
    community planning and, 480-81
    federal grant and loan programs, 478
    low- and middle-income projects, 478, 480
    public, 478, 481
    renewal projects, 478-79, 480, 481
    see also construction *and under countries*
hovercraft, 152
"humanization" of work, 75-76
human relations movement, 61-63
Human Use of Human Beings, The (Wiener), 636, 639
hump yard, railroad, 147
hybrid corn, 339-43
hydrocarbons, 185, 190, 477
hydroelectric power, 8, 237, 250-52
hydrofoil, 152
hydrogen, 166
hydrogen bomb, 546
hydroponics, 418-19
hypar shells, 211

ice-making machinery, 228, 229
"iconoscope" camera tube (television), 304

Idea of Progress, 3-10, 23, 695-96
Idemitsu Maru, 151
"image dissector" tube (television), 304
Imperial Chemical Industries, Ltd., 618, 645
imperialism and technology, 22-23
incandescent bulb, 17-18, 225-26
incendiary bombs, 563, 575
India, technical research in, 526
indigo, synthesis of, 187-88, 189
Industrial College of the Armed Forces, 560
Industrial Development Center, U.N., 527
industrial engineering. *See* automation, distribution, industrial research and development, labor, mass production, production, Scientific Management, work
industrial research and development
    analysis and testing, 621
    basic standards, 621-22
    cold war developments, 633-34
    Depression of the 1930's and, 631-32
    early examples of, 620 ff
    electrical industry, 624-27
    France, 618
    Germany, 615-16, 617
    Great Britain, 615, 617-18
    research institutions, 623-24
    Japan, 618-19
    post-World War I developments, 628-31
    post-World War II developments, 633-34
    Soviet Union, 619
    United States, 620
    World War I effects on, 627-28
    World War II effects on, 632-33
Industrial Revolution, 4, 5, 22, 39, 64, 96, 217, 288, 433, 699, 702, 703, 705
industrial unionism, 66 ff
Industrial Workers of the World (IWW), 503
industrialism, social effects, 465
"inflated balloon" process, shell concrete construction, 213
Influence of Sea Power upon History, The (Mahan), 592
Ingalls (Transit) Building, Cincinnati, 205
Inland Steel Building, Chicago, 216
Inland Waterways Commission, 445, 446
innovation, 18-19, 20, 21-22, 194, 602
Insecticide Act (1910), 380
insecticides, 368, 576
    chemical pesticides, controversial aspects of, 378-82
    DDT, 368, 375-76, 381, 382
    inorganic, 373-74
    organic, 371-73
    organic poisons, synthetic, 374-75
installment credit, 90
Institute Centroamericano de Investiga-

ción y Technología Industrial, 525
Institute for Defense Analysis, 547
institutions, educational, research. *See under specific names*
intelligence technologies, 573-75
interchangeability, concept of, 40 ff, 51, 55
intercontinental ballistic missile (ICBM), 556, 580, 582, 584, 585, 587, 588, 677
Interior Department, U. S., 381, 424, 439, 440, 443, 448, 489, 508
intermediate range ballistic missile (IRBM), 584
internal-combustion engine, 119, 120, 123, 126-27, 132, 135-36, 157
International Association for the Exchange of Students for Technical Experience, 525
International Association of Machinists, 65
International Business Machines Corporation (IBM), 105, 318, 318, 605
International Council of Scientific Unions, 678
International Geophysical Year (1957-58), 677, 678, 680
International Harvester Company, 359, 361
international manufacturing systems, 527
interstate highway program, 135, 476
ion-exchange process, water desalination, 424
iron production, 38, 196-97
irrigation, 415-17, 433, 435, 487
Israel
    economic progress, 531
    technical research, 526
Italy, automobile industry, 129

Jablockhoff candle, 224
Jacquard loom, 318, 319
Japan, 22-23, 52
    automobile industry, 129
    economic progress, 531
    fish industry, 403, 404
    industrial development, 518
    industrial research, 618-19
    labor-intensive techniques, 526
    technological flexibility of, 523
    in World War II, 561
jeep, 132-33
Jersey Central Power and Light Company, 274
Jesperson system, precast housing units, 209
jet aircraft, 566-67, 570, 578, 579, 585, 674
    development of, 176 ff
    engine, 158, 159, 608
    propulsion, 567, 632
Jet Propulsion Laboratory, 494, 677
Jodrell Bank Experimental Station, 681
Johns Hopkins University, 547, 621

Joint Research and Development Board (JRDB), 543-44
Journey to the Center of the Earth (Verne), 23

Kaiser Motors Company, 133
Kaiser Wilhelm Society, 14, 617
Kenya, technological research institutions in, 525
kerosene, 223, 243, 245, 254, 372
kitchen appliances, 221-22, 233
klystron, 305
Korean War, 128, 352, 580 ff, 585, 592, 598
Koslov system, precast housing units, 209
Krupp industries, 184, 617

labor
    division of, 38
    Scientific Management and, 64-66
    shift in demand for, 109-11
    technology and, 64-76
    see also unions
Lake Shore Drive Apartments, Chicago, 214, 215
lamp
    arc, 224, 225
    electric, 17-18, 224-26
    fluorescent, 226
    oil, 222-23
Land-Grant Agricultural College Act (1862), 492
land management, 442-43
Langley, 168
Lawrence College, 630
lead arsenate, 373-74
legislation, patent, 490-91
Lehigh University, 621
leisure, 99-101, 665-66

Liberia, technical research in, 525
lift-slab system, 208, 212-13
light attraction fishing, 409
lighter-than-air ships, 165-67
lighting, 218
    early sources, 222-23
    electric, 17-18, 224-26
    gas, 223, 224-26
lime-sulfur, 374
Limited Nuclear Test Ban Treaty (1963), 587
Lincoln Laboratories, 307
liquefied gas, 247
livestock, 345-48
Lockheed Aircraft Company, 173, 174, 175, 176
locomotive, 8
    articulated, 138
    diesel, 143-46
    electric, 143
    gas-turbine, 145-46
    Krauss-Maffei, 145
    Mallet, 138, 139
    refinements and improvements, 138 ff
    steam, 137-38, 143

locomotive (*Cont.*)
  superheater, 137 ff
  "super power," 139
  Union Pacific 4000-class, 140
  Zephyr, 143
logarithms, 312, 313
London purple, 373
Los Alamos Scientific Laboratory, 494
Lowell, Massachusetts, 465, 466
lubricating oils, 243
Luftwaffe, 565
lumber industry, 438, 439
Lusitania, 148

machine gun, 551-52, 554, 591
machine tools and computer, 315-16
Machinery Hall, Paris Exposition (1900),
  204
Macy department store, 80, 81
Maginot Line, 560
magnesium bomb, 575
magnetic mine, 572
magnetohydrodynamics (MHD), 255
magnetron, 305 ff
mail-order houses, 79, 82-85, 86
malathion, 377
maleic hydrazide, 378
Mallet locomotive, 138, 139
Manhattan, 150-51
Manhattan Project, 259, 261, 542
Manpower Development and Training
  Act (1962), 460
manufactured gas, 237
margarine, 189, 394
mariculture (sea farming), 412-13
marine diesel engine, 149
Mark I computer (1944), 319-20, 321,
  605
marketing
  chain stores, 79, 81, 85-86
  charge and credit system, 90
  department stores, 80
  distribution of goods, 78 ff
  handling of goods, 89-90
  in 1900, 79 ff
  mail-order houses, 79, 82-85
  organization of, 77-91
  shopping centers, 88-89
  supermarkets, 86-88
Marmon-Herrington Company, 132
Marshall Plan, 579
maser, 307
Massachusetts Institute of Technology,
  515
mass media
  audience, 328-29
  communication process, 329-31
  content, 331-32
  criticisms, 329
  education and, 332-34
  see also communication, radio, *etc.*
mass consumption, 38, 43, 44, 49, 102-3,
  107-9, 697
mass culture, 703

mass market. *See* mass consumption *and*
  mass production
mass production, 19-20, 25, 92-93, 577,
  697
  American success in, 40-42
  auto assembly line, 42-48
  definition of, 92
  early experiments, 38-40
  extension of, 48-49
  extractive industries, 49-51
  of firearms, 40-41
  flow of materials, 38-39
  from Industrial Revolution to 1900,
    10 ff
  fundamentals of, 37, 93
  mass consumption and, 102-3
  in process industries, 98-99
  social effects of, 91-103
  spread of, 48 ff
  in textile industry, 95-98
  work environment, 93-95
Mass Transportation Demonstration Project, Massachusetts, 477
Matabele War (1893), 551, 552
materials, synthetic. *See under individual
  materials and* chemical industry
Materials Testing Reactor, 263-64
mathematical calculator
  abacus, 310 ff
  digital calculator, 310 ff
  mechanical adder, 313-14
  odometer, 311
  and origins of computer, 310 ff
  slide rule, 313
  see also computer, Heron of Alexandria
Mauritania, 148
Max Planck Society, 14
McGraw-Hill Building, New York City,
  201
meat-packing industry, 41, 391-93, 648
mechanical engineering. *See* automobile,
  engine, gas, internal-combustion engine, locomotives, machine tools and
  computer, motors, production, railroads
Mechanical Smoke Generator, 576
mechanization of agriculture, 353-68
  abundant society and, 368
  airplane and, 368
  automobile and, 365-66
  early, 354-56
  electricity and, 366-67
  harvester, 362, 363-65
  increased productivity, 354
  steam power, 356-57
  tractor and, 357-63
mechanization of war (1880-1919), 548-
  61. *See also* World War I
medical technology. *See* chemical industry *and individual drugs*
Megalopolis, 7, 457, 481-82
Mellon Research Institute, 623
Menlo Park Laboratory, Edison's, 14, 625
Mercury space flights, 683

Merrimack Manufacturing Company, 620
metallurgy. *See* alloys, coal, mining, *and individual metals and minerals*
metal cans, 397-98
metal tubes, collapsible, 397
methanol, 185
Metropolitan Community, The (McKenzie), 473
metropolitan region. *See* urban planning and development
Miami-Dade County, Florida, 475
microorganisms, petroleum-based, 426-27
microwave and shortwave, 304-5
migration, 459
  migratory farm workers, 457
  Negro, 456, 457
  suburban, 478
mileage meter. *See* odometer
military aviation, 167-68
military research
  Atomic Energy Commission, 545-46
  basic research, 543
  co-ordination of, 541
  and development, 543-45
  government research contract, 541
  and "knowledge" industries, 547-48
  National Aeronautics and Space Administration, 546-47
  National Defense Research Committee, 540-41
  National Science Foundation, 543
  Office of Scientific Research and Development, 541-43
  organization of, 535-48
  regression between World Wars, 538-40
  in World War I, 537-38
military technology
  since World War II, 583
  in Space Age, 589-90
  transfer to civilian use, 601-12
milk concentrates, 394
Miller Amendment (1954), 380
Milwaukee Line, 143
mineral lands, conservation program, 444, 447
mineral oils and tars, 372
mines (weapons), 572, 576, 591
mining industry, 50-51, 237-39
Ministry of Automation, Russian, 638
Ministry of Technology, British, 618
Mirex (Kepone), 384
missiles, 170-71, 546, 556, 568-69, 572, 573, 580, 582, 584, 585, 587, 674, 677, 684
MITRE Corporation, 547
Model T Ford, 45, 46-47, 51, 93, 125, 126, 365, 629
Mohole project, 21
Monadnock Building, Chicago, 196, 197
Morrill Land-Grant Act (1862), 621
motion pictures, 4, 8, 31, 326-27
motors
  electric, 247, 254, 367

gasoline, 358
multi-packaging, 399

Nagasaki, 256, 260, 575
napalm bomb, 575
"Napier's rods," 312-13
Nashville-Davidson County, Tennessee, 475
National Academy of Sciences (NAS), 438, 493, 497, 536, 537-38, 539, 540, 543, 562, 678
National Advisory Committee for Aeronautics (NACA), 161, 493, 497, 538, 539, 541, 542, 546
National Aeronautics and Space Administration (NASA), 493, 546-47, 609, 610, 633, 680
National Bureau of Standards (NBS), 13, 303, 493, 496, 539, 622
National Commission on Technology, Automation, and Economic Progress, 641, 695
National Conservation Commission, 446
National Defense Research Committee (NDRC), 514, 540-41, 562
National Electric Light Association, 622
national forests, 442, 444
National Institute for Physical and Chemical Research, Japan, 619
National Inventors Council, 495, 541
National Irrigation Congress, 434
National Labor Relations Board (NLRB), 68
National Physical Laboratory, British, 622
National Planning Association, 460
National Reactor Testing Station, Idaho, 263, 264, 268
National Recovery Administration (NRA), 509-11
National Research Council (NRC), 497, 538, 539, 540, 562, 619, 628, 631
National Resources Committee, 489, 497, 511
National Resources Planning Board, 460, 497-98, 511, 631
National Science Foundation (NSF), 490, 493, 495, 543, 545
National System of Political Economy (List), 491
natural gas, 223, 237
  pipelines, 246
  supplies of, 283-84
  tanker transport, 246-47
  see also petroleum
natural resources. *See* conservation, energy resources
Naval Consulting Board, 537, 538
naval power, 554-58
Naval Research Laboratory, 537, 539, 542, 545, 678
Navy, U. S., 166, 171, 265, 544-45, 546, 555, 576, 582
Navy Bureau of Steam Engineering, 497
neutrodyne receiver, 302

New Deal, 67, 366, 436, 448, 459, 460, 504-14, 540, 632
Newlands Act (1902), 435
newspapers, 324-26, 328
New Towns program, 477, 479, 483
New York City, 199, 200-201, 214, 218, 219, 464, 470, 474
New York Metropolitan Area, 478
nicotine, 372
Nigeria, technical research in, 526
nitrates, 185
nitric oxide, 477
nitrogenous fertilizers, synthetic, 351-52
Normandy invasion, 570
North American Aviation, Inc., 267
North Atlantic Treaty Organization (NATO), 582, 586
Northrup automatic loom, 500
nuclear dilemma, 592-93
nuclear reactor
    development plans, 262 ff
    for electrical generation, 261, 263, 266 ff
    Experimental Boiling Water (EBWR), 268, 270, 273
    Experimental Breeder Reactor, 263, 264, 268, 270, 273
    experimental models, 262 ff
    European, 265-66, 270-71
    first, 259-60
    gas-cooled, 273
    Homogeneous Reactor, 264-65, 268, 270
    Materials Testing, 263-64
    Pressurized Water, 266, 267, 269-70, 272
    Sodium Reactor Experiment (SRE), 267
    water-cooled, 259-60
    see also atomic energy
nuclear submarines, 265, 546, 584
Nuclear Test Ban Treaty (1963), 546, 684
nuclear weapons. See atomic weapons
nylon, 192, 631

Oak Ridge, Tennessee, laboratory, 264, 265, 268, 270
oceans, exploration and development of, 21
odometer, 310, 311, 314, 323
Office of Manpower, Automation and Training, 641, 664
Office of Naval Research (ONR), 545
Office of Scientific Research and Delevopment (OSRD), 498, 541-43, 544, 547, 562-63, 595
Ohio State University, 630
oil
    catalytic cracking, 245
    drilling rig, 241
    lamp, 222-23
    pipelines, 152-53
    recovery of, 242

refining, 243
scientific methods of exploration, 240-41
oil shales, 284
thermal cracking, 243-44
see also petroleum
open-pit mining, 50
Operations Evaluation Group, 547
Opinion Research Corporation, 101
organic insecticides 371-73
Orly Airport, Paris, 210, 211

Pacific Gas and Electric Company, 273
packaging (food), 386, 395-400, 577
paperback books, 328
parathion, 377, 382
parcel post, 82
Paris green, 373
Paris International Exposition (1900), 6-7
Parke-Davis, pharmaceutical company, 626
passenger cars, railroad, 142
Pasteur Institute, 193
pasteurization, 389, 393
Patent Office, U. S., 489
patent system, 309, 488-90, 513, 630
payload technologies, 575-76
Pearl Harbor, Japanese attack on, 561
penicillin, 194, 577, 632
Pennsylvania Electric Company, 273
Pennsylvania Railroad, 142-43
personnel administration, 71-73
pest control, 369-85
    non-chemical, 382-84
    problems of, 369-71
    see also insecticides
petrochemicals, 189-90
petroleum, 253, 283
    exploration, 240-42
    as food source of the future, 426-27
    industry, 50
    oils, 372
    production, 240-42
    reserves, 281-83
    as source of energy, 240-46, 280-83
    thermal cracking, 243, 245
phenol 186, 187, 191
Philadelphia, Pennsylvania, 464
Philadelphia Centennial Exposition (1876), 120
Philadelphia Electric Company, 273
Philadelphia Savings Fund Society Building, 201, 202
Philco Corporation, 629
phosphate, 349
phylloxera, 370, 382
Physikalische-Technische Reichanstalt, 622
phytoplankton, 425
Piggly Wiggly self-service stores, 87
piggyback service, rail, 146-47
pipeline transmission
    gas, 221, 246
    oil, 152-53

piston engine, reciprocating, 157, 159
Pittsburgh, Pennsylvania, 467, 469, 472, 474
Pittsburgh Survey, 467
Place Victoria Building, Montreal, 215
plankton, 425-26, 427
plastics industry, 9, 15, 186, 190-92
plastic wrappers, 398
plow, 355, 366
plutonium, 257-58, 262
pneumatic tire, 122, 129
poison gas, 553
poisons, See pest control
Pollopases, 186
polymer chemistry, 631
Pope Manufacturing Company, 123, 129
population explosion, 31-32, 183, 275, 288, 414-15, 427
Populist Movement, 435
port cities, 464-65
Portland (hydraulic) cement, 204, 206, 207-8
Port of New York Authority, 475
Post Office Department, U. S., 173, 178
potash, 350
Poulsen arc, 298
power. See energy resources
power blackout, 233, 253
"power pools," 252
Power Reactor Development Company, 268
precision chronometer, 310
predatory insects and diseases, 382-83
prefabricated building systems, 209 ff
Presidential Commission on Automation, Technology and Economic Progress. See Automation Commission
President's Research Committee on Social Trends, 502
President's Scientific Research Board, 498
pressurized cans, 397
Pressurized Water Reactor, 266, 267, 269-70, 272
printed circuits, 321
printing press, 323, 324, 325
private enterprise, federal grants to, 494-95
private interests, public policies and, 519
process industries, mass production in, 98-99
product design, underdevelopment and, 521
production
    automatic, 642
    factor combinations in, 519-20
    organization of, 520-21
    rationalization of, 37-52
production machines, automatic, 642-44
production technologies, 577-78
Project Plowshare, 605
Project SCORE, 307, 608
Project Vanguard, 678
propaganda, 599-600
protective tariff, 490-91, 496, 497

protective technologies, 576-77
proximity fuse, 563, 570, 574
psychological warfare, 599-600
Public Health Service, 476
Public Lands Commission, 442, 443
public-opinion polls, 594
public policy
    in Classical civilizations, 487
    economic pressures and, 495-97
    governmental advisory organizations, 497-98
    grants to private enterprise, 494-95
    laissez-faire, 491
    patents, 488-90
    policy-making, 497-98
    private interests and, 519
    in the Renaissance, 488
    restrictive legislation, 490-91
    17th to 19th centuries, 494 ff
    social dislocation, 495-97
    technical education, 491-94
Public Works Administration (PWA), 448, 509
Public Works and Economic Development Act (1965), 461
pulley-block machinery, 642
punch card control system, 317-19, 645
purification of water, 218-19
pyrethrum, 371

Queen Elizabeth, 149
Queen Mary, 149

radar, 152, 305-6, 563, 564, 570, 573-74, 578, 608, 632
radar-navigation aids, 178-79
Radburn, New Jersey, 472, 478
radiant heating, 226, 228
Radiation Laboratory, M. I. T., 573
radiation preservation of food, 391
radiator, 227
radio
    amplitude modulation (AM), 301
    audion, 297 ff
    development of broadcasting, 302 ff
    development of triode, 300
    frequency modulation (FM), 304-5
    industry, 629
    in mass communication, 326-27
    prehistory of, 293-94
    receiver, 295-97, 301
    transmitter, 297-99, 301
    transistor, 306-7
    see also microwave and shortwave, L. De Forest, G. Marconi and individual companies
Radio Corporation of America (RCA), 302-3, 304, 309, 630
railroads, 3, 8, 30, 130, 137-48, 153, 454, 494, 631
    boxcar, 147
    electrification of, 142-43
    freight car, 142
    hump yard, 147

railroads (*Cont.*)
  passenger car, 142
  piggyback service, 146-47
  signalling, 141
  steam locomotive, 137-40, 143
  technology applied to, 147 ff
  transcontinental, 432
  TOFC (trailer-on-flatcar), 146-47
  see also locomotive
rails and ties, 140-41
RAND Corporation, 494, 547
rayon, 189
Raytheon, 629
reaper, 355
reclamation, 434-37
Reclamation Act (1902), 434, 443, 446,
  459
Reclamation Fund, 436
Reclamation Service, U. S., 435-36, 437,
  448
Red Army, 579, 580
Red China, nuclear tests by, 589
refining, oil, 243-46
refrigerator, 49, 87, 90, 222, 224, 229, 401
regional planning and development, 449-
  61, 698
  approaches to, 449-50
  basic problems, 458-59
  in the Northeast, 452
  in recent decades, 459-61
  recent social and economic changes,
    455 ff
  redistribution of population, 457
  regional growth, early policies influ-
    encing, 453-55
  regional specialization, early, 450-53
  in the South, 451
  in the 20th century, 455-58
  in the West, 450
  see also urban planning and develop-
    ment, urbanization
Regional Planning Association of
  America, 472-73
reinforced concrete construction, 204-10
renewal projects. *See* housing
Report on the Lands of the Arid Region
  (Powell), 433, 442
Republican party, 454
research and development, 13-15, 18,
  493-94, 623-24. *See also* industrial
  research, military research, *indi-*
  vidual technologies and specific
  research and technical institutions
Research and Development Board
  (RDB), 544
reservoir management, crude oil, 242
residual oil, 245
resins, synthetic, 186-87, 191-92
resources. *See* energy resources
restrictive legislation, 490-91
retarder, 148
reverse-cycle heating and cooling, 230
reverse-osmosis process, water desalination, 424

Rhodesia
  irrigation in, 417
  technical research in, 526
Riddle of the Sands, The (Childers), 556
river transportation, 151-53
roads
  freeways, 135-36
  highways, 129, 132, 133-35
  limited-access, 134-35
  traffic control, 134
Robert E. Lee, U.S.S., 584
Robinson-Patman Act (1936), 86
Rockefeller Brothers Fund, 528
Rocket Propulsion Laboratory, 546
rockets, 159, 170, 171, 567, 568-70, 573,
  578, 580, 675-78
room air conditioner unit, 230, 231
rotenoids, 371-72
Royal Air Force (RAF), 566, 573
rubber. *See* chemical industry
Rural Electrification Administration
  (REA), 225, 247, 366-67, 459
Russian Academy of Sciences, 619
Russo-Finnish War, 561
Russo-Japanese War, 551

sapodilla, 372
Sabine's equation, 232
St. Peter's Basilica, 210
St. Petersburg-Tampa Air Boat Line, 173
Salvarsan, 188
satellite relays, 307
satellites, 584, 587, 590, 600, 674, 678-81
  communication, 608, 609, 674, 698
  weather, 674
Saturn rocket, 684
Savannah, 151
Schnorkel, 572
science and technology, relations of, 15-
  18, 153 ff. *See also* research and development
Science Advisory Board, 505, 540
Science, 691
Science—The Endless Frontier (Bush),
  696
Scientific American, 691
Scientific and Industrial Research Department, British, 617
Scientific Management, 9, 28, 41-42, 46,
  696, 697, 707
  and assembly line workers, 55-61
  contributions of, 63-64
  criticism of, 65-66, 68-69
  disadvantages, 59 ff
  economics of, 25
  and growth of unions, 61
  human relations movement, 61-63
  and labor force composition, 25-26
  methods of, 54
  rise of, 52-55
  and steel industry, 52 ff
  underlying assumptions of, 60-61
  see also F. W. Taylor
Score, 307, 608

screwworm fly, 383
sea farming, 412-13
sea power, 554-58
Sears, Roebuck & Company, 82, 83, 86,
  89
secondary recovery, 242
Sectra system, precast housing units, 209
selenium, 374
self-service food stores, 86-87
sequence-controlled calculator, automatic,
  316-17
Servel Company, 229
sewage, 219-20, 420
sewing machine, 49
sex attractants, pest control by, 383
shale oil, 255
Shantytown, 466, 469
sheet steel, 49
shell structures in concrete, 210-13
shopping centers, 88-89
shortwave and microwave, 304-5
signals, railroad, 141
Silent Spring (Carson), 379, 381
silicones, 192
Singer Building, New York City, 199
Sinox, 378
skeleton-frame construction, 196, 197,
  199, 204
skyscraper 9, 197-204, 205, 214-17, 227
slide rule, 313
slip-form system, concrete construction,
  208
slum clearance, 478, 480
Smith Corporation, A. O., 650
Smithsonian Institution, 492-93, 539
smog, 477
smokescreen, chemical, 576
soap as insecticide, 372-73
social control
  failure to plan, 514-15
  idea of, 499-500
  New Deal, 504-6, 507, 508-9, 510-11,
    512, 514
  problem of, 499-515
  and Technocracy, 502-5
social effects of mass production, 91-103
social sciences in the new warfare, 595-
  96, 692-93, 694
Society of American Foresters, 439
Society of Automotive Engineers, 126
"sociosphere," 688-89
sodium fluoride, 374
sodium nitrate, 350-51
Sodium Reactor Experiment (SRE), 267
Soil Conservation Service, 448, 508
soilless farming, 418-19
solar cell, 307, 609
solar energy, 286
solar system, 682
solvent method, water desalination, 424
sound barrier, 164
Southern Pacific Railroad, 145
Soviet Union, 29
  atomic energy program, 259, 266, 271,

272, 274
coal mining, 238
dehydration of food, 391
electrical transmission, 250
fish industry, 403-5
food processing, 387
frozen food, 390
industrial research, 619
mechanization of agriculture, 354
natural gas industry, 247
nuclear tests, 546, 579, 582, 586
postwar policy of, 580-81
prefabrication systems, 209
rocket development, 677
social and economic planning, 502
social control of technology, 499
space information co-operation program, 681
space satellites, 546, 678
soybeans, 344-45
space exploration, 20, 673-86
Space Age, 493, 546, 580, 606, 607, 673,
  674, 678, 680, 681
  military technology in, 589-90
Space Treaty (1967), 684
Spanish-American War, 536
spectrophotometers, 409
Spirit of St. Louis, 172
Sputnik, 582, 678, 679
stainless steel, 184
standardization, 40, 41, 43, 51, 55
Standard Metropolitan Area (SMA), 474
Standard Metropolitan Statistical Area
  (SMSA), 474
Standard Oil Company, 622, 630
Stanford Research Institute, 547
Stanley steamer, 124
starting system, electric, 127
State Fair Arena, Raleigh, North Carolina,
  214
State Technical Services Act (1965), 461,
  611
steam car, 119-20, 123-24
steam power
  engine, 119 142, 145, 148, 152, 603
  on the farm, 356-57
  locomotive, 137-40, 143
  steam shovel, 50
  turbine, 148, 248
  vessels, 137, 148
steel construction, 196, 197-204, 213-17
steel industry, 49, 53
sterilization in pest control, 383
sterilization of food by radiation, 391
Stockholm City Planning Commission,
  480
storage of food, controlled-atmosphere,
  390
storage mill, computer, 317
Strategic Air Command, 170, 585
street lighting, 223, 224
streptomycins, 194
strip mining, 239
styrene, 191

submarine, 557, 558, 572, 573, 584
submerged-tube process, water desalination, 421-22
Suez crisis (1956), 150
sulfa drugs, 192-93
Sunnyside Gardens, Long Island, 472
superheater, 137-38
superheterodyne receiver, 301
supermarket, 86-88, 401
supersonic speed, 177, 584, 697
supertanker, 150-51
supplemental irrigation, 416
surface irrigation, 416, 417
surface mining, 239
Survey Research Center, University of
    Michigan, 328, 332
suspension bridge, 9
Sweden
    automobile industry, 129
    community planning and housing, 480,
        481
    electrical transmission, 249
    social control of technology, 499
    unemployment, 531
    uprban planning, 479-80
switches, remote-controlled rail, 147
synthetic materials. See materials, synthetic
"systems approach," 19-22

tank (warfare), 553-54, 560, 561, 565,
    570-72, 577
tank car, 147
tanker, 149, 150-51
tape control system, 645, 646
tariff, protective, 490-91, 496, 497
tar sand, 255, 284
Taylor Act (1933), 448
Taylorism. See Scientific Management
Technocracy, rise and fall of, 502-4
technological civilization, 27-28
technological unemployment, 504, 512-13
technological work, 11-22
    methods of, 15-19
    professionalization of, 12
    progress of, 3-10, 695-96, 707
    specialization of, 12-13
    "systems approach," 19 ff
technology transfer, 256
    in underdeveloped countries, 516-31
    see also transfer of military technology
Telefunken Corporation, 302
telegraph, 3, 8, 30 325
telephone, ship-to-shore, 152
telephony, 300, 304
    transatlantic, 300-301, 307
television, 31, 326, 327, 328, 331, 632,
    698
    development of, 303-4
    transmission, 293, 303-4, 305, 307
Telstar relay satellite, 307, 308, 327, 633,
    674
Temporary National Economic Committee (TNEC), 511-14

Tennessee Valley Authority (TVA), 350,
    351, 448, 460, 506-8
TEPP, 377
Tersons system, precast housing units,
    209
textile industry, 465-66, 500, 642
    mass production in, 95-98
thallium compounds, 374
thermal cracking, 243, 245
thermionic valve, 296
thermite bomb, 575
thermoelectricity, 255
thermonuclear weapons, 580, 585
theories of warfare, 500-501
    "balance of terror," 592-93
    "command of the air," 592
    guerilla warfare, 599 ff
    "strategy of force," 590-91
    war of attrition, 591
    see also warfare
third rail power transmission, 143
Thomson-Houston Electrical Company,
    625
three-dimensional warfare, 561-78
    delivery technologies, 565-72
    human factor in, 578
    intelligence technologies, 573-75
    new elements in, 562-64
    payload technologies, 575-76
    production technologies, 577-78
    protective technologies, 576-77
    weapons systems, 562, 579, 585
    see also World War II
threshing machine, 355-56
tidal power, 285
tilt-up method, concrete construction, 208
Time Machine, The (Wells), 23
time-payment plans, 90
time study, 54
tires, pneumatic, 122, 129
TOFC (trailer-on-flatcar) service, 146-47
toilet facilities, 220
Tokyo, Japan, 575
toll road, 135
Tomorrow: A Peaceful Path to Reform
    (Howard), 471
torpedoes, 572, 576
Torengebouw, Antwerp, 200
Torpex, 576
towboat, 152
Town Development Act (1952), British,
    479
Toxaphene, 377
tractor, 8, 357-63, 366
trade agreements, 491
trade associations, 502
Trade Expansion Act (1962), 460
traffic control, 134, 141
tramp steamer, 148
transfer machine, 643-44
transfer of military technology to civilian
    use
    by analogy, 603, 604
    contemporary problems in, 605-8

by imitation, 608 ff
indirect applications, 610-12
time lag, 603, 604
transistor, 306-7, 321
transit systems, 477
transmission of natural gas, 221, 246
transmitter, radio, 297-99
transportation
  commercial and specialized vehicles,
    129 ff
  distribution of goods, 78 ff
  freight, 89, 153
  metropolitan, 475-78
  river, 151-53
  water, 148-53
  see also automobile, aviation, locomo-
    tive, railroad, roads
Treasury Department, U. S., 493
Tribune Tower, Chicago, 200, 201
tricycle, 129
triode, 297, 298, 300, 301, 302, 305
truck, 129-30, 131, 146
tuna fishing, 402-3, 405
turbine, 148, 149, 248
turbojet, 158-59
TWA terminal, Kennedy Airport, 212
Twenty Thousand Leagues under the Sea
  (Verne), 23
*Two Cultures and the Scientific Revolu-
tion* (Snow), 686

Uganda, technical research in, 525
underdeveloped countries, 516-31
  agriculture, 527-28
  aid to, 109
  challenge of, 531
  economic environments, 517
  factor combinations in production, 519-
    20
  government-industry co-operation, 526-
    27
  interchange of people and institutional
    relations, 524-25
  international manufacturing systems
    in, 527
  organization of production in, 520-21
  physical endowment, 518-19
  product design for, 521
  social transformation, role of technol-
    ogy in, 523-24
  technical research institutes in, 525-26
  United Nations research program, 527
unemployment, 76, 110-11, 114, 509, 531
  automation and, 70, 659
  Negro, 110-11
  technological, 504, 512-13
  unemployability, 110-11, 114-15
unions
  automation, collective bargaining, and,
    69-71
  craft, 70
  growth of, 61
  "humanization" of work, 75-76
  industrial, 66-68

legislation and, 73-74
mutual accommodation, 68-69
outside the U. S., 74-75
personnel administration and, 71-73
Scientific Management and, 61, 64-66
unionization, 64
Union Pacific Railroad, 140, 143
United Auto Workers, 638
United Mine Workers, 67
United Nations, 421, 424, 579, 582, 587,
  680, 681
  General Assembly, 266
  research program, 527
United States, 149, 150
United States Steel Corporation, 102
University of Chicago, 621
University of Wisconsin, 439
uranium, 257-58, 274
urbanization, 29, 32, 386, 387
  central city and suburb, 473 ff
  early city building, to 1920, 462-73
  growth of suburbs, 482-83
  influence of technology on, 461-62,
    473
  see also urban planning and develop-
    ment
Urban Mass Transportation Act (1964),
  477
urban planning and development, 461-83
  backwardness of building industry,
    470-71
  capital city, 464
  communitarian settlements, 462-64
  environmental problems, 233
  first phase of, 462
  foreign programs, 479-80, 481
  Garden City principle, 471-72, 473,
    479
  growth of central city and suburbs,
    473 ff
  Homestead, Pennsylvania, example,
    467-69
  housing, 478, 480-81
  megalopolis, 7, 457, 481-82
  mill town, 465-68
  New Towns program, 477, 479, 483
  Pittsburgh, Pennsylvania, example, 467
  port cities, 464-65
  problems of metropolitan region, 475-
    77
  quanta planning, 465, 471-72
  reform in, 471
  renewal projects, 478-79
  special district authority, 475 ff
  superblock, 480
  transportation problems, 477-78
urea-formaldehyde resins, 186-87, 191-92
urethane, 192
utility services, 217

V-1, 567, 568, 569-70, 574
V-2, 170, 563, 567, 569-70, 580, 582,
  677, 678
vaccines, 576

vaccum-contact drying, 391
vaccum tube, 296-97, 300, 302, 307
Vällingby, Sweden, 479-80
Van Allen belt, 678
vapor-compression distillation, water de-
    salination, 423
Vietnam, 585
vitamins, 189, 193-94, 394, 426
Volkswagen, 122, 128
Vom Krieg (On War), Clausewitz, 590

wage structure in mass production, 95
Wagner Act (1935), 67
Waltham Watch Company, 643
Wanamaker department store, John, 80,
    224
War Department, U. S., 508
warehouse operation, 89-90
warfare
    change in, 27
    contemporary spectrum of, 578-90
    new warfare, 593-601
    three-dimensional, 561-78
    weapons for limited war, 585-86
    see also World War I, World War II,
        mechanization of war, theories of
        warfare
warheads. See nuclear weapons
warm-air heating systems, 227-28
war on poverty program, 114, 460
washing machine, 49, 221-22
water
    brackish, 424, 427
    conservation program, 444-46
    desalination of, 419-24, 427
    filtration, 420
    fresh, 419-24
    hydroelectric power, 237
    irrigation, 415-17, 433, 435, 487
    pollution, 413, 420
    power, 284-85
    purification of, 218-19
    supply systems, 218-19
    waste, reclamation of, 420
Water Power Act (1920), 447
Water Quality Act (1965), 461
water transportation
    ocean trades, 148-51
    river transport, 151-53
Wealth of Nations (Smith), 491
weapons. See individual weapons
weapons systems, 562, 579, 585
Weapons System Evaluation Group, 547
weather satellites, 674
weed control, 377-78
Welwyn, England, 472, 479
Western Electric Company, 61, 301, 626,
    653
West German Federal Republic, 617
    atomic energy program in, 274
Westinghouse Electric Company, 265,
    302, 303, 625, 629, 630
Westinghouse foundry (1890), 42
West Point Military Academy, 492, 497

whale oil, 223
wheat, new varieties of, 343-44
Wheeler Dam, 507
When William Came (Saki), 556
white arsenic, 373
White Motor Company, 124, 130
White Sands Proving Ground, New
    Mexico, 677
Williamsburg, Virginia, 464
Willys-Overland Company, 132, 133
wind power, 285-86
wireless telegraph, 8, 178, 293, 294-95
women, emancipation of, 4, 24-25
wood, source of energy, 237
Woods Hole Oceanographic Institute, 563
Woolworth Building, New York City,
    199-200
work
    "humanization" of, 75-76
    and leisure, 99-101
    mechanical pacing of, 93
    See also Scientific Management,
        technological work, time study,
        unions
work-engineering systems, 69
worker displacement, 71
Works Progress Administration (WPA),
    448, 509, 631, 632
World's Columbian Exposition (1893),
    221, 224
World Trade Center Towers, New York
    City, 216
World War I, 12, 16, 32, 61, 72, 90, 129,
    131, 157, 158, 166, 168, 171, 179,
    183, 240, 243, 301, 457, 497, 506,
    536, 537-38, 562, 563, 570, 590, 591,
    598, 704
    homefront, 558-60
    industrial research, 627-28
    leadership, 549
    mass production of weapons, 551, 560,
        561
    mechanization of agriculture, impor-
        tance of, 560
    mobilization timetable, 549-51
    new weapons and problems, 551-53
    postwar industrial research develop-
        ments, 628-31
    romantic view of, 553-55
    sea power, 556 ff
    theories of warfare, 556 ff
    war propaganda, 555
World War II, 12, 28, 32, 68, 72, 90, 97,
    128, 137, 145, 158, 160, 168, 170,
    173, 174, 179, 183, 193, 240, 245,
    256, 259, 263, 304, 337, 343, 351,
    352, 361, 368, 378, 387, 390, 457,
    493, 498, 540, 541, 542, 544, 545,
    549, 554, 579, 591-92, 596, 597, 605,
    677, 697, 699
    air warfare, 565 ff
    amphibious assault, 572
    co-ordination of research, 562
    delivery technologies, 565-72

ground warfare, 570-72
human factor in, 578
industrial research during, 632-33
intelligence technologies, 573-75
medical research, 576-77
operations analysis, 563
payload technologies, 575-76
postwar industrial research developments, 633-34
production technologies, 577-78
protective technologies, 576-77
radar, 573 ff
three-dimensional war, 561-78
warfare at sea, 572
weapons systems, 562, 579

wrapping materials, food, 398

X-1 rocket plane, 584, 697
X-rays, 9
Xerography, 632

Yale School of Forestry, 439
Yale Technology Project, 93
Yankee Atomic Electric Company, 268,
  269, 273

Zeiss Planetarium, 210, 211, 212
zeppelins, 165-67
zoning regulations, 200-201
zooplankton, 425

Name Index

Adams, Henry, 6-7
Agassiz, Louis, 340
Aiken, Howard, 316, 318-19, 320, 321
Aiken, R. N., 208
Alcock, Captain John, 172
Alexanderson, E. F. W., 299
Alexander the Great, 487
Alifas, N. P., 65
Allen, E. C., 83
Allen, W. C., 360
Almond, F., 211
Anderson, John W., 45
Anderson, Captain O. A., 165
Anthony, Susan B., 24
Appert, François, 605
Aristotle, 488
Arkwright, Richard, 39
Armstrong, Edwin Howard, 300, 301,
    302, 304, 309
Arnold, Harold D., 300, 626
Arnold, General Henry H. ("Hap"), 168,
    170, 585
Arnold, Thurman, 505
Astin, Allen V., 497
Atterbury, Grosvenor, 209
Aus, Gunvald, 199
Avery, Clarence, 45

Babbage, Charles, 315, 316-17, 319, 320,
    321
Bache, Alexander Dallas, 536
Bacon, Francis, 9
Baekeland, Leo, 186, 695-96
Baeyer, Adolf von, 14, 187-88
Baird, John L., 303
Baker, A. H., 228
Ballinger, Richard, 447
Bardeen, John, 307
Barger, Harold, 79
Barkin, Solomon, 97
Barredo, Ricardo, 211
Baruch, Bernard, 579
Bauer, Catherine, 480
Bauersfeld, Walter, 210
Beachey, Lincoln, 157
Beal, William James, 340

Beck, James, 620
Beecher, Catherine E., 221
Bell, Alexander Graham, 16, 493
Bellamy, Edward, 4
Bentham, Samuel, 39
Benz, Karl, 120
Berkner, Lloyd V., 679-80
Berliner, Emile, 13
Besserdich, William, 132
Bessey, C. E., 373
Beuth, Peter, 492
Biekart, H. M., 418
Birdseye, Clarence, 390
Bissaker, Robert, 313
Blake, Arthur, 228
Blanchard, Thomas, 644
Bland, Theodorick, 343
Blauner, Robert, 99
Blériot, Louis, 157
Bleucher, Field Marshal von, 27
Bohn, René, 188
Bollens, John C., 475
Bonaparte, Napoleon, 27, 605
Boole, Edward, 321
Boot, H. K. H., 305
Booth, James, 620
Boveri, Theodore, 339
Bowen, Rear Adm. H. G., 545
Brandeis, Louis D., 512
Branly, Eduard, 294, 296
Brattain, Walter H., 307
Braun, Karl Ferdinand, 303
Bridge, Adm. Sir Cyprian Arthur George,
    557
Brooks, Harvey, 263
Brown, Lt. Arthur W., 172
Brunel, Marc Isambard, 39, 642
Brush, Charles F., 224
Bryce, James W., 319
Buckingham, Walter, 659
Burbank, Luther, 339
Burroughs, William S., 315
Burton, William M., 623
Bush, Vannevar, 320, 513, 514, 540, 541,
    543, 544, 696
Byington, Margaret, 467-68

Candela, Felix, 211
Cannon, Joseph G., 492
Carlo, Charles de, 105
Carlson, Chester, 632
Carnegie, Andrew, 468, 621
Carothers, Wallace H., 15, 631
Carrier, Willis H., 229
Carson, John R., 627
Carson, Rachel, 379
Carty, John J., 626, 627, 628
Case, J. I., 360, 361
Cato the Censor, 374
Champagnat, Alfred, 426-27
Chaplin, Charlie, 32
Charles, J. A. C., 165
Chatelier, Henri le, 185
Chesterton, G. K., 6
Childers, Erskine, 556
Churchill, Sir Winston S., 565, 569, 579, 586, 593
Clark, W. C., 203
Clausewitz, Karl von, 27, 590, 591, 594, 595, 596
Clavier, André, 305
Clay, Henry, 454
Cleveland, Grover, 438
Cobden, Richard, 491
Cohen, Benjamin, 512
Coignet, Edmond, 210
Colt, Samuel P., 41
Columbus, Christopher, 686
Compton, Karl T., 504, 505, 510, 514, 515, 541
Comstock, John H., 370
Conant, James B., 262, 540
Connors, C. H., 418
Conrad, Captain R. D., 545
Considière, A. G., 204
Coolidge, Calvin, 501, 539
Cooper, Peter, 126
Corcoran, Thomas G., 512
Correns, Karl, 338
Cotton, R. T., 374
Coville, Frederick V., 443
Cramer, Stewart W., 229
Crane, Stewart W., 228
Cugnot, Nicholas Joseph, 119
Culmann, Carl, 199
Curie, Pierre and Marie, 4
Curtiss, Glenn, 156, 157

Daimler, Gottlieb, 120
Dana, Samuel L., 620
Daniels, Josephus, 537
Darwin, Charles, 340
Darwin, Erasmus, 374
Davidson, W. M., 375
Davis, Charles Henry, 536
Deacon, Henry, 185
Deere, John, 355, 359
De Forest, Lee, 296-300
Delaney, John, 380
Diebold, John, 636-38, 639
Dischinger, Franz, 208

Doering, Otto, 19
Domagk, Fritz, 193
Domenjoz, R., 375-76
Doolittle, General James, 575
Dornberger, Maj. General Walter, 568
Douhet, Guilio, 592
Doxiadis, Constantine, 531
Dudley, Charles Benjamin, 621
Duncan, Robert K., 623
Dunlap, John T., 664
Dunlop, John B., 122
Dunning, John R., 257
Dunwoody, H. H. C., 296
Dupire, A., 376
du Pont, Francis Guerney, 623
du Pont, Lammot, 620
Dupree, A. Hunter, 543
Durant, William C., 43-44, 49, 125
Durfee, B. M., 319
Duryea, Charles and Frank, 120

East, Edward M., 340-41
Eckert, J. Presper, 320
Edison, Thomas Alva, 9, 11, 13, 14, 16, 17, 18, 19, 123, 296, 535, 537, 624-25
Edward VII, 6
Edwards, Alba, 91
Edwards, George H., 359
Ehrlich, Paul, 188
Eiffel, Gustave, 203
Einstein, Albert, 257, 681
Eisenhower, Dwight D., 266, 268, 271, 570
Elliott, Sterling, 122
Elsässer, Martin, 211
Erlenback, Arnold, 375
Evans, Oliver, 40, 119-20, 489, 649, 650

Fageol brothers, 130
Fairless, Benjamin J., 639
Faraday, Michael, 16, 293, 294, 376
Farmham, R. B., 418
Farnsworth, Philo, 304, 632
Feddersen, Wilhelm, 294
Felt, Dorr E., 315
Ferguson, Gordon B., 212
Ferguson, Harry, 361
Fermi, Enrico, 256, 257, 262, 268
Fernow, Bernhard, 438
Fessenden, Reginald, 298-99, 301, 302
Fleming, Sir Alexander, 194, 577
Fleming, John Ambrose, 296-97
Flemming, Arthur S., 381
Föppl, August, 210
Forbes, R. J., 487
Ford, Edsel, 45
Ford, Henry, 12, 19, 25, 41, 44-45, 46, 47, 49, 52, 55, 92, 93, 120, 126, 360, 365, 648, 696
Ford, Henry, II, 103
Fortas, Abe, 505
Fourdrinier, Henry, 647
Fourneau, Ernest, 193

Frasch, Herman, 622
Frankfurter, Felix, 505, 512
Franklin, Benjamin, 227, 344, 492
Fraser, James, 426
Freyssinet, Eugene, 208, 210, 211
Fricke, Frederick J., 212
Froelich, John, 358
Fujitani, J., 371
Fuller, General J. F. C., 598
Fuller, R. Buckminster, 213
Fulton, Robert, 496
Furer, Rear Adm. J. A., 545

Gabor, Dennis, 109
Galileo, 674, 681
Gandhi, Mahatma, 22, 28, 531
Garfield, James R., 444, 445, 446, 447
Gargarin, Yuri, 683
Gaudi, Antonio, 206
Genghis Khan, 32
Geoffroy, E., 372
Gericke, E. F., 418
Gibbons, Thomas, 496
Gibbs, Josiah Willard, 4
Gilbert, Cass, 199
Gilman, Glenn, 98
Gindraux, Louis, 376
Glenn, John, 683
Goddard, Robert H., 568, 676, 677
Goldschmidt, Rudolph, 299
Gompers, Samuel, 66
Gordon, J. P., 307
Gorrie, John, 228
Gottmann, Jean, 457, 481
Gray, Asa, 340
Grazia, Sebastien de, 99
Green, William, 66
Gropius, Walter, 205, 480
Gunter, Edmund, 313
Gutenberg, Johannes, 38, 324

Haber, Fritz, 185, 352
Hahn, Otto, 256
Hahn, Philipp Mattheaus, 315
Haines, Kinnard, 359
Halban, Hans von, 257
Hale, George Ellery, 537, 540
Hall, Albert, 573
Hall, Charles Martin, 184, 623
Hall, John N., 40
Hamilton, Alexander, 454, 495
Hamilton, E. W., 359
Hamilton, F. E., 319
Handley, Hunter, 205
Harder, D. S., 635
Harding, Warren G., 539
Hare, Robert, 620
Harrison, Benjamin, 437
Hart, Charles W., 359
Hayes, Augustus A., 620
Hayes, Herbert Kendall, 341
Haynes, Elwood, 120
Hazeltine, Alan, 301-2
Heilbroner, Robert, 108

Heising, R. A., 301
Helmholtz, Hermann von, 16, 641
Henderson, Leon, 503, 504, 510, 512
Hennibique, François, 204
Henry, Joseph, 16, 232, 294, 536, 620
Henson, Victor, 425
Heron of Alexandria, 310, 313, 314, 323
Héroult, Paul Louis Toussaint, 184
Herrington, Colonel Arthur W. S., 132
Hertz, Heinrich, 16, 294, 573, 603
Hewitt, Abram S., 126
Hewitt, Edward R., 126
Higbee, C. H., 374
Hippodamos, 488
Hitchcock, E. A., 444
Hitler, Adolf, 23, 32, 166, 170, 561
Hollerith, Herman, 315, 318
Hood, Raymond, 201
Hoover, Herbert, 501, 502, 622
Hopkins, Harry, 509
Houdry, Eugene, 245
Howard, Ebenezer, 471-72, 473, 479
Howe, Charles S., 431
Howie, Captain Robert G., 132
Hoxie, Robert F., 65
Hubbert, M. K., 279, 285
Hull, A. W., 303
Humberstone, J. T., 350
Hussey, Obed, 355
Huxley, Aldous, 32

Ickes, Harold, 448, 509

Jacquard, Joseph Marie, 645
Jahnz, Edwin, 315
James, William, 601, 684
Jefferson, Thomas, 39, 355, 489
Jenkins, Charles Francis, 303
Jenks, Joseph, 488
Jenney, William Le Baron, 197
Jerome, Chauncey, 41
Jewett, Frank B., 540, 628
Johnson, Hugh, 509-10
Johnson, Louis, 582
Johnson, Lyndon B., 490, 641
Jones, Donald F., 341
Josephson, Matthew, 17
Justinian, Emperor, 490

Kant, Immanuel, 185
Kármán, Theodore von, 163
Kelvin, Lord, 320
Kendrick, John W., 78
Kennedy, John F., 28, 273, 379, 659, 681
Kettering, Charles Franklin, 12, 127, 130, 499, 513, 514, 629
Keynes, John Maynard, 103, 110, 512
Kilgore, Harley M., 543
King, Charles B., 120
Kingston, J. L., 203
Kitchener, Lord, 551
Klapper, Joseph, 332
Knight, Charles Y., 127

Knipling, E. F., 383
Knudsen, William S., 48
Kögl, Fritz, 378
Kompfner, Rudolf, 307
Kowarski, Lew, 257
Kurchatov, Igor V., 259

Laffaile, Bernard, 211
La Forge, F. B., 371, 372
Lake, C. D., 319
Lancaster, Frederick W., 121, 163
Land, Edwin H., 13, 632
Lane, John, 355
Langley, Samuel P., 7, 492
Langmuir, Irving, 300, 576, 627
Lavoisier, Antoine Laurent, 4
Lawes, Sir John B., 349, 350
Lawrance, Charles L., 172
Lawrence, T. E., 548
Le Corbusier (Charles Édouard
    Jeanneret-Gris), 205
Le Grand, Rupert, 635
Leibniz, Wilhelm von, 314-15
Leighton, Marshall O., 445
Leland, Henry M., 44
Lenoir, Etienne, 120
Levassor, Emile Constant, 121
Lévy, Lucien, 301
Levy, Maurice, 199
Lewis, John L., 67
Lick, James, 370
Liebig, Justus von, 13 16, 348-49, 350
Lilienthal, David, 506
Lincoln, Abraham, 492, 496
Lindbergh, Charles A., 172
List, Friedrich, 491
Little, Arthur D., 194, 623
Livingston, Robert, 496
Lodge, Oliver, 294, 296, 298
Long, Russell, 490
Lorain, John, 339
Loughead (Lockheed), Malcolm, 127
Lovell, Sir Bernard, 681
Lovenstein, Meno, 107
Lynd, Robert S., 501

McAdam, John Loudon, 133
McCormick, Cyrus H., 355
McGee, W J, 445, 446
MacKaye, Benton, 472
McKenzie, R. D., 473
McKinley, William, 6, 441
Maclaurin, W. R., 309
McLuhan, Marshall, 327-28
MacMahon, Brien, 546
Mahan, Alfred Thayer, 592
Malthus, Thomas, 354, 414
Mann, Floyd, 664
Mao Tse-tung, 594
Marconi, Guglielmo, 16, 294-95, 296,
    298, 603
Marcovitch, S., 374
Marcus, Siegfried, 120
Marmon brothers, 132

Marsh, James, 212
Marx, Karl, 6
Mauchly, John W., 320
Maudslay, Henry, 39
Maxim, Hiram Percy, 120, 123, 129, 551
Maxim, Hudson, 626
Maxwell, James Clark, 293-94
May, Ernest, 480
Mayo, Elton, 61, 62, 97
Mees, C. E. K., 626
Meikle, Andrew, 355
Meissner, A., 300
Mendel, Gregor Johann, 338, 340
Mendelsohn, Erich, 206
Midgley, Thomas, 243
Mies van der Rohe, Ludwig, 205, 214,
    215
Mihaly, D., 303
Millardet, M., 384
Miller, Arthur L., 380
Millikan, Robert A., 537, 538, 539, 540
Mitchell, Broadus, 507
Mitchell, General William ("Billy"), 168
Mörsch, E., 204
Mohr, Otto, 199
Moley, Raymond, 505
Moltke, Helmuth von, 549-50, 551
Mond, Ludwig, 11
Monier, Joseph, 204
Montgolfier, Joseph, 165
Moore, William, 374-75
Morgan, Arthur E., 506, 507, 508
Morgan, H. A., 506, 507
Morgan, Thomas Hunt, 339
Morgenthau, Henry, 512
Morley, T. B., 230
Morse, Samuel F. B., 11, 492
Moulton, F. C., 373
Mueller, Johannes, 425
Müller, Paul, 375
Mumford, Lewis, 7, 472, 482, 498, 699
Munroe, Jay R., 315
Murray, Sir John, 425
Nagai, K., 372
Napier, John, 312-13
Neff, Wallace, 213
Nehru, Jawaharlal, 28
Nernst, Walter, 185
Neumann, John von, 321
Newbold, Charles, 355
Newell, Frederick H., 434-36, 441, 442,
    444, 445
Newlands, Francis G., 435
Newton, Sir Isaac, 314
Nipkow, Paul, 303
North, Simeon, 40-41

Oberth, Hermann, 677
Ogden, Aaron, 496
Ohain, Hans von, 158
Olds, Ransom E., 43, 44, 120, 125
Oppenheimer, J. Robert, 262, 575
Orteig, Raymond, 172
Otis, Elisha Graves, 203

Otis, William Smith, 50
Otto, Nicholaus A., 358
Oud, J. J. P., 480
Oughted, William, 313
Owen, Robert, 72

Parr, Charles H., 359
Pascal, Blaise, 314-15
Pasteur, Louis, 219
Patterson, William, 359
Pauly, H., 188
Peierls, Rudolph, 258
Penney, J. C., 85
Perkins, Sir William Henry, 11, 16, 615
Perret, Auguste, 205
Perry, E. J., 347
Peter the Great, 619
Peugeot, Armand, 120
Philip II of Spain, 492
Pickard, G. W., 296
Pierce, J. R., 608
Pillitan, Pierre, 423
Pinchot, Gifford, 438-48
Pitt, William, 491
Pitts, Hiram and John, 356
Pliny, 355, 372
Polhem, Christopher, 39
Pollak, Fritz, 186
Polo, Marco, 372
Pope, Colonel Albert A., 123
Porsche, Ferry, 128
Potter, Albert, 440
Poulsen, Valdemar, 298
Powell, John Wesley, 433, 434, 436, 437,
    442, 443, 445, 447, 448
Prandtl, Ludwig, 163
Priestley, Joseph, 4
Pupin, Michael, 623

Rabi, Isadore I., 262
Randall, J. T., 305
Rankine, W. J. M., 199
Ransome, E. L., 204
Rateau, C. E. A., 228
Raucourt, M., 376
Rautenstrauch, Walter, 503
Raymond, A. A. 205
Reese, Charles L., 626
Reid, Robert, 340
Reitschel, Hermann, 228
Reuther, Walter, 638, 640
Reynolds, Osborne, 163
Richardson, O. W., 300
Richmond, Captain Herbert, 597
Rickover, Admiral Hyman G., 171, 265,
    266
Riley, C. V., 382
Riquet de Bonrepos, Pierre-Paul, 494
Roark, R. C., 374
Rodgers, Calbraith P., 157
Roebuck, A. C., 83
Rogers, Will, 503
Roosevelt, Franklin D., 366, 504-6, 511,
    512, 514, 540, 541, 543, 562

Roosevelt, Theodore, 431, 433, 435, 441-
    42, 444-48
Root, Elihu, 536
Rosendahl, Admiral Charles, 167
Rosenwald, Julius, 83
Rosing, Boris, 303
Ross, Commander M. D., 165
Round, Henry J., 301, 303
Ruffin, Edmund, 348
Ruskin, John, 700
Rutherford, Ernest, 296
Ruzicka, Leopold, 371

Saarinen, Eero, 212
Sabin, Wallace C., 232
Saki, 556
Santos-Dumont, Alberto, 165, 167
Saunders, Sir Charles, 344
Saunders, Clarence, 87
Schlesinger, Arthur M., Jr., 509
Schottky, Walter, 301, 303
Schrader, Gerhard, 377
Schumpeter, Joseph A., 77
Scott, Howard, 503
Seaborg, Glenn T., 258, 275
Sears, Richard W., 83-84
Selden, George B., 120, 125-26
Serpollet, Leon, 123
Sforza, Ludovico, 488
Shepard, Alan, 683
Shockley, William, 307
Shull, George Harrison, 340, 341
Siemens, Werner von, 11, 13, 16, 18, 19
Silliman, Benjamin, Jr., 620
Sims, Admiral William S., 558
Skinner, C. E., 627
Slick, Thomas B., 208
Sloan, Alfred P., 44
Smith, Adam, 93, 491
Smith, L. R., 650
Snow, C. P., 686
Snyder, John I., Jr., 639, 640
Sorensen, Charles E., 45, 126
Southworth, G. C., 305
Speer, Albert, 577-78
Spillmann, W. J., 343-44
Stalin, Josef, 561, 580
Stanley brothers, 124
Starley, J. K., 122
Staudinger, Hermann, 371
Stein, Clarence S., 472, 478
Steinmetz, Charles P., 14, 299, 502, 503,
    625
Stephens, Donald P., 212
Stevens, Captain A. W., 165
Stevenson, A. R., 230
Stine, C. M. A., 631
Stolz, F., 188
Stout, William B., 173
Strassman, Fritz, 257
Strauss, Siegmund, 300
Sullivan, Louis, 198, 199, 215
Sundstrand, Oscar, 315
Sutton, W. S., 339

Swope, Gerard, 504
Szilard, Leo, 257

Taft, William Howard, 447
Tagore, Rabindranath, 22
Takamine, J., 188
Tattersfield, F., 374
Taylor, Frederick W., 9, 25, 26, 41, 52-
    55, 60, 63, 64-65, 696, 697, 698
Tereshkova, Valentina, 683
Terry, Eli, 41
Thomson, Elihu, 625
Thomson, William (Lord Kelvin), 320
Tirpitz, Admiral von, 557
Tizard, Sir Henry, 563, 573
Tomlinson, Charles, 642
Torres y Quevado, 315
Torroja, Eduardo, 211
Townes, C. H., 307
Trouvelot, Leopold, 370
Truman, Harry S., 543, 575, 579-80
Tschermark, E. von, 338
Tsiolkovsky, Konstantin E., 676
Tugwell, Rexford, 505, 510
Turner, Frederick Jackson, 450
Twining, General Nathan F., 582

Upham, J. B., 232

Vail, Theodore N., 626
Van Allen, James A., 678
Van der Bijl, H. J., 301
Varian, R. H., and S. A., 305
Vaucanson, Jacques, 645
Veblen, Thorstein, 502-3
Verne, Jules, 23, 30
da Vinci, Leonardo, 488, 647
Vitruvius, 232, 310
de Vries, Hugo, 338

Wachsmann, Konrad, 213
Wallace, Henry A., 341, 354, 448, 500,
    515, 540
Wallis, Dean, 659
Ward, Montgomery, 82, 83, 86, 89

Washington, George, 492
Watt, James, 15, 119, 603
Wayss, G. A., 204
Weagant, Roy, 301
Webb, Walter Prescott, 451
Webber, Melvin, 481-82
Webster, Noah, 325
Wehnelt, Arthur, 300
Weinberg, Alvin M., 264
Wells, H. G., 4, 23
Westinghouse, George, 13
Whipple, Squire, 199
White, Edward H., 685
White, Lynn, 602, 705, 706
Whitehead, Alfred North, 696
Whitney, Eli, 11, 19, 39, 40, 41, 52, 535
Whitney, Willis R., 626, 627
Whittle, Frank, 158, 567
Wiener, Norbert, 636, 637, 638, 639, 655
Wiesner, Jerome, 379
Wigner, Eugene P., 263-4
Kaiser Wilhelm II, 554
Wilson, Woodrow, 447, 511, 537, 539,
    562
Winthrop, John, Jr., 494
Winton, Alexander, 120, 129
Withrow, Robert, 418
Wolfe, Alfred R., 229
Wood, Robert C., 476
Woodhouse, James, 620
Woollard, Frank G., 654
Woolworth, F. W., 85, 87
Wright, Frank Lloyd, 205-6
Wright, Henry, 472, 478
Wright, Wilbur and Orville, 12, 155-7,
    167, 179, 674, 697

Yamasaki, Minoru, 216
Yountz, Philip N., 208

Zachow, Otto, 132
Zeidler, Othmar, 375
Zeppelin, Count Ferdinand von, 165-7
Zinn, Walter H., 263
Zworykin, Vladimir K., 303-4